The History of the Rifle Brigade (the Prince Consort's Own) Formerly the 95th

THE RIFLE BRIGADE

LONDON: PRINTED BY
SPOTTISWOODE AND CO., NEW-STREET SQUARE
AND PARLIAMENT STREET

Plate I.

RIFLE CORPS,
1800.

THE HISTORY

OF THE

RIFLE BRIGADE

(THE PRINCE CONSORT'S OWN)

FORMERLY THE

95th

BY

SIR WILLIAM H. COPE, BART.

LATE LIEUTENANT RIFLE BRIGADE

WITH MAPS AND PLANS

London

CHATTO & WINDUS, PICCADILLY

1877

TO

FIELD-MARSHAL

HIS ROYAL HIGHNESS

THE PRINCE OF WALES, K.G.

&c &c

COLONEL-IN-CHIEF

THIS RECORD OF THE SERVICES OF

THE RIFLE BRIGADE

IS

BY HIS GRACIOUS PERMISSION

MOST RESPECTFULLY

DEDICATED

PREFACE.

A WISH had long been entertained and often expressed by Riflemen, both by those serving in the Regiment and by those who had formerly served in it, that a detailed record of its services should be compiled. It was suggested to me by many of my friends that I should undertake this task. The will certainly was not wanting; but the ability to carry out their wish has not, I fear, been equal to their partial opinion, or to my own desire to do justice to the subject.

The materials for such a compilation were not wanting. The late Colonel Leach published a very brief sketch of the Services of the Regiment,[1] and his 'Rough Notes'[2] give many and accurate particulars of events during the time he served in it. The Autobiography of Quarter-Master Surtees[3] is a most valuable record of the events in which he took part. Surtees came as a private into the 95th from the 56th Regiment in 1802. His good conduct raised him through the various grades of non-commissioned officer to Quarter-Master of the old 3rd Battalion.

[1] 'Sketch of the Field Services of the Rifle Brigade from its Formation to the Battle of Waterloo.' London, 1838, pp 32.

[2] 'Rough Sketches in the Life of an Old Soldier.' London, 1831

[3] 'Twenty-five Years in the Rifle Brigade' Edinburgh, 1833

His book I have found, on comparing it with other records, most accurate in every particular. As the 3rd Battalion was disbanded before the order for drawing up and preserving regimental records issued from the Horse Guards, no formal record of its services exists;[1] and had it not been for the facts and dates preserved and recorded by Surtees, I should have found it difficult, if not impossible, to have given any detailed account of the actions of that Battalion in the Peninsula and at New Orleans. Though tinged with the peculiar religious opinions which Surtees adopted, and which perhaps scarcely have place in a military record, his work is written with a distinctness and in a style which do him honour. And the high character of the man which breathes through his work has led me to place every confidence in his statements.

Very different are Sir John Kincaid's two books.[2] These, though written in too jocular and light a strain for regular history ('ad jocos forte propensior quam decet') contain many anecdotes and facts of which I have gladly availed myself. And I have found his dates and statements confirmed by other and more formal materials to which I had access.

Costello's little work[3] has also afforded me much information; and he has recorded many circumstances unnoticed or lightly touched upon by others.

The 'Recollections of Rifleman Harris'[4] have

[1] The order for keeping regimental records is dated September 1822 The 3rd Battalion was disbanded in 1818

[2] 'Adventures in the Rifle Brigade' and 'Random Shots from a Rifleman'

[3] 'Adventures of a Soldier.' London, 1852.

[4] Edited by Henry Curling. London, 1848.

also been of considerable service to me in compiling this record, especially as preserving many particulars, elsewhere unnoticed, of the retreat to Corunna and of the expedition to Walcheren. His editor, however, seems to have used the materials Harris wrote or dictated without any attempt at arrangement; so that it is difficult, and in some cases almost impossible, to disentangle the narrative, or to arrange the events he describes in chronological order

The valuable List of the Officers of the Regiment, compiled by Mr. Stooks Smith,[1] has also been of much use to me; and I have to thank that gentleman for some additional information, and for permission to republish that list with continuation to the present time, of which I hope at some future period to avail myself.

Nor can I close this list of printed works bearing on the history of the Regiment without mentioning the 'Recollections of a Rifleman's Wife,' by Mrs. Fitzmaurice, to which I am indebted for many facts and anecdotes, many of them especially valuable because they relate to the less stirring times of peace; nor without expressing my thanks for her permission to use the materials she has thus preserved.

When I proceed to acknowledge the personal recollections and the journals of services in the Regiment which have been placed at my disposal, I scarcely know how adequately to express my obligations to those who have aided me. Everyone who

[1] 'Alphabetical List of the Officers of the Rifle Brigade from 1800 to 1850.' London, 1851.

has worn the green jacket, from Generals to private Riflemen, to whom I have applied, or who has heard of my endeavour to preserve a record of the services of the Regiment, has, almost without exception, most kindly placed journals and letters in my hands, or assisted me by personal reminiscences.

The aid of my friend Lieutenant-General Sir Alfred Horsford procured for me the transcript of many valuable records and the elucidation of many points which I could not otherwise have obtained. Lieutenant-General Sir Arthur Lawrence not only communicated to me many particulars of the services of the 2nd Battalion in the Crimea, but placed in my hands his private letters written from thence, which afforded me most valuable information. Major-General Hill was so good as to draw up for me a detailed statement of the services of the 2nd Battalion, which he commanded during the Indian Mutiny. To Major-General Leicester Smyth I am indebted not only for a narrative of the battle of Berea, but also for the perusal of a private letter written by him directly after, and describing that engagement, and for much valuable information. By permission of Brigadier-General Ross, Lady Ross transmitted to me his letters to his family both from the Crimea and from India, to the perusal of which I cannot attach too great importance.

Colonel Smith, now I believe the oldest officer of the Regiment living,[1] has freely and kindly communicated to me his recollections of services in the Peninsula and elsewhere, and has patiently borne with my many enquiries which his accurate memory has enabled him to

[1] He joined the 1st Battalion in April 1808.

answer. To Colonel Dillon I am indebted for much valuable information which he kindly obtained for me. Lieutenant-Colonel Alexander was so good as to write out for me from his journals a detailed account of the movements and actions of the 3rd Battalion in India, in which he took part. Lieutenant-Colonel Sotheby had the kindness to transcribe for me his journal during the Indian Mutiny, and to illustrate it with sketch-maps. Lieutenant-Colonel FitzRoy Fremantle, Lieutenant-Colonel Eyre, Captain Percival, Captain George Curzon, and Major Harvey placed in my hands their valuable journals and diaries. Colonel H. Newdigate and Captain Austin favoured me with detailed and important particulars as to the services of the companies of Riflemen who formed the Camel Corps. To Lieutenant-Colonel Green I am indebted for his own narrative and that of Mr. Mansel (drawn up at the time) of the affair at Jamo in which he was so desperately wounded. I have to thank Captain Boyle for allowing me to see his continuation to the year 1860 of Mr. Stooks Smith's List of Officers, and for much other information. To Captain Moorsom I am under great obligations, not only for the three plans (of New Orleans, of Cawnpore, and of Lucknow) which he has contributed to this work, but for materially aiding me in obtaining important information. And to Surgeon-Major Reade I am indebted for an accurate and interesting account of the march to Cawnpore of Colonel Fyers' detachment, to which he was attached.

Sergeant-Major Bond, of the Sligo Militia, and formerly of the 1st Battalion, gave me a detailed account, from his journal, of the Kaffir War of 1847–9; and Corporal Scott, late of the 1st Battalion, communicated to me a most minute and accurate journal which he kept in short-hand during the Kaffir War of 1851–52, during the Crimean campaign, and during his service in Canada. It is not too much to say that without the valuable contributions of these two non-commissioned officers it would have been impossible to give any detailed account of the doings of the 1st Battalion during these wars Sergeant Fisher, late of the 2nd Battalion, placed in my hands an interesting journal kept during the Indian Mutiny, and Sergeant Carroll, of that Battalion, has communicated many particulars respecting the Camel Corps.

To these and to other Riflemen I owe my thanks, not only for the documents they have communicated to me, but for the kindness with which they have entertained, and the courtesy with which they have replied to my many questions for further information or details.

The officers commanding the four Battalions have given free access to, or transcripts of the several Battalion Records. These, though drawn up in obedience to an order issued in 1822, do not seem to have been compiled till some years afterwards.

That of the 1st Battalion appears to have been written by, or under the eye of, Sir Amos Norcott, who then commanded it, and by whom the transcript transmitted to the Horse Guards is signed. For it is very full and explicit in relating the actions in which he was personally engaged (as, for instance, the account of the engagement at Buenos Ayres, which bears internal evidence of having been drawn up by an eye-witness) but is rather slight and meagre in the narrative of many Peninsular and other victories.

The Record of the 2nd Battalion, transmitted to the Horse Guards, and dated March 10, 1831, is a model of what such a document should be. It has been compiled with great accuracy; and the movements and engagements of the Battalion, the lists of killed and wounded, and the distinctions won by its officers and men, are recorded under separate heads and with great minuteness.

These Recordshave been continued to the present time, for the most part with great accuracy and precision.

The Records of the 3rd and 4th Battalions have also been placed in my hands. The latter, containing, of course, only the movements of the Battalion, calls for no comment; that of the 3rd Battalion has been, in the earlier parts, kept irregularly, probably in consequence of the Battalion being broken up and constantly in the field; and no one perusing it could form an idea of, or trace accurately the distinguished service of that Battalion during the Indian Mutiny.

Nor is it to Riflemen alone that I am indebted for assistance. I have to thank Major-General Sir John Adye for permission to use the plan of Cawnpore, published in his account of those eventful days, Major-General Payn for an interesting letter on the same subject; the author of the articles on Ashantee in 'Colburn's United Service Magazine' for his liberal and unsolicited authority to use them as materials for my narrative; and especially Lieutenant-Colonel Home, R.E. for his kindness in giving me tracings of the plans of the operations at New Orleans deposited in the Quarter-Master General's Office, and for permission to have copies made of the plans prepared in the topographical department of that office for the Record of the 52nd.

I have expressed in another place the assistance I have derived from the accurately kept journal of the late Major George Simmons, and from his separate memoir on Waterloo, which were placed in my hands by his widow

I have not attempted to trace the strategical or tactical movements of the armies of which the Battalions have formed part, for two reasons: my own inability to record what has been so well described by abler pens; and also because any attempt to have done so would have swelled this book to an extent altogether disproportionate to its object.

For it must be borne in mind that I profess to be the historian, not of wars, but of this particular Corps only, and of that part it alone bore in them.

So, in like manner, I have not recorded the deeds of other regiments which may have acted with the Riflemen, save in a very few instances where it was impossible to separate the narrative of their movements from that of the movements of regiments which fought beside, or supported them. In the case of their old and most frequent companions in arms, the 43rd and 52nd, it was unnecessary that I should record their actions, since the histories of both these distinguished

Corps have been fully and well written.[1] And if others who have fought, and fought well, beside the Riflemen are here unnoticed, and as yet without a special history, they must believe that their gallant deeds, albeit unrecorded here, live in the recollection and the praise of many Riflemen.

To some readers some of the facts and anecdotes I have here recorded may appear trifling and unworthy of mention. But it must be borne in mind that I write for Riflemen, at the desire of Riflemen, and to preserve the memory of the deeds of Riflemen By them I am sure nothing will be considered trivial, nothing out of place in a history of the Regiment, which records the valour, the acts, the sufferings or even preserves an anecdote of any (of whatever rank) of the members of that brotherhood.

W. H. C.

BRAMSHILL *December* 1876

[1] 'Historical Records of the 43rd Regiment.' By Sir Richard G A. Levinge, Bart 1868.

'Historical Records of the 52nd Regiment.' Edited by Capt. W. S. Moorsom. 1860.

CONTENTS.

CHAPTER I

CHAPTER II.

CHAPTER III.

CHAPTER IV.

CHAPTER V.

CHAPTER IX.

CHAPTER X.

CHAPTER XI.

CHAPTER XII.

CHAPTER XIII.

CHAPTER XIV.

LIST OF PLATES.

[1] The position of the troops on this plan is that of November 27, 1857; but the plan will explain the actions on the other days.

*** I have not inserted plans of the Crimean actions, as accurate and detailed plans of these battles are to be found in Mr Kinglake's 'Invasion of the Crimea,' and in other works of the period, which are generally accessible.

Erratum.

Page 337, line 31: the name of the sergeant who distinguished himself is James Harrywood

THE RIFLE BRIGADE.

CHAPTER I.

TOWARDS the close of, the last century Colonel Coote Manningham and Lieutenant-Colonel the Honourable William Stewart addressed a representation to the Government, pointing out the importance of having a corps furnished with arms of precision, and the advantage of training such a corps in the special duties of Riflemen. It would have been interesting to preserve the text of this document; but I regret that it does not now exist. Every search has been made in the records of the War Department, by the kindness of Mr. Denham Robinson, of the War Office, but, I regret to say, without success; and it has been suggested that it may probably have been transferred to the Small Arms Department, and may have perished with the records of that office in the fire at the Tower of London in 1841.

However, in consequence of the suggestions it contained, the following Circular was issued to the commanding officers of fourteen regiments of infantry:—

CIRCULAR.

HORSE GUARDS *January* 17, 1800

Addressed to Officers Commanding the 2nd Battalion Royals, the 21st, 23rd, 25th, 27th, 29th, 49th, 55th, 69th, 71st, 72nd, 79th, 85th, and 92nd Regiments.

SIR,—I have the honour to inform you that it is His Royal Highness the Commander-in-Chief's[1] intention to form a corps of detachments from the different regiments of the line for the purpose of its being instructed in the use of the rifle, and in the system of exercise adopted by soldiers so armed It is His Royal Highness's pleasure that you shall select from the regiment under your command 2 sergeants, 2 corporals, and 30 private men for this duty, all of them being such men as appear most capable of receiving the above instructions, and most competent to the performance of the duty of Riflemen These non-commissioned officers and privates are not to be considered as being drafted from their regiments, but merely as detached for the purpose above recited, they will continue to be borne on the strength of their regiments, and will be clothed by their respective colonels.

[1] Frederick, Duke of York.

His Royal Highness desires you will recommend 1 captain, 1 lieutenant, and 1 ensign of the regiment under your command, who volunteer to serve in this corps of Riflemen, in order that His Royal Highness may select from the officers recommended from the regiments which furnish their quota on this occasion a sufficient number of officers for the Rifle Corps These officers are to be considered as detached on duty from their respective regiments, and will share in all the promotion that occurs in them during their absence

Eight drummers will be required to act as bugle-horns, and I request you will acquaint me, for the information of His Royal Highness, whether you have any in the — Regiment qualified to act as such, or of a capacity to be easily instructed

I have, &c.
HARRY CALVERT.
A. G

Thus we see that the Regiment was formed as a *corps d'élite*; and as regards the officers there was a double selection, eight of each rank of company officers being selected from the fourteen originally recommended.

The detachments so selected assembled at Horsham, in Sussex, in March 1800, and their first parade as 'An Experimental Corps of Riflemen' took place there on April 1 in that year; Lieutenant-Colonel the Honourable William Stewart being apparently in command.

The following is the Return of the state and strength of the Corps on this its first formation:

	Lieut.-Colonel	Captains	Lieutenants	Ensigns	Sergeants	Drummers	Rank and file
1st Foot	...	1	1	1	2	1	32
21st ,,	...	...	1	1	2	1	32
23rd ,,	...	...	...	..	2	1	32
25th ,,	...	...	1	..	2	...	32
27th ,,	.	1	1	1	2	1	32
29th ,,	...	...	1	1	2	1	32
49th ,,	...	1	1	1	2	1	32
55th ,,	...	...	1	..	2	1	32
67th ,,	1	...	1	...	..	...	...
69th ,,	...	1	1	...	2	1	32
71st ,,	...	1	..	...	2	1	32
72nd ,,	..	1	...	1	2	1	32
79th ,,	...	...	1	1	2	1	32
85th ,,	.	...	...	...	1	..	27
92nd ,,	...	..	1	1	2	1	32
Total	1	6	11	8	27	12	443
Wanting to complete					1	1	5
Establishment	1	6	11	8	28	13	448

The Corps being now formed marched to a camp of exercise at Swinley in Windsor Forest in May, and proceeded actively with their training as Riflemen. They are mentioned with great approbation by Mr. W. H. Fremantle in a letter, dated July 15, 1800, to the Marquis of Buckingham, as being 'good, and much more useful' than some other regiments then in that camp.[1] The camp broke up at the end of July, and at the request of Lieutenant-Colonel Stewart three companies of the corps (Captains Travers',[2] Hamilton's, and Gardner's) were ordered to embark, under his command, with the expedition against the north coast of Spain, under Lieutenant-General Sir James Pulteney, Bart, and Admiral Sir John Borlase Warren, K.B.

The expedition arrived before the harbour of Ferrol on August 25, and immediately commenced its disembarkation. This was effected without opposition in a small bay near Cape Prioriño; but on the troops proceeding to occupy a ridge of hills adjoining the bay, the Rifle Corps, which covered the advance, just as they gained the summit fell in with a party of the enemy which they drove back. In this skirmish Lieutenant-Colonel Stewart was dangerously wounded through the body. On the next morning, at daybreak, the position was attacked by a considerable body of the enemy, who were repulsed with much loss, and the English troops remained in complete possession of the heights. But in this action Captains Travers and Hamilton, and Lieutenant Edmonston, attached to the Rifle Corps, and eight rank and file were wounded. Sir James Pulteney being, however, of opinion that Ferrol could not be taken, or the ground he occupied be held, re-embarked the troops.[3] It was subsequently stated in the House of Lords that at the very moment he did so the proper officer was on his way with the keys of the place, to surrender it And Mr. Ford affirms that 'had the expedition sailed boldly up to the Ferrol, the Gallicians were only waiting to surrender, being, as usual, absolutely without means of defence.' He attributes the failure to the combined indecision of the leaders.[4]

[1] 'Memoirs of the Court and Cabinet of George III,' vol iii 88.

[2] Major-General Sir Robert Travers, C B, K.C M G, died at Cork, December 24, 1834.

[3] Sir James Pulteney's Despatch, August 27.

[4] 'Handbook of Spain.'

Of this, the first affair in which the Regiment was engaged, it may be observed that it has the high honour of having shed its first blood before its actual embodiment, and while it consisted only of detachments experimentally assembled for instruction. It was the only corps engaged on the day of disembarkation, and (with the exception of one officer of the 52nd) the only officers wounded were attached to it. August 25, the day on which it was first engaged, was the date of the commissions of its first officers when it was formally embodied.

The expedition then proceeded to Malta; and an order was issued by the Commander-in-Chief for all officers and men of the Rifle Corps, whose regiments formed part of the expedition, to rejoin them, and for those whose regiments were not so employed to be attached to corps serving with the expedition

Lieutenant-Colonel Stewart, Captain Travers, and Lieutenant Edmonston returned to England

The Rifle Corps was immediately re-formed, principally from detachments of fencible regiments serving in Ireland, and I presume also, on the return of the expedition, from the men originally selected as Riflemen. These detachments began to assemble at Blatchington in Sussex, near Lewes, about the end of August, and continued to join during the autumn The whole of the officers who had been attached to the experimental corps were appointed to it; their commissions being ante-dated, as I have observed, to August 25, the anniversary of which has been since observed as the foundation-day of the Regiment A second lieutenant-colonel and two majors were appointed, and some others were added to complete the Corps to eight companies, with a captain and two subalterns to each. The establishment was, therefore, on December 25, returned as follows .

Colonel	Lieut.-Colonels	Majors	Captains	First Lieutenants	Second Lieutenants	Paymaster	Adjutant	Quarter Master	Surgeon	Assistant Surgeon	Staff Sergeants	Sergeants	Buglers	Corporals	Privates
1	2	2	8	8	8	1	1	1	1	1	5	40	18	40	760

The officers on its formation were :

Colonel.

COOTE MANNINGHAM.

Lieutenant-Colonels.

THE HONOURABLE WILLIAM STEWART.
ALEXANDER HOUSTON.

Majors.

GEORGE CALLANDER.
HAMLET WADE.

Captains.

ROBERT TRAVERS.
CORNELIUS CUYLER.
THOMAS CHRISTOPHER GARDNER.
HENRY SHEPHERD.
THOMAS SIDNEY BECKWITH.
TIMOTHY HAMILTON.
ALEXANDER STEWART.

Captain-Lieutenant.

ALEXANDER D. CAMERON.

First Lieutenants.

BLOIS LYNCH.
J. A. GRANT
JOHN STUART
PETER O'HARE.
THOMAS STIRLING EDMONSTON.
ROBERT DUNCAN.
ALEXANDER CLARKE.
NIEL CAMPBELL.
JOHN ROSS
EDWARD BEDWELL LAW.
HENRY POWELL.
WILLIAM COITER.
JOHN CAMERON.
— DOUGLAS.
L. H. BENNET.

Second Lieutenants.

HENRY GOODE.
JAMES MACDONALD.
THOMAS BRERETON.
LOFTUS GRAY.
JOHN JENKINS.
PATRICK TURNER.
SAMUEL MITCHEL
GEORGE ELDER.
JAMES PENDERGAST.
JOHN BURTON.

Paymaster.

JAMES INNES.

Adjutant.

J. A. GRANT

Quarter Master.

DONALD MACKAY.

The Regiment, as it has existed since, and as it has won lasting renown in so many fields, as 'a Corps of Riflemen,' 'the Rifle Corps,'[1] 'the 95th,' and 'the Rifle Brigade,' was then and thus organised under Lieutenant-Colonel Stewart. For though Manningham was the colonel, and justly shares the honour of its formation, he seems seldom to have been present with it; for he was equerry to George III, and often at Court.

William Stewart was the fourth son of John, seventh Earl of Galloway, and at the early age of thirteen was appointed Ensign in the 42nd Regiment, but subsequently served in the 22nd and 67th, and with the former had seen service at the capture of the French West India Islands in 1793. We have seen that it was owing to Manningham's and his suggestions that the Rifle Corps was formed; and after its embodiment he also addressed a long letter to the Adjutant-General on the discipline and internal economy of such a corps. His recommendations (which were adopted) were: that it should first be formed of volunteers from infantry battalions which best could spare them, and by men from the undrafted part of the Irish militia; and he added the (rather singular) opinion that Irishmen were preferable for Riflemen, as 'perhaps from being less spoiled and more hardy than British soldiers, better calculated for light troops.'[2]

He now set himself vigorously to organise and discipline the Corps thus formed at his suggestions. The standing orders of the Regiment, which, though issued of course in Manningham's name, were probably principally compiled by Stewart, testify not only to his capability for organising and disciplining it, but in a most remarkable way to his pre-eminence above and beyond the military ideas of his time. The germs, if not, indeed, the actual existence of most of the late improvements for the training and advantage of the soldier are found in these orders. The good-conduct medal; the medals for acts of valour in the field; the attention given and the methods adopted to secure accurate shooting, dividing men into classes according to their practice at the target, and instituting a class of Marksmen; the rules for a regi-

[1] It was popularly known as 'Manningham's Sharpshooters.'
[2] 'Cumloden Papers,' 23.

mental school, and for periodical examination of its scholars; the institution of a library; the provision for lectures on military subjects, tactics and outpost duties; the encouragement of athletic exercises; these and many other plans, carried out in the British army only after the middle of the nineteenth century, are inculcated in the original standing orders, and were adopted in the Regiment from its formation.[1]

Sir Charles Napier, who was appointed to a lieutenancy in the Rifle Corps, December 25, 1800, and joined it at Blatchington, in his letters to his family, bears high testimony to Stewart's ability in organising the Corps; though he seems not to have liked him, and eventually to have quarrelled with him. 'Stewart makes it a rule to strike at the heads With him the field-officers must first be steady, and then he goes downwards: hence the privates say: "We had better look sharp if he is so strict with the officers."'[2]

In 1801 Colonel Stewart was selected to command the troops (the 49th Regiment and a company of the Rifle Corps) ordered to embark on board the fleet commanded by Admiral Sir Hyde Parker And on February 28 Captain Beckwith's[3] company, consisting of 1 captain, 2 first lieutenants, 1 second lieutenant, 5 sergeants, 2 buglers, 1 armourer, and 101 rank and file, embarked at Portsmouth on board H.M S. 'St. George,' bearing the flag of Vice-Admiral Lord Nelson. On arrival in Yarmouth Roads the right platoon of Captain Beckwith's Riflemen was shifted to the 'London,' Sir Hyde Parker's flag-ship But the men of the Rifle Corps seem to have been distributed, on arrival in the Baltic, among the ships of Nelson's squadron, which on April 2 attacked and reduced the Danish fleet at Copenhagen.

In this action First Lieutenant and Adjutant Grant was killed 'whilst gallantly fighting the quarter-deck guns of H.M.S. "Isis."' He was the first officer of the Regiment killed in action. He had volunteered for this service. His head was taken off by a cannon-ball as clean as if severed by

1 'Regulations for the Rifle Corps formed at Blatchington Barracks by Colonel Manningham' London, 1801 Stewart also published 'Outlines of a Plan for the General Reform of the British Land Forces.' a pamphlet, of which a second edition, enlarged, appeared in octavo London, 1806.

2 'Life of Sir C J. Napier,' i 19.

3 Lieutenant-General Sir T. Sidney Beckwith, K C.B., died January 19, 1831.

a scimitar Stewart recommended Second Lieutenant Pendergast, who was in the expedition, for the vacancy, and he was accordingly promoted on May 9. Two rank and file were also killed; and 1 sergeant and 5 rank and file wounded, of whom some subsequently died of their wounds.[1]

Lord Nelson, in his despatch, says: 'The Honourable Colonel Stewart did me the favour to be on board the "Elephant;" and himself, with every officer and soldier under his orders, shared with pleasure the toils and dangers of the day.'

It is said in the Record of the 1st Battalion that 'an appropriate medal was issued upon this occasion by Admiral Lord Nelson to the non-commissioned officers and several soldiers.' I have not been able to find any trace of this medal, which does not seem to have been given to the officers. For it appears from a correspondence between Stewart (then Lieutenant-General Sir William Stewart), Earl St. Vincent, and Lord Sidmouth in 1821-2, that Nelson had been desirous of obtaining a medal for the captains of his squadron who were engaged at Copenhagen, and had recommended Stewart for one; but that Lords St. Vincent and Sidmouth opposed the issue of any such medal, on the ground that it would be a very invidious distinction from those captains who, being with Parker's fleet, were not engaged. Stewart advanced a request for this medal in 1821, on the plea that, being a military man, his case was essentially different from that of the captains. But though his application was then supported by Earl St. Vincent, it was refused (in very flattering terms however) by Lord Sidmouth[2]

The Regiment marched to Weymouth in the early part of the summer, and was encamped there. Their being near Windsor the year before, and now at Weymouth, the

[1] Lieutenant-Colonel Stewart's Despatch, 'Cumloden Papers,' 41.

[2] 'Cumloden Papers,' 50, 51, 52 This service seems to have established a friendship between Stewart and Nelson, which terminated only with the great admiral's life. Several letters from him, written in very affectionate terms, to Stewart, are printed in the 'Cumloden Papers,' the last dated only thirteen days before his death off Trafalgar. Stewart also mentions incidentally that his son Horatio (who served in the Regiment) bore that name 'by the express wish of that great man who fell off Trafalgar.' He must have wished him to call his first son after him, for Horatio Stewart was not born till after Nelson's death.

summer residence of George III., was probably due to Manningham's being attached to the person of that sovereign. They returned to Blatchington barracks in the autumn.

On June 25 the establishment of the Corps was again changed, and companies were given to the field-officers, as was then the case in line regiments. But this arrangement was of short duration, for on March 27 following field-officers' companies were abolished, and effective captains were appointed in their place

In the autumn of 1802 the Regiment marched to Chatham. On this march, at Maidstone, some of the men broke open the plate-chest of the officers' mess. One of the offenders was discovered, and being tried by court-martial, was sentenced to receive 800 lashes, the whole of which were inflicted at one time.

The Regiment appears, even at this early period, to have been a favourite one with volunteers from the line and militia; and Surtees mentions four men in the ranks who had been commissioned officers; one of whom, indeed, was drawing half-pay, and was eventually recalled to full pay as lieutenant.

After a short stay at Chatham, the Regiment was moved for the winter to Shorncliffe and forts in the vicinity.

On December 25, 1802, the Rifle Corps was ordered to be numbered as the 95th Regiment, and thus assumed the name under which it was long known, and which its services on the continent of Europe made famous

In May 1803, the head-quarters, with five companies, returned to their old quarters at Blatchington, and in November moved to Colchester, and eventually to Warley and Woodbridge barracks, the other five companies, under Colonel Beckwith, remaining during the summer at Shorncliffe, where, on Colonel Stewart's promotion to Brigadier-General and command of a district, the head-quarters and other five companies joined them. Here they formed part of that camp of instruction under Sir John Moore, the marvellous results of which have been so truly and eloquently described by Sir William Napier,[1] and here they first met and were brigaded with their compeers, the 43rd and 52nd, in united action with whom, as the Light Division in the Peninsula, so many of their laurels were won.

[1] 'Life of Sir Charles Napier,' i. 58, 59

During the time the Regiment was encamped at Shorncliffe, Colonel Manningham, carrying out the intentions of his own standing orders, delivered a course of lectures on the duties of Riflemen in active service, which he published.[1]

On the breaking up of that camp, the Regiment moved into Hythe barracks till April 1805, when it appears to have returned to Shorncliffe.

On May 6, 1805, the 2nd Battalion was formed by the transfer of 21 sergeants, 20 corporals, 7 buglers, and 250 privates from the original Corps (now the 1st Battalion); the remainder of the proposed establishment being made up by volunteers from the militia; 1 major (Gardner), 6 captains and 3 first lieutenants being promoted from the 1st Battalion, which also supplied the adjutant. The command and formation of the Battalion was conferred on Wade,[2] of the 1st Battalion, who was promoted to the rank of lieutenant-colonel; and so vigorously did he proceed in its organisation, that in less than three months it wanted only 7 sergeants,

[1] 'Military Lectures delivered to the officers of the 95th (Rifle) Regiment, at Shorn-Cliff Barracks, Kent, during the Spring of 1803.' By Coote Manningham, Colonel of the 95th (Rifle) Regiment. Octavo, London, 1803, pp. 70. And see p. 7.

In the same year appeared 'Regulations for the Exercise of Riflemen and Light Infantry in the Field,' octavo, pp. 70, with diagrams and two pages of bugle sounds. What share, if any, Manningham or Stewart had in these books, I am unable to trace. A preface (signed by the Adjutant-General) states that it is founded on a work written by a German officer of distinction.

[2] Hamlet Wade was one of the original members of the Regiment, having been promoted to a majority on its formation, from captain in the 25th Foot. He was an extraordinary, gallant, dashing Irishman (he was one of the Wades of Clonabraney, County Meath), and anecdotes of him were still rife when I was in the Regiment. Surtees mentions Wade's praise and his rewards to him for his good shooting, when he joined as a volunteer. He was an admirable shot with the rifle himself. He and a private of the name of Smeaton used to hold a target for each other at 150 yards; and it is said (Smith's 'List of Officers,' 58) that he and John Spurry, a private in the Regiment, held the target for each other at 200 yards: a wonderful feat, while the Baker rifle was still in use. There used to be a story of him at an inspection by the old Earl of Chatham, who expressed a wish to see some practice with the rifle, and having made some remark on the danger of the markers, Wade said: 'There is no danger,' and calling one of the men (no doubt Smeaton or Spurry), bade him hold a target, and he himself taking a rifle fired and hit it. Lord Chatham's horror at this was extreme, on which Wade said: 'Oh, we all do it.' And bidding the other to take a loaded rifle, he ran out himself and held the target for the soldier's fire. Probably no other men in the Regiment but themselves could have done this. Colonel Wade, C.B., died February 13, 1821, having retired from the army.

6 buglers, and 98 privates to complete its full strength. It was formed at Canterbury, but moved to Brabourn Lees, near Ashford, in June, where it was brigaded with the 1st Battalion.

It was while the two Battalions were stationed at Brabourn Lees that a singular instance of self-control and magnanimity was shown by Sidney Beckwith, then commanding the 1st Battalion. Some men, volunteers from the Irish militia, meeting Mrs. Beckwith, with her child and nurse, on the Ashford Road, most grossly insulted them, proceeding to such lengths (Surtees says) as delicacy forbids to mention. The culprits were discovered, but not punished, for Beckwith next day on parade forming the Battalion into square, addressed them; and, after relating the outrage, added: 'Although I know who the ruffians are, I will not proceed any further in the business because it was my own wife whom they attacked; but had it been the wife of the meanest soldier in the Regiment, I solemnly declare I would have given the offenders every lash to which a Court-Martial might have sentenced them.' It is no wonder that by such acts of generosity, as well as by his leading them in the field, this man 'won the heart of every soldier in the Battalion,' as Surtees tells us, who served in the ranks under him.

So rapidly and effectually had the 2nd Battalion been organised, that it was in September of this year ordered on service, the right wing being marched to Dover to embark for the Continent, and the left wing to Winchester, to prepare to embark for the Mediterranean. However, it was subsequently countermanded, the right wing, from Dover, being marched to Hailsham in October, and the left from Winchester to Eastbourne; and both in November assembled at Bexhill, where they were quartered till March 1806.

In October 1805 the head-quarters and five companies of the 1st Battalion, under Beckwith, marched to Deal, and embarked at Ramsgate for Germany, in the expedition commanded by Lord Cathcart. After a stormy passage, in which some part of the Battalion seems to have been in great danger from the misconduct of the master of a transport,[1] they reached the Elbe in November, and on the 18th disembarked at Cuxhaven, and marched at once for Dorum, a village twelve or

[1] Surtees gives the story at length, 53–55.

fourteen miles distant, and proceeded by Osterholz and Bremerlehe to Bremen, the Riflemen forming the advanced guard. On their arrival before Bremen on the 24th, the barriers were shut, and the commandant of the Prussian garrison refused to let the troops enter; the Senate of Bremen also demurring to General Don's request for a passage through the place, on account of its neutrality. However, Beckwith, who commanded the advanced corps, was not the man to be daunted by such refusals He accordingly informed the Prussian commandant that unless his corps was admitted he should force an entrance. This he did on the morning of the 26th, opening the barriers by force, apparently without any armed resistance; and the refusal of the Senate seems to have been prompted rather by coyness than dislike, for the authorities of the town and the inhabitants generally received the advanced guard with expressions of friendship and satisfaction, the Prussian garrison alone looking on these tokens of welcome with great dissatisfaction. The Riflemen passed on, still in advance, to Delmenhorst, a Prussian regiment accompanying them through the city and across the bridge over the Weser, in order to guard their magazine of corn at Bremen for the use of their army on the Weser. From Delmenhorst the Riflemen were detached: three companies at Oldenburg, and two, under Major Robert Travers, at Wildeshausen, on outpost duty. These last were soon moved back to Delmenhorst, and shortly after reunited to the other three companies at Oldenburg Here they were welcomed and entertained by the inhabitants, and by none more than by the reigning Grand-Duke of Oldenburg, who became extremely fond of the Regiment, officers and men. In consequence of the battle of Austerlitz in December, and the powerful armies set free by that event, and by Mack's surrender of Ulm, to act against us in the North of Europe, the outposts were withdrawn to Delmenhorst, and eventually into Bremen; and on their march from Oldenburg the Duke sent forward plentiful refreshments for the Riflemen, both officers and men.

They continued at Bremen till February 1806, when the army moved towards a place of embarkation, Beckwith's force covering the retreat; but as great numbers of the Germans, who formed part of the British army there, were deserting, the 95th were directed to remain in the villages in order to intercept them However, eventually Beckwith's Riflemen also retreated, and embarking at Cuxhaven, arrived and landed at Yarmouth on the 19th ; thence they marched, by Lowestoft, to Woodbridge barracks, where they rejoined the remainder of the Battalion. During this abortive expedition they had never, I believe, been engaged with the enemy

From Woodbridge the Battalion marched, in the spring of 1806, to Deal, and afterwards to quarters at Ospringe and Faversham, where they joined the 2nd Battalion, which had moved there from Bexhill.

On June 13 three companies of the 2nd Battalion (Captains Macdonald's, Elder's, and Dickenson's), under the command of Major Gardner, marched from Faversham and embarked at Portsmouth, as part of the force under Sir Samuel Auchmuty, destined for service in South America. The transports in which the troops were embarked were in such bad condition that they were obliged to put into Rio ; and it was not until January 16, 1807, that a landing was effected at Maldonado, near the mouth of the river La Plata This operation was not accomplished without opposition, in which one bugler was killed and Lieutenant Chawner wounded The General moved forward and occupied the suburbs of Monte Video, with a view to investing the place On the morning of the 20th the enemy made a sortie, and attacked our troops with a force of 6,000 men. They advanced in two columns, one of which pressed our picquet so hard, that Colonel Gore Browne, of the 40th, who commanded the left of our line, ordered up three companies of that regiment in support. These companies fell in with the head of the enemy's column and very bravely charged it. The charge was as bravely received, and great numbers fell on both sides. At length the column began to give way, when it was suddenly and impetuously attacked in flank by the Riflemen and by a light battalion which Auchmuty had ordered up. The column then gave way on all sides, and was pursued with great slaughter to the town. The other column, observing the fate of their companions, retired without coming into action. In this sortie the Riflemen lost 5 men killed and 25 wounded

A breach having been effected, Auchmuty resolved to

assault the place, and an hour before daybreak on the morning of February 3 the attacking column moved forward It was headed by the Riflemen under Gardner; the storming party being led by Captain Dickenson at the head of his own company They got near the walls before they were discovered, when a destructive fire was opened from every gun that could bear on the column and from the musketry of the garrison. The enemy had piled up hides in the breach; and unfortunately, in the darkness, its situation was not immediately discovered, and the troops remained under a heavy fire for a quarter of an hour At last the breach was discovered and pointed out by Captain Renny, of the 40th (which formed part of the attacking column), who fell in the assault. Our troops at once mounted it, led by Dickenson and the Riflemen, and forced their way into the town; and though cannon placed at the head of all the principal streets opened a destructive fire, the place was taken and occupied.

In this gallant affair Dickenson fell gloriously at the head of his company; 10 rank and file were killed, and Lieutenants Scanlan and Macnamara, 4 sergeants, and 15 rank and file were wounded. The Riflemen engaged were specially thanked in General Orders; and eleven sergeants received silver medals under the sanction of the Duke of York, Commander-in-Chief, for their gallantry on this occasion.

The three companies under Gardner remained in La Plata until they were joined in May by a wing of the 1st Battalion

This force, consisting of five companies (Norcott's,[1] O'Hare's,[2] Jenkinson's, Ramage's, and Bennett's), under the command of Majors M'Leod and Travers, and numbering 25 sergeants and 370 rank and file, marched from Faversham on July 23, 1806, and embarked at Gravesend on the 26th on board the 'Chapman,' armed transport Their voyage was a slow one They sailed on the 27th, remained at anchor in the Downs from the 30th till August 4, arrived on the 21st in Plymouth Sound, were disembarked on September 2, and encamped on Buckland Down till the 13th, when they re-embarked, Norcott's and Bennett's companies being placed

[1] Major-General Sir Amos G R Norcott, K C.H, died January 8, 1838.

[2] Major O'Hare was killed at Badajos

on board the 'Alexander' transport. They did not sail, however, till October 6, and then only to Falmouth; the other ship, with the head-quarters, having preceded them on September 28.

On October 24, Brigadier-General Robert Craufurd (under whom the Regiment served subsequently so long and so gloriously in other fields) arrived at Falmouth and took command of the troops assembled in that harbour for (as it was then called) 'the remote expedition'

It sailed on November 12, and arrived in Porto Praza Bay, in the island of St. Jago (Cape Verde) on December 14. Here Craufurd, with the zeal for discipline which always distinguished him, minutely inspected the troops forming the expedition, on board the several transports The companies of the 95th were frequently landed for exercise during their stay at this island They sailed from St. Jago on January 11, 1807, and anchored in Simon's Bay, Cape of Good Hope, on March 14, and in Table Bay on the 20th.

Here General Craufurd received instructions to proceed, not to the coast of Chili, to which the expedition was originally destined, but to the river La Plata to join the force under Sir Samuel Auchmuty. The troops therefore sailed on April 6, and arrived at St. Helena on the 21st, sailed again on the 26th, and anchored in the river La Plata on the 27th. They were not, however, disembarked; and on June 4 a most violent gale drove the ships out to sea, and they did not reach Monte Video till the 14th. Every preparation having been completed for the service on which it was about to be employed, the expedition, comprising the troops under General Craufurd and those already at Monte Video under Sir Samuel Auchmuty, sailed on June 17. General Whitelocke had been appointed to command the whole force, most unfortunately, as the event proved, and assumed his command at Monte Video. On the 27th they arrived at Ensenada de Barragon, about thirty miles to the eastward of Buenos Ayres, where they disembarked on the morning of the 28th, at nine o'clock[1] After some fatiguing marches through a country much intersected by swamps and muddy rivulets, the army reached Reduction, a village nine miles distant

[1] The five 1st Battalion companies had thus been *eleven months* on board ship.

from the bridge over the Rio Chuello, on the opposite bank of which the enemy had constructed a formidable line of defence The General resolved to cross the river higher up and to turn this position On the evening of July 2, the light division of General Gower's column crossed at the ford of Passo Chico; the Chuello was about waist-deep, and the Riflemen carried their pouches on their shoulders. They were soon seriously engaged with the enemy. They charged rapidly, and overthrew their opponents in a few minutes, with great loss, taking twelve guns. In this affair Major Travers and the officers and men of both Battalions serving with this force greatly distinguished themselves. One sergeant and 1 private of the 1st Battalion were killed, and 2 sergeants and 10 rank and file wounded; and 1 private of the 2nd Battalion was killed, and Captain Elder and 10 rank and file wounded.[1]

The left column, with the Commander of the Forces, united with that under Major-General Gower in the suburbs of Buenos Ayres on the afternoon of July 3, and the whole army was placed in position. Two companies of the 1st Battalion, under Major Norcott, were immediately detached to occupy an advanced post, and became warmly engaged until dark; by which time they had completely dislodged a very superior force of the enemy from every point in their front which they were ordered to occupy

On the morning of the 4th this picquet was furiously attacked by several hundreds of the enemy, whose continued exertions to dislodge it proved fruitless. Major M'Leod joined the post about the middle of the day, and distinguished himself by his gallantry and judicious arrangements. This affair lasted until dusk, and our loss amounted to 2 officers (Lieutenants James Coane and Charles Noble) severely wounded, 1 sergeant and 1 rank and file killed, and 2 sergeants and 2 rank and file wounded. The two companies were relieved at night by a detachment of the 36th, and joined the army in its position.

[1] The three companies of the 2nd Battalion at Monte Video had been engaged, on June 7, at San Pedro, when Major Gardner and Assistant-Surgeon Turner, 1 sergeant and 26 rank and file were wounded. I find no particulars of this affair beyond the mention of it, and the casualties, in the Record of the 2nd Battalion

Orders were received during the early part of the night for the attack of the town at daylight on the 5th. The five companies of the 1st Battalion formed a part of the column of attack under Brigadier-General Craufurd and Lieutenant-Colonel Packe, leaving one company as an advanced guard to each division, supported by a light company. Major Travers commanded the advance of the right column and Major Norcott that of the left.

The companies of the 2nd Battalion seem to have been attached to Sir Samuel Auchmuty's division, the light battalion of which was divided into wings, each followed by a party of the 95th These troops were all unloaded, and were directed not to fire until the columns had reached their final points and formed

At the appointed signal the troops were in motion. The right column proceeded down the line of street it was directed to take, until it nearly reached the river; when, turning to the left, with the view of making for the Franciscan Convent and taking possession of it, it was assailed from the parapets and windows of every house along the whole street in so vigorous a manner as to render it impossible to penetrate further without the probable loss of every officer and man. Orders were at this moment given to retire, and General Craufurd took post in the great Convent of St. Domingo, occupying as many houses as his means enabled him to break into, on the flat parapetted tops of which the troops formed. Every possible effort was made to assail the enemy from all parts of the Convent, but without success; for those points which the men were enabled to reach were mostly commanded by the neighbouring houses on one side, which the Riflemen had not been able to force open, and from which fire they suffered dreadfully. With the exception of the operations of the force under Sir Samuel Auchmuty, and of the 45th Regiment, every point of attack failed.

The capture of the 88th Regiment, together with the Light Brigade under Lieutenant-Colonels Packe and Cadogan, and the immense loss of killed and wounded, furnished the enemy with such powerful means of attack that at three o'clock he had dislodged our force from every house they occupied, and confined our operations entirely to one or two points of the Convent. The loss of officers and men at this time increased most considerably. Every effort was made to preserve the posts, but, finding his troops deprived of all means of succour, or prospect of success in holding out, having ascertained the fate of the neighbouring columns, and further resistance proving quite useless, the Brigadier surrendered with his column at four o'clock in the afternoon, and the officers and men were immediately marched as prisoners to the citadel and other buildings. Major M'Leod, of the 95th, however, on Craufurd consulting the field-officers in the Convent, was the only one who demurred to the necessity of surrendering. But when Craufurd offered, if M'Leod was decidedly of opinion that they could force their way out, to head the column with him, he declined the responsibility.[1]

The left column moved as directed until it came in view of the river; it had scarcely approached the Franciscan Convent when, by an almost invisible fire, it lost nearly half its officers and men. Finding it impossible to penetrate to the objects of attack, Lieutenant-Colonel Packe acceded to Lieutenant-Colonel Cadogan's taking possession of some houses. This was effected, and they were afterwards defended to the last extremity by that officer and Major Travers; but they were at length compelled to surrender, having suffered most severely in killed and wounded, and all chance of further resistance being deemed useless on account of the capture of the column on their left. Nothing could exceed the persevering gallantry and conduct of every officer and man of the Regiment engaged on this unfortunate day.[2]

The loss of the five companies of the 1st Battalion was Captain Jenkinson, 2 sergeants, 2 buglers, and 36 rank and file, killed; Captain O'Hare, Lieutenants Cadoux, Macleod, and Turner,[3] wounded severely; Majors Travers and M'Leod, and Lieutenant M'Cullock, wounded slightly; and

[1] 'Brigadier Craufurd's Evidence on Whitelocke's Court-martial,' p. 335-6.

[2] Two majors, 5 captains, 19 subalterns, 3 staff, 24 sergeants, 12 buglers, and 495 rank and file of the Rifle Corps (including the wounded) surrendered to the enemy. 'Return in Whitelocke's Court-Martial,' Appendix, p. 45.

[3] Lieutenant Patrick Turner died of his wounds.

8 sergeants, 2 buglers, and 73 rank and file wounded; and 2 sergeants, 2 buglers, and 39 rank and file missing

Of the three companies of the 2nd Battalion the loss was 3 sergeants, 1 bugler, and 46 rank and file killed; and Lieutenants Hill[1] and Scott, 6 sergeants, and 40 rank and file wounded.

In consequence of the treaty which had been concluded on the 7th, the prisoners were released on the morning of the 8th July, and joined the different posts occupied by the army.

Every arrangement having been completed for the evacuation of the country on the south side of the river La Plata, the army was embarked by the 12th, sailed on the 13th, and anchored at Monte Video on the 15th.

On August 8 the five companies of the 1st Battalion sailed for England, and arrived at Falmouth on November 9. They proceeded to Dover by sea about the end of January, 1808, whence they marched to Shorncliffe barracks, and soon after to Colchester to join the other five companies of the Battalion, to which station they had moved after their return from Germany.[2]

The three companies of the 2nd Battalion embarked also, under Major Gardner, on July 12th. They landed at Portsmouth on December 2, and joined the Battalion at Hythe on the 18th.

But we must return to the companies of both Battalions which remained in England. In July, 1807, five companies of the 1st Battalion, under Colonel Beckwith, and five companies of the 2nd Battalion, under Colonel Wade, embarked at Deal with the expedition to Denmark under Lord Cathcart. They arrived in the Sound on August 18, and disembarked at Veldbeck, about ten or twelve miles from Copenhagen, on the 16th. Immediately on landing, the Riflemen of both Battalions were sent on in advance towards Copenhagen. And here first they served under the immediate command of the great chief, who commanded the advance; under whose eye they were so often to fight; whose praise they were so

[1] Major-General Sir Dudley St Leger Hill, K C B., died February 21, 1851.

[2] 'Annual Register,' xlix, 'London Gazette,' September 13, 1807; and Record of the 1st Battalion This narrative is evidently drawn up by an eye-witness · no doubt Sir Amos Norcott, by whom the regimental Record is signed.

often to receive: their future Colonel, then Major-General Sir Arthur Wellesley.

To this march no opposition was offered by the enemy; a small patrol of cavalry appeared in their front, but retired on the approach of the Riflemen. They halted for the night at Lingbye, rested on their arms all night, and early next morning again advanced, and about mid-day took up a position within a long gunshot of Copenhagen, and invested the place.

About three o'clock on that day (August 17) a considerable body of the enemy advanced from the town and attacked the picquets on the left of the line towards the seashore. This small force, consisting of four companies of the 2nd Battalion and six of two line regiments, in all not more than 1,000 men with two light field-pieces, were opposed to about 3,000 of the enemy. But almost as soon as they came in contact the Danes gave way and retired into the town, leaving a good many dead and wounded. The detachment of the 2nd Battalion lost 1 man killed, and 2 men were wounded.

On the 19th the 2nd Battalion was moved further to the right, and nearer to the town; and from this day till the 24th a constant fire was kept up between the advanced posts and the place; by which, however, no loss seems to have been inflicted on the Riflemen. On the 24th they were under arms at two o'clock in the morning, and immediately advanced, driving in the Danish outposts; in this operation they encountered considerable opposition, and had some skirmishing among the gardens and suburbs. During the 25th a constant fire both of artillery and small arms was kept up from the place, by which a battalion of the German Legion suffered rather severely. They were relieved on outpost duty a little before dark by the 2nd Battalion, who did not lose a man at this post. On the 26th a division was formed, under Sir Arthur Wellesley, to which the two Battalions of the 95th were attached; and they were ordered to proceed into the interior to disperse a large body of militia and armed peasantry. They marched about three P.M., and made their way through the country on the left of the great road to Roeskild. They halted that night at Cagstrup, and next morning continued to advance towards Kioge, halting in the evening at a village near Roeskild. The troops were now, or just previously, formed into two brigades, the five companies of the 1st Battalion being attached to that under the immediate command of Sir Arthur Wellesley, and those of the 2nd Battalion to General Baron Linsingen's brigade.

On the 29th Sir Arthur Wellesley attacked the Danish army, which was established in position on the north side of the town and rivulet of Kioge. He sent round Baron Linsingen's brigade to cross the rivulet at Salbye and fall upon the enemy's left flank, while Sir Arthur himself advanced on his front, covered by the 1st Battalion skirmishers. The enemy gave way at once before an attack by the 92nd, and retreated in disorder, 'followed in the most gallant style by the 1st Battalion of the 95th,'[1] and eventually by the whole infantry. Major-General Oxholm, the second in command of the Danish army, attempted to make a stand with the rear-guard in the village of Hervolge, but was briskly attacked by some German hussars and a company of the 2nd Battalion; and though he took up a strong position in the churchyard, which was considerably higher than any other part of the village, he was, after a short resistance, compelled to surrender with several officers and about 400 men. In this action at Kioge the loss suffered by the 95th appears to have been inconsiderable; no mention of casualties appears in the 2nd Battalion Record; Sir Arthur Wellesley says that 'a few men of the 95th fell.'[2] They must have belonged to the 1st Battalion. The conduct and steadiness of the 1st Battalion of the 95th, under Colonel Beckwith, are 'mentioned particularly' in Sir Arthur Wellesley's despatch.[3]

The two Battalions were engaged all the remainder of the 29th and during the 30th in scouring the woods near Kioge, in order to complete the dispersion of the Danish force and to prevent its reassembling. They reached Ringstæd on the 31st; and as the regular portion of the troops of the enemy had retired into one of the islands, and the militia had entirely disbanded itself, they halted here till after the surrender of

[1] 'Wellington Despatches,' iv. 4.

[2] 'Supplementary Despatches,' vi. 10. It is strange that no mention of their services in this expedition appears in the 1st Battalion Record. That of the 2nd Battalion mentions only the casualties on the 17th before Copenhagen.

[3] 'Wellington Despatches,' iv. 4.

Copenhagen on September 7. But during this halt detachments were occasionally sent out to search for and disperse any lurking parties of the enemy, and to bring in arms or stores. One of these detachments, consisting of 100 men of the 2nd Battalion, mounted in light German waggons, scoured a considerable tract of country, and took possession of ten guns of small calibre, forty rifles, and a number of muskets.

The terms of the capitulation of Copenhagen extended only to the British and Danish forces in the Island of Zealand, and the troops were, therefore, still liable to attack from any Danish force which might be reassembled on the mainland or in the other islands. Strong outposts were therefore established in the towns and villages along the Belt, and the two Rifle Battalions were employed on this service; the 1st Battalion occupying Callundborg, Slagelse, Corsoer, and Skielskior; and the 2nd Battalion, Nestved, Lundbye, Wordingborg, and Præstoe. They remained in their cantonments till October 15, when they retired towards Copenhagen, which they reached on the 17th The two Battalions embarked on board the 'Princess Caroline,' 74, a Danish prize, sailed on the 21st, arrived in Yarmouth Roads in November, and (after a stormy passage) at Dover on the 15th, landed next day at Deal, and joined their Battalions at Hythe[1]

On April 8, 1808, three companies of the 1st Battalion (Major Norcott's, Captains Ross'[2] and O'Hare's), under the command of Major Gilmour, marched to Harwich, embarked the next day, sailed the following day, and joined the troops assembled in Yarmouth Roads destined for the Baltic, under Sir John Moore, to co-operate with Sweden. They arrived at Gottenburg on May 17, but owing to misunderstandings with the King of Sweden they never landed; and having remained on board their transports nearly ten weeks, they sailed at the latter end of July, and eventually landed in Portugal, at Peniche, at the end of August, and formed a junction with the force under Sir Arthur Wellesley.

But previously to their arrival there, two companies from those of the Battalion remaining in England (Captains

[1] Surtees, 60-72 Leach, 28-38 'Wellington Despatches,' iv. and Supplementary Despatches,' vi

[2] Major-General Sir John Ross, K C.B, died April 31, 1835

Cameron's[1] and Ramage's), under Colonel Beckwith, embarked at Harwich early in July. The strength of this detachment was about 180 men;[2] these landed on August 19, a few days before Major Gilmour's force, which was immediately united to it.

About the same time four companies of the 2nd Battalion, under the command of Major Robert Travers, had embarked at Dover on June 8, and formed part of the force destined for Portugal under Sir Arthur Wellesley The transports assembled in Cork harbour early in July. The strength of the detachment of the 2nd Battalion was 1 field-officer, 4 captains, 13 subalterns, 1 staff, 20 sergeants, 8 buglers, and 399 rank and file.[3] These disembarked at Figueira, in Mondego Bay, on August 1, 1808.

These four 2nd Battalion companies were attached to General Fane's brigade, and, immediately after disembarkation, pushed on, keeping their right towards the sea, several miles over an unbroken plain of white sand. The men, who had been many weeks on board ship, were much fatigued by this their first day's march, as the weather was hot, and the sand so loose that they sank ankle-deep every step They encamped at night near the village of Lavaos, to which the rest of the army moved up as soon as they disembarked. On August 9, these companies, forming part of the advance, marched from Lavaos about three o'clock in the morning Their destination was Leiria, and their orders were, if the enemy were in strength at Leiria not to drive him out till the 10th, but to halt in the pine-woods which cover the country between Lavaos and Leiria. And General Hill was ordered to let 200 Riflemen and a few dragoons feel their way into Leiria, and if they obtained possession to support them with his whole corps[4] However, the French had evacuated Leiria before the Riflemen entered it, and it bore terrible marks of their cruelty and excesses.

The army marched hence towards Lisbon, the Riflemen still forming the advance, and daily expecting to fall in with the enemy, who were gradually retiring before them. The first meeting took place at Obidos on the evening of August 15, where, after a long march, a party of French

[1] Major-General Sir Alexander Cameron, K C.B , died July 20, 1850

[2] 'Wellington Despatches,' iv 28 [3] Ibid iv. 27 [4] Ibid. iv. 77.

cavalry and infantry were found These were immediately attacked by the Riflemen under Major Travers, together with some of the 60th, and forced to retire. In the eagerness of this first encounter the pursuit was continued too far, and the Riflemen pushed on to a distance of three miles from Obidos, and quite away from any support. They were then attacked by a superior body of the enemy, who attempted to cut them off from the main body of the detachment to which they belonged, which now advanced to their support Larger bodies of the enemy appeared on both flanks, and it was with some difficulty that General Spencer, who had gone out to Obidos, when he heard that the Riflemen had advanced, was able to extricate them [1] In this sharp skirmish Lieutenant Bunbury and 2 men were killed, and Captain Pakenham [2] and 6 men wounded. Ralph Bunbury was the first English officer who fell in the Peninsula. Harris says that he was 'the first man that was hit;' and he was much regretted by his brother officers. It is painful to add that this first blood was spilt, in Sir Arthur Wellesley's opinion, unnecessarily. 'The affair,' he writes to Lord Castlereagh, 'was unpleasant, because it was quite useless; and was occasioned solely by the imprudence of the officer and the dash and eagerness of the men; they behaved remarkably well, and did some execution with their rifles.' [3] And to the Duke of Richmond he says, 'that it was foolishly brought on by the over-eagerness of the Riflemen in the pursuit of an enemy's picquet, the troops behaved remarkably well, but not with great prudence.' [4]

They held possession that night of an extensive knoll near the road by which the enemy had retired, and were under arms till morning, when they occupied the village of Obidos till the morning of the 17th.

Early on that day they advanced towards Roleia,[5] where,

[1] 'Wellington Despatches,' iv. 94.

[2] Afterwards Major-General Sir Hercules R. Pakenham, K C.B. The Duke of Wellington, applying for his promotion on October 15 following, mentions his being wounded in this affair, and adds 'that he is really one of the best officers of Riflemen that I have seen' ('Supplementary Despatches,' vi 160) He was his brother-in-law He remained in the Regiment till 1810

[3] 'Wellington Despatches,' iv 95

[4] 'Supplementary Despatches,' vi 115.

[5] Properly *Roliça* I retain the name granted to the Regiment, and borne on its badge

after a march of two or three hours, they found the enemy, under General Laborde, posted in a strong position on high ground, having Roleia and several passes into the mountains in his rear. The four companies formed part of General Fane's brigade, which attacked the enemy's position in front; but some were detached to cover the advance of General Ferguson's brigade, which operated on the right of Laborde's posts at Roleia. As soon as the army moved, the Riflemen of Fane's brigade were sent into the hills on the left of the valley, in order to keep up the communication between the centre and the left columns, and to cover the advance of the former; and the enemy's outposts were rapidly driven in. He was pressed by the attacking force in his front; Hill's division advanced against his left, and the Riflemen were in the hills on his right. From this position he extricated himself by a rapid retreat by the passes into the mountains, where he took up a formidable position. The Riflemen were already on his right, and no time was lost in supporting them and attacking the different passes. These were all difficult of access, and it is well known that they were forced with great courage and impetuosity, especially by the 9th and 29th Regiments. Here, however, I have only to do with the part borne by the 95th; and their conduct during the day elicited the approval of Sir Arthur Wellesley. They were almost all young soldiers, and few of them had ever been under fire; yet, engaged with the French light troops during an intensely hot day, they succeeded in driving them before them from pass to pass, and mountain to mountain, in spite of a destructive fire from thick heath and brushwood, which hid their opponents from them. During this fight the Riflemen were fearfully galled by the fire from two houses which the French light troops occupied, and some high ground in front of the buildings gave them a further advantage. At last the Riflemen could stand it no longer, and one of them, jumping up and rushing forward, exclaimed, 'Over, boys! over, over!' In a moment every one of them was dashing forward, repeating the cry, 'Over, over!' and fixing their sword-bayonets as they ran up the rising ground. The voltigeurs could not stand this, but turned and fled; and the Riflemen soon entered and cleared out the houses. Their loss was 17 rank and file killed, and Captain Creagh and Lieutenants Hill and Cochrane, and 30 rank and file wounded. It was during this action that an incident occurred, which I give in Leach's own words, who records it[1]:

'Having driven the enemy from one of the highest mountains, and in the act of collecting our men on its summit to renew the attack on a second position to which they had retired, one of my brother officers, whilst holding his canteen to my mouth to give me some wine, well mulled by the sun, received a musket-shot through his hand and through the canteen, which latter it split, splashed my face thoroughly with wine, spoiled my draught, gave me a sharp blow, which cut my mouth, and spun me round like a top. For a few moments I concluded that I was wounded; but the mystery was soon explained by my seeing my friend on the ground bleeding profusely, and the broken canteen at his side. I sent a soldier with him to the rear; and notwithstanding that his wound was for a length of time afterwards painful and troublesome, we had the pleasure to see him rejoin us in a few weeks. A more gallant soldier, sincere friend, or a more independent, straightforward, manly fellow than Cochrane, never wore His Majesty's uniform. In proof of the high estimation in which he was held by his Corps, suffice it to say, that his brother officers erected a monument to his memory in Ireland,[2] where he died a few years after the termination of the war in the Peninsula and Waterloo, in both of which he was actively engaged.'

[1] Leach, 47.

[2] At Kinsale, where is this inscription in the church

SACRED TO THE MEMORY OF

LIEUTENANT THOMAS COCHRANE

OF THE RIFLE BRIGADE.

HE DIED IIND OF JULY MDCCCXXIII., AGED XXXIV. YEARS.

AS A SOLDIER

HIS ZEAL, GALLANTRY, AND INTELLIGENCE

RENDERED HIM VALUABLE TO HIS COUNTRY;

AS A MAN

HIS PRIVATE VIRTUES, EMBRACING EVERY ENNOBLING AND ENDEARING QUALIFICATION,

SECURED TO HIM THE ESTEEM AND LASTING ATTACHMENT OF HIS BROTHER OFFICERS, WHO HAVE RAISED THIS MONUMENT TO HIS MEMORY

On the 20th the two companies of the 1st Battalion which had embarked at Harwich, and had landed at Maceira on the day before, joined the army, which was then in position near Vimiera.

On the night of the 20th, a detachment of the 2nd Battalion, with some of the 60th, in all about 200 men, were on picquet in a large pine wood, on the road from Lourinha to Torres Vedras. About eight in the morning of the 21st, a cloud of light troops, followed by a strong column of the enemy, entering the wood, vigorously attacked this picquet and drove it in on the 97th, which was in support. As soon as the Riflemen had cleared the front of this regiment, passing by its right flank to the rear, the 97th poured a steady fire on the advancing column and held it in check, while the 52nd took it in flank and drove it back in confusion.[1] This picquet, on being driven in, rejoined the other 2nd Battalion companies. With this attack began the Battle of Vimiera. The Riflemen were soon assailed by a swarm of light troops, who covered the advance of large masses of infantry. These pressed on up the hill on which the Riflemen were posted, in spite of a deadly fire which they poured upon them, until, the Riflemen running in, the 50th received them with a destructive volley and a furious charge, which sent them, broken, down the hill in confusion, with the loss of seven guns and many prisoners. In this fight, three brothers of the name of Hart, privates in the 2nd Battalion, pressed on the French with such daring intrepidity, that Lieutenant Molloy, who himself was never far from his opponent in action, was obliged repeatedly to rebuke them: 'D—n you!' he cried, 'keep back and get under cover. Do you think you are fighting with your fists, that you run into the teeth of the French!'

In the meanwhile the enemy were attacked in flank on our left by General Acland's brigade, to which the two 1st Battalion companies were attached.

In his despatch of this victory and in General Orders Sir Arthur Wellesley particularly notices the valour and discipline of the 2nd Battalion of the 95th under Major Travers.[2]

[1] Leach, 50, who was on this picquet.

[2] 'Wellington Despatches,' iv. 111; and 'Supplementary Despatches,' vi. 121.

In this battle the 2nd Battalion suffered severely; 3 sergeants and 34 rank and file having been killed, and Lieutenants Manners, Hill, James Johnson, William Cox, 3 sergeants, and 40 rank and file wounded As they had left England about 400 strong, and had suffered at Obidos and Roleia, about one-fourth of their effective strength was put *hors-de-combat* at Vimiera.

No record exists of the casualties, if any, of the 1st Battalion companies on this day

The two 1st Battalion companies, which had landed with General Acland's brigade, were immediately after the action transferred to General Fane's brigade, where they joined the four 2nd Battalion companies.

As I am the historian not of the War but of the Regiment, I need only add that, owing to the evacuation of Portugal by Junot's army, and the Convention of Cintra, the portion of the Corps in the Peninsula was not actively employed for some months.

But at the end of August, the three companies of the 1st Battalion, which had been to Sweden with Sir John Moore, and had been disembarked in the Mondego on the 28th, joined their comrades in camp at Torres Vedras There were now, therefore, five companies of the 1st and four of the 2nd on active service.

Early in September the five 1st Battalion companies moved across the Tagus to Villa Viciosa, where they were quartered, and the four 2nd Battalion companies soon after drew towards Lisbon, and encamped near it. The French army had not yet embarked, and the best feeling existed between our men and their late opponents, Riflemen and French soldiers walking about the streets of Lisbon and drinking together in the wine-shops.

Sir John Moore soon after assumed the command of the army, and moved from before Lisbon at the end of October. The Riflemen, marching with the central division, under Moore himself, on the 27th, by way of Abrantes, crossed the frontier into Spain on November 12, and proceeded by Ciudad Rodrigo to Salamanca, where they arrived about the 13th.

Meanwhile, five companies of the 1st Battalion still at home, embarked, under Major Norman M'Leod, to join the other companies already in Portugal; and four of the remaining companies of the 2nd Battalion embarked at Harwich, under Colonel Wade. After a short detention at Falmouth, they sailed for Spain, and disembarked at Corunna on October 26.[1] They were attached to the force under the command of Sir David Baird, and the Riflemen of both Battalions formed the advanced guard. A day or two after landing they marched to Betanzos, and thence through Lugo, Villa Franca, and Cacabelos, to Astorga, which they reached on November 26. Already on this march they experienced great privations, owing to the defective arrangements of the Commissariat; and it was not until they reached Celada, a village a few miles in advance of Astorga, where they halted for some days, that they were sufficiently supplied with provisions. They were then sent forward to La Bañeza; but after a few days' halt they were, on account of a report that the enemy were in force in their front, recalled to Celada. Hence, on account of the utter rout of the Spanish armies, under Palafox and Castaños, at Tudela, Moore ordered Baird's force to retire again to Corunna; and they retreated, the Riflemen now forming the rear-guard and halting at Cacabelos, while the army moved on to Villa Franca. But after a few days, Baird's force was again ordered forward, and the Riflemen, now again forming the advanced guard, moved up through Astorga and La Bañeza to Benevente, which they reached on December 15. They marched again on the 17th, through Valderas, Mayorga, and Sahagun, and reached the Convent of Trianon, about a league from the latter place, on the 20th.

The companies of Riflemen were here reunited with those already in the Peninsula; the five companies under Major M'Leod joining the five head-quarter companies of the 1st Battalion under Colonel Beckwith; and the four companies of the 2nd Battalion, under Major Travers, which had served at Roleia and Vimiera, uniting themselves to the head-quarter companies under Colonel Wade, which had come out with Sir David Baird. When these men met, a few miles from the Trianon Convent, the new comers gave a loud cheer to the 'heroes of Portugal,' as they called their comrades who

[1] Surtees, 74. I take the dates from Surtees, who was with this force. The dates in the 2nd Battalion Record are here in inextricable confusion.

had fought at Roleia and Vimiera; which was heartily returned[1] The worn and sunburnt appearance of the one set of Riflemen contrasted strangely with the trim and neat look of the other. They were soon all to be alike in the tokens of toil, want and suffering A new distribution of the army taking place, consequent on the junction of Moore's and Baird's forces, the 1st Battalion were attached to the reserve, under Sir Edward Paget; and the 2nd Battalion, with a battalion of the 43rd and one of the 52nd, formed a brigade under Brigadier-General Robert Craufurd.

I will first trace the services of this Battalion till their separation from Moore's army On the evening of December 23 the Battalion was called to arms, with a view it was believed of attacking Soult in his position on the Carrion. In a cold and bitter night they moved forward; but had not marched far when they were countermanded, and returned to the quarters at Trianon. Surtees records an instance of Craufurd's severe and impartial discipline during this night march. An officer of the Battalion, who was unwell, in passing a brook, of which there were many on the road, left his section and went round it. Craufurd, who happened to be by, recalled him, and made him walk through and through it several times[2] The retreat commenced on the 25th, in terrible weather and over ground covered with snow. On that night they fell back to Mayorga, and the next day, though they started early, the state of the ground they had to get over was such that they did not reach the village of San Miguel till midnight The day following they marched to Castro Pipa, near Castro Gonzalo. Here there was a bridge, the passage of which Craufurd was to guard until the army, the stragglers and the baggage had passed over, and then to destroy it. During this operation, while half the brigade worked at its destruction, the other half held the enemy at bay, for his cavalry hovered all round and frequently attacked them, and the Riflemen had some smart skirmishing. At last, at midnight on the 28th, the brigade passed over in single file by planks laid over the broken arches, and fell back to Benevente.[3]

[1] Harris, 160. [2] Surtees, 80

[3] Surtees mentions that he crossed the Esla, at a ford a little way from Castro

On the next morning the 2nd Battalion left Benevente, and after a toilsome march of thirty miles, reached La Bañeza late at night; and on the following day moved on to their old quarter, Celada. On the 31st they marched into Astorga, and halted for an hour or two there while the magazine was destroyed; observing the road from Astorga to Leon, by which it was thought the enemy were advancing. However, they did not appear; and the Battalion moved on another wearisome march of twenty miles to Foncevadon. Here Craufurd's brigade, which had hitherto formed the rear-guard, was detached, and proceeded by Orense to Vigo, in order to seize the passage of the Minho should Moore's army find it necessary to retreat by that route On January 1, 1809, therefore, the Battalion marched by most difficult mountain roads to Ponferrada Here the men suffered great privation, the Alcalde having given all the bread to his countrymen of Romana's army, which was marching with ours, and thus left our people without provisions after their wearisome march.

On the next day they marched over rugged snow-clad mountains, and while they were toiling over them another instance of Craufurd's iron discipline occurred. The word being passed to open out to allow the General to pass, a hungry Rifleman called out that 'he had more need to give them bread' This, unhappily, reached the General's ears, who at once halted the brigade, ordered the offender to be tried by drum-head Court-Martial, and flogged on the spot: a terrible, perhaps a necessary, check to murmuring under such privations. So, labouring in hunger and fatigue, the Battalion toiled on to San Domingo-Flores, which they reached at ten o'clock at night, and after a scanty ration of black bread, lay down, wet and weary, till dawn, when another long and difficult march brought them at night to La Rua. These terrible marches caused many stragglers, many perished on the inhospitable hills; many fell into the hands of the yet more cruel enemy; and some, with the help of some refreshment from the sparse and poor population, dragged on wearily and rejoined the Battalion at Orense or Vigo.

Gonzalo, in a bullock-cart loaded with biscuit, while the brigade were occupied in destroying the bridge The time lost in its destruction might have been saved had Moore or Craufurd known the river was fordable.

In such want and sufferings the Battalion reached Orense on January 7, having pushed on a detachment by forced marches to secure the bridge over the Minho there. A halt on the 8th enabled the men to wash their linen and take off their clothing and accoutrements; a relief they had not had for many days; and a supply of provisions much refreshed the starving soldiers.

On the 9th they resumed their retreat, marching that day to Rivadavia, through roads inundated by the overflowing of the Minho and Avia, swollen by the incessant rains and melting snow. Three more such toilsome marches brought them to Vigo. And when they crowned the hills at some distance from the town, and, looking down on the bay and *ria* of Vigo, saw the ships which were there waiting to convey them home, the hearts of the weary, foot-sore Riflemen bounded for joy, and the rest of the day's march was performed with a long unwonted cheerfulness. They immediately embarked; and after waiting in the bay a few days to give a chance to stragglers to come in, sailed on the 21st, and landed on February 1 at Portsmouth, whence they marched to their old quarters at Hythe barracks.

Meanwhile, the 1st Battalion continued with the force under Sir John Moore; and being in the reserve, under Sir Edward Paget, which formed the rear-guard, besides the almost unparalleled sufferings from hunger, fatigue and exposure to unusually inclement winter weather, were daily engaged with the enemy.

On December 28 the reserve passed the Esla at Castro Gonzalo and fell back on Benevente, and the bridge (as we have seen) was destroyed During the whole day and night there was sharp skirmishing between the picquets of the Battalion and the enemy, who came up with the rear-guard for the first time on this day.

On the next day the outposts were withdrawn, and the infantry marched; but the cavalry was left in Benevente, with outposts on the bank of the river.

On January 3 the enemy again came up The Battalion, forming the rear-guard of the reserve, was formed in front of the village of Cacabelos. This place, scarcely more than a hamlet, is situated on the declivity of a high hill, sloping down to a deep stream, a branch or tributary of the Sil, which is crossed by a bridge at the foot of the village street. Two companies (Captains Norcott's and O'Hare's) and a small party of the 15th Hussars were detached to cover the retreat of the Battalion. These troops were soon warmly engaged with a very large body of cavalry, advanced by the enemy as a reconnoitring party; but, as this was soon after joined by a still more formidable force, they were directed to retire and follow the Battalion through the village, and to take post on the other side of the river and bridge, situated at the extremity of the street.

During the execution of this movement the enemy's cavalry pressed forward so rapidly and in such large masses that they compelled the 15th Hussars, who were in rear of the two companies, to retreat at full gallop. And Sir John Moore and his Staff also dashed past. The Riflemen, having opened to let them pass, immediately faced about, and forming across the whole breadth of the street of the village which they had now entered, poured on the enemy's cavalry such a rapid and well-aimed fire that many saddles were emptied and the pursuit instantly checked. But it was still necessary to go through the village to pass the bridge, and to gain the opposite bank of the river, and this was at length effected, not without great exertion and fatigue, and the loss of about 40 men, killed, wounded, or prisoners.

The Reserve formed in position on a range of heights about five hundred yards from the river, the 95th being advanced as a support to their rear-guard, and in that position awaited the enemy's attack. He was not long in fording the river to our right and left with a large body of cavalry and about a thousand Voltigeurs, which latter had not until then come up with the retreating army. They had been passed over the river on the horses of the cavalry.

The attack by this infantry began at about four o'clock in the now rapidly approaching evening, on the flanks of the Rifle picquets and on the Battalion of Riflemen formed for their support; and the enemy moved at the same time a large force of cavalry over the bridge on the high road to Villa Franca. After some severe skirmishing both with the picquets and the Battalion, these were obliged to fall back and occupy a more defensible position; and five companies extended behind the banks, and in the vineyards on each side of the road, on which the British cavalry and some guns were posted. Scarcely had this movement been effected when a warm attack was made by the Voltigeurs and cavalry against the Riflemen, the dragoons, and the guns. After an hour's hard fighting it was found impossible to withstand the superior force of the enemy, and the advanced wing of the Battalion was withdrawn, and joined the other five companies, with the view of following the main body of the Reserve, which had just before been ordered to retire.

It was now nearly dark; and General Colbert, who commanded the enemy's cavalry, conceiving probably that the Riflemen had retired, and that the English cavalry and guns were unprotected, made a most rapid and furious charge upon them with a mass of cavalry. The Riflemen again instantly threw themselves into the vineyards, and from the banks lining the road poured so hot and well-aimed a fire that the attacking cavalry were instantly checked. It was at this moment that Thomas Plunket, a private of the Battalion, noted for his excellent shooting, crept out with some expression that he 'would bring that fellow down,' and throwing himself on his back on the snow-covered ground he caught the sling of his rifle over his foot, fired with deliberate aim, and shot General Colbert dead. His orderly trumpeter rode up to assist him, but Tom Plunket had reloaded, and he also fell before his unerring rifle.[1] He had just time to jump up, and, amidst the cheers of his comrades, by running in upon

[1] I note Costello's assertion that General Paget offered his purse to any Rifleman who would bring down the French General, only to point out its improbability, not to say its impossibility. No one who knew the gallant Sir Edward Paget will believe that he bribed a soldier to slay a chivalrous and brave enemy; of whom Napier writes, 'his fine martial figure, his voice, his gestures, and, above all, his great valour, had excited the admiration of the British, and a general feeling of sorrow was predominant when the gallant soldier fell.' It is quite possible that, as Costello says, General Paget flung his purse (or some of its contents) to Tom Plunket, in admiration of two such unerring shots in the midst of a hot fight. But this is a very different matter from the previous offer of it. It is to be observed that Costello was not at Cacabelos, but was then a recruit at the Depôt; and no doubt the story did not lose, in the barrack-room or at the camp-fire, where he probably had heard it.

one of the rear sections, to escape the sabres of a dozen troopers who spurred after him in pursuit.

By the fire of the Riflemen the enemy's cavalry suffered severely. Besides their General, some two hundred horsemen were killed, wounded, or prisoners

Night had now fallen, and no further attack was attempted: the Riflemen retained the position till about ten at night, in order to give the rest of the army time to fall back They then retired, marching all night, a most difficult and fatiguing march, part of it through vineyards, and arrived at Curtro about daybreak.

This most gallant action may be said to have been fought altogether by the 1st Battalion; for no troops assisted them except a few of the 15th Hussars, who, being hard pressed by the enemy, rode through the two rear companies at the first onset, and formed on the rising ground beyond the bridge on the Villa Franca road; and 'a few of the 52nd,'[1] who, as night fell, appeared on that ridge to their assistance; but Colbert's final charge had then been checked by the Riflemen. Mr. Moore, in his Life of his brother, says that 'to arrest the enemy, four hundred Riflemen, with a small detachment of horse, were posted,' while the Reserve crossed the bridge; but in fact scarce half that number remained on that side of the river Only two companies (Norcott's and O'Hare's) were there posted; and their strength would not have been a hundred men each after the casualties of several days' march, in weather of unusual severity, and amidst almost unparalleled toils.

The march was resumed in a few hours; the weather was intensely cold, the road rugged and difficult, and the snow knee deep, and the fatigue and exhausted state of the men were extreme, yet amidst all these sufferings the Reserve preserved order, 'covered the retreat, and protected, as much as lay in their power, the stragglers.'[2]

On the road from Villa Franca to Herrerias the French patrols during the night attacked the Rifle picquets, and wounded a few men; but the Riflemen drove them back, and the enemy did not ascertain that the retreating army had aban-

[1] 'Napier,' Book iv chap. v

[2] 'Life of Sir John Moore,' ii 210.

doned the position. After a march of eighteen miles the Reserve reached Herrerias on the morning of the 4th. A forced march of thirty-six miles brought them on the 5th to Nogales. Thence they started again, and towards evening of that day, when near Constantino, the enemy came up with them. Moore was with them, and his position was difficult. A river was to be crossed, and a hill overlooking and close to the bridge would, if the enemy should occupy it, give him such an advantage as would render the passage of the Reserve very difficult. Moore posted a battery on the top of the hill, 'and guarded it, as usual, by the brave Rifle Corps.'[1] They held the enemy in check while the Reserve defiled over the narrow bridge; as soon as they were safely over, the guns were limbered up, and trotted down the hill; the Riflemen followed at the double, and passed the bridge without the loss of a man. The French rushed on in pursuit; but when they reached the bridge the Reserve were in position, and after maintaining the post till nightfall General Paget fell back towards Lugo.

During all this retreat Moore accompanied the Reserve, and rode beside his friend General Paget, their chief. His cheerful demeanour sustained the spirits of the way-worn, suffering soldiers; he praised their superior discipline on the march, and warmly applauded their gallant conduct in action.

The whole of Sir John Moore's forces were now in position in front of Lugo. On the 6th the French came in sight, and collecting in considerable numbers, took up a position in front of the rear-guard. On the next day the outposts were attacked, and the enemy repulsed. And on the 8th another attack was made, and with a similar result.

On the 9th Sir John Moore drew up his whole force in position, and offered battle. After waiting in line of battle till towards evening, the General ordered the army to retire in the night, the Reserve covering their march. They kept up bright fires to deceive the enemy, and then, in a night of terrific weather, and in drenching showers of rain and sleet, they fell back towards Betanzos. Near this town the enemy came up with them, and attacked them during their passage over a bridge, with some loss.

The sufferings of the Battalion in the next few days were

[1] 'Life of Sir John Moore,' ii. 201.

terrible. The men were in a state of starvation; many without shoes, and almost all in rags. The officers were, many of them, barefooted; and some, from hunger and fatigue, so incapable of further exertion that they had to be carried on mules. In this state they arrived, on the 11th, at El Burgo (the main body of the troops having entered Corunna), their discipline unimpaired and their courage undismayed. 'For twelve days,' says Napier, 'these hardy warriors had covered the retreat, during which time they had traversed eighty miles of road in two marches, passed several nights under arms in the snow of the mountains, were seven times engaged with the enemy, and now assembled at the outposts, having fewer men missing, including those who had fallen in battle, than any other division of the army: an admirable instance of the value of good discipline.'

As soon as they had passed the river at El Burgo the bridge was blown up, and two companies of Riflemen, under Major Norcott, were posted in the village, the remainder of the Battalion being, with the Reserve, cantoned upon the high road to Corunna, at a little distance.

The enemy's cavalry again came in sight on the morning of the 12th, and, after reconnoitring, dismounted a part of their force, and attacked the companies at El Burgo vigorously. This skirmishing continued during the day; but their efforts to drive the Riflemen from the post were ineffectual.

On the 14th, however, this post was withdrawn, as the enemy had forded the river on our left. The Battalion therefore joined the Reserve in the position taken up by the army on the heights about two miles in front of Corunna; while the enemy was employed in concentrating his forces on a very strong range of hills opposite and nearly parallel to the British line, and distant from it about five hundred yards.

The Battalion was advanced, in the course of the morning, about half-a-mile in front of the Reserve, in order to occupy several detached and commanding pieces of ground, on the right of Lord William Bentinck's brigade, and just opposite a battery of guns on the left of the French position.

The enemy's troops continued to pour into his position during the whole night. Their bands played, and shouts, plainly heard by the Riflemen, announced their joy at the certainty of a general action on the morrow, and the anticipated destruction or capture of the British army.

On the 16th several movements of cavalry, artillery and infantry were observed in the French lines, and about two o'clock in the afternoon the Riflemen could distinctly see their first line getting under arms on the brow of the hill. The assault was not long in coming. At three o'clock a furious onset of three thousand skirmishers burst upon the whole line of English picquets, which, although at first driven back, rallied under cover of the numerous stone walls which intersected the valley, and kept the enemy in check for a considerable time; particularly at the village of Elvina, which was watched by the brigade under Major-General Coote Manningham.

The enemy finding his first efforts to drive in our picquets unavailing, reinforced his first line with several battalions, and compelled them to fall back to their respective brigades. The action immediately became general, and the attacks particularly severe from the Corunna road to the extreme British right (comprising about half the English forces) It was evidently Soult's great object to turn the right, whilst on the left and left centre the attack was not pushed with much energy, and was intended only as a feint. Lord William Bentinck's brigade was so roughly handled about five o'clock, and was losing so many men by the fire of the enemy's guns on our right (by which Sir John Moore fell at this time), that Colonel Beckwith pushed on with the whole Battalion; and dashing into the very midst of the enemy's artillery, would inevitably have captured or destroyed them in a few minutes, had not two battalions of Voltigeurs moved out so rapidly from the second line to their assistance, that the Riflemen were obliged to fall back for the moment. They were checked, not quelled, a sharp skirmish, kept up for two hours between the Riflemen and the Voltigeurs, ended in the complete repulse of the latter, with considerable loss, leaving seven officers and one hundred and fifty-six men prisoners in the hands of their opponents, whom the Battalion took on ship-board and brought to England

By this time the enemy had been completely defeated at all points, and retired to his position.

The troops embarked during the night. The 1st Battalion of the 95th was the last corps that entered the gates of Corunna, having acted as the rear-guard ; and scarcely had it reached its ship, when the enemy made his appearance, with several guns, on the heights commanding the bay, from which he fired on all the vessels within range. The fleet, however, was soon under sail, and arrived at Spithead on the 21st. The Battalion was landed and marched to Hythe

I have reserved till now the details of its losses during that memorable retreat.

At Cacabelos, on January 3, 2 sergeants and 17 rank and file were killed ; and Captain Bennett, who died of his wounds on the 11th, and Lieutenant Eeles were wounded ; and on that occasion 4 sergeants and 44 rank and file were taken prisoners In the skirmish on the 5th, 1 man was killed and 1 man also on the 10th. One sergeant, 1 bugler, and 13 rank and file died of want, sickness, or fatigue during the retreat; and 31 men, wounded or exhausted, fell into the enemy's hands. In the final fight before Corunna on the 16th, Lieutenant Charles Noble, 1 sergeant, and 10 rank and file were killed, and 8 rank and file were taken prisoners Thus the total loss of the Battalion in twenty days was 2 officers, 8 sergeants, 1 bugler, and 125 rank and file dead, or prisoners in the hands of the enemy. Lieutenant Eeles, 1 sergeant, and 33 rank and file wounded disembarked in England.

But the condition of the survivors and unwounded was deplorable. The appearance of the Battalion was squalid and miserable. Most of the men had lost some of their appointments; many were without shoes ; and their clothing was not only tattered and in rags, but in such a state of filth and so infested with vermin, that on new clothing being served out it was burnt at the back of Hythe barracks.

Among the losses of the Regiment consequent on the retreat to Corunna, not the least conspicuous was that of their first Colonel, Major-General Coote Manningham, who died at Maidstone on August 26, 1809, in his forty-fourth year. A short sketch of the life of one who may be called the originator of the Regiment, may well be given in this place. He was the second son of Charles Manningham,[1] Esq., of Thorp, in Surrey, who was Governor of Bengal in 1758, by the daughter of Colonel Charles Hutchinson, Governor of St. Helena, through whom he was nearly related to two distinguished Generals, Sir Robert Boyd and Sir Eyre Coote, who had married her sisters. Under the former, and in his Regiment, the 39th, his services commenced at the siege of Gibraltar. On the breaking out of the war of 1793, Manningham, then a Major in the 45th, was appointed to a light infantry battalion, formed in the West India Islands, in order to join Sir Charles Grey, on his coming out to attack the French West India possessions. With it he took part in the reduction of Martinique, St. Lucia, and Guadaloupe. He soon after became Lieutenant-Colonel of the 41st, and in 1795 was appointed Adjutant-General to the force under General Forbes at St. Domingo. While on this service he was severely wounded by an ambuscade of the enemy. On or soon after his return to England he was, in 1798, appointed Aide-de-Camp to King George III., with the rank of Colonel, and soon after one of His Majesty's Equerries. He was promoted a Major-General in 1805; and after serving some time on the home staff, he was appointed to command a brigade in the division which went out with Sir David Baird in 1808. On the junction of this force with that under Sir John Moore, he had a brigade under Moore, and took part in the retreat; and, as we have seen, held the position of Elvina in the final action at Corunna. The fatigues and sufferings he had undergone during this campaign, acting on a constitution impaired by service and by wounds in the West Indies, brought on, soon after his return to England, an illness from which he never rallied. He is buried at Little Bookham,[2] in Surrey, where this inscription to his memory remains:

[1] His grandfather was Bishop of Chichester. See a full account of the family in Nichols' 'Literary Anecdotes,' i. 207–11.

[2] He had married the daughter of the Reverend George Pollen, Rector of Little Bookham.

In this vault are deposited the remains of
Major-General COOTE MANNINGHAM, equerry to the king
and colonel of the 95th or rifle regiment of foot;
This corps he originally raised and formed, and by his
unvaried zeal and exertion, as well as excellent discipline
and good example, brought to the highest state of
military reputation and distinction.

He died at *Maidstone*, on the 26th day of August 1809
in the 44th year of his age

An early victim to the fatigues of the campaign in *Spain*
operating on a constitution already enfeebled
by long service in the *West Indies*
and honourable wounds received in that climate

A monument to his memory was also erected in the North Transept of Westminster Abbey, by his friend Lieutenant-General Sir Thomas Hislop, in 1813, which records that 'In him the man and the Christian tempered the warrior;' and that 'He was the model of a British soldier.'

His only surviving child married Sir Edward Buller, Bart., and more than one of her sons has served with distinction in the Regiment, in which they may be said to bear the honourable distinction of 'founder's kin.'

CHAPTER II.

THE two Battalions, then stationed at Hythe, were ordered to be completed to a strength of a thousand men each; and active steps were taken to supply the losses occasioned by the retreat by obtaining volunteers from the Militia The Regiment had already become so famous and so popular, that not only were the deficiencies filled up in a very short time, but more than a thousand volunteers presented themselves beyond the numbers required.[1] It was therefore resolved by the authorities to add a 3rd Battalion to the Regiment. Colonel M'Leod was promoted to the Lieutenant-Colonelcy of it, and soon afterwards exchanged with Colonel Andrew Barnard, of the 1st Royals, afterwards Sir Andrew Barnard: a name indelibly connected with the subsequent achievements of the Regiment Only two or three other of the steps consequent on the formation of an additional Battalion were given in the Regiment, the services of those by whose valour and sufferings the Regiment had obtained the fame which attracted these volunteers and to whose exertions in recruiting their great number was due, being, with the usual injustice of the

[1] This return will show the actual numbers:

Return of 95th, May 10, 1809

	Effective April 1, previous to Militia volunteering	Volunteers from Militia		Remaining in Portugal	Total	Left in Spain	Grand total
		English	Irish				
1st Battalion	799	641	None	8	1448	88	1536
2nd Battalion	863	641	None	37	1541	38	1579

Thus leaving an excess of more than eleven hundred men, after completing the two Battalions to a thousand men each. This excess formed the 3rd Battalion

British Government to its military defenders, ignored. General Sir David Dundas, then Commander-in-Chief, became Colonel-in-Chief on August 31, 1809, in place of Manningham; and the Colonelcies of the three Battalions were bestowed on Major-Generals Forbes Champagné, Sir Brent Spencer, and the Honourable William Stewart, thus restoring to the roll of the Regiment the honoured name of its first Lieutenant-Colonel.

I now resume the history of the services of the 1st Battalion, which having been completed to 1,010 rank and file, marched from Hythe, under the command of Lieutenant-Colonel Beckwith, at two o'clock in the morning of May 25, 1809, and arriving at Dover about six, soon after embarked in three transports, the 'Fortune,' the 'Malabar,' and the 'Laurel,' and sailed immediately for the Downs. Here they were joined by a battalion of the 43rd and by the 52nd, which were to form the Light Brigade under Major-General Robert Craufurd, who embarked in the 'Nymph' frigate. Contrary winds kept them in the Downs till June 3, when they made sail; and arriving in the Tagus on the 28th anchored off Lisbon. Here they remained until July 2, when about midnight they were put into flat-bottomed boats, and towed up the river. The men and officers were very crowded, and experienced great inconvenience for twenty-four hours, until they were landed at Vallada on the right bank of the river, at or near which place they bivouacked on that night. On landing they were definitively formed, with the 43rd and 52nd Light Infantry Regiments, their constant companions in arms, into the Light Brigade, whose deeds of arms in Portugal, Spain and France, can never be forgotten while England has an army.

The Battalion marched on the 4th to Santarem, where they halted till the 7th, to allow the baggage animals, the ammunition, and the Commissariat to come up On that day they marched to Golegão, and on the 8th to Punhete and Tancos, still on the Tagus; on the 9th they passed through Abrantes, but, not halting there, crossed by a pontoon bridge to the left bank of the river, and bivouacked in extensive woods. All these marches were, in consequence of the extreme heat of the weather, performed in the night; the Battalion generally falling in about midnight, and arriving at their bivouack about eight or nine in the morning.

It was about this time that Craufurd issued standing orders to his Brigade of extreme strictness, not to say severity. This Draconic code made him at first very unpopular, but as time went on, its usefulness in maintaining discipline and repressing offences became manifest. It produced a perfection in the Brigade which the officers and the men themselves could not but recognise; and this, added to his own personal valour and reckless daring, eventually endeared him to the soldiers who followed him.[1]

At midnight on the 10th the Battalion moved to Gaviaõ, a march of thirteen hours, the greater part under a blazing sun. On the 12th they reached, through a bleak and high country, Niza On the next day they marched through the pass of Villa Velha, and crossing the Tagus by a bridge of boats, bivouacked on the opposite bank. On the 14th they advanced by mountainous and difficult roads to Sernadas, and on the 15th reached Castello Bianco Here they halted on the 16th and 17th to enable the 43rd and 52nd to join them. On the 18th the Brigade thus complete marched soon after midnight and bivouacked in the woods near Ladouira; on the 19th they moved through a desolate country to Zebreira; and on the 20th, crossing the Elgas, passed into Spain and encamped near Zarza Major On the next day, after a long and oppressive march, they reached Moralegua, and on the 22nd arrived at Coria, where they halted during the 23rd.

On the 24th the Battalion marched to Galisteo, on the river Alagon, on the 25th over a burning plain, with the Sierra de Gata, topped with snow, in view, to Malpartida, a village on the Calzones. On the next day, the 26th, crossing the river Tietar by a flying bridge, they had a most fatiguing march to Venta de Bazagona, and on the 27th arrived at Navalmoral, the heat being oppressive.

On the 28th they marched at daylight to the town of Calzada, where tidings reached Craufurd that an action was imminent between Sir Arthur Wellesley's army, with General

[1] For twenty years and upwards after the end of the war, every officer of the Regiment was required to learn and to know these standing orders.

Cuesta's Spanish troops, and Marshal Victor's army, then in close proximity. He determined, therefore, if possible, to unite his Brigade to Sir Arthur Wellesley before it should take place; and undertook the forced march which has rendered the name of the Light Division famous Accordingly, after a short rest at Calzada, he pushed on to Oropesa, two leagues, which he reached about noon A distant cannonade began to be heard, which, increasing as they approached it, acted as an incentive to speed and endurance. They marched on under a scorching sun to Oropesa, where they halted for four hours to cook. Here Craufurd desired the commanding officers to pick out of the ranks such men as they considered unable to continue a further march. Very few men of the Battalion fell out; these were left at Oropesa in charge of a subaltern. After this was done the bugles sounded the '*fall in*,' and the Riflemen moved onward till about ten at night; when, passing a cattle-pond, Craufurd halted to allow the men to drink. The parched soldiers eagerly drank the water, filthy and nauseous though it was. As soon as they had satisfied their thirst, the march was resumed and continued through the night, without check, through deep, sandy roads. Early on the morning of the 29th the Light Division marched across the field of Talavera, giving three hearty cheers for the victory of the day before.

They had thus, in heavy marching order, under a burning sun, and with a most insufficient supply of food, marched upwards of fifty miles, with only two short halts, in twenty-five hours. They thus arrived the morning after the fight at Talavera; but though the Battalion itself was not present, a detachment of the Regiment left in the Peninsula in 1808 took part in the action, and was mentioned in Sir Arthur Wellesley's despatches as having particularly distinguished themselves.[1]

As soon as it arrived at Talavera the Battalion was imme-

[1] 1st Battalion Record I do not find this in the 'Wellington Despatches' or in the 'Supplementary Despatches. It was probably noticed in Divisional Orders. The detachments under Colonel Bunbury are, however, mentioned with praise in the despatch of Talavera ('Wellington Despatches,' iv. 537) It may have formed part of these, for it appears by the return (p 42, note) that 88 men of the 1st Battalion and 38 of the 2nd Battalion had been 'left in Spain;' and 8 men of the 1st Battalion and 37 of the 2nd Battalion 'left in Portugal.'

diately ordered to occupy some woods in advance of the British position and to furnish the picquets, the sentinels of which were facing the position of the French army. Here the Battalion remained till August 3. During that time it suffered much from want of provision, not more than one ration of bread, and but little of other food, having been issued.

On the 3rd the British army began to fall back in consequence of information that Soult with a large force was moving towards the rear of the English with a view of cutting off their communications with Portugal. Before daybreak they marched and arrived at Oropesa, the 95th forming the rear-guard with the cavalry On the 4th they crossed the Tagus by the bridge of Arzobispo. It was during this march that Craufurd, knowing that his Division were famishing, allowed them to kill any animals which might be in the woods in which they halted that evening. A large herd of pigs being discovered was instantly set upon by the hungry soldiers, killed, cut up and eaten in an incredibly short time. About midnight they started again, thus refreshed, and pushed forward to secure the bridge of Almaraz, the rest of the army moving on Truxillo. It was of vast importance to secure this bridge, as it was feared Soult might occupy it. The Light Division, therefore, was pushed on with great rapidity. The Riflemen marched for fourteen hours through a hilly and barren country, still without food, except a kind of pea parched by the sun, and wheat found in such fields as remained ungleaned; suffering also from want of water, the streams being almost all dried up, and on the evening of the 5th the Battalion bivouacked in some woods in advance of the rest of the Division. Before dawn on the 6th they resumed their march under a burning sun, and with the same scanty provision, and after fifteen hours' march, during which there were many stragglers, faint from heat and want, they reached the bridge of Almaraz. Two companies of the Battalion were immediately sent on picquet at a ford a little below the bridge; and the remainder bivouacked near, in order to support the picquets in case of an attack. Here they remained till August 20, the Battalion being always in advance, and bivouacking in an olive wood near Rio Gardo, and furnishing the picquets at the ford. Every evening at sunset they moved out of the olive wood, and lay down with their arms on the bank of the river, and returned to the camp at sunrise. The remainder of the Light Division were encamped near the village of Las Casas del Puerto.

During this whole fortnight the scarcity, or rather the absolute want, of provision continued. Scanty rations of goat-flesh were issued during this time ; and a coarse kind of pea-flour, with bran and chopped straw, provided by the Commissariat, which the officers and men made into a kind of cake with water, and cooked on a camp-kettle lid or on a stone, was the only provision. Unless when the men found some ears of corn in a field, and by rubbing them in their hands and grinding the grains between stones, in this way supplemented the Commissariat allowance.

On the 12th the French picquets appeared on the heights opposite the bridge and the ford, but no shots were exchanged between them and the two companies of Riflemen always posted at the ford And indeed then, as throughout the war in the Peninsula, the best understanding existed between the Riflemen on outpost duty and the advanced posts of the French ; the officers frequently saluting each other And so far did this go that the Riflemen, when ordered to advance to drive in the French picquets, used to hold up their rifles and tap the brass bullet-box in the stock of the Baker rifle then in use, to show their opponents that they were in earnest, and that their adversaries were to stand on their defence.

The insufficient food and the unwholesome position of their camp near the Bridge of Almaraz, in a damp situation, with poisonous vapours arising from vegetable matter decaying, and swamps half-dried under a burning sun, soon began to tell on the men of the Battalion ; and fever and dysentery became prevalent among them.

At midnight on August 20 the Light Division marched from Almaraz and arrived at Deletosa on the following day, where a large portion of Sir Arthur Wellesley's force was encamped This and the whole British army (except the Light Division) marched on the 21st for Truxillo. On that evening the Battalion marched ; and about midnight lay down with their arms until daybreak, when they started again for

Caceres, where they arrived on the 23rd. And on the three following days they continued their march towards the Portuguese frontier, starting in the night and proceeding during many hours of the day. During this march the men suffered much both from the heat of the sun in a barren, treeless country, and the constant insufficiency of provisions. And it was not until they reached Valencia de Alcantara on the 26th, where they halted during the 27th, that they were able to procure bread, and the luxury of fruit and vegetables from the neighbouring gardens Late on the 28th they started again, and marching during most of the night crossed the rivulet which here divides Spain from Portugal on the 29th, and proceeding by Maravaõ, after a march of many miles encamped at Castello de Vide, where the Battalion halted for a week. On September 7 they marched to Portalegre, where they halted two days, after which, resuming their march, they arrived at Arronches on the 10th, whence one more march on the next day brought them to Campo Major, their winter quarter, where they remained three months. During these, sickness and death ravaged the Battalion; fever, ague and dysentery, the fruits of exposure, of want, and of the proverbially unhealthy climate of Alemtejo, in which Campo Major is situated, sent numbers into hospital; and it is said[1] that nearly three hundred men of the 1st Battalion died during their stay there.

I now return to the narrative of the services of the 2nd Battalion, which we left at Hythe barracks; whence, after a rest of five months after the fatigues of Moore's retreat, their losses being replaced by volunteers from the Militia, and their clothing and accoutrements renewed, they marched, about July 20, 1809,[2] about a thousand strong, under Colonel Wade, to Deal, and there embarked in the 'Superb,' 74, to join the expedition destined for Holland, under the Earl of Chatham. Subsequently they were shifted into the 'Namur,' on the 22nd, and formed part of the brigade of their former Lieutenant-Colonel, the Honourable William

[1] Costello, 24. He was himself in hospital and dangerously ill.

[2] The 2nd Battalion Record says that they embarked on the 23rd, but as Stewart ('Cumloden Papers,' 56) notes that they changed to the 'Namur' on the 22nd, this must be an error.

Stewart, with the 2nd Battalions of their constant companions in arms, the 43rd and 52nd. They sailed on July 30, and arrived off Flushing on the following day Two companies were immediately detached to act with the force under Major-General Baron de Rottenberg; and on that night Lieutenant William Humbley, being in charge of an advanced picquet, while going his rounds, was informed by a peasant that a party of French soldiers were at that moment plundering his house. Humbley, with great promptness, suspecting that while intent on plunder the look-out would not be very good, at once took with him a corporal and eight men of his picquet; and, under the guidance of the peasant, the night being very dark, made his way to the house, about 200 yards from his post. They moved in perfect silence, and arrived at the place without a '*qui vive*' from the only sentry there posted. Him a Rifleman knocked down at once with the butt of his rifle, the others instantly surrounded the house, and made prisoners the whole picquet, consisting of 2 sergeants, 2 corporals, and 20 privates. The officer in command of it alone escaping, by getting out of a back window, and in the darkness of the night getting away. The Riflemen broke the whole of the muskets of the French picquet, and conveyed their twenty-four prisoners into the British lines and forwarded them to head-quarters.[1]

The two companies to which Humbley's picquet belonged, on the next day repulsed a sortie made from the place; and in this affair Humbley received a severe wound in the head from a musket ball, and 1 sergeant and 9 rank and file were also wounded.

During the subsequent siege, a Rifleman named Jackman got close up to the walls of Flushing, and scooping out a pit with his sword, entrenched himself in it, and began to fire deliberately at the French gunners. He is said to have picked off eleven artillerymen, as they showed themselves at the embrasures; and having done so, he sprang out of his pit, ran across the open, and rejoined his Battalion unhurt.[2]

Five companies, with the rest of Stewart's brigade, were not landed till the 9th, when they disembarked on the Island

[1] Humbley's Letter, January 31, 1838, in Adjutant-General's Office.

[2] Harris, 131.

of South Beveland. The other companies, on the Island of Walcheren, took an active part in the siege operations until the capitulation on the 15th. During these operations the Battalion lost 11 rank and file killed, and Lieutenants Manners and Clarke, and 21 rank and file wounded. But the casualties from engines of war were trifling compared to the devastating effects of the climate of Walcheren and South Beveland. The officers and men were struck down by fevers; and on the 27th Stewart writes that the increase of the sickness in the 95th was at the rate of twenty cases daily. On September 8 the Battalion re-embarked, and this useless, abortive and mismanaged expedition came to an end. They landed at Dover on the 14th, and on the 18th the Battalion which had left Hythe barracks less than six weeks before, a thousand stalwart and hale men, staggered into them a gaunt and fever-stricken band of about seven hundred: many to be carried at once to hospital, and not a few to their grave. Thus in the space of nine months had the Battalion been twice more than decimated by fatigue, want and pestilence.[1]

The 1st Battalion having remained at Campo Major three months marched on December 12, forming the advance of the Light Division, to Arronches; and thence by Portalegre, Crato, Ponte de Sor, Abrantes and Punhete, to Thomar, which they reached on the 23rd They continued their march through Leiria, Pombal, Condeixa, and arrived at Coimbra on the 29th, and halted there during the next day. Resuming their march on the 31st, they passed through Ponte da Murcella, to Venda and Gallizes, in which villages they were quartered on January 1, 1810, arrived at Celorico on the 3rd, and at Pinhel on the next day; and crossing the Coa on the 6th, occupied the villages of Villar Torpim, Regada and Cinco Villas. In this position, with occasional shifting of quarters with the other regiments of the Division, they continued during the remainder of January, February and the early part of March. The Riflemen, with a few German hussars, were the only troops pushed across the Coa to observe

[1] There died between the date of their return, and January 10, 1810, 5 sergeants and 128 rank and file On February 10, 1810, the Battalion had 161 sick; on February 25, 140 sick The strength on embarkation was 70 sergeants, 988 rank and file.

the French outposts at St. Felices, immediately opposite the bridge and pass of Barba del Puerco, the remainder of the army being quartered on the left bank of the Coa.

On February 27 Captain Creagh's company was ordered to reconnoitre the village of Barba del Puerco, which he found occupied by a strong detachment of French cavalry; and after a skirmish with them fell back, according to his orders, to Escarigo, where he was joined by Captain Leach's company, while a third was moved in support from Villar Torpim to Vermiosa On the 28th Leach[1] made a fresh reconnaissance; and finding that the enemy had left Barba del Puerco, occupied it, sending a party to the bridge which spanned the Agueda at the foot of the pass. It was ascertained that the French occupied St. Felices with about 3,000 men of all arms, under General Ferey, having a picquet of cavalry and infantry at their side of the bridge. Thus it continued, three companies being posted in the village, and one on picquet at the bridge, on which were double sentries. At the same time the whole of the Battalion was pushed up to the Agueda, the whole line of which they (with the German hussars) occupied, with four companies at Villa de Ciervo on the left, one company at Almofela, and another at Escalhao on the right of the position of Barba del Puerco

On March 19 the French General Ferey attempted to surprise the post of Barba del Puerco. About midnight, leaving a strong force in support, at the head of six hundred grenadiers, chosen for this service, he approached the bridge, as the moon, rising behind him, threw a shadow from the high ground and made his approach invisible. The roaring torrent of the Agueda, swollen by recent rains and melting snow, overpowered the tread of the advancing column. Thus he came, unperceived, on the double sentries on the bridge. They had just time to fire their rifles, when they were both wounded and made prisoners. Ferey at once dashed across the bridge with his grenadiers, sweeping before him a sergeant's party at the bridge, and made for the pass. Here he was met and checked by O'Hare,[2] whose company happened

[1] Lieutenant-Colonel Leach retired from the army 1821.

[2] Captain O'Hare was very ill and in bed; but at the first alarm placed himself at the head of his company, which was previously in the charge of Lieutenant Mercer

to be on picquet, who defended the face of the hill, step by step and muzzle to muzzle, as overpowering numbers forced him up it. Meanwhile the three companies in the village sprung from their sleep, seized their arms, and without waiting for regular formation, fought hand to hand with their enemies as they met them. One company, Colonel Sidney Beckwith, who was in command of the post, immediately sent away to the right, thinking that the enemy might attempt to climb the hill by a pathway there and turn his flank; with the other two he reinforced O'Hare's picquet; and so they fought for half an hour, with such daring and such fury that the French turned and fled across the bridge, leaving 2 officers and 7 men killed, 6 prisoners and 30 muskets in the hands of their opponents

In this affair great deeds of valour were done. Beckwith, while lowering a piece of rock to hurl down on the advancing Frenchmen, received a musket-ball through his shako, without its wounding him. And James Stewart, then the Adjutant, was engaged in a hand-to-hand fight with two of the grenadiers, when a Rifleman named Ballard shot one, on which the other was overpowered by, and surrendered to, Stewart, who was specially mentioned by Sir Arthur Wellesley in his Despatches, and recommended by Beckwith for promotion, but it never came, and he was killed a year after in the advance from Santarem. Lieutenant Mercer and 3 Riflemen were killed, and 10 were wounded.

In repelling this night attack the Riflemen stood against more than double their numbers. Six hundred grenadiers crossed the bridge, and only three companies repulsed them, O'Hare's picquet and two under Beckwith; the fourth company occupying the post being detached to defend the path on the right, which was not attempted, never having been engaged.

This fight opened the campaign of 1810. The stern Craufurd, ever sparing of praise, issued the following divisional order:

D O Villa de Cierro *March* 25, 1810

Brigadier-General Craufurd has it in command from the Commander-in-Chief to assure Lieutenant-Colonel Beckwith and the officers of the 95th Regiment who were engaged at Barba del Puerco that their conduct in this affair has augmented the confidence he has in the troops when opposed to the enemy in any situation.

Brigadier-General Craufurd feels peculiar satisfaction in noticing the first affair in which any part of the Light Brigade were engaged during the present campaign. That British troops should defeat a superior number of the enemy is nothing new; but the action reflects honour on Lieutenant-Colonel Beckwith and the Regiment, inasmuch as it was of a sort which the riflemen of other armies would shun. In other armies the rifle is considered ill-calculated for close action with an enemy armed with a musket and bayonet; but the 95th Regiment has proved that the rifle in the hands of a British soldier is a fully sufficient weapon to enable him to defeat the French in the closest fight, in whatever manner they may be armed.

(Signed) V. GRAHAM, D A G.

Sir Arthur Wellesley also repeatedly mentions this gallant fight in his Despatches and letters. Besides the message thus conveyed by Craufurd, he tells Admiral the Honourable G. Berkeley that the French were 'repulsed in fine style' by the 95th; and in his Despatch reporting it to the Earl of Liverpool, he adds that 'this affair was highly creditable to Colonel Beckwith, and displayed the gallantry and discipline of the officers and troops under his command.'

But this discipline, which thus elicited the approval of the great commander, was not enforced by Beckwith with sternness or severity. It is recorded how, during their halts at Campo Major and near the Coa, during the preceding winter, he had let his Battalion repose from the fatigues of their long marches, and their sufferings from famine and disease; not worrying the soldiers with drills or barrack-yard parades; but rather encouraging amusements and sports which refreshed and reanimated them. This it was, added to their knowledge of his valour and experience when leading them in the field, that made him loved by the Officers and Riflemen of his Battalion, made them ready to 'follow him through fire and water when the day of trial came; for they well knew that he was the last man on earth who would give them unnecessary trouble, or, on the other hand, would spare either man or officer when the good of the service demanded their utmost exertions.'[1]

About this time the 1st and 3rd Caçadores of the Portuguese army were added to Craufurd's Division; the latter commanded by Lieutenant-Colonel Elder, one of the original officers of the Rifle Corps.[2] At the same time Ross'[3] troop

[1] Leach, 121

[2] Major-General Sir George Elder, K C.B., died December 3, 1836.

[3] Afterwards Field-Marshal Sir Hew Dalrymple Ross, G C.B.

of Horse Artillery and the 14th and 16th Light Dragoons were attached to the Light Division.

Soon after the attack on Barba del Puerco the troops (which had been reinforced with some of the 43rd and 52nd) were withdrawn to Villa de Ciervo.

Early in April, in compliance with orders from home, the ten companies of which the Battalion on service had hitherto consisted were reduced to eight, two captains with subalterns, non-commissioned officers, and a few men returning to England to form a Depôt. These eight companies were of about a hundred men each, as the Battalion which embarked a thousand and ten rank and file, had been reduced in about nine months, principally by disease, to about eight hundred men in all

Craufurd now maintained a long line of posts on the right bank of the Agueda, from Fuentes Guinaldo on the right to the junction of the Agueda and the Douro, near Escalhao, on the left. In May the French began the siege of Ciudad Rodrigo, distant a few miles from Gallegos, then the headquarters of the Light Division The 1st Battalion had picquets at Carpio, Molina das Flores, and Marialva The Battalion itself was every evening under arms, and took up a position in a wood situated on some high ground behind Gallegos, and towards Duas Casas , here they remained during the night, returning for the day to their quarters. It seems that Massena observed this movement, and supposed that these troops were reinforcements to Craufurd's Division. He therefore ordered Junot with a considerable force to cross the Azarva at the bridge of Marialva. This he did at daybreak on July 4, driving in the picquet at Marialva; the passage of his cavalry was gallantly disputed and checked by the German hussars; but Junot advancing in force, Craufurd resolved to fall back behind the Duas Casas. The Battalion, with some cavalry, covered this movement, and skirmishing with the French advanced troops, held them back until Craufurd had established himself behind the river. Junot, probably thinking Craufurd's force to be much larger than it was, did not follow up this advance; and the Battalion took up a position at Val de la Mula, behind the River Turon, here the boundary between Spain and Portugal, detaching two companies to Fort Concepcion in front of the position. On July 10 Craufurd resolved by a night march to surprise the French posts at Gallegos and Barquillo. Accordingly, seven companies of the 95th with two of the 52nd got under arms late on that night, together with the 14th Light Dragoons and some German hussars. The Riflemen were ordered to load, to march in silence, and not to light their pipes. The wheels of two of Ross' guns, which formed part of the column, were muffled. Thus they marched through a good part of the night, Craufurd himself accompanying them. On reaching some high ground, the Riflemen were ordered to lie down in some high standing corn Here they waited for dawn , when it appeared, the orders to fall in and to advance to the edge of the height were given, and the French appeared in the plain below. They consisted of about two companies of infantry and a troop of cavalry. Craufurd ordered Colonel Talbot to charge them with the 14th ; this he did gallantly, sabreing or making prisoners the cavalry , but the infantry formed square, and receiving the charge, brought down Talbot himself and several of his troopers, and then made good their retreat. Why Craufurd did not use his guns, or let loose the Riflemen at the French infantry, seems inexplicable. But so it was : and after remaining on the hill inactive spectators of the combat, they marched back to their position at Val de la Mula. But Ciudad Rodrigo having surrendered, Craufurd fell back on July 16 to Junça, about a mile and a half from Almeida, in Portugal, and on the right bank of the Coa.

At daybreak on the 21st the Battalion, with Ross' battery, advanced towards the Turon to support the cavalry who were driven from Val de la Mula and across the Turon by an advance of the enemy in great force. On this advance the mines which our engineers had formed under Fort Concepcion were fired. The two companies of Riflemen posted there, under Captain O'Hare, proceeded to rejoin the Battalion, and had not long left their position when the work fell with a tremendous explosion. On the 22nd Craufurd fell back to near Almeida, his left protected by the guns of that place, and his right resting on the Coa.

During the night of the 23rd the Division was exposed to a violent storm of thunder, lightning and torrents of rain.

Day had just begun to dawn on the morning of the 24th, and the troops, which had assembled at their alarm posts, were expecting an order to retire, as all seemed quiet, when the crack of the rifle of one of the advanced sentries announced the approach of the enemy. Marshal Ney, with an overwhelming force, was advancing by the road from Val de la Mula, and attacked and drove in the outlying picquet under Captain the Honourable Keith Stewart, which occupied that road. In resisting this attack, and falling back on the supports, Lieutenant M'Cullock, who was on this picquet, was sabred, and, with several men, taken prisoner.[1]

O'Hare's company were at once ordered in support, and he disposed them behind some walls. Here they waited till Stewart's picquet, slowly retreating and disputing their ground, came in upon them, followed by a swarm of French tirailleurs. A wing of the 43rd were about a hundred yards in the rear of these Riflemen; and at this moment a shell from Almeida, thrown of course at the French, burst close by, and killed and wounded several Riflemen.

O'Hare's company was now ordered to retire. Half the company did so, the remainder, under Lieutenant Johnston, were still engaged with the French advanced troops, when a troop or squadron of the enemy's hussars, whom our men, on account of the similarity of the uniform to that of the German hussars, had not noticed, swept round their left flank, and galloping between the Riflemen and their support the 43rd, sabred and rode down many, and caused great confusion.

It was but for a moment: for the 43rd, recovering from their surprise, fired a volley which emptied many saddles. The action now became general along the whole line. The French advance was for a time checked in the broken ground; but Ney's overwhelming force bore back the English towards the rocky defile which led to the one narrow bridge over the Coa. The ground was disputed inch by inch by the Battalion,

[1] M'Cullock refused to give his parole, and was marched towards the French frontier, and at Valladolid, being confined in a private house, his handsome person and his wounds excited the pity, or that which is akin to pity, of a young lady of the family. The old story: she laid plans for his escape, she procured him a disguise, she gave him a supply of money; and he succeeded in rejoining the Battalion.

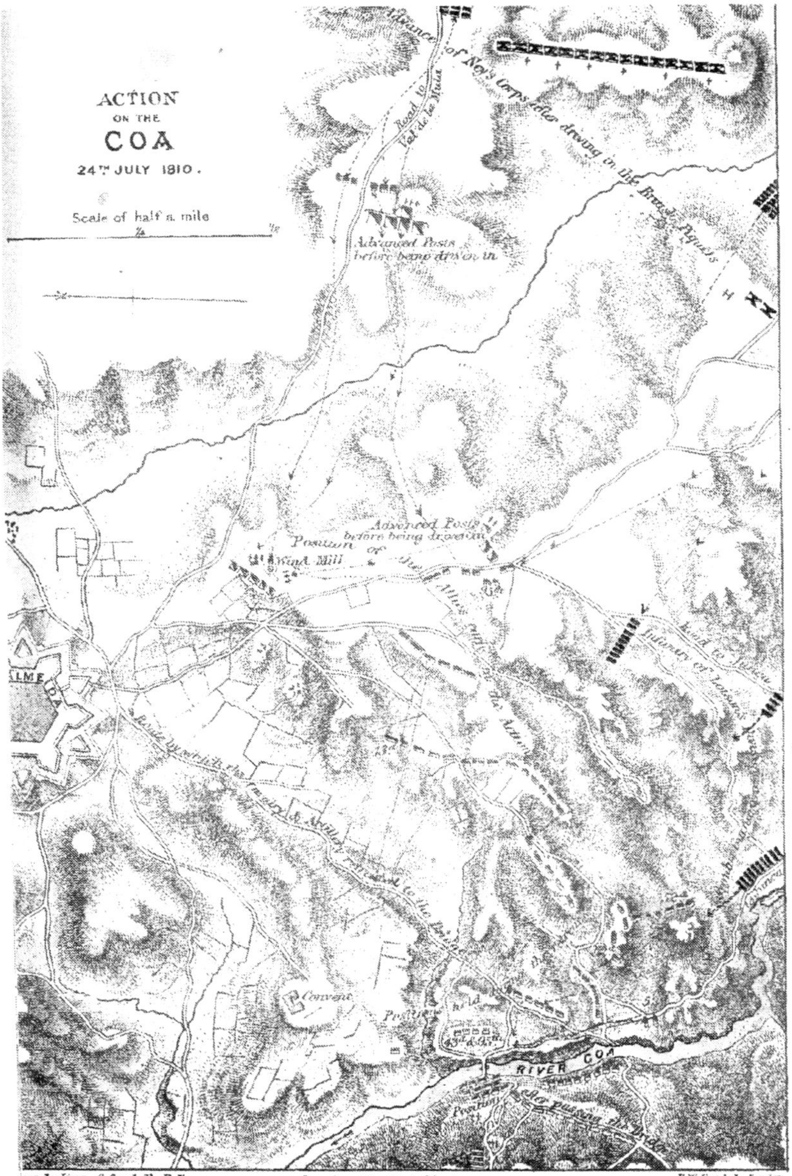

…wn by Lieut. G. Goodall, R.E. London: Chatto & Windus. E. Weller, lith. London

the 43rd and the 52nd, while the cavalry, the guns, the baggage, and the two Portuguese regiments attached to Craufurd's Division, descended the steep defile and crossed the bridge, about a mile to the rear

Thus the unequal contest had long and arduously to be maintained As they fell back to the hill which overlooked the Coa, it was perceived that some of the cavalry and artillery had not yet got across the bridge. Craufurd unhappily ordered a number of Riflemen, who occupied a position which prevented the enemy from cutting off the passage to the bridge, to evacuate it, before the 52nd, who were far on the right of the position, had made good their retreat. Beckwith at once saw the mistake, and ordered the Riflemen to retake the hill and the wall. This they did in fine style; but not without many officers and men falling. And about this time some skirmishers of the Battalion and a wing of the 43rd, led on by Major Mc Cleod of that regiment, the senior officer on the spot, not only held their ground, but, mixed together and gallantly headed, rushed against the French advanced troops, and checked them until the bridge was clear and the 52nd over, then, rushing down at speed, they got across the bridge. As soon as the regiment got over they formed along the bank of the river, among rocks, walls, and any ground that could afford cover. The Coa, swollen by the rain of the preceding night, and by that which had been incessantly pouring since noon, was not fordable, so that the only point to be defended was the narrow bridge Twice it was attempted by a valiant assault of French grenadiers; twice they were sent reeling back under our fire, almost all killed or wounded; the few who got across falling on the other side. Still a constant fire was kept up till about five o'clock; when the French ceased, apparently giving up all hope of forcing the bridge; and our men ceasing fire from exhaustion after about twelve hours' hard fighting.

The loss of the Battalion in this engagement was very severe. Lieutenant Donald M'Leod and 11 rank and file were killed, Captains Creagh, Samuel Mitchell, Lieutenants Matthew Pratt, Peter Reilly, Alexander Coane, Thomas Smith, and Second Lieutenant George Simmons were severely, and Lieutenant Harry Smith slightly, wounded; and 1 sergeant and 54 rank and file were wounded; and Lieutenant M'Cullock wounded and prisoner, 1 sergeant and 52 rank and file missing

Of these, Captain Creagh died the night of the fight; Reilly died the following day at Celorico; Pratt,[1] shot in the neck, died from the bursting of the carotid artery on August 1, on the Mondego river, near Fordaso; and many of the wounded men also died on their way to Lisbon.

In O'Hare's company alone, which, as we have seen, bore the brunt of the hussar charge, Lieutenant Alexander Coane was dangerously wounded, 11 men were killed and wounded, and 45 prisoners. Indeed, it is said that O'Hare's company only mustered 11 men on parade next morning.

A Rifleman, named Charity, in the cavalry charge received a sabre cut in the head, another in the body, and a musket shot through the arm; yet recovered and died a Chelsea pensioner many years afterwards.

In the Despatch reporting this action to the Earl of Liverpool, Lord Wellington states 'I am informed that throughout this trying day the Commanding Officers of the 43rd, 52nd, and 95th Regiments, Lieutenant-Colonel Beckwith, Lieutenant-Colonel Barclay, and Lieutenant-Colonel Hall, and all the officers and soldiers of these excellent regiments, distinguished themselves.'[2]

As soon as night had fallen Craufurd withdrew his Division from the Coa, and the Battalion bivouacked late on that night in some rocky ground near Valverde, the men suffering from the heavy rains of the preceding night and day.

Late in the night of the 25th they marched from Valverde, the rain still continuing to fall in torrents, and bivouacked near Freixadas. Here they were met by Lord Wellington, who came up from head-quarters at Alverca early in the morning, on hearing of the affair at the Coa. By him the Battalion were ordered into the village of Freixadas, where they were housed until the 28th.

On that day they arrived at Celorico, and hutted themselves by cutting down branches of the trees in a wood.

[1] 'As noble a fellow and as worthy a man as I ever met with.'—George Simmons' MS

[2] 'Wellington Despatches,' vi 293.

Here, on August 4, Craufurd's Division was divided into two brigades; one under Colonel Sidney Beckwith, consisting of the right wing of the 95th, the 43rd and the 3rd Portuguese Caçadores; the other, under Colonel Barclay of the 52nd, consisting of his own regiment, the left wing of the 95th and the 1st Caçadores. The Battalion remained at Celorico until August 5, when it was ordered to the front to support cavalry; and for about a fortnight or three weeks it was constantly on the move, the latter part of the time in heavy and continuous rain for three or four days. Early in September the army began its retreat, being covered by the Battalion and the other regiments of Craufurd's Division as a rear-guard. On the 20th they marched before daylight from Celorico, and crossing the Mondego by a ford, fell back by the road from Viseu to Coimbra. On the 23rd, the enemy's advanced guard pressing the cavalry of the rear-guard, Lord Wellington, who was present, ordered Craufurd to retire by the road leading to Busaco. This was effected during the two following days; on both of which the French pressed the rear-guard, composed of some companies of Riflemen and the 52nd and of some cavalry, with cavalry and infantry skirmishers intermixed, and some light guns, but the retreat was effected in good order and with little loss. The Battalion on both those nights threw forward picquets to support the cavalry.

On the 25th, when about a league and a half from Busaco, the enemy pressed the British cavalry so hard that the rear company of the Battalion had to face about and check them; and soon after the left wing of the Battalion was halted in a fir-wood, behind the village of Mora Morta, and effectually stopped them until the Light Division drew into the Sierra of Busaco, where the rest of the army were at this time assembled in position. This was an important and well-performed service, for Craufurd had kept his Division too long in an advanced position; and it was not without some difficulty that, protected by these four companies of Riflemen, he moved the Division into its position on the heights.

The right wing of the Battalion under Beckwith was halted in the village of Sula, at the foot of the hill of Busaco, where they were smartly cannonaded from the opposite heights, but without loss; and at night they were withdrawn from Sula, leaving a picquet in that village, and stationed among the rocks on the face of the hill, right and left of the road leading to Coimbra.

On the 26th Massena was engaged in bringing up his forces. Some infantry was pushed into a wood close to Sula, and skirmishing took place between them and the picquet of the Battalion there; and the companies attached to Barclay's brigade, in an adjacent village, were also attacked. This continued all the day; and as this constant interchange of fire was very harassing, the companies on picquet were relieved about every two hours. At last, at nightfall this skirmishing and fire ceased, and nothing indicated the presence of the vast hosts but the numerous watch-fires, which illuminated the sides of the mountains, divided only by a narrow valley.

It is not for me to describe the position of Busaco, or the particulars of the fight. It is enough for this record to note that in the centre of the side of the Sierra projects a hill forming a sort of natural bastion, and connected with the mountain itself by a neck, depressed below the level of the projecting hill. Among the rocks and broken ground on the sides of this hill were disposed the Riflemen of this Battalion; while in the hollow behind it Craufurd had concealed the 43rd and 52nd. Scarcely had day dawned on the 27th, when the enemy made his advance. Loison's division climbed the road leading up the face of the projecting hill, though galled by the fire of the Riflemen and Ross' guns. Yet they came on, the Riflemen, as the French pressed up the hill, running in on their supports and forming in the hollow between the spur and the mountain. At last the leading section topped the hill, and then, and not till then, Craufurd gave the signal; the bugles sounded, and eighteen hundred men sprang as from the earth. Instantaneously they gave a volley, the head of the column after one destructive fire from the leading section reeled; Craufurd ordered a charge; and soldiers, arms, knapsacks and caps rolled in a confused mass down the precipitous hill. The French column was wedged in the road, the leading sections were driven back on the still advancing rear, and all turned back in utter confusion. Then they came under the fire of the whole

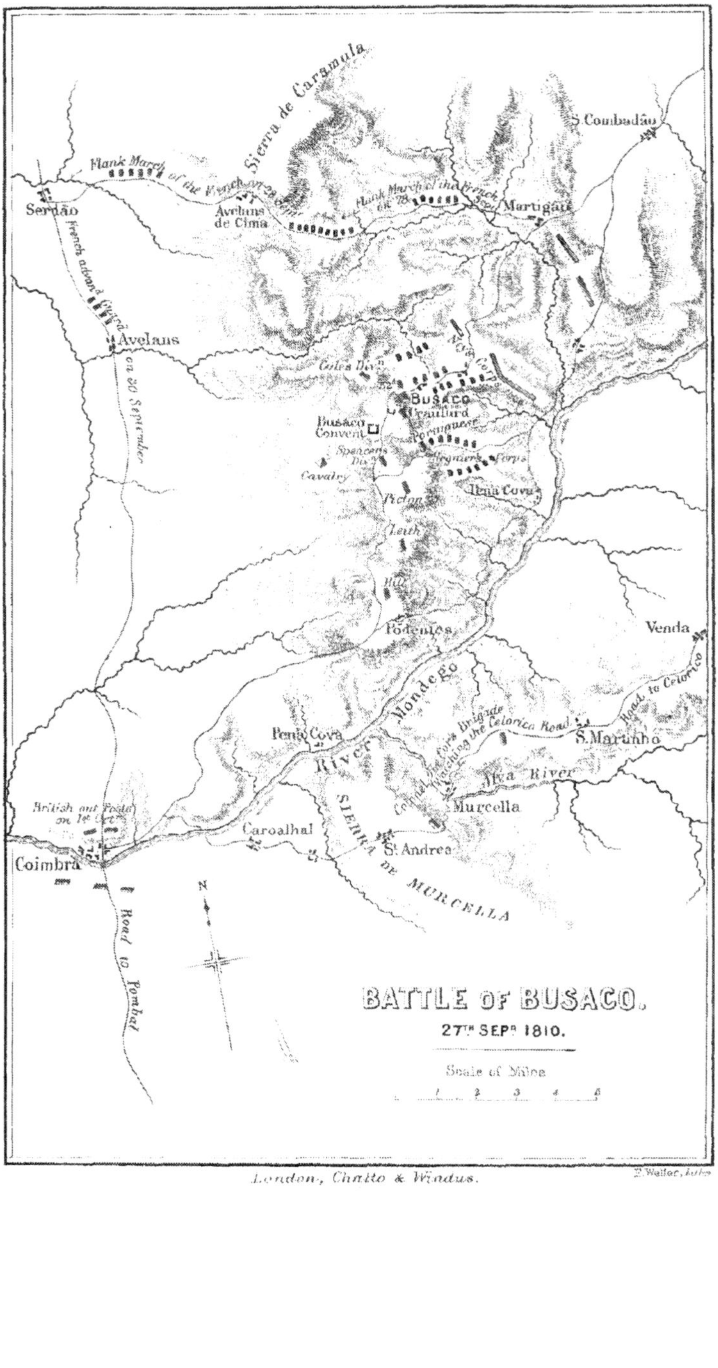

London, Chatto & Windus.

E. Weller, Litho

Division which far overlapped their flanks; and through the narrow street of Sula they fled, trampling the living and the dead. The Battalion and some Caçadores were ordered to pursue them; and General Simon, who commanded the attacking brigade, and many others were made prisoners by the Light Division.

No further attack was made on this position; but the enemy's skirmishers swarmed in the valley, and kept the Battalion employed till the afternoon, when Craufurd received a flag of truce with General Simon's baggage, and granted a temporary cessation of arms Leach mentions that, during that time, he went down into Sula, and met officers and men of Loison's division, who acknowledged their loss to be very heavy; one of them asserting that his company, which mounted the hill 120 strong, could only muster 27 men after their repulse.

The time limited for the truce having expired, the French seemed disposed to keep possession of the village of Sula; but Lord Wellington, who happened to be at hand, ordered a company of the Battalion to go down and drive them out: which they did in a very short time, and established a picquet there.

On the 28th no movement took place; but on the morning of the 29th, owing to an attempt on Massena's part to turn Lord Wellington's position by getting round by Coimbra, the English army broke up and fell back at a very early hour. About nine the Battalion followed, forming, as usual, part of the rear-guard, with some cavalry; and at night halted in a wood some miles from Busaco. On October 3 they reached Pombal; on the 5th Batalha; and on the succeeding days, in incessant rains, proceeded to Alemquer, where they arrived on the 9th. On the 10th they were pressed by the French advanced guard, and after a little skirmishing fell back to Arruda in a tempest of rain.

Thus they reached the Lines of Torres-Vedras, of which no description is needed here. The portion of the lines this Battalion occupied was on the right centre of the position, and on the fortified heights immediately behind Arruda, having advanced posts in front of the town. In very wet weather the Battalion were allowed to shelter themselves in

Arruda during the day, but always returned to their bivouack on the heights during the night.

While the Battalion remained in these lines the enemy made several reconnaissances, which occasionally brought on affairs of picquets. On one of these occasions, on October 14, a sharp affair took place near Sobral between the advanced guard of the 8th *Corps d'Armée* and the light troops of Sir Brent Spencer's division. In this skirmish a company of the 3rd Battalion, which had lately arrived from England and had been detained on its way to Cadiz by Sir Brent Spencer, as the Regiment was his,[1] was engaged, and Captain Percival and Lieutenant Eeles were severely wounded, and several men killed and wounded. These young soldiers (as George Simmons observes) 'behaved *like Riflemen*, and were complimented.'

On the 23rd, Simmons and Hopwood, being on picquet with Mitchell's company near Villa Matos, observed two French soldiers entering a house in their front in search of provisions. Taking three men of the picquet with them, they crawled to an avenue which screened them from a vedette who was stationed on a rising ground to give the foragers notice of any danger. Entering the house they seized the men, who were armed, and one of whom snapped his musket at his assailants, but it missed fire. The Riflemen found a large barrel of wine in the house; and the officers sending back one of the men for all the canteens he could find at the picquet while the others kept a good look-out, filled sixty, destroyed the rest of the barrel, and led off their two prisoners to the picquet.

The army remained in the lines of Torres-Vedras till November 15. Leach's company, which furnished the picquet in front of Arruda on the night of the 14th, discovered at daybreak on the next morning that the French army had fallen back during the night, leaving dummies of straw topped with a shako, and with a pole to look like a musket, to represent their advanced sentries. Soon after this was known at head-quarters the Battalion was ordered in pursuit; but did not come up with the French rear-guard, and halted that

[1] 'Wellington Despatches,' viii. 218. He was Colonel-Commandant of a Battalion.

night near Alemquer. On the 16th the Battalion continued the pursuit through Villa Nova and Azambuja; and though they never got sight of the rear-guard, they took many stragglers prisoners They first got sight of the French near Cartaxo, where they found them posted on some rising ground, having a heathy plain in their front. Craufurd, believing that a rear-guard only was opposed to him, was on the point of attacking, but Lord Wellington, who came up at the moment, forbade this attack, a whole *Corps d'Armée* being, in fact, concealed behind the heights on which the small force visible was posted. The Battalion halted that night in Cartaxo, and before dawn on the 18th again started in pursuit, and came up with the enemy's rear-guard, which retired before them across a plain to the Rio Mayor, which they crossed by a narrow bridge at the end of a long causeway. A company of the Regiment was pushed on as a picquet near the bridge. The enemy were occasionally exchanging shots with some dismounted dragoons whom the Riflemen relieved; and Simmons, who was on the picquet, taking three men with him, crept on the bridge, and lying down behind a dead mule, which gave them a good rest for their rifles, they took deliberate aim and evidently hit some of their adversaries, who became very chary of showing themselves. As the Riflemen had had a long march and a hard day's work, they were relieved at night by a company of the 52nd; and retreating to a grove of olive-trees near at hand, for they were to remain as a reserve, they kindled their fires and made themselves as comfortable as a rainy night allowed. But they were not long undisturbed. For Craufurd, fancying or hoping that the enemy were moving off, and ever anxious to be the first in pursuit, took two or three soldiers with him, and walked cautiously along the causeway so far that the French sentry challenged and fired; Craufurd ordered his escort to return it. And this alarmed the enemy; who, fancying probably that the English were crossing the bridge in force, opened a heavy fire, the balls of which rattled among the olive trees where the weary Riflemen were bivouacked, and rudely disturbed their rest. However, at last the uproar ceased; and when day broke on the 19th it was found that during the remainder of the night the French had formidably increased the strength of their position by placing *abattis* on the causeway and breastworks at the end of it. They had also placed guns on the high ground which rose behind, and which they had also fortified with *abattis*. The position, in fact, was a very strong one: in front the Rio Mayor, and swampy ground crossed only by the bridge and causeway; on the left the Tagus, with ground rising in bold and hilly eminences; and the considerable town of Santarem about a league in the rear. After bivouacking in a pine-wood near Valle, where, as in the previous night, they suffered from torrents of rain, they were ordered on the 20th to cross by a bridge near Valle to the left of the enemy's position and to attack his picquets. The Battalion was employed to drive in the enemy's advanced party, which they effected in fine style, and with but slight loss, though under sharp fire from the French light troops for about two hours The object of this reconnaissance was to ascertain whether Massena's whole force occupied the position or only a rear-guard; though, as Beckwith observed in his north-country phrase to a staff officer who asserted his certainty that it was but the latter, 'It was a *gay* rear-guard that built that *abattis* in a night.'

However, it being evident that the whole of Massena's army held this strong position, the Battalion was withdrawn and placed in houses, cottages and sheds, near the bridge. On it they had double sentries, close to it an outlying picquet of three hundred men; a large inlying picquet close by; and the rest of the Battalion, sleeping always by their arms, were ready, in case of an alarm, to turn out at a minute's notice.

As the Battalion remained thus posted at Valle, near the bridge to Santarem, during the winter, and there is nothing to record of them for four months, I shall return to trace the services of the 2nd and 3rd Battalions; observing only that General Craufurd at this time went on leave of absence to England, and that Sir William Erskine succeeded to the command of the Light Division during his absence.

We left the 2nd Battalion at Hythe on its return from Walcheren Its sufferings and casualties there prevented its taking part in any operations of the war for some time. But its losses were supplied with energy; and within a space of five months after its return from Flanders, two companies (Captain Cadoux's and Captain Jenkins') embarked on February 12, 1810, and formed part of the force assembled at Tarifa on February 25, under Lieutenant-General Graham, being then attached to Brigadier-General Dilkes' brigade. They served at Cadiz, and under the command of Colonel Norcott distinguished themselves at the Battle of Barrosa, as I shall more particularly mention when I come to detail the part taken by the 3rd Battalion in that action. Meanwhile, to trace the services of these companies.

One of these (Captain Jenkins') was detached to act with Ballesteros' Spanish force, and disembarked at Algeçiras early in September, and marched to Ximena; whence on the 18th they advanced to Alcalá de Gazules, and after some smart skirmishing with a French detachment from Chiclana, retired to Ximena. It remained in the neighbourhood of Algeçiras for two months; and after being constantly engaged with the enemy, it retreated (with Ballesteros' army) to Gibraltar.[1]

This company subsequently formed part of the garrison of Tarifa

On December 20 it was engaged in Colonel Skerrett's attempt to resist the investment of the place, and both companies took part in successfully repelling the assault on the breach which was made on the 31st, when their distinguished gallantry was very conspicuous. On the former of these occasions they lost 2 men killed, and had 10 men wounded. In the fight at the breach 1 man was killed and 1 wounded.

After taking their share in this 'great and splendid exploit,'[2] this company rejoined the other at Cadiz.

In July 1810, another company (Charles Beckwith's) embarked at Portsmouth, and, having landed at Lisbon, marched to join the army, then on its retreat from Busaco to Torres-Vedras. It joined at Coimbra, and was attached to the 1st Battalion in the Light Division.

This company thenceforward took part in the movements and actions of the 1st Battalion during the remainder of this and the first half of the following year

[1] 2nd Battalion Record

[2] 'Napier,' Book xv chap. v.

On July 5, 1811, another company (Captain Hart's) embarked at Portsmouth and joined the Light Division on the frontiers of Portugal in September. These two companies then, as we shall see, acted with the 1st Battalion and the Light Division, and distinguished themselves at the two great sieges (Ciudad Rodrigo and Badajos) of the next year.

A further reinforcement of two companies (Captains Duncan's and Ferguson's) left England in May 1812, and landed at Lisbon at the latter end of that month. They joined the army in July, shortly before the battle of Salamanca, and were attached to the Light Division. At Salamanca and during the advance to Madrid the four companies of this Battalion were commanded by Major Wilkins; but soon after they reached Madrid, Colonel Wade arrived from England with the Staff of the Battalion, and took command. And on the retreat from Madrid, the other two companies (Cadoux and Jenkins'), which had been in Andalusia with Skerrett, having, as we have seen, joined Lord Wellington's army early in November, the strength of the 2nd Battalion in the Peninsula consisted (as did the 1st Battalion) of six companies until the close of the war.

I have thus brought down the details of the movements of this Battalion to this period, because being enfeebled by the results of the disastrous Walcheren campaign, they were enabled only to join the army in the field by single, or at most by two, companies at a time, as their numbers were recruited and their health was restored. Its marches, its actions and its glories will henceforward form part of the general history of the Regiment, as will that of the 3rd Battalion, which, until its junction with the other Battalions, I will now proceed to particularise. But I will in as far as record or other information enables me to do so, distinguish the feats of arms and the losses of each Battalion.

The 3rd Battalion on its formation in 1809 was stationed at Brabourn Lees; and the drill and discipline of this new levy were carried on so vigorously and effectively that it was able early in 1810 to send three companies to Cadiz. And on July 11 in that year two more companies and the head-quarters, under the command of Colonel Barnard, embarked at Portsmouth on board the 'Mercury' frigate, and landed at Cadiz on the 29th Cadiz was at this time besieged by the army under command of Marshal Victor; who occupied all the surrounding towns and villages except Cadiz itself and the Isla de Leon, their advanced posts being pushed forward to near the river Santi-Petri, except near the bridge of Zuazo, the only communication with the mainland Here the English picquets were thrown forward beyond the bridge and on the road to Seville, which forms a causeway across the marshy plain intersected with saltpans And so well was it defended by our picquets, that, as Ford observes, this bridge was the *pons asinorum* of the French; for they never could get over it.

Here the 3rd Battalion, and the two companies of the 2nd under Norcott, remained until February 1811, when they embarked under the command of General Graham on the 18th, and landed at Algeçiras on the 24th. Having bivouacked on a height near Algeçiras, they moved the next day to Tarifa, where they halted until the 26th. The two companies of the 2nd Battalion were attached to the brigade of Guards commanded by Brigadier-General Dilkes, and the four companies of the 3rd Battalion,[1] with two companies of the 47th, were brigaded under Colonel Barnard.[2]

On March 1 they marched about twelve miles and bivouacked on some high ground; and the following day reached Casas Viejas, where they bivouacked on a hill, and suffered much from the bitterly cold weather. On the 3rd, having started before daylight, they reached about mid-day a lagoon through which was a ford. The Spaniards, who led the column, hesitated so long in attempting to cross, that General Graham, out of all patience, proposed to General La Peña to let the British troops advance The 3rd Battalion was the leading regiment, and at once entered the ford in column of sections, and marched straight through it, the water reaching about to their waist. The rest of the English force followed; and the Spaniards, shamed into imitation, followed their example. The troops marched for-

[1] The other company of this Battalion had joined the army under Lord Wellington ('Wellington Supplementary Despatches,' vi 569, 575), and was no doubt the company with Sir Brent Spencer's Division. See p. 62.

[2] 'Napier,' vol. ii. appendix ix. 2

ward, and halted that night in an olive-wood on very high ground, near Vejer, the soldiers suffering from the extreme cold, which was severely felt in consequence of their wetting in crossing the lagoon, and the scarcity of wood for firing. They halted here until the evening of the 4th, when a little after dark they marched to the village of Conil, and on the morning of the 5th reached the plain of Chiclana, and halted on the eastern slope of the knoll of Barrosa. This is a ridge running in from the sea-coast about a mile and a half, and overlooking the plain, which is bounded on one side by the shore, and on the other by the forest of Chiclana. In our front was a pine-wood. About twelve o'clock General Graham put his troops in motion, and the 3rd Battalion were ordered down the hill and into the wood in order to take possession of the height of Bermeja. But they had not long moved, when Graham was informed that the enemy had debouched from the forest, and having forced the troops left on the height, were ascending the hill of Barrosa. The 3rd Battalion were instantly countermarched, and ordered to get to the plain and engage the enemy as soon as possible. On emerging from the pine-wood they found themselves in front of two battalions of the 8th Regiment, one of grenadiers, the other of voltigeurs. Two companies under Barnard were left to cover and protect the guns, while the other Riflemen of this Battalion, inclining to the left, and extending as they came up the hill, soon became engaged with their opponents. In the same way Norcott, in command of the two 2nd Battalion companies forming the rear-guard, as soon as he heard from a sergeant of the German hussars of the appearance of the enemy, put his column to the right about, and extending his two companies, made his way out of the wood; and on getting out of it and seeing the enemy advancing, he put his right to the cliffs to cover the British regiments then filing out of the wood, and was soon engaged with the enemy's voltigeurs; and the Guards and 67th having advanced, he placed his Riflemen on the flanks of the brigade, and with them advanced against the enemy's line.[1]

About this time the grenadiers of the 8th French Regiment advanced, with drums beating, and the 54th (French) entered

[1] Norcott's Report. 'Wellington Supplementary Despatches,' vii. 128.

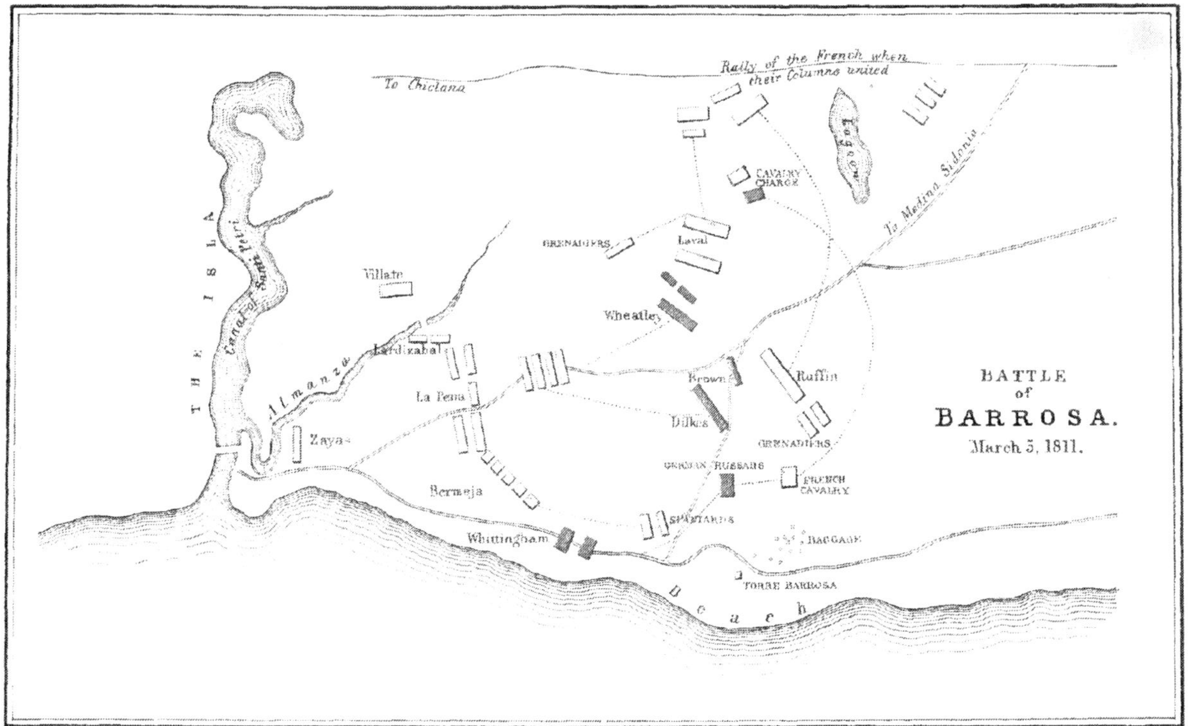

London. Chatto & Windus.

the pine-wood to endeavour to turn our left. Notwithstanding the fire of the 3rd Battalion on them in column, and at a short range, the grenadiers of the 8th pushed on and drove in our skirmishers; when the 87th, with some companies of the Guards, charging them with the bayonet, they gave way, and in a short time fled routed and in disorder; pursued by the Riflemen, who were engaged with the light troops which attempted to cover their retreat. However, as is well known, the Spaniards giving no help, but looking on as unconcerned spectators, Graham was unable to follow up his victory, and the Riflemen were recalled.

'In all my fighting,' says Surtees, 'I never saw an action in which the chances of death were so numerous as in this.'[1] And so the Duke calls it 'the hardest action that has been fought yet.'[2]

In the hour and a half during which it lasted, the two 2nd Battalion companies lost 6 rank and file killed, and Lieutenants Hope[3] and Thomas Cochrane (severely) and 1 sergeant, 1 bugler, and 26 rank and file wounded; and the four 3rd Battalion companies had Captain Knipe and 13 rank and file killed, and Lieutenant-Colonel Barnard, Lieutenants William Campbell (severely) and Hovenden, 3 sergeants, and 45 rank and file wounded. Barnard was severely wounded about the middle of the action, and was carried to the rear, and while the wound was being dressed, another shot struck him, and inflicted a wound more severe than the first. Surtees, who went to the rear to bring up fresh ammunition, says that the ground there was ploughed up by the enemy's round shot and musketry. The 3rd Battalion had four mounted officers in the field: the horses of two were killed; of another wounded.

In his despatch reporting this action General Graham says: 'Lieutenant-Colonel Barnard and the officers of his Battalion executed the duty of skirmishing in advance with the enemy in a masterly manner.' And he specially mentions Lieutenant-Colonel Norcott, whom he recommends for promotion.[4]

Soon after the action the British forces moved off, and crossed to the Isla, except the 3rd Battalion, which was left

[1] P. 127.
[2] 'Wellington Despatches,' vii 400.
[3] Lieutenant-Colonel John Charles Hope, K.H., died October 12, 1842.
[4] 'Wellington Despatches,' vii 396.

on the field to protect the wounded, and to give notice of any return of the enemy. But none appeared; and after dark Major Ross, who had succeeded to the command on Barnard's being wounded, moved the Battalion across the field, thickly strewn with dead and wounded of both armies, and formed it into square on a sand-hill on the beach, where they rested on their arms during the remainder of the night. It was severe service which fell to the lot of this young battalion; a march of sixteen hours in the preceding night; three hours' manœuvring, and half of it hard fighting; and all this without food; remaining under arms on the field till dark; and now only resting on their arms.

General Rousseau, who had been made prisoner, badly wounded, died in the course of the night, and was buried on the beach by the 3rd Battalion. In his pocket they found a leave of absence to return to France on account of ill-health, which his appearance clearly indicated, but of which this brave soldier had not availed himself

Towards morning Ross moved off his weary and famished Battalion; and passing by the beach and over the Santi-Petri river, they returned to their former quarters in the Isla de Leon

Here they remained till June 30, when, embarking at Cadiz, they reached Lisbon (after an unusually slow passage) on July 19, and marched up the country to join Lord Wellington's army. They arrived on August 21, and were attached to the Light Division, then cantoned in villages near the Agueda. At the same time the company of this Battalion which had been attached to Sir Brent Spencer's division was withdrawn from it, and joined the Battalion.[1]

[1] 'Wellington Despatches,' viii 218, and see p 62.

Plate II.

THE 95TH

CHAPTER III.

ON the night of March 5 it was ascertained that Massena had evacuated his position at Santarem, and had commenced a retreat, and the Light Division were ordered immediately in pursuit; and at three in the morning on the 6th they marched. The 1st Battalion, being in advance, on crossing the bridge came upon the dummy straw sentries (the old trick of the retreating enemy), and pushing on, arrived at Santarem at midday. This was found quite deserted, and after an hour's halt the Riflemen resumed their march, and that night occupied Pernes.

On the 7th they followed the retreating enemy to Torres Novas; and halted at night at Arga and La Marosa. Starting at daybreak on the 8th, the Riflemen first caught sight towards evening of the enemy's rear-guard, which occupied the village of Paralvo. The 1st Battalion were at once ordered to dislodge them, which, with the help of a couple of 6-pounders, they did very speedily. On the 9th they advanced early, and after five hours' march came up with the enemy's rear-guard at the junction of the roads from Leiria and Lisbon and that to Coimbra Here a large body of cavalry was posted, and infantry in force was halted in rear. An advanced squadron of the 11th *Grenadiers à Cheval* was charged by the German hussars, and some prisoners taken by them and the Royal Dragoons. About 40 prisoners, mostly stragglers, also fell into the hands of the Riflemen.

During these marches O'Hare's company were pushed forward, by mounting them behind the dragoons, and were on the 9th engaged all day in skirmishing, but without any loss.

On the 10th, the enemy having shown himself in great strength, in order to check the advance and to take up a position, the Battalion retired about half a league, and bivouacked in a pine-wood On moving forward on the 11th it was found that the French had taken up a strong position at Pombal, occupying the old castle situated on an eminence and the town with infantry; the rest of their force being posted on the heights behind the town. Two companies of the 1st Battalion, O'Hare's and another, with Elder's Caçadores, dashed over the bridge leading to the town, and found the enemy in some houses near the bridge, from which they kept up a brisk fire; which the Riflemen, entering the opposite houses, returned for some time Till at last Sergeant Fleming and a few men rushed into one of the houses held by the enemy and made several prisoners Then the Riflemen drove them out of the houses. Lieutenant Hopwood, as he was entering one of them, got a bad wound in the thigh; pushing on they carried the castle, the key of the position; and pursuing the enemy, after some sharp fighting with their voltigeurs, who obstinately disputed ground which from its nature was very defensible, drove them completely out of Pombal. But continuing their pursuit too far, some were taken prisoners, and others escaped with difficulty The combat continued till dark, which fell before Lord Wellington could bring up a sufficient body of troops to make a general attack. After this hard day's fighting the Battalion bivouacked in a ploughed field, exposed to torrents of rain.

In this skirmish the two companies captured a grey horse, which carried the baggage of Colonel Soult, the nephew of the Marshal; and the contents were sold by auction by the captors in the bivouack; except his medals, which the men presented to Captain O'Hare, whose company had been actively engaged.

They stood to their arms before daylight, and found that the enemy had retired in the night They immediately followed, and found the enemy posted in front of the town of Redinha; his right protected by some wooded heights; his left resting on the river Soure beyond Redinha, and well protected by ravines. In front was a large plain, which, when the Riflemen emerged from the defile leading to it, they found occupied by large bodies of troops It was a bright Spring day, and the sight of the one army advancing over the plain, the other in position on it, was splendid The woods on the right of the position were immediately attacked by the left wing (four companies) of the 95th, under Major Stewart, which carried them and cleared them from the enemy in gallant style. This enabled Lord Wellington to form his line in front of the defile. At the same time the left of the position was attacked by the right wing of the 95th, under Major Gilmour, while the other regiments of the Light Division supported their attacks. The French rear-guard made gallant attempts to check their advance, but after a stubborn resistance they were driven through the town of Redinha and over the bridge; the Riflemen pressing them so hard, that they and the flying enemy passed over mixed together. Many of the enemy were forced over the battlements of the bridge; many threw themselves over to escape from their pursuers, and not a few were slain in the hand-to-hand fight on the bridge. On passing the bridge the rear-guard attempted to form on the height beyond, but the Light Division allowed them no respite, and they were driven towards Condeixa. The enemy's guns occasionally gave our skirmishers some discharges of grape, but they pressed on till dark, when they were recalled, and bivouacked for the night on a height, the French army in the valley beneath, and the advanced sentries not more than two hundred yards from each other.

On this day Lieutenants Robert Beckwith and Chapman, of the 1st Battalion, were wounded; and of the 2nd Battalion, 4 rank and file were killed, and 9 wounded.

Lord Wellington, in his despatch, highly praises the conduct of the Regiment on this day, specially naming Majors Gilmour and Stewart; and in reference to driving the enemy's right out of the wood, he says: 'I have never seen the French infantry driven from a wood in a more gallant style;'[1] but by some mistake in Sir William Erskine's report, he gives the credit of this exploit to the 52nd, while it was really performed, 'to the admiration of the whole army,' by four companies of the 1st Battalion[2]

After some of the 1st Battalion skirmishers had towards evening driven the French before them, the officer commanding the latter held up his sword with a white handkerchief

[1] 'Wellington Despatches,' vii 356-7.
[2] MS Record 1st Battalion

tied to it; and on coming to a parley, he told the officer commanding the Riflemen that he thought both parties needed some rest after a hard day's work, and proposed a truce for the night. To this the Riflemen agreed; and asked him and his subalterns to share their rations They very readily accepted the invitation; and after a scanty dinner of ration beef, and a little rum for beverage, they separated; one party to resume their retreat, the other their pursuit, next morning.

Three months after, Lieutenant Fitz-Maurice of the 95th, who had been present, was on picquet at Duas Casas, near the Agueda, when he saw a French officer limping towards him, who saluted him as an acquaintance. '*Est-ce que vous ne me reconnaissez pas?* I was one of your guests at Redinha. One of your men wounded me next morning. No matter. I come now not as a spy; but we have heard that you are short of rations; and I come, in return for your kindness, to offer you a share of ours.' Fitz-Maurice was too old a soldier to admit that they were in want of supplies, though indeed they were; so, thanking him for his proffered kindness, which he declined (with great inward longing and regret, no doubt), they parted as good friends as they had been on the night of the fight at Redinha.

O'Hare's and Balvaird's companies being on picquet, an alarm was created by a Rifleman, Humphrey Allen, shooting a French sentry, in the hope of finding something in his mess-tin, because his own company had refused to share their provisions with him in consequence of his having skulked to the rear, carrying wounded, during the day. A general alarm took place, which brought Beckwith to the front.

On the 13th the Regiment marched to Condeixa and were left comparatively quiet on the roadside. For while some manœuvring took place to turn the enemy's position, he evacuated it, having set the town of Condeixa on fire As Lord Wellington was superintending these dispositions to turn the enemy's flanks from a knoll close to the Regiment, some French tirailleurs crept near unperceived and fired at him and his Staff without success Several Riflemen ran up to shoot or capture them, but they fled on their approach.

On the 14th at dawn the Light Division advanced against the enemy, who was posted on ground presenting many obstacles near the village of Casal-Nova. Other divisions of the army were sent to turn the flanks, while the Light Division attacked Ney's centre. The ground was much intersected with stone walls, which enabled the enemy to dispute every foot of ground. And this Battalion was skirmishing from early morning until night; but they drove the enemy from one post of advantage to another in spite of many checks, and eventually Ney's rear-guard fell back upon the main body at Miranda de Corvo. Early in the day a section of one of the companies was thrown forward among the skirmishers, and some rising ground being in front, Kincaid was ordered to take a man with him and occupy it, and to give notice of any movements of the enemy. He and the man who accompanied him, John Rouse, an old Rifleman, on getting to the top, ensconced themselves behind two large stones; but every time Rouse put his rifle over the stone to get a shot, a shower of French bullets rattled near them. After several attempts he gave it up, observing, 'There will be no moving among them till this shower ceases.' Kincaid observes that 'this was the hardest day's fighting he had ever known.'

As the French were retreating before our skirmishers, one man was observed to remain behind, deliberately loading and firing. Costello covered him and shot him. On coming up with him, a French sergeant, who lay wounded beside him, said: '*Hélas! vous avez tué mon pauvre frère.*' The cause of his having remained behind was evident; it was in the hope of protecting his wounded brother. Costello, much to his credit, as soon as the fighting was over, returned to look for the brothers; both were dead, stripped by camp-followers, by whom they had probably been murdered.

Major John Stewart was killed in this fight, and Lieutenant Strode received wounds of which he died. Stewart was a most admirable officer of light troops, skilful in handling them, experienced in outpost duty, and (after Beckwith's example), while strictly maintaining discipline, never harassing the men with matters of minute detail. Strode, who was also an excellent officer, always carried a rifle in action, and in the accurate use of it he excelled

This day's fighting lasted till sunset, when the picquets of the 1st Battalion occupied the village of Illama, which had been set on fire by the French; and the officers and men of the picquets saved many of the inhabitants and their children, who were too exhausted from famine to extricate themselves, from perishing in their burning houses. Some, however, were only saved from one death to die, when brought out, from want and exhaustion. Lord Wellington, in his despatch, specially mentions the conduct of the Regiment and the names of Colonel Beckwith and Majors Gilmour and Stewart.

The Battalion on going over the field after the action found that they had been opposed by the French 95th Regiment, and many buttons with that number were cut off the coats of the killed and preserved as trophies

On the morning of the 15th a thick fog prevented the army starting early in pursuit. When it cleared it was found that the enemy had evacuated their position, and the Battalion passed through Miranda de Corvo, which was in flames, having been set on fire by Marshal Ney's rear-guard, which had occupied it the night before.

The Battalion were halted beyond the village on a gentle slope, when Lord Wellington rode up; and Beckwith took occasion in conversation with him to mention that the Battalion were suffering much from having outmarched their supplies, and that some of his men from want and weakness had been unable to keep up. The Commander-in-Chief at once told them that they should have the first rations that came up. The men were just setting about cooking some provisions they had found abandoned by the French, when they were ordered to fall in at once and advance The truth is that Lord Wellington on going to the front had observed that the enemy were in a strong position behind the river Ceira, but had committed the fatal mistake of leaving the rear-guard under Ney in front of Foz d'Aronce on our side of the river, here crossed only by a narrow bridge. The Battalion at once attacked them, and after a short but hot engagement drove them over the river. By some mistake the bridge was destroyed before the whole of the rear-guard had passed; and these being hotly pressed, endeavoured to cross the river, and a large number of them were drowned in the attempt. It was almost dark before the action commenced and it was quite dark before it was ended. The Battalion occupied for the night the camping-ground thus suddenly vacated by the French rear-guard, and at their camp-fires resumed the cooking of their suppers which had been interrupted by the hasty advance from Miranda de Corvo, or, rather, they continued the cooking begun by the French, for they found their pots on the fire, and a good supply of biscuit.

In this affair Lieutenant M'Cullock was severely, and Kincaid slightly, wounded. The general orders of the 16th contain, besides expressions of approbation and thanks to the army in general, the following clause: 'The Commander of the Forces requests the Commanding Officers of the 43rd, 52nd and 95th Regiments, to name a sergeant of each Regiment to be recommended for promotion to an ensigncy, as a testimony of the particular approbation of the Commander of the Forces of these three Regiments.'[1]

In compliance with this order, Sergeant Simpson, then acting Sergeant-Major, was recommended, and was appointed an Ensign in the 2nd (Queen's) Regiment of Foot.

The 16th was a day of rest. The Light Division had outmarched their supplies; the men were fatigued and weak from hunger; and the bridge over the Ceira being destroyed Lord Wellington gave them a day's halt

On reaching the banks of the Ceira the Riflemen came upon a sight of such wanton cruelty as seemed to stand out in horrid prominence in a retreat where cruelty, rapine and slaughter were of daily occurrence. Nearly 500 donkeys were standing in mute agony, hamstrung by the inhuman enemy who had fled the preceding night. That they should prevent their falling into the hands of their pursuers was natural; that they should choose this alternative of rendering them useless, instead of killing them, was brutal.

On the morning of the 17th the Battalion crossed the Ceira at the ford of Alça Perna; the ford was so deep that the men with difficulty kept their legs; and having passed it they halted on high ground covered with wood, a little short of the Alva The next morning the enemy was found in a strong position on the rugged banks of the Alva, behind the Ponte da Murcella They had broken down the bridge. However, the Battalion was formed up opposite the enemy,

[1] 'Supplementary Despatches,' vii. 82.

and some 9-pounders being brought up, their fire and the advance of the Riflemen 'put them all in a bustle,' to use Lord Wellington's characteristic language;[1] and George Simmons says he never saw them go off in such confusion.[2] The Battalion halted on a swampy height covered with pine-woods, and bivouacked.

On the 19th, a temporary wooden bridge having been constructed, they crossed the Alva, and passing through Sabriera, halted for the night in a wood of pines.

On this day, amongst many other prisoners, an Aide-de-Camp of General Loison was taken, with a very handsome Spanish girl, dressed in a hussar uniform, who was said to be his wife. He was a Portuguese, a traitor to his country.

On the 20th, the Battalion advanced through Gallizes and halted in a fir-wood near Venda Nova. Here they found quantities of carts and waggons which had been abandoned by the enemy. On the following day they continued their advance and halted in fir-woods near Marusa. On the 22nd the Battalion went into houses in the town of Momenta de Serra in consequence of the inclemency of the weather. Here, as indeed during this whole advance, they found the dead and mutilated bodies of the people, and heard from the survivors heartrending accounts of the cruelties perpetrated by the retreating enemy. On the 23rd they advanced to S. Paio and bivouacked in a wood in front of it; on the next day they marched to and were quartered in the village of Mello, and on the 25th bivouacked in a wood near it.

During these days the Battalion was obliged to make these short marches in order to let the supplies come up. The men and officers suffered the greatest privation, only one ration of bread being given out in four days, and the country behind the retreating French being stripped of everything.

On the 26th the Battalion marched to Celorico, which the enemy had evacuated, and halted there the next day.

On the 28th the right wing of the Battalion by a forced march reached Avalans de Ribeira, and 100 men under Captain Charles Beckwith were sent to dislodge a strong rear-guard of the enemy from a mill in front of Freixadas.

[1] Letter to Marshal Beresford: 'Wellington Despatches,' vii 372.

[2] MS Journal.

They found the French busily at work, grinding corn, and soon drove them out of the mill and the village; taking several prisoners. In this affair the Adjutant, Lieutenant James Stewart, having dashed into the village with a few Riflemen, was shot, from a window, through the left breast and heart. He was acting as Brigade-Major to Colonel Beckwith, and was universally esteemed in the Regiment. 'It is not too much to say,' Leach observes, 'that no man in any corps ever filled the situation of adjutant better than he did, and very few half so well. He was open-hearted, manly, friendly and independent; a most gallant and zealous officer, and much devoted to his own Corps. He neither cringed to, nor worshipped any man, but did his duty manfully, and with impartiality: two qualities inestimable in adjutants. By the soldiers he was idolised, and very justly. When his duties as adjutant did not interfere, he was amongst the first to enter into any frolic and fun, and a more jovial soul never existed.' [1]

On the next morning at dawn the whole of the advanced guard, Riflemen, cavalry, and artillery, attended his funeral; and his body, wrapped in his cloak, and deposited in a chest, was buried in front of Colonel Beckwith's quarter, in the village of Alverca.

The left wing of the Battalion, with the rest of the Light Division, had on the 28th crossed the Mondego, and occupied the villages of Baracal and Mavashal.

On the 29th the army moved forward on the front and flanks of the strong position of Guarda, which stands perched on a high hill, and is said to be the most elevated town in Portugal.[2] Notwithstanding the strength of his position the enemy did not await our onset, but moved off in the direction of Sabugal, pursued by cavalry and artillery only. The Light Division was not now handled by the fiery Craufurd; and the enemy escaped with the loss of barely 200 prisoners, which fell into the hands of the pursuing cavalry.

The Battalion halted in Carapeta and other villages at the foot of the hill on which Guarda is placed.

On April 1 the Battalion marched by Adão to Pega,

[1] 'Leach,' 204-5.

[2] It is said to be more than 4,000 feet above the level of the sea.

where they halted about an hour in very heavy rain ; and then proceeded to Quintas de S. Bartolomeo on the banks of the Coa, and nearly opposite Sabugal, where the 2nd Corps of the French army, under Regnier, were posted in great force, having picquets on our side of the river.

The Battalion furnished the picquets, which were ordered to be extremely vigilant ; not to interfere with the enemy if he did not molest them ; but if attacked, to hold their post and never to quit it.

It was a very dark and stormy night, with heavy rain. George Simmons and Kincaid were on this picquet, and the latter relates a curious instance of the impossibility of a man's walking quite straight in the dark. On going to visit one of his sentries about midnight, he found the man absent from his post. Being an excellent old soldier he felt assured that he had not deserted, and after searching for him in vain he called him by name. The man's answer was instantly followed by the discharge of a French sentinel's musket ; and it then appeared that on every successive walk up and down his beat he had verged nearer and nearer to the French lines, which he was close to when called. The man, convinced that he had kept on his post, was astounded and incredulous that he had in the pitchy darkness edged away from it

On the 2nd the Battalion moved towards the right, and nearer to the bridge in front of Sabugal, and during this movement had some slight skirmishes with the enemy's advanced posts.

On the morning of the 3rd a thick fog hung over the banks of the Coa. Beckwith's Brigade of the Light Division was drawn up in close column behind the heights on the left bank of the river (in compliance with the disposition for the attack [1]), when a staff officer rode up and asked him 'why he did not cross ?' Beckwith was not the man to whom such a question should have been addressed, nor one to hesitate in giving a practical answer to it. He immediately ordered his brigade to advance. Four companies (the right wing) of the 1st Battalion led. The banks were steep and the ford at which they crossed deep, the water nearly up to the men's armpits. As soon as the Riflemen had climbed the opposite

[1] 'Supplementary Despatches,' xiii. 609.

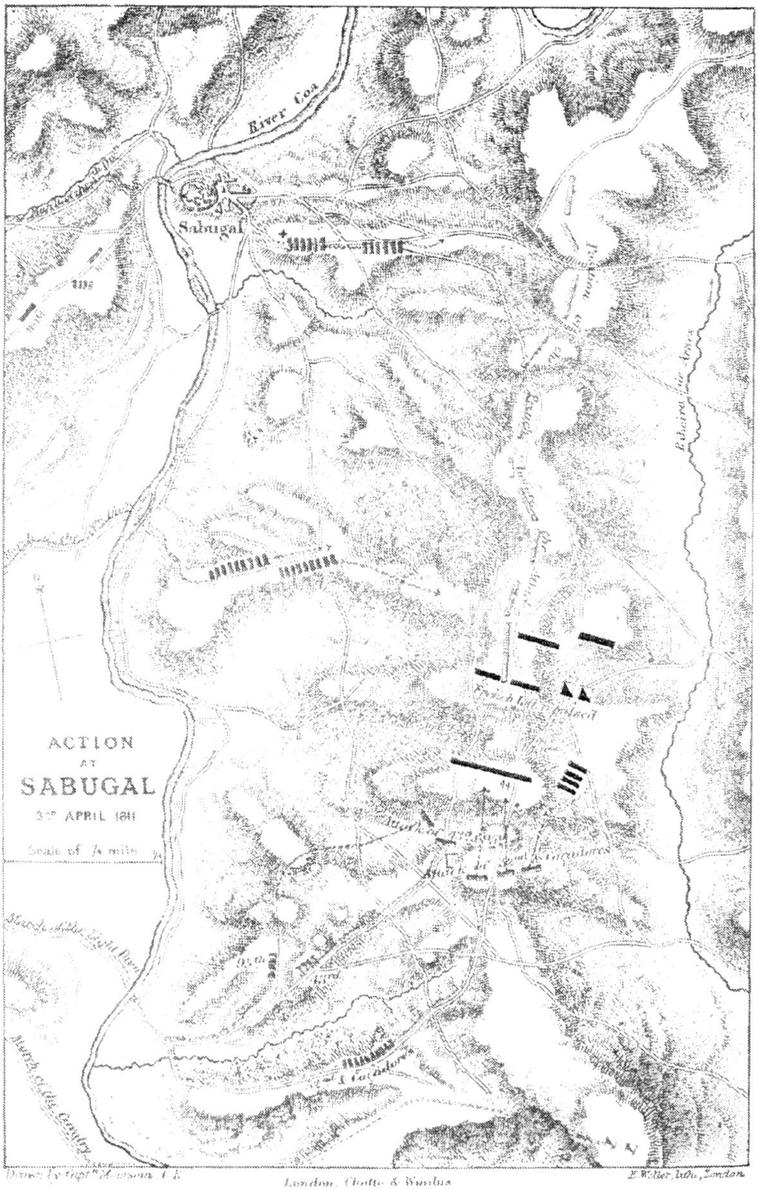
River Coa
Sabugal
ACTION
AT
SABUGAL
3rd APRIL 1811
Scale of ¼ mile
French left Defeated
Caçadores
95th
Caçadores
Ribeira dos Arrôes
London, Chatto & Windus
E. Weller, lith., London

bank they advanced in skirmishing order The officer in command of the French picquet ordered his men to fire as they retreated. Following the picquet, they soon came upon a regiment, and continued skirmishing till the rest of the brigade came up. Then they pushed the enemy through a chestnut-wood and up the hill ; a blinding rain came on, and on advancing Beckwith found himself, when the shower ceased, confronted by the whole of Regnier's *Corps d'Armée*. Their fire and overwhelming numbers forced back the four companies of the Battalion on the 43rd who were in support. Regnier followed with three strong columns ; but the 43rd received them with such a fire that they fell back, and the 43rd charging them, drove them down the hill and into their position. Here the enemy made a stand, and being reinforced, again obliged Beckwith to retire He got his Riflemen behind some walls, where he not only held and checked the enemy, but again drove the French back and pursued them ; but on reaching their original position, Beckwith was attacked by infantry on the left, while cavalry on the right charged the skirmishers A third time the handful of men were forced back by overwhelming numbers ; but now the other brigade of the Light Division, attracted by the fire, came up ; and the fog clearing off, the 3rd Division, under Picton, which had crossed the river lower down, came up on the enemy's right , and the 5th Division, having crossed the bridge, appeared debouching from the town of Sabugal , thus reinforced, Beckwith drove the enemy at the point of the bayonet into and through his original position, and the French retreated in confusion. Unfortunately, Sir William Erskine with the cavalry had lost his way in the fog, and had gone too far to the right , so that advantage could not be taken of the loose manner in which the enemy left the field ; yet some prisoners were made.

In this action, in which, as Lord Wellington states, 'the operations of the day were, by unavoidable accidents, not performed in the manner he intended they should be,' nothing could be more daring or more characteristic of British courage, than the way in which Beckwith, with a handful of men (the Riflemen, Elder's Caçadores, and the 43rd), withstood and thrice repulsed and pursued a whole *Corps d'Armée* placed in a strong position. And deservedly does the great captain go on to say that he considered 'the action fought by Colonel Beckwith's brigade principally, to be one of the most glorious the British troops were ever engaged in.'[1]

Beckwith's own coolness and gallant bearing in it are recorded by all the narrators of the action. When obliged by the overwhelming numbers and fury of the French to give the order to retire, he rode among his own Riflemen; and seeing some disposition to quicken the pace he would say: 'Don't run; I did not mean that; we will go steadily, and give them a shot as we retire' When he had reached his supports and could make a stand, he faced them about, and led them forward again, and was obeyed and followed as calmly and steadily as if he was marching them up and down the barrack square.

In this affair Lieutenant the Hon Duncan Arbuthnot and 1 Rifleman were killed. Beckwith was wounded in the forehead, and had a horse shot under him; and Second Lieutenant William Haggup and 12 rank and file were wounded.

And of the company of the 2nd Battalion present in this action, 1 man was killed and 2 wounded.

During the fight, as the Riflemen were driving the enemy's skirmishers through a chestnut-wood, a man of the 1st Battalion of the name of Flinn, was aiming at a Frenchman, when a hare started out of the fern with which the hill was covered Flinn, leaving the Frenchman, covered the hare, and fired and killed his game On the officer commanding the company remonstrating with him, his reply was, 'Ah! your honour, sure we can kill a Frenchman any day; but it isn't always I can bag a hare for your supper.'[2]

The fight was hardly over, when the fog dissolved in torrents of rain; and Lord Wellington, riding up at the moment, directed the Light Division, as an express recognition of its prowess during the day, to house themselves in the town

[1] 'Despatches,' vii. 445 He adds 'The 43rd Regiment particularly distinguished themselves; as did part of the 95th Regiment under Major Gilmour'

[2] I am indebted for the particulars of this anecdote (which I had heard old officers of the Regiment mention) to Mrs Fitz-Maurice's 'Recollections of a Rifleman's Wife.'

of Sabugal. They arrived just in time to anticipate the 5th Division, who yielded the much-coveted shelter, not without much murmuring Thus the Riflemen had a roof over their heads; but the houses were mostly shared with the former occupants, who were dying of hunger or of ill-usage

On the next day the Light Division moved through Quadrazaes, Valdespina, and Alfayates, and halted for the night at the frontier village of Forcalhos

On the 5th the Battalion marched to Albergucria (in Spain); Massena having crossed the Agueda, and evacuated Portugal, with the exception of a garrison in Almeida, which was immediately blockaded.

On the 8th they marched to Fuentes d'Onor, and on the next day took up their old line of outposts on the Agueda, at Gallegos, Espeja, and Fuentes d'Onor.

On the 10th two companies of Riflemen, consisting of 150 men, under Captain Cameron, were detached to San Pedro near Almeida, to shoot the cattle grazing on the glacis of that fortress. Daily until the 15th, before dawn, they marched to near Almeida, and taking a position among rocks, and firing at the cattle, compelled the garrison to withdraw them. They were daily saluted with the fire of the guns of the place, by which, on the 12th, 1 sergeant (McDonald) was killed. At dusk they returned to San Pedro, to resume their watch on the next morning

On the 23rd, a force consisting of two battalions of French infantry and a squadron of cavalry, marched by Carpio to the heights above the bridge of Marialva, on the Azarva, and halting there, sent forward a party to attack the picquets of the Light Division stationed at the bridge, then furnished by the 52nd. The pass was gallantly defended; and another company of the 52nd and some of the 1st Battalion coming to the assistance of the picquet, the enemy were repulsed, and retired towards Ciudad Rodrigo. Lord Wellington, in his 'Despatches,' mentions Lieutenant Charles Eeles as having distinguished himself on this occasion.[1]

On the 27th the Battalion marched early in the morning from the villages of Sesmero, Barquella and Villar de Puerco, which they occupied, to Alameda, and thence in rear of

[1] 'Wellington Despatches,' vii 515.

Gallegos, on which occasion another attack was made on the picquets, and again the enemy were repulsed

And again, on May 1, six squadrons of French cavalry and a column of infantry appeared on the old ground of the heights of Carpio and Marialva; but after making a demonstration for some hours, withdrew.

On the 2nd the French army was concentrated, and advanced with a view evidently of raising the blockade of Almeida, or of throwing supplies into it; and as Lord Wellington was not disposed to dispute their advance until they approached his position at Fuentes d'Onor, the Light Division fell back without firing a shot, and passing through the village of Fuentes d'Onor, took post behind the village of Alameda.

But though the 1st Battalion were not actually engaged on this day, the company of the 3rd Battalion which was attached to the 1st Division took part in resisting the furious attack made by the enemy's light troops on the village of Fuentes d'Onor, Lieutenant Uniacke was severely wounded, and 9 Riflemen were wounded

On the evening of the 4th, the Battalion were moved to the rear of the centre of the British position. On this day General Craufurd rejoined from England, where he had been on leave, to the great satisfaction of his Division, which had experienced the want of his leading on more than one occasion during his absence

On the 5th took place the Battle of Fuentes d'Onor. In the morning the Battalion was moved to the right and posted in a wood of oaks, throwing out skirmishers in front Here they were hotly engaged for some time with the French skirmishers, who, however, did not attempt to drive them through the wood, till a large body of cavalry appearing on their right, and the French skirmishers pressing them sharply through the wood, they were compelled to retire, as the flank of the 7th Division being turned, they were in great danger of being cut off Then it was that Craufurd moved them in close column, ready to form square in an instant had the cavalry charged them, across a plain nearly a mile in extent. This manœuvre was executed with all the precision and deliberateness of a field-day, while an enormous force of hostile cavalry hovered around them, but did not dare to

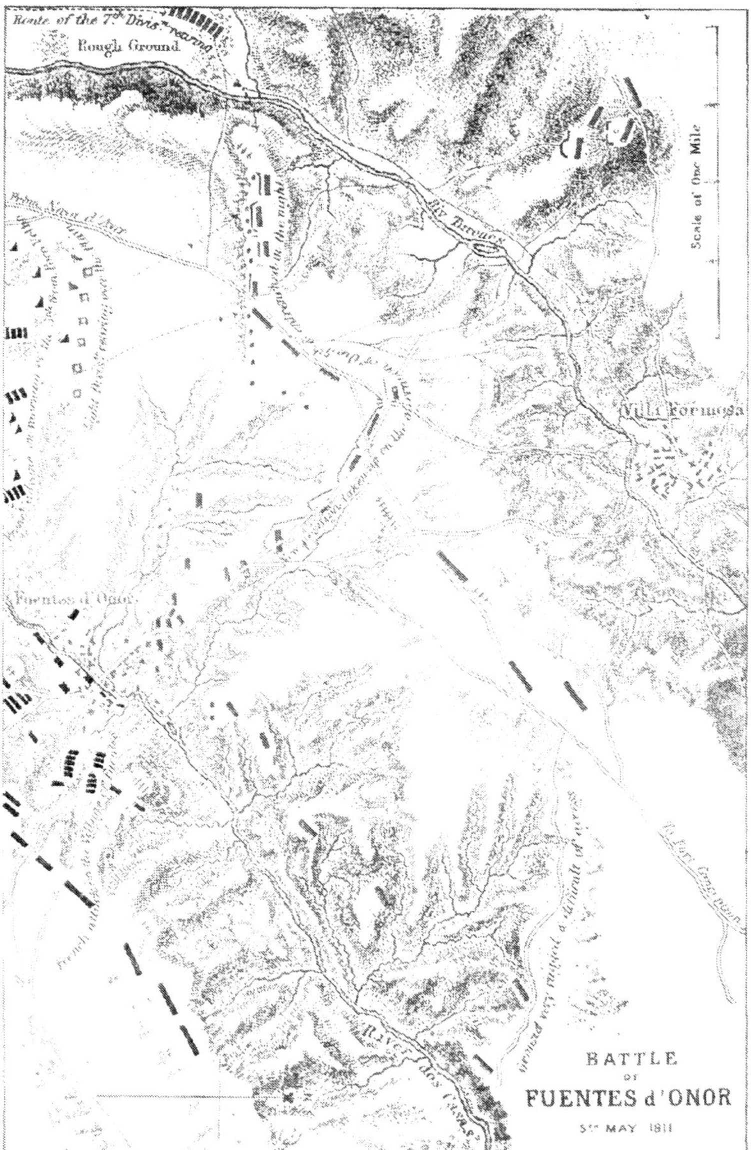

BATTLE
OF
FUENTES d'ONOR
5th MAY 1811

charge, so formidable was their formation, and so steady their movement, and while a furious cannonade assailed them. They marched to that part of the position where the Guards were formed in line, and they wheeling back a company, the Battalion marched through, and halting in column acted as a support to that part of the position. They were afterwards placed at a right angle to the right of the British position, with their own right resting on the river Turones; and getting behind and among some rocks and broken ground, they were menaced by a large force of French infantry, which endeavoured to push in between the 1st and 7th Divisions, but finding the position unassailable, and being vigorously attacked by four companies of the Battalion under Major O'Hare,[1] withdrew. Then a tremendous fire of artillery was opened upon the Riflemen

About two o'clock, as the enemy did not seem to threaten any further attack on this position, the Battalion were withdrawn, and placed in reserve in rear of the centre Here they remained, lying down, until near dusk, when the Battalion moved down into Fuentes d'Onor, to relieve the troops which had been engaged there.

While the Battalion were in position near the Turones, and the French infantry which threatened them kept out of rifle range, Flinn, whose sporting propensities at Sabugal I have recorded, was observed to leave the ranks, and, with his comrade, advance towards the enemy The officer in immediate command, fancying they were deserting, asked the sergeant of the company what it meant 'Oh no, sir,' he replied, 'they are only gone for some amusement.' Accordingly, 'on nobler game intent' than the hares at Sabugal, after stopping to drink at the Turones (for the May day was hot) they crept up to the French, and taking good aim, brought down each his man. Then, putting their caps on their rifles to receive the return fire, while they were well under cover, they deliberately walked back, and fell into their places in the Battalion[2]

In this action 1 sergeant and 6 Riflemen of the 1st Battalion were wounded, of the company of the 2nd Battalion, 2 were killed and 4 wounded; and of the company of the

[1] This gallant repulse is mentioned by Lord Wellington 'Despatches,' vii. 532.

[2] 'Recollections of a Rifleman's Wife.'

3rd Battalion, attached to Sir Brent Spencer's Division, Lieutenant Westby and 1 private were killed, 2 were wounded, and 1 sergeant and 1 private were missing.

Shortly after the Battalion occupied the village of Fuentes d'Onor, the French, whose picquets were at the other side of the bridge which spans the Duas Casas, sent over a flag of truce, with a request to be allowed to carry off their wounded. This was of course acceded to. Three French officers crossed the bridge, and while the wounded on both sides were being carried off had much friendly conversation with our officers, preceded by polite offers of '*une prise de tabac.*' They were loud in their praises of the gallantry of our troops, and presaged hard fighting on the morrow. One of them, alluding to the name of the place, observed to George Simmons that of that 'Fountain of Honour' many of their comrades and of ours had drank deep The wounded having been removed, they politely wished our officers 'good night,' and returned to their side of the river.

They had a captain's picquet posted near the bridge, and a strong column of infantry near a church, and two of their sentries were at the foot of the bridge, while ours were stationed on our side of it Great vigilance was necessary, and was exercised by our officers of the picquet, in consequence of the proximity of the posts.

A man of the Battalion of the name of Tidy, a blacksmith by trade, having found a forge in the village, set to work to shoe some of the officers' horses. A French grenadier, attracted by the light, crossed the bridge, and asked to be allowed to light his pipe, and having done so remained talking to our men. Craufurd, who had come down to visit the picquet (Costello says to see after the shoeing of his horse), caught sight of the red epaulette, and sternly asked 'What the man was doing there;' and being informed that he only came to light his pipe, ordered him to begone.[1]

In the course of the night the Riflemen on picquet in the village threw up earthworks in the gardens, and a strong breastwork across the street. Before dawn they stood to their arms, but when day broke they found that the French did not renew the attack; nor did any change occur in the position

[1] 'Adventures of a Soldier,' 82

of the two armies until the 10th, when it was ascertained at daybreak, by the Riflemen on picquet, that the French had retired, leaving only a small cavalry picquet at various points in the line of posts they had occupied. The Light Division and cavalry pursued them; but the superiority of the enemy in cavalry, which covered their retreat, effectually checked the pursuit, and the Battalion bivouacked in its old quarters at Gallegos and Espeja.

On the 12th three regiments of French cavalry moved from Ciudad Rodrigo by the heights of Carpio, and our cavalry picquets fell back, followed by a squadron towards Espeja. Beckwith at once turned out his brigade, and sent forward some Riflemen as skirmishers, and the enemy retired across the Azarva with the loss of a few horses.

On the 26th, the Battalion marched to Nave d'Aver and Aldea de Ponte, fully expecting to proceed to the Alemtejo; but the next day they were countermanded, and resumed from the 5th Division the line of outposts in front of Espeja, Gallegos, &c.

On June 3, Beckwith, having heard that the French cavalry were collecting on the Agueda, and not knowing where an attack might be made, moved his brigade before dawn out of Espeja, and occupied a wood in rear of it; but no attack being made he returned to his former post at noon.

On the 5th, the Light Division broke up from the line of posts it had occupied since the battle of Fuentes d'Onor, and marching by Aldea de Ponte, bivouacked in a wood near Alfayates. On the next day the Battalion crossed the Coa by the very same ford near Sabugal by which they had advanced to the fight of April 3, and bivouacked in a neighbouring wood of chestnut-trees. The night was very dark, and about midnight there occurred one of those strange panics which excite the terror even of those who never flinched in battle. Some bullocks straying among the piled arms knocked them over. Those awakened by the crash of the falling rifles raised the cry, 'The French are upon us!' In a moment all was confusion; the officers trying to assemble their companies; even Craufurd himself, it is said,[1] ordering the men to fall in and load; and the camp followers flying to the rear. After a time the panic died out; and on the morning of the 8th the

[1] Costello, 87.

Battalion marched to Memoa, and halting there to cook, proceeded to Penamacor in the evening.

On the 9th to S. Miguel d'Arch, and halted on the 10th

On the 11th, by some blunder of the Staff, they were ordered to commence their march under a burning sun, and a great many men fell out, necessitating frequent halts. By some further mistake the baggage and supplies did not come up, and the men were without provisions for forty hours. At night they arrived at As Caldas de Cima, and bivouacked in a wood.

On the 12th the Battalion passed through Castello Branco, and halted during the heat of the day at As Cornadas de Rodão, and in the evening advanced to the pass of Villa Velha.

On the next day, crossing the Tagus by a bridge of boats, they marched to Niza, and bivouacked in a wood; on the 14th marched to Alpalhão, and on the following day to Portalegre, where they halted until the 19th, when they moved to Arronches.

On the 23rd they took up their position with the army which Lord Wellington had concentrated, encamping on a most arid plain near Monte Raguinga on the Caya, and about three miles from Campo Major.

Here the Battalion remained for about a month, during which time Craufurd did not allow his Division to be idle, but frequently took it out for drill and exercise. During the time it remained here the Battalion suffered much from the baneful climate of the Alemtejo, and fever, ague and dysentery were rife amongst the officers and men. To add to the discomfort of this camp, it was infested with snakes, scorpions and other reptiles; yet it is strange that among so many men occupying it, no fatal or serious accident ever occurred from this nuisance, at least among the Riflemen

At last, on July 21, they were released from the life, to them after active service, so monotonous and every way so disagreeable; and on that day marching about a league and a half only, bivouacked, and on the next day marched into Portalegre On the 23rd they proceeded to Castello de Vide, where they occupied several quintas round the town. Thence they marched northward by much the same route by which they had moved to the Alemtejo, passing Niza on the 29th, and on the next day crossing the Tagus at Villa Velha, by a pontoon bridge, and bivouacking in an olive-grove. Thence to Castello Branco on August 1, to Lausão on the 2nd, Bemposta on the 3rd, Mauras on the 4th, whence they moved to the neighbouring heights on the 6th, and continued their march towards the northern frontier of Portugal on the 7th. On the 10th the Battalion crossed the Agueda at the ford of Vado de Carros, and occupied the villages of Martiago with the right wing, and Langella with the left. On the 11th they started, with Lord Wellington, to make a reconnaissance on Ciudad Rodrigo. On their approaching it some hundred infantry with a few field-guns, came out of the town, but did not venture beyond the protection of the guns of the place. The reconnaissance having been effected, the Riflemen returned to their cantonments.

During the march from the Alemtejo the men of the Battalion had suffered much from the heat, and many of the marches had to be performed in the evening, or before sunrise, or during the night On August 21 the four companies of the 3rd Battalion which had been at Barrosa, joined the Light Division, and a fifth company, which, as has been mentioned, was attached to Sir Brent Spencer's Division at his request, as a Colonel Commandant of the Regiment, also joined, thus forming five companies of the Battalion, under the command of Colonel Barnard. They were placed in Beckwith's brigade of the Light Division. About the same time another company of the 2nd Battalion, which had embarked at Portsmouth on July 5, and had landed at Lisbon on the 14th, under the command of Captain Hart, also joined the Light Division

Sickness, no doubt contracted in the Alemtejo while encamped on the Caya, still made great ravages among the troops of the Light Division; three officers and many men of the Regiment having died while it occupied these cantonments on the Agueda.

At the end of August the Regiment (or at least the 1st Battalion) marched to Villa Rejo, on the 28th to Zamarra, and on the 29th to Atalaya.

On that evening George Simmons was sent forward with a company, and a corporal and three men of the German hussars, with orders, by moving through a woody country and by a circuitous route, to strike on the road leading from Salamanca; and then to proceed at his discretion, in order to ascertain, if possible, whether any convoy was on its way to throw provisions into Ciudad Rodrigo. He reconnoitred Tenebrun, and bivouacked for the night in a wood.

The next morning he moved to Boca de Carro and S. Spiritus, and ascertained from Don Julian Sanchez's guerillas that a convoy had left Salamanca for Ciudad Rodrigo, but had been compelled to return, several parties of guerillas having formed across the road and attacked it The company therefore returned to its quarters at Atalaya

On September 9, Leach with his company and one of Portuguese Caçadores was sent over the Sierra de Gata to occupy two villages, Las Herrias and Aldea Juella, in the heart of the mountains, to observe some roads by which it was thought that Marmont might attempt to move light cavalry or infantry, and to obtain information as to the movements of the enemy. Here they remained a fortnight, daily patrolling and reconnoitring, but unable to ascertain anything of the enemy's doings.

Marmont having determined to throw provisions into Ciudad Rodrigo, assembled his whole army and crossed the mountains from Plasencia The Regiment, as part of the Light Division, was posted on the heights near Horquira. The enemy's cavalry watched them, and entered Atalaya on September 23. Here the Riflemen remained three days; and on the 25th the combat at El Bodon took place between the Hon General Colville's brigade and the enemy's cavalry. At this time the Riflemen were on the right bank of the Agueda, occupying the line of the Vadillo, a tributary flowing through a rocky channel into the Agueda, and falling into it about three miles from Rodrigo. Their position was a most dangerous one; for unless the troops on the left bank of the Agueda could hold the French in check they would have been cut off. Their safety was further endangered by the obstinacy of Craufurd, who though he received orders to retire, and join the rest of the army at or near Guinaldo, at two o'clock in the afternoon of the 25th, marched only to Cespedosa, one league from the Vadillo. On the next morning, however, at daybreak, they marched; and crossing the Agueda by a ford, and taking a circuitous route joined the 3rd and 4th Divisions near Guinaldo about three o'clock in the afternoon.

On that night the whole army retired, leaving the Light Division as a rear-guard. The Riflemen having made up their fires to deceive the enemy, and to lead them to believe that they were still in bivouack, followed about midnight. They marched through Casillas de Flores to Forcalhos, and were on the march during the whole of the 27th, with the exception of a short halt. General Craufurd having remained behind with a troop of cavalry to reconnoitre, was sharply pressed and pursued by the enemy's chasseurs, and came galloping into the middle of the Riflemen with the enemy's troopers at his heels. But the Riflemen, throwing themselves into rocky ground and cover, which fortunately was on each side of the road, soon brought the French cavalry to a check; but these dismounting and acting as infantry skirmishers, a smart skirmish took place between some companies of the Regiment and these dismounted men, which continued the greater part of the day. In the evening the Regiment joined the other Divisions at Aldea de Ponte.

Again forming the rear-guard, the Regiment marched at midnight, and about eight o'clock on the morning of the 28th reached a position on the height near Soita in a wood of enormous chestnut-trees, many of which were hollow from age and of such dimensions that men might have been and were sheltered in them. Lord Wellington was here in a very strong position; and Marmont having effected his principal object of re-victualling Ciudad Rodrigo, declined to give battle, and retired.

The Regiment on October 1 marched to Aldea Velha, and resumed its cantonments on the Agueda at Castellejo de Duas Casas, Martiago, Atalaya, Robleda, etc.

The Regiment now (with the Light Division) maintained the blockade of Ciudad Rodrigo, and there is little to record of its movements until the commencement of the more active operations of the siege.

On November 2, however, information having been received that a considerable body of French troops were in motion to escort a new governor to Rodrigo (the former one, General Renaud, having been taken prisoner near the place by Don

Julian Sanchez and his guerillas), the Regiment moved up nearer to the fortress on this morning; but it having been ascertained that the governor had succeeded in entering the place, and that the escort was bivouacked two leagues in its rear, the Regiment fell back to its former cantonments.

On the 20th Lord Wellington inspected the Regiment (with the rest of the Division) between El Bodon and Fuente Guinaldo. The Regiment had marched from its cantonments in the morning and returned to them after the inspection

About this time, or rather earlier, Colonel Beckwith went to England on account of his health, and Barnard (commanding the 3rd Battalion) took command of his brigade.

On January 4 the troops intended to carry on the siege of Ciudad Rodrigo were moved up near the place In an incessant fall of cold rain the Riflemen forded the Agueda; the water being nearly up to their shoulders, the men were obliged to put their pouches on the top of their knapsacks and to hold on to one another to prevent their being swept away by the current The Light Division occupied Pastores, La Encina, and El Bodon No sufficient arrangements having been made for their quarters, houses were with difficulty obtained, and officers and men were huddled together wherever they could find shelter. Next day, however, better arrangements were made, and the companies of Riflemen were housed separately.

On the 8th the Regiment crossed the Agueda before daylight on a bitterly cold morning at the ford of Cantarona, near the Convent of La Caridad; the water was about knee-deep; and passing round a hill to the north of the town near San Francisco and out of range of the enemy's guns, they halted. Several French officers appeared and spoke to the officers of the 95th with great politeness, being anxious to ascertain, as it seemed, what this movement meant.

It was not long before they learned; for at nine o'clock that evening a party of 300 men of the Light Division, under Colonel Colborne of the 52nd, stormed the detached fort of San Francisco. Captain Crampton's company of the 1st Battalion first formed upon the crest of the glacis, followed by Travers's company of the 3rd Battalion, and another company, commanded by Lieutenant Macnamara, of the 1st

Battalion. In a moment they were in the ditch and swarming over the parapet. Three guns were taken, 2 captains and 48 men made prisoners, and the rest of the garrison were killed. In this attack Second Lieutenant Rutherford Hawksley, 'a most promising young man,' was severely wounded, and died of his wounds. The officer commanding this outwork, a smart, talkative little Frenchman, was, when made prisoner, brought to General Craufurd. He had been stripped by the Portuguese and had nothing on but trousers, and was bleeding from the nose and mouth. Craufurd having expressed regret that he could not furnish him with clothing, Tom Crawley, a well-known private in the 1st Battalion, stepped forward, and saluting, said, 'He may have my great coat, your honour.' Craufurd, who was much pleased, said, 'You are very good, Rifleman; let him have it' Almost at the same time a sergeant was brought in, stripped naked by the Portuguese; he embraced his captain and burst into tears. Harry Smith, then on Craufurd's Staff, gave him his handkerchief to cover his nakedness.[1]

The capture of this work enabled the working parties immediately to begin the first parallel The garrison kept up an incessant fire of shot and shell, but by daylight the men were well covered Early on the 9th the Light Division were relieved by the 1st. The French from the old square tower of the cathedral had a good view of this relief, and a furious fire was kept up on the advancing and retiring Divisions.

On the 12th the Light Division again occupied the trenches, fording the Agueda up to their waists, and continuing in this wet state, half-frozen, till relieved next day. Some worked at the approaches; some kept up a fire on the works of the place; and in the evening, under cover of a fog, thirty men of the 1st Battalion, under Kincaid, were sent forward to dig holes as near as possible to the crest of the glacis, in which to shelter themselves, and to pick off the gunners This was not difficult for a good marksman, as, by having his rifle ready, he was able to aim at an embrasure and fire at it the moment he saw the flash of the gun. But the garrison threw fire-balls among them, however, the men crouching in their rifle-pits, lay hid until the fire-balls burned out, and then springing up again, picked off their gunners in the embrasures.

[1] Costello, 93

At ten the next morning the Division was relieved, and marched back to its cantonments. The fording of the Agueda, now partly frozen, on coming to and returning from the trenches, was very trying to the men. Not only the depth and the cold of the river; but now large blocks of ice carried down by the current bruised and incommoded them. In some measure to obviate this, cavalry were ordered to form across the ford above the infantry, and under this shelter the Riflemen crossed, if in the cold, at least unmolested by the floating ice.

On the 16th they again resumed their place in the trenches. The enemy had now got the range so accurately that their shells literally dropped into the trenches So murderous and incessant was the fire from the place, that on their relief the next morning a new expedient was devised to escape its effect. The relieving division came up by small parties and the Light Division in like manner retired a few men at a time. But strange is the confidence given by constant exposure to danger: the Riflemen having discovered that by crossing the river close to where they then were, and running the gauntlet of the enemy's fire for about a mile, instead of going round behind the hill near San Francisco, they would save both time and distance in getting to their cantonments, they did so

Two breaches having been pronounced practicable on the 18th, the troops were ordered to assemble on the 19th for the assault of the place. The storming party consisted of a hundred men from each Regiment of the Division. The officers of the Regiment who volunteered for this duty were Captain Mitchell[1] of the 2nd Battalion, and Lieutenants William Johnston and Kincaid of the 1st Battalion. The Regiment forded the Agueda as usual, and halted for about an hour near the Convent of La Caridad. Thence they moved forward, and halted again behind the Convent of San Francisco.

The order of attack was as follows:

Four companies of the 1st Battalion, commanded by Major Cameron, who were to line the crest of the glacis and keep down the fire of the place;

[1] Colonel Samuel Mitchell died June 3, 1833

Portuguese, carrying hay-bags, which they were to throw into the ditch, and ladders;

The forlorn hope;

The storming party, commanded by Major George Napier, of the 52nd;

The main body of the Division, commanded by Craufurd.

While waiting behind the Convent for the order to advance, Harry Smith came up to the Regiment, and said, 'Some of you must come and take charge of some ladders;' George Simmons at once stepped out and offered to go; and, having picked out the number of men required, followed Smith to the Engineer camp and obtained them. When he returned, Craufurd fiercely attacked him; 'Why did you bring these short ladders here?' 'Because I was ordered by the Engineers to do so, General.' 'Go back, Sir, and get others; I am astonished at such stupidity.' Simmons returned and procured others; and on his way back finding a Portuguese Captain wishing to be useful with his company, he handed over the ladders to him with strict injunctions as to how to place them, and rejoined his Battalion.

It is pleasanter to record Craufurd's last address to his Division, almost his last words, as they stood waiting to attack, words never forgotten by some who heard them.

'Soldiers,' he said, in a voice which seemed to be peculiarly impressive, 'the eyes of your country are upon you. Be steady; be cool; be firm in the assault. The town must be yours this night. Once masters of the wall, let your first duty be to clear the ramparts, and in doing so keep well together.'

At last the signal was given, and the leading Riflemen issued from behind the Convent of San Francisco and turned to the left to ascend the glacis. The night was clear enough to enable the defenders to perceive them; and no sooner had the head of the column appeared, than a furious fire of shot, shell and musketry lit up the ramparts in a sheet of flame, while fire-balls enabled the enemy to direct their aim on the advancing columns. Cameron's Riflemen extended along the glacis, and opened their fire. The stormers rushed up to the ditch, and without waiting for the hay-bags or ladders carried by the Portuguese, who were nowhere, leaped into the ditch, a descent of ten or twelve feet, and made for the breach. Kincaid, by mistake, turned to a ravelin which he fancied to be a bastion, and finding one angle of it a good deal battered, thought it was the breach, and mounted it; but soon perceiving his error, was about to return, when a shout from the other side of the ditch announced that the breach had been found. He dropped from the ravelin, and on coming to the breach found the head of the storming party just ascending it.

But not the stormers only: the rest of the Regiment were pouring into the ditch. George Simmons finding ladders reared against the *fausse-braye* (for the Portuguese by this time had found their way to the ditch) mounted it with many others, fancying it to be the breach; but discovering his mistake, slid down the other side and mounted the breach. As he was ascending the ladders, Uniacke of the 1st Battalion accosted him. 'This is the way.' 'Impossible,' replied Simmons, 'here are the ladders.' Uniacke left him, turned to the left, and just as he reached the rampart an expense magazine exploded, and blew him and many others up.[1]

Then was there furious fighting at this breach, but it was soon won. The men, true to Craufurd's orders, cleared the ramparts, and within an hour the place was in our hands. Then began that furious tumult, and that loosening of all the bands of discipline which mark the sack of a place captured by assault. The town was set on fire, but by the exertions of Barnard, Cameron and others it was extinguished. Barnard and Cameron with some of their officers seized broken gun-barrels, of which many French ones were found, and by force and even blows compelled the men to refrain from brutality and madness. By one o'clock in the morning Barnard had got the Regiment together and formed them on the ramparts, where, kindling fires, they lay down and slept soundly after this din of arms.

And many slept to wake no more. Captain Uniacke, as I have said, was blown up on reaching the rampart; his arm

[1] Just before the attack he had been twitted by a brother officer (Fitz-Maurice) with having dressed himself in a new pelisse for such a night's work. 'Never mind,' he said, 'I shall be the better worth taking.' 'Recollections of a Rifleman's Wife.'

was torn from the socket, and he was fearfully scorched He was carried to Gallegos, where he died a few hours after, surrounded by the men of his company, by whom he was beloved.' 'Though young in years,' says Costello, who served in his company, 'he was gallant, daring, and just to all whom he commanded His affability and personal courage had rendered him the idol of the men of his company.' Fairfoot, who was Pay-sergeant of his company, was resolved that he should be buried in consecrated ground, but he found an obstacle in the prejudices of the clergy, who considered him a heretic. However, Fairfoot (with pardonable equivocation) assured the priests that his Captain was an Irishman, which to the Spanish priests implied that he was a Catholic. Their scruples gave way; 'and I chose,' said Fairfoot afterwards, 'the finest tree in the church-yard of Gallegos' At its foot he was laid; the whole of his company attending, under the command of Thomas Smith, his subaltern. Lieutenants John Cox and Hamilton, of the 1st Battalion, were also severely wounded, 1 Rifleman was killed, 1 sergeant and 15 rank and file wounded; in the 2nd Battalion, Captain Mitchell, and Lieutenants Bedell and M'Gregor were wounded, the two former severely; 8 rank and file were killed, and 22 wounded,[1] and 2 sergeants and 7 rank and file of the 3rd Battalion were wounded

Besides these losses in the Regiment they had to regret the loss of their leader in so many glorious fields, Major-General Robert Craufurd, who, soon after starting them from the San Francisco Convent with the inspiriting words, 'Now, lads, for the breach,' was struck down mortally wounded, and died on the 24th. He was buried with military honours at the foot of the breach his Division had so gallantly carried, borne to the grave by four Sergeant-Majors of his Division, and followed by Lord Wellington, his Staff, and the officers of his

[1] The following nine non-commissioned officers of the 2nd Battalion volunteered for the forlorn hope.

Sergeant Bowley, wounded	Sergeant Spencer
,, Comerford, ,,	,, Tuite
,, Derby, killed	Corporal Larkins, wounded
,, Ecke, ,,	,, Nesbitt, ,,
,, Fairfoot,[*] wounded	

[*] Afterwards Quartermaster

Division. Though not of the Regiment, he had led them in so many a glorious field that he seemed to be of them. At Buenos Ayres, in the retreat to Corunna, and now in Portugal and Spain, he had been their Brigadier or divisional General. At first dreaded and disliked for his strict rules of discipline and for his unswerving punishment of all breaches of them, he had come to be beloved by men and officers, who saw to what a pitch of excellence that code and that enforcement of it had brought the Division he commanded, making it the admiration or the envy of the whole army; who recognised that if he was exacting, he always was just; who felt that he cared for their wants or their comfort, and who knew that he always led them bravely, always to conquer.

I am not writing a memoir of General Craufurd; yet two anecdotes connected specially with the Regiment I may here record.

On one occasion he was riding in front of the lines when two Riflemen rushed out of a house, pursued by a Spanish woman calling out '*Ladrone! ladrone!*' They had stolen bread. Craufurd with his orderly immediately pursued them, the guard was turned out, and they were made prisoners. The next day they were tried by a brigade Court-Martial, found guilty, and sentenced to a punishment of a hundred-and-fifty lashes. One, a Corporal Miles, was of course to be reduced to the ranks They were brought out to a wood to be punished. As soon as the Brigade Major had read the proceedings, Craufurd addressed the men on their cruelty to the Spaniards. Then, turning to the Regiment, he upbraided them in no measured terms. 'You think that because you are Riflemen, and more exposed to the enemy's fire than other troops, you may rob the inhabitants with impunity; but while I command you, you shall not.' Then addressing Corporal Miles, he said in a stern voice, 'Strip, sir.'

When Miles was tied up to a tree to receive his punishment, he turned his head and said: 'General Craufurd, I hope you will forgive me.' Craufurd answered: 'No; your crime is too great.'

On this Corporal Miles, in a quiet and most respectful voice and manner, addressed the General: 'Do you remember, sir, when you and I were taken prisoners, when under the command of General Whitelocke at Buenos Ayres? We were marched prisoners to a sort of pound, surrounded with a wall. There was a well in the centre, from which I drew water in my mess-tin, by means of canteen-straps which I collected from the men who were prisoners like myself. You sat on my knapsack; and I parted my last biscuit with you. You then told me that you would never forget my kindness to you. It is now in your power, sir. You know how short of rations we have been for some time'

These simple words, and the soldier's respectful manner, affected not only Craufurd but every man in the square. Meanwhile the Bugle-Major gave the fatal nod, and Miles received a lash. But before a second fell, Craufurd called out: 'What's that? who taught that bugler to flog? send him to drill, he cannot flog. Stop, stop, take him down; I remember it well, I remember it well!' Then he paced up and down the square, evidently much moved In a dead silence Miles was untied; and at last the General said to him: 'Why does a brave soldier like you commit these crimes?' and calling his orderly, he mounted, and rode off without a word more. The other man was pardoned, and Miles had his corporal's stripes restored in a few days

On one occasion during Moore's retreat, Lieutenant Thomas Smith, then a very young officer who had but lately joined, was accompanying ammunition which was in charge of a Quartermaster (Ross). On their arrival at Craufurd's head-quarters, the wily Quartermaster advised Smith to go and report their arrival to the General. The other demurred; saying that he was not in charge of the ammunition, but only accompanying it However, the Quartermaster urged him, reminding him that he must be hungry; they had not, in fact, tasted food for twenty-four hours; and that the General would probably ask him to dinner. Thus counselled by his senior and impelled by his hunger, he presented himself at the General's quarter and saw his Aide-de-Camp, who going upstairs returned with an order to proceed at once a further march of some three leagues. Smith returned to the Quartermaster with this woful order, adding that as he was in charge of it, he might remain with it, for that he should go on and overtake his Battalion. The Quartermaster declared he should do no such thing, and after a sharp argument they both started and joined the Battalion. In the morning as Smith was sitting down to breakfast, an order came from Craufurd, who had come up, that he and the Quartermaster should attend him. On being ushered into the General's presence they found him warming himself before a comfortable brazier, while breakfast stood on the table. In a voice of great severity he asked which of the two had received his order the night before.

'I did, sir,' said Smith, 'but'——

'No *but*, sir,' interrupted Craufurd; 'consider yourself under arrest, and,' adding a tremendous oath, 'I will smash you.'

Poor Smith—for Craufurd would not hear a word more—returned in dismay to his brother officers, whom he found at breakfast; but hungry as he was and pressed by them to be of good heart, food had now no charms for him.

Eventually Beckwith represented to Craufurd that the offender was but a boy just joined; and his pleadings, coupled perhaps with the fact that they were just going to fight, when every available officer would be wanted, induced Craufurd, contrary to his wont, to relax his severity and to release Smith from his arrest.

Long afterwards as Craufurd was standing talking with the officers of the Battalion, round a camp fire, he turned to him.

'Smith,' said he, 'did I not once put you under arrest?'

'Yes, sir, you did.'

'And do you know,' he continued, 'what became of the ammunition? I found it steadily going towards the French lines, and had but just time to put spurs to my horse and to turn it back. So that through your default I had nearly lost my ammunition.'[1]

On the 20th the Regiment marched back to its cantonments. Nothing could exceed the extraordinary appearance

[1] This anecdote, which I had often heard in the 1st Battalion, was related to me with graphic distinctness by Colonel Smith. As may be imagined, his relation differed somewhat from the story, which, passing through many mouths, I had heard in the Battalion. It was strange to hear it from the lips of one of the actors in it, when the other had slept more than sixty years in the breach at Rodrigo.

it presented. The men were dressed in every possible variety of costume which they had found in the houses. Some wore French uniforms, some breeches and jack-boots, some cocked hats; many had pieces of salt beef, hams and any provisions they could lay hands on stuck on their swords fixed to their rifles. In fact so strange was their appearance that Lord Wellington, who saw them on their march, asked 'What regiment that could be.'

One of the Riflemen, a day or two after, playing the game of 'nine-holes' with what he fancied to be a cannon-ball brought from the place, was blown to pieces. It proved to be a live shell, which passing over some hot ashes, exploded just as he had it between his legs.

The Regiment soon after the fall of Rodrigo moved to Ituera. And while here a military execution took place of some deserters of the Light Division who had been found in the place. They had been tried by a Court-Martial, of which General Sir James Kempt was president, and were shot in the presence of the whole Division. Two of them were Riflemen; one was in the highland company, which was then kept up in the 3rd Battalion, of the name of M'Guinniss, a shoemaker by trade. He had once been a man of good character, but had been led away by another, named Hudson, of Uniacke's company.

To conclude this painful subject I will add here that a month later when the Regiment was at Castello de Vide another man of the 1st Battalion was shot for desertion. His name was Arnal, and he was, or had been, a Corporal. When Ciudad Rodrigo was taken he in some way escaped and endeavoured to join the French troops at Salamanca, but in crossing the country he fell in with some Spanish soldiers, who made him prisoner and marched him back to the Regiment. He had been a man of good character, and it was hoped that this might have weighed in his favour, but discipline had to be vindicated, and so great a crime as desertion to the enemy could not be condoned. This man met his death with amazing firmness; settling his accounts with the Pay-sergeant of his company, and distributing his balance among his comrades the night before his death. When brought out to execution he refused to have his eyes bound, saying to the Provost Sergeant. 'There is no occasion; I shall not flinch,' nor did he.

On February 14 the Regiment marched to Portalegre, on the 15th to Arronches, and on the 17th to Elvas.

On March 17 the Regiment marched out of Elvas, the band playing 'St Patrick's Day,' to take up their position before Badajos, and after dusk began to break ground. A very heavy rain came on, and the weather continued very broken during the whole time of the siege operations. The ground to be occupied being extensive, and the force employed comparatively small, the men were required to be in the trenches six hours by day, and as many in the night; and this amount of time, with the addition of the marches to and from their camp, and the continued inclemency of the weather, made the period of the siege one of unusual hardship to the men and officers of the Regiment.

On the 19th the enemy made a sortie with about 1,500 infantry and some cavalry at the moment when the relief of the working parties in the trenches was taking place. The weather being, as usual, dull, and a drizzling rain falling, these troops got very close before they were perceived; and their cavalry, being mistaken for Portuguese, made their way through the camp of the Light Division. The men flew to their arms, and the sortie was repulsed; but the enemy succeeded in carrying off intrenching tools from the Engineers' camp, and in injuring the works of the approaches. In this sortie Lieutenant Freer, of the 1st Battalion, was wounded.

On the 22nd, the enemy having brought some field-guns out of San Cristobal, and placed them in position enfilading the trenches, some Riflemen were ordered out, to get as near the Guadiana as possible, and to fire across the river, and shoot their gunners. This they did so effectually that the guns were soon withdrawn, many of the men working them being killed or wounded.

On the 26th Fort Picurina was attacked and carried a little after dark, and a party of Riflemen, taken from the working party, was ordered to carry the ladders. Lieutenant Stokes, then of the 3rd Battalion, who was in command of this party, was the first man in the fort; and it was owing to these men (with others of the Light Division) that, according to Napier, the capture of the place was effected They were provided with axes, and broke down the palisades and gates of the fort It being evident that the enemy, as soon as they knew the place was in our hands, would redouble their fire, the working parties were urged by their officers to work hard to cover themselves. The Riflemen did so; and so effectually, that when at daybreak the enemy opened a furious fire of shell and grape, the men had made such good cover that they were comparatively uninjured.

On April 4 George Simmons with a party was in an advanced sap, and observing that some large guns of the place were doing much injury to our artillery in an advanced battery, he selected some of the best shots and directed them to fire steadily into the embrasures. In half-an-hour he found that the guns were not fired so regularly as before, and soon gabions were brought and stuffed into the embrasures. These were withdrawn when the guns were about to be fired. The Riflemen took note of this, and the moment the gabions were removed fired steadily into the embrasure. Very soon the gabions began to be replaced without the guns having been discharged They were thus effectually silenced. And from daylight till dark Simmons kept up this practice with 'forty as prime fellows as ever pulled trigger.' A French officer, probably a celebrated marksman, half hidden, lying on the grass of the parapet, set up his cocked hat some way in front of him to deceive our people, and to draw their fire. Some soldiers by him handed him loaded muskets to enable him to fire more rapidly. Simmons, leaning over the top of the trench, got a good view of this man; he selected a good shot, and being anxious that he should see the Frenchman, desired him to lay his rifle over his shoulder and steady his aim. The Rifleman fired; and nothing more was seen of the Frenchman, whom, no doubt, he killed or wounded, though the cocked hat remained in position until dark. But Simmons, in his anxiety, had forgotten that the priming of the old Baker rifle was close to his ear, which was much burnt and the whole side of his head singed.

Some of the best shots in the Regiment were selected also to occupy pits which had been dug between our approaches and the crest of the glacis, in order to pick off the gunners. This was most arduous and dangerous work, for not only were the men exposed to a deadly fire in running out to the pits, and in returning when relieved, but sometimes a man was wounded or killed in the pit, and the relieving Rifleman had to pull him or help him out before he could shelter himself, all the time exposed to a murderous fire from the place.

The breaches being reported practicable on the 6th, the assault was ordered to take place on that evening. It is needless, after Napier's magnificent description of this combat, to do more than specify what part the Regiment took in it The Light Division, under the command of Barnard, formed at about eight o'clock in close column of companies, left in front, about 300 yards from the ditch. They were detailed to attack the breach in the Santa Maria bastion. Four companies (the left wing) of the 1st Battalion, under Major Cameron, were in front, with orders to extend to the left on reaching the covered way, in order (as at Ciudad Rodrigo) to keep down the fire from the ramparts. Next came six volunteers of that Battalion, under Lieutenant William Johnston, provided with ropes, to endeavour to pull the *chevaux-de-frise*, with which it was known the garrison had defended the breaches, out of their place. Then followed the forlorn hope,[1] and then the storming party, consisting of 100 men from each regiment of the Division. The officers of the Regiment with this party were Captains Crampton of the 1st Battalion; Hart of the 2nd, and Diggle of the 3rd; and Lieutenants Bedell, Manners, Coxen, and M'Gregor, of the 2nd Battalion. The rest of the Division followed. So noiselessly did Cameron's four companies advance, and so accurately had he reconnoitred the ground, that he reached the place indicated for the head of his column, and extended along the covered way to his left, without being perceived by the garrison. Every man as he got into his

[1] The following non-commissioned officers of the 2nd Battalion volunteered for the forlorn hope

Sergeant Cairns	Corporal Coward, wounded
,, Fairfoot, wounded	,, Derby, killed
,, Kennedy, ,,	,, Mc Cordell, wounded
,, Taggart, ,,	,, Nesbitt
,, Fritte	

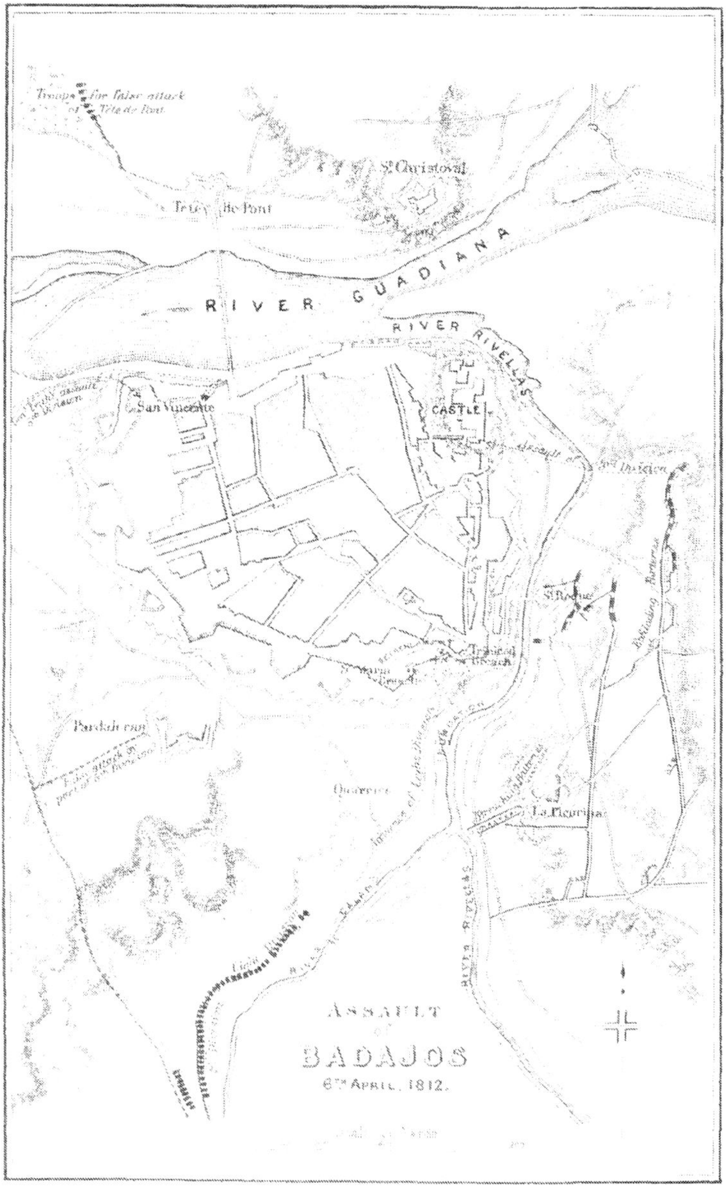
Troops for false attack of Tête de Pont
St. Christoval
Tête de Pont
RIVER GUADIANA
RIVER RIVELLAS
San Vicente
CASTLE
St. Roque
Trinidad Breach
Pardaleras
Quarries
La Picurina
RIVER RIVELLAS
ASSAULT
OF
BADAJOS
6TH APRIL, 1812.

place, silently lay down, placing the muzzle of his rifle through the palisades, and at the edge of the ditch. The men could see the heads of the troops lining the rampart: for the night was clear, though a sort of haze rising from the ground and the dark dress of the Riflemen enabled them to get into position unperceived. Yet a French sentry challenged twice; and his '*qui vive*' being unanswered, he fired, and drums were heard, beating to arms. Yet Cameron reserved his fire for about ten minutes, till the forlorn hope coming up, he began while the heads of the troops lining the rampart could still be seen immovable. Then began from the place that murderous and unceasing fire of grape, shell, and musketry which has been compared by more than one of those who saw it, to the central fires of the earth, or even hell itself, vomiting forth their fury. Surtees, who as Quartermaster of the 3rd Battalion and a non-combatant (though he wished to be in the fray and was hardly restrained) witnessed it from the quarries, between the Picurina and the Pardeleras, says that it was so bright and so incessant that he could plainly see the faces of the defenders, though nearly a mile off Yet Johnston with his volunteers, the forlorn hope and the stormers advanced, slid down the ladders or leaped into the ditch. The rest of the Division followed, tore up the palisades and ran up the glacis There Captain Charles Gray was shot in the mouth, and many officers and men fell. Yet all pressed on; even the firing party in the covered way, carried away by frenzy, seeing their comrades fall, and their aim baffled by the smoke, leaped into the ditch, and passing, how they could, the drain cut in it and filled with water, in which not a few were drowned, they surged like the wave of a raging sea up the breach. But as the wave is repelled from the rock, so were they checked by the insuperable obstacles; the *chevaux-de-frise* of sword-blades fixed in beams; the murderous fire from behind the wall of sand-bags, the planks studded with nails and fixed at the upper end; the shells, powder-barrels, grenades and even cart-wheels, which were hurled down upon them Again and again as one wave fell or melted away under that slaughtering shower, another took its place. O'Hare fell in the breach, shot through the breast with two or three musket balls His sergeant, Fleming, who had stood by him in many a bloody field, fell at his side. Many officers of the Regiment and many valiant Riflemen lay dead or wounded, or pressed down by those who were so, in that heap which extended from the top of the breach to the counterscarp. At last, after two hours of this murderous work, Lord Wellington gave orders for the Light Division to draw off. Still the intrepid Barnard, who had more than once himself ascended the breach, was unwilling to give way; and it was not till after renewed attempts had been made, and till he saw all hopeless, that he gave the order for his Division to withdraw. Even then in that deafening turmoil the order was imperfectly heard; and many officers were keeping their men from retiring. At last, however, almost all that lived and could move came away, and the remnant of the Regiment was formed a little distance from the place between midnight and one o'clock. Here Surtees found them, having posted off as soon as he knew (for he was near Lord Wellington when Picton's hurried note was brought to him) that the 3rd Division had stormed, and was in possession of, the Castle He was scarcely believed; so incredible did it seem to the assailants of these impregnable breaches, that any troops could have entered the place The men and the officers were lying down, in gloomy sullenness, after their terrible conflict. A staff officer brought word, 'Lord Wellington desires the Light Division to return immediately and attack the breach.' The men leaped up, resumed their formation, and advanced as cheerfully and as steadily as if it had been the first attack. Proceeding past, and often over, their fallen comrades, they again mounted the breach; but now the defenders having been called away, the resistance was slight, and they soon established themselves on the ramparts. Then Cameron formed his Regiment there, and told them that when all danger from the enemy was over, he would let them fall out; but that, until then, if a man left the ranks he would have him put to death on the spot They remained under arms and perfectly steady till between nine and ten next morning, when, as the whole garrison were prisoners and being marched out, he dismissed them, and they joined in that madness of intemperance, rapine and lust, on which it is more agreeable to their historian to draw a veil

Great were the losses of the Regiment. Twenty-three officers and 292 non-commissioned officers and Riflemen fell, killed and wounded in that fatal night

In the 1st Battalion (eight companies), Major O'Hare and Lieutenant Stokes, 3 sergeants, and 24 rank and file were killed; Captains Crampton, Balvaird, Charles Gray, and M'Dermid, Lieutenants William Johnston, Gardiner, McPherson (who died of his wounds), Forster, and FitzMaurice, 15 sergeants, 3 buglers, and 136 rank and file were wounded In the 2nd Battalion (two companies), Captain Diggle, 1 sergeant and 20 rank and file were killed; Lieutenants Bedell and Manners, 3 sergeants, and 31 rank and file were wounded. In the 3rd Battalion (five companies), Lieutenants Hovenden, Cary, Allix, and Croudace, and 9 rank and file were killed; and Lieutenants Macdonell (who died of his wounds), Worsley, Duncan Stewart, Farmer, and volunteer Lawson,[1] 2 sergeants, and 45 rank and file were wounded

Well may Sir William Napier sum up his glowing description of the assault with this stirring appeal. 'Who shall measure out the glory of . . . O'Hare, of the ninety-fifth, who perished on the breach at the head of the stormers, and with him nearly all the volunteers for that desperate service? Who shall describe . . the martial fury of that desperate soldier of the ninety-fifth who, in his resolution to win, thrust himself beneath the chained sword-blades, and there suffered the enemy to dash his head to pieces with the ends of their muskets?'[2]

O'Hare, a gallant soldier, beloved by his men, had a foreboding of his death. As the stormers assembled, he observed, in conversation to Captain Jones of the 52nd, that 'he thought that night would be his last.' To George Simmons, with whom he shook hands as the stormers were moving off, his last words were: 'A Lieutenant-Colonel or cold meat in a few hours' He was found the next morning by Simmons on the breach, naked. Cary was found by Surtees next day under one of the ladders, shot through the head. He had, no

[1] He was appointed to a second-lieutenancy in the Regiment May 9 following He left it in 1814, and died at Sligo, March 1874

[2] Book xvi chap v This incident is also mentioned by Kincaid It is to be regretted that the name of this heroic Rifleman has not been preserved.

doubt, been wounded in ascending it, and fallen from it. He also was stripped. He still breathed, and Surtees pressed some of the soldiers about the place to carry him to the camp. They were so drunk that they let him fall; but he was past all feeling, and died soon after he was laid in his tent. Croudace also was brought out alive, but died almost immediately. Of the wounded officers, McPherson died a few days after. He was a man of herculean stature, and great bravery. 'He had been true to man and true to his God, and he looked his last hour in the face like a soldier and a Christian.'[1]

Macdonell died a few months after he received his wound.

Some personal anecdotes of the storm may be given. George Simmons, on going into the town, went into a house, the Spanish owner of which told him that the French Quartermaster-General had been billeted there. He showed him the room he had occupied; and there he found on the table a paper on which he had made a sketch of the two breaches, showing the line by which our columns would probably move to attack, and the spot where our ladders might best be planted to avoid the fire from the place and the inundation in the ditch. The owner of the house informed him that the French officers had left it in great alarm, on being informed of our attack. There were also a bottle of wine and some glasses on the table; and, as Theodore Hook somewhere observes, eating and drinking must go on, whatever the vicissitudes of life, George Simmons sate down, ordered some eggs and bacon to be fried, and drank the French officers' bottle of wine.

Kincaid was acting Adjutant with Cameron's four companies who lined the glacis. When they were established in the place, he went to post picquets in streets leading to the ramparts. While so engaged, a Rifleman brought him a French officer prisoner, who he said was the Governor. The officer at once said that he was not, but that he had passed himself off as such to ensure the soldier's protection and better treatment. He added that he was Colonel of a regiment in the garrison; that his officers were all assembled in a house near at hand, to which he would conduct Kincaid,

[1] Kincaid, 'Random Shots,' p. 288.

and who would give themselves up as prisoners to anyone who would ensure their safety Taking a few men with him to guard against surprise, Kincaid accompanied him, and found fifteen or sixteen officers assembled, who professed great astonishment at our being in possession of the town. As in Simmons' case refreshment was to be thought of; and Kincaid and his prisoners discussed some cold meat, and sundry bottles of wine which their chief placed upon the table At last Kincaid marched them off; and before parting the French Colonel told him that he had two good horses in the stable, of which he advised him to take possession. This counsel was not lost on Kincaid, who thus became the owner of a black mare, which carried him till the end of the war As he was making his way to the ramparts, many French soldiers, who were skulking in out-of-the-way corners to escape the fury of the British troops already in the town, joined him And marching at the head of this party, he was very nearly fired on by a picquet of our men whom Barnard was placing across a street, and who, seeing so many French uniforms together, fancied it was a rallied party of the enemy. Happily the challenge of the picquet, which owing to the noise of his prisoners he had not heard, was repeated and answered; and he handed over his prisoners to be marched with others to Elvas.

Surtees was occupied in a more benevolent work. Directly the place was in our hands, he and Percival, who was in command of the 3rd Battalion, set about finding and removing the wounded of the Regiment This was an arduous work; for the wounded were numerous, and their claims for assistance incessant. And Percival was lame, from his wound at Sobral, and not well able to move about; yet they were obliged to carry the wounded themselves, for of the soldiers they called on to help them many were drunk; and even those whose help they secured, soon went off to share in the rapine of the town. Many are the heartrending details Surtees relates; and many are the horrors he and all the Riflemen who were present record of the plunder of the town. No doubt the men were furious with the inhabitants, who had here assisted the French, while at Rodrigo they had resisted them; no doubt they were frenzied with the difficulty of the assault, and savage at the wholesale slaughter of their comrades. These envenoming motives, added to the usual and (so to say) admitted license in a town taken by storm, have made the sack of Badajos one of exceptional violence. Yet all that men could do to resist it was done. Barnard, commanding the Division, opposed not only his commands but even his great personal strength to the plunderers He endeavoured to prevent the men from entering the town, but they rushed past him, and while striving to wrest a musket from a soldier of the 52nd, he fell and was very nearly thrown into the ditch. He then, with others, went into the streets, and strove to check the madness of his men; but in vain.

Cameron, as I have said, got the men of the 1st Battalion together after the assault and kept them formed on the ramparts till between nine and ten; he then thanked them for their conduct throughout. 'And now, men,' he added, 'you may fall out and amuse yourselves; but I expect you all to be in camp at tattoo to-night.' It was a vain hope; and it was two days before the absentees returned, and discipline was restored

On the day after the assault two officers of the 1st Battalion were talking over the events of the past night at the door of a tent, when two ladies approached from Badajos, and claimed their protection. They were evidently, from their appearance and manner, of the upper class of Spanish society. Both were handsome; and the younger, then about fourteen, very beautiful The elder, though still young, addressed the Riflemen, and said that she was the wife of an officer in the Spanish service, who was in a distant part of Spain; that the young lady with her was her sister, who, having just completed her education in a convent, had been placed under her charge; that yesterday she had a comfortable house and home, that now it was in the possession of an infuriated and insane soldiery; that they had already suffered violence, as their bleeding ears, from which the ear-rings had been rudely torn, bore witness; and that to escape greater violence and dishonour worse than death, they had fled, and had resolved (however strange the step might seem) to throw themselves upon the honour and the protection of the first English officers they might meet. It need not be told that it was freely given, and chivalrously observed, and that they were conveyed to a place of safety. Nor will it seem strange to add that the acquaintance begun in so romantic a manner ripened into a warmer feeling; and that within two years, the younger of them, Donna Juana Maria de los Dolores de Leon, became the wife of him who had saved her, Harry Smith, then a Captain in the Regiment, and was long known in English society as Lady Smith, the honoured wife of the conqueror of Aliwal.

CHAPTER IV.

SOON after the capture of Badajos the command of the Light Division was given to Baron Charles Alten, and the two Brigades of which it consisted were commanded, one by Barnard, and afterwards by Sir James Kempt, and the other by General Vandeleur. On Craufurd's death and Vandeleur's wound at Ciudad Rodrigo, the command of the Division had devolved on Barnard How well he handled it, and how gallantly he led it at Badajos, has already been recorded.

I may here note that Barnard, who had hitherto commanded the 3rd Battalion, soon after this period was transferred to the command of the 1st Battalion, in Beckwith's place, who had, as already noted, gone home on account of his health, and did not again return to the Peninsula. He was one of the original officers of the Regiment, and a most excellent Rifleman. In here parting from him as a regimental officer, I may add Kincaid's testimony to his merits 'He was,' he says, 'one of the ablest of outpost generals. Few officers knew so well how to make the most of a small force. His courage, coupled with his thorough knowledge of the soldier's character, was of that cool, intrepid kind, that would at any time convert a routed rabble into an orderly, effective force. A better officer probably never led a brigade into the field.' [1]

On April 11, the Regiment broke up from the camp before Badajos and marched to the north Before doing so the men were ordered to give up the articles which they had plundered in Badajos; and to prevent their secreting any of them, their packs were examined Whatever was found was collected in heaps and burned But for two or three days

[1] 'Adventures,' 143.

before, the men had been selling what they had taken ; crowds of country people thronged the camp to purchase ; and it presented almost the appearance of a fair. On the 11th, however, the Regiment marched to Campo Major On the next day they proceeded to Arronches and bivouacked in a wood The 13th they marched to Portalegre, and on the 14th to Niza. On the next day they crossed the Tagus at Villa Velha, the 1st Battalion being in Monte de Senhora and the 3rd Battalion at Sernadas On the 16th the Regiment marched to Castello Branco. Here they halted one day to allow the supplies to come up and to rest the troops, and the day following moved to As Caldas de Cima and Loisa. Here they came very close to the rear-guard of the French , and as they were informed by the peasants at S. Miguel d'Arch, which they reached on the 20th, that the enemy were in force, they moved with great caution to Penamacor on the 21st, San Bartolomeo on the 22nd, and passing through Sabugal on the 23rd, bivouacked near Alfayate. The British force on the north of the Tagus being as yet small, and the enemy falling back in force, their march had to be conducted with great caution.

On the 24th they proceeded to Ituera, where they halted for two days, and from thence the Regiment occupied cantonments on the Agueda ; the 1st Battalion being between Ituera and Castellejo de Azarva , and the 3rd Battalion at La Encina. Here every exertion was made to get the Regiment equipped for taking the field ; the clothing was repaired, and shoes provided ; and everything was done that could be done to turn the men out in good order for a summer campaign. Nevertheless, when the Regiment was reviewed by Lord Wellington on May 27 between Guinaldo and El Bodon, the clothing of the Riflemen was patched with pieces of many colours, and the dress of many of the officers was little better. But Lord Wellington, whose soldier's eye measured not the spic-and-span appearance, but the endurance and daring of the men, told them that they 'looked well and in good fighting order.'

On June 6 the 1st Battalion moved to El Bodon, and on the 11th the whole Regiment left their cantonments on the Agueda, and bivouacked in a wood near Ciudad Rodrigo ;

on the 13th, moving on Salamanca, they advanced to Alba de Yeltes; on the 14th to Sancho Bueno; and on the 15th to Matilla. On the next day they marched to within about five miles of Salamanca; and having crossed the Rio Valmusa, bivouacked near some low hills extending from that stream to the city On the 17th they moved towards Salamanca; but the enemy having constructed forts which commanded the bridge over the Tormes, they were obliged to cross by a deepish ford about a mile further up the river, and bivouacked in a wood on the plain a little way from the ford

On the 18th the Regiment moved from this bivouac to Aldea Seca, about a league and a half from Salamanca; and the enemy fell back after skirmishing with our cavalry.

On the following day the Regiment was suddenly called to arms, the enemy having appeared in force in front of the position; but no fighting took place, and the Regiment moved from the plain and occupied Monte Rubio.

Here they remained some days. And one evening about this time stormers were called for from the Light Division to lead the assault on San Vincente, the strongest of the three forts constructed by the French near Salamanca. Two men per company, the first for duty, were selected for this service; but after being marched down to the fort, they were countermanded. An assault had been attempted, and had failed on the 23rd, and on the 27th the forts surrendered. On the fall of the forts, the enemy fell back, and the Regiment made a forward movement, and marched to Castillonos. On the 29th they bivouacked at Prada de Rubiales; on the next day at Castrillo d'Aquarino; and on July 1, marching through Alejos, they were billeted in the town of Nava del Rey, where the beds in their billets were the first they had occupied for a very long time. On the 2nd they moved forward to Rueda. A pretty strong force of the enemy, of all arms, was evacuating Rueda as the Regiment entered it. This was in fact the rear-guard, which was to hold us in check till his column could file over the bridge, across the Douro, at Tordesillas. But our cavalry and Horse Artillery coming up, the latter fired some shrapnells, which did much execution, and the cavalry had a slight affair with them.

Our Regiment also sent out some skirmishers, who made a few prisoners, amongst them a Sergeant-Major of hussars, whose abject terror, even to tears, excited the surprise of those who saw him. Yet this man must have been a good and probably a brave soldier; for his exchange for one of our sergeants in their hands, was asked for by a flag of truce, on the ground that he was about to become adjutant of his corps. He was accordingly exchanged a few days afterwards.

All the march hitherto from the frontier of Portugal to this place had been through an open country, devoid of trees, abounding indeed with corn, and near the rivers with vines, but with little water except in the great rivers, which were far apart. The men had therefore suffered much, marching under the full blaze of a Peninsular mid-summer sun. Their occupation of the town of Rueda, and the delicious coolness of its great wine-vaults, excavated in the sides of the hills, were a great refreshment. Unhappily the wine these vaults contained was as great a temptation, to which many yielded. So had their enemies, who had preceded them; for many of their bodies were found in the cellars: some hideously mutilated by the Spaniards.

The Regiment remained here for a fortnight; the only movement in that time being that they were on July 3 moved opposite to Tordesillas, on the left bank of the Douro, the enemy being massed in large force on the opposite bank. This movement was probably a feint, and they returned to their cantonments at Rueda.

On July 16 the Regiment marched from Rueda about nine in the evening and halted next day near Castrejon On the evening of the 17th Kincaid had a picquet in front of the Division. Soon after sunrise a smart cannonade began behind a hill to the right of the picquet. In fact Marmont had recrossed the Douro at Tordesillas, and was making an attack on our position at Castrejon. While the picquet, alert at the sound of cannon, were earnestly watching the ground in front of them, no enemy being visible, a terrific turmoil suddenly arose behind some rising ground on their left. Uncertain whence this noise might proceed, Kincaid at once placed his picquet behind a deep ditch about a hundred yards in his rear. He had scarcely done so when a confused *mêlée* of horsemen dashed over the hill: two squadrons of our cavalry, two guns of Horse Artillery, and a strong body of the enemy's cavalry, all cutting at each other; and among the rush Lord Wellington, Lord Beresford, General Bock, and their Staffs. These and the two guns took shelter behind our picquet, who could not fire, for friends and foes were mixed up in an inextricable tangle. The cavalry swept past the front of the picquet; but finding a reserve squadron of heavy dragoons, they returned again at a gallop, the French now flying before those they had lately pursued.

Some companies of the Regiment were thrown out as skirmishers to support the 14th Light Dragoons. One of these brought in a French prisoner, badly wounded, who in conversation with Lieutenant Gardiner, who was a proficient in French, was vehement in asserting that he would not have been taken, had he had a better horse On this being repeated to his captor, he said to Gardiner: 'Then, sir, tell him if he had the best horse in France I would bring him prisoner if he stood to fight me' The prisoner assured Gardiner that his horse had not been unsaddled for a week; and the state of his back, when the saddle was removed, too surely corroborated his assertion

The army was now ordered to retire; and the country being an open plain was very favourable for cavalry. The British troops therefore were formed in quarter-distance column ready to form square at any moment. The Regiment marched in this way for upwards of ten miles, with all the regularity and steadiness of a field-day, taking up distant points to march on; and avoiding the villages in order not to lose time in passing through them. For it was a race between the two armies to gain some high land beyond the Guareña. And the French moved on our right during the whole day; often coming within 500 yards of our flank. Occasionally the enemy opened a cannonade; but on the whole this day's march was effected without fighting. The men, oppressed by the heat, and suffocated by the clouds of dust which arose from the sandy plain, were tormented with thirst. But there was no time to halt, nor water at hand to quench it. At last, arriving at the edge of this table-land, they looked down into the vale of the Guareña, and the Riflemen hurried their pace to reach the water. The French instantly unlimbered their guns on the height above and sent some round shot among them. But our men drank of the muddy stream as they passed through it, and suffered little from the cannonade; and they bivouacked on the high ground beyond the river.

During the early part of the 19th the Regiment continued at rest on the ground of their bivouack; but in the afternoon (with the rest of the Division) they were suddenly called to arms, and commenced a movement to the right, in order to defeat Marmont's plan of interrupting our communications with Salamanca. During this march the enemy cannonaded sharply, and one shot knocked off the head of a Rifleman, who had but just joined. When night put a stop to the march and the firing, the Regiment lay by their arms, close to the enemy's columns. On the morning of the 20th no enemy was to be seen, as Marmont had moved forward to turn Lord Wellington's right flank; and some intervening ground hid his troops from the Riflemen; they were put in motion and soon came in sight and in close proximity to them. Thus they marched as they had done on the two preceding days with all the regularity of a barrack-square drill, parallel to the enemy, and close to him. There was a short halt in the afternoon to refresh the men: for the heat was sultry, and the dust suffocating. With this exception they continued to march till a late hour in the evening.

On the 21st they again started at dawn, and continued to march as before till about two o'clock, when they halted near the village of Villa Moresco. A little before dark they were again in motion; and they forded the Tormes about two miles above Salamanca. The river here was very deep, and the men were nearly up to their shoulders. Hardly had they got across when rain began to fall in torrents, the night grew suddenly dark, the lightning flashed with unusual vividness, and played on the men's arms; and the thunder crashed so close and so loud, that scared horses broke from their picquet-ropes, and rushed into the ranks of the enemy. In this turmoil the Riflemen groped their way through the murky night, up to their knees in mud, to their bivouack in a field not far from the Tormes; where they lay by their arms, without any shelter from the rain which fell heavily and incessantly during the whole night.

On the 22nd occurred the Battle of Salamanca, the only one of Wellington's great victories in which the Regiment did not bear a prominent part. They were under arms at daylight and occupied a position on the extreme left of the British position; and during the greater part of the day the only duty they were called upon to perform was to keep the French right in check. But about five o'clock, after Lord Wellington had taken advantage of his enemy's blunder and driven him from the field, the Regiment was ordered to advance in pursuit. They did so, and continued to press on the rear of the retreating foe till about eleven at night, when they halted near the village of Huerta. Had there been a few hours more daylight, or had the Spaniards held, as Don Carlos de España was directed to do, Alba de Tormes, Marmont's whole army must have fallen into our hands. In this action the losses of the Regiment were inconsiderable; being 2 men of the 1st Battalion wounded, and 2 missing; and a sergeant and 4 men of the 2nd Battalion wounded.

During the pursuit on this evening a partridge was started, and ran between the line of the retreating and pursuing forces. George Simmons caught it, and committing it to his havresack, found it an agreeable addition to his supper at Huerta.

On the first streak of daylight on the 23rd the Regiment was again in pursuit, and fording the Tormes, came up with the French rear-guard of cavalry and infantry, commanded by General Foy The infantry immediately formed three squares, which their cavalry covered; but these flying on the advance of General Bock's German cavalry, and leaving the squares unprotected and unprepared, the Germans dashed into two of them, and, not without terrible loss, broke them and cut them up The third square being at an elbow of roads leading to high ground, retired in good order. The Regiment was ordered to advance, but the enemy's rear-guard having been thus disposed of by Bock's Germans, their only office was to follow in pursuit; and soon after they found the rear-guard, consisting of the three arms, posted on some high ground near a village. Lord Wellington, who then happened to be with the Regiment, gave immediate orders for an attack; but on their advance the French broke up and melted away before they reached them.

On the 24th the Regiment moved to Flores d'Avila, passing on the way through Penaranda. After halting during the 25th to refresh the men, as this march had been extremely hot and fatiguing, they proceeded on the 26th to Aldea Seca; on the 27th to Montejo Viejo; on the 28th to Pedrajo de Portellio, and on the 29th to Olmedo. A little beyond this place was buried the body of General Fercy, who had died at Olmedo on this retreat, of wounds received at Salamanca. This was the same man who had attacked the 1st Battalion at Barba del Puerco in March 1810. He had been interred apparently with honour, and a canopy of laurel had been erected over his grave. But the Spaniards, as soon as the French were gone, had dug up his body, and mutilated it, severing his head—noble and soldierlike even in death—from it. But his old foes of Barba del Puerco were more generous. They re-interred his remains, replaced the canopy of laurel which had covered his grave, and exacted a promise from the people of the place that they would respect the remains and the tomb of the fallen warrior.

On the 30th the Regiment forded the Douro and halted on its right bank about six miles from Valladolid until August 1. This halt on the bank of a large river where they could bathe and have their clothes washed, was a great boon to men and officers; for from July 16 they had been almost daily on the march or in action

On August 1 they proceeded to Tudela del Douro; and passing through Aldea Major, where they recrossed the Douro, and Matta de Qualiaz, bivouacked on the 7th on the right bank of the Penrone.

Marching at daylight on the 8th and passing through Carbonero, they bivouacked on the Eresma not far from Yangues On the 9th they marched by Madrona and bivouacked at or near a hunting place of the kings of Spain, El Palacio del Rio Frio. On the next day they marched to near Otiro and Madrona-Segovia, not far from the city of the latter name.

On the 11th they crossed the Guadarrama mountains, by the Puerto de Guadarrama, and by an excellent winding road leading over the Sierra and descending the southern slope, and bivouacked in the Park of the Escurial.

Scarcely had the Riflemen taken off their knapsacks when two wild boars made their appearance; and scared at the number and the noise of the men, dashed in among them and knocked over several. But in a moment they had received stabs or cuts from a hundred swords, and in a very few minutes their carcases were cut up and distributed.

On the 12th they halted; and on the 13th Lord Wellington made his entry into Madrid, amidst the congratulations and acclamations of its inhabitants of all ranks. On that day the 1st Battalion marched to Rosas; and a day or two after to Gatafe, about eight miles from the capital. Here, in or about Madrid, the Regiment remained for more than two months.

I have now to resume the account of the two companies (Cadoux's and Jenkins') of the 2nd Battalion, which we left at Cadiz. These embarked there and landed with Colonel Skerrett at Huelvas. Thence advancing to San Lucar la Major on August 24, and having driven the French corps of observation from that place, they took post there. On the 26th they marched to the heights of Castileja de la Cuesta, near Seville, where they arrived on the morning of the 27th, about six o'clock. They advanced to the bridge of Seville under a heavy fire of grape and musketry, the two companies of the 2nd Battalion forming the advanced guard. Captain Cadoux, who commanded the Riflemen, with great judgment made a flank movement to the left, and the result was that the enemy fled through the streets of Seville, which were strewn with their dead and wounded The conduct of this Detachment of the Regiment is mentioned with praise by Colonel Skerrett in his despatch.[1]

These companies subsequently effected a junction with the force under General Hill, near Toledo, in October; and were engaged in repelling the attack made by a large body of troops under Soult on Sir Lowry Cole's Division at the Puente Larga, near Aranjuez, on October 29 This gallant

[1] 'Supplementary Despatches,' Appendix xiv. 108-9.

defence of the bridge fell entirely on the 47th Regiment and our two companies, and their loss in it was 1 sergeant and 2 rank and file killed; and Lieutenant Budgen and 8 rank and file wounded.

After these companies joined the army under Lord Wellington, the 2nd Battalion in the Peninsula consisted of six companies.

On October 21 the 1st Battalion marched to Rivas, and on the 22nd to Villa Coaxa. And as a large force of the enemy was approaching, at four o'clock on the morning of the 23rd, the Regiment was ordered to form on its alarm post, and marched to the city of Alcalá de Henares. On the 27th it proceeded to Arganda; but assembling at dark, marched back during the night to Alcalá, which it reached at daylight; and after resting in the streets made another march; and on the 30th again moved to near Madrid and halted near the Segovia gate. It was now determined to evacuate Madrid and to retreat on Salamanca, as Soult's army was approaching in force. On the 31st, therefore, they left the neighbourhood of Madrid to the great regret of its inhabitants, the men showing by gloomy sullenness, and the women by contemptuous sneers, their opinion of our leaving them to the tender mercies of the French. The regret was shared by officers and men of the Regiment, to whom the sojourn in the capital was long one of the most pleasing recollections of their Peninsular service. They halted, on November 2, in the park of the Escurial, and on the 3rd recrossed the Sierra de Guadarrama and bivouacked near Villa Castin. Here General Hill took the command of the retreating army, Lord Wellington being engaged on the siege of Burgos On the 4th they bivouacked near Lanza, and on the 5th marched to near Fuente de Baños. The next day they fell back to the heights between Flores de Avila and Penaranda On the 7th the Regiment bivouacked about a league from Alba de Tormes, and next day crossing the river at the bridge of Alba, bivouacked in a wood. During this portion of the retreat their march had been without any circumstances of note; and the advanced guard of the French had not come up with them. The weather however broke up, and rain set in, and continued during the remainder of the retreat, with great violence.

At this time the portion of the army which had retreated from Burgos on the unsuccessful attempts to storm it, effected a junction with the troops falling back from Madrid, and Lord Wellington resumed the command.

On November 10 the Regiment moved into the city of Salamanca, and was quartered in the Irish College While they remained here, on the evening of the 13th, about eight o'clock, George Simmons, being orderly officer, was ascending the stairs in order to see the men's lights out He met Lieutenant Firman, of the 3rd Battalion, who was on the same duty. As the stairs were extremely slippery, and the men had torn out portions of the balustrade for fuel, he advised Firman not to move further until he returned with a light. He fetched one, and as he was ascending the stairs, he was horrified at hearing a slip, and a crash below. Firman had fallen a great depth, and Simmons found him with his skull frightfully fractured and several ribs broken He was immediately removed to his billet, where, after continuing insensible for two days, he died.

On the 14th the Regiment left Salamanca, and crossing the Tormes, took post on the heights near the Arapiles, and occupied the ground of the great victory of July 22 It was thought indeed that a second battle would be fought on the same spot; but the enemy's forces being greatly superior to ours, Lord Wellington resolved to continue the retreat And on the 15th, about three o'clock, the Regiment resumed its march and bivouacked that night in a wood about four miles from Salamanca. The weather still was dreadful; the rain had made the roads ankle-deep with mud, and streams, which in better weather might have been stepped over, had swollen to torrents which the men had to pass through knee-deep They were also without provisions, and ravenous with hunger, they searched for something to eat. They found some bullocks, dead or half dead, which had fallen on the road, unable to drag the carts any further These were immediately cut up with their swords and eaten half-toasted at the camp fires. For the soldiers were famished, and the wet wood kindled too slowly for them to wait Some, too, groped about the wood on their hands and knees, searching for the acorns which had fallen from the oaks and cork trees, and devoured them voraciously; and though bitter and unpalatable, they stayed the pangs of hunger. Nor were these wants confined to the men; few of the officers had even a biscuit; and Costello relates how he saw Lord Charles Spencer, then a Second-Lieutenant in the Regiment, standing on some branches to keep him out of the wet, and earnestly watching a few acorns which he was trying to roast in the embers. As the only means of keeping themselves dry, the men cut down the branches of the trees and lay on them. And as the Regiment formed part of the rear-guard on this retreat, it was of course among the first under arms in the morning and the last at night, often not reaching the bivouack till some hours after the other regiments were in theirs.

On this and the preceding day, the French appeared in force on their right flank, threatening the communication of the army with Ciudad Rodrigo.

On the 16th the retreat was resumed in the same weather and under the same privations. Many of the men lost their shoes in the sticky slime of the roads, and had to march barefoot. The French cavalry hovered close behind the Regiment, but did not attack; and after dark the Riflemen bivouacked, again glad that in a wood they had at least acorns to assuage their hunger.

On the 17th they fell in before dawn. The rain still fell in torrents. Early in the day the French cavalry pressed the rear-guard, and the 1st Battalion took possession of some high and broken ground on each side of the road, and one or two companies were thrown out as skirmishers to check their advance. But as the enemy continued to press on, and were very numerous, the skirmishers were called in. When running in on the Battalion they passed Lord Wellington; he called out to them: 'Be cool, my lads; don't be in a hurry.' But the French were close upon them; and they, as well as the Commander-in-Chief, were obliged to retire.

While this was happening the Riflemen were surprised to hear the sharp crack of rifles in their rear. The occasion of this was that some of the French dragoons crept, under shelter of a wood, near the baggage and made a dash across the road at it, took some, and made prisoner Lieutenant Cameron, who was on the baggage-guard. But as the head of the Division appeared almost immediately, they let him go. Riflemen were immediately sent into the wood on each side of the road, and a few shots from them soon drove off the dragoons. This was the same party which afterwards made a similar dash at Sir Edward Paget as he was riding alone in an interval between the 5th and 7th Divisions, and took him prisoner.

In the afternoon the Regiment reached the edge of the table-land, whence the ground fell with a long open slope to the Huebra. As soon as they began to descend it, the enemy, who had assembled a large force of infantry and artillery under cover of the wood, opened a severe fire of cannon and musketry, while their cavalry hovered on the flank, watching for an opportunity of dashing at them, if any confusion had occurred. Nevertheless the Light Division went down that hill with all the deliberation and all the steadiness of a field-day They forded the Huebra, which was rapid and breast-high, near San Munoz, under this fire; followed down the slope by the French skirmishers, whom one company of the 1st Battalion, extended, kept in check; and these were the last men who passed the Huebra on that day. On reaching the other side the Division formed column of battalions, and showed such a front that the enemy evinced no disposition to venture further. The loss of the Regiment was considerable, and would no doubt have been larger, but the ground was so soft from the continued rain that many of the shells buried themselves in the mud and were harmless.

This day's march was even more harassing than the preceding ones. The constant marching in slushy mud, and continuance in wet shoes, had made the men's feet very sore; and they often struck them against the stumps of small trees, which had been felled, but, being covered with mud, were not seen. This added much to their sufferings: many men fell out from sheer inability to march, and were made prisoners; and some died.

When the Regiment had passed over, it was discovered that Lieutenant Joseph Simmons, who was sick, was absent; and he was seen sitting on the ground on the other side of the Huebra, too weak to walk or to mount the mule which was beside him His brother George at once dashed into the ford;

lifted him on the mule, and led him over, under the fire of shot and shell which still continued from the height.

In a forest near the steep bank of the Huebra the Regiment bivouacked that night, the picquets being only divided by the river from those of the enemy. The rain and the discomforts of the preceding nights still continued. But at last the commissaries brought in a few half-starved bullocks, and the Riflemen looked forward to a meal, albeit a scanty one. The animals were very soon slaughtered and divided; fires were lighted, and, with much persuasion, even the damp wood began to burn. Then men and officers gathered round their fires, and endeavoured to toast the meat on the points of their swords, but, just then, the wind rose; the gusts shook the heavy drops from the loaded leaves, and most of the fires were extinguished; and they were obliged to resort to the now familiar food of acorns.

The other divisions were to have marched in the night, and the Regiment being part of the rear-guard could not move till they were on the road. But such was the state of the roads and such the fatigue of the men, that these troops had made scarce any way when the Riflemen stood to their arms at dawn. A thick haze hung over the river and the high ground beyond, and they were momentarily expecting an attack which they must have resisted at all hazards to enable the army to make good its retreat. But none took place, and it was not till they had retired some distance, and found no foe in pursuit, that they ascertained that the French, overcome by the fatigue and want which they had borne, had fallen back from the Huebra to Salamanca.

However, though they had no material enemy to contend with, their fatiguing march through slimy roads, and their want of food continued; only the weather improved. The rain ceased; and the sun, which they had not seen for many days, shone out. After a long march they bivouacked on the side of a hill near Santi Spiritus.

During this retreat the casualties of the Regiment were: in the 1st Battalion, 1 sergeant and 1 private killed, and 5 rank and file wounded; in the 2nd Battalion, 1 private killed, and 5 wounded, 1 bugler and 8 rank and file missing; in the 3rd Battalion, 1 private wounded and 9 missing.

On the 19th they marched to near Ciudad Rodrigo, and bivouacked on the banks of the Agueda. And this put a period to their sufferings. For bags of biscuit and other provisions were brought out to them. Yet such was the ravenous hunger of the starved soldiers, that sentries with swords fixed had to be posted over the provisions during their distribution.

Great was the relief officers and men experienced by rest, and by being able to change their clothes, which they had not done since they left Salamanca, a week before. So swollen were the feet, and so hard the boots from constant moisture, that some officers and men had to cut them from their feet.

On the 25th the 1st Battalion moved to Villa de Puerco, and on the next day to Alameda, while the 3rd Battalion were cantoned at Espeja. These villages on the Agueda, so often occupied by them, had come to be looked upon as a home by the Riflemen (at least by those of the 1st Battalion); and in these cantonments they continued during the winter

Thus closed the campaign of 1812, in which the Regiment had taken part in the storm of two fortresses, in one general action; in three combats, and in many skirmishes and affairs of outposts.

A good deal of sickness, the unfailing consequence of exposure, want and fatigue, prevailed among the Riflemen on their going into winter quarters. And the Record of the 1st Battalion makes special mention of 'the indefatigable exertions of Surgeon Burke' during this time. Many of the men, and some of the officers, suffered from a numbness in the limbs and extremities, which was said to result from the change from exposure to comfort, and from want to plenty.

Soon after their entering their cantonments a circular was issued by Lord Wellington to Officers Commanding Divisions and Brigades[1] commenting in very strong terms on the bad conduct of the men, and the neglect of duty of the officers, during the late retreat This caused great dissatisfaction and regret in the Regiment, for it was felt to be undeserved. That many irregularities took place, and much duty was neglected in some divisions and corps, may be as

[1] See it in 'Wellington Despatches,' ix. 582, Nov. 28, 1812 Leach and Kincaid both mention this regret and dissatisfaction.

freely admitted, as that armies become disorganised in retreats. But in the Light Division Craufurd's strict orders were still observed 'Being dead he yet spoke:' and in the Regiment, Manningham and Stewart's standing orders so strictly defining the duties of company officers were still observed ; and Beckwith's and Barnard's admirable system prevailed, and among them no such irregularities took place. The circular also stated that the army had 'suffered no privations which but trifling attention on the part of the officers could not have prevented,' and had 'not suffered any hardships but those resulting from the inclemencies of the weather.' Yet anyone who reads the last few pages, compiled from Journals of Riflemen who were present, may think the sufferings of the troops are under-estimated by their great Leader. Still less did the sweeping accusations of want of discipline and neglect of duty seem deserved. Both Leach and Kincaid state that not a man of the Regiment (nor, as they believe, of the Division) was left behind, except those too badly wounded at San Munoz, or too utterly exhausted and moribund from hunger or fatigue, to be brought over the Huebra. Had the great Commander, like Moore, exempted from censure those who deserved praise, he would not have wounded the feelings and the *esprit de corps* of men who had so bravely fought and suffered, and were yet to fight and suffer, under his eye and at his side

While on the subject of discipline I may perhaps mention an incident which occurred while the Regiment was in these cantonments, as well because it shows the confidence of the officer in the right judgment of the men, as because it evinces the opinion of the soldier concerning deserved punishment.

A man of the 1st Battalion, a *vaurien*, had robbed his comrades and deserted He was intercepted and brought back by some guerillas, and having been tried by a regimental Court-Martial was sentenced to receive 150 lashes. As soon as the Adjutant had read the proceedings of the court, Colonel Cameron, who then commanded the Battalion, observing on the infrequency of corporal punishment in it (Costello says that not more than six men were punished in the six years they were in the Peninsula), said that he would forgive the culprit if the Battalion would be answerable for his good behaviour. After a pause, during which not a man spoke or made a sign, Cameron ordered him to strip, and he received twenty-five lashes Before the next bugler began, Cameron again addressed the men. 'If,' said he, 'this man's company will speak for him, he shall be no further punished.' Still not a word was said, nor a man moved; and twenty-five more lashes were inflicted. A third bugler was about to begin, when Cameron again spoke, and said that if one man of the Battalion would come forward in his behalf he would forgive him No one answered, and the bugler laid on three or four strokes, when a man called out: 'Forgive him, sir,' and, being ordered, stepped out of the ranks 'Is it you, Robinson?' said Cameron, 'I thought as much; a man no better than himself. But I will keep my word. Take him down' When the prisoner had been released, Cameron spoke again: 'Your bravery in the field, men,' he said, 'is known to me and to the army. Your moral worth I know now. I am glad that not a man of the Battalion would come forward for that prisoner, except one; and what he is you know as well as I do.'

At Alameda the officers of the 1st Battalion, for the first time for some years, resumed their Battalion mess. A large barn formed the mess-room, in which they constructed two fire-places and chimneys; and dishes, plates, platters, and cups, which had been used by the different company messes in the field, brought into common stock, formed a sufficient if not a very magnificent service.

About this time a number of Spaniards joined the Regiment as recruits An order had been issued in the May preceding[1] to enlist 100 Spaniards in each Battalion, and Surtees had been sent into the country about to endeavour to obtain these recruits. But unsuccessfully; for though many gave their names, and promised to come in and be attested, yet none appeared. But now it seems they were obtained. They told Costello that they were compelled by their government to serve, and that they preferred enlisting with us. They were divided among the different companies, furnishing about ten or twelve to each company. They made excellent Riflemen, and were distinguished for their bravery,

[1] 'Wellington Despatches,' xi 153

degenerating often into ferocity, prompted by revenge for the injuries they and their families had suffered from the French. Some of them were made corporals; and all these men, according to the terms of their enlistment, were discharged when the Regiment passed the Spanish frontier in 1813.

Great exertions were made to equip the Regiment for the ensuing campaign. The clothing was got up from Abrantes, not before needed, for the Regiment had become, during the campaign and after the retreat, 'a thing of shreds and patches'

For the first time, too, in this war tents were provided for the Regiment, three per company for non-commissioned officers and privates, and one for the officers of the company. In the last campaign indeed a sort of '*tente d'abri*' had been extemporised by making the men sew loops on the corners of their blankets. Two blankets being looped together, and the ends fixed to stands of arms, four men could creep under them But with this disadvantage, that as two blankets were used for the covering, the four men had only two blankets to wrap themselves in. Yet they were ordered to pitch these new company tents always behind rising ground and out of sight of the enemy.

The Light Division was divided into two brigades. The 1st and 3rd Battalions of the 95th, consisting respectively of six and five companies, with the 43rd and some Portuguese, formed the 1st brigade under the command of Major-General Kempt

The 2nd Battalion, consisting of six companies, were with the 52nd, and some Portuguese regiments in the 2nd brigade, commanded by Major-General Vandeleur

On May 21 the Regiment broke up from its cantonments, and marching to Molina des Flores and fording the Agueda near the mill, encamped that night near San Felices el Chico Marching at daylight next morning, they passed S. Espiritus and Martin del Rey, and encamped near it on the banks of the Yeltes. On the 23rd, after a long march, they encamped on the left bank of the Huebra at San Munoz, which they repassed by the very ford where they had their hard fight with the French six months before But the face of nature and their own feelings were indeed different. The slushy swamps were now green meadows; the then sullen, swollen river now glistened under a bright sun ; the constant, chilling rain was replaced by warm spring sunshine. And they, then fatigued and faint, now rested and restored ; then famishing with want, now amply supplied ; then depressed by the pursuit of an enemy, now gallantly going to seek that enemy, and exulting at the prospect of driving him before them. Here they halted during the 24th ; and on the 25th, passing through Aldea Quella de Penida and Castro, and crossing the Matillo, encamped near Robleza. On the next morning they marched to the banks of the Valmusa, where about mid-day they halted and cooked And then resuming their march, arrived in the evening at the ford of El Canto on the Tormes, about two leagues below Salamanca, where they encamped that night and remained during the following day On the 28th they moved, and having forded the Tormes, passed through Monte Rubio, and after a march of twenty-four miles encamped at Aldea Nueva de Figueira, where they remained until June 2. On that day marching early they arrived at Villa Buena, where they cooked and rested ; and in the afternoon proceeded to Toro ; where finding that the enemy had blown up the principal arch of the bridge, they encamped in some fields on the left bank Marshal Jourdan now abandoned the line of the Douro, and fell back on Palencia. And in order to follow the line of retreat of the enemy, the Regiment on June 3 crossing the Douro by the bridge of Toro, which had been hastily made passable by planks laid across the broken arch, advanced to Terra Buena, where they encamped. On the next day they moved by Casa Sola and La Mota de Toro, and after a march of about eighteen miles encamped at night on some high ground overhanging the Convent of Espinaz.

On the 5th, passing through Castromonte, where they halted an hour, they encamped at Muderra ; and on the next day they marched through Villa Alba to Ampudia, their camping place. On the 7th, marching early, they reached the city of Palencia, and passing through it amidst the acclamations and rejoicing of its inhabitants, encamped close under the walls on the banks of the river Carrion. On the 8th, advancing through Valdepero and Mongen, they encamped at Tamara. The weather now broke up, and from having been hot and fine, now became chilly with much rain. The next day they moved to La Peña de Campos, and encamped near the Rio Cieza On the 10th they crossed the river by a stone bridge, and passing by the villages of La Peña and Francoen, and across the canal of Castile, encamped near Lantadilla on the right bank of the Pisuerga. During the last few marches the weather had been unfavourable, and the supply of food scanty. The country was devoid of wood, and fuel was with difficulty procured for cooking. The peasantry, too, seemed poor, and their dwellings inferior to those in other parts of Spain. Yet the villagers everywhere welcomed our men with shouts of joy, and the women danced before them, in their national manner doubtless, but it seemed absurd and ridiculous to our people. Yet this amused the tired soldiers, whose heavy load and rapidity of march were lightened by the antics of the rejoicing peasantry.

On the 11th they crossed the Pisuerga by a stone bridge, and passing by Pallacio encamped near Villa Sandino on the river Brullo

Since leaving Toro in pursuit of the enemy they had never seen a French soldier; but on the 12th, after marching a few miles, and when near the village of Isar, they came upon a rear-guard, composed of a pretty large body of cavalry drawn up on some high ground, and a division of infantry formed in squares. On the cavalry attached to the Light Division advancing, the enemy's cavalry at once withdrew. The Regiment was drawn up on some high ground over the river Hormaza, and when the squares of the infantry were cannonaded by our guns, though without much effect, they retired towards Burgos. But when passing under the height our men were on, they halted and gave them a volley. This they could do, being in square, and the 95th so much above them Yet their fire was ineffectual by reason of distance. They moved across the plain, and as soon as they were clear of their guns, these opened a smart cannonade, without, however, doing any harm. The Regiment then continued its route, and encamped at Hornila de Camino, near the river On the 13th, as the Regiment was starting early on the march, a tremendous explosion, which seemed to shake the ground on which they stood, and which the soldiers fancied was an earthquake, was heard. This was, as they subsequently found, caused by the enemy blowing up the castle of Burgos, on their evacuating that place. Continuing their march through Villa Nueva, Organda and Villa Rejo, they encamped that night at Tovar.

On the next day, passing through Guermathes, Quintanaleia sobre la Sierra, to Quintanajuar and Poza, they encamped in a wood near these two villages.

On the 15th, after a long and wearisome march through Villa Alta, Pesados and El Almunc, and over a most uninteresting country, they came to the edge of the heights overlooking the vale of the Ebro And the sight of that noble river, fringed with verdant meadows and fruitful orchards, and dotted with farms and country-houses, inspirited them. For from the day they had left the neighbourhood of Salamanca till now, their route had lain through an unwooded, arid country, sometimes indeed bearing great crops of corn, but always uninteresting. Wood for firing could scarcely be found ; provisions ran short, and when they were issued, consisted only of tough ration beef and hard biscuit. But now they were descending into a fruitful valley, teeming with everything which could supply their wants. The spirits of the men were elated, and coming to the village of Puente Arenas, they crossed its long stone bridge, the band of the 1st Battalion playing 'The Downfall of Paris,' and encamped close to the village.

At dawn of the 16th they started again, and winding along the left bank of the river for about a league, and then ascending the heights which shut it in, marched through a mountainous country, the rugged hills clothed with wood to their summits, and passing the villages of Encinillas and Bisquesas, and crossing the river Nela, encamped a little beyond Medina de Pomar, on the Trueba river.

On the 17th their march was through mountain tracks impassable for artillery. They were in fact striking across the country to the great road from Burgos to Vittoria, in order to intercept the enemy who were proceeding by that road, and after a fatiguing march encamped in a woody height near the river Loza. Picquets were thrown out, as the enemy was supposed to be not far distant, and the Regiment was placed in thick wood, where there was hardly room to pitch the tents.

On the 18th they moved very early. A troop of German hussars led, and then came the 1st Battalion, one company being in advance. After marching about two leagues they arrived at the point where the road by which they were moving struck into the great road, which by a steep descent between high banks, enters the village of San Millan. Here they came upon a strong rear-guard of the enemy who were coming down the hill towards San Millan. The German cavalry first attacked a force of cavalry which was with the rear-guard, and which made a stand, but they soon routed them, and brought in many prisoners Then Barnard extending the 1st Battalion came down upon the infantry, through the wooded height which overhung the road, and with a sharp and destructive fire put them into confusion. The 3rd Battalion also became actively engaged; and the enemy being broken, retired rapidly, through San Millan and up the hill beyond it, closely pursued by our people. When the Riflemen were beginning the attack Lord Wellington rode up, and directed their movements. As he had another division ready to intercept the French, at Espejo, some distance in advance towards Vittoria, he desired Quartermaster Surtees to go and fetch a peasant who was supposed to be with the 1st Battalion, to guide him to Espejo But the guide not liking the fire, was nowhere to be found, and on Surtees reporting this to him, Lord Wellington galloped off towards Espejo, without a guide. The Riflemen continued the pursuit of the enemy, who on getting on the height above San Millan, again showed front, and formed up some battalions. But the inexorable Riflemen again pressed them so hard, that they fled through Villa Nueva and Villa Naña; and the country being admirably suited for Riflemen, they inflicted on them great loss.

During this fight an officer of the 3rd Battalion was chased round and round a tree by a French hussar, who cut at him repeatedly, and would undoubtedly have cut him down had he not spied the rifle of a man who had been killed; and as it was fortunately loaded, he shot his antagonist 1 sergeant and 2 privates of the 1st Battalion were killed;

Lieutenant Haggup was desperately, and it was thought mortally wounded, being shot through the belly; yet he recovered; and 10 privates of the 1st and 2 of the 3rd Battalion were wounded.

While the 1st and 3rd Battalions were pursuing the enemy, the second brigade of the Light Division came up to San Millan, and as the rear brigade of the French rear-guard, following their companions, arrived there at the same time, they were attacked by the 2nd Battalion, and handled much as their first brigade had been by the 1st and 3rd. They broke and fled at once, abandoning their baggage, and took to the mountains, where they were pursued and many of them taken by the Spaniards. The 2nd Battalion had 1 sergeant killed and 1 private wounded, in this affair. This was the first time the Regiment had been actually engaged in this campaign.

The 1st and 3rd Battalions having returned from their pursuit, the Regiment encamped on the Jumillo, between San Millan and Villa Nueva.

On the 19th they proceeded by the same road by which their opponents on the preceding day had fled; and halted at the village of Salinas The day was hot, the march ascending the hill fatiguing; and the clear sparkling rills at Salinas were eagerly resorted to. Every man dipped his mess-tin; every man, when he had tasted it, made a wry face. The water was salt The earth all around is strongly impregnated with saline matter. And one of the men observed. 'We must be near the sea now; for we have got to the salt water.'

Continuing their march they encamped that night, after crossing the river Bayas by a moveable bridge, at Pobes, on the bank of that river.

On the 20th the Regiment did not move, but continued in the same encampment.

General Alten directed the baggage taken from the French at San Millan to be sold by auction, and the proceeds to be divided among the soldiers. Not only horses, mules and carts, and the usual baggage of an army were thus disposed of, but a variety of female attire was also found and sold; several Spanish ladies, the wives or *chères amies* of French officers, having been among the prisoners taken The proceeds of this sale were divided only among the men of the

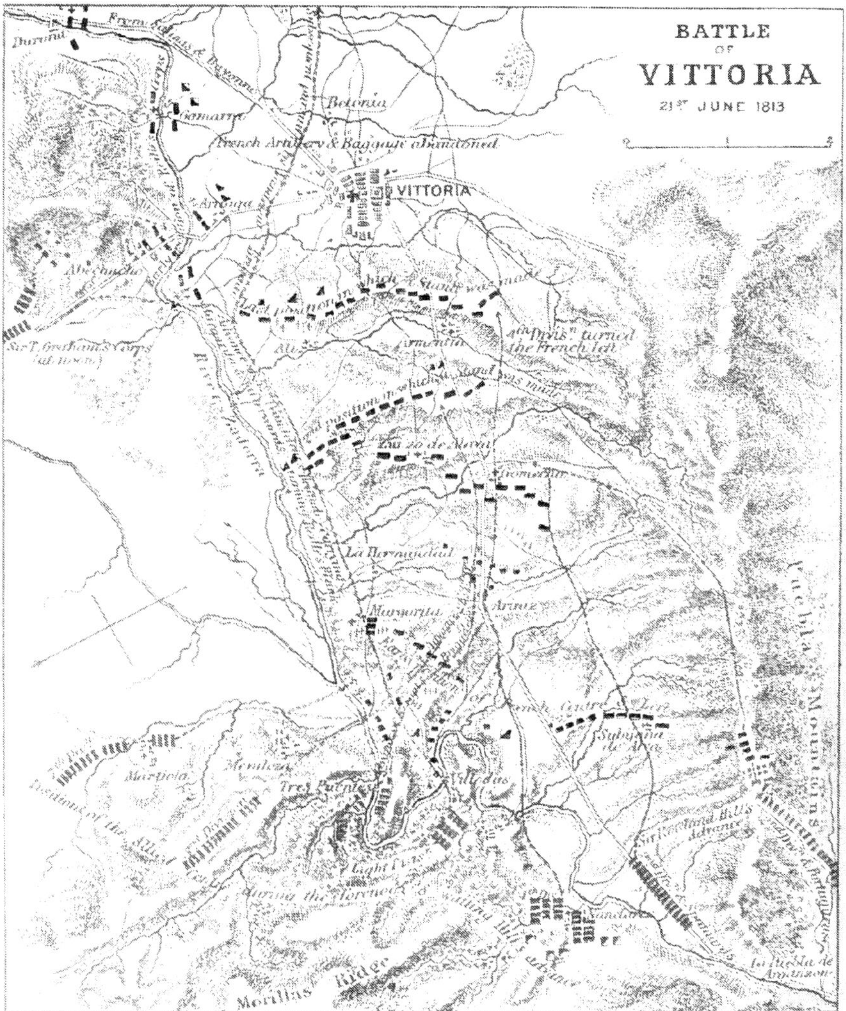

London: Chatto & Windus

E. Weller, lith., London.

second brigade, who were in fact the actual captors; very much to the discontent of the soldiers of the 1st and 3rd Battalions, who maintained that, if it had not been for their attack and discomfiture of the first French brigade, this booty would never have been taken.

On the 21st the Regiment fell in at daylight and advanced, the 1st Battalion leading, over some high ground; and having arrived early near the river Zadorra, which flowing from near Vittoria turns at nearly a right angle towards Miranda, were ordered to pile arms. The river was thus in their front, flowing from their left to their right, and then again turning round their right flank. While they were thus resting with piled arms, Lord Wellington rode up, and advancing to the very bank of the river, observed the enemy's position. This was not unnoticed by the French, who detached a cloud of voltigeurs, who, rushing across a bridge at the village of Villodas, seized a woody height on the side of the river our men occupied, and opened a fire on the Staff. The 3rd Battalion and two companies of the 1st Battalion which stood next to them, were immediately ordered to stand to their arms, and drive them back. This they did in a very short time; and thus they, and not General Hill's division, as has been generally said, began that memorable battle.[1] They drove the French out of the woody height, through the village and over the bridge; but not having orders to cross, they extended along the river's bank, as did the voltigeurs on their side, and many men fell, for the river was not broad, and a desultory fire was kept up. And as soon as the French were clear of the village a cannonade was opened from a battery on some high ground beyond the Zadorra, by which many men were killed. For the ground was rocky, and our men were dispersed among the rocks, and the fragments splintered off by the cannon-balls wounded them almost as much as the balls themselves. One shot took some Riflemen, who were lining a garden-wall, in flank and swept off several men at once.

Their task having been accomplished by clearing the village, some of the officers and half a company of the 3rd Battalion took post at the church of Villodas, and observed

[1] Surtees, 203, 4. Costello, 153.

the course of the battle. General Hill's force had now possession of the range of hills on the enemy's left; while the smoke and booming of cannon on the right of their position showed that Sir Thomas Graham had commenced his attack on that flank. At this moment, about twelve o'clock, a peasant gave information that one of the bridges over the Zadorra was undefended, and the 1st and 3rd Battalions, moving to their left along the bank of the river, crossed by it (the bridge of Tres Puentes) at the point where the Zadorra bends with a right angle, and ascending the high ground halted just under the brow of the hill. While they were there the 3rd Division were seen advancing to the bridge of Mendoza next on the left to that by which the Riflemen had crossed; and the French observing them sent down some cavalry and light troops to oppose them, while a battery of French guns opened fire upon them. At this moment Barnard, with great promptitude, led his Battalion to the left, between the French cavalry and the river, and took the light troops and artillerymen in flank with such a severe fire, that he drove them off and enabled the 3rd Division to cross the river without opposition or loss. But the English gunners, who from the opposite bank were replying to the fire of the French battery, not distinguishing the dark dress of our men, who were in close contest with the enemy's skirmishers, continued to pound them, and several men thus fell by the fire of our own guns. Nor was it till the head of Picton's Division came over the bridge and joined the Riflemen that they ceased their fire.

The Light Division covered by the skirmishers of the 1st and 3rd Battalions, and the 3rd Division covered by two companies of the 1st Battalion, now advanced and pushed up the conical hill in front of Arinez, the centre of the enemy's position. In this advance Lord Wellington rode close behind the two 1st Battalion companies, which were heading the 3rd Division,[1] calling out to the men 'That's right, my lads; keep up a good fire.' The Battalion soon cleared the hill, and were going down the other side, when they were stopped

[1] See his private letter to Sir Thomas Picton, 'Despatches,' x 529. He says, 'The Riflemen of the Light Division were the first to ascend the hill, and I went up immediately after them.' He mentions that these were the 95th.

by a wall at the entrance of the village of Arinez, behind which the enemy had posted some battalions of infantry, who on our men coming over the hill opened a sudden blaze of fire, which checked them. But only for a moment; for running forward they occupied one side of the wall while the enemy held the other And in the few minutes they were there two officers and thirty men of the Battalion fell. Then some of the 3rd Division, having deployed into line, gave the French a volley, which dislodged them ; and the Riflemen clearing the wall, rushed into and through the village, and took three guns, the first which were captured that day. The first of these was taken by Lieutenant Fitz-Maurice and two privates of the 1st Battalion. Observing that the French artillery, a battery of six guns, was retreating, and believing that he could intercept it, Fitz-Maurice started with his company, but they being in heavy marching order, were not able to keep up with him. Five guns had passed before he reached the road ; he caught the leading horses of the sixth, and stopped them The driver drew a pistol and fired at him, but the bullet passed through his cap. He called on the two men who were with him to fire, and one of the horses fell, which completely checked the gun. Then the rest of the company came up, cut the traces, and made the three drivers and four gunners prisoners. However, just beyond Arinez the enemy rallied a strong battalion, who advancing on the Riflemen forced them to retreat about a hundred yards, and to give up possession of the captured guns. But as our men had cut the traces with their swords, taken away the horses, and killed many of the gunners, when they saw the head of the 3rd Division advancing, they went forward again ; and thus reinforced, drove the enemy finally from the village, and recaptured and retained possession of the guns

In the meantime the 2nd Battalion with the 2nd brigade of the Light Division were hotly engaged at the village of Margarita, to the left of Arinez ; but that village being carried and the enemy being driven off, they also advanced on the left of the other two Battalions

The whole Regiment then continued to advance in the direction of Vittoria. On their right a large body of the enemy, which had been driven by General Hill from the high ground on that flank, were marching in a parallel direction They were at first supposed to be Spaniards, and on its being ascertained that they were French, it was a question with the commanding officer of one of the Rifle Battalions whether he should not attack them But his orders were to make the best of his way to his front; and he did not like to depart from them. Moreover the intervening ground was bad, and it might not have been easy to close with them So hurrying on and outstripping our people, they joined their main army in retreat.

As the Riflemen advanced they came to a village where there was a French battery which cannonaded them severely. They formed lines of Battalions and lay down in some ploughed fields, still exposed in some degree to the enemy's fire. In about half-an-hour they moved on; and with little check passed through the city of Vittoria and proceeded about three miles beyond it, the enemy having abandoned all their positions and flying before them. Here they bivouacked, having been on foot since three o'clock in the morning, and having fought almost all that time, over about twenty miles of ground.

Surtees being the only quartermaster up with the Regiment, was sent back to look for its baggage. He repassed Vittoria, and after a long search amongst the carriages of all descriptions which blocked up the road, at last found it. But it was impossible to get it forward, or to extricate it from that wonderful tangle of every kind of vehicle and impediment which blocked the road to and through Vittoria Wherefore, directing those in charge of it where to find the Regiment next morning, he returned through Vittoria and joined the bivouack For the tents had not come up. And men and officers slept by the camp fires, having supped on provisions obtained from the well-filled stores of the flying foe.

On this day 1 sergeant and 3 rank and file of the 1st Battalion were killed; and Lieutenant-Colonel Cameron, Lieutenants Cox, Hopwood, and Gairdner were severely, and Lister slightly, wounded; 1 sergeant and 36 privates were also wounded: of the 2nd Battalion, Captain Jenkins and 8 men were wounded: of the 3rd Lieutenant Campbell and 7 privates were killed, and 16 wounded.

One of the first who fell was Lieutenant Leckie Campbell, who was shot through the forehead at the affair in the early morning at Villodas. Colonel Cameron was so severely wounded in the thigh that he was obliged to proceed to England.

A man of the name of Hudson of the 1st Battalion (one of the deserters found in Ciudad Rodrigo, who had been pardoned) received a shot in the mouth, which knocked out several teeth, and passed out at the back of the ear; yet from this wound he recovered. I have mentioned the Spanish recruits who joined the Regiment One of them, by name Blanco, in this battle was distinguished not only for his bravery, but for his cruelty; stabbing and cutting the wounded French whenever he came upon them. This so exasperated an old Rifleman that he felled him with the butt-end of his rifle The other men could scarce withhold Blanco from stabbing him on the spot.

On the 22nd, about mid-day, the Regiment moved in pursuit of the French, but did not come up with them; and they bivouacked that night near Salvatierra

On the 23rd the Regiment again started in pursuit at daylight, and arriving at the river Borunda, found the enemy posted on it. The wooden bridge over it had been set on fire. But some shrapnell shells fired by Ross' guns soon made them move off. The Regiment then forded the river, and pressed the rear-guard so hard that they could not destroy the bridges they passed. They now set every village on fire, with a view of delaying our pursuit, the passage through the flaming villages and falling houses not being easy, and the country round them being generally enclosed. But this did not much delay the Riflemen. At Echarri-Aranaz they had a skirmish with the enemy's voltigeurs, but they soon moved off. They came up with them again at the village of La Cuenca; here they drew up, but our Horse Artillery having opened upon them, they resumed their retreat through Huarte. The Regiment encamped at La Cuenca

On the 24th at daylight they marched, the 3rd Battalion leading, and after proceeding eight or ten miles found the French rear-guard in a strong position on the side of a mountain behind the river Araquil. The banks were rocky and rugged, and the stream swollen by recent rains. A narrow bridge, therefore, afforded the sole passage. The 1st and 3rd Battalions of the Regiment were the only infantry up at the time. The two Battalions were halted; and the men were ordered to put their knapsacks behind the troopers of the German Legion (who accompanied them) in order that they might move more rapidly. Then the 3rd Battalion were ordered by General Alten to mount a hill to the left of the road in order to fire down upon the right of the French, while the 1st Battalion lined the banks of the river and opened a smart fire. Under this attack the enemy gave way; and our people crossing the bridge, pursued them in a kind of desultory skirmish for about two miles But they retired slowly, and fighting hard, to enable the troops behind them to make good their retreat The road by which they were moving soon struck the great road, the 'Camino real,' leading from Madrid to Pamplona The enemy detached one battalion to the right, which moved down a valley and was soon out of sight It was ascertained afterwards that they fancied that this valley had an outlet to the road further on, where they might take up a position to receive our people. At the end of about two miles, where there was a narrow pass between two overhanging rocks, the enemy halted, and soon advanced upon our two Battalions. A sharp attack now again took place; and the battalion which had left the road emerged from a wood among our skirmishers. It was roughly handled, and suffered severely before it regained the road. It seems that, finding no way out of the valley they had entered, they returned to help their companions.

At this moment two of Ross' guns came up, and opened on them; and a general fight of all three arms (the Riflemen, the German hussars, and Ross' guns) took place, which drove the French from their position, through the pass and on to the open country beyond. Here the road is carried on an embankment with very steep sides And when they had proceeded about two miles, the fire of Ross' guns killed two and wounded one of the horses of the French gun, an 8-pounder.[1] They were so hard pressed that they had no

[1] Letter from Field-Marshal Sir Hew D. Ross, G C B.

time to disentangle the horses, and they flung the gun, with the horses, over the embankment, here about fifteen feet deep Thus the Riflemen, who had taken the first gun at Vittoria, took the last and only gun which the French carried off from that field. 'The French entered Pamplona, therefore, with one howitzer only'[1] The Riflemen (some of them mounted behind the troopers of the Royal Dragoons)[2] continued to pursue them till they were under the walls of that fortress; and they occupied that night the villages of Aldava, Santa Barafra, and Berrioplano.

On the 25th, at an early hour, the Regiment advanced towards Pamplona, and arriving about a mile and-a-half from it, they moved to the left, just out of range of the guns of the place, and proceeding by a mountain road to Villaba, encamped near that village.

On the 26th Lord Wellington intending to intercept General Clausel, who having learnt the rout of the main French army at Vittoria, was endeavouring to make good a retreat into France by the east of Spain, the Regiment (with some other divisions of the army) moved to Noain and past the aqueduct of Pamplona, and encamped near Muro, at the junction of the roads from Tudela and Zaragoza.

Next day they started early, and near Barasoain halted to cook and refresh. Then passing through Tafalla, where they crossed the Zadacos river by a stone bridge, and where the inhabitants received them with acclamations of joy, they encamped in an olive-grove near Olite.

On the 28th passing through the town of Olite and striking out of the Zaragoza road they took that to San Martin. And after crossing a barren plain, halted to cook in a pine-wood near Murillo del Fruto. They had then marched about four leagues; but their labours were not nearly over For starting again they skirted the river and got to Gallepienza, where they crossed it by a stone bridge; and proceeding by a mountain track, where darkness overtook them, they encamped in a ploughed field, near Caseda, about midnight in tremendous rain The whole march had been about twenty-four miles; and they had been pushed on in the hope of intercepting Clausel, but

[1] 'Wellington Despatches,' x 456. [2] Letter from Sir Hew D. Ross.

it was here reported that the Alcalde of Tudela had given Clausel notice of the movements of the column, and that he had effected his retreat by another road.

Therefore the Regiment halted on the 29th; and on the 30th beginning its return to Pamplona, crossed the Aragon at Caseda and marched to Sanguessa, near which they encamped, and halted during July 1.

On the 2nd they resumed their march towards Pamplona; passing Narden and Andoain, and encamped near Monreal.

On the 3rd the Regiment returned by Noain to Villaba, and moving past it, encamped at the village of Berissa near Pamplona. On the next day it furnished working parties to throw up works to shelter our picquets from the fire of the place, or from a sortie of the garrison.

On the 5th the Regiment commenced its march into the Pyrenees; and proceeding up a narrow valley to Ostiz, encamped near a rivulet.

And on the 6th, penetrating into the mountains, they marched by Olague to Lanz, which is situated at the foot of the Pyrenean range

At daybreak on the 7th the Regiment began to climb the mountains and halted on a mountain side near Gustella and Lagassa, where they were about to encamp for the night. But in three hours they got a fresh route and were ordered to move into San Esteban.

Here they halted in very pleasant quarters until the 14th. During this time Major-General Skerrett was appointed to the command of the second brigade of the Light Division, in which was the 2nd Battalion, in succession to General Vandeleur, who was transferred to the command of a cavalry brigade.

On the afternoon of the 14th the Regiment marched from San Esteban, and encamped on the heights above Sumbilla.

On the 15th at daylight they marched down the Bidassoa, by a road which sometimes skirted its bank, and sometimes rose upon the mountain side over it. On getting near the bridge of Lezaca the enemy's advanced post was discovered near it, on the heights of Sta. Barbara. And the 1st Battalion was ordered to dislodge them. They climbed the mountain slowly; for it was very steep, and they were obliged to husband their strength for the fight which might take place at the top. The French gave them some shots; but when they arrived on the crest, they quickly drove them down the other side. And as they stood on the top the Riflemen had a view of the enemy's position; and of the Bidassoa, which here makes a sharp bend to the left, and flows thence through a rocky channel to the sea. Below them was the town of Vera and the road which, leading into France through Vera, is called La Puerta de Vera To defend this pass the French had thrown up strong works And here also the Riflemen looked, far to the left, upon the sea; and a simultaneous cheer burst forth at the sight of that ocean which seemed to connect them with their native land, and which, for some years, most of them had not seen.

The 43rd drove the enemy out of the town of Vera; but they still kept a picquet in some outhouses near it, and our picquets were posted in Vera. The Regiment encamped on the heights they had gained.

It remained in this position, furnishing the picquets, and keeping up the communication between the army under Sir Thomas Graham, which was besieging St. Sebastian, and that under Sir Rowland Hill, which was investing and covering Pamplona.

On July 25 Marshal Soult, who had assumed command of the French army, attacked the positions of Roncesvalles and Maya, with a view to raising the siege of Pamplona or throwing provisions into it; and after several hardly-contested fights had obliged Hill to fall back. It therefore became necessary for the Light Division also to retire, though the enemy in front made no sign of advancing Accordingly on the 26th the Regiment marched from their encampment, and crossing the Bidassoa, and passing through Lezaca and Jansi, encamped for the night on high ground near Sumbilla.

They did not move from this till nightfall on the 27th, when they resumed their retrograde movement; and marching all night did not reach Zubieta (a march of only two leagues and-a-half) till after daylight. For the route was by mountain tracks and in the dark, and was accomplished with difficulty and fatigue So dark and dangerous was the way, that at a stream on the road, which dashed down from the mountain side, a Corporal of the Regiment placed himself in mid-stream, and taking each passer by the hand guided him to the other side. On arrival at Zubieta, about a league to the right of San Esteban, their late quarter, they encamped for the day, and starting again at nine in the evening arrived at Salin next morning. This night march, though not so harassing as the last, for the road was less difficult, was yet not free from danger. For Lieutenant William Eeles, the Adjutant of the 3rd Battalion, having had his cap knocked off by the bough of a tree, in endeavouring to catch it as it fell, pulled his horse off the road, and both rolled down a precipitous declivity. Fortunately it was not very deep; and horse and man were recovered unhurt At Salin they encamped for the day And on the 30th proceeded by a long march, by day, to Lecumberri, and were moved into a wood *à cheval* on the great road from Pamplona to Bayonne, and about equidistant from the former and Tolosa. They were again to keep up the communication between Hill's corps and that before St Sebastian; and also to bar the way to any of the enemy's troops which might move by that road. During the last few days they had heard heavy firing in the direction of Pamplona, but were without intelligence of the result of the fight. But late on the 31st, their anxiety was relieved by the arrival of a staff officer, who informed them of the complete defeat and repulse of the French in the battles of the Pyrenees, and who also conveyed orders that they were to advance over the ground by which they had retired Wherefore, falling in on the evening of that day, they marched to Larissa and encamped there.

On the 1st August they marched early, and passing by Esema, Zubieta and Irurlia, heard that they were to push forward to intercept the retreat of the French They proceeded by a mountainous and rough road, under a burning sun, and about three o'clock reached some high ground on the left bank of the Bidassoa It was a long march and the heat was oppressive. They had marched about thirty miles, when, about three o'clock, they arrived on the heights overhanging the river near the bridge of Jansi Then the knowledge that they were near the enemy revived the spirits of the wearied Riflemen; and declaring that they 'would knock the dust out of their hairy knapsacks,' the 1st Battalion descended the hill on the left, while the 3rd Battalion held a wood above. Then the disordered column of the enemy was seen approaching on the opposite bank, faint and weary; and the 1st Battalion, concealed among the brushwood at the foot of the hill, received them with a raking fire Many, pointing to the wounded who were borne with them, by their gestures implored quarter, and the generous Riflemen withheld their fire, and called to one another to spare them Yet many, as they passed, fired at our men, but without much effect; for they were so effectually concealed in the brushwood, that the flash of their rifles was the only guide for the aim of the enemy. Thus pursued by the 4th Division, they had to pass this fiery ordeal. Some throwing off their knapsacks, and casting away their arms, strove to climb a hill on their right; but it was inaccessible, and on the hill-side the fire of our men picked them off. Then they pushed some light troops across the river, who became engaged with the 3rd Battalion; but they were soon driven down, and across the bridge. In the evening two of our companies got possession of the bridge, and then the rear of the column had to pass in front of their fire. At last they got a battalion into line behind a stone wall beyond the river; this somewhat checked our fire, and the remainder of the flying enemy passed with less loss. Yet arms, knapsacks, baggage and wounded were abandoned

In this affair the Regiment lost but few men. Captain William Percival of the 3rd Battalion was wounded, being at the very close of the day shot through the right wrist The left hand had been before contracted by a wound in that wrist; and he was also lame from a wound in the hip.

This day's march was most fatiguing, being made under a hot sun, and with frequent want of water. The whole distance was about eight leagues, and considering that it was made in the heat of an August sun, and that at the end of the march the men had four or five hours' hard fighting, it may hold its place with the famous march from Calzada to Talavera. Napier gives a frightful picture of the sufferings of the men. It was said that 200 men of one regiment of the second brigade of the Light Division fell out. But the Riflemen had a resolution to excel; and many held on till they died.

Yet when the roll of the 3rd Battalion was called just before the fight began, only *nine* men were absent

On the 2nd, the 1st and 3rd Battalions moved after the French by the road to the pass of Vera; the 2nd Battalion by Jansi and Lezaca; and the Regiment took up the line of picquets it had held a week before without firing a shot. On the march they met Lord Wellington, who, in recognition of their long march and hard fight of the day before, honoured them with an approving nod and smile, which much pleased the soldiers.

In the afternoon, it being observed that the enemy held the mountain of Echalar, which standing on the right of our position was in fact in our line of posts, it was resolved to dislodge them. And the 1st and 3rd Battalions supported by the 43rd were ordered to take the position The 1st Battalion extended to the right, and the 3rd advanced up the face of the hill A thick fog came on, and though the French kept up a pretty brisk fire they did the Riflemen no harm For their aim being probably rendered uncertain by the mist, they fired over their heads, and any of their shot which took effect, fell on the 43rd, who were much lower on the hill-side. The 3rd Battalion, advancing up the hill in the fog, found themselves against a rock the top of which was thronged with Frenchmen, who gave them a biting fire As the Riflemen were unable to climb the precipitous face of the rock, the Frenchmen called upon them with gibes, in the Spanish language, to come on The Riflemen retreated for an instant to the rocks around, among which finding cover, they kept up a telling fire on the occupants of the rock. And one of the Spanish recruits before mentioned, enraged at the insults of the French, replied to their sneers in most bitter words, which he accompanied with constant shots. But he was soon killed. Now gathering courage they made an advance against the 1st Battalion, but the Riflemen with a shout of defiance repelled them, and they turned and fled; and descending their side of the mountain retreated to their own position

The men, while the Regiment remained in the neighbourhood, called this mountain 'Barnard's Hill;' in memory of the valour with which Sir Andrew, who commanded on the occasion, had carried it.

An officer of the 1st Battalion had a strange escape in this fight. When the enemy advanced on that Battalion, they made a rush at him, which in trying to avoid, he fell into a bush. They seized his sword, which was not drawn, to drag him out; but it broke away from the belt, and he escaped

A Portuguese regiment took up the ground the Riflemen had gained; and they encamped near Vera and the Bidassoa.

On the 3rd another division having relieved them, the Regiment returned to their old encampment on the heights of Sta. Barbara, where they remained for about two months

On August 25, the three Battalions being together, it was resolved to commemorate the anniversary of the formation of the Regiment A trench was dug round a parallelogram of greensward, which served for the table, while the *convives* sat on the opposite bank, with their legs in the trench Many patriotic toasts and many healths were drunk. And the cheering that followed them must have astonished their French neighbours. Indeed they are said to have remained under arms part of the night, expecting an immediate attack. This was, I believe, the first 'Regimental Dinner.'

On the 31st the storming of St Sebastian took place. Fifty men under a subaltern of each Battalion of the Regiment were allowed to volunteer for this duty. Lieutenant James Perceval of the 1st Battalion claimed this duty by right of seniority, but William Hamilton, a Second Lieutenant, obtained Sir Andrew Barnard's permission to accompany the stormers also. Lieutenant Eaton commanded the stormers of the 2nd Battalion. I regret that I am unable to ascertain who led those of the 3rd.

About noon, they moved forward from the trenches, and after five hours' desperate fighting—for the breaches were found to have fallen in such large fragments as to be almost impregnable, and the resistance of the enemy was most gallant—they entered and took possession of the place. Perceval was severely wounded at the foot of the breach; and Hamilton was also desperately wounded in two places; one ball entered the eye, passed down through the mouth, and was cut out at the shoulder-blade Both recovered; but Hamilton was never again able to join the Regiment, and was placed on full-pay of it (as First Lieutenant) some time afterwards. Of the 1st Battalion, besides these officers, 2 Riflemen were killed, and 2 sergeants and 4 Riflemen were wounded, of the 2nd Battalion, 3 Riflemen were killed, and 6 wounded; and of the 3rd Battalion, 2 Riflemen were killed and 2 wounded.[1]

But on that same day the Battalions from which these volunteers had been detached had also hard fighting. They had, as usual, been under arms before daybreak, but after dawn the mountains were covered with a thick mist, and as nothing appeared they broke up, and had just returned to their encampment, when the bugles sounded the 'assembly;' and a breeze having carried off the mist, the hills on the French side of the river were seen covered with troops These soon began to descend, and forded the Bidassoa a little below Vera. Some columns also approached Vera in order to cross by that bridge; but the 2nd Battalion were posted here, having two companies at the bridge and in a loop-holed house near it, and the other four in the town. They resisted and defeated the attempt to cross at that point. Meanwhile the 1st and 3rd Battalions, seeing the enemy advancing, thought the attack would be on them. For the French crossed in force, preceded by numbers of skirmishers under cover of the fire of some mountain guns. This fell short at first, and instead of reaching our people some shells fell among their own skirmishers, and caused no little confusion; while the Riflemen, who were looking down upon them, burst forth into a loud and derisive cheer, as each shell fell among them. But when they came across, and our people were to

[1] 'London Gazette.' Either, however, this list is incomplete, or the Record of the 2nd Battalion erroneous: for that Record gives the names of Sergeant-Major Adams, Corporal Port and 14 privates who volunteered on the forlorn hope Of these Corporal Port and 5 Riflemen were killed and 6 wounded. 12 disabled out of 16 Nevertheless, even this list is not perfect For Mr. Kenneth Stewart Mackenzie of Seaforth is in possession of a medal with clasp granted to Sergeant John Himbury of the 2nd Battalion for gallant conduct on the forlorn hope at St Sebastian. This medal was presented to him by the General commanding his brigade. It bears on the *obverse* 'ST SEBASTIAN, 31 DE AGOSTO DE 1813;' on the *reverse*, a bugle, the cords attached to a crown, '95 in the centre, 'RIFLE CORPS' on a ribbon above * And the clasp is inscribed 'FORLORN HOPE' J H SERGEANT.

* This was the old badge of the Regiment before the Maltese cross was adopted

receive them, they turned to their right, and proceeded towards St Sebastian to attack some Spanish troops on the left of the position the Riflemen occupied, leaving some troops about Vera to keep them in check

Thus matters remained till the afternoon; the 1st and 3rd Battalions suffering, but a little, from the fire of the enemy's mountain guns. About three o'clock three companies of the 1st Battalion with part of the 43rd, crossed by the bridge of Lezaca, and proceeded along the heights above the river, in a direction parallel to the French; they were afterwards followed by the remainder of Kempt's brigade, and moved from hill to hill, in the evening occupying a height above Lezaca where they remained for the night But a picquet was left on the heights of Sta Barbara, with orders, as soon as it was relieved by a Spanish regiment, to follow the Battalion across the Bidassoa. But this was no easy matter. For a tremendous storm of wind, thunder and lightning came on; and it was extremely difficult for the picquet to thread their way by mountain paths along the hill-side

The rain also fell in torrents And as is always the case in these mountains every rill rapidly became a torrent, and the Bidassoa rose and ere long became unfordable. That portion of the enemy to the left of the British position had, on being defeated, recrossed the river But General Clausel's force, which was nearer to Vera, was unable to do so Clausel himself, indeed, with two brigades, did repass the river early in the evening, leaving General Vandermaesen with the other divisions on the left bank Then the Bidassoa rose rapidly, and night set in Some of his troops attempted to ford the angry river, but were swept away and drowned. Then the only chance was to force the bridge of Vera. Here Cadoux's company and part of Hart's company of the 2nd Battalion were posted under command of the former, in a loop-holed house about thirty yards from the bridge, having double sentries posted on the bridge itself Thomas Smith, the Adjutant of the 2nd Battalion, having reported to General Skerrett that the bridge was held by this detachment, Skerrett sent his Brigade-Major, who was sleeping in the same room with him, to Cadoux, desiring him to evacuate it, probably in consequence of Vandermaesen's overwhelming numbers. This Cadoux refused to do; saying that he could hold the bridge-house. Meanwhile, about two o'clock in the morning, the French, silently drawing near the bridge, made a rush. The two sentries on the bridge snapped their rifles to give the alarm; but the priming was wet from the heavy rain, and they were at once shot down or bayoneted. Cadoux, by his fire from the bridge-house, kept the head of the advancing column in check. At this fatal moment General Skerrett sent a fresh order to Cadoux, and in such terms as he could not disobey, to leave the bridge-house and join his Battalion. He of course complied; but with the memorable words that 'but few of his party would reach the camp.' Even so it was. They at once became exposed not only to the fire of the troops on the bridge, but to a cannonade from the guns of the French reserve on a height near Vera. Cadoux was killed; 2 sergeants and 14 rank and file were killed; and Captain Hart, Lieutenants Llewellyn and R. Cochrane, 9 sergeants and 34 rank and file were wounded. So that every officer present was either killed or wounded besides 11 sergeants and 48 rank and file, out of a total strength of about 100 men. And it is to be noted that until the party left the bridge-house Cadoux had not lost a man, except the double sentries on the bridge.[1] The opposition being thus withdrawn the French crossed the bridge, and returned to their position. Whereas had Skerrett not only left Cadoux at the bridge-house, but supported him with the remainder of the Battalion, or with the 52nd, who were close at hand, not a man of Vandermaesen's division could have recrossed the Bidassoa. One company of the 3rd Battalion indeed and some Portuguese troops came up about daylight, but it was then too late, and the passage had been effected.[2]

For this neglect and for the sacrifice of Cadoux and his gallant band General Skerrett has been greatly and deservedly blamed; in which censure Sir William Napier (though apparently not fully aware of Skerrett's fault) concurs.

[1] The particulars of this affair of the bridge of Vera have been related to me by Colonel Thomas Smith.

[2] Lord Wellington, in his despatch ('Despatches,' xi. 69) states that the passage of the bridge 'was made under the fire of a great part of Major-General Skerrett's brigade.' This mistake has been pointed out by Napier (Book xxii. chap. 3); the truth is, only the two 2nd Battalion companies resisted it.

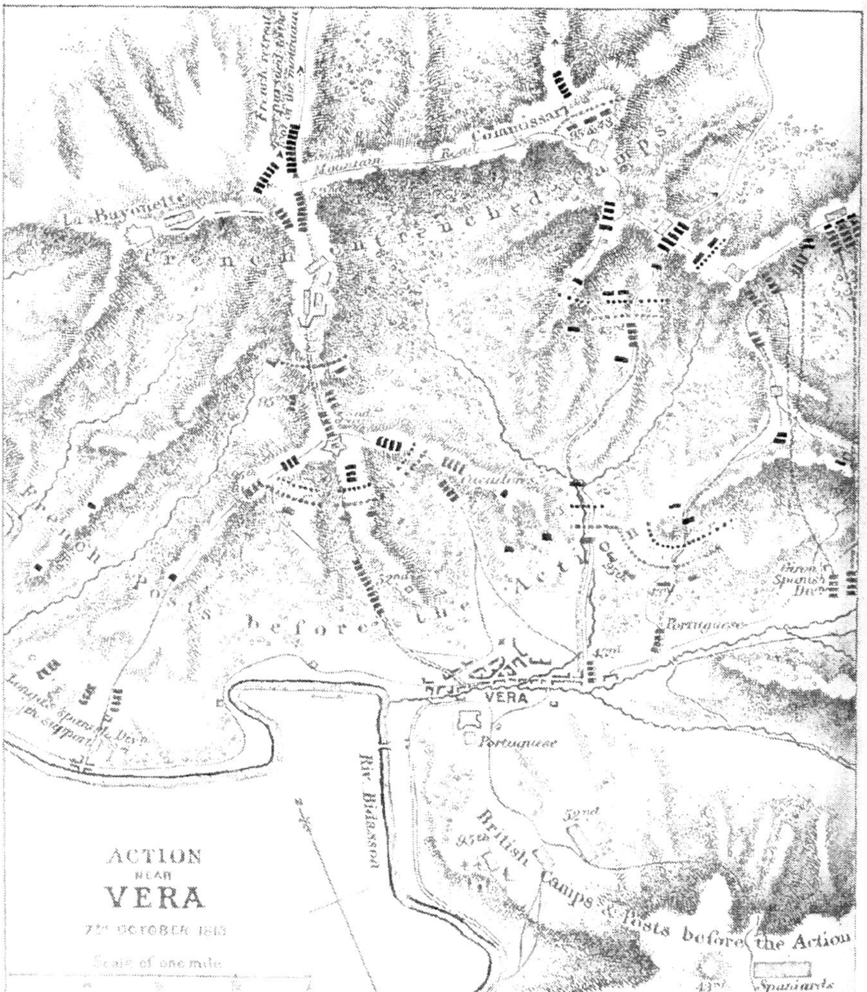

London: Chatto & Windus

E. Weller, lith. London

Besides the great loss of Cadoux's party at the bridge-house, Lieutenant Nicholas Travers, who commanded the company of the 3rd Battalion which came up at dawn, was also wounded, and 2 men of it were killed and 10 wounded.

But if the Riflemen suffered, the loss they inflicted on their assailants was enormous. The bridge next morning was strewn with their bodies; and the river full of them; while many wounded had been removed General Vandermaesen, who commanded the force, was killed.

In the course of the following day the Regiment returned to their former encampment, and took up the line of picquets they had previously furnished. Here they remained in quiet until October 6, on which evening Barnard arrived from head-quarters with the welcome intelligence that they were to force the pass of Vera on the ensuing morning. Early in the night a thunderstorm set in; but it rolled away in the course of the night, and the morning was fine when the Regiment fell in Leaving the tents standing to deceive the enemy as to the object of the movement, the three Battalions, with the other regiments of the Division, formed at the foot of the heights behind the town of Vera. A little to the right was an isolated hill, standing out in front of the great Pyrenean chain on the north of the valley of the Bidassoa, to which the soldiers had given the name of 'the Boar's back.' This was to be occupied as a preliminary measure And Colonel Ross, extending the 3rd Battalion, began to ascend it Without firing a shot, though exposed to the fire of the enemy who crowned the crest, the Riflemen climbed to a pine-wood more than half-way up the mountain side, whence, after they had rested for a few minutes, they issued again At this time the French crowded behind the crest; and it was thought by their brother Riflemen in the plain below, who could see the ground beyond, that the enemy would charge down the slope. But it was not so, for pursuing their way with all the steadiness of a field-day, Ross and his gallant Battalion gained the ridge. Then its defenders turned and fled; and then the Riflemen plied their rifles, which they had not before discharged, and poured a fire into them as they hurriedly descended the reverse slope This exploit and the manner in which it was executed excited the admiration not only of their own comrades still standing in the plain below, but of the whole 4th Division, which had been moved up as a support to the Light Division.

This being accomplished, the other two Battalions moved forward. The 1st, with General Kempt's brigade, advanced into the pass, and though at first sight their task seemed a difficult one, yet the steadiness and gallantry of the men carried all before them ; and with little loss they stood on the top of the pass Some descended the other side. For George Simmons and Cox with about sixty Riflemen, following the retreating enemy down the pass, took some prisoners, among whom were a commissary and two bandsmen. These the soldiers ordered to play some French tunes , but from the alarm and the pace at which they had retreated, their music was neither very coherent nor melodious.

But the 2nd Battalion had a more difficult task to perform. The second brigade was on that day under the command of Colonel Colborne[1] of the 52nd (Skerrett being absent from the field on account of ill-health), and to them was allotted the duty of carrying a high hill on the left called La Bayonette, which bristled with the enemy's entrenchments. The Riflemen ascended the lower slopes of the hill, and coming out of a wood which there girded it, advanced with a quick fire to a redoubt The French who filled it, waiting until the Battalion was within a few yards, then opened a murderous fire, which checked the Riflemen and obliged them for a moment to retire. But the 52nd at that moment coming up in support, they again advanced, and together they cleared the redoubt of its defenders and drove them before them to a second line of works. Here they did not experience any serious resistance. But at the crest the enemy had constructed a formidable work, from which they not only poured forth a blaze of fire, but rolled great pieces of rock on the climbing soldiers While these were endeavouring to storm the work, the 1st Battalion, with the first brigade, gained the top of the pass on their right ; and the enemy's left flank being thus turned, and his retreat threatened, he abandoned the entrenchment and retired down the reverse slope of the mountain.

[1] Afterwards Lord Seaton , and Colonel-in-Chief.

As the French were retiring a curious circumstance took place. Colonel Colborne, accompanied by a small escort of Riflemen of the 2nd Battalion, came suddenly on a battery of mountain guns and some three hundred men, who were retreating from the right flank of the French position. He called to them peremptorily to lay down their arms, which they did, thinking he had a large force at hand.

The loss of the 2nd Battalion was very severe, amounting to nearly one-third of its strength. They fell principally at the Star redoubt, which they first attacked. Captain Gibbons, Lieutenants Alexander Campbell and John Hill, 4 sergeants, and 23 rank and file were killed; Captain Hart, Lieutenants Budgen, Ridgeway, Fry and Madden, 6 sergeants, and 128 rank and file were wounded; and 1 Rifleman was returned 'missing' The 1st Battalion had 10 Riflemen wounded, and the 3rd Battalion 4 killed and Lieutenant Vickers and 17 wounded.

The Regiment, now encamped on the ridge, looked over the steppes of the Pyrenees and the vast plain at their feet St Jean-de-Luz seemed also beneath them, and Bayonne could be seen in the distance; while the Bay of Biscay bounded their view to the left, and a richly-tilled and well-wooded country stretched away far to their right.

Towards evening the 3rd Battalion went down into the plain below on outpost duty, relieving Longa's Spanish troops.

The whole range of mountains was now in our occupation, except one: the extreme projection on the right called La Montagne d'Arrhune This the French retained till the 8th; the Spaniards not having succeeded in dislodging them On that day the second brigade of the Light Division having been sent to assist in carrying it, the enemy evacuated it, and it was thenceforth occupied by a picquet of three companies of the Light Division.

Beyond it was an outlier separated by a valley, and called 'La Petite Arrhune,' though itself a mountain of very considerable elevation. This the French occupied; and their advanced sentries were posted at the foot of the slope, and ours on the opposite slope of the valley, not more than 200 yards apart.

CHAPTER V.

THE Regiment remained now encamped for more than a month on the slope of l'Arrhune. Extremely inclement weather set in, rain, wind, and sometimes snow Occasionally tents were blown away, or falling on their sleeping occupants buried them under the wet canvass. The men on picquet also suffered severely But notwithstanding the altitude and exposure of their camp and the severity of the weather, the health of the Regiment was uncommonly good, not one man, in the 1st Battalion at least, being sick. But this immunity from illness did not extend to all the officers; for Colonel Ross was obliged to leave the camp and the command of the 3rd Battalion, and to take up his residence in the village of Renteria

During this time the French were busily employed in fortifying and throwing up entrenchments on La Petite Arrhune. The officers with these working parties frequently interchanged civilities with our officers, saying. 'You will not be able to remain on these bleak mountains. You will have to retire into Spain' To which the reply was: 'We will do so, if we are ordered.' At last La Petite Arrhune exhibited a truly formidable appearance. Stone walls were built with loop-holes to fire through; the ground was escarped where it appeared accessible, and redoubts were built at intervals.

Pamplona surrendered at the end of October, and Lord Wellington being thus relieved from any enemy in his rear, immediate measures were adopted to advance into France. Heavy rains and the consequent impracticability of the roads postponed this movement, which was resolved upon in the first days of November, until the night of the 9th. On that day the commanding officers of the three Battalions had been taken up to the top of l'Arrhune, and from that commanding

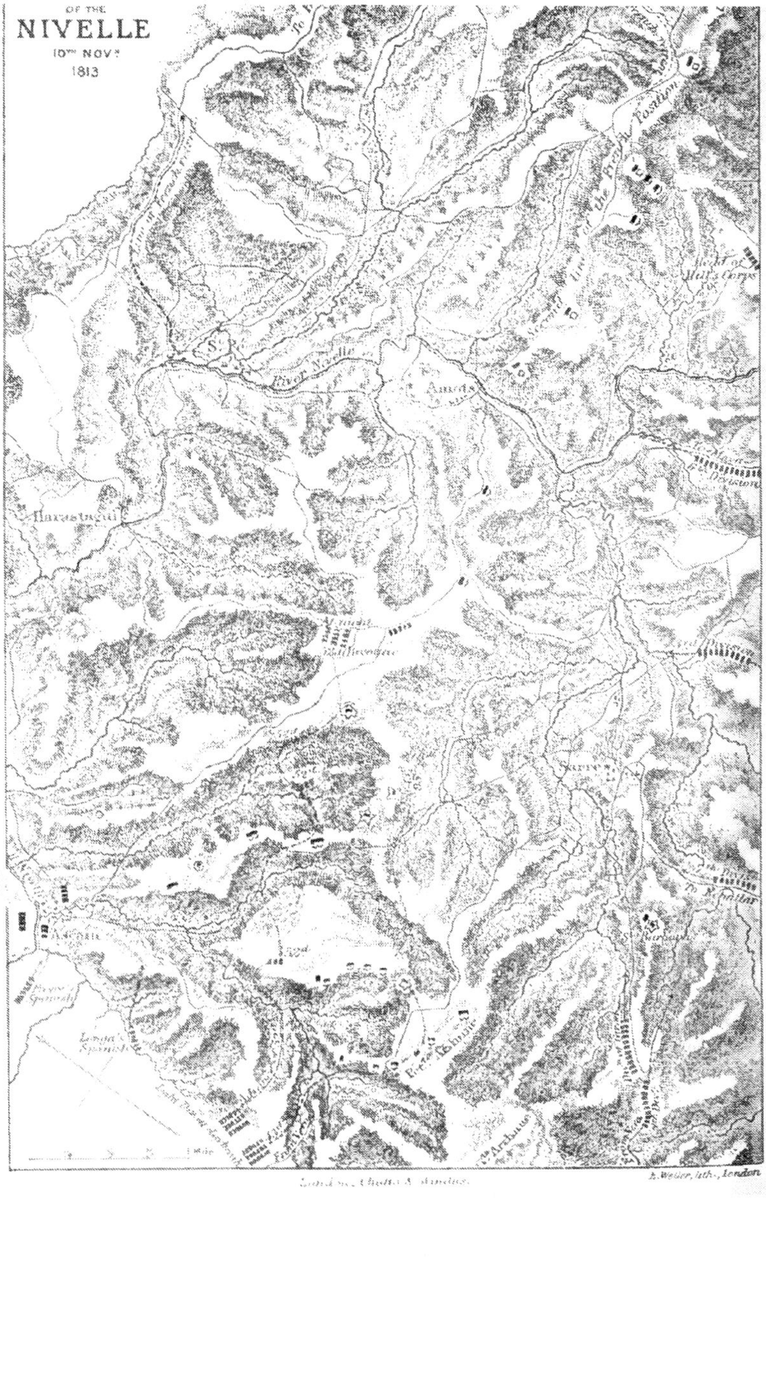
OF THE
NIVELLE
10TH NOVR
1813
River Nivelle
Amots
Head of Hill's Corps
6th Division
3rd Division
Sarre
To St Pe
Ascain
London, Chatto & Windus.
E. Weller, lith., London

position the task laid out for each of the Battalions, and the ground over which they were to move, had been pointed out to them. After nightfall on that evening the Regiment moved to its ground, and about midnight took up its position, crouching behind the rocks within half-musket shot of the enemy's picquet. All this was done in profound silence. No horse, nor even a dog, was allowed to go with the Regiment, lest their neighing or their barking should reveal the movement.

The signal for attack was a gun on the left. A little before daylight the Riflemen assumed their arms, and watched with anxiety the first tinge of sunlight on the peaks of the mountains. At last that streak appeared, the gun pealed forth among the hills, and the Riflemen sprang up from their lair. The enemy, though surprised (for their picquet was found seated round the fire), were not unprepared, but flew to arms and to man their works. The 1st and 3rd Battalions crossed the valley separating the two Arrhunes, and ascended and forced the steep sides of La Petite Arrhune. The 2nd Battalion, with the mountain guns, was stationed near the hermitage at the top of the greater Arrhune; but when the other two Battalions had advanced, they also moved forward and took their part in the fray. The French fought here with great determination, and clung to the works they had constructed with resolute tenacity. The officers were observed by the Riflemen to stand on the walls, and urge their men by their gesture and example to remain. One young man in particular excited their admiration by prodigies of valour, and refusing to the last to retire, fell forward pierced by a bullet. Later in the morning, when La Petite Arrhune had been carried and cleared of its defenders, General Alten led his Division across and attacked the enemy's entrenchments on the opposite range. These were carried with less difficulty than those they had fought for in the morning. But towards the close of the day the 1st Battalion charged the right flank of the French, near a redoubt called the Signal redoubt; and the enemy being taken in flank at the same time by other troops, turned and fled, closely pursued by the Riflemen.

At this moment Barnard, who led them, fell from his

horse, wounded through the right breast by a musket-ball George Simmons, who was close to him, was at once at his side, and placed his head on his breast. It was evident that the lung was penetrated ; for blood and air issued from the wound, and blood came from the mouth also. His first words were : 'Do you think I'm dying? Did you ever see a man so wounded recover?' Simmons assured him that though his wound was dangerous, yet that there were many instances of recovery from such wounds, and that his pulse indicated no appearance of sinking.[1] 'Then,' said the gallant chief, 'you give me hopes. If any man can recover, I know that I shall.' While he lay here, as at Barrosa, the enemy seeing they had brought down an officer of rank plied their fire on him and those who surrounded him He was at once carried by four soldiers into a farm-house, whence three days after he was borne by his band of the 1st Battalion through the pass to the town of Vera, where he slowly recovered

The loss of the Regiment in this action, known as the Battle of the Nivelle, was very severe Of the 1st Battalion, Lieutenant-Colonel Barnard, Captain Charles Smyth, Lieutenants Haggup and Fensham were severely wounded ; 2 sergeants, 1 bugler, and 3 Riflemen were killed ; and 42 wounded.

Of the 2nd Battalion, Captain William Cox was slightly, and Lieutenants Charles Eaton, Henry Scott, and Doyle were severely wounded. Doyle died of his wounds. Five Riflemen were killed ; 3 sergeants and 23 Riflemen wounded ; and 3 missing.

Of the 3rd Battalion, there were Lieutenants Kirkman slightly, Loftus Jones severely, and 8 Riflemen wounded.

The Regiment bivouacked that night on the ground it had taken in front of Sarre. It rained hard all the following day, and for some days subsequently, and the troops suffered severely from the state of their camp On the 15th the Regiment moved to Arbonne, where the men were quartered in houses, and on the 17th proceeded to Arcangues. Here the 1st Battalion occupied the château and some houses near it ; while the 3rd Battalion were placed in some houses near the church, about a quarter of a mile to the rear. The village of Arcangues is built on high ground, from which three tongues or spurs run out like a trident. The enemy's pic-

[1] George Simmons had been brought up to the medical profession.

quets were at the village of Bassussari, about 400 yards from our picquets posted on these tongues of land; and in fact the sentries of the opposing armies were so close that the reliefs passed each other. There were some houses in this line of posts in the possession of the enemy which it was important to take from them, and so to connect our picquets on the tongues by a line of sentries extending across the valleys between them.

Accordingly, on November 23 the Light Division was ordered to attack the houses. This task was given to the 43rd. They at once attacked and carried these houses, but unfortunately the officer commanding the company engaged went beyond, and attacked a fortified house which the French occupied in strength on their reinforcing their post there, and the 43rd became seriously engaged The 1st Battalion were then ordered to move forward and cover this officer's retreat. But he was made prisoner with many of his men, and his Lieutenant was killed The 1st Battalion then held the houses which it was the object of this movement to secure.

While this was happening on the left projection, there were some houses also on the right in the possession of the enemy, which it was essential to take in order to secure access to a causeway, which ran along a marsh, and to some high ground near the Nive, occupied by another Division of the army; and on which stood a château, called, from the owner of it, 'Garrat's House.'

This task was also assigned to a company of the 43rd, supported by some other companies of that regiment, and by the 3rd Battalion The houses were at once taken, but an order immediately arrived to evacuate them, and the 43rd retired. But ere long a counter-order was issued that they were to be held; when a company of the 3rd Battalion took possession of them. They had not, however, been long in them when a third order was given that they were to retire. Scarcely had they begun to obey it when they were charged by some cavalry, supported by a column of infantry. The officer in command of the company, anxious perhaps to fulfil the last orders, and not unnecessarily to engage himself with a superior force, ordered his company to run to the rear. He thus brought them off safely, with the exception of one man wounded ; but rather to the offence of his brother Riflemen, who felt that he might have resisted, and punished the cavalry, and then have slowly withdrawn before a superior force of infantry.

One man of this company I have said was wounded. He was shot in the head ; and came to the surgeon who was with the other 3rd Battalion companies in reserve, to have his wound dressed As the surgeon was sponging it with water from a mess-tin held by the hospital orderly, a ball struck the tin, knocking it out of the hands of the orderly ; but without injuring any of the party. There were also wounded of the 1st Battalion, Lieutenant Stilwell, 1 sergeant and 3 Riflemen, and of the 3rd Battalion, 1 sergeant and 1 other man

The houses so often taken and evacuated were retaken next day by another company of the 3rd Battalion, who held them in spite of all attempts of the enemy to dispossess them In taking them a young officer, George Cary, then a Second Lieutenant, advanced with his men on the enemy, who withdrew for some distance without much resistance ; but on reaching a hedge some way in front of the principal house, they called to him to come no further, or they would fire. Cary, having placed his men under cover, called out to them (for he spoke excellent French) that they might begin their fire when they liked , but that he must have the house. They made no more resistance , but walking off planted their sentries within about forty yards of it

This is but one of many instances of the good and chivalrous feeling that existed between the Riflemen and the French troops on outpost duty. On another occasion soon after, some French officers made signs of peace to those of our 3rd Battalion on picquet. These being courteously returned, the French officers advanced, and informed our officers that some of the inhabitants who had fled from their homes within our lines were desirous to return to them ; and requested our officers to pass them through our outposts unmolested. This was of course readily agreed to, and promptly executed ; and the officers on both sides parted with mutual expressions of esteem 'But the most remarkable instance'—(though it occurred a little later than the period of which I am writing, I will give it here, in the words of Sir William Napier)—'happened on the occasion of Lord Wellington's being desirous of getting to the top of a hill occupied by the enemy near Bayonne. He ordered the Riflemen who escorted him to drive the French away, and seeing the former stealing up, as he thought too close, called out to commence firing. With a loud voice one of those old soldiers replied "No firing!" and then holding up the butt of his rifle towards the French, tapped it in a peculiar way At the well-understood signal, which meant "We must have the hill for a short time," the French, who though they could not maintain would not have relinquished the post without a fight if they had been fired upon, quietly retired And this signal would never have been made, if the post had been one capable of a permanent defence. So well,' concludes the historian, 'do veterans understand war and its proprieties'[1]

The well-known signal was holding up the butt, and tapping the brass tool-box which was in the stock of the Baker, as it was also in that of the Brunswick rifle It signified 'We are in earnest;' and was used by the Riflemen when they approached the French outposts to drive in picquets or with other hostile intent Without this signal made they were unmolested.

On December 9 the Light Division was ordered to advance with a view to the troops under General Hill passing the Nive. The 1st and 3rd Battalions drove in the enemy's outposts, the latter advancing along a ridge in their front. The 2nd Battalion was also actively engaged. A heavy fire was kept up by the French, to which the Regiment was more or less exposed all day. In the evening the Regiment fell back to the cantonments at and near Arcangues which they had before occupied. On the morning of the 10th no immediate fighting was anticipated, so little indeed that the Light Division had orders to fall back to Arbonne about four miles to the rear, and part of the second brigade had already marched; but General Kempt, not being satisfied with the look of things in his front, delayed his movement. The morning dawned with a thick drizzling rain; and the troops, having been as usual under arms at daylight, had turned in, when a sudden order was received to fall in and support the picquets, for the enemy were advancing The position of Arcangues has been already described: the church, the château, the adjacent houses, the three tongues of hilly land,

[1] 'Napier,' Book xxiii. chap. 3.

and there was a table-land, a sort of open common, at the top. The left tongue was occupied by picquets of the 52nd, the centre by those of the 43rd; the right by those of the 1st Battalion; and that near Garrat's House by those of the 3rd Battalion. As soon as these Battalions turned out, they found the picquets vigorously attacked. The numbers of the assailants were overwhelming, and they had to retire. But though this had to be effected at the double—for there was much ground to get over to reach the plateau in front of Arcangues—and though they moved over bad ground, yet the moment they reached the flat ground at top, these apparently flying skirmishers resumed their formation, and presented a steady and impenetrable front to the advancing enemy. But some of the 1st Battalion retiring from the right-hand tongue were unable to head the enemy, who moving by the ravine, arrived at the plain before them. Some men[1] and one officer, Second Lieutenant James Church, were then made prisoners.

Two companies of the 3rd Battalion were pushed forward to cover the retreat of the picquets, and having done so, they retired gradually as the enemy advanced. This Battalion then lined a coppice at the foot of the high ground on which the church is situated and connecting the church with the château, whence the 1st Battalion, having loop-holed it and strengthened it with *abattis* and a kind of rude rampart, kept up a galling fire upon the enemy. This *tiraillade* continued till dark.

In this affair Lieutenant Hopwood of the 1st Battalion, Sergeant Brotherton and Private Patrick Mahon were killed by one ball, which passed through the heads of all three as they were standing one behind the other. They fell near a hedge which the Battalion had defended as they fell gradually back from one defensible point to another. During the day several French soldiers came through the hedge and approached their bodies; but as our men supposed that it was with the intention to plunder them, they shot every man who passed the hedge. For they were unable from the violence of the fire to go out themselves to remove their bodies. At

[1] Nineteen men of the 1st Battalion, and 1 bugler and 12 men of the 2nd Battalion, were returned as 'missing.'

last towards evening a French officer approached through the hedge waving a white handkerchief, and when our firing ceased, he brought out some of his men with spades, who buried Hopwood and the sergeant in one grave.

On this day the losses of the Regiment were: 1st Battalion: 4 Riflemen killed; 2 Sergeants, 1 Bugler and 21 Riflemen wounded; 2nd Battalion: 4 Riflemen killed, 3 Sergeants, 1 Bugler and 24 Riflemen wounded; 3rd Battalion: 1 Rifleman killed, 1 Bugler and 22 Riflemen wounded.

On that night the 1st Battalion continued of course in its occupation of the château d'Arcangues, while the 3rd Battalion bivouacked on the ridge extending from it to the church.

On the 11th the Regiment was not engaged. And on that day some French officers, continuing the good feeling which I have mentioned, and doubtless anxious to show their confidence, brought out some chairs and a table from a house occupied by their picquet; and having carried them into the middle of the adjoining field, within 100 yards of our sentries, placed some wine and glasses on the table, and sitting down saluted the officers of our picquet; bowing and holding up their glasses, as if drinking to their healths.

Yet this security of the outposts was sometimes broken through. For on this night a Sergeant of the 3rd Battalion surprised the French picquet. Taking a few men with him he stole past the sentries and got up to the picquet house undiscovered; and seizing their arms, which he found piled outside, broke them. And while the picquet, utterly surprised, were turning out, he and his companions ran back to their lines. I do not know the name of this daring soldier. He lost an arm at the battle of Toulouse, and was consequently discharged.

On the other hand: some of the 1st Battalion were, in one of the affairs of outposts about this time, ordered to drive in the French picquets in front of them. Lieutenant Gardiner, who commanded the party, observed that he would not shoot the French sentries. So, calling to them to begone, he told them that he was going to attack the post. I have already noted that he spoke French fluently. They retired; but had hardly done so, when the French officer ordered his picquet to fire on Gardiner, who was making his men fall in for the attack. The discharge was ineffectual; and the Riflemen were glad to hear afterwards that the officer in charge of the French picquet was not a real soldier, but one of the national guard.

On the 12th the enemy made a show of strengthening his position; constructing a six-gun battery on the height in front of Arcangues, which however his gunners never could have served, as the Riflemen would have shot them before they could have fired a second round. While therefore our people were strengthening the château of Arcangues by *abattis* and throwing up a breastwork, the older heads declared that it was all a sham. And so indeed it proved. For though some fighting was anticipated on the 12th, and though in the afternoon the 1st and 3rd Battalions fell in with the supposed intention of driving the enemy's outposts further back from the ridge in front of Arcangues, yet nothing was done. And in the night between the 12th and 13th, the sentries of the picquets having reported that the enemy's fires were burning more brightly than usual, the *ruse* was suspected. And an officer with a patrol, having crept up to their lines, found them almost abandoned. The truth is that Soult had withdrawn his force in front of the Riflemen, to attack General Hill's force on their right.

In the morning the Riflemen moved forward to the ridge of Bassussari, and had some little firing with the rear-guard, which had not yet cleared off; but one of the known signals being made (an officer holding up his cap on the top of his sword), the firing ceased; and the Riflemen were suffered without any opposition to advance their outposts to the ground they had occupied before the attack on them on the 9th

On this night an untoward event occurred, which gave the officers of the Regiment some annoyance. After dark, a French officer accompanied by two men, approached our position; when the Corporal in charge of the advanced post of the picquet at the *abattis* took up his rifle and shot the French officer, whom the two soldiers carried into their picquet. It was feared that this would endanger the good understanding of the French outposts with the Riflemen.

For it was not known whether they came on a friendly visit, as they sometimes did; or whether it was a patrol sent forward to ascertain if we had withdrawn the picquets pushed forward in the afternoon. If the latter (and the presence of the two soldiers makes it probable that it was), of course those composing the patrol, risked the chances of war. However, no retaliation was attempted, and the outposts continued as friendly as before.

Here the Regiment remained without any other matter of moment worth recording for some weeks, during which they were hospitably entertained by the owners of the château of Arcangues, an aged lady and her grandson.

On January 3, 1814, they were moved to the right; and crossing the Nive advanced a league or two, in order to support some operations of the army on the Adour. These being effected they fell back to the Nive; and were cantoned in the villages of Ustaritz and Aurantz; the 3rd Battalion occupying the latter.

The weather now became very severe; rain, sleet and snow fell; and the roads were knee-deep for foot-passengers, and up to a horse's girths.

On January 24 the 1st Battalion was transferred to the second brigade of the Light Division, and the 2nd Battalion was placed in the first brigade. This was in consequence of Barnard, commanding the 1st Battalion, being given the command of the second brigade.

On February 16 the Regiment moved from its cantonments, and may be said to have commenced the campaign of 1814. Crossing the Nive at Ustaritz, they moved to within a league and a half of La Bastide de Clarence and encamped on a wild heathy plain Next day they marched to La Bastide itself, and encamped on a hill beyond it.

On the 18th they were moved into houses in consequence of the weather; which beginning with rain, changed through sleet into snow.

On the 19th the 1st Battalion marched for St. Jean-de-Luz to get their new clothing, for they were almost in rags; and the means of transport were not forthcoming, nor the roads easy for its conveyance. Therefore the Regiment went down to St. Jean-de-Luz, one Battalion at a time, to obtain it.

Having received it on the 23rd the Battalion started on the 24th to rejoin the army, and passing though Ustaritz, La Bastide and Garris, arrived at St. Palais on the 28th. Here they were very much disappointed to find that the regiment which occupied it had orders to move to the front, leaving the 1st Battalion at St. Palais till a fresh regiment relieved them. For they had heard firing on the 27th, and now the tidings of the hard fight at Orthez had reached them. Here they remained some days, in a state of great anxiety and excitement, until, as they were trying to persuade some detachments which came up that they were a relieving battalion, an order reached them to move forward And marching as rapidly as possible, they reached Sauveterre on the 7th March, Orthez on the 8th, and rejoined the other two Battalions at Barcelonne on the 11th

But while the 1st Battalion was absent for re-equipment in clothing, the two other Battalions had moved from La Bastide to Esturi on February 21st, and to St. Palais on the 22nd, and on the 23rd they encamped near La Chere and Charite. And it was found that the enemy had blown up a bridge over the Bidouze. It was necessary therefore on the 24th to cross two branches of that river by fords. The first, the Gave de Mauleon, they passed at Nabes; and then moving forward to Gave d'Oleron, they found some French cavalry drawn up on the opposite bank to dispute the passage. A small cottage was on the bank; and George Simmons,[1] taking a few Riflemen into it, kept up a smart fire from the windows to cover the passage of the two Battalions through the ford. As it was very deep, they were halted, and made to take off their pouches and strap them on the top of their knapsacks, and then plunge in, Captains Miller and Duncan of the 2nd Battalion leading the way. The water was above the men's waists, and they were obliged to link themselves together to avoid being swept away; while some of the men clung to the stirrup-leathers and tails of the horses of the mounted officers. On arrival at the opposite bank they found that the enemy had endeavoured to obstruct their mounting it, by drawing harrows with the point upwards to the slope. The cavalry

[1] He was, while the 1st Battalion were absent, temporarily attached to the 2nd Battalion; being employed on the telegraph of the Light Division.

however did not molest them. One man indeed galloped towards the bank, but he was instantly shot down by one of the 2nd Battalion men in the cottage. Under their fire, and that of a couple of guns, brought up to the left bank, they gave way and retired. This ford was near Villeneuve; and having passed through that village the Riflemen halted till the rest of the Division had crossed and formed up. While here George Simmons, being wet to the shoulders and very cold, entered a respectable house, and sitting down by the fire, asked the people to get him some wine and something to eat. Some ran to execute his orders, while the rest watched him with terror and aversion A little child being present, he took it up on his knee and fondled it, and (as the people refused to be paid for the refreshment he had asked for) he put some money into its hand. On his setting it down a general feeling of relief seemed to pervade the bystanders, who then told him that Soult and his emissaries had informed the peasantry that the English were barbarians, who would carry off and murder their children.

On their march after crossing the Gave d'Oleron, they came in sight of a body of the enemy's infantry moving parallel to them, and apparently making the utmost haste to escape from them. It was at first proposed to fall on them; but some wiser man having observed that their supports were probably not far off, they were allowed to depart in peace. The two Battalions bivouacked on a bleak exposed common not far from Orion

The next day they passed through Orion; and on arrival there learned that it had been occupied as Soult's head-quarters the night before. The wisdom of not attacking the retreating column the day before was now apparent; for the French being in force at Orion, would have moved out to their succour; and possibly might have overpowered, and certainly would have harassed, the soldiers weary with a long march and the passage of two fords.

Pursuing their march they arrived near Orthez and soon heard a loud explosion, which proved to be the destruction by the enemy of the stone bridge over the Gave de Pau. The two Battalions advanced to some high ground looking over the town of Orthez. Some troops of the enemy were observed filing through the town; and some guns being brought up opened on them, which induced them to quicken their pace, and their officers were seen riding up and down and urging them on. They also brought forward some guns which returned the cannonade without, however, doing much harm. The Riflemen bivouacked on this height.

On the 26th Lord Wellington after reconnoitring the enemy's position ordered them about twelve o'clock to fall in. And they were soon after directed to move to the right, and cross a ford a little above the destroyed bridge. This promised to be a most deadly business as the French infantry were massed, with heavy guns, directly in front of the ford. However the Riflemen marched off, the 3rd Battalion leading. On the way a staff officer overtook them, and ordered them to conceal themselves as much as possible behind any irregularities of the ground. This they did and crept on; and just as they got to open ground leading down to the ford, and expected the artillery to open upon them, they were suddenly countermanded, countermarched, and moved far to the left. The truth is that this was a double feint. First, to make the enemy believe that our people were going to attempt the ford; and then, lest they should have suspected that any open demonstration to do so was a feint, to make them fancy, by our stealth and getting under cover, that it was hoped to conceal the movement from them. By occupying the enemy's attention with this skilful manœuvre, three divisions of the army were enabled to cross the river by a pontoon bridge at a point near Salles, below Orthez. By this bridge the Riflemen were also to pass; and marching all day they bivouacked near the village of Salles and close to the pontoon bridge at night.

On the 27th they early crossed the Gave de Pau; and moved by the great road which leads from Peyrehorade towards the town of Orthez; and when within about two miles of it, turning to the left, they ascended the ridge which runs parallel with the river and in front of which the French were posted in a very strong position. Whether it was that the Light Division was weak, two of its regiments being absent, or that they were not needed, the two Battalions were not actively engaged. Lord Wellington was in front of them during the afternoon, and ordered that advance of the 52nd which, as is well known, broke through Soult's centre and decided the fate of the day

Then the enemy fled, and then the Riflemen were ordered in pursuit, but did not come up with the retreating columns. Their march continued for about two leagues, in the course of which they passed the river Lys de Béarn and bivouacked near the village of Bonne Garde. They were entirely without covering and suffered much; for it froze hard. The Commanding Officer of the 3rd Battalion (whether Ross or Balvaird, I am not sure) did indeed contrive to get into a hut; but there being no bed unoccupied, he lay down in a kneading-trough or flour-bin, and appeared in the morning more like a miller than a Rifleman.

On the 28th the two Battalions started early, and after crossing the Lys de France, arrived at Duerse, where they halted for the night.

On March 1, they passed the Adour, and after a long march entered Mont-de-Marsan, which the enemy evacuated just before they reached it. Here they were quartered in good houses, and had comfortable beds: a change very refreshing to them after their long marches, often in very bad weather, and after their exposed bivouacks.

On the next day the 2nd Battalion marched to Bertam, and the 3rd Battalion to St. Maurice; the march was through the pine forests and by the sandy roads of the Landes; and being made in a snow storm was very painful to the soldiers.

On the next day the 3rd Battalion moved on to St. Sever, where Lord Wellington had fixed his head-quarters. Here they continued till the 8th, furnishing the guards and duties of head-quarters On the 4th the 2nd Battalion had marched to Bascom, where they remained till the 9th, when both Battalions re-united near Aire, whither the 3rd Battalion had marched, crossing the Adour on the 8th and moving to Grenade; and next day to Barcelonne opposite Aire on the right bank of that river.

On the 10th both Battalions marched at daylight to some poor cottages near Arblade, and on the 11th entered Tarsac, where they halted for the night. The 1st Battalion now rejoined the Light Division, and the Regiment was re-united.

On the 14th, as Soult assembled a considerable force and threatened General Hill's corps, the Regiment was moved back through Tarsac and formed on the high road near a wood, where they remained the whole day expecting to be engaged, but the enemy retiring after making a demonstration only, they marched back to Tarsac and re-occupied their quarters there.

The enemy had left a rear-guard of cavalry, and as they remained during the next two days, it was determined on the 16th to attack them. The 15th Hussars were with the Riflemen at Tarsac; and accordingly on that morning this regiment moved out to attack the French cavalry. This consisted of the 13th French Hussars, and they sent one squadron in advance, the rest of the regiment being formed in support. The English cavalry adopted the same formation, and a squadron under Captain Hancox, supported by the 2nd Battalion, advanced to meet their opponents. The French were rapidly charged and upset; many of them sabred, and about twenty-five made prisoners, among whom was the French Captain. He was badly wounded, and died of his wounds in his father's house, to which he was taken. For he was a native of the place, which it was said he had not visited for many years. The rest of the French cavalry rapidly retired and escaped.

On the 18th the Regiment advanced by the road by which the French had retreated, and crossing the Adour by a bridge at Arros (or La Rose) proceeded to St. Germain; whence, after a short halt, to Plaisance, where they remained for the night, three companies of the 1st Battalion being pushed across the river.

On the next day the Regiment marched to Obregon, where they halted for some hours; and in the evening halted at Aget.

The French were now falling back on Tarbes, and on this day the Riflemen heard much firing on their right, which was caused by the attack of Picton's light troops on the retreating enemy near Vic en Bigorre.

On the 20th the Regiment marched early, and moving along the ridge on which they had last night encamped, arrived at Rabastens Here learning that the enemy had taken up a position near Tarbes, they moved to the right, by the road leading from Auch to Tarbes. On approaching this town the French were found posted in a formidable position on a hill, or rather a succession of heights intersected with ditches and hedges, which gave it almost the form of entrenchments. It being at first supposed that no considerable force was engaged, for on marching along the road only a small party were observed, a company of the 2nd Battalion was sent to dislodge them. But when it was ascertained that the position was occupied by a considerable part of General Harispe's division, the whole Regiment advanced to the attack. The 3rd Battalion were on the right, the 2nd in the centre, and the 1st Battalion on the left. The front of the enemy was covered by clouds of light troops, whom it was not easy to dislodge, for they had the protection of hedges and banks; and the Riflemen had to force their way in skirmishing through some covert of considerable growth. Then they emerged at the foot of the hill, and the enemy's ranks rose 'tier above tier' as one eye-witness describes it, on the side of the mountain. But the Riflemen rushed forward; and though their opponents fought desperately, and their fire was delivered from one rank above another like the guns on the decks of a three-decker, yet the Riflemen drove them from the hill, over it and into the plain below. 'The French,' Napier relates, 'charged with great hardiness, and being encountered by men not accustomed to yield, they fought muzzle to muzzle; and it was difficult to judge at first who would win.' It was not long to decide; for within an hour this hill was taken; its face cleared of all but the dead or dying, and the French in disordered flight over the plain beyond. Napier supposes that the French mistook the Riflemen, on account of their green dress, for Portuguese, and therefore fought with more perseverance than was usual against English troops. Yet one would suppose that the veterans of the Peninsula had too often fought with the green-jackets to be ignorant of their nationality or their endurance in fight Be that as it may, all agree that this was an unusually hard-fought field. Surtees says 'the firing was the hottest I had ever seen, except perhaps Barossa.' And Costello observes 'I never remember to have been so warmly engaged as on this occasion, except at Badajos.'

The odds too were very great. I am not able to say how many French crowded that hill-side; but sixteen companies of Riflemen only drove them from it. For though the other regiments of the Division were in reserve, and would doubtless have supported the Riflemen, had they been repulsed; yet not a shot was fired on that hill except from a 95th rifle. Lord Wellington in his despatch notes the loss of the enemy as being considerable; that of the Regiment was 11 officers and 80 men.

Of the 1st Battalion, Captain Loftus Gray and Lieutenant John Cox were severely, and George Simmons slightly, wounded; 2 Riflemen were killed, and 5 sergeants and 21 Riflemen wounded. Of the 2nd Battalion, Captain Duncan was killed, Lieutenant-Colonel Norcott, Captain Miller, and Lieutenant Dixon were severely, and Lieutenant Humbley slightly, wounded; 1 sergeant and 2 Riflemen were killed; and 14 wounded. And of the 3rd Battalion, Captain William Cox and Lieutenant Farmer were severely, and Lieutenant Sir John Ribton and Quartermaster Surtees slightly, wounded. 1 Rifleman was killed, and 3 sergeants and 32 Riflemen were wounded

Colonel Norcott was conspicuous, riding about on a tall black mare: he was early in the day wounded in the shoulder. George Simmons late in the day was wounded in the knee. When he was down the French continuing to fire at him, his servant, Henry Short, a brave Rifleman, ran up and deliberately placing himself in the line of fire, said 'You shall not hit him again except through my body.'

Amongst this carnage some curious, some almost ludicrous, circumstances occurred. A captain of the Regiment was struck by a ball on a flask or drinking-horn which he carried at his side. The force of the ball knocked him down and for the moment stunned him. The men thinking he was killed, or desperately wounded, were carrying him to the rear, when he revived and called out 'Stop, let me feel;' when finding he was unhurt except by the blow, he leaped out of their arms, and again headed his company. His return was heralded by shouts of laughter, so ludicrous was the whole episode, though the fight was at the thickest, and the men falling fast.

When the Riflemen were occupying their camp on the

Pyrenees, an owl had taken up its quarters with them, and always pitched on the tent of Lieutenant Doyle, who was killed at the Nivelle. Its accustomed haunt being gone, it transferred its perch to Captain Duncan's tent. The joke ran, in the rough mirth of the camp, that he must be next on the roster; a joke of which he neither liked the point, nor saw the wit. Yet so it was that he fell in this day of Tarbes.

This fight was a strictly regimental one, for (as I have said) the Rifle Battalions only were engaged. It excited the admiration of their companions in arms. One of them, an eye-witness, thus speaks of this action: 'Our Rifles were immediately sent to dislodge the French from the hills on our left, and our battalion was ordered to support them. Nothing could exceed the manner in which the ninety-fifth set about this business. Certainly I never saw such skirmishers as the ninety-fifth, now the Rifle Brigade. They could do the work much better and with infinitely less loss than any other of our best light troops. They possessed an individual boldness, a mutual understanding, and a quickness of eye in taking advantage of the ground, which, taken altogether, I never saw equalled. They were in fact as much superior to the French Voltigeurs as the latter were to our skirmishers in general. As our regiment was often employed in supporting them, I think I am fairly qualified to speak of their merits.'[1]

The enemy having been driven from the hill retreated across the plain, which was covered with the pursued and the pursuers. As they were crossing it, the Riflemen came upon a considerable body of the French who were retreating from the town of Tarbes, whence they had been driven by the 3rd Division; and it was proposed that the Riflemen, quickening their pace, should fall upon their flank and intercept them. But the French were too quick for them. For perceiving their intention, they inclined to the right and got away.

The enemy having crossed the plain took up a strong position on some heights at the extremity of it; but while Lord Wellington was making dispositions to attack them, darkness came on, and the Riflemen bivouacked that night on the plain. The French cannonaded the bivouack from the height, but the fire was almost harmless; and as the troops

[1] 'Twelve Years' Military Adventure.'

did not move from the ground on which they had bivouacked, it gradually ceased. And in the night the enemy abandoned the position and continued their retreat; pursued in the morning by the Riflemen, who halted that night at Lannemazen. The next day they proceeded, still in pursuit, to Castelnau. And starting early in the morning of the 24th, halted that night at L'Isle-en-Dodon. And on the next day (moving on Toulouse) reached Mont Ferrand On the 27th they advanced to the village of Tournefeuille, a little beyond which the enemy still held some ground, occupying some hedges and enclosures, in front of a bridge about half a mile from the village The 3rd Battalion and a Portuguese regiment were ordered to dislodge them. And the Riflemen extending to the left while the Portuguese moved on the road, the French gradually fell back towards the bridge and crossed it, taking the road to Toulouse; and the Riflemen did not pursue. The loss was trifling. But a most curious circumstance occurred during this skirmish. A Rifleman of the name of Powell was shot in the mouth, the ball knocking several of his teeth out. One of these struck a Portuguese and wounded him in the aim. The surgeon of the 43rd who happened to be at hand, dressing the wound of the Portuguese, found in it not a bullet but a tooth. On this the cry went among the Riflemen that 'The French were firing bones and not bullets'

On enquiry being made and the relative positions of the Portuguese soldier and Powell being ascertained, no doubt remained that his tooth had caused the wound. Powell was afterwards killed by a cannon-ball near New Orleans. I relate this extraordinary circumstance on the authority of Surtees, who was near Powell at the time he was wounded, and who minutely examined into the circumstances at the time. I ought to add that I have invariably found Surtees' statements corroborated in every particular by the relations or journals of others; and as he was a man of strong religious impressions his veracity cannot I think be questioned.

On the 29th the Regiment moved forward to near Toulouse, and occupied some villages and châteaux in the neighbourhood. On the 31st the engineers attempted to throw a bridge over the Garonne above its junction with the

Ariège above the town, and the Regiment was assembled to pass it; but the number of pontoons being insufficient, and it not being possible to construct a bridge on trestles, they returned to their cantonments. But it would seem that the 3rd Battalion did cross (ferried over probably)[1] and were left as a picquet in one of the villages on the bank.[2]

On April 2 all had recrossed the Garonne, and again occupied cantonments, on this occasion the houses occupied being lower down the river than those in which they were formerly cantoned; the 3rd Battalion were quartered in a wine-store, amongst the casks of which the men slept. During the time they occupied it no depredation whatever was committed, nor was any man of the Battalion found to be drunk. On the 6th the Regiment moved down the river towards Grenade, and encamped near the village of Seilh. A bridge of pontoons had been thrown across the Garonne here, and some divisions had crossed; but the river having risen, and fallen trees having been floated down the river, the pontoons broke away from the right bank, and were swung round with the stream, being still fast to the left bank. Though exertions were made to re-establish it, it was not practicable till the 9th. And early in the morning of the 10th the Regiment with the other troops of the Light Division crossed it, and moved up into position in front of Toulouse. The roads were excellent, and they quickly attained the position they were to occupy. Their right, the 3rd Battalion, was to touch Picton's left, and the left was to communicate with the Spanish force under General Freyre. In front of the Riflemen the enemy occupied some houses, and they had constructed a battery near the bridge over the canal of Languedoc; and at the end of the bridge stood a Convent which they had loop-holed and fortified in a very effective manner. The Riflemen commenced by driving the enemy from the houses, and keeping up their attention during the day. But some of the 3rd Battalion (and of Picton's division on their right) pushed on too far, and getting under the fire of the defenders of the Convent, they suffered severely. To cover

[1] See Napier, Book xxiv. chap. 5.

[2] Surtees, 296, 297. The context is very confused, the editor not having been able to decipher or to arrange Surtees' MS.

themselves they had to leap into an open sewer; and detestable as was this position, they had to remain in it for some time, so severe was the fire of their opponents. But on the left of the Riflemen a different scene was taking place. The Spaniards had claimed, as a place of honour, to lead the attack on the Calvinet. Their rout and their flight under the fire of its defenders are well known. The Riflemen, and the other regiments of the Light Division, were mainly occupied during the day in covering the retreat of the Spaniards, who re-formed more than once and advanced to the attack; but always to be repulsed by the French fire, and to fly from it. As often as the English troops interposed, the French retired; as often as they left the fight to the Spaniards, the French pursued them.

When the left of the Division was thus occupied in shielding the flying Spaniards the French rushed out again with loud cries, in front of the 3rd Battalion, and only with hard fighting were again driven in. So the battle raged till about four o'clock, when Beresford having carried the heights on the left of the Riflemen, the French withdrew within the place, and the battle ended.

Captain Michael Hewan of the 2nd Battalion was severely wounded. 14 Riflemen of that Battalion were killed; and 3 Sergeants and 23 Riflemen wounded.[1]

The Regiment bivouacked on the ground they had occupied, being saluted from time to time by shot or shell from the place.

On the 11th the Regiment remained perfectly quiet, and on the 12th entered Toulouse, Marshal Soult having in the previous night retreated from the place in the direction of Carcassonne. On the same day Colonel Cooke and Colonel St. Simon, as English and French commissioners, arrived with intelligence of the abdication of Napoleon. This was at once communicated to Marshal Soult; but as he refused to acknowledge the authority of those making the communication, the Regiment with other troops was started in pursuit, and marched on the 16th towards Villefranche. On the second

[1] Record, 2nd Battalion. As the return in the 'London Gazette' does not distinguish the regiments of the non-commissioned officers and privates, I am unable to give the casualties of the other Battalions.

day's march, as they were halted on the roadside, loud huzzas were heard in front, and a carriage approached containing Count Gazan, the bearer of intelligence that Soult recognised the abdication of the Emperor, and acceded to a suspension of arms. The Regiment, therefore, at once returned to Toulouse and occupied their former quarters.

Towards the end of April the Regiment moved out of Toulouse, and descending the Garonne were quartered in Castel Sarazin and the neighbouring villages, the 1st Battalion occupying Castel Sarazin, and the 3rd Grisolles. The 2nd appear to have been at Castelnau d'Estrettefons.

Here they remained until the 1st June, when they forded the Garonne and halted at Grenade. On the next day they reached Cadours near Cologne, at which the 2nd Battalion halted. On the 5th they marched to Leitoure; and passing next day through Condom and Nerac halted at Castel Jaloux. On the 11th they reached Bazas and on the 12th arrived at Langon. The next day they proceeded to Barsac. On the 14th they halted at Castres, and the next day entered Bourdeaux. They were not however quartered there, but merely passed through it, and marched on to Blanquefort. On the road the Riflemen were reviewed by Lord Wellington, and the men and officers as they passed saluted with loud cheers the chief who had for six years led them to victory.

They remained at Blanquefort till the 13th July, when the 1st and 2nd Battalions embarked at Paulliac on board H. M. ship 'Ville de Paris' and disembarked at Portsmouth on the 22nd.

The 3rd Battalion embarked on the 8th July on board H. M. ship 'Dublin,' and sailing on the 9th arrived at Plymouth on the 18th, and disembarking there occupied the barracks.

I have been unwilling to interrupt the narrative of events in which the Regiment was engaged in the North of Spain and the South of France; but I have now to turn to operations in Holland in which detachments of the three Battalions were engaged.

An expedition to that country having been decided on,

under the command of General Sir Thomas Graham [1] (afterwards Lord Lynedoch), some companies of the Regiment, from the depôts of each Battalion at Shorncliffe, were selected to form part of it.

Of the 1st Battalion, Captain Glasse's company; of the 2nd, Captain M'Cullock's; and of the 3rd, two companies, Captains Fullerton's and William Eeles', formed the detachment to accompany this expedition.[2]

They marched from Shorncliffe on November 28; but in consequence of the continuance of easterly winds, did not embark from Deal until December 9. In this embarkation the Deal boat which was conveying Captain Glasse's company on board H M. ship 'Grampus' was swamped; but the men, after being in considerable danger, were all saved. Yet their dangers were not over; for on that or the next night the 'Grampus,' in which the Rifle companies were embarked, came into collision with the 'Monarch' These dangers being overcome, the Riflemen disembarked at St. Martin's dyck in the Island of Tholen on December 17; and made a night march to Wosmaer. On the next day they proceeded to Halteren, and thence to near Bergen-op-Zoom, near which they halted. At this time Bergen was partially invested, and the Riflemen were moved up on the 23rd close to the walls. But on the 24th they made a night march to Steenberghen; and on the next day proceeded to Oudenbosch. Here they halted some days; and on the 29th an attack was anticipated, but none took place.

Early in January 1814 a combined movement was arranged between Sir Thomas Graham and General Bulow, who commanded the Prussian force with which Graham's was to co-operate, by which the French were to be dislodged from

[1] It is evident from Sir Thomas Graham's letters to Lord Bathurst and Lord Wellington ('Supplementary Despatches,' viii. 376-7) that he undertook this command very unwillingly and only from a sense of duty. To Lord Wellington he says 'I cannot look forward to it otherwise than an irksome service, with scarce a chance of any material success'

[2] It would appear from a private letter from Lord Bathurst to Lord Wellington, that the strength of the detachment of the 3rd Battalion was 250 men. 'Supplementary Despatches,' viii. 390 This is a clerical or typographical error for 'of the three Battalions.' The depôt companies were at this time very weak, and the strength of the whole detachment was about 250 men.

Hoogstraten, and a reconnaissance was to be made on Antwerp. Accordingly the Riflemen moved to Roosendael on January 9, and thence to Calmthout, where they arrived at daybreak on the 11th. The combined movement of the English and Prussians was to have taken place on the 12th; and on that day the enemy threatened an attack; but learning from their patrols that the Prussians were also approaching, they fell back, and being reinforced from the garrison, took up a position in front of Antwerp, their left resting on the village of Merxem, their right on Bergerhout. The Riflemen on the enemy retiring had advanced in pursuit to Capellen

On the 13th they advanced towards Antwerp, and soon came up with the enemy's rear, as they were retiring into the place. There was a smart skirmish, and the enemy were driven into Antwerp. The Riflemen distinguished themselves in this affair; and Sir Thomas Graham in his despatch particularly mentions 'the rapid but orderly advance of the detachment of the 3rd Battalion of the Rifle Corps under Captain Fullerton's command,' with great praise [1]

In this affair one Rifleman of the 3rd Battalion was killed, and one wounded.

On the 14th they fell back to Calmthout, and on the 15th marched to Eckeren, where they remained for some days The Riflemen had suffered much from the extreme cold; and on January 26 it reached its maximum, the thermometer marking 13° of frost.

During the month of January the army under Sir Thomas Graham, which originally amounted to hardly 6,000 men, was increased by reinforcements of about 3,000 men. And at this time Major and Brevet Lieutenant-Colonel Cameron of the 1st Battalion arrived in Holland and took command of the detachments from the three Battalions.

As the French had 12,000 men in Antwerp under Carnot's command, no regular siege could be attempted with this force and with the means at Graham's disposal; it was resolved therefore to attempt to set fire to the enemy's ships at Antwerp. With this object the troops were moved forward. And the Riflemen returned on January 30 from Eckeren to Calmthout; on the 31st marched to Braeschaet, and on February 1

[1] Graham's Despatch, 'Annual Register,' lvi, 154.

advanced to Donk On that evening the picquets had some fighting with those of the enemy. On the 2nd the enemy advanced to Merxem, which had been strengthened with field works, and the Riflemen had some hard fighting in and about that village, and at Schooten Merxem was carried in gallant style; and Graham specially notes the conduct of 'the detachments of the three Battalions of the Rifle Corps,' under Colonel Cameron's command, 'for the distinguished manner in which they attacked the left and centre of the village, forcing the enemy from every stronghold.' [1]

On this day Lieutenant Wright of the 1st Battalion was returned as wounded,[2] as were Captain William Eeles, Lieutenants Ferguson and Fitzgerald of the 3rd Battalion. One bugler and 2 Riflemen of the 2nd Battalion were killed, and 6 wounded.[3]

The attempt to burn the ships in the Scheldt and in the docks was unsuccessful; for our mortars numbering only seventeen, two-thirds of which were Dutch or French ones found on the ramparts of Willemstadt (where part of the force had disembarked), were unserviceable, and unable to throw shells a sufficient distance The enemy too nightly flooded the decks with water, which the intense frost converted into a thick coating of ice, which, at that range, helped to resist the shells thrown by the imperfect mortars And the enemy were able at once to extinguish any fire among the shipping which might take place

On the 3rd the Riflemen occupied the château of Merxem, where they remained until the 6th, when the partial investment of Antwerp and the attempt on the ships having

[1] Despatch, 'Annual Register,' 157

[2] I am informed by Mr Wright that he was *not* wounded on this occasion. This is a curious illustration of Byron's remark about 'Gazette fame' ('Don Juan,' canto viii, stanza 18 and note) The officer of the 1st Battalion who was wounded at Merxem on February 2 was Lieutenant Church He had been taken prisoner in one of the fights at Arcangues on December 10, 1813 (see p 160); but had made his escape, had found his way across France without being discovered, and had joined Glasse's company in Holland Like M'Cullock after the Coa (p 56) he had trusted himself to the fair sex, who had assisted his disguise, and favoured his escape

[3] 'London Gazette,' and 2nd Battalion Record As the 'Gazette' does not distinguish the regiments of the non-commissioned officers and lower ranks, I am unable to state the losses of the detachments of the other two Battalions.

been found a failure, they moved to Braeschaet. On the next day they were again moved forward to Donk to repel a sortie of the garrison, which having effected they returned to Braeschaet; and on the 9th fell back to Klein Zundert, and on the 15th to Loenhout

About this time the Prussians, having received orders to proceed to the south, separated from the British force; and Graham's position on the frontier of Holland was far from secure He fell back, as we have seen, from Antwerp, and occupied ground between that place and Breda. He eventually resolved to attempt the capture of Bergen-op-Zoom The Riflemen moved on February 28 to West Wesel. In the storm of Bergen and its failure they had no part; for on March 8 (the day on which the attempt was made) they marched in the evening towards Antwerp, it being understood that their destination was to attack Fort Lillo. They marched all night, and towards morning were countermanded and halted; and some hours afterwards heard of the failure at Bergen-op-Zoom. However a picquet of the 3rd Battalion was left near Bergen; and on the failure of the attack on it, they were ordered late in the night of the 8th to retire, and to make the best of their way to their companies This they effected; but with barely sufficient time to call in their advanced sentries[1]

On the 9th the Riflemen halted at Stabroek, and on the 11th moved to Capellen.

Another sortie was made by the enemy from Antwerp on March 26, and the Riflemen were under arms expecting an attack, but none took place on them, the enemy having retired. Such alarms and affairs occasionally occurred, for on the 30th the Riflemen pursued a foraging party of the enemy, but unsuccessfully, for they made good their return into Antwerp before the Riflemen could intercept them. But all really active operations of this expedition terminated with the failure at Bergen-op-Zoom. Some further operations were contemplated; but as Graham was on the point of executing them, news reached the Riflemen on April 4 of the entrance of the Allies into Paris on March 31

[1] I derive this information from Michael Mappin, a pensioner in the Royal Hospital at Chelsea, who served in the 3rd Battalion from April 1813 till it was disbanded, and afterwards in the 2nd Battalion, and who was himself on this picquet. He was wounded before Antwerp

However by the Treaty of Paris the Kingdom of the Netherlands was to be established; and pending the details of that measure being arranged by the Congress of Vienna, an Anglo-Hanoverian force was to remain in the country. The Rifle detachments formed part of it.

Early in April a detachment of one company was sent to occupy Fort Batz, and on April 15 the Riflemen moved from Capellen to Braeschaet and Schooten; on the 29th they marched to Contich, and on the 30th to Mechlin, where they remained about a fortnight. On May 14 they arrived at Brussels, where on the 30th they were reviewed by the Prince Sovereign of the Netherlands, as he was then styled, afterwards the King of the Netherlands.

On Sir Thomas Graham, then Lord Lynedoch, returning to England, the Anglo-Hanoverian force was placed under the command of General the Prince of Orange. The Riflemen remained at Brussels until August 29, when they moved to Ypres, and on the 31st arrived at Courtrai. On September 5, they marched to Menin; but returned to Ypres on October 12. Remaining there till November 22, they moved on that day to Dixmude, and to Furnes on December 9. About this time the Rifle detachments received some reinforcements Captain Logan, Lieutenant Robert Cochrane and 45 men of the 2nd Battalion embarked at Deal on November 7 to join them. On March 8, 1815, they were at Nieuport, with a detachment of two companies at Furnes; their strength being then 4 captains, 14 subalterns, 2 staff, 21 sergeants, 9 buglers and 388 rank and file, under the command of Captain Glasse of the 1st Battalion. But on March 24 they were re-united at Menin[1]

On the renewal of hostilities in 1815 the companies of the 1st and 2nd Battalions joined those Battalions on their arrival in Flanders The 2nd Battalion company joined at Leuze on April 18; and the two companies of the 3rd Battalion were (with the 2nd Battalion) in Sir Frederick Adam's brigade at Waterloo.[2]

[1] 'Wellington Supplementary Despatches,' x 704-5-6, and 718.

[2] I owe almost all the particulars of this expedition to the kindness of Lieutenant Wright, on half-pay of the Regiment, who served in it, and who survives in good health and perfect memory, whose acquaintance I had the pleasure of

I have said that the five companies of the 3rd Battalion, on their return from the Peninsula disembarked at Plymouth, and moved into barracks there On September 18, 1814, exactly two months after their arrival in England, they re-embarked for service; the commanding officer, Major Mitchell, and three companies on board the 'Fox,' and the other two companies on board the 'Dover' frigates. Their destination and the nature of their service were kept a profound secret, but they were, in fact, intended to effect a descent on the American coast near New Orleans They reached Madeira on the 8th October, where they remained till the 11th, and having touched at Barbadoes early in November, anchored in Negril Bay, Jamaica, on the 25th Here they were joined by four line regiments, and two West India regiments; and setting sail on the 29th, arrived off the American coast near Mobile on December 10, and on the 11th anchored near the Chandeleur Islands near the entrance to Lake Borgne.

New Orleans is situated on the left bank of the Mississippi, here about 800 or 1,000 yards across; below the town are great marshes, covered with reeds six or seven feet high While on the river bank runs a strip of firm ground, varying from one to three miles across, and mostly under sugar plantations. From this the marsh extends six or seven miles to the shores of Lake Pontchartrain, which communicates by Lake Borgne with the sea.

It was deemed impossible to approach New Orleans by the Mississippi, as well because very strong works existed at its mouth, and on the way up to the city, as because the course of the river is so tortuous that no wind would have carried the ships up, without considerable delay. It was therefore resolved to disembark the troops on the shore of one of the lakes. But it was ascertained that the Americans, already cognisant of the intended invasion, had placed gun-boats on these lakes to prevent the landing. The previous destruction of these was therefore necessary; and this was effected in

making while these sheets were passing through the press The information and papers he communicated to me enable me to supply many details of this campaign, which, squeezed out between the Peninsular and Waterloo campaigns, and eclipsed by the latter, has never had its history sufficiently written. Yet it was arduous service, albeit unsuccessful.

very fine style and in a very short time by the boats of the fleet under Captain Lockyer.

On the 15th the Riflemen were moved from the ships of war into brigs, which drew less water, but in which they were so crowded as to be unable to lie down or almost to turn. But even these were too deep for the shoal waters of the lake, and they were transferred into long boats, from which they were landed on the 19th on the Île au Poix (or as our men called it Pearl Island), formed by the branches of the Pearl river. The weather in moving from the ships to the island was very bad; and on arrival at it, it was found to be a perfect desert. Nothing but reeds grew on it, except a few scrubby pine-trees at one end. To add to their discomfort, a severe frost came on at night; the men were without shelter of any kind, and they suffered severely. And as all their supplies had to be furnished from the fleet, want of provisions was added to their other hardships.

On the 22nd the Battalion (which formed part of the advance under Colonel Thornton) embarked in boats, and about two o'clock pushed off to land on the mainland. The place decided on for their disembarkation was at the head of a creek called Bayou Catalan in Lake Borgne. The distance was between thirty and forty miles, and the men were so crowded in the boats that they could not move. They did not reach the entrance to the creek till after dark. As a picquet of the enemy was posted about half a mile up the creek, Captain James Travers, with his company, were placed in small boats and pushed forward. The picquet was stationed at some huts; near these Travers landed, and having moved his men to both ends of the huts, prevented the escape of the picquet, which was secured without a shot being fired. This was admirably effected, and was a most important service. For had this picquet escaped or raised an alarm, the landing would have been opposed. And this would have been a serious check; for on the morning of the 23rd, when the leading boat reached the narrow part of the Bayou it was found impracticable to ascend higher, and the boats being drawn up one after another the men passed over them as a bridge. This of course was a very slow operation, and one which, if opposed, would have been very difficult. The

Battalion disembarked about an hour after daylight, having been upwards of sixteen hours cramped in the boats.

As soon as the whole advance were on shore, they marched, Travers' company leading, and to give their force as imposing an appearance as possible, and to scour the country, they advanced with extended files. They moved in this order through a wood which skirted the swamp on this side, and as soon as they had cleared it, came upon a house, surrounded with out-buildings and huts for slaves, belonging to a M Villeroy. The Battalion advancing at the double, took possession of it; and in this and some neighbouring houses took about thirty prisoners, and a good many stand of arms, belonging, as was supposed, to the local militia. Unhappily M. Villeroy escaped, and probably gave information to the enemy; this, before the night was over, entailed very disastrous consequences. The Battalion then advanced, and turning to the right, marched for about a mile on the road to New Orleans, and then bivouacked in a green field in quarter distance column

The road ran near the river's bank which was on the left; and an embankment about three or four feet high was thrown up to keep the overflow of the river from the cultivated ground, here about three-quarters of a mile or a mile broad, beyond this was a strip of wood, the way through which was, in fact, impracticable, the ground under the trees being wet and swampy. The cultivated land was much intersected with wet ditches, and divided by strong wooden palings five feet high.

On arriving at the bivouack Travers' company, which had formed the advanced guard on the march, was pushed forward about a mile to the front, on the main road, as a picquet.

The troops halted somewhat after mid-day; and as the men had been without provisions since the morning before, they began as soon as dismissed to cook. While doing so, between three and four o'clock, firing was heard in the front from the picquet, it turned out to be in consequence of an American officer, attended by some mounted men, riding up to the picquet to reconnoitre. However, the Riflemen saluted him with a few shots, one of which wounded him, and another killed the horse of one of the party, on which they retired, getting off the wounded officer with them.

At nightfall, Captain Hallen's company relieved Travers at the advanced picquet, and the men of the rest of the Battalion, being much fatigued by their uncomfortable night in the boats, their tedious landing, and their march, lay down in bivouack. They had torn down some of the palings dividing the fields, and had made good fires which then burned brightly. While they were thus, as they fancied, secure, a schooner dropped down the Mississippi, and guided by the light of their fires, opened a heavy cannonade upon them with great effect. The men of course were aroused and dispersed; but no shelter could be found, in this dead flat, except by crouching under the embankment by the river-side. Hallen had seen the schooner pass his post and had sent a man off to alarm the Battalion, but the schooner having the current of the river in her favour reached the bivouack before the Rifleman could get there.

While in this state of alarm from the sudden cannonade from the schooner, heavy and continued firing was heard in the front. A body of 5,000 Americans had attacked Hallen's picquet, detaching 1,500 men through the wood to turn the right of the troops. Nobly Hallen kept them at bay; but being himself wounded, and his picquet threatened by such overpowering odds, reinforcements advanced from the Battalion. Meanwhile the enemy made way through the garden of a house on the right, where a picquet of the 85th had been placed, and the night being very dark, a hand to hand fight took place. Every deception was practised by the enemy; and having discovered (from prisoners probably made in the *mêlée*) the regiments opposed to them, they would call out, 'Come on my brave ninety-fifth (or eighty-fifth),' and then make those who advanced prisoners.

But this *ruse* was not always successful; more than once they found that instead of making Riflemen prisoners, they had themselves 'caught a Tartar.' On one such occasion an officer and some men of the Battalion made a body of the Yankees prisoners, and when they were desired to lay down their arms, the cowardly officer who commanded them made a stab at the 95th officer with a knife. He was summarily disposed of, for a Rifleman instantly shot him through the body.

Meanwhile the fight continued at Hallen's post. Two battalions came up and fired volleys by word of command as at a drill Not much to their advantage, for the Riflemen, warned by the words, 'Ready! Present!' took care to lie pretty close before the word 'Fire!' which, having been pronounced and obeyed, they sprang up, and gave them a severe return before they could reload This continued for some time; but at last, the picquet was obliged to give way before superior numbers Yet they only retired a little way to get under cover and re-form. Eventually the Riflemen advanced again, attacked their assailants, repulsed them, and regained the post. Hallen, as I have said, was wounded, so was Lieutenant Forbes, who held a separate post, and about forty men were killed or wounded. This defence by Hallen has truly been characterised as 'an affair of posts but rarely equalled, and never surpassed in devoted bravery.'[1]

'Had the expedition terminated more favourably,' he who makes the foregoing remark goes on to observe, 'it is to be presumed that the brave commander of the company would not have gone unrewarded' It may be so: this is the presumption, the fact is, that Hallen retired from the Service in 1824 with the rank of Captain, which he had obtained fifteen years before. Thus England rewarded acts of valour performed by all but her superior officers.

When the fire was first heard at Hallen's picquet, Major Mitchell, taking with him twenty or thirty Riflemen, had hurried to the front to reinforce it. On the way, however, he fell in with a body of the enemy, whom, in consequence of the darkness of the night, he could not distinguish, and he and the men with him were made prisoners Altogether the loss of the Battalion on that night was 6 Sergeants and 17 Riflemen killed, Captain Hallen, Lieutenants Daniel Forbes, (severely), and W. S. C. Farmer (slightly), 5 Sergeants and 54 Riflemen wounded; and Major Samuel Mitchell, 2 Sergeants, and 39 Riflemen missing A total (exclusive of officers) of 123, or one-fifth of their whole number

The loss of the Americans, who were finally driven off

[1] Leach, 'Sketch of Field Services,' 27.

about midnight, must have been very great, for the field was strewn with their dead.

Yet still the schooner, and a ship which had joined her, inflicted amazing annoyance on our people. With a brutality happily unknown among European nations, they fired into the houses to which the wounded had been carried. One shot struck a house in which a wounded Rifleman was lying, and knocked away his knapsack, which he was using as a pillow, without doing him any actual injury.

However, this savage warfare was to end. On the night of the 25th a battery was constructed close to the river's edge, and furnaces erected for heating red-hot shot. At daybreak on the 26th the battery commenced its fire on the schooner. Its crew, whose courage did not equal their cruelty, at once took to their boats and fled; the fourth shot set her on fire, and she soon afterwards blew up. While the ship, warned by her fate, and esteeming discretion as the better part of valour, had herself towed, as rapidly as possible, out of the range of the little English battery.

In this bivouack the Riflemen continued till the 28th. But it was toilsome work The picquets were continually fired at; the reliefs waylaid; the officers going round their sentries exposed to chance shots from a concealed marksman. How different this from the courtesies and chivalry of their European enemies, which I have so often had occasion to narrate!

Early on the 28th the army advanced towards New Orleans, the Riflemen leading, by the high road along the river's bank. They drove in the enemy's picquets, and proceeded along the road here called '*Le détour des Anglais*,' till, on turning round some houses on the left, they suddenly found themselves in front of a strong work the enemy had thrown up, and from which they opened a cannonade from four guns; while their old enemy the ship, now moored a little in advance of the work, brought a flank fire to bear on them. The Riflemen, leading and extended, did not suffer so much;[1] but the 85th which followed in close formation were mown down by this fire. Some houses were on the right, which might have afforded some temporary cover; but

[1] Their loss between December 25 and 31 was 1 Rifleman killed, 1 Sergeant and 3 Riflemen wounded; and 1 Rifleman missing

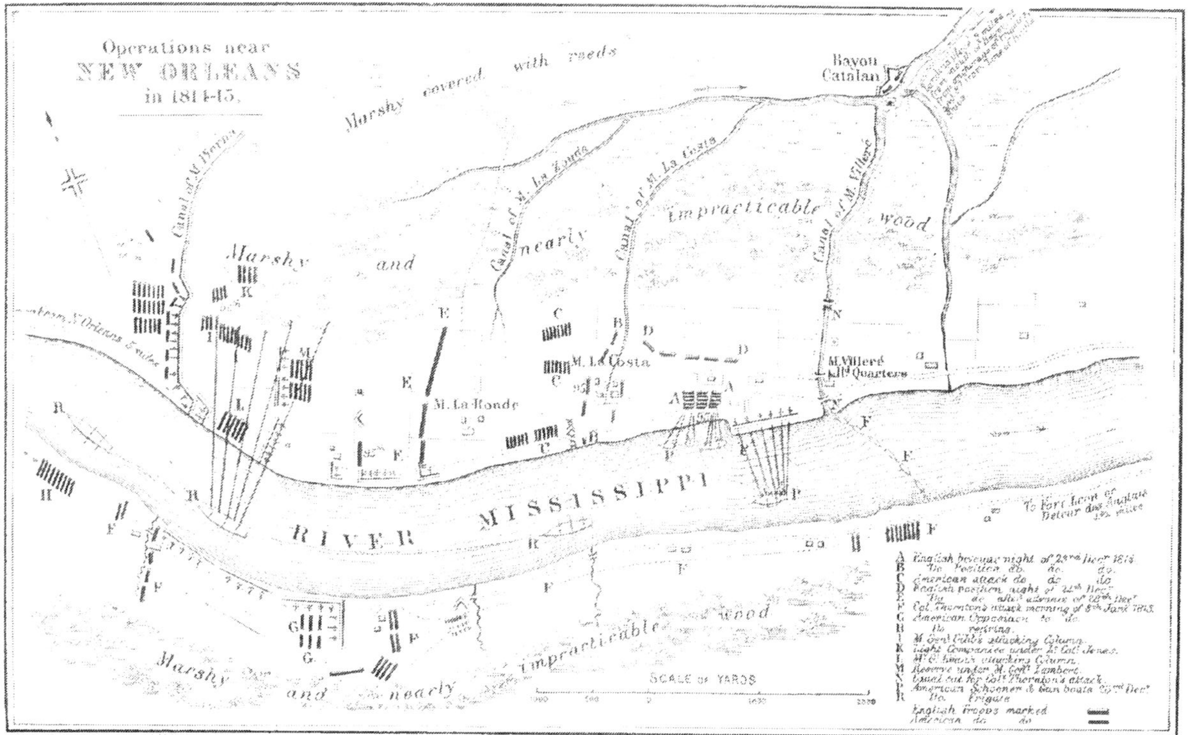

London, Chatto & Windus.

E. Weller, Litho.

the enemy, by their shells, set them on fire, and the flames added to the confusion. To escape in some measure from the effects of the fire the regiments were deployed to the right, while the Riflemen advancing about a hundred yards got into a ditch, which in a great degree sheltered them. In the afternoon the regiments moved off by wings, so as to present as small a body as possible to the enemy's fire. The Riflemen, however, did not move off till after dark, nor till some of the Yankees had ventured out of their works 'in a very triumphant manner.' But a few shots from the Riflemen immediately produced the conviction among them that it was more advisable to return to the protection of their rampart. This work was a stout parapet, in front of which was a wet ditch or canal. Its extent was about 1,000 yards, and its left touched the river, while its right was defended by the wood

The army now took up a position about a mile and a half or two miles from this work. The Battalion was placed in a house rather in advance, and on the left of the line. This was exposed, not only to the fire from the work, but also, as it was near the bank, from a redoubt which the enemy had constructed on the opposite side of the river. The men were placed in a sugar house belonging to this farm, the floor of which being sunk below the level of the natural ground afforded some protection. Yet on one occasion at least their cooking utensils were knocked off the fire by shot passing through this house.

So matters continued until the 31st. It was resolved to bring up some of the ships' guns and to place them in battery against the enemy's work Accordingly on the night of the 31st strong working parties were employed in constructing two batteries near it ; one with the object of keeping down the flank fire from the ship, the other with the view of breaching the centre of the rampart. The night was dark ; the men worked in silence ; and before daylight the batteries were completed, and the guns in position.

Early in the morning of January 1, 1815, the troops were moved up, with the object of attacking the enemy's work. A thick fog favoured their advance, and concealed their movements from the Americans. About nine o'clock the fog rose, and our batteries at once began their fire. This threw the Yankees, who were seen on parade, into utter confusion; and had a charge on the works been made at that moment, no doubt it would have been successful But unhappily the orders were that the attack was not to be made till the enemy's fire had been silenced, and his works breached. When, therefore, the Americans saw that nothing took place but a cannonade, their courage returned, and after about twenty minutes they began to return our fire; and gradually increased to a vigorous cannonade, which effectually overpowered our guns, and dismounted some of them. The flank fire too from the battery on the opposite bank of the river, in which they had placed their ship's guns, was very galling.

After being kept under this fire inactive till between two and three o'clock in the afternoon, the troops were withdrawn and bivouacked on the ground, and some occupied the houses they had held during the last few days. At night the troops were turned out and employed in withdrawing the guns from the batteries in which they had been placed. This was hard work; and some of the guns had to be buried, it being found impossible to remove them before daylight Thus the men had been up, and at hard work, two nights; and in the intervening day had been for many hours under the enemy's fire, without the chance of fighting them The loss of the Battalion was, 1 Rifleman killed, and 2 missing.

Things continued in this state till the 7th, the picquets being as before constantly harassed by the enemy.

No other course remained but to carry the enemy's work by an attack *de vive force*, and it was decided that this should take place on the 8th. Three companies of the Battalion were to precede the advance of the right column under General Gibbs, consisting of the 4th, 21st and 44th regiments; while the other two companies were in like manner to act with the left column. The Riflemen were to extend along the edge of the canal or ditch in front of the enemy's rampart, and both parties so extended were to occupy the whole of the bank, or as it might be called, the crest of the glacis. At four o'clock in the morning the troops paraded, and by daylight the Riflemen were in their place. But the 44th

Regiment, which had been appointed to carry ladders and fascines to enable the attacking force to cross the ditch, had come without them. Their commanding officer, the Hon. Colonel Mullens, had said loudly the night before when the regiment was detailed for this duty in orders, that 'his regiment was sent on a forlorn hope' and 'was doomed.' And on the regiment returning to fetch the ladders and fascines, he prudently did not come back to the front with them. The enemy meanwhile opened a furious fire on the troops, specially destructive to the Riflemen who were extended within 100 or 150 yards of the work. One regiment of the right attack, finding itself exposed to this fire, and without the fascines and ladders they had been led to expect, wavered, broke up, and fled to the rear, throwing the regiment which was following in support into confusion. Sir Edward Pakenham, who commanded, in trying to rally this column was killed; General Gibbs, who commanded it, was mortally wounded; and General Keane, who commanded the left attack, was wounded. This attack succeeded better, and for a time the troops composing it held a redoubt which the enemy had constructed in front of the ditch, and which they had stormed. But in the end they were obliged also to give way. Thus the Riflemen, extended in skirmishing order along the edge of the ditch, were left unsupported, and were obliged to retire as best they could. As their files were extended they presented a less prominent object for the enemy's guns, and they eventually got away with comparatively small loss. Some of them had got quite to the edge of the ditch, and reported that they could have passed it, but the attacking columns which they expected never came up, and to have entered the enemy's work without them would, of course, have been certain destruction.

A gallant and successful diversion was made on the right bank of the Mississippi by a column under Colonel Thornton; but as the Battalion did not form part of it, it is not my province, as historian of the Regiment only, farther to notice it.

It was regretted by the Riflemen, that Pakenham, himself a Peninsular soldier, did not employ troops who had seen fighting more prominently in so arduous an operation as storming this work. The 7th and 43rd had arrived just before; beside both these regiments the Riflemen had fought in Spain and Portugal; the latter were especially companions in arms, and they had hailed their advent with delight. Yet these he held in reserve, while he advanced comparatively unseasoned troops to the fire of the Americans

The Battalion retired at last, sorrowful and weary, to its bivouack. It lost 1 Sergeant and 10 Riflemen killed, and Captains James Travers (severely) and Nicholas Travers (slightly), Lieutenants John Reynolds, Sir John Ribton, John Gossett, William Backhouse, and Robert Barker (severely), 5 Sergeants and 89 Riflemen wounded [1]

During the night the wounded were removed, and a truce for two days, to enable the dead to be buried and the wounded cared for, was made between General Lambert (who succeeded to the command) and General Jackson who commanded the American force. This truce was effected, not without difficulty, by Major Harry Smith, Assistant Adjutant-General, who passed and repassed frequently between the opposing armies.

During this truce every attempt was made by the Yankees to induce our men to desert The non-commissioned officers were promised commissions, the men land, if they would enter the American service. On one such occasion two Sergeants and a private of the 95th were accosted by an officer of American Artillery, who with such large promises invited them to enter the American service. The Riflemen heard the tempter out; and then, in language perhaps rather forcible than complimentary, assured him that they would rather be privates in their own Corps, than officers with such 'a set of ragamuffins' as they saw before them; assuring him that if he did not move off, he should have a taste of their rifles. On that hint, he fled; but getting into the work turned a gun on them and fired, knocking over the private, whom however he only wounded.

A Rifleman on sentry was exposed to the solicitations of another of these gentry. He heard all his generous offers of money, land, and promotion, but pretending he did not, he

[1] Major James Travers, K H, died February 5, 1841 The ball received at New Orleans had never been extracted, and is said eventually to have caused his death. Lieutenant Backhouse died of his wounds.

begged him to come a little nearer and 'tell him all about it.' The Yankee elated at his success walked up to the post, and when he was well within range, the Rifleman levelled and shot him in the arm. Then walking forward, he led him prisoner to the guard-room; on the way informing him what a real soldier thought of such sneaking attempts on his fidelity[1]

These attempts were not always unsuccessful, and much desertion took place; but Surtees records with natural pride, that as far as he knew not a single instance took place among the Riflemen of the 3rd Battalion.

During this truce an officer of the American army was observed plundering a wounded soldier. This excited the ire of Corporal Scott of the 3rd Battalion, who (with the permission of his officer) took a shot at the marauder, and tumbled him over the man he was plundering.

The last duties having been paid to the dead, and all the wounded that were capable of being moved having been withdrawn, a retreat was effected on the night of the 18th. The fires were trimmed, and the men fell in and marched in silence. The weather had latterly broken up; heavy rains by day, and sometimes thunderstorms, were often followed by frost at night. As it was impossible, owing to the narrowness and shallow water of the Bayou Catalan, to embark the troops where they had landed, a road, or an attempt at a road, had been constructed across the marsh, from the great road to New Orleans, along the river's bank to the shore of Lake Borgne. This extended some miles, and was made of reeds, which it was thought would support the men across the morass, and where it crossed open ditches, as it frequently did, the reeds were laid on boughs of trees brought with great labour from the wood This road, a bad one at the best, was much injured by the rains, and sunk in with the tramp of the head of the column, so that this night march was very fatiguing, the men often sinking in to the knees, and sometimes in the dark slipping off into the marsh, from whence they were with difficulty rescued

However at last on the 19th they reached the shore of

[1] Gleig, 'Campaigns of the British Army at Washington and New Orleans,' p 186 He regrets that he has forgotten, or did not know, the name of this soldier; a regret in which all Riflemen will join.

the lake about one mile from its entrance. Here they were ordered to hut themselves; but this was no easy task, the place being a desert, and almost the only material the reeds which grew on the marsh.

Here they remained till the 25th, when the Battalion embarked on board the 'Dover,' which had brought out two of its companies The Battalion was reduced by its losses in the field to almost half its strength on landing. On the 27th they set sail; and it was resolved to attempt the capture of Mobile. This place, lying about 100 miles to the eastward of New Orleans, is situated in a bay, the entrance to which is defended by a work called Fort Boyer, which therefore had first to be reduced. In order to effect this the 4th, 21st, and 44th Regiments were landed, and commenced the investment of and approach to the place While on the 8th February the Riflemen and the rest of the troops were disembarked on Île Dauphine at the other side of the bay, till the reduction of Fort Boyer should enable them to move up to Mobile. Here the men hutted themselves; for the island, though otherwise almost a desert, is well covered with pine wood, while the officers, or some of them, had tents

During the time that they were here, General Lambert inspected the troops by regiments On making his inspection of the 3rd Battalion, James Travers (in Mitchell's absence, who had been taken prisoner) was in command. 'Well, Travers,' said the General, 'I hear your Sergeant-Major ran away on the night of the 23rd December.' 'Nay, General,' answered Travers, 'that he did not. He fought as well as any man could, and was towards the end of the affair severely wounded But,' added he, 'I think I know what may have given rise to that report. A sergeant of ours was in or near one of the houses where the wounded were taken, and the surgeon made him remain there as Hospital Sergeant I did all I could to get him back to the Battalion, but I could not succeed.' 'Well,' said the General, 'since I had done the Sergeant-Major some wrong, I must see what I can do to make him amends.' He did procure him an ensigncy in a West India Regiment, to which he was gazetted soon after.

While the Battalion was on Île Dauphine, a gallant act was performed by Sergeant Thomas Fukes. He, with four or five Riflemen, was sent over to the mainland to shoot bullocks. Fukes with a couple of Riflemen went inland, leaving the other men in charge of the boat. Here one Shiel of the American navy (who had captured a boat in bad weather with some of the 14th Light Dragoons, when embarking at Lake Borgne, and who in consequence fancied himself a hero) came upon them round a jutting point, and having captured them, put them in charge of some of his own crew into their own boat, and dispatched them to an American ship or post Then waiting for the sergeant, the other two Riflemen, and the Commissary, he of course made them prisoners, since their boat and the rest of their party had disappeared. The Commissary was placed aft with Mr Shiel; Sergeant Fukes and his two men forward; and they were being rowed off. When well off the shore the Commissary seizing Shiel by the thighs chucked him overboard, while Sergeant Fukes at the same instant sent one of the boat's crew to follow him, and the Riflemen disposed of the rest. They now recovered their rifles, and having taken security of Mr. Shiel for his good behaviour, admitted him at his urgent importunity into the boat, from whence they landed him, a moist and dispirited prisoner of war, on Île Dauphine.

The approaches to Fort Boyer being completed, Harry Smith was sent in with a summons to surrender. The poor Yankee commandant, sadly puzzled, asked Major Smith what he would advise him to do He strongly recommended him to surrender immediately, as the place must be taken by assault. Acting on such good advice, which fell in probably with his own sinking courage, he surrendered with his garrison, and signed a capitulation on the 11th February.

This important work having fallen, immediate preparations were made for re-embarking the troops, and attacking Mobile. But on the 14th news arrived of the preliminaries of peace between England and the United States having been settled at Ghent on December 24. All warlike operations of course terminated; and the troops only awaited on Île Dauphine the ratification of the treaty by President Madison. Intelligence of this reached them on the 5th March, and on the 15th the officers and Riflemen who had been made prisoners rejoined the Battalion, having been released under the terms of the treaty. Major Mitchell had been roughly treated by General Jackson, because he refused to furnish him with information of our strength or movements

On the 31st March the Battalion embarked on board the 'Dover,' some few men being placed on board the 'Norfolk' transport. On the 4th April they set sail, and, having called at the Havannah, arrived at Plymouth, whence they were ordered round to Dover, where they disembarked on the 2nd June and moved to Shorncliffe, where they found three companies of the Battalion, the remaining two being in Flanders, as is now to be narrated.

CHAPTER VI.

I NOW return to the narrative of services of the 1st Battalion, who had marched to Dover on their return from the Peninsula in 1814 Napoleon having landed from Elba, on the resumption of hostilities against him, six companies of this Battalion, under the command of Sir Andrew Barnard, embarked at Dover on the 25th April 1815 on board the 'Wensleydale' transport and landed at Ostend on the 27th

The officers present with these six companies were:

Colonel SIR ANDREW BARNARD.	Lieutenant GEORGE SIMMONS
Major and Brevet Lieut - Col. CAMERON	„ STILWELL.
Captain LEACH, *Brevet Major.*	„ HAGGUP.
„ CHAS. BECKWITH, *Brevet Major.*	„ FITZMAURICE.
„ GLASSE.	„ E. D JOHNSTON.
„ LEE.	„ ORLANDO FELIX
„ SMYTH.	2nd Lieutenant CHURCH.
„ CHAWNER.	„ ALLEN STEWART.
Lieutenant LAYTON.	„ WRIGHT.
„ MOLLOY.	Volunteer CHARLES SMITH.
„ ARCHIBALD STEWART.	Lieutenant and Adjutant KINCAID.
„ FREER.	Paymaster MCKENZIE.
„ GARDINER.	Quartermaster BAGSHAWE.
„ LISTER	Surgeon BURKE.
	Assistant-Surgeon ROBSON.
	„ „ HETT.[1]

As soon as the companies were all landed at Ostend they embarked in large boats on the canal, and arrived at Bruges about dark. The next morning at four o'clock they proceeded (towed by horses) to Ghent, where they arrived at three o'clock. Here they disembarked and were billeted

[1] This list (copied from Simmons' 'Narrative') is not perfect Captain William Johnston was at Waterloo He was probably with the detachment which had been in Holland, and which joined on the advance from Ostend to Brussels Captain Glasse, who was acting as Deputy Judge Advocate, did not join till after the battle of Waterloo

until the 10th May; on which day they marched to Alost, and thence on to Wella, where they halted during the 11th. And on the 12th marched to Brussels, where they arrived about eleven o'clock, and went into billets.

Either at this time or soon afterwards they were placed (with the 28th, 32nd and 79th) in Sir James Kempt's brigade of General Picton's division. Sir James Kempt having commanded one of the brigades of the Light Division during the latter part of the Peninsular war, the Riflemen of the 1st Battalion felt themselves at home under his orders.

Leaving the 1st Battalion at Brussels I proceed to note that five companies of the 2nd Battalion, consisting of 2 Field Officers, 5 captains, 14 subalterns, 4 staff, 50 sergeants, 16 buglers, and 480 rank and file, under the command of Colonel Wade, marched from Dover Castle at five o'clock P.M. on March 25, and embarking at eleven P.M. on board packets, reached Ostend on the next day, disembarked at two P.M. and marched immediately, three companies to Saas and two to Sluys. On the 28th the whole marched to Bruges, on the 29th three companies marched to Piethem and two to Eeghem. The next day the five companies marched to Courtrai, and on the 31st to Tournay. The 1st April they marched to Leuze. Here they remained, with detachments at Villers St. Amand, Villers Notre Dame, Ligne, Moulbaix and Grammont, till June 12.

Meanwhile, on April 18 the company (1 captain, 5 subalterns and 100 men) which had been with Sir Thomas Graham in Holland joined, making the strength of the Regiment in Belgium six companies; and on April 20 they were inspected by the Duke of Wellington.

On April 29 Colonel Wade left the Battalion to take command of the consolidated depôts, and on May 2 Major and Brevet Lieutenant-Colonel Norcott took command of the Battalion.

On June 12 the Battalion marched to Tourpe, Ellegnies and Auberhies. On the 16th it marched to Nivelles, and on the 17th marched to Waterloo and bivouacked there.

About the same time that these Battalions embarked, Major and Brevet Lieutenant-Colonel Ross proceeded to Belgium to take command of the two companies of the 3rd Battalion, which had been in Holland, the Head-quarters being still in America, or on their way back. These as well as the

2nd Battalion were placed in Sir Frederick Adam's brigade of Sir Henry Clinton's division, with their old companions in arms the 52nd and with the 71st Light Infantry.

The 1st Battalion being, as I said, at Brussels and in billets, were startled from their sleep on the evening of June 15, by their bugles sounding the 'assembly.' The companies immediately assembled on their alarm posts. Here two days' rations of biscuit and meat were served out to the men, and they marched to near the Park, where the Battalion was formed in quarter-distance column. This was effected, though the men were billeted all over the town, by eleven o'clock, whereas the other regiments of the division were not formed up till two o'clock in the morning. The Battalion being thus assembled, piled arms; the men took off their packs, and using them as pillows, were soon fast asleep. The officers following their example and reposing on a doorstep, or wherever else they could, were frequently disturbed by the ladies and others returning from the Duchess of Richmond's ball, which, it is well known, took place on that night. However, the other regiments of the division having assembled, about dawn they left Brussels by the Porte-de-Namur, and marched to Waterloo. Here they halted among some trees on the left side of the road. The men cooked, and after a rest resumed their march by the Charleroi road towards Quatre Bras. The heat was intense; and one man, struck by a coup-de-soleil, went raving mad, struck the man next him with his rifle, and fell down dead. After passing Genappe the companies extended as they came up, passing through fields of high standing corn. A few round-shot now greeted them, but they proceeded till brought up by a thick quickset hedge. The enemy fired at this, and wounded one man. The Riflemen poked their rifles through, but hesitated to force themselves through it on account of the sharpness of the thorns. So strange it is that these men, who feared no fire of the enemy, hesitated before a prickly hedge. Then it was that George Simmons, seeing the check, went back a few paces, and rushing at Sergeant Underwood, hit him on the knapsack and butted him through. Both rolled on the ground on the other side, which was much lower; but they soon sprang to their feet, and, the gap once made, the men poured through.

It was now about two o'clock when FitzMaurice, who was in Leach's absence at Brussels commanding the leading company, and who was posted on some high ground, observed a horseman, apparently in deep thought, coming up the road. As he drew near he recognised the Duke of Wellington, who raising his eyes, and seeing the 95th uniform, called out quickly, 'Where is Barnard?' The word was passed for him; and when the Colonel galloped up, the Duke said, 'Barnard, these fellows are coming on; you must stop them by throwing yourself into that wood' Barnard immediately ordered FitzMaurice to take the company into the wood, and 'amuse' them, until he brought up the rest of the Battalion As FitzMaurice was moving off, the Duke called to him to go round a knoll which would shelter him from the enemy's fire.[1]

General Bachelu had occupied the wood of Piermont, and was pushing forward to obtain possession of another small wood which would have interrupted the communication between Quatre Bras and Ligny. But the Riflemen anticipated them 'Here, for the first time in this campaign, the troops of the two nations became engaged. The skirmishers who successfully checked the further advance of the French, and secured the wood, were the 1st Battalion of the British 95th Rifles,[2] whom the old campaigners of the French army, at least those who had served in the Peninsula, had so frequently found the foremost in the fight, and of whose peculiarly effective discipline and admirable training they had had ample experience'[3]

Besides the occupation of this wood the Battalion kept possession of the Namur road, which they lined[4] Charles Beckwith's company, commanded by Lieutenant Layton, lined an embankment with a ditch in front of it, and kept up a smart fire on the enemy, which was as smartly returned. Layton himself was hit in the wrist and side. Yet the enemy forcing the Riflemen, by increased numbers, out of the wood, made furious endeavours to turn the left flank of the English line, on which the Battalion was posted. They had already

[1] General FitzMaurice's letter to the 'Times'

[2] Leach's company, under the command of FitzMaurice, who thus 'opened the ball' on that memorable day

[3] Siborne, i. 106 [4] Ibid. 109

gained the road, when the Riflemen at last received the glad summons to advance, and leaping over the bank and ditch, dashed in among them, and drove them from the road and from some houses on it which they had occupied.

Marshal Ney was now checked at every point; the wood of Piermont on his right, that of Bossu on his left, and the plain in the centre, were all occupied by the Allies or cleared of the French.

The losses of the Battalion at Quatre Bras were Lieutenant Lister,[1] 2 sergeants and 6 rank and file killed; Captain Smyth[2]; Lieutenants Layton, wounded in the wrist; Gardiner, severely wounded in the leg; FitzMaurice,[3] wounded in the leg; 3 sergeants and 48 rank and file wounded.

At nightfall the ground won by the Riflemen was given over to Sir Charles Alten's division, and the Battalion retired to the rear of the farm of Gemioncourt, where, having formed open column of companies and piled arms, the men lay down in their ranks, the officers on the inner flanks of their companies; ready, all of them, to take their arms and assume order of battle on any alarm.

Before the Battalion left the ground on which it had fought, Sir Andrew Barnard called attention to a Rifleman lying in their front, with both his legs shattered, adding, 'Gentlemen, if one of you would remain here with two or three men, and bring that poor fellow off, it would be a glorious act indeed' George Simmons at once volunteered. After the Battalion had moved off, he set up two sticks in the direction of the wounded man and laid another at top. When it was getting dark he sent a man forward in this alignment, and marching upon him, and past him, soon reached the wounded man. He told him not to make a sound, hoisted him on the back of one of the men who remained with him, and, the poor fellow suppressing a groan or a sound, he took him away. Luckily while he was thus engaged the sentries of the French picquet were being visited, so that their attention was occupied. On nearing our lines he and his suffering burthen were challenged by the Germans of Alten's division,

[1] He was shot through the abdomen, and died, in a house at Quatre Bras, next morning

[2] He died of his wounds.

[3] Major-General FitzMaurice, K H, died December 24, 1865.

and it was not till an officer and twenty men had advanced and examined him, that he was suffered to pass, and to deposit the wounded man in a house at Quatre Bras. After which he rejoined his Battalion.

Before daylight a sharp fire took place between the picquets, owing to a patrol of cavalry having by some mistake got between the advanced sentries At dawn on the 17th a company of the Battalion was sent forward to occupy the farm-yard of Gemioncourt at Quatre Bras, and they detached a picquet of two officers and twenty men to the front These were placed, some in a ditch and some behind a wall, with orders not to fire, and the French, finding their fire not returned, by degrees ceased firing. The men now cooked; those in rear cooking for those in front.

The retreat of the Prussians having rendered a similar movement on our part necessary, the troops at Quatre Bras began a retrograde movement on the morning of the 17th. The 1st Battalion received orders to cover the retreat, and was the last infantry that fell back. Before the picquet retreated Sergeant Fairfoot, a brave Peninsular man, who had been wounded in the breach at Badajos, was struck by a musket ball, which fractured his right fore-arm. Yet with amazing bravery, before going to the rear, he took a shot with his rifle (rested on the shoulder of the officer of the picquet), at the French, firing from his left shoulder and with his left arm

The Battalion had now fallen back, and, the French advancing, this picquet retreated also; and came up with the Battalion at Genappe, where it was halted in column at the entrance to the town The Duke and his Staff were on the rising ground near; the Duke watching intently through his telescope the advance of the enemy. At this moment rain began to fall heavily, and the men were ordered to shelter themselves in the houses on each side of the village street; but they had not been long in them when some shots which were heard between the enemy's advancing and our retreating cavalry, soon produced the order to 'fall in;' and passing with the cavalry through Genappe, they reformed column on some high ground at the end of that village. While they were so posted they had the satisfaction of witnessing that charge of the Life Guards down from that height, which rolled up the

French Lancers, and jammed them up with the cuirassiers in the narrow street of Genappe The retreat continued, through incessant torrents of rain, which made the ground and the trampled corn so difficult to move over, that the Riflemen did not reach the position of Waterloo till a couple of hours before dark There they bivouacked, with the right wing of the Battalion resting on the Charleroi road, behind La Haye Sainte, and near a small cottage where Sir Andrew Barnard had established his quarters, and where he dispensed the provisions he had received from Brussels to many of his officers

The enemy coming up on the opposite heights opened a cannonade, but without effect, at least on the Battalion ; and at nightfall they discontinued it.

While the Battalion lay by their arms, the rain still fell in torrents; there was a thunderstorm in the evening, and through the night it rained heavily; but towards morning dwindled to a thin small rain, and finally ceased before daybreak.

The morning of the 18th dawned heavily, the heavy moisture of the night rose from the heated ground in mist and haze, which, as the sun gained power, ascended and left the ground and prospect clear, yet kept the day cloudy

At daylight the men sprang to their feet, and took their arms; cleaning them and their accoutrements, moistened and rusted by so many hours of wet

This done, the Battalion took up its position.

The road from Brussels, passing through the forest of Soignies and the village of Waterloo, reaches the hamlet of Mont St. Jean, where it bifurcates · the one to the right leading to Nivelles, while that which goes straight on leads through Genappe to Charleroi. Nearly three-quarters of a mile from this fork the Charleroi road is crossed at right angles by a cross-country road, leading on the left to Wavre, on the right to Braine-la-Leud. About a quarter of a mile from this cross, and on the right-hand side of the road to Charleroi, is the farmhouse of La Haye Sainte, with a garden or orchard running along the road. On the opposite side of the road was a knoll with a sandpit at its base, and behind this sandpit was a strong hedge running parallel to the Wavre road for about 140 yards. In the sandpit were placed two companies of the 1st Battalion under Brevet Major Leach; another company, William Johnston's, lined the hedge; and the remaining three companies lined the Wavre road from its junction with that leading to Charleroi

As the Battalion formed column to move up to this position, a shot from one of the enemy's guns struck a rear-rank man of the rear company He was the first man of the Battalion who fell at Waterloo.

A party of men under George Simmons were sent to cut wood to form an *abattis*, which the Riflemen constructed on the Charleroi road, at the point where the hedge abutted on it.

The battle began, as is well known, with an attack on Hougoumont. But about two o'clock D'Erlon's corps moved upon La Haye Sainte. They advanced in four columns. The left central column moved in a direction parallel to the Charleroi road, as they approached the sandpit, which was hidden from them, both by its depression below the level of the surrounding plain, and by the height of the standing corn, they became exposed to the fire of the Riflemen stationed in it This obliged them to incline to their right; but they then became exposed to the fire of Johnston's company lining the hedge, which not only threw them farther to their right, but checked them. So that not only was the interval between their columns diminished by the fire of the Riflemen driving them to the right, but the distance between that column and that which succeeded it was also diminished by the fire of Johnston's company checking their advance. Donzelot's brigade, however, continued to press forward, and out-flanking the advanced companies of the Riflemen, obliged them to run in on the other three companies of the Battalion Still the French pressed on, for a Belgian brigade on the left of Picton's division had fled, leaving a gap in our line. But Picton brought up his infantry; and pouring in a terrific volley while the French were attempting to deploy, led his division to the charge (in doing which he himself fell), and completely routed them. At this moment, as they were going down the slope, a body of cuirassiers crossed from their right, pursued by the 2nd Life Guards. The French infantry flung themselves on the ground, while pursued and pursuers passed over

Pl. I.

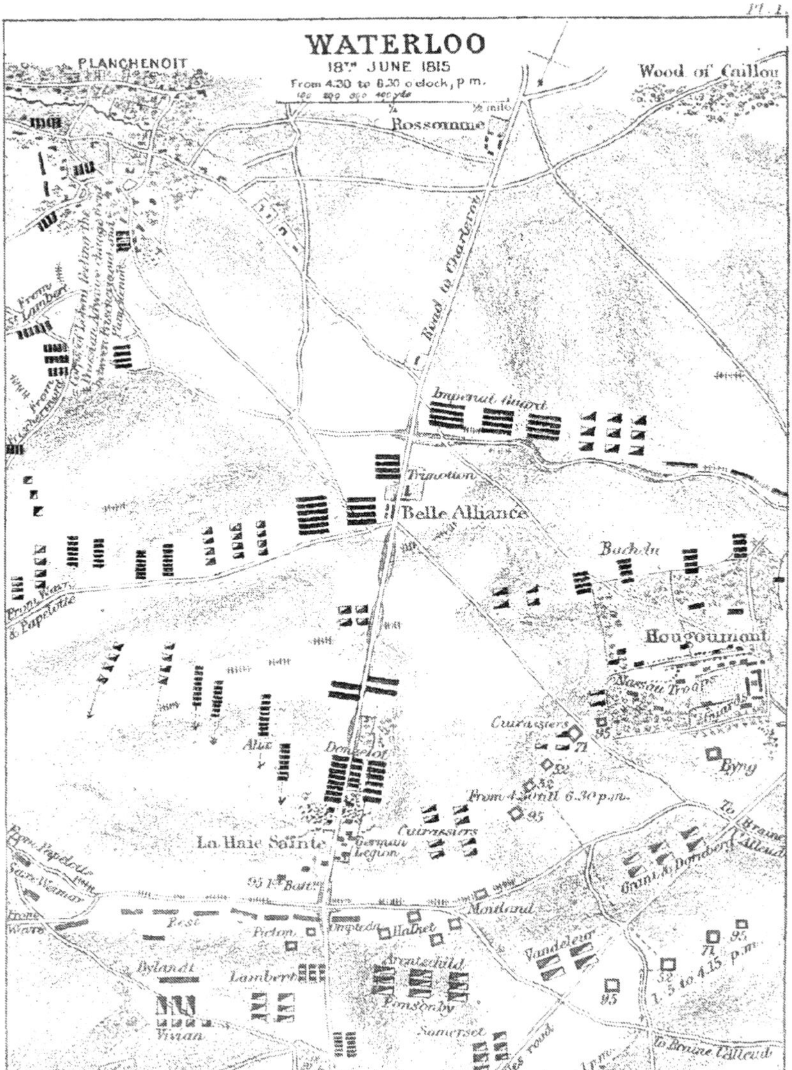

London: Chatto & Windus

F. Weller, lith. London

them, and Leach's two companies and Johnston's company running out to and beyond their former positions in the sand-pit and at the hedge, slew many men, and made many prisoners. But the Duke's orders were peremptory that the troops were not to quit their positions, and the Riflemen, having disposed of their prisoners, returned to theirs.

For some hours after this first attack the 1st Battalion was left comparatively quiet A constant and fierce cannonade was indeed kept up, from which they suffered , but no direct attack was made upon them till about six o'clock, when the French again advanced against La Haye Sainte. As the ammunition of the Hanoverians who occupied it was exhausted, they succeeded in obtaining possession of it. Having established this post, close to the companies in the sandpit and lining the hedge, they kept up an incessant fire from loop-holes and from the windows of the farmhouse on these companies ; who being thus raked by a fire on their right flank, and being also pressed hard in front by the advancing columns, were obliged to fall back and join the remaining companies of the Battalion, who were lining the Wavre road. Thus the enemy were able to establish on the knoll and along the crest a line of infantry ; who kneeling or lying down, showed only their heads, but delivered a most murderous fire against the Riflemen and the other regiments of Kempt's division Frequent endeavours were made by the French officers to induce their men to leave this shelter, and to charge the English line; and now and then a few gallant spirits seemed inclined to try it. But as often as they did so, the rifles of the 1st Battalion swept them off. The enemy also brought up two guns by the garden hedge of La Haye Sainte to the back of the Charleroi road, and opened fire along it at those lining the Wavre road, but the Riflemen taking deliberate aim slew the gunners before they could fire a second round

At this time the Hanoverian regiment, commanded by Colonel Von Ompteda, while attempting to deploy (in obedience to the Prince of Orange's injudicious orders), was attacked by a body of cuirassiers, rolled up, and cut to pieces. Though this took place in front of the ground occupied by the Riflemen, and within range, they could not fire, through fear of shooting the unfortunate Hanoverians as well as the slaughtering cuirassiers. But just as these last were being charged by an English regiment of cavalry (the 23rd Light Dragoons), they opened upon them a well-directed fire which sent both parties flying, and the ground so lately crowded with combatants was entirely cleared, except of the dead and wounded Hanoverians, and the many cuirassiers brought down by the rifles of the 95th Sir Andrew Barnard was wounded early in the day. The command of the 1st Battalion then devolved on Major and Brevet Lieutenant-Colonel Cameron; and on his being also wounded later in the day, Captain and Brevet Major Leach commanded it

Leaving the 1st Battalion, for a time lining the hedge of the Wavre cross road, and exchanging fire with the French in La Haye Sainte, and the adjacent ridge, let us trace the actions of the 2nd Battalion, and of the two companies of the 3rd Battalion during the day They were, I have already noted (with the 52nd and 71st), in Sir Frederick Adam's brigade. Their station at the commencement of the action was between the village of Merbe-Braine and the road to Nivelles, near where that road is intersected by one leading to Braine-la-Leud. But as soon as the battle began, by the first attack on Hougoumont, they advanced across this last road, and stood in column of companies at quarter-distance on the plateau overlooking the Nivelles road. Subsequently they moved more forward still, and from the plateau drew up close to the road to Nivelles

About four o'clock, when an attack was made on Hougoumont, a crowd of French skirmishers pressed up the hill in their front. The Duke of Wellington, who was close to the brigade, ordered it to form line four deep. This they did at once, the 2nd Battalion on the left, the 71st in the centre, and the two 3rd Battalion companies on the right. For the 52nd in this formation into line were pushed out for want of room, and formed in rear as a reserve. Then the Duke, pointing to the French skirmishers, bade them 'Drive those fellows away' This they did speedily. For springing up the slope with a cheer, they drove the French before them over the crest, and down the slope on the other side; bringing up their right shoulders, and halting in a hollow which extends from the ridge towards the south-east of Hougoumont. Here they were threatened with an attack of cavalry, and at once formed square. They were soon charged by *carabiniers* and *grenadiers-à-cheval* of the Guard. In one of these Captain William Eeles formed his company of the 3rd Battalion in line with the rear face of the square of the 71st, and ordered his men not to fire till he gave the word. Then allowing the *carabiniers* to approach within thirty or forty yards of the angle of the front on which they were charging, he gave them such a volley as, combined with the fire of the square, brought half of them to the ground; some dead, some wounded; and many entangled among the dead or dying horses.

During the intervals between these charges the 2nd Battalion suffered much from a furious cannonade kept up on them.

About this time Colonel Norcott, commanding the 2nd Battalion, was wounded, and Major Miller succeeded to the command; and on his being wounded soon afterwards, the command of the Battalion devolved on Captain Logan At the same time that Colonel Norcott was disabled, Colonel Ross, commanding the companies of the 3rd Battalion, was wounded; Major Fullerton succeeded to the command, and on his being wounded about an hour afterwards the command of these companies devolved on Captain Eeles.[1]

Thus each Battalion of the Regiment had, on this day, its two senior officers disabled by wounds

When the last attack was made upon Hougoumont, Adam's brigade, with the 2nd Battalion and the two companies of the 3rd, was withdrawn, first to the crest, and subsequently to the reverse slope, so as to be in some measure protected from the cannonade directed against it.

At seven o'clock a column of the Imperial Guard advanced against this part of the position. It was covered by a cloud of skirmishers; and in order to check them, a company of each of the regiments of Adam's brigade was thrown out in skirmishing order The enemy's advancing column suffered so severely from the English guns, that a body of cuirassiers were sent forward to endeavour to silence these guns. The gunners

[1] 'Supp. Desp.' x. 751.

ran in in rear of the infantry, and the cuirassiers not only drove in the skirmishers of the 2nd Battalion, but came upon Adam's brigade, then in line. The Duke was then with them, and the 52nd, the regiment most threatened, came to the 'Prepare to receive cavalry.' But the cuirassiers did not face them, and their further attempts were checked by some English cavalry sent against them. The Riflemen were then on the road leading along the crest of the ridge.

As the column of the Guard came forward, Sir John Colborne, in command of the 52nd, at once wheeled up its right shoulder, so as to throw it on the flank of the column. The Duke, who was present, approving of this movement, immediately ordered up the 2nd Battalion on its left; the 71st moved up to its right, and the two companies of the 3rd Battalion formed the extreme right of the line. These owing to the rapidity of the movement were not quite in line, but a little retired from the alignment of the 52nd. The attacking column of the Imperial Guard, having Maitland's brigade of Guards in its front, was evidently staggered by finding Adam's brigade on its flank It halted, and wheeling up its left sections, began to fire Colborne also halted the 52nd and fired into the column, and the 2nd Battalion coming up at that instant on the left, poured a deadly fire into the Guard. Then Colborne checked the fire, and calling out 'Charge! Charge!' led his men against the column. The 2nd Battalion joined vigorously in this charge; which, as Siborne observes, 'was remarkable for the order, the steadiness, the resoluteness, and the daring by which it was characterised.' The Imperial Guard wavered, reeled, and then breaking up, fled in inextricable confusion, in spite of attempts made by its officers and some brave men in its ranks to stem its flight But they were swept away in the torrent of fugitives, and the brigade continuing its triumphant march across the field, and bringing its left shoulder, the 2nd Battalion, rather forward, halted near the Charleroi road, with the left of the 2nd Battalion close to the orchard of La Haye Sainte The Duke, who came up that moment, suggested to Adam to attack some squares of the Guard, which appeared disposed to make a stand, but Adam observed that his men had marched far, over heavy ground encumbered with dead and wounded, and

Pl. II

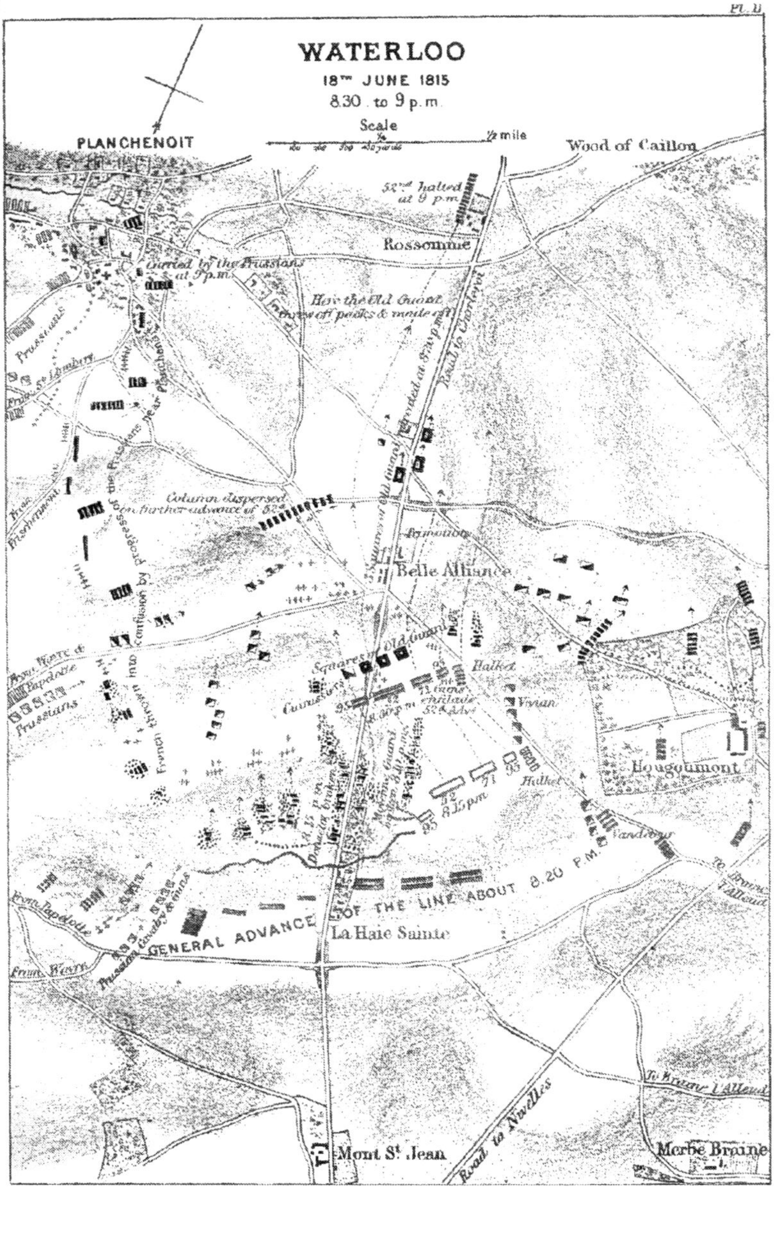
WATERLOO
18TH JUNE 1815
8.30 to 9 p.m.
Scale
½ mile
PLANCHENOIT
Wood of Caillou
Rossomme
Carried by the Prussians at 9 p.m.
Road to Charleroi
Column dispersed on further advance of 52nd
Belle Alliance
Squares of Old Guard
Halket
Vivian
Hougoumont
Vandeleur
GENERAL ADVANCE OF THE LINE ABOUT 8.20 P.M.
La Haie Sainte
Prussians
From Wavre
Mont St. Jean
Road to Nivelles
To Braine l'Alleud
Merbe Braine

required a short halt To this the Duke assented; but in a few moments—knowing by old Peninsular experience that the French once routed never rally—he called out, 'Better attack them; they won't stand.' Nor did they. For although they opened fire when Adam's brigade approached them, the moment these appeared in earnest and determined to charge, they faced about and retired by word of command. The Duke was with the brigade as they ascended the hill to the French position, and having seen the only standing squares of the Guard thus disposed of, or, as he said himself, having seen 'those fellows off,' he rode away. Then Adam crossed the Charleroi road, and bringing up the 2nd Battalion, his left, he proceeded, skirting it, to drive the enemy before him.

While the 2nd Battalion and the two companies of the 3rd are thus employed, let us return to the 1st Battalion, which we left on the Wavre road, exposed to and thinned by the musketry fire from the heights near La Haye Sainte. When the Duke saw the decisive movement of Adam's brigade and the failure of the last attack of his enemy, he ordered a general advance. The first intimation the 1st Battalion had of it was a pealing cheer, beginning on the right and rolling along from brigade to brigade, from battalion to battalion. As the Riflemen were taking it up, the Duke rode up behind them; the cheers were redoubled at his appearance, but he said. 'No cheering, my lads; but go on and complete your victory.'

'This movement,' says a Rifleman who was with them, 'had carried us clear of the smoke; and to people who had been so many hours enveloped in darkness, in the midst of destruction, and naturally anxious about the result of the day, the scene which now met the eye conveyed a feeling of more exquisite gratification than can be conceived. It was a fine summer's evening, just before sunset. The French were flying in one confused mass. British lines were seen in close pursuit, and in admirable order, as far as the eye could reach to the right, while the plain on the left was filled with Prussians.' [1]

The 1st Battalion, after marching across the field of battle, halted about half a mile in front of it, and bivouacked there.

[1] Kincaid, 'Adventures in the Rifle Brigade,' p. 353.

The 2nd Battalion and the two companies of the 3rd bivouacked near La Belle Alliance.

The losses of the Regiment at Waterloo were:

OF THE 1st BATTALION.

Killed

Lieutenant Stilwell, 4 sergeants, and 16 rank and file.

Wounded.

Lieutenant-Colonel Sir Andrew Barnard.

Major and Brevet Lieutenant-Colonel Cameron, severely.

Captain and Brevet Major Charles Beckwith (Staff), severely, leg amputated.

Captain Chawner, severely in the leg.

„ W Johnston, severely.

Lieutenant Molloy, severely

„ George Simmons, shot through the liver and two ribs broken.

„ Gairdner, severely.

„ E. D Johnston, severely.

„ Felix.

„ Allen Stewart, stabbed through the arm and wounded in the shoulder.

„ Wright, severely.

„ Church, severely.

„ William Shenley, severely.

7 Sergeants, 1 bugler, and 116 rank and file.

OF THE 2nd BATTALION.

Killed

2 Sergeants, 1 bugler, and 31 rank and file

Wounded.

Major and Brevet Lieutenant-Colonel Norcott, severely.

„ „ Wilkins, severely.

Captain and Brevet Major Miller, severely.

„ M'Cullock, severely

Lieutenant Humbley, severely.

„ Coxen, severely.

„ D Cameron.

„ R. Cochrane.

„ Ridgeway, severely

Lieutenant Fry.
,, Webb.
,, Lynam, severely.
,, Eyre, severely.
,, Walsh, severely.

6 Sergeants, 2 buglers, and 171 rank and file. And 20 rank and file, *missing.*

Of the 3rd Battalion.

Killed.

Captain Charles Eeles, 3 rank and file.

Wounded.

Major and Brevet Lieutenant-Colonel Ross, severely.
Captain and Brevet Major Fullerton, severely.
Lieutenant Worsley, severely.
,, G. H. Shenley, severely.

1 Sergeant, 1 bugler, and 34 rank and file. And 7 rank and file, *missing.*

The strength of these Battalions on the morning of June 18 was as follows:[1]

	Field officers	Captains	Subalterns	Staff	Sergeants				
					Present	Sick		Wounded	Total
						Present	Absent		
1st Battalion 6 companies	1	3	7	6	27		11		38
2nd Battalion 6 companies	2	6	20	6	37	1		3	41
3rd Battalion 2 companies	1	2	5	2	11			1	12
Total of the regiment	4	11	32	14	75	1	11	4	91

	Buglers			Rank and file				
	Present	Sick absent	Total	Present	Sick.		Wounded	Total
					Present	Absent		
1st Battalion 6 companies	10	2	12	364		185		549
2nd Battalion 6 companies	17		17	567	10	3	5	585
3rd Battalion 2 companies	6		6	176	2	2	8	188
Total of the regiment	33	2	35	1107	12	190	13	1322

[1] I have extracted the above return from the 'Wellington Despatches,' xii. 487, and it is signed by Lieutenant-Colonel Waters, Assistant Adjutant-General,

Of the wounded Lieutenant Johnston had been brought with Simmons to the farmhouse of Mont St. Jean, a little in rear of the position of the Battalion Some Riflemen procured two horses, which had belonged to French cavalry soldiers, on which they set these officers to take them to Brussels, and as they were turning out of the gate a cannon shot, many of which were bounding along the road, struck Johnston and killed him on the spot.

Of Worsley, Kincaid relates that he had at Badajos received a shot in his ear, which came out at the back of the neck, which on his recovery had the effect of turning his head to the right; and that now he received exactly a similar wound in the left ear, the ball coming out near the exit of the former, which restored his head to its original position.[1]

M'Cullock had been wounded in the shoulder on Massena's retreat from Portugal in March 1811, and this wound deprived him of the use of the arm. At Waterloo, by a shot fired very late in the day, he lost the other arm He was promoted, 'having no longer an arm to wield for his country,' as he told the Duke of Wellington, 'but being anxious to serve it,' to a majority in the 2nd Garrison Battalion in Dec. 1815, and died in London in 1818.

Charles Beckwith had his left leg shattered by grape-shot shortly before the end of the battle. It was amputated a few days afterwards He exchanged to half-pay in 1820; and some years subsequently, having had his attention directed to the Waldenses, he, after frequent visits to the Pignerolo valleys, eventually settled in that country Here his career was one of great usefulness. He found the people in a state

but it is certainly incorrect as regards the 1st Battalion. Two Field Officers were certainly present, Barnard and Cameron both were wounded, and are so returned ('Army List,' August, 1815), nor is it easy to account for the number (185) reported as 'sick absent' A note to the original states that the large number of 'sick absent' in this (and some other regiments) is owing to their losses at Quatre Bras, yet the 1st Battalion had only forty-eight men wounded there It will be seen on comparing this return with the lists of casualties that the 1st Battalion lost of all ranks in killed and wounded more than three-eighths of its numbers, the 2nd Battalion rather less than one-third; and the 3rd Battalion a little more than a fifth, and the whole Regiment (fourteen companies) about a third.

[1] I presume as Kincaid calls Worsley, then residing on his estate in Nottinghamshire, as a living witness to the truth of this statement, it may here be recorded. It has been confirmed to me by independent testimony

of great depression, poverty and ignorance; and by untiring devotion to their interests, temporal as well as spiritual, conferred on them inestimable benefits. He established schools for primary education, and seminaries for more advanced instruction And he taught the people self-reliance, and led them to join in and contribute to the good works he originated for them. After a career of great usefulness he died (having then the rank of Major-General) at Torre, on the 19th July, 1862, attended to the grave by the love and lamentations of the people for whom he had done so much.[1]

Lieutenant Allen Stewart was stabbed through the left arm by a French officer 'whom he finished in an instant,'[2] he was subsequently wounded by a musket-ball which lodged in the shoulder. After long suffering at Brussels, where he experienced, as did many other Riflemen, very great attention and kindness from the inhabitants on whom they were billeted, he returned to England[3] with George Simmons, who had also long been detained at Brussels by his dangerous wounds[4]

Sir James Kempt, who succeeded to the command of the 5th Division on Picton's death, says in his report to the Duke of Wellington. 'I lost in my brigade major, who was killed, Captain [Charles] Eeles, 95th, a most valuable officer. . . . I shall take the liberty of bringing under your Grace's notice the particular claims and merits of the officers commanding regiments, in a separate report, but I cannot close this one without mentioning that Colonel Sir A. Barnard and the next in command, Colonel Cameron of the 95th, were both wounded'[5]

And Sir Henry Clinton, in his report to Lord Hill, says:

[1] A memoir of General Beckwith has been published by M Meille, of which there is an English translation, London, 1873

[2] Simmons' MS Narrative

[3] He was placed on half-pay at the reduction of the 3rd Battalion, and after serving in some other regiments, died in the Norwich Military Lunatic Asylum, July 6, 1847

[4] I cannot mention George Simmons' name here for the last time without recording how much I have been indebted to his Journal in the Peninsula from 1809 to 1814, and to his Narrative of Quatre Bras and Waterloo, in compiling this History. After a service of nearly thirty years in the 1st Battalion he left it in 1838, on promotion to an unattached majority, and died March 5, 1858

[5] 'Supplementary Despatches,' x. 537

'The manner in which the several regiments . . . . the 2nd and 3rd Battalions 95th, under Lieutenant-Colonels Norcott and Ross, discharged their duty, was witnessed and admired by the whole army.' [1]

And on the 26th June he writes thus to Lord Hill: 'I beg leave to add the names of officers, which from the favourable reports made of them by the officers commanding brigades, it is my duty to request you will lay before the commander of the forces, in the hope that his Grace will recommend them for promotion. The names of these officers are: . . . .

'Captain Logan, Lieutenant Humbley,[2] and Lieutenant and Adjutant Smith, 2nd Battalion, 95th Regiment.

'Captain [William] Eeles and Lieutenant Hope, 3rd Battalion, 95th Regiment.' [3]

It appears also, by a letter from Sir Henry Torrens to the Duke of Wellington, February 29, 1816, that the Duke had on the 12th strongly recommended Lieutenant-Colonel Norcott, on account of his conduct at Waterloo. For after stating that his obtaining the honour of Commander of the Bath, in his then rank, was contrary to regulation, he goes on to add: 'You may be assured that I shall pay every attention in my power to the high opinion you have expressed of him, and to your desire that his claim should be attended to' [4]

On June 19, 1815, the Regiment began its march to Paris. On the 24th the 1st Battalion moved from Bavay to Engle-fontaine, and encamped or was cantoned in that neighbourhood, and on the 25th at Maretz. On the 26th the 2nd Battalion moved from Nauroy and Magny, and encamped near Beauvoir and Lanchy, and the 1st Battalion halted at Nauroy, Magny, and Bellenglise. On the next day the 2nd Battalion crossed the Somme at Villecourt and moved by Nesle to Roye, and the 1st Battalion advanced, and encamped between Douilly and Villers On the 28th the 2nd Battalion marched by Montdidier to Petit Crèvecœur: on the next day from that place to Clermont; and the 1st Battalion from Roye,

[1] 'Supplementary Despatches,' x 545

[2] Colonel Logan, 63rd Regiment, died September 1, 1844. Lieutenant-Colonel Humbley (retired) died 1857

[3] 'Supplementary Despatches,' x 624

[4] Ibid xi 311

where it had halted on the 28th, to Gournay on the road to Pont St. Maxence. On the 30th this Battalion crossed the Oise at Pont St. Maxence, and was pushed on as far as Fleurines on the road to Senlis; while the 2nd Battalion and companies of the 3rd moved from Petit Crèvecœur to Chantilly. On July 1 this Battalion relieved the Prussians near Aubervilliers, and the 1st Battalion moved by Senlis and Louvres, and encamped between Louvres and Vauderlan. On the 6th both Battalions were encamped near Neuilly. On July 7 the army marched into Paris, and the 2nd Battalion had the honour of being the first corps which entered; Lieutenant and Adjutant Thomas Smith, riding in front of the Battalion, being the first British officer who entered Paris on that famous day.

The 1st Battalion was encamped at the village of Clichy until October 30, when it was cantoned in and near the village of Vaux. On December 19 it was moved into the city of Paris, and occupied barracks in the Rue de Clichy. On the entry into Paris the 2nd Battalion was encamped in the Champs Elysées, where it remained till October 29, when it went into quarters at Versailles; and on December 8 marched to St Leu Tavernay and St Prix and Moullinor.

On July 10 the Head-quarters of the 3rd Battalion (five companies, 300 men) embarked at Dover, and landing on the 13th at Ostend, moved through Bruges, Ghent, Oudenarde, Mons, Bavay, Le Catelet and Peronne, and thence by the route before traversed by the other Battalions through Roye, Pont St. Maxence and Louvres to Paris. On arrival they were placed, with the 2nd Battalion, in Sir Frederick Adam's brigade, to which their two detached companies were already attached, and were encamped with them in the Champs Elysées. It was subsequently removed to another brigade and cantoned at Montmartre

The three Battalions being thus re-united in the neighbourhood of Paris, the officers observed the anniversary of the formation of the Regiment by a 'Regimental Dinner' at St. Germain-en-Laye, on August 25. This seems to have been the second 'Regimental Dinner.'

At the end of November, a new arrangement of brigades was made, under which the 1st Battalion, then consisting of six companies and 577 men, was placed in Sir John Lambert's brigade of Sir Lowry Cole's division The 2nd Battalion, then consisting of 534 men, was placed in Sir Manley Power's brigade of Sir Charles Colville's division. And the 3rd Battalion (480 men) was ordered to return to England It quitted Paris on December 3, and halted that night at St. Denis. From thence passing through Beaumont, Noailles and Beauvais, it arrived at Abbeville on the 11th It reached Montreuil-sur-Mer on the 14th, and embarked at Calais on the 20th, landed at Dover on the 22nd, and marched on the next day to Shorncliffe

On January 16, 1816, the 1st Battalion marched from Paris, and having halted some days at Louvres, proceeded to the neighbourhood of Cambrai, having its Head-quarters at Bourlon, with detachments at Inchy-en-Artois, Proville, Baralle, Buissy Baralle, and Sains-lez-Marquion. Its strength was 30 officers and 503 men of all ranks.[1]

On December 26, 1815 the 2nd Battalion marched from St. Leu to Gonesse, the next day to Claye, and the day following to Crecy, where they remained until January 23, on which day they marched by Compiègne, Noyon, Ham, St Quentin, Le Catelet and Cambrai, to villages near Valenciennes, in which they were billeted on January 31, and on February 1 moved into cantonments, with Headquarters at Lecelle, and detachments at Rumegies and Rosult Its strength was 29 officers and 553 men[2]

By an order dated Horse Guards February 16, 1816, the 95th was removed from the regiments of the line, and styled THE RIFLE BRIGADE.

On July 15 the 1st Battalion was at Bapaume,[3] but soon marched and encamped on a common at Bourlon ; and on the 24th the 2nd Battalion marched to and encamped on a common near St. Amand.

On October 24 the 2nd Battalion marched from camp and resumed its cantonments at Lecelle, Samcon, Rumegies, and Rosult.

[1] Return, April 10, 1816, 'Supplementary Despatches,' xi. 357

[2] Ibid xi 360.

[3] I copy this from a French return in the 'Wellington Supplementary Despatches,' xi 412-3, where it is styled *Brigade de Carabiniers, le 1 Bataillon. Le 2 Bataillon* was still at Lecelle.

Early in 1817 this Battalion was removed from Sir Manley Power's to the 3rd Brigade under the command of Sir Thomas Brisbane; and marched to join that brigade through Aberchicourt, Gavrelle, Aubigny to St. Pol; where it was cantoned with detachments in fourteen surrounding villages.

On July 4 it marched from these cantonments, and encamped at Helfaut near St Omer, where it remained till August 31, when it marched to Valenciennes, and encamped on the glacis of that place; but on October 4 went into barracks at Valenciennes for half-yearly inspection. On the 8th it moved to camp at Denain, which however broke up on the 16th when the Battalion marched to St. Pol, where it arrived on the 20th and resumed its quarters there and in the neighbourhood.

On May 31, 1818, the Battalion was again encamped at Helfaut till August 15, when it marched to and encamped near Valenciennes. On October 17 it marched to Neuville near Bouchain, preparatory to a grand review by the Duke of Wellington in the presence of the Emperor of Russia, the King of Prussia and other Sovereigns and Princes; which took place on the 23rd.

The Army of Occupation being now to leave France, the Battalion marched on the 25th to Auberchicourt, and thence through Lens, Lillers, Blendecques, Peuplingue, near Ardres, whence they marched at two o'clock in the morning of the 30th to Calais, where they arrived and embarked at ten o'clock, and sailing immediately arrived at Dover in the night. On the 31st they disembarked and marched to Shorncliffe.

The 1st Battalion also moved into camp and changed its cantonments during the time it formed part of the Army of Occupation; but I am not able to give its movements with equal minuteness, as the regimental Record for that period has not been kept with the same accuracy as that of the 2nd Battalion. It was moved into the 7th Brigade under the command of Major-General Sir W. O'Callaghan; and I find that on September 27, 1818, it was encamped near Cambrai.[1] It marched to Calais, where it embarked on October 31,

[1] 'Supplementary Despatches,' xii. 706.

and sailing on the same day arrived at Dover and marched to Shorncliffe on November 1.

I have now to trace the movements of the 3rd Battalion, which had returned to Shorncliffe in December 1815 Soon afterwards it was ordered to Dublin, where it was quartered for two years and three months Whilst the Battalion was in Dublin a melancholy event took place, on August 16, 1817: the death of Lieutenant Amphlett from hydrophobia, resulting from the bite of his dog. The details of this sad case are very fully related by Dr Ridgway, Surgeon of the Battalion, in the *United Service Journal*, vol. i. part i p. 577. The Battalion afterwards proceeded to Birr; and at the end of 1818, a diminution of the army having been resolved upon, this Battalion was reduced. The junior officers of each rank, who thereby became non-effective, were placed on half pay on December 25, 1818; but the actual disbanding of the Battalion did not take place till towards the end of January 1819; when some of the men were drafted into the 1st and 2nd Battalions and the remainder were discharged. Its strength when disbanded was 810 men[1]

[1] 'Annual Register,' lx 168

RIFLE BRIGADE.
TO 1833.

CHAPTER VII.

THE 1st Battalion marched from Shorncliffe in three divisions on December 24, 26 and 28, 1818, for Chichester; and after halting there for two days proceeded to Gosport, and was quartered there, and at Haslar barracks.

It remained here till the autumn, when the disturbed state of the northern parts of the kingdom requiring the presence of a military force, the 1st Battalion embarked at three or four hours' notice, on board the 'Liffey,' frigate, and the 'Hind,' sloop, on September 18, 1819, and landed at Leith on the 27th; and marching from thence on the next day arrived at Glasgow, the principal seat of the disturbance, on the 30th and was quartered in the Infantry barracks. Here they remained during the rest of the year.

On its arrival in England the 2nd Battalion received orders the very day after reaching Shorncliffe to march to Hastings; and starting on November 2, 1818, and halting successively at Romney and Rye, arrived there on the 4th. Its stay at Hastings however did not much exceed a month For marching on December 7, through Hailsham, Lewes, Shoreham, Arundel, and Chichester, it arrived at Hilsea on December 12. On the 24th of that month it was inspected, previous to embarkation, by Major-General Lord Howard of Effingham; and on the 26th embarked at Portsmouth on board the 'Fame' and 'Sir George Osborne' transports; and sailing on the 28th arrived at Cove on the 31st; and disembarking immediately marched to Middleton. And on the day following, January 1, 1819, it marched to Fermoy, and after three days' halt here, on the 5th the Battalion proceeded by Mitchelstown, Cahir, Thurles and Roscrea, and arrived at Birr barracks on the 9th; relieving there the 3rd Battalion which was being then disbanded, and from which the 2nd Battalion received by transfer on January 11, 213 non-commissioned officers and privates

From Birr the Battalion detached two companies to Roscrea, one company to Maryborough, and smaller parties to Frankford and Banagher In August another company was detached to Tullamore, and three companies under a major to Mullingar. These companies proceeded to Athlone on February 18, 1820; and three other companies with the Staff of the Regiment under Lieut-Colonel Mitchell re-inforced them at Athlone on the 24th in consequence of the disturbed state of the country On this account too the companies at Maryborough and Roscrea were pushed forward to Loughrea on the 27th; and another company from Birr followed them there on March 27. Meanwhile, three of the companies at Athlone had marched to Tuam.

On February 19, in this year, Field-Marshal The Duke of Wellington was appointed Colonel-in-Chief of the Regiment, on the death of Sir David Dundas. On this occasion the Officers of the Regiment presented to him the following address:

'May it please your Grace,

'We, the Lieutenant-Colonels Commanding, Field-officers, Captains and Subalterns of the two Battalions of the Rifle Brigade, beg leave to represent to your Grace with what feelings of pride and satisfaction we viewed your appointment to be our Colonel-in-Chief.

'Assuredly so high a distinction could not fail to make a deep impression on the minds of any corps in His Majesty's service; but we cannot conceal from ourselves that, in the breast of the majority of us, every sentiment of joy and exultation was in no slight degree augmented when memory recalled the days of active service under your Grace's command, as well in that series of brilliant campaigns which terminated in the emancipation of the Peninsula, as during the last grand struggle, which, sealing the destruction of the common enemy, purchased for Europe tranquillity and for your Grace the title of its deliverer.

'Whatever henceforth may be the destinies of this Corps—whether its exertions shall be for some time confined to the humbler, less inspiring, but not less imperative duty of protecting our fellow-citizens against the criminal attempts of flagitious and designing men in our native country, or whether our better fortune shall again direct us to the more enviable and spirit-stirring occupations of foreign war—we entreat your Grace to believe that the lustre of your high example will ever be present before our eyes, animating us all, each in his degree, and within the sphere of his activity, to renewed exertions; imparting to our humble efforts a character of a loftier emulation, and teaching us unceasingly to aim at results not unworthy to be associated with a name which history will indissolubly blend with the fairest and most enduring triumphs of a free and independent people.

'We have the honour to be,

'Your Grace's most obedient humble servants,

'1st and 2nd Battalions Rifle Brigade.

A NORCOTT, Col. and Lieut-Col. Com
D. LITTLE GILMOUR, Lieut-Col.
J. ROSS, Major and Lieut.-Col
S MITCHELL, Major and Lieut-Col.
J. LEACH, Major and Lieut-Col.
GEO MILLER, Major and Lieut.-Col
W. GRAY, Capt and Major.
MORGAN BRENT, Major'[1]

This address was forwarded to the Duke by Colonel Gilmour, then commanding the 2nd Battalion, with the following letter:—

'Tuam, May 31, 1820.

'My Lord Duke,

'As senior Lieutenant-Colonel of the Rifle Brigade, I have the honour of forwarding to you a letter from the officers composing the two Battalions of it, and in doing so I beg leave to express the high sense I entertain of the honour which has now devolved upon me, as also to embrace this opportunity of acknowledging the many obligations personally conferred upon me by your Grace, and which I beg leave

[1] 'Despatches and Correspondence,' i. 126

to assure you shall ever be held in my most grateful recollection.

'I have the honour to be
&c., &c
'D. LITTLE GILMOUR,
'Lieut.-Col., 2nd Battalion Rifle Brigade.'

During the time the 1st Battalion remained at Glasgow, they were frequently engaged, if not in actual conflict with the insurgents, yet in repressing acts of violence by the populace of Glasgow and Paisley, during the political excitement, then known as 'The Radical War.' Thus, among other occasions, I find that on April 2, 1820, the people of Glasgow, Paisley and the surrounding villages having left work and assembled for illegal and riotous objects, the Battalion was under arms from before day-break and posted in St George's Square, but the assemblage dispersed without acts of overt violence.[1]

On the removal of the Battalion from Glasgow, it received, by District Order dated November 12, 1820, the approbation of Major-General Reynell, commanding the district, for its conduct 'upon those trying occasions when its steady, temperate deportment was so mainly conducive to the restoration and maintenance of tranquillity in that populous city'[2]

A letter from the Provost of Glasgow, dated October 28, conveyed to Colonel Norcott the approbation of the magistrates of that city of the conduct of the Officers, Non-commissioned Officers and Privates of the Battalion, 'during a period of great anxiety and alarm,' for their 'admirable discipline and propriety of conduct under very trying and harassing circumstances.'

The 1st Battalion left Glasgow in three Divisions on November 15, 16 and 17, 1820, and arrived at Belfast on the 24th and 27th and were there quartered, furnishing detachments to Downpatrick, Carrickfergus, Coleraine, Castle-Dawson, Bally-castle, Dungiven, Maghera, Newtown-Glens and Ballymoney.

[1] 'Annual Register,' lxii 98.
[2] 'Record' 1st Battalion

About this time reference was made to the Duke of Wellington as to the Peninsular actions the names of which were to be borne by the Regiment, and on December 7, 1820, the Duke addressed the following letter to the Adjutant-General:

'Sir,—In returning to you the letter of Colonel Norcott, commanding the 1st Battalion Rifle Brigade, which I had the honour to receive from you some time ago, I beg leave to state, for the Commander-in-Chief's information, that, according to the rule to which I have confined myself in recommending regiments for honorary distinctions, I conceive that the Rifle Brigade may be permitted to bear on its appointments the following inscriptions, in commemoration of the distinguished services of the several Battalions of that Brigade on those occasions, viz: Roliça and Vimiera; Busaco; Barrosa; Fuentes de Honor, Ciudad Rodrigo; Badajoz; Salamanca; Vittoria; Nivelle; Nive; Orthes, Toulouse.[1]

'I have the honour to be, &c.,

'WELLINGTON.'

In compliance with this recommendation an order was issued from the Horse Guards dated January 4, 1821, directing the names of those victories to be borne on the appointments.

A further order dated Horse Guards, March 1, 1821, authorised the Regiment to bear the word 'Corunna' on its appointments in commemoration of its gallantry on January 16, 1809. And a third order, dated Horse Guards, March 22, 1821, authorised the words 'Copenhagen' and 'Monte Video,' in commemoration of the distinguished services of the Corps in the action of April 2, 1801 (its *first* service at Copenhagen), and of three companies of the 2nd Battalion at Monte Video in January 1807.

On March 7, 1821, the 1st Battalion marched from Belfast

[1] 'Despatches, Correspondence, and Memorandums,' i 154. The Regiment had already been authorised to bear the word WATERLOO on their appointments, in compliance with a memorandum of the Duke of Wellington, dated 'Head-quarters, Paris, November 7, 1815' 'Supplementary Despatches,' Appendix, xiv 600.

and the several detached stations, and arrived at Armagh on the 9th, whence it furnished detachments to Strabane, Lifford, Omagh, Monaghan, Aughnacloy, Derg-bridge, Gortin, Dungannon, Cookstown and Clones.

On November 13 the Battalion marched from Armagh and the neighbouring cantonments, and arrived at Naas on the 18th, sending out detachments to Kilcock, Baltinglass, Maryborough, Philipstown, Wicklow, Carlow, Glencree, Laragh, Gold-mines, Aughavanagh, Drumgoff and Leitrim, and subsequently to Athy.

The Head-quarters, consisting only of two companies, marched from Naas on December 20, and arrived at Kilkenny on the 22nd, where some of the detachments soon afterwards joined them, and whence they subsequently sent out detachments to Duncannon Fort and Callan.

The 2nd Battalion having had detachments from Tuam (where Head-quarters were stationed) besides those before mentioned, at Kilcurren, Moylagh, Mount Bellew, Cong, and Shrule, moved in two divisions on April 9 and 10 through Athenry, Loughrea, Portumna, Nenagh, Limerick, Bruff, Charleville and Doneraile, and arrived at Fermoy on the 19th where they were quartered, and shortly afterwards sent out detachments to Youghal, Dungarvan, Mitchelstown, Killorglin, Ross-Castle, Bantry, Bere Island, Mill Street, Cloyne, Buttevant, Kilworth, Tralee and Dingle.

On September 15 the Head-quarters, consisting of three companies, marched from Fermoy, through Clogheen, Clonmel, Callan, Kilkenny, Carlow and Ballitore, and arrived at Naas on the 22nd, furnishing detachments to some of the out-stations, which the 1st Battalion afterwards occupied from the same head-quarter station. On November 12 the Head-quarters of the Battalion returned by the same route to Fermoy, being relieved at Naas, by the 1st Battalion. On its arrival at Fermoy on the 18th it sent out detachments to Kildorrery, Castletownroche, Liscarrol, Newmarket and Mitchelstown; and subsequently to Kanturk and Doneraile.

The Head-quarters of the 1st Battalion consisting of two companies marched from Kilkenny on February 3, 1822, (having previously detached one company to Mitchelstown) and arrived at Fermoy on the 6th, sending out a detachment to Cappoquin. Soon afterwards, some of the detachments from Kilkenny having joined head-quarters, four companies marched from Fermoy to Charleville and detached parties from thence to Kilmallock, Bruree, Kilfinane and Gibbon's Grove.

The Head-quarters of the Battalion marched from Fermoy on February 16, and arrived at Newcastle on the next day. On this march a most violent outrage occurred Some non-commissioned officers' and soldiers' wives preceded the Battalion on three jaunting cars. About half-past six in the evening of Sunday, the 17th, when about a mile and a half from Kildorrery, the cars were stopped by about a dozen men, and some of the women, being seized and dragged off the cars, were violated by more than one man Others of them fled from their assailants and ran back and met the Battalion. For this outrage three men were tried at the ensuing Cork assizes, and being clearly identified by the women were found guilty, and executed.[1]

One of the victims of this outrage, the wife of a non-commissioned officer, was with the Battalion when I served in it She was flighty; having lost her senses in consequence of the violence inflicted on her, and never perfectly recovered. This assault was intended as a direct affront to the Regiment, for the miscreants enquired whether any officer's wife was on the cars; whether there was any ammunition in them; and on leaving said that they would let the Riflemen know that they were Captain Rock's men.

The late hour of the march, and its being on Sunday, show that it took place in consequence of the disturbed state of the country.

On its arrival at Newcastle the Battalion furnished detachments to Abbeyfeale, Athea, Drumcollogher, Ruskey, Mount Catherine, Hospital, Ballygran, Kilmedy and Glenduff

The Head-quarters of the Battalion marched from Newcastle to Rathkeale on July 23, and, the former detachments being withdrawn, sent out parties to Ballingarry, Croome, Shanagolden, Glyn, Youghal, Askeaton and Kildemo.

[1] 'Annual Register,' lxiv. 67

Early in the year some of the detachments furnished by the 2nd Battalion formed part of a moveable column under Colonel Straton, 6th Dragoons, and two companies of the Battalion marched from Fermoy to Cork.

On January 24 Colonel Mitchell with a party consisting of Captain Pemberton and fifty men of his company, a subaltern and a few men of the 11th Foot, and a few men of the 6th Dragoons, were engaged with a large body of the insurgents, about a thousand in number, posted on the hills near Carrigamanus, and completely routed them, some being killed and wounded, and twenty-two taken prisoners

On the next day Colonel Mitchell received information from a magistrate of the County that the insurgents were in force on the hill of Dasure, and would attack his party on his march from Fermoy to Macroom He therefore reinforced his small force with Captain Macnamara and Lieutenant Woodford's detachments and Captain Eaton's company, with his two subalterns, making his force of Riflemen three captains, three subalterns, four sergeants and 110 rank and file. They marched towards Dasure and found the insurgents posted on that hill, fully a thousand strong, while an equal number occupied the surrounding hills. As Mitchell's small party approached, they rushed furiously down the hill with the object of surrounding them. But Mitchell had thrown out skirmishers in his front, and to his flanks, and completely defeated their attempt. They fired a few shots; but finding that their proposed charge had failed, fled panic-struck, leaving many killed and wounded (some accounts made the number forty, others from twenty to thirty) and about thirty were made prisoners. This attack on the Riflemen was made with a fury and determination not usual in combats of this kind,[1] and their steadiness and zeal called forth the warm commendations of Colonel Mitchell.

Two more companies moved at this time to Cork; and parties were detached thence to Macroom, Inchigeelagh, Firmount, Derry, Larchfield, Mount-rivers, Warren's-court and Nettleville.

And on January 27 the Head-quarters of the Battalion marched from Fermoy to Bandon, leaving the heavy

[1] 'Annual Register,' lxiv. 15

baggage at Cork, and sent out detachments to Dunmanway, Skibbereen, Rosscarbery, Clonakilty and Bantry.

At this time a party of the Battalion proceeding in charge of cars conveying ammunition from Macroom to Bandon was attacked by the insurgents at Clara Mountain, near Kilmurry; but they were driven off with the loss of some killed and wounded.[1]

On March 12 the Head-quarters, consisting of one company and some attached men only, marched from Bandon to Kinsale, the detachments continuing as before with occasional reliefs and changes; and additional parties being sent to Crowhowley, Millstreet and Ballyvourney.

On August 25, 1822, Sir Andrew Barnard, who had been promoted Major-General from the command of the 1st Battalion on August 12, 1819, was appointed Colonel Commandant of a Battalion.

The 1st Battalion, besides the detachments already mentioned, furnished parties to Abbeyfeale, Tarbert, Athea and Mountpleasant.

The Battalion marched from Rathkeale and the outstations in two divisions on October 25 and 27, 1823, and arrived in Dublin on November 1 and 3, and occupied Richmond barracks until December 30, when they moved into the Royal barracks.

Previous to their leaving Rathkeale Major-General Sir John Lambert, who then commanded the district, issued a district order very complimentary to the discipline and services of the Battalion during more than a year and a half, during which it had been under his command, and stationed in a part of the county of Limerick which had been in a most disturbed state

On July 23 the 2nd Battalion marched from Kinsale in two divisions which arrived at Limerick on the 28th and 30th, being again broken up in detachments to Newcastle, Glyn, Athea, Drumcolliher, Mayne and Glenduff, and subsequently to Abbeyfeale and Rathkeale.

[1] 'Annual Register,' lxiv. 19.

The 1st Battalion marched from Dublin in three divisions on September 7, 8 and 9, 1824, and arrived at Belfast on the 16th and furnished detachments to Downpatrick, Carrickfergus and Ballymena.

The Head-quarters of the 2nd Battalion marched from Limerick on May 29 by Tipperary and Cashel, and arrived at Templemore barracks on June 1, where they remained until September 6, when they marched by Mountrath, Monasterevan and Naas and arrived in Dublin on the 9th and occupied Richmond barracks. Here the detachments left in the county of Limerick shortly afterwards joined, and the Battalion was at last re-united; and soon after the 1st Battalion, also re-united, arrived in the same barracks, and for many months both were quartered in Dublin

By an order from the Horse Guards dated April 25, 1825, the strength of the two Battalions was augmented from eight to 10 companies each, and those of the 1st Battalion were divided into six Service and four Depôt companies. This division was carried into effect on July 25; and on the 28th 29th and 30th the six Service companies embarked at Belfast for Nova Scotia, on board the 'Arab,' 'Speke,' and 'Joseph Green,' and arrived at Halifax about September 1, and were quartered in the South barracks

The Depôt companies remained at Belfast until August 24 when they marched for Newry, arriving there on the 26th. After a brief stay there they marched on September 17, and reached Cavan on the 20th, where they were quartered during the remainder of the year.

The 2nd Battalion marched from Dublin in four divisions on July 5, 6, 7 and 8, detaching two companies to Cavan, and a party to Maguire's bridge. After a three months' station at Enniskillen, these detachments having been called in, the Battalion marched in three divisions, on October 3, 4 and 5, and arrived at Birr on the 10th and proceeded to Buttevant which they reached on the 16th.

Here the division into Service and Depôt companies took

place on October 25, and on the 27th the six Service companies (leaving the Depôt at Buttevant) marched to Cork, and were there quartered. The Depôt on December 12 marched from Buttevant to Kinsale.

During the year 1826 the Service companies of the 1st Battalion continued to occupy the South barracks at Halifax, Nova Scotia.

The Depôt companies marched from Cavan on March 23, and arrived at Drogheda on the 25th sending a Captain's detachment to Dundalk, another to Trim, and a small party to Kilcock.

On May 4 they marched to Naas, the detachment from Dundalk having previously rejoined; but the other detachments remained out, and a party was also detached to Robertstown.

On August 8 the Depôt companies marched from Naas to Dublin, and occupied George Street barracks; but they returned to their former quarters at Drogheda, on October 14 sending out detachments to Swords and Garristown.

On January 10, 11 and 13 the Service companies of the 2nd Battalion embarked at the Cove of Cork, on board the 'Vibilia,' 'Cato,' and 'Sovereign,' transports, for Malta where they arrived on February 22, and were placed, four companies in the Lazaretto and two companies (Head-quarters) in Fort Manuel under quarantine. On receiving pratique they removed to Fort St Elmo; where they were quartered, with detachments at Fort Manuel, Fort Tigné, and a company at Gozo.

During the general election in this year a company from the Depôt of the 2nd Battalion under Captain Ferguson, stationed at Tralee, were called out on June 24, in consequence of a riot and attack on some of Lord Ventry's tenantry. The Riflemen were ordered to fire, and five of the rioters were killed and thirteen wounded, many of them dangerously. At an inquest held on two of the persons killed, a father and son named Sullivan, a verdict was returned that the order to fire was 'unjustifiable and unnecessary.'[1] I do

[1] 'Annual Register,' lxviii. 105.

not know whether any further proceedings were taken; but the conduct of the Riflemen was approved by the Duke of York, Commander in Chief; and Sir Herbert Taylor, then Military Secretary, states in a letter dated July 14, that 'The cool and determined conduct of Captain Ferguson, and the detachment of the Rifle Brigade under his orders at Tralee, appears, from the reports made to His Royal Highness, to have been deserving of his entire approbation, which he desires may be communicated to them.'

On January 27, 1827, Major-General Sir Thomas Sidney Beckwith, K.C.B., who had so long served in the Regiment, and had so gallantly led it in many a hard-fought field, was restored to its roll as Colonel Commandant of the 2nd Battalion, Sir Andrew Barnard becoming Colonel of the 1st Battalion by the death of the Honourable Sir William Stewart, at his residence, Cumloden, Kirkcudbright, on January 7.

On July 27, the Service companies of the 1st Battalion moved from the South to the North barracks at Halifax, and furnished detachments to Annapolis, Prince Edward's Island, Windsor, Cape Breton, and York redoubt

The Depôt companies of this Battalion marched from Drogheda on October 9 to Dublin, and on their arrival there were quartered in George Street barracks.

On the departure of the Depôt from Drogheda the Mayor and Corporation presented Major William Eeles, who commanded it, with the freedom of their Corporation, 'not only as an evidence of their personal regard for him,' but also 'to record their high sense of the gentlemanlike demeanour of the officers, and steady, soldier-like conduct of the non-commissioned officers and privates.'

The Depôt companies marched to Kingstown on October 21, and embarked in the 'Amphitrite' and 'Maria' transports for Devonport, where they arrived on the 31st, and occupied Stonehouse barracks.

The Service companies of the 2nd Battalion remained at Malta during this year; no change beyond the reliefs of detachments taking place until December 21, when they removed from Cottinera district to the lower St. Elmo barracks at Valetta, with a small party detached to Fort Tigné.

The record of this Battalion does not specify the movements of the Depôt companies; but I find that they were stationed at Clare Castle in March, and had moved before June to Cashel.

The Service companies of the 1st Battalion remained at Halifax during the year 1828, the various detachments mentioned in p. 228 rejoining the Head-quarters in May, June and August.

On July 29 His Royal Highness, the Duke of Clarence (afterwards King William IV.) on his visit to Plymouth as Lord High Admiral, reviewed the Depôt companies of both Battalions, with the other troops in garrison.[1] The day was very unfavourable, the rain falling in torrents; but His Royal Highness went through the review, which occupied some hours. Addressing the Riflemen, he traced the history of the Regiment and its principal deeds of arms from its foundation (as was his wont on such occasions), concluding with these words: 'And what more can I say to you, Riflemen, than that wherever there has been fighting you have been employed, and wherever you have been employed you have distinguished yourselves?'

Immediately after this review the Depôt companies embarked on board the 'Amphitrite' transport at Devonport, and on the 31st landed at Gosport, and occupied Forton barracks. On December 21 they furnished detachments to Tipner and Hilsea.

No change (except the relief of detachments) took place in the Service companies of the 2nd Battalion, which remained at Malta; but its Depôt companies were (with those of the 1st Battalion) at Devonport during the spring and summer; and in September were stationed at Portsmouth; but before the end of the year returned to Devonport.

The Service companies of the 1st Battalion remained at

[1] The Duke of Clarence had also reviewed the two Depôts on a previous visit to Plymouth on December 21 preceding

Halifax until October 1829, on the 17th and 18th of which month they embarked in the 'Ann,' 'Amelia,' and 'Wellington,' transports; and sailing on the 21st, arrived at St. John's, New Brunswick, where they disembarked on the 29th and 31st. They immediately furnished detachments to Fredericton and St. Andrew's; and on November 7 the Headquarters with Captain Hope's company embarked on board the 'St George' steam-boat, and moving up to Fredericton, occupied the new barracks with the detachment of the Battalion already there.

On March 13 the Depôt companies calling in the detachments at Tipner and Hilsea, moved to Cambridge barracks, Portsmouth On August 11 they embarked on board the 'Amphitrite' and disembarked at Dover on the 13th, where they occupied the Western heights barracks.

The 2nd Battalion remained at Malta during this year, changing its quarters on December 18 from the St. Elmo to the Floriana barracks.

During the year 1830 the 1st Battalion remained at St. John's and Fredericton, New Brunswick; and the Depôt continued in its quarters at Dover

The only change in the quarters of the Service companies of the 2nd Battalion this year was their removal from Floriana barracks to the Cottinera district on December 20.

The Depôt companies moved about April to Deal and soon afterwards to Dover, where they were quartered with the Depôt of the 1st Battalion.

No change took place in the quarters of the 1st Battalion during the year 1831; the Service companies continuing in New Brunswick, and the Depôt at Dover.

The Service companies of the 2nd Battalion remained at Malta during the whole of this year, and the Depôt continued at Dover.

Lieutenant-General Sir T. Sidney Beckwith, K.C.B., Colonel Commandant of the 2nd Battalion, died January 19, 1831, at the Mahabuleshwar hills, Bombay, of which Presidency he was Commander-in-Chief. He was the last of the original officers of the Regiment remaining in it.

The Head-quarters of the 1st Battalion with three companies left Fredericton in two divisions on August 14 and 17, 1832; and the whole of the Service companies embarked at St. John's in H M.S. 'Winchester,' and the 'Arachne' and 'Chebucto,' brigs, on the 21st and 22nd and disembarking at Halifax, Nova Scotia, were quartered in the North barracks.

The Depôt companies continued at Dover, furnishing a detachment for a short period to Shorncliffe.

On February 12 the Head-quarters of the 2nd Battalion with two companies embarked at Malta for Corfu, where they landed on the 19th, and on the 23rd the remaining six companies embarked, landing at Corfu, two on the 1st March and two on the 6th.

On April 6 the Battalion moved to the Island of Vido, sending out small parties to the Lazaretto Island, Paleo Castrizza, Fano and Paxo.

On August 1 the Battalion returned to Corfu, calling in these parties; but, shortly afterwards sending out a detachment to Cephalonia.

The Depôt of the 2nd Battalion remained at Dover.

On April 1 in this year a change was made in the clothing of the non-commissioned officers and private Riflemen, the coats being made double-breasted, instead of single-breasted as heretofore; black horn-buttons being substituted for white metal; and black lace and chevrons being adopted instead of those before worn by sergeants.

No change took place in 1833 in the station of the Service companies of the 1st Battalion, which continued to occupy the North barracks at Halifax.

Early in the year 1833 Captain Horatio Stewart's Depôt company was ordered to proceed from Dover by forced marches to Hastings The whole of that part of the coast was in a state of great excitement in consequence of the proceedings of smugglers, who had not long before had an affray with the coastguard, in which one of the latter was killed and others wounded. On the arrival of the company at Hastings the men, after being allowed to rest and refresh themselves for about an hour, were ordered to fall in, and were divided into parties, under officers and non-commissioned officers, which were directed to patrol the beach for many miles in various directions during the night. This unpleasant duty continued for six weeks; patrolling by night and target practice by day. This was watched by numbers of the people; and no doubt the practice made at the target was observed with good effect by the smugglers and their friends; for no smuggler was ever met with by the patrols, nor was any attempt made, while the Riflemen continued at Hastings, to land contraband goods. The company then rejoined the Depôt.[1]

The Depôt companies, calling in the detachment at Shorncliffe, marched from Dover to Chatham on April 1, whence they furnished in June a strong detachment under a Field officer to Gravesend, in aid of the Civil power. And 'their excellent conduct,' and 'the unceasing attention of the officers,' received the thanks of the Mayor in behalf of the inhabitants.

These companies embarked at Chatham on November 11 on board H.M. steam-vessel 'Salamander,' and arriving at Jersey on the 14th, disembarked at St. Aubin's, from whence they proceeded to occupy quarters in Fort Regent, at St. Helier's.

The Service companies of the 2nd Battalion were moved from Corfu to Vido on August 1, sending out detachments to Lazaretto Island and Fano; but on December 1 returned to Corfu. The Depôt companies continued at Dover.

In consequence of the breaking out of cholera in the 1st Battalion, the Service companies were moved from Halifax on August 24, 1834, and encamped at Sackville, whence they returned to their former quarters in the North barracks, Halifax, September 30. In this outbreak of cholera the Battalion lost 31 men, 6 women and 5 children.

[1] 'Personal Narrative of Military Travel and Adventure in Turkey and Persia,' by Robert Macdonald, pp. 22–25. The writer, a sergeant in the 1st Battalion, was selected with his brother Peter Macdonald to proceed to Persia in 1836. See p. 234

The Depôt remained during the whole of this year at Fort Regent, Jersey.

The Head-quarters of the Service companies of the 2nd Battalion embarked at Corfu for Cephalonia on October 8, and landed there on the 9th. Two companies had preceded them on June 20, and two others on September 26. From hence detachments were furnished to Calamos, to Ithaca, to Paxo, to Lixuri, to Fort San Georgio and Sta. Euphemia About March the Depôt companies removed from Dover to Guernsey.

During the year 1835 no change of quarters took place in either Battalion or in their Depôts

The Service companies of the 1st Battalion sailed from Halifax, Nova Scotia, in the 'Stakesley' and 'Katherine Stewart Forbes,' on August 20 and 26, 1836, and arrived at Chatham and disembarked on September 15 and 29, and occupied quarters there.

The Depôt companies had sailed from Jersey in the 'Katherine Stewart Forbes' on May 24, and arrived at Gosport on the 28th, where they disembarked, and were quartered in Fort Monckton till June 17; when they crossed to Portsmouth, and occupied Forehouse barracks, with detachments at Tipner and Hilsea.

On August 1 the Depôt companies marched from Portsmouth, through Chichester, Petworth, East Grinstead, and arrived at Chatham on the 8th to await the arrival of the Service companies; and on their landing on September 15 and 29, they were again reunited into a Battalion of ten companies.

No change took place in the quarters of the Service companies of the 2nd Battalion, except the occasional relief of the many detachments they furnished from Cephalonia. But the Depôt companies in September embarked at Guernsey for Dover, where they awaited the arrival of the Service companies, and were reunited with them on their arrival in June following.

Early in the year 1836 Lieutenant Wilbraham,[1] then Adjutant of the 1st Battalion, was selected to proceed to Persia, with eight sergeants of the Rifle Brigade, in charge of two thousand stand of rifles, intended by the Foreign Office as a present to the Shah on his accession to the throne. Four of these sergeants, belonging to the 1st Battalion, were sent out from England; the other four, belonging to the 2nd Battalion, joined the expedition at Cephalonia, where their Battalion was then stationed

Lieutenant Wilbraham was promoted in July 1836 to an unattached company, and subsequently the local rank of Lieutenant-Colonel was conferred upon him. For nearly three years he and the eight sergeants were employed in organising and instructing the Persian troops, but at the end of that time a rupture took place between England and Persia, in consequence of the Shah's advance upon Herat, and they returned to Europe. The rifles had under one pretext or another been withheld, as it was foreseen that they would probably be used against ourselves, but as they were too bulky to be carried, they were rendered useless by the removal of the locks, which were brought away

Of the sergeants who were selected for this duty Sergeant Peter Macdonald afterwards rose to the rank of Lieutenant-Colonel, and retired from the Service in 1865; and Colour-sergeant Johnson, 2nd Battalion, subsequently became Captain in the 41st Regiment, and died at Balaclava as Provost-Marshal of the Army.

The 1st Battalion marched from Chatham in two divisions on May 1 and 2, 1837, and arrived at Woolwich and Deptford on the 2nd and 3rd. Seven companies with Head-quarters were stationed at Woolwich, and three companies at Deptford.

During the time the Battalion was quartered at Woolwich, Lieutenant-Colonel William Eeles died in command of it on October 11 He had served in the Regiment thirty-two years, having been appointed to it in 1805; and had accompanied it through its Peninsular and other campaigns, and had been present at Waterloo. He was succeeded

[1] Now Lieutenant-General Sir Richard Wilbraham, K C B.

in the command of the Battalion by Lieutenant-Colonel Hope, who had been promoted after twenty-eight years' service in the Rifles to the Lieutenant-Colonelcy of the 21st Fusiliers; and was now brought back to his old Corps.

On April 8 and 13 the Service companies of the 2nd Battalion embarked at Cephalonia on board the 'Parmelia' and 'Prince Regent,' transports, and landed at Dover on June 3 and 13

And on August 14, 15 and 16 the Battalion marched from Dover to Portsmouth in three divisions, arriving there on the 24th, 25th and 26th, and detaching one company to Tipner Magazine.

The 1st Battalion embarked in steam-vessels at Woolwich early in the morning of June 28, 1838, and attended the Coronation of Queen Victoria This and the 2nd Battalion lined Piccadilly from Hyde Park Corner to the corner of St. James' Street in extended order.

After the procession had returned from Westminster Abbey to Buckingham Palace the 1st Battalion marched back to Woolwich and Deptford.

On July 9 the Battalion again embarked in steam-vessels and was conveyed to London, and took part in the review in Hyde Park on that day under the command of General, the Marquis of Anglesey, and in presence of the Queen. Marshal Soult was present at this review.

At its conclusion the Battalion was billeted in the neighbourhood of Hanover Square until the 11th, when it marched to the Tower of London and was there quartered. Three or four days after their arrival there the Battalion was inspected by the Colonel-in-Chief, Field-Marshal the Duke of Wellington, accompanied by Marshal Soult. They proceeded down the ranks and inspected the Battalion together.

On June 16, 17 and 18, the 2nd Battalion marched in three divisions from Portsmouth to Chelsea and was there billeted. And on the 28th attended the Coronation of Queen Victoria as above stated; and on July 9 was present at the review in Hyde Park.

On the next day, it moved from Chelsea to Woolwich

relieving the 1st Battalion, and like it, having Head-quarters and seven companies at Woolwich and three companies detached at Deptford.

The 1st Battalion marched on February 1 and 2, 1839, by wings, from the Tower to Paddington, and thence proceeded by Railway to Windsor, where they were quartered in the Infantry barracks.

On March 11 and 12 the left wing of the Battalion marched from Windsor and arrived at Weedon on the 15th; and they were followed by the right wing and Head-quarters which left Windsor on the 18th and arrived at Weedon on the 22nd.

In consequence of the disturbed state of the country, detachments were furnished by the Battalion to aid the Civil power, to Birmingham, Nottingham and Warwick; the two former continuing detached (with occasional reliefs) for about a year; the latter from July till December. During the chartist disturbances the detachment at Birmingham was on more than one occasion called out to disperse the mob. Rioting having more or less continued from the 4th to the 8th July, the detachment was called out on the latter evening, and took their station in the Bull-ring. Here fighting with the police took place, and the mob, having got the worst of it, assembled in the Holloway road The Riflemen were ordered to disperse them, and were pelted with stones. Then an order to load and to make ready was given; but fortunately before they fired, the 4th Dragoon Guards arrived and dispersed the people, taking many prisoners

A few days later similar harassing services were required of them On July 15 a mob assembled in the evening, in the Bull-ring, and attacked the houses of several citizens and tradesmen and set some of them on fire. The mob would not let engines approach, and compelled the firemen, under pain of death, to take off their horses and retreat. At this moment a party of 200 Riflemen made their appearance (accompanied by a magistrate), and under their escort the firemen brought up, and worked their engines, while the 4th Dragoon Guards charged the people and cleared the streets.

Among the parties sent out to clear the neighbouring

streets was one consisting of a section commanded by Sergeant Robert Macdonald. It was arduous work, for the mob assailed them with stones and every description of missiles. The men became so exasperated under this provocation (for some were severely hurt) that they could hardly be restrained from retaliating by attacking their assailants with their swords, which were fixed on their rifles. Sergeant Macdonald did what he could to prevent mischief; but in the tumult one or two persons were killed or died of wounds, and several were wounded A coroner's inquest, however, returned a verdict of 'justifiable homicide,' thereby exonerating Macdonald, who was amenable as having been in command at this post, from all blame.[1]

On the next day, the Riflemen were engaged in patrolling the town ; and in the evening, it having been announced that another chartist meeting was to be held, they were brought down in force, accompanied by a Squadron of the 4th and some artillery with guns The mob did not care to come into collision with them, and the riots subsided.

On this detachment returning to Weedon, a very strong and favourable representation was made by the mayor and magistrates of Birmingham to the Home Secretary of its services and conduct, and of the indefatigable zeal and humanity with which it had performed the duties required of it. This was transmitted by the Marquis of Normanby, then Home Secretary, to General Lord Hill, Commanding in Chief, and by him to the Commanding Officer of the 1st Battalion, both adding their expression of satisfaction and approval of the conduct of the detachment.

The following address was also forwarded by the Mayor of Birmingham to the Commanding Officer :

'To the Officers, Non-commissioned Officers and Privates of Her Majesty's Rifle Brigade, now stationed at Weedon barracks.

'We, the undersigned the Mayor and magistrates of the borough of Birmingham, having heard with regret of your intended early removal from this neighbourhood, cannot permit your departure to take place without tendering to you this cordial and respectful assurance of our esteem and

[1] 'Personal Narrative of Military Travel and Adventure,' pp 286-7.

gratitude. For a considerable period during which we were indebted to you for aid and protection, we had frequent occasions to admire the order, courage and humanity which marked your performance of some of the most painful duties which it falls to the lot of a British soldier to fulfil. Nor can we forget that alike by officers and men these duties, often dangerous and always irksome, were discharged with uniform cheerfulness and alacrity.

'As a very inadequate, though warm and grateful return, allow us to repeat the expression of our heartfelt thanks and to offer our best and earnest wishes for your future happiness and welfare.

'Signed by the Mayor and ten magistrates.

'Birmingham, April 30, 1840'

In November 1839, the flint-lock Baker rifle was replaced by the percussion Brunswick rifle, a supply of which was forwarded from the Tower to Weedon, together with swords, &c.

The 2nd Battalion marched in two divisions from Woolwich on October 9 and 10, for Windsor and arrived there on the 12th and were quartered in the Infantry barracks.

On November 1 the Battalion was reviewed in the Home Park by Queen Victoria.

In consequence of the disturbed state of South Wales, and the attack on Newport in November, two companies of the Battalion, under the command of Major Irton,[1] were ordered to march from Windsor on December 18 to Monmouth, where they arrived on the 28th of that month

The 1st Battalion remained at Weedon till November 1840, when an order having been received to prepare for foreign service, the Battalion was divided into six Service companies and four Depôt companies.

And on November 9 and 10 the Service companies proceeded by rail-road to London; and embarked at Deptford on board the 'Abercrombie Robinson' transport for Malta, where they arrived in January following.

The Depôt companies continued to be quartered in Weedon barracks during the remainder of the year.

[1] Lieutenant-Colonel Irton died June 9, 1847.

The trial by Special Commission of the ringleaders of the attack on Newport having concluded, the two companies of the 2nd Battalion which had been detached to Monmouth, marched on March 2 and rejoined Head-quarters at Windsor on the 10th of that month.

On May 22 a company of the Battalion marched to Esher to furnish guards and duties at Claremont, during the Queen's residence there; and returned to Windsor on the 25th, and on June 1 a similar detachment proceeded to Esher, for the same duty, rejoining Head-quarters on the 5th.

South Wales continuing in a disturbed state, two companies marched from Windsor to Brecon, one to Pontypool, one to Swansea, and one to Merthyr Tydvil on August 22, and arrived at their destinations on September 1 and 2. And on August 24 the Head-quarters marched to Newport, Monmouthshire, and arrived on September 1; furnishing additional detachments to Newtown and Montgomery.

On October 26 the detachment at Brecon was broken up, one company marching to Abergavenny, and the other to Usk.

The Service companies of the 1st Battalion disembarked at Malta on January 13, 1841, and were quartered at Fort Manuel, with detachments at St. Salvador and another to the Zabbar gate.

On January 28 the Head-quarters moved to Fort Ricasoli, detaching another company to St Salvador. But the Battalion only remained in these quarters till February 13, when they removed to Isola barracks, with one company at St. Francis de Paolo, and one at St. Salvador.

On May 7 the Battalion left the Cottinera district, and moved to lower St. Elmo barracks, with a company detached at St James' Cavalier.

The Depôt companies removed from Weedon to Chester Castle on May 5, and were there quartered until 20th of the same month, when they proceeded to Liverpool; and embarking for Dublin, arrived there on the 21st They disembarked on the following day and occupied Beggar's-bush barracks until the 25th when they moved into Richmond barracks.

On July 10 a detachment of five officers and about a hundred men were sent to Wicklow, in aid of the Civil power, during an election. They returned to Richmond barracks on the 23rd.

No alteration of quarters (except the change and relief of detachments) took place in the 2nd Battalion until August; on the 28th, 30th and 31st of which month the Battalion left its cantonments in Monmouthshire and in Wales, and was reunited at Bristol preparatory to embarking for foreign service.

On this occasion an address was presented to the Commanding Officer, signed by the Mayor of Newport and five other magistrates, commending the 'peaceable, orderly and soldierlike manner in which the men had conducted themselves.' An address was likewise presented, signed by five magistrates of Newtown, thanking the detachment there for its 'efficient assistance in preserving the peace of the town,' and for 'protecting the property of many of its inhabitants.' And another signed by forty inhabitants (magistrates and tradesmen) testified to the good conduct of the detachment stationed there.

On September 3 the Battalion was divided into six Service and four Depôt companies; and on the 9th and 10th (leaving the Depôt companies at Bristol) the Service companies proceeded by Great Western railway to Paddington, and thence to Deptford, where they embarked on board the 'Abercrombie Robinson' for Bermuda They arrived on November 5 and disembarked at St. George's.

The 1st Battalion remained in its quarters at Malta during the whole of the year 1842, furnishing detachments to Forts Ricasoli and Tigné.

The Depôt companies marched from Richmond barracks to the Pigeon-house Fort, near Dublin, on January 20; where they remained until October On the 17th of that month the first division marched for Drogheda through Ashbourne, and on the 19th the Head-quarters through Balbriggan; and on arrival at Drogheda were quartered, three companies in Millmount barracks, and one company in Fair Street barracks.

On May 7 an order was issued from the Horse Guards increasing the 2nd Battalion to twelve companies, six of which were to be called the Reserve Battalion. The Depôt companies were therefore increased to six companies, eighty men having volunteered from the 1st Battalion to complete them. This was effected at Dover.

The six companies at Bermuda embarked on board the 'Java' transport on July 30, and landed at Halifax, Nova Scotia, on August 12.

On September 6 the Reserve Battalion arrived at Halifax And in October the Battalion, thus completed, sent out detachments to Prince Edward's Island, Cape Breton, and Annapolis.

Lieutenant-General Sir Dugald Little Gilmour, K.C.B., who had served in the Regiment nearly twenty years, during many of which he had commanded the 2nd Battalion, was appointed Colonel Commandant of it April 25, 1842.

The right wing of the 1st Battalion, recalling the detachments, embarked at Malta, on board the 'Boyne,' transport, on March 2, 1843, and landed at Corfu on the 6th. The left wing did not leave Malta till April 1, when it embarked, also in the 'Boyne,' and arrived at Corfu on the 7th. The Battalion furnished detachments to Santa Maura, Vido, Paxo and Fano.

The Depôt companies continued at Drogheda, whence a detachment of 3 officers and about 70 men marched to Carrickmacross on April 5, in aid of the Civil power, and rejoined on the 27th.

A detachment consisting of one company proceeded on May 23 to Dundalk, and occupied quarters, with the cavalry, in the barracks there. On June 7 it marched to Carrickmacross, to aid the Civil power, and returned to Dundalk on the 15th. Two months afterwards, on August 15 it marched to Castle Blaney again to aid the Civil power; but returned the following day. On September 12 it moved to Longford, and on the same day another company marched from Drogheda to Granard; and the Head-quarters of the Depôt followed to Longford on the 16th, arriving there on the 21st, where they occupied the Line and the Artillery barracks. In the meanwhile a detachment had been sent to Trim, to aid the Civil powei ; and this rejoined at Longford on October 3.

Detachments were soon afterwards sent out to Athlone and to Roscommon ; and that at Granard was called in.

The numerous detachments, in aid of the Civil power, and the frequent removals of the Depôt, were caused by the Repeal agitation, which was at its height during this year ; and by the 'Monster Meetings' held by O'Connell at Trim, Roscommon, and other towns.

No change seems to have taken place in the quarters of the 2nd Battalion during this year, when it continued at Halifax.

The Service companies of the 1st Battalion continued at Corfu during the year 1844, the only changes in them being the relief of detachments, and the furnishing an additional one to the Lazaretto

The Depôt companies marched from Longford on January 8 to Athlone, where they arrived on the following day, and were soon joined by the detachment from Roscommon.

The 2nd Battalion continued at Halifax, the detachments at the out-stations being relieved, by another regiment, and rejoining Head-quarters in July.

The Service companies of the 1st Battalion remained at Coifu during the year 1845; the only change in its quarters being the occasional relief of the detachments.

The Depôt companies marched from Athlone on April 14 and 15, and arrived in Dublin on the 19th and 21st, and were quartered in Beggar's-bush barracks, furnishing a detachment for a short time to the Pigeon-house fort. The Depôt Head-quarters removed to this fort on June 2, leaving a small detachment only in the Beggar's-bush barracks. But to these barracks the Head-quarters returned on October 27.

The 2nd Battalion remained during the whole of this year stationary at Halifax.

About the beginning of August 1846 the Service com

panies of the 1st Battalion were directed to hold themselves in readiness to proceed to Jamaica; but very shortly afterwards a letter was received from Lord FitzRoy Somerset, Military Secretary to the Commander-in-Chief, stating that the destination of the Battalion was changed; that it was to be held in readiness to embark for the Cape of Good Hope; and that steamers were on their way from England to convey it to Gibraltar.

The Detachments at Lazaretto, Santa Maura and Fano were therefore immediately called in; and the Battalion prepared for active service.

Shortly before embarkation the Service companies were inspected by Lieutenant-General Lord Seaton, then Lord High Commissioner of the Ionian islands, who after witnessing a few battalion movements ordered square to be formed and thus addressed them:

'Rifle Brigade, or old 95th, I have known the Regiment more than forty years and have taken part with them in battles and sieges in the Peninsular war, and at Waterloo. My old regiment, the 52nd, and the 43rd, formed the famous Light Division under his Grace the Duke of Wellington, who always led them to victory. Your Queen and country now call upon you to uphold her honour in Southern Africa, against hordes of savages; and I feel quite sure that the Battalion will sustain the undying fame that it gained in the Peninsula and at Waterloo, and add more laurels to its wreath. Riflemen, old 95th, I bid you good bye with my heartfelt and best wishes for you all.'

Lord Seaton also issued a farewell order, highly commending the state of their discipline and general good conduct, and expressing his regret at their removal from his command, and his wishes for their future welfare.

The Service companies were ordered, by letter from the Horse Guards, July 23, 1846, to embark 560 strong including musicians, and to take out only 540 rifles and accoutrements; and the supernumerary men and arms were to be sent to England to form part of the Depôt.

Though the Service companies were thus reduced to 560 men, the total strength of the Battalion was actually increased by 200 men, by a Horse Guards order dated March 27, 1846.

On August 21 the Service companies embarked; the Headquarter division under Major Egerton[1] in H.M. steamship 'Retribution;' and the left wing, under Captain Horsford,[2] in the 'Terrible;' and steaming away at once (through the Straits of Messina) arrived at Gibraltar at twelve P.M. on the 27th and disembarked on the following day, and occupied barracks.

[1] Colonel Buller (now General Sir George Buller, G C B) had left Corfu for England before the order to embark arrived.

[2] Lieutenant-General Sir Alfred H Horsford, G C B

CHAPTER VIII.

ON August 31, 1846, transports having arrived from England for the conveyance of the 1st Battalion to the Cape, they re-embarked, Head-quarters on board the 'Equestrian' transport, consisting of Captains Macdonell's, Rooper's, and Stewart's companies, with Staff and band; and the left wing consisting of Captains Horsford's, Murray's, and Gibson's companies, on board the 'Fairlie' under Captain Horsford.

The latter vessel arrived first, reaching Table-bay on October 30. Here an order was at once given to land the women and children; and to take in supplies and camp-equipments. This being done the left wing sailed on November 4, for Algoa bay, where they arrived on the 12th and anchored opposite the town of Port Elizabeth.

On the day following their departure the 'Equestrian' arrived at Table-bay, and having in like manner landed heavy baggage, women and children, and taken in stores and camp-necessaries, proceeded to Algoa bay on the 11th and arrived there about November 20.

On the 14th the 'Fairlie' having drawn as near the shore as possible, surf-boats came alongside, and were soon filled and rowed to the shore until they took the ground. Then Fingoes carried the Riflemen pick-a-back to the dry sand. As soon as all were landed, they marched through the town of Port Elizabeth, and piled arms and encamped about half-a-mile beyond it to the left of the Graham's-town road The necessary supplies and equipments having been procured, not without difficulty which Horsford's energy and perseverance surmounted, this wing began its march under a burning sun for Kaffirland. They reached Graham's-town, a distance of about 100 miles, on the 23rd.

They halted here on the 24th and on the following day moved to Manley flats; on the 26th to Cawood's post; and on the 27th reached Waterloo-bay. The next day, after receiving a field ration of rice, salt, sugar, and green coffee (these troops being thus supplied with that valuable but unusable berry in its natural state, as they were afterwards in the Crimea) they marched to Newton Dale; on the 29th to Fort Peddie; on the 30th to the Chalumna river; and on December 1 joined the 2nd Division of the army, which was commanded by Colonel Henry Somerset of the Cape Mounted Rifles. In this march the men suffered severely from the sun; their faces being almost skinned as their forage-caps had no peaks; and their shakos had been given into store at Graham's-town, and were never returned to them.

The Head-quarter wing disembarked at Port Elizabeth, on November 25; commenced their march, by the same route, on the 24th, and joined the 2nd Division of the army, then encamped on the Buffalo river, on December 12.

On December 21 the Battalion marched, and on the 25th encamped near the great Kei river, and during the rest of the month furnished frequent patrols on both banks. One Rifleman was killed, and one wounded by the Kaffirs on December 31 in the performance of these duties.

The Depôt companies embarked on January 28, 1846, at the North Wall, Dublin, in the steamer 'Albert' for Liverpool, where they landed on the following day; and proceeded by rail-road to London, and thence to Dover, which they reached on the following day, and were quartered in the Castle; furnishing a subaltern's detachment to Sandgate Castle.

On May 18 they marched to Chatham; and after a short stay there proceeded in a steamer to Sheerness on June 1.

The 2nd Battalion left Halifax, in H M.S. 'Belleisle' on August 1, and arrived at Montreal on the 22nd and were there quartered during the remainder of the year.

The Service companies of the 1st Battalion with the exception of Captain Gibson's company which was left on the other side of the Kei river not having returned from a previous expedition, marched on January 2, 1847, at three P.M., with the Division commanded by Lieutenant-General Sir Peregrine Maitland, for the Kei river, and arrived within about two miles of it at seven in the evening, and halted for the night. The march had been a very hot one; but soon after sunset a tremendous storm of thunder, lightning and hail came on; this was followed by a deluging rain, which drenched the men to the skin in a few minutes. They had no tents; no fires; not even pipes were allowed to be lighted, nor was a word permitted to be spoken above a whisper. For the Kaffirs were near them; and had they known exactly where the troops were bivouacked would have attacked. But the night was very dark, and they remained unmolested.

On the 3rd the Riflemen in advance forded the Kei river, here about 350 yards wide, and knee deep, and waited on the other bank for the Division After breakfast, rifles were fired off and cleaned from the effects of the last night's rain, and they marched towards Butterworth. On reaching a hill, afterwards well known to Riflemen by the name of Mount-Misery, they halted and bivouacked for the night. On the next morning at daylight they resumed their march, and arrived at the Missionary Station of Butterworth at six in the evening: a distance of nearly thirty miles. The Missionary's house and the church were in ruins, having been burnt down; but every wall and corner which remained was occupied by the weary soldiers, glad of even such insufficient shelter. For scarcely had the outlying picquets been posted, when heavy and continuous rain came on, and lasted throughout the night.

On the 5th Captain Gibson's company rejoined. The rain still continuing the men suffered much. They were glad to gather stones on which to lie, to keep them off the streaming ground; and even these were sometimes washed away by the rills formed in paths and tracks. This rain continued during the whole of the 6th and until the afternoon of the 7th; nearly seventy hours of incessant rain.

On the 6th five days' ration of biscuit, which had from December 29 been reduced to six ounces a day, was served out to the men; but hunger takes no account of Commissariat measurement, and long before the expiration of the five days, the Riflemen were picking gum off the trees, and eating it to assuage their need.

At this time Sir Peregrine Maitland being recalled, left the army, and the command of the division again devolved on Colonel Somerset.

Fine weather having at last come on, the men wrung out and rinsed their wet shirts and dried them in the sun. In the evening the rifles were inspected and the ammunition examined, for much of it had been damaged by the wet. On the 8th at six in the morning, they marched for Spring-Flats where they arrived at eleven. After a halt of three hours, during which the weakly men and those who had sore feet fell out of the ranks and were marched to the Kei under an officer of another regiment, they resumed their march for Kreili's Corner, and halting at six o'clock, bivouacked for the night.

At dawn on the 9th, intelligence having come in of a quantity of cattle, said to be a few miles ahead, they marched towards Kreili's Corner; and with a halt of one hour for breakfast, and two for dinner, continued their march till eight in the evening, when they bivouacked.

Next day at daylight they moved on in the hope of coming up with the cattle, but nothing being seen of them, the cavalry pushed on at ten o'clock; while the infantry continued their march till two in the afternoon. At four the cavalry appeared with 12,000 cattle which they had captured at Kreili's Corner, and 100 men of the Battalion were detailed as a cattle guard. Rain now began again, and the ration consisted of fresh beef only, the biscuit being all consumed, and that without salt to season it. Firewood too was scarce; and there were no tents.

On the 11th the Riflemen halted in bivouack, rain still continuing; and on the 12th marched for Spring-Flats under a burning sun Many Kaffirs were on the surrounding hills; but few ventured within range. One however was shot by one of the cattle guard, when attempting to steal cattle. On the 13th a company of the Rifle Brigade and one of another regiment were sent to the Kei river with the captured cattle; but on their arrival the river was found to be unfordable, and the current running at a rapid rate They had therefore to return, and on their arrival at the second hill (Mount-Misery) an order reached them to send out a patrol in search of

Captain Gibson, for whom great fears were entertained. This officer, and Assistant-Surgeon Howell, had accompanied the party of weakly and disabled men which had marched from this place on the 8th. While this party were halted on January 11 near the ford of the Kei, waiting for the fall of the river to enable them to cross, some cattle were observed grazing on the hills about three miles off. Captain Fraser, of the 6th Foot, who was in command of these invalids, directed all the men who were able to march to proceed, under Captain Gibson, to endeavour to capture these cattle, which were beyond the bank which reached from the river half way up the hills.

After the party, which was accompanied by Assistant-Surgeon Howell and by Lieutenant the Honourable W. J. G. Chetwynd of the 73rd Regiment, had marched about an hour by a rather wide path through the bank, they arrived at a bend in the path. Unhappily the officers, unsuspicious of any attack, were marching ahead of their men, between seventy and 100 yards from the leading files. When therefore they took the bend in the road, they were entirely hidden from them. At this moment the Kaffir Chief, Pato, observing their defenceless position, rushed upon them with about 200 of his followers, and before the detachment could come up, killed all three officers.

The little detachment under a sergeant of the 6th Foot, made good its retreat, gradually retiring, and whenever the Kaffirs attacked, turning round and firing a volley.

The patrol sent out to recover the remains of these officers, after marching about three hours through thick bush, came upon their bodies which they brought into the bivouack at Spring-Flats, where they arrived about nine in the evening. They were interred by the officers and men of the Battalion on the next day at a place called Shaw's fontein; bushes being burnt over the graves, to prevent the Kaffirs discovering the place of their interment, and exhuming and desecrating their remains.

The Riflemen who had acted as this patrol marched again on the 14th for the Kei river, it having been reported that it was fordable; but this proved to be a mistake, at least as far as infantry was concerned; though the cavalry had forded; not, however, without some loss. Again, therefore the Riflemen had to return and bivouack on Mount-Misery. And the rest of the Battalion was moved up to the same place.

They remained here during the next three days, suffering great privations. For the swollen state of the river did not admit of supplies being brought over. In consequence, too, of a soldier of another regiment who had gone out for water having been found killed and stripped, a stringent order was issued that no men were to go for water, except in armed parties of thirty, under an officer, and accompanied by two non-commissioned officers This water duty was exceedingly fatiguing; as the men had to go down two very steep hills into a kloof,[1] about a mile distant, and to reascend them loaded with water Want and exposure too began to tell heavily on the men; and the seeds of much subsequent disease were to be traced to this bivouack. At last on the 18th the Riflemen marched at ten o'clock from this hill and bivouacked near the banks of the river. It had fallen sufficiently for the Commissariat to get over some stores; and the famished Riflemen on reaching their bivouack found coffee, sugar, salt, and a ration of biscuit awaiting them; and what they welcomed almost as much, tobacco, which for many days they had not had, and the want of which they had vainly tried to supply by smoking leaves of the Kaffir tea-tree dried in the sun On the 19th the cattle were driven through the river by fifties at a time; and at two o'clock the Battalion began to ford it. The water was still deep, and the current running six or seven miles an hour. A stout rope was made fast to each bank, and reeved through three waggons placed at equal distances in the bed of the river. This made a good hand-rail for the men But the leading files having difficulty in stemming the current, and the succeeding files crowding on them, a sort of animated dam was formed which had the effect of sending the current boiling between them; and the water, which was but little above the hips on the lower side, was dammed up nearly to the armpits on the upper. However all got over in safety except one man (Private James King) who, letting go the rope, was swept off by the current with arms and accoutrements, and never afterwards

[1] *i.e.* A wooded ravine or valley.

seen or heard of. The succeeding companies, not crowding so much, got over with less difficulty. After fording the river the Battalion marched about six miles, and then bivouacked near the Commissariat waggons. Yet this short march took them about four hours to accomplish: so much were they weakened by their late privations.

On the 20th they halted to rest; and to clean arms and accoutrements. In the afternoon there was a general parade; but it was of a motley crew. The clothing was some of it in rags; some patched with leather; some men had no shoes; some wore sandals made of raw hide and fastened with thongs. And those who had seen the smart Battalion three months before could scarcely have recognised it in the gaunt, unshaven, and ragged warriors on this parade.

On the 21st they marched about fourteen miles and joined the division in the general camp.

On the 25th the Battalion marched to King William's-town and arrived there on the following day.

On the 31st two companies, Captain Horsford's and (late) Gibson's, commanded by Lieutenant Hardinge,[1] crossed the Buffalo river and marched for Fort Peddie, being ordered to join the camp of the 6th Foot, to form a force under Lieutenant-Colonel Michel, the Head-quarters and remaining four companies of the Battalion continuing at King William's-town.

On February 4 the two detached companies marched to Tamaka; and on the next day, crossing the Keiskamma river at the Line drift, proceeded to Buckraal

On the 6th they started about four in the morning, and marched to the Fish river bush, a few miles to the right of Fort Peddie, where they arrived about ten and halted for breakfast. But just as the Riflemen were lighting their fires, an order was issued that the two companies were to skirmish through the bush; and if no enemy opposed them to skirmish on to Trumpeter's drift.[2] Leaving their untasted breakfasts, they dashed into the bush and made their way through it in extended order, until two in the afternoon, when they halted and breakfasted. And at three, falling in again, proceeded through the bush till they emerged from it on the

[1] Lieutenant-Colonel Henry Hardinge, retired.

[2] *i.e.* A ford.

Graham's-town road about a mile from the great Fish river; to which they advanced, and forded it, the water reaching to the middle, just at sun-set After this hard day's work they marched into the barrack built on the bank of the river; and were hospitably received by a detachment of the 91st which then occupied it.

A private, who had been missing when they fell in after breakfast, made his appearance here about eleven at night; and his arrival unharmed was a sufficient proof that no Kaffirs were lurking in the bush. On February 7 these two companies marched to Fort Peddie.

On February 1 the Head-quarters consisting of four companies had marched from the Kei river to King William's-town, where they encamped on the 3rd, forming part of the 2nd Division, of which Lieutenant-Colonel George Buller, who had arrived from England, assumed the command. But the Battalion was broken up into numerous detachments on the frontier for the purposes of patrols and escorts

On the 9th one of the companies at Fort Peddie under the command of Lieutenant Hardinge marched to Newton Dale (leaving Horsford's company at Fort Peddie). A few days after their arrival there an officer of the Cape Town volunteers applied for a patrol to pursue Kaffirs, who, eluding the vigilance of the troops on the frontier, had driven off almost all the cattle to within a few miles of Graham's-town. He stated that he had tracked them to the Fish river, where he had left his men, who were utterly unable to follow them further. A patrol of 2 sergeants and 40 men under Lieutenant Oxenden[1] was immediately turned out; and after a quick march of three hours came up with the Kaffirs in the bush. They were about seventy in number, and were broiling the flesh of one of the cattle, which they had just killed, over their fires; some were sitting on the ground smoking; and all had their wallets, or leathern bags, taken off and laid on the ground, while the stolen cattle were feeding in the dell. The Riflemen, creeping up, poured in a volley which killed seven and wounded eleven; the rest running into the bush escaped. The patrol, recapturing the cattle, marched back with them to Newton Dale, where they arrived about eleven at night, bring-

[1] Colonel Charles Vernon Oxenden died April 26, 1868.

ing with them the assegais and leathern bags of the Kaffirs. This was the first occasion on which the Riflemen and the Kaffirs were in such close quarters.

This company was employed until June 18 escorting supplies to the frontier as far as Fort Peddie It then proceeded to Line drift, where it had the duty of escorting supplies from that place to King William's-town. On September 9 it rejoined the Battalion.

On February 10 two companies under Captain Rooper marched for the river Temacha, where they arrived on the same day; and on March 20 proceeded to Fort Peddie.

On March 24 Horsford's company removed from Fort Peddie to the Goolah heights, where it was employed on patrol duty, until June 17 when it rejoined Head-quarters

On the 25th Rooper's company left Fort Peddie for Wesleyville arriving there on the 29th, on April 7 proceeded to Chalumna post, and on June 14 marched for Head-quarters at King William's-town where they rejoined on the following day.

On April 5 Macdonell's[1] company left Head-quarters at King William's-town for Mount Coke, arriving there on the same day; and returned to Head-quarters on September 14. On the 6th Murray's company marched from Fort Peddie on escort duty, and arrived at the Goolah heights on the Keiskamma on the 19th, whence it rejoined Head-quarters on September 14.

During the time these companies were employed on patrol duty, a private belonging to a party sent out in search of cattle, having lost his way in the bush, came near a kloof, in which he heard the voices of Kaffirs. Lying concealed he watched their movements. Some Kaffirs arrived with arms, which they handed to their companions, who concealed them in a ravine. The Rifleman, still contriving to escape observation, watched his opportunity and made his way back to the camp, and, on his report of what he had seen, a party of Cape Mounted Rifles were sent out to search for the concealed arms.

An attack on the Amatola mountains having been decided on, supplies of all kinds were collected at King William's-town On August 2, during a hurricane, a fire broke out which for some time threatened the destruction of the

[1] Major-General Alexander Macdonell, C.B

place and of the stores there collected. But by the exertions of the Battalion, the fire was got under and the greater part of the stores and ammunition saved from destruction. On this occasion Lieutenant-General Sir George Berkeley issued a General Order commending 'the coolness and judgment displayed by Lieutenant-Colonel Buller,' and 'the discipline and energy of the troops, by which a great calamity was averted;' and conveying to them 'his best thanks for their exertions.'

On September 17 the detached companies having all rejoined, the Battalion under command of Lieutenant-Colonel Buller marched from King William's-town towards the Amatola mountains, halting on that night on the Deba Flats, and on the 18th near Fort White. On the 20th the Battalion (with about 300 of the Burgher force) accompanied by fifty mules carrying provisions for six days and ammunition, marched to Fort Cox, situated on a high projection over the Keiskamma river, which winds round its base; and arriving there at eight o'clock in the evening, bivouacked for the night.

Before daybreak on the 21st the Battalion marched; and after fording the Keiskamma, without opposition or loss, though not without difficulty, advanced through a dense wood to the valley of the Amatola, and encamped at the head of the valley. During this march no attack was made by the Kaffirs, who retreated as the Riflemen approached; and their huts were burned by the troops, the flames lighting up the valley on every side.

On this evening Colonel Buller's force was joined by another column under Colonel Campbell

On the morning of the 22nd at dawn the Battalion, as well as the other troops, marched to the Amatolas, and crossing their lofty and precipitous ridge, forded the Wolf river, a tributary of the Keiskamma, and ascended another ridge, where a third column under Colonel Somerset joined them. From this point Colonel Buller detached the Burgher force; and advanced with his Battalion to a valley on the Goolah river, where they encamped for the night, with the other two columns

On the 23rd the troops under Colonel Campbell having returned to the rear, those under Colonel Somerset and the

Riflemen under Colonel Buller moved into the Keiskamma basin; and Colonel Somerset's division having soon afterwards marched to the great Kei river, the Battalion remained in the Keiskamma basin, constantly engaged in active pursuit of the Kaffirs who were starved out and everywhere driven out.

The nature of the ground Sandilli and his people occupied, a deep valley near Wolf river, rendered it unapproachable by cavalry, but was exactly suited to the operations of Riflemen. And by their constant patrols, acting from camps well stored with provisions, Sandilli was completely foiled; his cattle destroyed or scattered; his followers driven away; and he himself hunted from place to place. And the result of these operations[1] was that Sandilli the Gaika chief, the principal leader of the Kaffirs, surrendered himself, with ten of his principal men, on October 19 to Colonel Buller After his capture Sandilli stated that on October 12 he had been nearly made a prisoner by a patrol of the Regiment. They lost their way in skirmishing in the bush, and by this chance he escaped. He admitted that he must otherwise have been taken or killed.

This terminated that campaign, and the four companies, Head-quarters of the Battalion, were afterwards kept unoccupied in the Keiskamma basin, though perfectly efficient for the field. While on the Great Kei river, where operations were still going on, their presence and assistance would have been of great consequence. However the arrival of Sir Harry Smith soon changed the face of affairs, and brought the war to a termination.

On November 14 Captain Murray's company marched from Fort Stokes to the Kei river and was employed in active operations against the Kaffirs.

On December 4 part of the Battalion under Colonel Buller left the Amatola mountains for King William's-town, and arrived the same day.

And on the 25th the remainder, under command of Captain Horsford, followed them to King William's-town.

[1] 'It was,' says an historian of the war, 'the useful green jackets, the untiring Rifle Brigade, who worried Sandilli out of his hiding-place among the mountains.' ('Five Years in Kaffirland,' ii. 240, 2nd edition.)

From hence the Battalion was again broken up into detachments; and a company under Lieutenant Cartwright marching from King William's-town on the 29th for Mount Coke, arrived there the same day and occupied it as a post.

On December 23 Sir Harry Smith was received at King William's-town, the band of the Battalion playing 'God save the Queen,' and 'See the Conquering Hero comes.' When the cheers of the assembled concourse subsided, Sir Harry rode up to the Battalion and complimented Colonel Buller on having the command of such a body of men, and the Riflemen on their advantage in having such a commander; and he noticed 'that bravery and endurance which they had displayed during the long and harassing warfare through which they had struggled.' [1]

The Depôt companies remained at Sheerness during the early part of this year, detaching one company to Canterbury on March 26.

On July 13 and 14 the Depôt companies, in two divisions removed from Sheerness to Bristol, the detachment from Canterbury joining them on the way at Maidstone; and arriving on the 15th and 16th they were quartered at Bristol during the remainder of the year.

The 2nd Battalion continued at Montreal till August 1847, on the 10th of which month the Head-quarter division marched to Lachine; and there embarking proceeded to Toronto. The left wing under Captain Wilkins on the 17th embarked at Lachine and proceeded to Kingston.

Sir D L. Gilmour, Colonel Commandant, having died at Rome on March 22, Major-General Sir Harry Smith, Bart., G C.B, succeeded him as Colonel Commandant of the 2nd Battalion, April 16, 1847.

The 1st Battalion were stationed at King William's-town, with one company detached at Fort Murray and another at Fort Waterloo, and no changes, beyond the occasional relief of these detachments, took place during the first half of the year 1848.

But scarcely had the war with the Kaffirs been brought

[1] 'Five Years in Kaffirland,' by Mrs Ward, ii. 329-30.

to a successful conclusion, when the Dutch Boers, not only within the colony but beyond the Orange river and in Natal, who, during the months of June and July had exhibited unmistakable symptoms of disaffection, broke out into open rebellion; and being headed by one Pretorius, a Dutch colonist of some influence and of considerable ability, assembled in great force beyond the Orange river

Sir Harry Smith at once took energetic measures to attack them. A force consisting of two companies, Captains Murray's and Hardinge's, of the 1st Battalion, two of the 45th, two of the 91st and two squadrons of the Cape Mounted Rifles, with two six-pounders, was ordered to proceed at once to Colesberg. Colonel Buller was in command of the whole force and Major Beckwith of the infantry. The two companies of Riflemen were made up to a strength of eighty rank and file each; each man carried sixty rounds of ammunition, and all were in light marching order, carrying their great coats or blankets, but not their knapsacks.

On August 4 the Riflemen marched; and, though delayed by the state of the river Buffalo, which was swollen by the rains, and which they passed by india-rubber pontoons, arrived on the 21st at Colesberg, within about twenty-one miles of the Orange river

On the next morning they continued their march and halted on the high-ground on the left bank of the Orange river, there between 250 and 300 yards broad, and then unfordable.

Several attempts were made unsuccessfully to construct a raft; but, at last, a hawser was thrown across and fastened to a tree on the opposite bank, and then a lighter rope was passed over, by which the india-rubber pontoon, which had been brought up by the Riflemen from King William's-town, was worked backwards and forwards. On the 23rd Captain Murray's company was carried over. And on the three following days the remainder, and the baggage were taken across; not without difficulty, on account of the steepness of the banks leading to the place of embarkation, and the rapidity of the current. The embarkation was superintended by Colonel Buller; the disembarkation by Major Beckwith. However by sunset on the 26th the whole force was conveyed across, and encamped on the right bank of the river.

On the 27th the troops marched at daylight, the Riflemen leading the infantry (the Cape Corps being in advance), and after a march of about twenty miles, encamped on the plains near Phillipolis, at Benlois Hoek.[1]

On the 28th, marching at daybreak, the Riflemen encountered swarms of grey locusts which actually obscured the light of the sun. They proceeded past Phillipolis, a village of the Griqua Kaffirs, and after a march of about twenty miles encamped for the night.

On the 29th they continued their march at dawn; and after proceeding about ten miles, halted at some deserted farm-houses to breakfast. These were situated on the slope of a hill overlooking an extensive plain, called the Boemplaats, which extending about twelve miles was terminated by a range of low, rocky hills, rising one above another in height. Those on the right projected into the plain. Through these hills the road or track wound; and on them the Boers, estimated at about 2,500 or 3,000 in number, had taken up their position, adding to its natural strength a kind of breastwork of piled stones. Had it been defended by disciplined troops, under a competent leader, it would have been if not impregnable, at least not to be forced without most serious loss. While the Riflemen were at breakfast the tidings reached them that they were soon to meet their enemy; and when breakfast was over, rifles were looked to, and packets of cartridges loosened As soon as they fell in, Sir Harry Smith addressed them. No one could do so, on such an occasion, with more authority and experience; for he had fought in their ranks (or, while on the Staff, at their side) from Monte Video to Waterloo, in the Peninsula, in America, in Holland, in Belgium. He reminded them of the glorious deeds there done, ending an inspiriting address by declaring that he would drive the arch-rebel Pretorius and his followers like rats from those hills. He was answered by such a cheer as Riflemen can give to an old Rifleman who leads them into the fight.

Resuming their advance about eleven o'clock they arrived at the foot of the hills between one and two P.M. Colonel Buller then ordered the Cape Corps to advance and to endea-

[1] Hoek, i.e. an inlet from a plain to high land, and from which there is no outlet.

vour to turn the position in front and by both its flanks. But the Boers receiving them with a heavy fire, and some mistake having occurred in executing the order, they retired, and cleared the front for the Riflemen, who in extended order advanced and drove the enemy at the point of the sword from the first, and through the second range of heights; and kept up a galling fire on them, as they retreated to the third and highest crest. Here they rallied their whole force, and delivered a telling fire, under which men and officers fell fast. But nothing could stand the dash of the Riflemen; this last position was carried; and at the end of two hours' hard fighting, the Boers fled after a short attempt at resistance behind the walls of a kraal.[1]

Then the troops were formed at quarter distance behind the guns, which opened with grape and shrapnel, on the flying enemy; delivering their fire; limbering up and advancing to the front; then firing again. Thus the pursuit was continued for about eleven miles; until from sheer inability to proceed further the troops halted at Culverfontein for the night.

The loss of the Riflemen in this action was severe. Colonel Buller was severely wounded, and his horse was killed under him; Captain Murray and 6 rank and file were killed or died of their wounds; Captain Hardinge and 8 rank and file were wounded, and Lieutenant and Adjutant Julius Glyn[2] had his horse killed under him.

Murray was leading his company when he was hit in the shoulder and his arm was shattered Glyn, who was near him, ordered some men to take him to the rear; but before he could dismount, another shot struck him, which passed through the body and injured the spine. He lived till about midnight; and was buried under a peach-tree at Boemplaats. Sir Harry Smith in communicating his death to his father, Major-General the Honourable Sir Henry Murray, says that 'he proved himself a most gallant officer; his loss deeply regretted by the men of his company.'

In this letter Sir Harry Smith observes that 'this outburst of rebels has cost as smart an affair as I ever witnessed.' Yet he had witnessed many; and some of them very smart

[1] *i.e.* An enclosure, generally for cattle.

[2] Major-General Glyn, C B.

affairs. 'Your son,' he continues, 'led an attack as bold as it was successful, under a storm of fire, in a difficult position, but fell an honour to his father and to his country.'[1]

The wounded were left at Boemplaats, except Colonel Buller, who was conveyed with the troops

About ten o'clock at night the tents arrived and the Battalion encamped. It had marched more than twenty-six miles; had fought a sharp action; and followed the enemy with a most active pursuit.

But they were not long to rest. They paraded at one o'clock on the morning of the 30th and by two o'clock leaving blankets, tents and all that could impede rapidity of march behind them, were again following up the Boers. Both the companies of Riflemen were now commanded by 2nd Lieutenants, the Hon. Henry Clifford[2] and W. W. Knight, and they led the column as an advanced guard.

About daylight they arrived at a place called Welman's Pass, where it was thought that the enemy might make a stand. Accordingly the Riflemen were extended, and skirmished over the hills on each side, which commanded the defile. However nothing was seen of the Boers, who were in fact utterly disorganised and demoralised by their defeat at Boemplaats, and who never attempted to rally.

The Riflemen continued their march and halted for the night at a Dutch farm-house, named Bethany.

Pursuing their march they arrived at Bloem-fontein on September 2; and halted there until the 4th. During this time a General Court Martial was held to try some rebel Boers, and an English deserter from the 45th, who had acted as a leader of the revolted Dutch, and they were sentenced to death. On the 4th (the sentence having been executed) the Riflemen marched at daybreak for Weinberg, a settlement on the Vial river, and arrived there on the 7th. Here Sir Harry Smith received the unconditional submission of the rebellious Dutch; and fell back to Bloem-fontein on September 14 The Governor having directed a field-work to be erected here the Riflemen worked at it, until its completion, when it was garrisoned by the 45th and 91st detachments;

[1] 'Annual Register,' xc 248.

[2] Colonel the Hon. H H. Clifford, C.B , V C

and the Riflemen marched for King William's-town on October 16.

In the expedition thus concluded, the Riflemen had marched between 1,100 and 1,200 miles; had crossed several difficult rivers with insufficient means of transit, had worn their clothing to shreds and their shoes off their feet. General Orders highly laudatory of the conduct of the officers and men were issued by Sir Harry Smith, both on August 30, immediately after the fight at Boemplaats, and also on his leaving the troops at Bloem-fontein on September 15. Colonel Buller was appointed Companion of the Bath, and Major Beckwith received the brevet rank of Lieutenant-Colonel.

During the time the Battalion was near King William's-town the men were employed in building 'They built a town, they built barracks, they built houses for their officers, some of "wattle-and-daub," some of bricks, and roofed with various materials They also made an aqueduct some three or four miles long to supply the camp with water, and for the purpose of irrigation. When we left they had more than half built permanent barracks of stone. That was all done by one battalion, without neglecting any of its military duties. . . . We had a daily parade, inspected arms, &c, and saw that the men were in proper order, and then dismissed them to their working parties'[1]

The Service companies being reunited at King William's town furnished a detachment on October 18, to Fort Murray; and another, of a company, on November 3, to Forts Grey and Glamorgan.

The Depôt companies continued at Bristol during the whole of this year, the only change being that a subaltern's detachment proceeded to Trowbridge on May 10 and rejoined the Depôt at Bristol on July 6.

No change took place in the quarters of the 2nd Battalion during the year 1848, which remained with one wing, Head-quarters, at Toronto, and the other at Kingston: the Reserve Battalion companies being still at Quebec.

[1] Colonel Evelyn (formerly of the Rifle Brigade) in the 'Journal of the Royal United Service Institution,' vol xiv p. 103

The 1st Battalion continued in 1849 at King William's-town, without other change than the occasional relief of its detachments.

The Depôt companies were during the whole year stationary at Bristol. And on September 27 they furnished a guard of honour, consisting of a captain, 3 subalterns, 5 sergeants, 2 buglers, and 100 rank and file, to attend Her Majesty Queen Victoria, at the Gloucester Railway Station, on her return from Scotland.

No event worth recording occurred in the 2nd Battalion, which continued at Toronto and Kingston with its Reserve at Quebec, until November 20; when a detachment consisting of 1 subaltern, 3 sergeants, 2 buglers, and 80 rank and file proceeded from Toronto for Mina bay, under the command of Captain Cooper, with the object of quelling disturbances at the Bruce mines

The eventful history of this detachment cannot better be given than in the words of a letter addressed by Captain Cooper (now Sir Astley Paston Cooper, Bart) to the Assistant-Adjutant-General at Kingston :—

'Sault Ste. Marie, Hudson's bay Company's Fort,
'December 16, 1849

'Sir,—I have the honour to report for the information of the Major-General commanding, that bad weather and the lateness of the season, combined with various accidents and delays, having frustrated our efforts to make Mina bay, we have been obliged to return to the Sault Ste. Marie, where we have now been obliged to go into quarters for the winter. Our failure is however the less to be regretted as the ring-leaders in the affair have been captured, and all the Indians, to the best of my knowledge and belief, have left Mina bay, and returned to their homes for the winter.

'I stated in my last communication that the captain of the "Propeller" had engaged to be ready to start from the Sault river on the evening of Thursday, the 4th inst., but about four o'clock that afternoon a gale commenced that rendered it impossible for the boats to continue to take the freight on board, and eventually swamped a scow that we had engaged for the purpose. The wind did not abate sufficiently to allow us to assume our operations till the Friday following; and we completed the embarkation of men and stores on that day. Just however as we were about to start, a fresh delay occurred, arising from a dispute between the captain of the vessel and the engineer, who being the only one left at the Sault, felt himself at liberty to make his own terms, and who refused to go at all unless he got 237 dollars for his trip, paid in advance. The captain refused to give it him, and at one time it seemed very doubtful whether we should not be obliged to return again to the Hudson's bay Company's Fort. This settled, we started about seven P.M to a place about seven miles up the river, called Wood Dock, where we were to take in more wood, it having been found impossible to provide a sufficient quantity at the Sault. On arriving there we found that the ice had collected in such quantities in the bay that it was impossible to approach the "Propeller" to the wharf. After making a variety of attempts to cut through the ice, carry the boats on &c. to no purpose we were obliged to give it up for that night.

'The following morning we managed to land nearly the whole of the troops, by pulling them round the ice to a place where the wind and current had broken it up sufficiently to allow us to get through. Carrying the wood from the wharf to the boats and thence to the ship occupied about eight hours; and we did not get under weigh again until about four P M.

'During the whole of the time we had been thus delayed, the weather had been perfectly fair; but we had scarcely started when a wind sprang up, which gradually increased to such a height, that the funnel was bent, one of the stays gave way, the stove and everything else in the cabin was overturned, and the binnacle and compass upset and rolled about the deck.

'Not being able, from the rolling of the vessel, to put back the compass properly in its place, the helmsman was steering partly by guesswork, and we drifted about five points out of our course. At half-past eleven P.M. the ship struck hard on a point of land on the American shore, called White Fish point, the bottom happening fortunately to be sandy, and the sea right on, the captain got the foresail on her and allowed her to drive up into the shallow so far as she would, to obviate the heavy bumpings, to prevent her broaching to, receiving the seas on her broadside. The conduct of the men, when the ship struck, was most admirable, inasmuch as the general rocky nature of the coast along the shore of the Lake Superior was well known to everyone on board No one knew where we were , and White Fish point was perhaps the only place on Lake Superior where such an accident could have occurred without the vessel being instantaneously broken up. Had the men not obeyed the command to stand still, but had they rushed on deck, as the captain of the ship afterwards told me he fully expected they would have done, at least one half of them would have been washed overboard and drowned ; as the deck was as slippery as ice could make it, and there was no bulwark round it other than a slight open railing, scarcely a foot high. Both the captain and subordinate officers of the vessel afterwards expressed their astonishment at the coolness and discipline the soldiers displayed. We remained at White Fish point till about half-past three P.M. Monday without any apparent possibility of getting the ship off, occupying ourselves in the meantime with landing the freight for the purpose of lightening the vessel, and making what arrangement we could for passing the winter where we were. About that hour, however, by working the vessel back with all the steam the engine would bear, and rigging a derrick, they got us off again ; and about ten A M Tuesday, we again proceeded towards Mina Bay and had arrived to within eight miles of the place, when the wind shifted to the SW. and commenced blowing again with such violence, that they were obliged to put about and return to White Fish point for shelter. After remaining there till noon, Wednesday, and the weather not at all improving, the captain represented to me the impossibility of reaching the bay this fall.

'I then wrote to him requesting his opinion in writing ; his answer to which I enclose. We anchored in the Sault river on Wednesday evening, and I am now getting the men settled in quarters in the store-houses of the Hudson's bay Company's Fort ; and I trust that in a few days they will be made tolerably comfortable for the winter. From the time the men left Toronto till we returned to the Sault, they had never slept in a bed, or taken off their clothes; yet in despite of that, and of the cold and wet they have daily endured, we have no sickness whatever I am also happy to be able to inform you that the conduct of the detachment continues to be exemplary.

'I have the honour to be,
&c &c. &c.,
'A. P. COOPER.
'Capt Commanding detachment.'

On December 3, the left wing of the Battalion removed from Kingston and joined Head-quarters at Toronto.

In March 1850, the 1st Battalion being ordered home, were relieved on the frontier by the 6th Foot, and on April 2, three companies marched from King William's-town to Fort Glamorgan, there to await the arrival of H.M. steam-vessel 'Hermes' for conveyance to Table-bay.

And on May 20 the remaining three companies, with Head-quarters, marched from King William's-town to Fort Glamorgan, and arrived there on the next day.

On the departure of the Battalion from the frontier, a very complimentary District Order was issued by Colonel Mackinnon, commanding at King William's-town, thanking the officers, non-commissioned officers and men for their excellent conduct while under his command.

Free discharges having been offered to such of the men as desired to settle in South Africa, 165 non-commissioned officers and men availed themselves of them; and being paraded on April 30, were there and then handed their discharges by Lieutenant-Colonel Beckwith.

On May 25 the Head-quarters, with three companies, embarked at Fort Glamorgan, in surf-boats, and were conveyed on board the 'Hermes,' which started for Table-bay, at which place they disembarked on the 29th.

On the 31st they were inspected at Cape Town by Sir Harry Smith, previous to their embarkation for home, who took leave of his old Corps in the following characteristic General Order.

'Head-quarters, Cape Town, May 31, 1850

'The 1st Battalion Rifle Brigade will be held in readiness to embark for England on board the ship, "Duchess of Northumberland," having completed a colonial tour of ten years' service, throughout which it has maintained the character for discipline, bravery and interior economy which distinguished it during the eventful period of the Peninsular War, under His Grace the Duke of Wellington.

'At the Cape of Good Hope in the Kaffir War and in a rapid, long, and harassing march over the Orange river, for the suppression of rebellion, the Riflemen were ever as distinguished for good fellowship among their comrades of other regiments, as they were formidable to their foes. Colonel Mackinnon the Commandant of Kaffraria, thus reports of the Regiment:

'"Nothing can have been more satisfactory than the conduct of the Battalion ever since it has been in this district, and it has been most ably commanded by Lieutenant-Colonel Beckwith"

'In 1805 the Commander-in-Chief Sir H. Smith, joined this Battalion then commanded by a Colonel Sidney Beckwith, (the uncle of the present,) an officer of great military renown.

'He has served with it during the most eventful period of its career, and has never worn the Regimental uniform of any other corps. The veteran and truly commendable affection, which is thus created, leads His Excellency therefore fervently to hope for the future welfare and honour of the Regiment.

'"The true test of real excellence is not immediate success, but durable fame;" and Sir Harry Smith trusts, with all his heart, that this may ever be applicable to his old comrades of the Rifle Brigade.'

On June 6 the Head-quarter division embarked at Cape Town in the 'Duchess of Northumberland,' and sailed the same day; and after touching at St. Helena for water on the 19th, proceeded for England.

But the other division of 8 officers and 100 men of other ranks were still at East London, where they embarked in surf boats on June 10 and 11, and were conveyed on board the 'Hermes' They disembarked at Falk bay on the 17th, and proceeded to Cape Town, where they were quartered until July 11.

On that day they embarked on board the 'Himalaya,'[1] and sailed on the 12th for England.

We must now return to the movements of the Depôt companies which left Bristol in two divisions on April 8 and 11, and arrived at Brecon on the 9th and 11th.

They removed in three divisions from Brecon on June 17, 18 and 19, and proceeded to Canterbury, where they arrived on the 19th, 20th and 21st, and were there stationed until the arrival of the Service companies.

The first division of these disembarked at Gravesend on Sunday, August 11, and proceeded by railroad to Rochester, and marched into Brompton Barracks Chatham, and on the 13th marched to Canterbury, where they arrived the next day.

The second division did not reach Gravesend till September 23, when they disembarked, and marched to Canterbury, where they arrived on the 26th. Thus the whole Battalion was reunited; but owing to the free discharges given in Africa it was greatly below its strength; and recruiting was actively carried on and the staff and parties at the principal stations in England, and at Edinburgh, Glasgow, and Newry were directed, by order from the Horse Guards, to raise 160 men at once for the Battalion; yet up to the end of the year it had only succeeded in obtaining 114 recruits.

On December 30 and 31 the Battalion marched in two divisions from Canterbury to Dover, where they were quartered; Head-quarters with five companies in the Western heights, and five companies in the Castle.

By an order from the Horse Guards dated February 6, 1850, the Reserve Battalion of the 2nd Battalion was to be done away; and the 2nd Battalion and Reserve, of six companies each, were from April 1 to be absorbed into one Battalion of ten companies. The officers (1 Lieutenant-Colonel, 2 Captains, 2 First Lieutenants, 2 Second Lieutenants and an Adjutant), who thus became supernumerary, were retained *en second*, until vacancies occurred. Pursuant to this arrange-

[1] Not the steam Troop-ship of that name; but a sailing Barque.

ment the six companies which formed the Reserve Battalion left Quebec, where they had been stationed since their formation in August 1846, and proceeded to Kingston in two divisions, the first, consisting of three companies under Major Norcott, leaving Quebec on May 1, and arriving at Kingston on the 3rd; the remaining three companies leaving on the 8th, and arriving on the 11th.

The 2nd Battalion itself left Toronto, where it had been quartered since August 1847, in two divisions on May 22 and 24, arriving at Kingston on the following days respectively. Thus the Battalion and its Reserve were amalgamated; and at Kingston reunited into one Battalion.

CHAPTER IX.

DURING the year 1851, when the 1st Battalion was stationed at the Western heights, their Colonel-in-Chief, the Duke of Wellington, reviewed them for the last time. Arriving from Walmer in September, he saw the Battalion put through a field day by Colonel Buller.

The fresh outbreak of the Kaffirs and the accounts which reached England from the Cape having necessitated the despatch of reinforcements to that colony, the 1st Battalion which remained at Dover was, by letter from the Adjutant-General dated December 17, 1851, directed to be formed into Service and Depôt companies; and the former were desired to hold themselves in readiness for immediate service. Accordingly one Major (Horsford), 6 Captains, 6 First, and 6 Second Lieutenants, with the usual Staff, 30 sergeants, 24 corporals, 11 buglers and 614 privates were detailed for embarkation under the command of Colonel Buller; and were on December 29 inspected by Major-General Brown, Adjutant-General of the Forces, on the Western heights, who expressed his satisfaction at their appearance.

The 2nd Battalion remained during the whole of this year stationed at Kingston, Upper Canada.

On the morning of January 2, 1852, the Service companies of the 1st Battalion were conveyed, in three small steamers, on board H.M.S. 'Megæra;' which in the evening proceeded to, and anchored in the Downs.

Nothing could exceed the discomfort of this wretched ship. The men were crowded; but Buller had wished his whole Battalion to go out together; and, no doubt, eventually this saved many lives. For the fate of the 'Birkenhead,' which took out detachments of other regiments, and would probably have taken Riflemen had not all been pushed into the 'Megæra,' is well known.

The 'Megæra' steamed from the Downs on the morning of the 3rd and off Beachy Head and the back of the Isle of Wight encountered a heavy gale, which much damaged her. She caught fire twice, but it was each time happily extinguished, and on the 5th she put into Plymouth harbour utterly disabled.

Here intelligence reached the Riflemen of the disastrous fight of November 6, 1851, when Colonel Fordyce of the 74th was killed and his regiment severely handled by the Kaffirs. And the 'Megæra,' hardly refitted, was desired to put to sea immediately. Stores were incomplete; but the only reply to all such representations was the repetition, by telegraph, of the order 'Put to sea.'

So on January 7, at ten at night, the 'Megæra' again started; and arrived at Madeira on the 24th. After coaling, and taking in supplies here, she left on the 27th and arrived at Sierra Leone on February 6. She steamed from this at midnight on the 7th and after some severe gales, and being on fire again more than once, this unhappy ship at last reached Simon's bay on the night of March 24 having taken nearly two months to make the passage.

After coaling here, and landing women and children and six sick men, who were sent to Cape Town in charge of a sergeant, the 'Megæra' again put to sea on the 27th and anchored in Algoa bay on the 30th.

The Riflemen were immediately landed, by means of surf boats and the help of Fingoes, as they had been at the same place six years before As soon as they were ashore they marched by companies to the hill above Port Elizabeth where they were encamped; each company pitching tents for that following it, so that the men were at once under canvass as soon as they reached the ground. At the back of the camp was a sort of ravine, through which flowed a stream, in which the men washed everything, great-coats, clothing kits, in order to cleanse them from the smoke and dirt of the 'Megæra.' On April 2 about two in the afternoon, camp was struck, and the Battalion commenced its march for the frontier; halting that night at the Swart Kop river.

The next morning they resumed their march, the last three hours being under heavy rain, and encamped. On the

Coega river on the 4th they started at half-past four in the morning, and after marching about ten miles, halted for breakfast, and then continued their march, the intention being to cross Sunday river; but it was so swollen with the rains as to be impassable. On its bank they remained encamped therefore until the 8th On that day about noon the river was reported to be fordable, and the Battalion having passed it, and marched about two miles and a half encamped for the night at Commando's kraal.

On the 9th, starting very early, they halted for breakfast at Addo bush. On this day's march they passed a well where the Battalion had halted during a similar march in November 1846, and where the date, then carved by them on a post, was still to be seen; and at night encamped at Quagga Flats.

On the next day again marching very early, they advanced a good way over the flats, and then again continued to ascend; for the road for the whole march had been almost a constant rise, and after the usual halt for breakfast, and a further march, arrived at Sidbury and encamped on a hill-side.

On the 11th marching, as usual, about half-past four, they went forward about eleven miles through the Assegai bush, and halted for breakfast near a river of the same name; and marching on about seven miles further encamped near the Karraga river, which however was hid from the camp by a wooded declivity.

On the next day after the usual early march of about six miles, in which they crossed the river, after a fatiguing descent to it, and an equally fatiguing ascent on the opposite side of a ravine, they halted for breakfast in a spot covered with mimosa bushes, with fine grass between them, which had rather the appearance of an artificial lawn than of unreclaimed wilderness. Soon after starting again, they met such crowds of people coming out from Graham's-town to meet them, that they fancied themselves close to it; but after a toilsome march of six miles further, over a very rough road, they encamped in the Drostdy barracks.

During the two following days they halted, but on the 15th starting from Graham's-town about eleven, accompanied by numbers of the inhabitants, they marched to Botha's Hill, where they encamped for the night.

On the 16th marching about five, over the Ekka heights, they entered the Fish river bush, by a newly-cut path called the 'Queen's road.' Proceeding about five miles, on emerging from the bush, and passing over some flat country to Fort Brown, they crossed the Fish river by a wooden bridge, and proceeding about three miles further, they encamped about three o'clock near the Koonap, a tributary of the Fish river

On the next day they marched about six miles to their breakfast halt, on some very high ground; and after crossing the Koonap at a shallow ford, ascended the Koonap heights; and, after a short march, reached their camping ground at Liew fontein early and untired.

On the 18th starting at five, they had a long march to Mildenhall, where they breakfasted, and where three houses had recently been destroyed by the Kaffirs. After this halt crossing the Chumie river, and afterwards the Kat river by a shallow ford, they marched through the town of Fort Beaufort amidst the hearty welcomes of its inhabitants, and encamped on a plain on the other side of it.

Here they halted for three days in very inclement weather; the heavy rain on the 19th obliging the men to turn out at night to dig trenches round the tents, and to bale out the water which had flooded them

On arrival at Fort Beaufort the Battalion was placed in the 1st brigade of the division under Major-General Somerset. The brigade, which was commanded by Colonel Buller, was composed of detachments of the 74th, Cape Corps, and Artillery, with two six-pounders and rocket apparatus, and some Fingoe levies.

The Battalion, having been inspected by General Somerset on April 21, marched about half-past six on the morning of the 22nd for the Waterkloof, accompanied by eight of the Cape Corps, and a detachment of Artillery with a six-pounder, drawn by twelve oxen.

They halted for breakfast at Gilbert's farm 'Klu-klu,' which had been burnt by the Kaffirs. Resuming their march to Yellow-wood they encamped for the night on the Kroome river, where plenty of long grass afforded them excellent beds. The day's march had been very fatiguing, for though part of it was through a fine grassy country, and on a hard road, yet this had in places been broken up by mountain storms into gullies, sometimes resembling steep steps of stairs, and sometimes the loose *débris* of a stone quarry.

On the 23rd they started soon after 5, and after passing some ruined houses halted for breakfast at McMaster's canteen, which, like the buildings they had passed, bore evident marks of Kaffir depredation and destruction. After a rest of about two hours, they resumed their march towards the banks of the Koonap, and pitched their tents at a place called Haddon's post; but which the men called Stony camp, from the difficulty they experienced in driving in the tent pegs; near a thickly wooded ravine called Bushneck.

Hardly had the camp been pitched when a storm of wind, rain and hail, accompanied with thunder and lightning, came on, which threw tents to the ground, and obliged men and officers to turn out with shovels and mallets to dig trenches, and drive tent-pegs. And even after the violence of the storm abated, rain continued at intervals during the night. Kaffirs were seen at a distance on the hills near the camp.

On the 24th when they were preparing to advance, the conductor declared that the oxen could not go forward, consequently the Battalion halted for the day, Captain Glyn's company going out on patrol, and bringing in a horse, which was claimed by the Fingoes

On the 25th they started in a fog so thick that they lost their way in the first half-hour; and had to halt. Then resuming their march, they literally felt their way to the banks of the Koonap, which they crossed five times in the course of this day's march. They halted for breakfast at Nell's Farm, where one end of the house only was standing. On resuming their march, after twice crossing the Koonap, they ascended a hill of exceeding steepness, by a road formed by the dry and rocky course of a mountain torrent The advanced guard shot one Kaffir and made two women, mother and daughter, prisoners. They burnt some Kaffir huts also, but they were empty. On getting to the top the Riflemen were halted to get their breath. This hill forms one of the Winterberg Mountains, the Chumie range forming the opposite side of the Waterkloof. After a short halt they resumed their advance; and, after marching some distance, were halted in a pretty but irregular valley, where it was intended to camp. But it was found that the oxen with the tents and baggage had been unable to ascend the hill as fast as was expected; and consequently the Battalion was ordered to countermarch (an unwelcome order, after so fatiguing a march) and after descending again about a mile and a-half, encamped on some stony and uneven ground. A strong guard was formed round the camp, and the picquet were sent down the hill with the dinners of the men at the bottom, and to form a guard while they ate it. For one company was sent down the hill to bring up the waggons, and all were not up till 2 o'clock in the morning On the next day the Battalion marched forward to a place called Bear's farm, about 5 miles from the Waterkloof valley To reach this it was necessary to go down a road almost as steep as that ascending the opposite side of the ridge from the Bushneck valley, and equal difficulties were experienced in getting the baggage forward.

On April 29 Captains Somerset's,[1] Lord Alexander Russell's[2] and Woodford's companies (with some Fingoes, and Cape Corps) fell in at 4 in the morning, and were ordered to move forward in perfect silence Somerset with a 6-pounder went round by a road; while the remaining two companies advanced over most rough and broken ground to the edge of the Waterkloof, which, in consequence of its being perfectly dark, rendered the march extremely difficult. Daylight was just appearing when they caught sight of some Kaffir fires. Colonel Buller passed the word to extend, and the two companies advanced. The Kaffir 'Whoop' was soon heard, and firing commenced when they were about 200 yards from the first kraal. From this the Kaffirs fled to the bush and the rocks, taking cover behind the rocks as the Riflemen came on. They set fire to the huts, and still advancing and searching every bush and hiding place, emerged on the plain beyond Somerset's company with the gun now joined them on the left. They soon came in sight of another kraal, and the gun was unlimbered and a shell thrown into it. The Riflemen still advanced; and the

[1] Major-General Edward Arthur Somerset, C.B.
[2] Major General Lord Alexander Gordon Russell.

Kaffirs kept up a brisk fire from the bush, and from a hill just beyond. Here the three companies made a halt, and eventually returned to camp, as the force was not strong enough to attempt the hill, where the Kaffirs greatly outnumbered them.

In this patrol, Lieutenant Godfrey and 3 men were wounded. The place was called Mundell's Krantz, and was in fact the place where Colonel Fordyce had been killed.

The three companies reached the camp about 2 o'clock after a march of 18 miles. Kaffirs hovered on their rear during their march back; but did not venture within range.

On May 3 another patrol, consisting of four companies started at half-past two A.M., as some Kaffirs were said to be in Engelbrecht's kloof. Of these one company joined a party of the 74th Regiment at Post Retief, and starting thence at 3 in the afternoon marched about 12 miles along the Koonap, which they forded seven times, and occupied for the night a ruined farm-house which they reached at dark. On the next morning they marched about 5, again crossing several streams, some of them very dangerous from the slippery state of the rocks, in falling from which one Rifleman dislocated his knee. At 9 o'clock they fell in with the remaining companies, which were posted on a hill in front of them; but the scouts came in with intelligence that the Kaffirs had all left the kloof, and the patrol returned to the camp at Bear's farm.

On the 5th one company proceeded with a party of the 74th as a covering party to protect those engaged in road-making in the Blinkwater. The scouts reported traces of cattle near Bushneck, and on the 6th Captains Rooper's and Woodford's companies, accompanied by a party of the Cape Corps and some Fingoes, started at 4 A.M. under command of Major Horsford, and after marching round by the hills and destroying many huts so hurriedly left by the Kaffirs that they found them full of necklaces, and various utensils, and even one young child left behind, they returned to camp about 2 o'clock.

On the 8th a patrol under command of Colonel Buller, accompanied by two guns, proceeded early to the hills at the mouth of the Waterkloof. However the Kaffirs, though occupying it in great strength, would not show themselves. And after firing about twenty rounds from the guns into the kloof, the patrol returned to camp It seemed that the Kaffirs by watching were aware of every movement made by the Riflemen, and so avoided an attack But it was thought that these frequent patrols harassed them as much as if they had been brought to an actual engagement.

On the 17th four companies, Lord Alexander Russell's, Woodford's, Hardinge's and Glyn's, moved before daylight for the Waterkloof; and arriving near the scene of the skirmish on April 29, burned several huts and captured three horses, several shots being fired from the kloof. No enemy then appeared. But as the patrol began to retire they showed themselves in all directions. Several men had been left in ambush near the burning huts; and they were soon busily engaged. The patrol was extended, and retired by companies, each company facing the enemy in turn, while the rest moved to the rear. As soon as they left a position, or passed over rising ground, it was taken possession of by the enemy who kept up a smart fire from their large elephant pieces Happily their aim was generally too high, but three of the Riflemen were wounded. They were about four hours engaged; and retired fighting over about 5 miles. Twice they halted and endeavoured to bring the Kaffirs to close quarters; but they declined meeting them on the plain.

The Battalion remained at Bear's farm without any important occurrence until the 27th, when three companies, Rooper's, Somerset's and Glyn's, proceeded on patrol at 5 A.M. under the command of Major Horsford, for Ingilby's farm; and discovered numerous traces of cattle but did not come upon any Kaffirs.

On the 29th a patrol of 70 men with Lieutenants Elliot[1] and Coote Buller, proceeded to Ingilby's farm, in order to ascertain whether the spoor[2] observed on the 27th was caused by the Kaffirs grazing their cattle by night. They had nearly reached the place where they were to make this examination, when a sharp fire opened from an unseen enemy, by which four men were wounded. The fire was immediately

[1] Lieutenant-Colonel the Hon Gilbert Elliot, d e l May 25, 1865

[2] i e track

returned into the bush, but its effect could not be ascertained, and the patrol returned to camp.

On the evening of the 30th the Battalion paraded for patrol at tattoo, it being important to ascertain whether the Kaffirs did, as reported by the scouts, bring out their cattle to feed at night. Strict orders were given for perfect silence, no lights were to be struck or pipes lighted They marched about 8 miles, and then were ordered to be ready to fall in at three minutes' notice. About 5 A.M. they stood to their arms, extended, and advanced to the edge of the bush, where they again halted and lay down till daylight As soon as it appeared they dashed rapidly into the bush downhill to a valley. Two Kaffirs were seen, and both brought down by the Riflemen. They came on smouldering fires, and many traces of Kaffirs, but saw no more. The valley was well cultivated as a garden; and full of fruit, with which the men filled their haversacks. Having halted there for breakfast, they marched back to camp; where they arrived about 10 o'clock on the 31st, and were mustered as they stood, in their accoutrements.

On June 3, four companies, Lord Alexander Russell's, Woodford's, Hardinge's and Glyn's, paraded at 6 in the morning and marched towards the Waterkloof, in order to meet General Cathcart, and to accompany him on a reconnaissance to the Waterkloof and the Blinkwater. Having reached the place fronting the Kloof called the Horse-shoe, they piled arms and awaited the General. The Kaffirs were soon seen in motion in every direction, wondering probably what was intended by this demonstration by daylight, and they lit two large fires on the opposite side of the Kloof apparently as signals. On the General's arrival, accompanied by his Staff, some of the Cape Corps, and a troop of the 12th Lancers, they proceeded with him to examine the different parts of the Kloof to which the Riflemen had patrolled on former occasions. As they moved along the Kaffirs accompanied them, keeping within the edge of the Kloof They proceeded towards the Blinkwater, from whence the General went on to Post Retief, while the Riflemen returned to their camp, after a most fatiguing day's march, in consequence of the slipperiness of the grass, and the necessity of their keeping up with the mounted force. On the 4th it was seen that the Kaffirs had set fire to the grass round the camp; and watch had to be kept all night to see that it did not approach too close. On the morning of the 5th three parties were despatched to beat out the fire with bushes; which they did effectually owing to the shortness of the grass.

On the 8th two companies proceeded on a reconnaissance towards the Waterkloof, and returned without doing anything; but one man was killed.

On the 11th Lord Alexander Russell's, Woodford's and Hardinge's companies started at 4 in the morning in the direction of Bushneck; not proceeding by the usual road, but directly across country, up and down hills, some of them extremely steep, with large projecting rocks, which the men had to climb, and to slide down on the other side. Part of the march also was over the burnt grass, the dust from which was extremely annoying, and at times almost prevented their seeing anything. They marched fully 18 miles, not even halting for breakfast. They came on traces of Kaffirs, who as usual disappeared, unless surrounded before daylight.

On July 3 a patrol of Captain Somerset's company started at 5 A.M. and examined the valleys in the neighbourhood of the Waterkloof in search of cattle; but the sun rose before they had found them, and rendered their efforts unsuccessful.

An escort marched towards the Blinkwater on July 5 to deliver the guns to a party of the 91st and some of Lakeman's volunteers. As they were returning they saw some Kaffirs driving off a cow. The officer in charge would not allow the company to go, but gave permission for ten volunteers to attack them; who immediately doubled to cover. The Kaffirs observing the company did not see the detached party, who cut them off from the bush. There were three men and two women; who seemed so destitute and starved that it was not worth while to make them prisoners.

At midnight on the 6th a patrol left the camp, and after marching a considerable distance, were halted, divided into watches, and ordered to conceal themselves. The object was to intercept cattle, supposed to be on the move. But after lying down in concealment during a very cold morning, at sunrise they returned to camp without having effected their object.

On the 7th the camp at Bear's farm was struck, and the tents and baggage placed in the farm-yard under the charge of Captain Woodford's company The remainder paraded a little before midnight, with coats and blankets and three days' rations, which the men were recommended to cook before starting Soon after they moved off, and marching, in a cold sleet, by the southern heights of the Waterkloof, were joined by another division under General Cathcart[1] They then proceeded to the ridge separating the Waterkloof valley from Fuller's Hoek, and after firing shell, shot, and rockets into the bush, bivouacked on the night of the 8th at the head of the pass, after having been fourteen successive hours on the move. They had seen many Kaffirs, who kept close in cover, occasionally firing on our skirmishers. In this affair one Rifleman was killed, shot through the brain while taking aim over a rock. The weather during the time the Battalion was engaged on this reconnaissance was extremely inclement, rain, sleet and snow falling almost incessantly

During the absence of the Battalion the Kaffirs rushed out of the Kloof, and drove off seven oxen feeding near Bear's farm The company there immediately stood to their arms; but could not leave their position, as the Kaffirs appeared in number on the neighbouring hills. The waggoners were despatched to secure the oxen; and the Kaffirs at first retired. But seeing that they were only waggoners not soldiers, they returned and made off with their prize.

The Battalion returned about noon on the 9th and found the tents pitched and everything made ready for them by their comrades in charge. They were accompanied by two 12-pounders, with the men and horses.

On the morning of the 14th the Battalion finally left its camping-ground at Bear's farm, and proceeded to Mount-Misery, marching by the edge of the Waterkloof into which shells were occasionally dropped. The Riflemen had scarcely reached their position, when a waggoner came running in and informed them that his span[2] of oxen had been seized by the

[1] Lieutenant-General the Hon. G. Cathcart had succeeded Sir Harry Smith as Governor of the Cape.

[2] i e team.

Kaffirs. The cattle-guard which was in the act of mounting, set off at the double; the best runners taking the lead, and soon came up with the cattle, which they recovered, shooting one Kaffir

Here a standing camp was formed, and two redoubts were built, as a base from whence General Cathcart operated in the final attacks on the Kaffirs. On the morning of the 15th the outlying picket at the head of Fuller's Hoek had just lit their cooking fire at daybreak, when the fuel was knocked about by a ball from the bush Several more shots were fired ; but no mischief done And some men of the picquet, crawling into the bush, shot one Kaffir and took three horses

The Riflemen were engaged till the 23rd in assisting in building the redoubts, and strengthening the camp; which was placed on the ridge commanding and cutting the communication between Fuller's Hoek and the head of the Waterkloof.

On the 24th the Battalion started at half-past four in the morning accompanied by all the available force at Colonel Buller's command, leaving a party in charge of the forts. They marched in the direction of Mundell's Krantz, near which they burned a number of Kaffir huts, and captured several horses. Several shells were fired into the Kloof into which the Kaffirs had fled, and from which they kept up a smart fire by which two men of the Battalion were wounded, one dangerously, the other, the Colonel's orderly, shot in the face and neck. Sergeant Green had a very curious escape; the bullet passing behind his ball-bag, and bending the brasses of his waist-belt.

The General Order of which the following is an extract, was issued by General Cathcart on the next day:

'General Order No 59.

'Head-quarters, Fort Beaufort, July 25, 1852.

'3. The Commander of the Forces has received with much satisfaction Colonel Buller's report of his attack on the 24th inst. at daylight on the Kaffir kraals of the Waterkloof near Mundell's Krantz, which were destroyed, as well those above as those below the krantz [1]

'In this attack, which Colonel Buller conducted with much

[1] i.e. the upper rocky margin of a ravine

ability, a considerable loss of life was inflicted on the enemy, many of their arms and some ammunition destroyed in burning the huts, and twelve head of cattle and eight horses taken.

'Colonel Buller speaks in terms of marked praise of the manner in which Major Bedford, commanding the 60th rifles, and Major Horsford, Rifle Brigade, led their battalions, &c. . . .

(Signed) 'A. J CLOETE,
'Q. M. Gen.'

On their return to camp the Riflemen were warned, that, as they were to start on an expedition across the Kei river against Kreili, they were to take out of their knapsacks any article wanted for the road; and the knapsacks were to be conveyed in waggons to Fort Beaufort, to be kept in store till their return.

At daybreak on the 25th four companies under the command of Major Horsford started for Fort Beaufort, leaving two companies with Head-quarters to occupy and complete the fort.

Horsford's column, after bivouacking one night near the Blinkwater, reached Fort Beaufort, by a mountain road, on the 16th. The band, which had been stationary at Beaufort, met the Battalion about a mile from the fort; and the familiar strains of 'Ninety-five' greeted and enlivened the men after their fatiguing march They encamped on the same spot occupied by the Battalion in the war of 1847–9. And remained there till the 29th, when they marched, returning to and camping near the Blinkwater, where they were joined by the remainder of the forces for the Kei expedition.

On the 30th they marched at half-past six, and followed the windings of the Kei river for about twelve miles; and, after fording it, halted for breakfast about two o'clock. Resuming their march, they halted at Fort Armstrong where they encamped.

On the next day having but a short march of seven miles to accomplish, they did not start till after breakfast—and encamped for the night in an acacia grove about a mile from Eland's post. On August 1, the Riflemen having to escort the waggons, did not start till about eight, and after a march of four miles, halted at the foot of the Winterberg mountain. The ascent of this occupied the remainder of the day; and the road after reaching the summit being very circuitous, it was late before they reached their camping-ground.

Marching the next day about eight o'clock, they passed over an undulating plain, covered with burnt grass, and after a very fatiguing march, though not more than eight miles, encamped after dark at the Katsberg mountain. The place was so utterly devoid of wood, that the men were obliged to collect dry dung for the fires.

On the 3rd they marched about ten o'clock, and after a most fatiguing march, climbing and sliding down steep hills, reached their camping-ground about six. During this march twenty of the draught oxen were lost from fatigue and starvation.

The day following, marching early they crossed a sandy plain, and in the course of the march passed near some settlers' houses and encamped on a fine stream near Shiloh.

On the 5th starting about ten, and marching eight miles over a fine grassy plain bounded on each side by ridges of mountains. they encamped near the Klaas Smidts river, which they crossed. And on the next day, accomplishing a march of about twenty miles, encamped at Umvani. On the 7th after an easy day's march of about eight miles which they got over at a rapid pace they encamped for the night at Balotta. During this day the Riflemen could see from the high ground parties of burghers, levies, and waggons making by different roads for the general *rendezvous* of the expedition

On the 8th at an early hour the 'alarm' and 'assembly' were sounded; and in less than five minutes the Riflemen were all under arms, standing in front of the tents, and expecting the appearance of an enemy. It proved however only to be a trial by General Cathcart of in how short a time he could have his force under arms Horsford's party afterwards formed line, and after being inspected by the General, were dismissed and halted that day and the next.

On the next morning a march of about ten miles brought them to the Kei river, which they crossed at a very shallow place, the stony bed being in some parts exposed. They encamped at Sabella half a mile from the White Kei. The General here manifested his extreme regard for the Regiment, which continued till his death. Their tents were next to those of the Staff, and the Riflemen were specially attached to his person The General divided his forces into two columns, one under Colonel Michel, of the 6th Regiment; the other under Colonel Napier. Each consisted of one regiment of infantry, mounted burghers, and levies, Africandos, Dutch and English, native levies, Cape Corps and Lancers. These two columns were to patrol in Kreili's country The four companies of the Regiment were to hold the camp; to act as the General's body-guard; and to form escorts for the cavalry-patrols and cattle.

On the 14th an alarm was given from the outlying picquet that the Kaffirs were taking the cattle. The Riflemen were cleaning their belts, but before the bugler could sound the 'assembly' they had slipped on their belts, seized their rifles, and were off over the hill. It was a false alarm; a party of mounted Fingoes coming in from Balotta had fired off their pieces near where the cattle were grazing. On seeing the Riflemen, they turned tail and fled, and were hotly pursued by them. It was a fine chase, till Major Horsford, galloping forward, ascertained the real state of the case, and brought the Riflemen back to camp.

They continued in this camp without any material occurrence until the 20th; on which day two companies, Somerset's and Woodford's, started at four o'clock in the morning, carrying two days' rations, to cover a patrol of cavalry. They arrived about ten at Crouch's post, and halted in a large wood. As the cattle captured from the Kaffirs were brought in by the mounted parties, the Riflemen in parties of twelve or twenty taking them over, drove them to the camp, where they arrived about sundown. About 12,000 head of cattle were said to have been taken on this day.

On the 21st the tents were struck and these companies commenced their return march, in order to cross the Kei before the rains set in. The Riflemen on reaching the river were ordered to conceal themselves in ambush. About two o'clock they made a rapid dash back to the site of the camp.

in the expectation that they might come upon some Kaffirs. Some men were seen in the distance, who were immediately pursued by some of the Cape Corps who accompanied the Riflemen, while they took prisoners a few women who were foraging about the place where the tents had stood. However these were afterwards released; and the Riflemen, moving off, reached Balotta about dark. The next day the column halted, as a division of the captured cattle was made among the burghers and others. On the 23rd resuming their march about nine o'clock, after ascending the high ground from which they had observed the assembling forces on the 7th, leaving their old track to the right, they struck into a valley; and after passing over an undulating country encamped on the bank of the Swart Kei, having made a march of about twenty miles. The Riflemen on this march presented a curious appearance; many of them leading colts, calves or kids.

The following day they did not march till two o'clock in the afternoon, being detained by the difficulty of getting the waggons across the river After fording it, they ascended the steep range of the Windvogelberg. The Kaffirs still hung on their rear, occupying their camping grounds as soon as the Riflemen were out of range. They marched about eight miles, the latter part of it in torrents of rain; and encamped near the Windvogel river. On the 25th they marched at eight o'clock; and still ascending, moved forward about seven miles after reaching the top of the range of mountains, and encamped on the Thorn river. During these marches great difficulty was experienced in getting the waggons up the hills. On this night some of them did not reach the camping-ground till eleven o'clock, and as some of the Riflemen had to escort, and some to help forward, the oxen, these marches were most toilsome. After a halt on the 26th devoted to cleaning arms and accoutrements and mending clothing, they resumed their march on the 27th, and did not reach their camping-ground on the Klip-plaatz river till after dark. This day's march was partly over snow-covered ground; and the Kaffirs knowing where they would have to halt for water, had burned the herbage, so that fodder and wood were scarce. In consequence of these wants, they started at half-past five on the morning of the 28th and refording the Klip, passed through a mountain ravine, the Klipclowberg; and afterwards marched about four miles through a bog, and after fording the Mud river, halted for breakfast under Gaika's kop, in order to allow the oxen, who had had no food for two days, to graze. Resuming their march they passed over the range; and descending a most precipitous mountain-side about six miles in length, where the Riflemen had to hang on to the rear of the waggons to prevent their overturning, they encamped that night within about a mile and a half of Eland's post From hence, proceeding by the route by which they had advanced, and encamping at the same points, they reached Fort Beaufort on the 31st.

In the meanwhile the two companies and Head-quarters had left their standing camp at the Waterkloof on August 29, and had arrived at Fort Beaufort on the day following, where they occupied quarters. The four companies which formed part of the Kei expedition were encamped near the fort. These men had not shaved since they started; and their appearance and their patched and many-coloured garments contrasted strangely with the neat aspect and new clothing of the two Head-quarter companies On the 26th Colonel Buller had been appointed to succeed Major-General Somerset in command of the 1st Division of the army, so that the command of the Battalion devolved on Major Horsford

General Cathcart, commanding the forces, having decided on a general operation in order to clear the Waterkloof, four columns were appointed to move simultaneously from various points, and to converge to a common centre. In accordance with this arrangement the Battalion, having been re-equipped, was ready to take the field again on September 6; but the rains having rendered the rivers unfordable, they did not move until the 10th. On which day, starting early, they breakfasted at Klu-klu, and halted for the night at Yellow Wood. On the 11th they marched at five, and after halting for breakfast at McMaster's canteen, reached Haddon's post in the evening. At all these stations the houses were in ruins, the gardens devastated; and marks of the incursions of the Kaffirs everywhere visible.

On the morning of the 12th a strong patrol advanced into the Bushneck to select a spot for a camp; and returned to Haddon's post in about an hour, having shot the only Kaffir who was seen. On the 13th the Battalion marched at daylight to Nell's farm in the Bushneck, opposite the principal entrance to the Waterkloof. General Cathcart came to look at them on the march, and highly approved the appearance of the Battalion. One Kaffir and three women were made prisoners, and handed over to the Fingoe levies.

On the 14th an order was given that one company should always sleep fully accoutred, and ready to stand to their arms at a moment's notice. The remainder of the Battalion were engaged in building a fort. On the 15th the Battalion paraded two hours before daylight, with three days' rations, and moving up the Waterkloof reached Mundell's Krantz, a distance of about four miles, by daybreak. As soon as it was light, they entered the Kloof and commenced burning the huts and shooting the occupants. Some of the other troops were above, pouring rockets and shell into the Kloof, and the Riflemen picked off the Kaffirs, whom these missiles dislodged from their cover. About sixty Kaffir women, besides children, and some rebel Hottentots, were taken prisoners. These last were immediately hung. The Riflemen, pushing forward through the Kloof, met the 73rd, who had penetrated from the head. These, their companions in the former war, on first catching sight of the Riflemen from the top of a rock, set up a ringing cheer, which was heartily returned by the greenjackets. The troops on the Chumie and the adjoining heights took it up, and the whole Kloof re-echoed it. The columns had met in the centre, having penetrated from all points. But the Kloof was not taken yet; the various krantzes and gorges were to be searched.

Later in the day, two companies, Somerset's and Woodford's, accompanied by the Grenadier company of the 73rd, proceeded to clear a krantz. The troops on the opposite side of the Kloof could see the Kaffirs gathering on the top, and shouted in warning to our men. Colonel Eyre, in command of the party, desired the men to go slowly up, and to keep their wind till they were fired on; then to give a cheer and rush to the top. On a ledge about half-way up screened from below by trees, they found a village, which they immediately burned; and the ascending flames and smoke from these burning huts seriously incommoded them as they clambered up the remainder of the cliff When they got near the top firing commenced; and they dashed to the top amidst the cheers of the troops on the opposite heights The Kaffirs flew before them into the adjoining bush. Lieutenant Lindsay and four Riflemen pursued them, and had penetrated some distance into the bush, before they realised the weakness of their party, and the fact that they had lost their way. After wandering about for some time, they caught the sound of the bugle, and following its direction, they eventually rejoined the Battalion, which bivouacked that night in a small clump of trees on the Iron Rock

The 16th was occupied in searching for Kaffirs, most of the huts having been already burnt The Riflemen, guided by Fingoes, searched the bush and the caves up the Kloof and back again to their bivouack of the night before, which they did not reach till a late hour, and in heavy rain

The Battalion was off before daylight on the 17th, the men shivering with cold and wet. As they were passing along the edge of the Kloof they were informed that Macomo was in Fuller's Hoek; and they immediately started to the bush over Blakeway's farm. Troops surrounded every part of Fuller's Hoek which men could reach; and the Riflemen patrolled the ridges and Kaffir tracks in every direction; sometimes passing over ground so steep that it was difficult for them to keep their feet. Some huts were found securely concealed, which were immediately burnt. Though numerous traces of Macomo and his attendants were found, he himself was not unearthed. For it was impossible to search every foot of a kloof miles in extent, covered with dense bush, and which abounded with places of concealment. The Riflemen, much fatigued with this harassing work, bivouacked early in Harris' Kloof, and some cattle captured during the day were killed and served out to the Riflemen by Major Horsford's order.

On the 18th they started early, again taking the road to the Hoek; but heavy rain coming on, Colonel Eyre's intention of again searching it was defeated, the ground being soon so slippery that neither men nor horses could stand. He therefore dismissed the column, and the Riflemen turned homeward, passing over the Iron Rock and the lower part of the Waterkloof. It was a long way, and it took them six hours' quick marching to get over it There was a short halt; but the men's rations being exhausted, there was nothing to cook. The officers emptied their saddle-bags among the men; but this was insufficient. However Horsford sent on a Cape Corps man with an order to get the tents up, and as the Riflemen came in sight of their old camping-ground at Nell's farm they found their houses all standing

The Battalion remained in their camp on the 19th, but on the 20th four companies proceeded to the Waterkloof in which they encamped at Brown's farm at the foot of Mundell's Krantz; one company (Somerset's) proceeding to the top of the krantz, and Rooper's company remaining at Nell's farm, in occupation of the fort built there.

On the 22nd every available man started at two o'clock A.M. on a patrol to Stuart's Kloof, a Hottentot prisoner captured the day before being led in front by a halter as a guide. Reaching the kloof about sunrise, and perceiving smoke issuing from it, the Riflemen surrounded it and skirmished through it; but finding nothing but Hottentot women and children, returned to their camp at Brown's farm about two

Heavy and almost continuous rain prevented active operations for some days, and the Riflemen were engaged in building a fort near their camp, and in a very central position in the Waterkloof

But on the 30th, spies having reported that Macomo was in the Kroome hills, a patrol started soon after midnight; and after fording a river and ascending the hills, scoured the kloofs, but did not find any Kaffirs, and returned by the Bushneck to camp about noon

On October 4 a patrol proceeded to the Iron Rock; two companies going to the top of it, while the others extended at its foot. Two Kaffirs were shot; one an amazingly powerful man, quite six feet three in height.

On the 10th and following days the Battalion was employed, a company at a time, making roads through the

Waterkloof, and opening up communications between the forts lately erected. The men for this duty starting at day-break and working till sunset.

On the 14th the company left at Nell's farm captured several head of cattle, which were almost driven into their hands by the Kaffirs, who appeared to be ignorant that a party were there stationed.

On the 20th all the available men started at three A.M. over Mundell's Krantz, but were soon enveloped in a mist so thick that they could not see many yards on any side They were compelled to halt till it cleared off; when they perceived a party of the 91st and some of Lakeman's volunteers in a similar difficulty. They proceeded together to Post Retief, which they reached about two; and were ordered to draw four days' rations, and to be ready to start again at ten o'clock at night. Marching all night they reached, towards sunrise on the 21st, the very steep range of the Zoorberg mountains. The road was most difficult, and the ascent so sharp that many men fell out On reaching the summit the Riflemen were ordered to fall in by comrades and to lie down to rest. Afterwards the companies were despatched in different directions; some to skirmish through the bush; others to extend along its edge, keeping a good look-out for any Kaffirs who might bolt out of it. This sort of patrolling continued during the whole of the day and until late on the 22nd; the men having lain down in their ranks and snatched a very few hours' sleep. Towards that evening the companies assembled on one of the mountain ridges; and halted for a time to refresh the men, wearied and thirsty from having been the greater part of three days on the move. The Battalion then marched on, and bivouacked in the night in a position where they found plenty of wood and water.

On the 23rd, starting about four A.M., they proceeded, at a rapid pace and by the most direct route, to Mundell's Krantz, descended by the road made obliquely down the face of the krantz by Captain Somerset's company, and reached their home at Brown's farm in the afternoon.

The Battalion continued engaged in road-making and the usual duties of the camp till November 3; on which day Captain Somerset's company proceeded from Mundell's Krantz to Fort Beaufort, where it arrived on the following day; and on the 11th marched to Eland's post, and was there stationed.

On the 5th Captain Woodford's company marched for the Blinkwater, where it arrived on the following day; and having built huts, and entrenched the position, was there stationed.

On the 12th the Battalion, with the exception of these companies, marched to Fort Beaufort and occupied quarters.

On November 19 two companies, Lord Alexander Russell's and Captain Hardinge's, marched to the Chumie-neck and occupied that post

General Cathcart having determined to proceed with a force to the North-Eastern Frontier, to demand satisfaction from, or to punish, Moshesh, chief of the Basuto tribe, for his incursions and depredations on the settlers near the Orange river, had intended to take with him four companies of Riflemen; but the Kaffirs and Hottentots having shown themselves in force near Fort Beaufort, General Cathcart resolved to take one company only as a camp body-guard. Rooper's company was the first for duty; and as he had lately been appointed to an official situation in the colony, the command of it devolved on Lieutenant the Hon. Leicester Curzon.[1] They were ordered rather unexpectedly late in the evening of November 17, to march at daylight on the following morning. The rest of the troops had started about a week before under Colonel Eyre, and General Cathcart was to overtake them at Burghersdorp, about 160 miles from Fort Beaufort. The Riflemen therefore made forced marches, their orders being that they must camp at night with the General. The men's packs were however carried for them in mule-waggons.

Passing the Blinkwater, Fort Armstrong, Eland's post, Whittlesea, and Shiloh, they crossed the Brak river, and going through the rocky defile called Klaas Smidts Poort, and over an extensive plain, ascended the Stormberg mountains. After descending this lofty ridge and crossing the Stormberg Spruit,[2] a tributary of the Orange river, they arrived at

[1] Now Major-General the Hon. Leicester Smyth, C.B.

[2] *i.e.* a rill, a rivulet.

Burghersdorp, where the rest of the troops were assembled, on the 27th.

The whole force was inspected on the next day by the Commander-in-Chief, and divided into brigades, the Riflemen being attached to that under Major Pinckney of the 73rd, consisting of that regiment, the 43rd, and two guns. This was first in Colonel MacDuff's division; but on his being left behind at the Caledon river, was placed under the command of Colonel Eyre They marched at daybreak on the 30th, and after a long and fatiguing march of 20 miles, during which one of the Riflemen had a *coup-de-soleil*, reached their halting-place. On December 1 after another hot march they forded the Orange river without much difficulty; it being lower than it had been for many years. Yet the water reached almost to the middle, and the men were obliged to carry their pouches on their shoulders They pitched their tents in the plain a little beyond the river. They proceeded the next day over a desert plain to a place called Ranakin, and the day following forded the Caledon river at the Commissie drift, and encamped on the other side Here they remained until the 8th, when they marched about five A.M., and continuing their advance during the two following days, encamped on the evening of the 10th, after twenty miles' fatiguing march, at Sanna Spruits. Marching on the following morning through a country not quite so desert as that passed over in the last few days, they forded the narrow but rapid Lieuw river on the afternoon of the 12th, and encamped on the opposite side. On the 13th they proceeded to the Wesleyan Missionary Station of Platberg, and encamped on a fine grassy plain near it. They were now not far from Thaba Bossiou, the stronghold of Moshesh, situated on a lofty hill, very defensible, and considered by his people to be impregnable During the halt here, which continued until the 16th, Moshesh's two sons, and afterwards the chief himself, visited the camp. General Cathcart named as his *ultimatum* that Moshesh should deliver 10,000 head of cattle within three days, reckoning from the 16th, as a compensation for the depredations he had committed. On the 16th the General reviewed the whole force at six o'clock in the morning; which, after marching past, was put through various evolutions: no doubt as a demonstration to overawe Moshesh.

On the afternoon of the 19th, the last of the three days, a herd of cattle were brought into camp by an escort of Basuto horsemen, under the command of one of Moshesh's sons. On their being counted and found to number only 3,500, this Prince was desired by General Cathcart to inform his father that, unless the remainder were delivered the next morning, he would come and seize them. No more cattle appearing, Cathcart, to show that he was in earnest, ordered Eyre, with the cavalry, two guns and a brigade of infantry, with the Riflemen to move forward on the 19th and form a flying camp on the Caledon river. This demonstration being unheeded, Eyre received orders to advance at dawn, to find his way across the mountain of Berea, and, having swept the plateau at the top, to join Cathcart, who with some other troops proceeded round the base of the mountain by its Southern and Western sides. About three therefore, on the morning of the 20th, Eyre advanced, sending forward the light company of the 73rd and the Riflemen When they had marched about four miles they saw a great number of Kaffirs on the mountain on their right. This hill stands up isolated in a plain, and its sides are steep and craggy. Eyre ordered the light company of the 73rd under Lieutenant Gawler to mount the hill, and halted the Riflemen. Then after a brief interval, he ordered Curzon to lead them on, to get to the top, bring his right shoulders forward, and take the cattle Thus the Riflemen were in echelon on the left of the company of the 73rd. The ascent was desperately steep, and in parts almost impracticable; but the Riflemen pushed on They had not advanced far when the Kaffirs gave them a volley, which the Riflemen avoided by lying down flat on the ground Again they pushed on, seeking cover among the rocks which dotted the side of the mountain. While in this cover one of them, armed with the Lancaster rifle, brought down a Kaffir as he was taking deliberate aim at some of the Riflemen, who were blown and could not climb up the steep mountain-side as fast as their comrades. Three more Kaffirs were brought down before the top was gained, without one Rifleman being hit. On reaching the summit, a table-land of two or three square

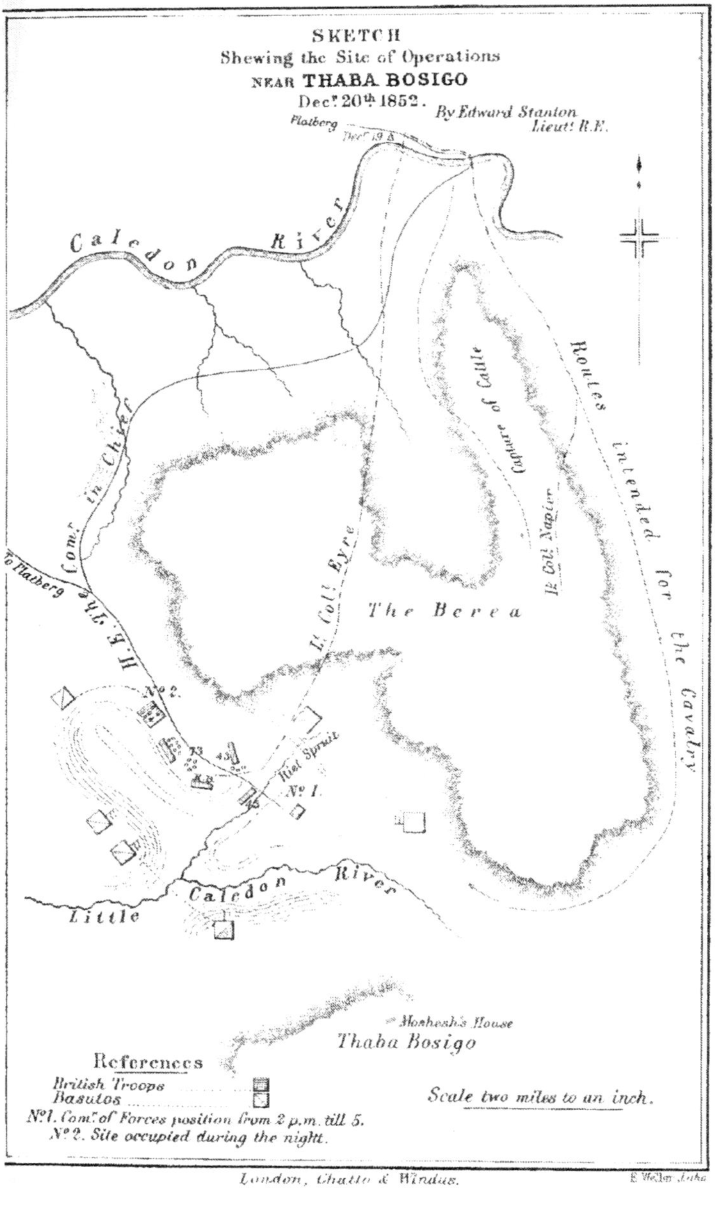

London, Chatto & Windus.

miles, they found the 73rd company on their right; and on their advancing together the Kaffirs bolted, a number of them being killed by the fire of the Riflemen, as they crossed their front at about sixty yards. But as Curzon and Gawler found themselves separated from the main body, they moved forward in search of it, keeping together for mutual support. For they were surrounded by hordes of mounted Basutos, who hovered near, appearing and disappearing, and watching for any straggling or irregularity in their formation, which might give them a chance to charge. These were well mounted, organised, and armed with assegais and elephant guns. And after attempting to terrify the little band they almost encompassed, with yells and pretended charges, they dismounted and fought on foot. They were repulsed however, and driven off the plateau, and Curzon and his Riflemen joined the main body in the afternoon, to their great relief and satisfaction: a satisfaction much enhanced when Eyre came up to them, and told them that they had done their work well. But they had scarcely joined the rest of Eyre's division, when he was obliged to descend the further side of the mountain with his whole force (abandoning 30,000 head of cattle which he had driven into a corner whence they could not escape), in order to assist General Cathcart, who had gravely compromised himself. The junction with Cathcart's force was effected about five in the afternoon; and the weary Riflemen thought they were now to halt for the night, for they had been fighting and without food for twelve hours. Far from it. They were charged with great fury by about 7,000 mounted Basutos; they had to fight retreating, and were in a critical position till between eight and nine at night, when a round of canister at point-blank range from two guns under Captain Stapylton Robinson, Royal Artillery, effectually checked the Basutos who were pressing on them, and who left the field. The Riflemen bivouacked on the ground where they then halted; Eyre telling them that, if attacked they must fight to the death there, as he neither could nor would retreat further. However they were left to their repose; much needed and well earned after being under arms about eighteen hours, and fighting during most of them.

In this affair the Rifle company which numbered 90, lost

three men; Privates Boffin and Case, who were killed, and Acting-Corporal Howard who died of his wounds on the next day. Lieutenant H. G. Lindsay behaved with great gallantry; and three Riflemen particularly distinguished themselves: Acting-Corporal Bateman and Privates Ricketts and W. Hayward.

Colonel Eyre in his despatch dated 'Camp Platberg, December 28, 1852,' says, writing of Lieutenant Gawler and Lieutenant the Hon. L. Curzon, 'These two young and promising officers led their companies in the most spirited manner up ground all but inaccessible, though opposed and immediately fired upon by the enemy above. Covering themselves as they advanced, they reached the summit with little loss, and drove the enemy before them in good style.'

And he adds 'I beg to return my thanks to' (among others) 'Lieutenant the Hon L. Curzon commanding a detachment of the Rifle Brigade.' And in the General Order issued by Sir George Cathcart on December 22, 'The noble conduct of the company under Lieutenant the Hon. Leicester Curzon' is specially mentioned.

'Company No 9 Letter I,' writes General Smyth, 'always looked upon Berea as *the* day of their life; and were not a little proud of the way Sir W. Eyre wrote of them and spoke of them. For he was a man who worked hard and exacted hard work; and soldiers had reason to exult when they received his praise.'[1]

In the course of the night a flag of truce arrived, bearing a letter of submission written by Moshesh, and suing for peace.

The object of the expedition being thus fully attained, the Riflemen after a few days' halt, began their downward march and reached Head-quarters at Fort Beaufort on January 21, 1853.

[1] Letter of January 17, 1875 For the account of the affair at Berea, I am indebted to Major-General the Hon Leicester Smyth, with some information gathered from Captain W. R. King's 'Campaigning in Kaffir-Land,' and from the 'Correspondence of Lieutenant-General the Hon. Sir George Cathcart, K.C.B.,' published (after his death) in 1856 And a remarkable letter of Sir William Eyre which appeared in the 'Morning Herald' of October 23, 1856 (to which my attention was kindly drawn by General Smyth), commenting on some statements in the 'Cathcart Correspondence' as to the action at Berea, has also afforded me important information.

On the embarkation of the Service companies, the Depôt companies of the 1st Battalion had been moved to Walmer, where they arrived on January 1, 1852. During the time they were there, the Colonel-in-Chief, the Duke of Wellington, when at his adjacent residence, Walmer Castle, used frequently to come into the barrack square with his grandchildren. These were his last visits, for he died there on September 14. From that day until November 10 a party consisting of 1 officer, 2 sergeants, 2 corporals, a bugler and 36 Riflemen, was daily furnished by the Depôt to guard his honoured remains at Walmer Castle. At nine o'clock on the night of November 10 their great Chief was removed to London; and on that occasion the whole Depôt escorted his body to the Railway station at Deal by torchlight.

The Depôt companies remained at Walmer during the rest of this year.

In May the 2nd Battalion left Kingston and proceeded in steam vessels to Quebec; where they embarked on June 1 on board H M S 'Simoom;' and starting for England on the 3rd arrived at Portsmouth on the 26th. On disembarkation they moved by Railway to Canterbury and occupied barracks.

Soon after their arrival there the Battalion was inspected (on July 13) by their former Lieutenant-Colonel, Sir George Brown, then Adjutant-General of the Forces.

On November 17 they proceeded to London in order to be present at the funeral of the Colonel-in-Chief, the Duke of Wellington, and were billeted at Chelsea. On the 18th they headed the funeral procession from the Horse Guards to St. Paul's.[1] And the following day they returned to their quarters at Canterbury.

Field Marshal His Royal Highness, Albert, Prince Consort, succeeded the Duke of Wellington as Colonel-in-Chief on September 23.

No change took place in the stations of the 1st Battalion until June 13, 1853, when Captain Glyn's company, under

[1] A full-page engraving of the Battalion marching along Piccadilly is in the 'Illustrated London News,' vol. xxi. p. 477.

the command of Lieutenant the Hon. H. Clifford, marched from Fort Beaufort to the Blinkwater post; relieving Captain Woodford's company which joined the Head-quarters on the same day.

On June 29, Captain Rooper's company marched from Fort Beaufort to the Chumie-neck; relieving Captain Hardinge's company, which left the Chumie on the next day and joined Head-quarters.

On October 8 the Battalion having received orders to be concentrated previous to returning to England, Captains Rooper's, Somerset's, Lord Alexander Russell's, and Glyn's companies came in from their several detachments on the 10th, 11th and 12th, and joined Head-quarters at Fort Beaufort.

Previous to the Battalion quitting this Station the following General Order was issued.

'General Order, No 238 'Head Quarters, Graham's-town.
'October 10, 1853.

'1. The Rifle Brigade, having been ordered to return to England, will march to Port Elizabeth for embarkation on board H.M. Steam Troopship 'Simoom,' under such arrangement as will be made by the Deputy Quarter-Master General.

'2. The departure of this distinguished Corps from the command after their valuable services which contributed so materially to the successful termination of the recent war, calls forth the Commander of the forces' warmest acknowledgments The uniform excellent conduct and high discipline of the Corps in quarters have been only equalled by their gallantry in the field.

'3. To Colonel Buller, C.B., who relinquishes the command of the 1st Division, and his appointment of Colonel on the Staff, in order to proceed with his Corps, His Excellency is much indebted for the able, zealous, and soldier-like manner in which he has conducted the command held by him.

'(Signed) A. J. CLOETE
'Colonel, Deputy Quarter-Master General.'

Accompanied by a large assemblage of the inhabitants of

Fort Beaufort, and amidst the expression of their best wishes, the Battalion, under the command of Lieutenant-Colonel Horsford, started on the 20th and encamped the same day at the Koonap river. On the 21st they forded the Koonap, and proceeded to Fingoe Pole. The next day they encamped on Graham's-town Flats within about three miles of that place. On the 22nd they halted, it being Sunday. The day following, passing through Graham's-town they encamped on the Karrega river. On the 24th, passing Sidbury they reached Quagga Flats. The next day, as it had been raining all night, they pushed on to cross the Sunday river. It was much swollen, the water being up to the men's waists, and rising fast. On the 26th, still pushing on they encamped near the Swart Kop river. Having halted during the 27th, they reached Salt Lake on the day following. The 29th being Sunday they again halted, and on the 30th reached Port Elizabeth; and, the 'Simoom' not having arrived, remained encamped on the heights. Colonel Buller having resumed command, the Battalion embarked on the 10th, and sailed from Algoa bay on November 12, arriving at Table bay on the 15th, and finally starting for England on the 16th.

The Depôt companies continued at Walmer till August 20, 1853, when they removed to Dover.

The 2nd Battalion proceeded by railroad to Guildford on June 13, and marched from thence to Chobham, where they encamped and formed part of the brigade under the command of Major-General Sir De Lacy Evans. They continued to take part in the evolutions of this camp of instruction till July 14. On which day they marched from Chobham to Woking; and proceeded thence by rail to Portsmouth, where they occupied quarters in Clarence barracks.

CHAPTER X.

THE Service companies of the 1st Battalion arrived in Cowes Roads on January 7, 1854, and disembarking on the 10th at Portsmouth, proceeded direct by South Coast and South Eastern Railways to Dover, where they joined the Depôt companies and occupied the Western Heights barracks.

On March 12 and 13 the Battalion moved, by railroad, to Portsmouth in two divisions and occupied Clarence barracks.

Previous to this move an order was received that a hundred men should be transferred to the 2nd Battalion, then under orders to embark for Turkey. The men readily volunteered for this service, and many veterans who had served through both Kaffir wars were thus added to the 2nd Battalion, and formed a valuable nucleus of old soldiers in that Battalion, which since Waterloo had not been engaged in the field. The 1st Battalion being subsequently ordered to hold itself in readiness for embarkation, received an augmentation of 1 staff sergeant, 10 sergeants, 10 corporals, 1 bugler and 240 rank and file. These numbers were made up by a hundred volunteers from the 60th, and many from other regiments. Most of these were very young soldiers; many of them not dismissed drill.

On May 16 the Battalion was augmented to twelve companies, which were to be distributed as follows:—

Augmentation, dated May 16, 1854.

	Field Officers	Captains	Lieutenants	Ensigns	Staff	Staff Sergeants	Sergeants	Buglers	Corporals	Privates
8 Service companies .	3	8	10	6	6	7	50	21	50	950
4 Depôt companies .	—	4	4	4	—	—	20	8	20	380
	3	12	14	10	6	7	70	29	70	1330
									1400	

On June 6, 1854, an order was issued that the junior subalterns of the regiment should in future be ranked as 'Ensigns' and not 'Second Lieutenants,' as they had been ever since the formation of the Regiment—a singularly inappropriate designation. for Dr. Johnson defines as 'Ensign' 'the officer of Foot who carries the flag;' whereas this regiment had never had any flag or colour to carry. This absurd anomaly continued until 1872.

The Battalion having received orders to hold itself in readiness to join the army under Lord Raglan in the East, was inspected on June 9 by Major-General Simpson, who expressed his entire satisfaction with its appearance and discipline.

At this time the Battalion, which hitherto had been armed with the Brunswick rifle, received the Minié In order to supply a sufficient number, in this emergency, those which had been issued on approval to various regiments at home were handed over to the Riflemen.

The Service companies of the Battalion under the command of Lieutenant-Colonel Beckwith, embarked from the Dock-yard at Portsmouth on July 13 on board the steamship 'Orinoco,' and steamed out of harbour on the 14th The strength of the Battalion on embarkation was 20 officers, 4 staff, 54 sergeants, 21 buglers, 50 corporals, 850 privates. Total non-commissioned officers and men 975.

On the embarkation of the Battalion, the Depôt companies under command of Captain and Brevet-Major Lord Alexander G. Russell, removed from Clarence to Colewort barracks; and continued at Portsmouth, occupying different quarters, till about August 1855, when they moved to Winchester.

The Battalion arrived at Malta on the 24th, and there received orders to proceed at once to the East. The 'Orinoco,' having coaled, started the next day for Constantinople; where having arrived on the 30th, orders were received to proceed forthwith to Beicos bay, there to await further instructions.

On August 2 pursuant to orders then received the 'Orinoco' started for Varna; but after passing through the Bosphorus she was recalled and returned to her former anchorage.

The cholera having broken out on board, one Rifleman dying on August 6 and another on the 9th, it was decided to land the Battalion; on the 9th four companies, and on the 10th the remainder of the Battalion disembarked, and encamped on a range of heights on the Asiatic side.[1] The cholera however continued its ravages; and the Battalion lost during its stay here 1 colour-sergeant (Brown), 1 sergeant, 1 bugler and 24 privates. While in this camp the Riflemen were frequently exercised in the use of the new arm, which they had received before their departure from England.

On August 24 the Battalion was inspected by H.R.H. the Duke of Cambridge, who expressed his satisfaction with its state and its fitness for immediate service

On September 2 the 'Orinoco' having two transports in tow, proceeded out of the Bosphorus; but on rounding the point into the Black Sea, encountered so heavy a sea, and so strong a head wind, that she was unable to proceed And as it became dark and the wind increased, she put back and anchored in Buyukdere bay The transports barely escaped shipwreck, the tow-ropes having broken.

On the 5th the 'Orinoco' again started, having now but one transport in tow, and passing out of the Bosphorus, arrived off Varna the following day, and anchored in the evening. During this voyage the Battalion was in great jeopardy, the 'Orinoco' having been on fire by the ignition of the patent fuel which she was carrying As she was conveying the ammunition of the 4th Division, the danger for a time wa very great; and the transport in tow was cast off in order to avoid the risk of her taking fire, or being destroyed by the explosion of the 'Orinoco.' At Varna the rest of the expedition was assembled; and the 1st Battalion was placed in General Torrens' brigade and attached to the 4th Division, commanded by Sir George Cathcart a great gratification to the Riflemen, who had served under him at the Cape.

The 2nd Battalion being by this time at Varna, I have now to trace its movements.

[1] An engraving of this camp of the 1st Battalion will be found in the 'Illustrated London News,' vol. xxv. p 320

On February 23 it was inspected at Portsmouth by Major-General Simpson previous to embarkation. On the next day the Head-quarters consisting of six companies under the command of Lieutenant-Colonel Lawrence[1] embarked on board H.M S. 'Vulcan.' The total numbers embarked were 20 officers, 6 staff, 37 sergeants, 12 buglers and 703 rank and file. On the same day two companies proceeded to Southampton and embarked there on board H.M.S.S. 'Himalaya.' The numbers were 6 officers, 1 staff, 9 sergeants, 3 buglers and 195 rank and file.[2]

The Head-quarters reached Malta on March 11, and immediately disembarked and occupied quarters in the Ropewalk barracks, where they found the two companies, from the 'Himalaya,' who had arrived previously.

On the 17th the Battalion was inspected by Major-General Ferguson. And on the 23rd it paraded in review order for the inspection of the French General Canrobert

On the 30th the Battalion embarked on board the S.S. 'Golden Fleece,' with the exception of Captain Newdigate's[3] company, which (for want of room) proceeded in the 'Sir George Pollock' sailing transport.

This expedition was commanded by their former Lieutenant-Colonel, Sir George Brown, who, with his Staff, was on board the 'Golden Fleece.'

On April 6 the Battalion arrived at Gallipoli, and disembarked on the 8th And each company as soon as assembled on shore, marching eight miles to Balahar, near the Gulf of Xeros, there encamped The Riflemen were employed until the 21st in making roads and digging wells. On the 18th two regiments came up from Gallipoli and formed brigade with the Battalion, of which Colonel Lawrence took command. From the 21st the Riflemen were employed in the construction of the English half of the Lines, from the Gulf of Xeros to the centre of the position.

On May 6 the Battalion marched to Gallipoli; and after

[1] Lieutenant-General Sir Arthur J. Lawrence, K C B.

[2] Being a total of 33 officers, and 959 of inferior ranks With these numbers the 'Medical History,' i 452, nearly agrees: it enumerates 32 officers and 961 of inferior ranks.

[3] Colonel Newdigate, Commanding Rifle Depôt.

having been inspected by Sir George Brown with General Canrobert and Prince Napoleon, re-embarked on board the 'Golden Fleece.' They arrived on the 7th at Scutari, and having disembarked on the 9th occupied part of the new barracks until the 11th, when they pitched camp between the Hospital and the barracks, having been obliged to turn out of the barracks, on account of the fleas by which they were infested

On the 18th an order was received for the augmentation of this Battalion (as well as the 1st) to twelve companies.

At this time the Light Division was formed under the command of Sir George Brown, and the Battalion was attached to it.

On the 25th being the celebration of the Queen's birthday, the Division was reviewed by the Sultan and Lord Raglan Commanding the forces On the 29th the Battalion re-embarked on board the 'Golden Fleece' and proceeded to Varna, where they arrived on the following day; and on disembarking, the brigade encamped outside the town near the Shumla gate, the Battalion being nearest to the town.

On June 5 the Battalion marched to Aladyn nine miles on the road to Shumla, where they encamped on a hill with a lake in front and another in rear. And on the 30th marched to Devna seven miles further inland, where they encamped on a plateau near a marsh of some extent. On July 23 the Battalion was reinforced by a draft of 1 subaltern (Lieutenant Churchill), 2 sergeants and 150 rank and file, who arrived from England. On the next day, cholera having appeared in the Division, the Battalion marched four miles further to Monastir, where it encamped on an elevated plateau in hopes of finding healthier quarters. But without success; as on the 27th the scourge broke out in the Battalion, and two Riflemen died. And many others were ill. The men, probably to divert their attention, were engaged in learning to make fascines and gabions

On August 17 preparatory to moving to the Crimea, the Battalion was inspected by Sir George Brown, who came up from Varna to see them.

On the 26th they marched to Yuksarood, and having halted during the next day, on the 28th proceeded to Karagola, and on the 29th marched into Varna, and embarked on the same afternoon.[1]

The Battalion was broken up into companies which embarked in the following sailing transports:

The Head-quarters under Lieutenant-Colonel Lawrence with Captain Hammond's company in the 'Pride of the Ocean.'

Capt. Elrington's[2] company in the 'Monarchy'

Capt the Earl of Erroll's in the 'Echunga.'

Capt. Inglis' in the 'Caliope.'

Capt. Fyers'[3] in the 'Marianne.'

Capt Newdigate's in the 'Harkaway.'

Capt. Forman's in the 'Lord Raglan'

Capt. the Hon. W. J. Colville's[4] in the 'Talavera.'

Three ships started on September 7 for Battchick and three sailed on the 9th for the *rendezvous* at Cape Tarkan.

On the 13th the whole fleet anchored in Kalamita bay; and on the next day the landing commenced. Leaving their knapsacks on board, and taking with them a light kit folded in their blankets, the 1st Battalion landed about three in the afternoon, and bivouacked on the beach. The men were without tents, and heavy rain fell at night. The Battalion remained in this position (save that the tents were landed) until the 19th the Riflemen assisting in landing stores. On the 16th Sir George Cathcart saw the Battalion, and presented each man with a piece of black oil-cloth, which covered the blanket, keeping it dry and concealing its colour. These were also afterwards found very useful in keeping the men off the damp ground, when spread under them. Sir George, in addressing them, most kindly told them that he had considered what he could give them; and had thought these the most useful gift. On the 17th three companies, forming a patrol, marched about twelve miles inland: as they had to keep up with the cavalry they had little or no rest, the cavalry starting again almost as soon as our men came up with them. These companies did not get back till midnight, and the men

[1] During the months of July and August, while the Battalion was in Bulgaria, it lost thirty men from cholera. 'Medical and Surgical History of the British Army,' ii. 50.

[2] Major-General Elrington, C B

[3] Colonel Fyers, C.B. (retired).

[4] Colonel the Hon. W. J. Colville.

had suffered much, their feet being sore from the salt which had got into their boots. However they brought back with them carts, camels, &c., taken in a village which the Cossacks had left about two hours before they reached it.

On the 18th the tents were struck and sent on board the fleet.

On that night the whole Battalion, fully equipped for the march, fell in to form a circle round some captured horses. About midnight the men had leave to sit down, front and rear rank alternately. This harassing duty continued till the general advance on the morning of the 19th.

The 2nd Battalion also landed on the 14th, and being disembarked by eleven in the forenoon, and marching from the left of the line along the front of the other regiments towards the right, were sent on in advance, after being broken up into wings; the right wing consisting of four companies under Colonel Lawrence; the left wing, also of four companies, under Major Norcott.[1] They advanced about five miles, the former moving to the eastward occupied the village of Kentúgan; the left wing advancing to the northward occupied Kamishli. On this march the right wing captured a convoy of seventy arrabas (country carts) drawn by oxen, and laden for the most part with flour. Colonel Lawrence appropriated two dromedaries, part of the spoil, for the use of his wing; where they did good service as baggage animals till the drivers contrived to elope with them in the winter. During the time that the Riflemen occupied Kentúgan and Kamishli they made friends of the inhabitants. 'Their chief favourites, it seems, were the men of the Rifle Brigade. Quartered for a day or two in one of the villages, these soldiers made up for the want of a common tongue by acts of kindness. They helped the women in their household work; and the women, pleased and proud, made signs to the stately Rifles to do this and to do that, exulting in the obedience which they were able to win from men so grand and comely. When the interpreter came, and was asked to construe what the women were saying so fast and so eagerly, it appeared that they were busy with similes and metaphors, and that the Rifles were made out to be heroes more strong than lions, more gentle than young lambs.'[2]

[1] Major-General Norcott, C.B.

[2] Kinglake, vol. ii. 187.

The wing at Kentúgan occupied the residence of a person of some substance whose property they protected from the ravages of the French, who however pillaged the village.

During the stay of the Battalion in these villages, some amusing alarms from Cossacks took place. They were seen hovering about in the distance, and a night attack being expected, the companies of the right wing manifested their vigilance by very nearly firing into one of their own reliefs; while in the left wing a stray horse or a cow was taken for the expected Cossacks

On another occasion an Aide-de-Camp from the Commander of the cavalry having demanded immediate assistance, the four companies under Lawrence were soon under arms, and went at the double to afford the required aid. They were met however by a message of thanks, and an assurance that their help was not needed. It appeared afterwards that the vedettes had mistaken their front, and that the supposed enemy was some of their own force

'But,' writes Sir Arthur Lawrence, to whom I am indebted for these anecdotes, 'we were all pretty new at soldiering at that time, and we were kept on the *qui vive* for some hours before we marched on the 19th by the Russians burning forage in our front.' This Battalion, which had not seen a foreign foe for nigh forty years, was to learn soldiering, and to attain the prize of victory, in a severe school before the week was out.

On the 19th the whole army got into order of march at daylight. The 1st Battalion was divided between the two brigades of the 4th Division, four companies being attached to each. As the protection of the rear of the army was entrusted to this Division, the Riflemen did not leave their ground till about nine A.M. They then proceeded over the plain in the rear and on the left of the army. This march, although not more than twelve miles, was very fatiguing, on account of the heat and want of water. Vast numbers of men fell out; but those of the 1st Battalion all rejoined at nightfall after the heat of the day. During the advance the left flank was covered by Riflemen in skirmishing order, and a line of their skirmishers protected the rear. The Battalion reached the river Búlganak about six in the evening and bivouacked for the night. One company, Major Rooper's, being detached to the left to protect that flank. On this night Lieutenant-Colonel Beckwith was attacked by cholera, and Lieutenant-Colonel Horsford assumed command of the Battalion.

On the same day the 2nd Battalion advanced and were present at the cavalry affair on the Búlganak They were moved forward in support of the cavalry and to protect the guns, but were not engaged. The Battalion bivouacked on the heights south of the river Búlganak.

On the 20th the 1st Battalion, being provided with three days' rations, was ready to move at daylight, but did not leave its ground till a little before eight. It then advanced, covering, as on the day before, the left and rear of the army. On approaching the banks of the river Alma, a large force of the enemy's cavalry was observed on the left flank, which he repeatedly extended with the view, apparently, of turning the flank; but Sir George Cathcart answered the movement by throwing out skirmishers of this Battalion, which kept them in check during the engagement. The enemy having been repulsed at all points in the battle of the Alma, their cavalry also retired The Battalion then forded the Alma and ascended the heights on its south side, the enemy being then in full retreat. After a short halt the Battalion was ordered to bivouack on the bank of the river, and redescending the hill took up a position for the night. The 4th Division having been in reserve, the Battalion was not actually engaged; two men were however wounded.

But the 2nd Battalion was actively engaged. They were ordered to be ready to move by seven o'clock in the morning. I will first follow the movements of the right wing, consisting of four companies under Colonel Lawrence. At the hour appointed he extended two companies to cover the advance. But no order to move arrived for some hours; and it was not till about noon that the army was ordered to advance. The Riflemen then began to descend from the ridge the long slope which led to the Alma, two companies extended in skirmishing order, and two in support. As they drew near it the village of Búrhúk which they had not before noticed, for it was enfolded in a dip of the ground, burst into flames. They were sharply plied with grape from the batteries on the opposite slope, and with musketry from the village; while the smoke from the burning houses was so blinding that the Riflemen could hardly fire a shot.

As they could make no effectual use of their rifles, they inclined to their left and got some shelter from a dip in the ground. Meanwhile the Light Division behind them had deployed into line, and were ordered to lie down. Then Lawrence told his skirmishers to fix their bayonets, and to take two or three houses which were near them with a rush. On getting up to them however it was found that the enemy had evacuated them; and the Riflemen found shelter behind the smoking ruins. They then received the order to advance; and the Riflemen rushed into the vineyards which line the bank of the river, and which afforded some cover from the enemy's fire. Meanwhile Major Norcott with the four companies of the left wing had attacked the Russians so vigorously that he had made the place too hot for their skirmishers, and the right wing skirmishers and supports passed through the vineyards, and forded the river without difficulty, though saluted with a shower of bullets in their passage of it The 19th Regiment followed them. After passing the river they found some shelter under the slope of a bank: shelter from the shot and musketry which the enemy were pouring down from the redoubt, and the troops on the slope which rose from the crest of the bank which sheltered them: but not complete shelter; for the enemy had a battery on their right, which enfiladed them The left wing of the Battalion had passed on, and the 19th Regiment was preparing to advance. Lawrence therefore accompanied by his Adjutant, Lieutenant Ross, rode up the bank and the Riflemen followed, exposed to a tremendous fire, for as soon as they left the shelter of the bank they came under the full fire of the Russians However they advanced up the slope. When within a few yards of the redoubt Colonel Lawrence's horse was killed by a discharge of grape, nearly rolling its rider under the breastwork of the redoubt, under which he found shelter when he had extricated himself, as did his Adjutant whose horse also was killed. These Riflemen were soon mixed up with their comrades of the left wing and with the men of the 19th Regiment, all firing indiscriminately at an advancing column of Russians For we must now accompany Norcott's wing, and see how he had got to the redoubt where he met Lawrence's four companies

Descending the slopes of the right bank of the Alma, Norcott's Riflemen entered the vineyards, and at once were exposed to the fire of the Russian artillery and became engaged with their light troops. Fyers' company was extended on the extreme left, with Lord Erroll's company in support. The Riflemen inclining to the left to avoid the burning village of Búrliúk, which as we have seen had been fired by the Russians, forded the river and, ascending the other bank and passing through the vineyards, halted at a wall : a low wall which separated the cultivated ground from the slope beyond Here Norcott moved up and extended Erroll's company on the right of Fyers' ; and then, or soon after, he advanced ; and inclining to the right, on observing that Codrington's brigade had disarranged or lost its formation and was threatened by a Russian column, he poured such a searching fire from his line of skirmishers, that the enemy were checked and hindered from taking full advantage of the want of regular formation of Codrington's brigade. Still inclining to the right, the Riflemen approached the proper right flank of the great redoubt, where as I have said both wings met. As these Riflemen were rushing into the redoubt Norcott's horse was wounded. Soon after they had attained the redoubt a Russian column was seen descending the hill beyond. By a most unfortunate mistake these were thought to be French, and some officer (of what regiment is unknown) desired a bugler to sound the 'cease fire ;' and (it is said) afterwards the 'retire.' The men then began to leave the redoubt when their very existence seemed to depend on clinging fast to its bank, or boldly facing the enemy. In vain the officers of the various regiments endeavoured to check the stream, by calling on the men to halt or to return to the position they had won They slowly and orderly moved down the hill. The Riflemen, carried along with this rolling mass, sought shelter under the bank from which they had first emerged on the slope. They rallied at the sound of the regimental call, and the companies of both wings, Lawrence's and Norcott's, united and advanced again to the redoubt. The enemy then fled. And on the final retreat of the Russians part of the 2nd Battalion were ordered to take off their packs (or rather their coats and blankets), to leave them there, and marched with the cavalry and guns in pursuit of the retreating Russians; but after proceeding about a mile they were recalled, and on their return the Battalion bivouacked on the heights above the Alma on the ground they had won.

The casualties in this Battalion were 2 sergeants and 9 rank and file killed, and Captain the Earl of Errol, 1 sergeant 3 buglers and 34 rank and file wounded.

Lord Raglan in his despatch praises the conduct of the Regiment, and states that the capture of the great redoubt was 'materially aided by the advance of four companies of the Rifle Brigade under Major Norcott.'

He was also recommended for the Victoria Cross by Sir George Brown; who adds: 'Major Norcott's conduct on that occasion was not only conspicuous to the whole Division, but attracted the notice of the enemy; for the Officer in command of the Russian Battery, who was subsequently made prisoner, informed Lord Raglan, that he had laid a gun specially for the "daring officer in the dark uniform on the black horse."'

On the 21st the 1st Battalion moved at daylight, and ascending the heights halted on the ground which had been occupied by the enemy's right. Here they bivouacked; and were engaged on this and the following day in burying the dead and conveying the wounded to the field-hospitals. The cholera, which had disappeared from the time the Battalion left the Bosphorus, reappeared directly after they landed, and the Battalion suffered much from it about this time; having lost 1 assistant surgeon (Mr Shorrock) 1 sergeant and 9 privates.

The 2nd Battalion on these two days was similarly employed in the burial of the dead and the assistance of the wounded.

On the 23rd both Battalions, being under arms from seven o'clock, left the heights of the Alma and advanced to the Katchka, which they reached at sunset, and there bivouacked. The 1st Battalion formed the rear-guard of the army. The 2nd Battalion, in front of the rest of the army, passed through the vineyards and a village, and crossing the river, approached the position with caution; but it was found to be evacuated.

On the next day both Battalions were under arms at seven o'clock, but were kept hanging about till near twelve while a reconnaissance was being made. The 2nd Battalion, again covering the advance of the army, then mounted the ridge, and advancing over a level plateau, descended to the valley of the Belbek, through vineyards and gardens; fording the river and pushing on, they covered with their skirmishers the crossing of the Belbek by the army They ascended the opposite height, and at dusk their skirmishers were drawn in and they bivouacked on these heights, and furnished a picquet of two companies.

On the 25th the army made a further advance; but the 1st Battalion (with the rest of the 4th Division) remained on their ground to protect the wounded, and to cover the supplies. The Riflemen were ordered to conceal themselves in the bushes and to keep as quiet as possible. And at night occupied the bivouack of the night before. On this day Sidney Beckwith, who had been conveyed on board the 'Orinoco,' died; and thus the roll of the Regiment for the first time since its formation was without the honoured name of Beckwith.

On this day the 2nd Battalion under the command of Lawrence, its wings being now reunited, was ordered to place itself at the disposal of Lord Lucan, and to cover the flank of the cavalry on the advance from the Belbek towards Mackenzie's farm. The men were ordered to place their shirts and boots wrapped in their great coats (for they had not their packs) on the limbers of the guns; and starting at half-past eight four companies preceded or were on the flank of the cavalry, and four brought up the rear. Soon the wood became so thick that it was with some difficulty that the connection between the files—for they were in skirmishing order—could be kept up. As they approached Mackenzie's farm Lord Lucan and Lord William Paulet, Deputy-Adjutant-General, dismounted to look at a map; and while they were poring over it the sound of a gun startled the party. A second soon succeeded, the cavalry hurried forward, and the Riflemen followed, their pace quickened not only by their desire to be 'first in the fight,' but by a message from Lord Raglan to push on as quickly as they could. A few minutes at the double brought them out on the road, and on the baggage of Menchikoff's column. They pursued the rear-guard, but not far; and the men helped themselves to provisions, wine and whatever they could lay hands on; some horses amongst the rest; of which a piebald, taken out of a team, replaced Norcott's charger disabled at the Alma.

Subsequently this Battalion crossed the Tchernaya by a stone bridge and bivouacked on the height beyond. The men were much fatigued, having been on the move from an early hour till after dark without anything to eat.

On the 26th the 1st Battalion moved at 5.30 A.M., and throwing out skirmishers marched along the high road to Sebastopol for about three miles. They then turned to the left and proceeded with great caution through the forest to Kútor Mackenzie, where they halted for a very considerable time to allow the baggage and supplies of the army to precede. From Mackenzie's farm the Battalion descended to the valley of the Tchernaya, the whole road covered with loaded waggons and the remains of the Russian baggage train, which had been surprised the day before. On arriving at the banks of the Tchernaya about half-past six they bivouacked; having been thirteen hours under arms.

On this day the 2nd Battalion led the advance on Balaklava. The approach was by a narrow gorge, with high bare hills on each side Colonel Lawrence detached his majors, Norcott to the right, Bradford [1] to the left, while he himself with two companies kept the centre. Thus they approached Balaklava, throwing out skirmishers. No opposition was offered till they had advanced some distance, when some musketry fire was opened; but this was only from a few men on the heights who were soon driven in; and the advance continued. A staff officer then reported to Lord Raglan that the road was clear, and he rode forward and was just entering the gorge, when Lawrence observed to him that he still saw some of the enemy on the hills, and asked permission to send a company in advance This was granted, and Fyers' company was taken by Norcott towards the town. On their approaching it and the Battalion appearing on the heights, a few harmless shots were fired from the old Genoese fort; and soon after on their advancing nearer a white flag was hoisted. Fyers,

[1] Major-General W. H. Bradford.

who mistrusted the sincerity of the Governor, directed his subaltern to halt with one subdivision, whilst he, with the other, advanced by a narrow road engineered between the high ground and the sea. On Fyers' men entering the fort, the Governor left it by another side; and meeting Egerton and Ross surrendered, handing his sword to the former. Then Fyers taking his company into the town, a baker, evidently in great terror, came out of his house and, notwithstanding the early hour of the morning, produced a roast turkey which he offered him, and a great number of loaves These Fyers desired him to break in two, and to give half to each man. So that all the men of his company had a good meal.

The Battalion subsequently occupied Balaklava, posting sentries for the protection of the inhabitants, and at night bivouacked among beautiful vineyards two miles outside the town.[1]

Some spoil was found in the fort; Lawrence became the possessor of a fur coat, by gift from one of the Riflemen, and Ross obtained a remount in place of his horse killed at the Alma. On the next day this Battalion was moved about a mile nearer to Sebastopol, and encamped for some days

On the 27th the 1st Battalion was under arms at half-past six; but having to wait to allow the whole of the supplies and all the *impedimenta* of the army to pass over the Traktir bridge, did not themselves move until ten o'clock. They then followed, and advanced almost to Balaklava when they came up with the rest of the army; and passing it ascended the hill to the right and approached Sebastopol. They traversed the valley, and the quarries afterwards occupied by the 3rd Division, and advanced to the high ground overlooking the south harbour, becoming thus the most advanced battalion in front of the place. This was a great satisfaction to the Battalion, which had been so long protecting the rear; and the Riflemen greeted their change of position with hearty cheers. Here they bivouacked, throwing out one company as an outlying picquet. Shot and shell were thrown from the town, some reaching so near the bivouack that some rifles piled by the men were knocked down by the bursting of a shell.

On September 28 a Russian column having issued from

[1] Sir Arthur Lawrence's letters, and information from Colonel Fyers

the place, the Riflemen with the 4th Division advanced to meet it. The enemy however immediately retired, with the evident intention of drawing Cathcart in pursuit under the fire of the guns of the place; but finding the Riflemen declined the fight he returned to his camp. This was situated on a flattened limestone ridge extending in the direction of the city, a ravine separating it from the Inkerman heights and another from the ridge on which was placed the battery of the English right attack

On the 28th, in consequence of the gunners of the place having got the exact range of the position which the Battalion occupied, it was moved about 100 yards to the rear into a situation rather more sheltered.

On the 29th the 2nd Battalion, leaving their bivouack near Balaklava, advanced on Sebastopol, and took up ground on the left of the position towards Kamiesh And on October 1 moved its position to the right of the Woronzow road, and shortly after to near the Windmill, having a wing on each flank of the Light Division.

From the time the 1st Battalion left the position of the Alma till its arrival before Sebastopol it had lost by cholera, Lieutenant-Colonel Beckwith, Sergeant-Major Tucker, 1 colour-sergeant, 1 corporal and 7 privates.[1] Its strength on October 1 was—

Field officer	Captains	Subalterns	Staff	Sergeants	Buglers	Rank and file
1	5	11	5	43	19	691

On October 2 the Battalion being still exposed to the Russian fire, and many shells falling into the position, again moved to the rear and east of the stone quarries, and took up the position which it occupied during the remainder of the siege. On the next day the 2nd Battalion was kept on the alert all day by shot and shell thrown by the enemy into its position.

On the 4th the Regiment, which had hitherto since September 18 bivouacked without shelter, received tents, which the Riflemen brought up from Balaklava harbour.

On the 5th the 1st Battalion furnished a party to escort

[1] Record of 1st Battalion, and see p. 309. But Surgeon Bowen, in the 'Medical and Surgical History of the British Army,' states the total loss from cholera during the month to be thirteen, and that all, with one exception, occurred on the line of march.

Engineer officers making a reconnaissance and marking ground for the approaches. They started at three in the morning and returned soon after daylight.

On the 8th the 2nd Battalion furnished a picquet under Lieutenant-Colonel Lawrence, consisting of two companies, to cover the working parties at the five-gun battery. These companies held this battery for twenty-four hours under constant fire without a man being touched. The Battalion also furnished a covering party under Major Norcott at Gordon's battery.

On the 9th a similar party was furnished by the 1st Battalion to escort the Engineers marking ground at the Greenhill battery. The Riflemen descended the ravine about a mile, and lay down while the Engineers marked the ground. They had scarcely retired when the Russians were out looking at the same ground.

On the 10th the right wing of the Battalion went down to the trenches afterwards so memorable, to cover the working parties. They remained on for twenty-four hours, and were relieved at daylight on the 11th by the left wing. This duty in the trenches was thenceforward performed by wings alternately, with the other regiments of the Division.[1]

On the 12th Private Francis Wheatley of the 1st Battalion, being on duty in the trenches when a live shell fell among the party, having unsuccessfully endeavoured to knock out the fuze with the butt of his rifle, took up the shell with great deliberation and flung it over the parapet. It had scarcely fallen outside when it exploded. For this act of valour he afterwards received the Victoria Cross, and the cross of the Legion of Honour.[2]

On October 13 a man of the 2nd Battalion, Herbert, made a most remarkable shot. He was on outlying picquet, and observing a Russian officer on a white horse he took a shot at him, fixing the sight of his rifle at its extreme range. The officer fell, while the horse moved on. The distance at which he shot him has been variously estimated from 1300

[1] An engraving of 'Riflemen in the Trenches' is in the 'Illustrated London News,' vol. xxv. p. 573.

[2] Wheatley entered my service as lodge-keeper at Bramshill Park on his discharge, and died May 21, 1865.

yards[1] downwards ; the man himself told me that he thought the Russian whom he shot was about 1000 yards from him.

On the 14th the 1st Battalion lost its first man in the trenches; he was killed by a fragment of a shell.

On October 14 Fyers was with his company in the five-gun battery when he observed a column of Russian infantry advancing. Taking a rifle from one of the men, he put the sight at what he considered their distance, and fired, carefully watching the effect of the shot. When he perceived that it struck the ground a little in front of the column, he ordered his men to fix their sights for 750 yards, and to stand up on the parapet and 'give it them.' They had not been long firing when he found that he was under fire from the rear. Some of the Russians had moved up the ravine towards a house which was occupied by a picquet of another regiment, under a sergeant, which had retreated on their approach, and the Russians having taken possession of the house were firing on Fyers' party He therefore sallied with his company out of the battery and drove the Russians back, not before they had eaten the dinners of the former occupants of the picquet-house, and carried off their coats and blankets. Most of these they dropped on their way back, as they probably impeded their retreat, pressed as they were by Fyers and his party.

In this affair Hugh Hannan, the tallest man in the Battalion, was attacked by a Russian rifleman who turned upon him. Hannan fired , the shot was returned, and the Russian was preparing to fire again, but before he could find a cap, Hannan rushed upon him, and with a tremendous blow knocked him over a low wall, and leaped after him. They grappled , and a fierce struggle ensued in which Hannan was getting the worst of it For the Russian had drawn his short sword and was almost in the act of stabbing him in the thigh, when Hannan's friend and comrade, Ferguson, by a sure shot brought the Russian down dead.[2]

In this affair two Riflemen were wounded. Fyers took a

[1] 'Letters from Head-Quarters by a Staff Officer,' [Colonel the Hon. S. Calthorpe], p 101

[2] Hannan was one of a hundred men given by the 1st to the 2nd Battalion, before they embarked for the Crimea. He had been noted for his daring in the Kaffir War. He and Ferguson were fellow-countrymen, both being from the north of Ireland

sergeant and some men prisoners, of whom three were wounded; several others were carried off by their companions, and many were killed.

On the alarm Sir De Lacy Evans had moved up two regiments, and some of the 1st Division; and the rest of the 2nd Battalion were brought up and halted in rear of Gordon's battery, and some guns were ordered up; but before these troops came into action, Fyers had repulsed and effectually disposed of the Russian attack

On one occasion about this time, when a party of the Regiment had been pushed forward, four Riflemen crept up to within 500 yards of the place and fired into the windows of the grand barracks of Sebastopol [1]

On the 16th, while the left wing of the 1st Battalion was in the trenches, the enemy opened a murderous fire about ten A.M. on the whole length of the English trenches and continued it for half-an-hour, apparently determined to drive them from their position; however the Riflemen did not suffer much loss, but one colour-sergeant, James Powell, was disabled.

From this date the Riflemen were nightly thrown out in advance of the intrenchments, whatever regiments found the duties, they formed a line of double sentries, to watch and report any suspicious movements in the place.

On the 17th the Allies opened fire

On the 19th a man of the Regiment was seen to pick off eight men from a Russian battery.[2]

On the 25th the 1st Battalion was ordered out to repel the attack on Balaklava. They fell in between eight and nine o'clock, and starting at the double took up a position on the side of a hill The Russians had driven the Turks out of the forts in their occupation. The Riflemen arrived just after the heavy cavalry charge. After the light cavalry charge the 4th Division was ordered to advance, the 1st Battalion Rifle Brigade leading by wings. The right wing under Colonel Horsford took up a position with its left resting on the road from Sebastopol to the Traktir bridge; the 68th being de-

[1] 'Illustrated London News,' vol xxv p 466. The newspaper writer who records this, while doubting the accuracy of the estimate of the number of the enemy killed on the 19th, states this fact of the four Riflemen as 'certain.'

[2] Ibid. vol. xxv. p 487.

ployed in line on its right; and the left wing under Major Rooper being on the right of the 68th in support of Captain Barker's battery. The enemy brought forward a field battery of six guns and opened fire on the line. This fire became very troublesome on the right flank, and Lieutenant Godfrey with a few men was sent to try to silence these guns This they did most effectually in a very short time. The task was difficult, for the ground afforded no cover, the utmost shelter they could get being some slight undulation in the surface However the Riflemen lay down on their stomachs and picked off the gunners whenever they attempted to handle their guns, and in about twenty minutes forced the Russian guns to retire

The Battalion remained in the same order and in the same position until dark; but no further attack being made by the enemy, and it having been resolved to abandon these forts, the Battalion returned to its camp.

One man was wounded, being struck in the leg by a round shot.

On the 26th at noon the Russians came out from Sebastopol and attacked the extreme right of the English position, which was occupied by the 2nd Division. The enemy having advanced in a mass of columns, our guns opening upon them within easy range caused them such loss that they quickly retired. On this occasion the 1st Battalion, although the most distant from the right of the position, turned out so quickly, with Sir George Cathcart at its head, that it was on the scene of action in a very short time, but not till the enemy had retired

On this occasion a picquet, under Lieutenant W. T. Markham of the 2nd Battalion,[1] which was on duty in the five-gun battery, joining some men of the Guards under Captain Goodlake in the Careenage ravine, had an obstinate combat with a strong Russian column. They kept them back for a considerable time; and eventually the Riflemen succeeded in driving them out of the cave there, known as the Magazine Grotto; but not without a hard fight in which 5 Riflemen were wounded They however inflicted considerable loss on their opponents; and a Russian officer and many men were taken prisoners[2]

[1] Captain Markham retired (from the Coldstream Guards) December 23, 1858

[2] Nine men of the 1st Battalion were wounded in the trenches during the

On November 1 the morning state of the 1st Battalion was as follows:—

Field-officers	Captains	Subalterns	Staff	Sergeants	Buglers	Rank and file
1	5	11	6	38	18	550

showing a decrease of 5 sergeants, 1 bugler and 141 rank and file since the arrival of the Battalion before the place.

Early on the 2nd the enemy's batteries opened a cannonade, by which four men of the 2nd Battalion, forming part of a company which was going to relieve in the trenches, were wounded.

On November 4, four companies of the 2nd Battalion, the Earl of Errol's, Hammond's, Fyers' and Colville's, under Major Bradford (Major Norcott being sick), proceeded to the heights of Balaklava.

On the morning of Sunday, November 5, an hour before daybreak, the alarm was sounded through the English camp The greater part of the 1st Battalion had just returned from the trenches, and were still accoutred, though wet through; for it had rained the previous day, all through the night, and even then there was dense damp fog, with frequent showers As they were passing the head of the ravine, a bugle was heard sounding in camp, which these men at first fancied to be the usual parade horn It proved however to be the 'assembly' The remainder of the Battalion was soon under arms, and moved towards the fight, which the rattle of musketry and the roar of guns told them was going on, at the head of the 4th Division under Sir George Cathcart.

In like manner General Codrington, the first to give the alarm, turned out the Light Division, and the 2nd Battalion assembled at once Three companies only were on parade, one wing having gone on the previous day, as we have seen, to the heights of Balaklava, and Captain Forman's company being in the five-gun battery. Of these three companies, one had just come in after being twenty-seven hours in the trenches. However they at once advanced, and General Codrington having placed his brigade on the Victoria ridge, these Riflemen

month of October, of whom two died almost immediately, and one underwent amputation of the left thigh; and of the 2nd Battalion four men were killed in the trenches, and an officer and twenty-five men were wounded; of these five died.

extended along the left bank of the Careenage ravine on the extreme left of the line. Soon after they took up their position a column of Russians, part of Soimonoff's force, advanced up the Careenage ravine, and after opening fire on the Riflemen, attempted to ascend its left bank; but Captain Elrington, with two companies of the 2nd Battalion, at once attacked them, and drove them down at the point of the bayonet, they retreated by the bottom of the ravine, and did not again make their appearance in that part of the fight. In this attack a Rifleman named Hewitt, having put on a greatcoat and cap late the property of a Russian soldier deceased, followed the retreating Muscovites down the ravine, and picked off a number of them. He narrowly escaped however being shot by his own comrades. This man, as well as a brother in the same Battalion, afterwards died in the Crimea. This repulse occurred at the very beginning of the Russian attack. These companies under Elrington lost 5 men killed and 10 wounded in this gallant affair.[1]

Meanwhile the 1st Battalion were advancing with Cathcart towards the scene of the fight As they approached the end of the English line, manifest tokens of the battle greeted them The rattle of musketry in front, indeed apparently on every side; dead lying about, and wounded carried by; and tents thrown to the ground by the fire of the enemy's guns. On their arriving at the heights of Inkerman, where General Pennefather was maintaining a hard and unequal fight, Sir George Cathcart handed over to him the 1st Battalion which he so much esteemed, telling him that he had brought him 'a Battalion which could do anything.' Pennefather riding up to Lieutenant-Colonel Horsford, who was in command of the Battalion, and paying it a high compliment, informed him that he was hard pressed on the left of the centre ravine, and wished a reinforcement sent there The three leading companies were immediately detached for that purpose under Major Rooper who deployed them into line below the crest of the

[1] For this distinguished service Captain Elrington was recommended for the Victoria Cross; but Sir George Brown demurred to forward the recommendation, on the ground that the 2nd Battalion had not been engaged in the battle of Inkerman! The fact being that three companies were there, and suffered the casualties hereafter noted.

hill. They soon were confronted by a Russian column, part of Dannenberg's force. They were at a short distance, and the Riflemen halted and opened fire. For a short time the enemy returned their fire, then began to waver and eventually to retreat, hotly pursued by the Riflemen, who drove them down into the Quarry ravine. Those of them who were wounded, or who had not made good their escape into the ravine, were in a state of extreme terror, and called upon the Riflemen on their knees and with clasped hands raised in prayer to spare their lives [1]

Soon after Rooper's wing had been thus sent forward, the remaining three companies under Horsford moved to the right, deployed into line, and advanced to the Kitspur, and thence by the head of St. Clement's gorge they fought their way to the Barrier. On their way they opened their files to allow stragglers and wounded to pass through, and two companies of the Guards who were then retiring Finding themselves without support, and their ammunition beginning to fail, they halted But eventually both wings, that under Horsford which had worked round from the right, and that under Rooper, were posted at the Barrier. From thence Horsford with some men in extended order skirmished along the right bank of the Quarry ravine. About half-past twelve, Captain Somerset, who had been obliged to go to Headquarters on account of ill-health, with much difficulty found his way to the front, and joined a party of the Battalion whom he found in rear of the two-gun battery under Ensign Brett.[2] Soon Lieutenant Morgan brought him a message from Colonel Horsford that he wished to collect all the Battalion in front at the Barrier. Accordingly he brought up these men and joined Horsford under the ridge. During this terrible conflict many of the Riflemen fought independently, or by twos and threes. Sometimes they found themselves mixed up with men of other regiments, the mistiness of the day and their being all in greatcoats rendering it not always easy to distinguish their comrades. Some few Riflemen under Tryon joined the 57th Regiment in resisting an attack on the ridge.

[1] Kinglake, vol v p 298, quoting a letter from Lieutenant Bramston, Rifle Brigade

[2] Lieutenant-Colonel John Brett, retired full-pay.

The Riflemen got cover where they could among the scrub oak on the rocks. Some of them running short of detonating caps took them from dead Russians, and these, though large, exploded their rifles. These Riflemen getting cover in the brushwood on the left of the Barrier picked off the gunners of the Russian battery on the Shell hill.

About this period of the fight Colour-Sergeant Higgins,[1] collecting some thirty men of No. 2 company, formed them up on the left of the French division, and with them drove the Russians down the ravine.

Later in the day, and towards the close of the fight, Horsford with the remains of the Battalion, advanced from the Barrier, and pushed up the Shell hill to where a Russian battery had stood Ascending the hill, almost hand to hand with the enemy, these Riflemen fixed bayonets and charged, driving the Russians from the ridge, on whose retiring masses they kept up fire. Four tumbrils with ammunition remained in their hands; but the Russians had withdrawn the guns.

The Battalion, or the remnant of it, remained extended on the heights till about nine at night, when being relieved by picquets of the 2nd Division it marched to camp.

No. 2 company was brought out of the field in command of the Colour-Sergeant (Higgins), who indeed had been in charge of it from the time its Captain (Cartwright) had been killed.

The 2nd Battalion, after Elrington's exploit in the morning, continued posted on the left of Codrington's force on the Victoria heights They kept up fire on the Russians on the opposite height (Mount Inkerman) whenever they came within range Some Russian riflemen having come into the Careenage ravine and as far as the Magazine caves, took shelter there, and while the companies on the hill kept up a constant fire as often as they showed themselves, to prevent their emerging or escape, some of the Battalion descended into the ravine and made them prisoners. Three companies only of this Battalion were engaged, Elrington's, Inglis' and Newdigate's, mustering about 150 rifles. Forman's company was in the five-gun battery; and the other four companies were at Balaklava.

The losses of the Regiment were very severe. In the

[1] Captain William Higgins, Quartermaster, half-pay.

1st Battalion Captain Cartwright, 5 sergeants and 22 rank and file were killed. And Brevet-Major Rooper and Lieutenant Coote Buller[1] were severely wounded, and 5 sergeants and 26 rank and file were wounded Colour-Sergeant Noseley,[2] who was dangerously wounded, was taken prisoner.

Cartwright was killed late in the day, while sitting under the Barrier, which the men were then lining. He was shot through the eye and also in the chest. Colonel Horsford was also wounded by a shell, which exploded between his legs, and lifted him off the ground ; but not being disabled he did not return himself as wounded.

This Battalion also had to lament the loss of its kind friend Sir George Cathcart, under whom it had fought in Kaffraria, and who had from that time manifested great attachment to it.

In the 2nd Battalion Lieutenant Malcolm and 8 rank and file were killed and Captain Newdigate and 27 rank and file wounded.[3]

Of these Rooper died on the 11th on board the steamer 'Golden Fleece,' on his passage to Malta.

For some days after the battle of Inkerman the Riflemen were engaged in burying the dead Their other duties also were very severe. In consequence of four companies of the 2nd Battalion having been moved to Balaklava the 1st Battalion found duty both on the right and left attack. Even when other regiments were in the trenches they furnished a party a hundred yards in front ; and wherever there was an alarm or a position to be stormed the green-jackets were in request. During this time and while the duties were so constant, the men suffered much also from scarcity of rations. And even those issued were such as the men could scarcely use. Until the end of December the coffee was served out green ; there were no vegetables for a considerable time ; the biscuit when the weather was wet, was mouldy ; and fuel was scarcely to be procured. Even such supplies as were in Balaklava were but scantily brought up owing to want of transport ; and the

[1] Major Coote Buller died April 5, 1868

[2] Major G R Noseley, Paymaster, half-pay.

[3] 'Malcolm was shot through the head, a finer and more gallant young fellow never lived. . . . There is not an officer in the Regiment who does not sincerely regret him.'—Ross's Letter, November 7, 1854

position of the 1st Battalion being the most distant from that place, rendered their supply more scanty and precarious.

On November 14 occurred the memorable gale. The tents were blown down, and the hospital marquee of the 1st Battalion being torn to pieces the wounded had to be carried to such of the companies' tents as could be set up. On this occasion an instance occurred of the good feeling which has always existed in the Regiment between the Riflemen and their officers. Coote Buller was lying in his tent suffering from his wound, a broken thigh, at Inkerman. The men of the company held his tent during the gale, and thus, by preventing his exposure to the storm, rain and hail, probably saved his life.

The tents of the four companies of the 2nd Battalion at Balaklava, and everything belonging to them, except what they were standing in, were blown clean away, and were never heard of afterwards. At the same time the four companies of this Battalion on duty in the trenches were not relieved for forty-eight hours And one man of this Battalion died from exposure to the cold and to the storm.

The Russian riflemen having established themselves in some rifle pits in front of the left attack along some rising ground, annoyed our working parties as well as those of the French on the opposite side of the ravine by their fire. Lord Raglan determined to drive them back and to take possession of the pits. These pits, caverns, or 'ovens' as they were called by the men, are formed by the decay of softer portions of the rock between the harder strata, leaving caves in the sides of the hill. The duty of driving the Russians from them was confided to the 1st Battalion, and on November 20 a party consisting of Lieutenant Henry Tryon, in command, with Lieutenants Bourchier[1] and Cuninghame,[2] 4 sergeants and 200 rank and file, was detailed to carry it into execution. It was kept a secret what the service was to be till the party fell in about four o'clock in the afternoon. Then Tryon wheeled them round him and told the men what they were wanted for. He said that he intended to drive the Russians out, and that he was sure that they could do it And right

[1] Colonel Claude T. Bourchier, V.C, Aide-de-Camp to the Queen.

[2] Major Sir William J. M Cuninghame, Bart, V C, M.P., retired.

well they did it. Marching down to the trenches they lay down till dark. They then advanced stealthily, creeping along the broken ground which led first down a slight incline, and then up towards the enemy, who were completely surprised by the attack. Fifty men under Tryon formed the storming column; 50 the supports under Bourchier and 100 the reserve under Cuninghame. Eventually these parties became practically one. They quickly drove the Russian riflemen from their cover, though supported by a heavy column of Russian infantry. The occupants of the pits were evidently surprised. But soon the guns bearing on the pits poured grape and canister on the Riflemen, who had no cover, for the pits were open on the enemy's side. In the moment of taking possession of the pits the gallant Tryon fell shot in the head, Bourchier, who succeeded to the command of the party, maintained his advantage; and Cuninghame greatly distinguished himself by the energy with which he repulsed an attempt to turn the left flank of the advanced party, and thereby ensured the success of the capture. Repeatedly during that long night did the Russians attempt to retake the pits; sometimes by sending forward strong columns, sometimes by creeping up a few at a time, and when they got near making signals for their companions to come on. But this handful of Riflemen, under the command of these two young officers, bravely withstood them, and held the position until relieved next day by another party of the Battalion. In this affair Lieutenant Tryon and 9 men were killed, and 17 men were wounded. This gallant feat of arms, the first of the kind during that war, and never surpassed, was thus described in the despatch addressed by Lord Raglan to the Duke of Newcastle:

'Before Sebastopol, November 23, 1854.

'My Lord Duke,—The Russian advanced posts in front of our left attack having taken up a position which incommoded our troops in the trenches, and occasioned not a few casualties, and at the same time took in reverse the French troops working in their lines, a representation of which was made to me both by our own officers and by General Canrobert, a detachment of the 1st Battalion Rifle Brigade, under

Lieutenant Tryon, was directed on the night of the 20th to dislodge the enemy; and this service was performed most gallantly and effectively, but at some loss both in killed and wounded, and at the cost of the life of Lieutenant Tryon, who rendered himself conspicuous on the occasion: he was considered a most promising officer, and held in the highest estimation by all. The Russians attempted several times to re-establish themselves on the ground before daylight on the 21st, but they were instantly repulsed by Lieutenant Bourchier, the senior surviving officer of the party, and it now remains in our possession. Brigadier Sir John Campbell speaks highly of the conduct of the detachment, and of Lieutenant Bourchier and Lieutenant Cuninghame, and he laments the death of Lieutenant Tryon, who so ably led them in the first instance. This little exploit was so highly prized by General Canrobert that he instantly published an "Ordre Général" announcing it to the French army, and combining, with a just tribute to the gallantry of the troops, the expression of his deep sympathy in the regret felt for the loss of a young officer of so much distinction.

'(Signed) RAGLAN.'

The following General Order from Lord Raglan was also issued:

'General Order, November 24, 1854.

'The Commander of the Forces cannot pass unnoticed the attack, on the night of the 20th inst., of a detachment of the 1st Battalion Rifle Brigade under Lieutenant Tryon upon the advanced posts of the enemy, which had been pushed forward so as to enfilade the English trenches, and to take in reverse those of the French troops.

'The advance was made in the most spirited and determined manner, and was completely successful. And though several vigorous attempts were afterwards made by the enemy to dislodge the gallant band, they utterly failed, and the ground remains in our possession.

'Lieutenant Tryon, whose conduct was most conspicuous, was unfortunately killed, and several valuable soldiers shared the same fate.

'The General-in-Chief of the French army so highly

prized the achievement that he published a General Order eulogising the conduct of the detachment, and paying a just tribute to the officer who led it.

'(Signed) J. B B ESTCOURT.
'Adjutant-General.'

The following is the order referred to issued by the French General, a most honourable and unusual distinction :—

'*Ordre Général.*

'Dans la nuit du 20 au 21, sur la demande de concours que j'avais adressée au Commandant de l'Armée Anglaise, en lui faisant observer que les tirailleurs Russes s'établissaient à couvert en avant de ses lignes pour prendre à revers nos travailleurs, cent riflemen, conduits par le capitaine Tryon, sont sortis des tranchées Anglaises, ont tourné par la gauche les positions occupées par l'ennemi, et les ont enlevées après l'avoir débusqué Les Russes, formés en colonnes profondes, ont tenté trois fois de les reprendre à la baïonnette, après avoir fait pleuvoir la mitraille sur le détachment Anglais. Nos alliés ont tenu ferme avec l'énergie que nous leur connaissons, et sont restés maîtres de la position, où nous pouvons les apercevoir ce matin.

'J'ai voulu rendre hommage devant vous à la vigueur avec laquelle s'est accompli ce hardi coup de main, qui a malheureusement coûté la vie au vaillant capitaine Tryon. Nous lui donnerons les regrets dûs à sa fin glorieuse. Elle resserrera les liens de loyale confraternité d'armes qui nous unissent à nos alliés

'Au quartier général, devant Sébastopol le 21 Novembre, 1854.

'Le Général en chef,
(Signé) CANROBERT.

'Pour ampliation.
Le Général Chef d'Etat-Major général
E. de Martimprey.'[1]

[1] I am indebted to Marshal Canrobert for a copy of this order, which conferred so unusual and marked a distinction on the Regiment. In the letter which accompanied the transcript the Marshal expresses his appreciation of 'la magnifique conduite du detachment de la Rifle Brigade commandé par le Capitaine Tryon'

The following is the translation of the preceding General Order which was appended to Lord Raglan's orders on this occasion:

'Camp before Sebastopol, November 21, 1854.

'On the night of the 20th or 21st, on a request made by me to Lord Raglan, Commander-in-Chief of the English army, pointing out to him that the Russian riflemen had placed themselves under cover in front of the lines, from whence they could enfilade our workmen, one hundred Riflemen, under the command of Lieutenant Tryon, left the English trenches and, turning the flank of the enemy, charged and dispersed them. The Russians, formed in deep columns, attempted three times during the night to retake the place, after pouring in grape and canister on the English detachment. With that energy belonging to our allies, they held firmly their ground, and we can now see them where the enemy once stood.

'I wish before you all to render the homage due to so gallant an act, which unfortunately cost the life of the brave officer Lieutenant Tryon. We will give him all the regrets so glorious an end deserves It will be an additional link to the loyal fraternity of arms which unites us to our allies

'(Signed) GENERAL CANROBERT.'

For their gallant conduct in this affair Lieutenant Bourchier received the Victoria Cross, the Legion of Honour, the 5th Class of the Medjidie, and the Turkish Medal; Cuninghame the Victoria Cross, the 5th Class of the Medjidie, and the Turkish Medal; and Colour-Sergeant Hicks, who had volunteered for this duty, and was close to Tryon when he fell, obtained the French War Medal.

The gallant captors of the pits were relieved a little before daylight on the 21st by a party of the 1st Battalion, under the command of Lieutenant Flower, and accompanied by Lieutenant the Hon. G. B. Legge. The Russians kept up a very heavy fire on them all day, by which several men were wounded. So sharp was the fire, that it was impossible to go from one of the pits to the other without great caution. The ground, as we have seen, was rocky and crumbling, and most of the men who were wounded were struck about the face by fragments of rock. The position was so exposed to the enemy's fire that it was difficult even to get away the wounded; and Flower and Legge could only recover two wounded men, struck in the face and eyes and nearly blinded, by making them crawl on all fours into a pit where these officers had taken shelter. This party held the pits till nightfall, when they were relieved by another detachment of the Battalion. And for some days these pits, captured by Riflemen, were held by Riflemen, though occasionally a few men of other regiments may have been added to eke out the number required, which the diminished strength of the Battalion could hardly furnish.

The men of the 2nd Battalion were at this time called upon for very hard work, the right wing having been on duty on the 22nd three nights consecutively; and from the 26th the men were on duty five nights out of six. These duties, which were almost as severe in the 1st Battalion, the exposure to the weather; the shortness of food, rations being sometimes wanting for two or three days together; began to tell heavily on the Riflemen. Cholera and dysentery ravaged both Battalions. On November 27 Lieutenant Godfrey died, and the 1st Battalion, which had left England little more than four months before nearly a thousand strong, could only parade as fit for duty 275 men of all ranks.[1] And this, notwithstanding that it had received a draft from home of 154 non-commissioned officers and men. This shows a deficiency, even to this date, of 850 men.[2] The men of the 2nd Battalion at this time had for some days a ration of only a quarter of

[1] 105 men were employed on other duties connected with the service of the army.

[2] In order to show the state to which the Battalion was reduced by sickness and losses in the field, I may quote the Duty State of Woodford's company on January 19, 1855, which I owe to the kindness of the Hon. and Rev. George B. Legge. By this it appears that the company which left England six months before with a strength of about 100 men, had then present and nominally fit for duty just *one sergeant and eight men*. Of these some were in an exhausted and hardly efficient condition. Four non-commissioned officers and 25 privates were returned as 'in or attending hospital,' and 6 non-commissioned officers, 1 bugler and 42 privates were at Balaklava or Scutari, wounded or sick.

The 'Medical and Surgical History' states that during the month of November 2 officers and 29 men of the 1st Battalion were killed in action or in the trenches; and 3 officers and 131 men were wounded, of whom 13 died.

And that in the 2nd Battalion, 13 men were killed, and 1 officer and 33 men were wounded, of whom three suffered amputation.

a pound of salt pork and a pound of biscuit, owing to the difficulty of getting up supplies from Balaklava.

On the morning of December 2, about five o'clock, the Russians made a determined attempt to retake the 'ovens.' They advanced in considerable numbers. Surprising the sentries, they entered a trench which had been formed, after Tryon's party had taken the pits, into the second parallel, and driving out a party of another regiment who occupied it, took possession of it. At this moment a party of the 1st Battalion under Captain Churchill,[1] and accompanied by Lieutenant Blackett[2] and Ensign Brett, which formed the new guard of the trenches, came up and found the others retiring before the Russians. With the usual dash of the Riflemen, unabated in its energy by the severity of the weather or the urgency of their sufferings, they quickly attacked the Russians, drove them out, and took possession of the trenches, which they held as the guard for the day.[3]

The Riflemen lost in this affair one killed and two wounded, but the Russians left seven men dead on the field, and carried off seven wounded.

It was on this occasion that a *mot* is recorded of a non-commissioned officer of the Battalion, who, being asked how they came to be there, replied, 'If you please, Sir, the Russians relieved the —th, and we relieved the Russians.'

On December 12 a party of the 1st Battalion, under Captain Churchill (with Ensign Brett), being on duty in the trench near the Woronzow road, was violently attacked during the night by the enemy; but by showing a determined front and delivering an efficient fire they were at once driven off, and prevented from penetrating at this important point, which was the key to the British position.

On the 27th Colonel Horsford, who had commanded the Battalion at the Alma and Inkerman, and since Beckwith's fatal illness, had to return to Balaklava, and thence home on sick leave. And on the 29th Major Somerset, who had been on sick leave on board ship, arrived and assumed the command.

On the morning of December 30 the four companies of

[1] Lieutenant-Colonel C. H. S. Churchill.

[2] Lieutenant-Colonel E. W. Blackett, half-pay.

[3] 'Letters from Head-quarters by a Staff Officer,' 191, 3rd edition.

the 2nd Battalion, which were stationed on the heights near Balaklava, were ordered by Sir Colin Campbell to be under arms at half-past six. They paraded accordingly under Major Bradford, and after waiting till about eight o'clock, proceeded with a regiment of Highlanders to cover the flank of a considerable French force which made a reconnaissance. The Riflemen marched on, skirmishing through the woods and ravines They advanced to Kamara, and the French troops pushed on to the village of Tchorgúna, which they burned. However, the Riflemen were not actively engaged ; and after being under arms till the afternoon, returned to their camp.

The clothing which the Riflemen brought out from England being worn or torn by hard service, they presented a strange appearance. The greatcoat was always worn, and the blanket, with a hole cut through for the head, was put on under it. Over their shoulders they wore Cathcart's oilskins; and sand-bags, pieces of knapsacks, anything that would bend, were wrapped round the legs by way of gaiters. Some had loose Russian boots, which were worn over the trousers; for the cold was intense and food and fuel scanty, and everything that could give warmth, for comfort it could not be called, was pressed into service.

Great indeed were the sufferings of the men. During the whole month of December fresh meat was only served out two or three times, and they could not obtain vegetables of any kind. Some warm articles of clothing were indeed supplied, such as jerseys, drawers, blankets, socks and mitts; but these were not in sufficient quantities. The men were seven hours out of twenty-four in the trenches. Fifteen men of the 1st Battalion were wounded in the trenches during the month, of whom one died.

On January 4, 1855, by the efforts of the men of the 1st Battalion, assisted by two carts and six ponies from Headquarters, put at the disposal of the Battalion by the kindness of Lord Raglan and his Staff, the materials of the first wooden hut were brought from Balaklava to the front, but not without the loss of one horse, and the break-down of one cart, the Battalion, though probably weaker in numbers than any regiment at the front, showing a noble example, and proving the possibility (which some had doubted) of bringing a hut up at this season from Balaklava to the plateau on which the army was encamped. For driving snow and inclement weather continued for some weeks They proceeded as opportunity admitted to get up the huts, the 2nd Battalion beginning to erect theirs on the 22nd.

During this time of suffering and disease (for diarrhœa, dysentery and pulmonary complaints prevailed, and thirty-four men of the 1st Battalion died during this month) the camp of the Riflemen was frequently visited by Lord Raglan ; who on one occasion, finding a deficiency of port wine in the hospital marquee, immediately sent down four bottles from his own quarters [1]

On January 17, 1855, General Sir Andrew F. Barnard, Colonel Commandant of the 1st Battalion, died at his residence at Chelsea Hospital, of which he was Lieutenant-Governor. On his death Sir Harry Smith became Colonel Commandant of the 1st, and Lieutenant-General Sir George Brown, who had as Lieutenant-Colonel for seventeen years commanded the 2nd Battalion, became its Colonel Commandant.

On February 1, Colonel Norcott joined, and took command of the 1st Battalion, to which he succeeded by Beckwith's death , and thus the son of one of the earliest officers of the Regiment succeeded the nephew of another, both of whom had commanded it in many bloody fields.

On February 19 a party of the 2nd Battalion, under Colonel Macdonell, formed part of a reconnaissance in force under Sir Colin Campbell. They were under arms soon after midnight, and about four in the morning moved down towards the plain, and marched in the direction of Kamara and Tchorgúna. It was snowing heavily when they started, and the storm increased as the day broke. The Riflemen preceded the advance in skirmishing order. Orders were given not to fire if they came on the enemy, and it was hoped that they might be surprised ; but the density of the snow-storm prevented the men seeing many feet to their front. However, the skirmishers made three sentries prisoners, who were probably part of the picquet at Kamara. And it seemed that

[1] During this month eight men of this Battalion were wounded in the trenches, and one man, wounded in December, died of his wounds

the alarm was given; for the vedettes fell back firing their carbines into the darkness, the drums were heard beating to arms, and through the snow their battalions were dimly seen assembling on the heights over the Tchernaya. The snow fell more thickly than ever; the men could scarcely hold their rifles; the position and strength of the enemy were unknown; and Sir Colin gave the word to return. The Riflemen arrived in camp about eleven in the forenoon, suffering much from cold and fatigue.

On the 24th the 1st Battalion marched down to Balaklava and exchanged the Minié rifle for the Enfield. This was the long Enfield, for which the short Enfield was afterwards substituted.

On March 7 Major Macdonell took command of the four companies of the 2nd Battalion at Balaklava, Colonel Bradford having been promoted to the command of the 3rd Battalion, which was now again raised.

During this month the work in the trenches was, owing to the shortness of the numbers effective, most severe and harassing to the men. Many sank under it. But as regards provisions and comforts, things began to mend. For these were issued not only from Government stores, but were also provided from private sources. About the middle of March the climate much improved, and from that time, though the duties were still severe, the sufferings of the Riflemen much diminished.

On March 23 the Russians made a great attack on the whole length of the allied line. It was particularly severe on the right attack; Captain Forman's company formed part of the trench guard, and was actively engaged. This attack was led by a Greek in full dress who rushed at the magazine, and fired his musket into it, but it was empty; and he was immediately bayonetted in the trench

After this the enemy began firing shells into the camp of the 1st Battalion, but without doing any material injury.. During the month of March three sergeants and 82 men died, of whom 1 sergeant and 10 men died in camp, the remainder at Scutari or Kulalie.

During this month seven men of the 2nd Battalion were wounded in the trenches.

On March 19 the 1st and 2nd Battalions were augmented to sixteen companies, and were to consist of the following numbers:

Lieutenant-Cols.	Majors	Captains	Lieutenants	Ensigns	Staff	Staff-Sergeants
2	2	16	26	14	7	9

Sergeants	Buglers	Corporals	Privates
100	41	100	1,900

On April 9, fire was reopened and kept up till the 12th, and on the 13th volunteers were called for to man the rifle pits in front of No. 7 battery. Lieutenant the Hon. A. Anson [1] and eighteen men of the 1st Battalion volunteered for the duty. They occupied the pits from daylight until dark; but suffered a heavy loss, Sergeant Devitt and four men being killed. These pits were afterwards connected and formed the fourth parallel.

On April 22 a bandsman of the 2nd Battalion named Wright, who was on duty in the trenches, going to fetch water from a well in front of the advanced trench near the Quarries, was killed; it being impossible to throw up any cover near the well in consequence of the rockiness of the soil. This man being a great favourite of his comrades, a number of them rushed out determined to drive out the Russian riflemen, by whose fire he had fallen, from the pits which they occupied. Three men, Bradshaw, Humpston and MacGregor, were the first to reach them, and drove the Russians out, killing some while a few escaped. For this gallant deed these three Riflemen received the Victoria Cross, Bradshaw being also decorated with the French War Medal.[2]

About this time clothing of a new pattern was served out to both Battalions; a tunic being substituted for the old coatee for the men, and taking the place of the jacket and pelisse for the officers, which they had both worn with slight variations since the formation of the Regiment

The 1st Battalion received their new clothing April 1855, partly coatees and partly the new tunic.

[1] Lieutenant-Colonel the Honourable Augustus H A Anson, V.C, retired

[2] In the official notification of the grant of the Victoria Cross, MacGregor is said to have performed this act of valour 'in the month of July;' but I have been repeatedly assured by Bradshaw that he, Humpston and MacGregor were together, and won their crosses on this occasion.

In April two men of the 1st Battalion died of wounds received from the enemy.

The left wing of the 2nd Battalion embarked on May 3 as part of the Expedition destined for Kertch; but the order having been countermanded after they had arrived at the *rendezvous*, they landed again and joined the Head-quarters before Sebastopol on May 8.

On May 18 the Queen in person distributed the Crimean Medal on the Horse Guards parade, when the following officers and men of the Regiment received it from Her Majesty's hands:

Lieutenant-Colonels Bradford and Horsford; Majors Elrington, Hardinge, the Earl of Errol and the Hon. G. Elliott; Captains Inglis, Newdigate, Ross, Drummond, Nixon, C. Buller, Warren, Rowles, Lindsay, Bourchier, Deedes

Second Battalion: Corporal William Muggridge (wounded), Privates Thomas Palmer (wounded), William Careless (wounded) and T. Dulahan.

Third Battalion: Colour-Sergeant Andrew Holdaway, Sergeant James Johnson and Private John Titcombe

In May one man of the 2nd Battalion was killed, and 1 officer and 12 men were wounded in the trenches; of whom 3 died. One man was killed in action.

On June 7 the 2nd Battalion was engaged in the attack and capture of the Quarries, one of the principal outworks of the enemy, and had one Rifleman killed and 11 wounded. On that evening a working party of the 1st Battalion, consisting of all the men off duty, were employed to turn the works thus captured, and to make a covered way to the Mamelon. Several attempts were made by the enemy during the night to retake these works; and just before daylight a fierce attack was made. It was at first almost a hand-to-hand fight, and the Riflemen were for a time driven out of the works, but they eventually repulsed their assailants. These frequent attacks however seriously hindered their work, as the men were obliged to stand to their arms as often as the advanced sentries fell back.

On the evening of the 17th orders were issued to the 4th Division that it should attack the proper left face of the Redan. The 1st Battalion furnished 100 men under the command of Captain the Hon. James Stuart,[1] with Lieutenants Boileau and Saunders,[2] to act as a covering party. They were to get as near the works as possible and to pick off the Russians if they showed themselves above the parapet while the storming party advanced. This party left the camp at a quarter after one in the morning of the 18th, and occupied the trench round the Quarries until daybreak. But instead of issuing from the trench at once in extended order, they were moved down to the left, and passing a narrow opening between two rifle-pits, began to extend on the enemy's side of the cover afforded by the parapet of the trench. As soon as they appeared the enemy poured grape and canister, and opened musketry fire on them from the parapet of the Redan. The Riflemen were mown down like grass, but pushing on to the right advanced followed by the crew of the 'Leander' carrying the scaling ladders. Boileau, sword in hand, and shouting out 'Come on, Rifles!' gallantly led on his party, and endeavoured to get them below the line of fire from the guns But these brave men, not being supported, were eventually obliged to withdraw. They had got up to an *abattis* in front of the Redan and lay close under it until the middle of the day. For unfortunately they did not discover in time that the attack had failed; and there seemed no possibility of their crossing the open ground between their then position and the trenches in broad daylight without immense loss. Happily for them a sand-storm swept across the ground about mid-day; and screened by that they retired, regained the trenches, and returned to their camp.

The remainder of the Battalion, under Colonel Norcott, left camp about an hour after the covering party and occupied the trenches in front of the Redan, but were not moved out against the enemy.

The Light Division was directed to storm the right face of the Redan. And the 2nd Battalion furnished a ladder party of 100 men under Captain Blackett; a woolbag party of the same number under Lieutenant Fremantle;[3] a covering party of the same number under Captain Forman, and a

[1] Lieutenant-Colonel the Hon. James Stuart, died April 11, 1870.
[2] Captain Saunders (retired) died May 28, 1863.
[3] Lieutenant-Colonel Fitzroy Fremantle, Coldstream Guards.

working and gabion party under Colonel Macdonell. The attack was led by Captain Forman, who was killed. But these parties were only supported by the 34th Regiment; thus this attack likewise failed, and the troops were recalled and returned to their respective camps.

In the 1st Battalion Lieutenant Boileau was wounded, and died at Malta on August 1; one sergeant (Jerram) and 7 men were killed; and 11 men were wounded. And in the 2nd Battalion, besides Captain Forman, 2 sergeants and 23 rank and file were killed; and Captain Blackett (who lost his leg), Lieutenants Knox (who lost his arm) and Fremantle were severely wounded; and 3 sergeants and 75 rank and file were wounded.

At night the enemy made a general attack on the English lines; but were repulsed without any loss in the Regiment.

When parties were sent out to collect the dead on the 19th (a flag of truce having come in at four P.M.) the body of Sir John Campbell, who had led the attack of the 4th Division, was found inside the *abattis*, and that of Private Flannery of the 1st Battalion was found close to the ditch, and twenty yards in advance of where Sir John lay.

At night the cemetery was occupied and a communication carried down to it from the caves.[1]

On June 30 Lieutenant Woodford of the 2nd Battalion was wounded when on duty in the trenches, and died on the same day.

On July 3 Captain Fyers was coming off picquet in the advanced works with about 400 men. They were retiring by a zig-zag which by some oversight of the Engineers was directly enfiladed by a Russian gun. As soon as the men were well in the *boyau* a round shot was fired, which, bounding along, knocked down 13 men, of whom 8 were killed or died of their wounds.[2] The wounded were removed by Fyers, Colour-Sergeant Kemp, and some soldiers of another regiment who came to their assistance. The rest of the men turned into another zig-zag not exposed to this fire. The ball after

[1] One officer and 30 men of the 2nd Battalion were killed in action; and 4 officers and 125 men wounded during the month of June. Of these 12 cases proved fatal.

[2] Three privates of the 2nd Battalion are returned in the 'Gazette' as killed and 13 wounded on July 3.

this destructive course ran along the *boyau* and stopped against the bank of the parallel, a dead ball.[1]

On July 3 the body of Lord Raglan, Commander-in-Chief, who died on June 28, was conveyed on a gun-carriage to Kazatch bay, and was embarked on board the 'Caradoc' and taken to England. A party of 100 men of each Battalion accompanied his remains to the place of embarkation.

The siege continued during the months of July and August. The duties in the trenches were constant, and the Riflemen were engaged either in working parties or in covering them.[2] Almost nightly attacks were made on these parties; and they were vigorously plied with shot and shell.

On the evening of September 1 a party of the 2nd Battalion were ordered to cover a sap which was in course of construction from the fifth parallel towards the flank of the Redan.

At 7.30 Captain Balfour,[3] with one subaltern (Lieutenant Cary), 2 sergeants and 48 rank and file, left the camp for that duty. The Russians had erected a screen of stones about 80 yards in front of the head of the sap, as a protection to their sentries; and their reserves occupied a pit behind this screen and also a ravine on their left in which there was a cave. Captain Balfour detached Cary with one sergeant and 23 men to proceed down the ravine and turn the Russian left; while he himself with the remainder of the party made a rush at the screen of stones behind which the Russian riflemen were posted. After a short but sharp encounter the Russians abandoned the screen of stones and the pit, and retired towards the ditch of the Redan and to a small graveyard in the Karabelnaia ravine.

Lieutenant Cary and Sergeant Henry Wood much distinguished themselves in this affair, and were both wounded.

[1] For his conduct on this occasion Fyers recommended Sergeant Kemp for the Victoria Cross, but he did not receive it

[2] Three men of the 2nd Battalion were killed, and 43 wounded during the month of July, of these 6 terminated fatally. And 4 men, wounded in June, died in this month. Fourteen men of the 1st Battalion were wounded in the trenches in August, 2 of whom died. And 2 men of the 2nd Battalion were killed, and more than 80 wounded, 6 of whom died.

[3] Major Walter Francis Balfour, retired March 10, 1857.

One Rifleman was killed and 14 were wounded. Cary died at Malta, from the effects of his wounds, on November 9.

On September 8, when the assault was to take place, one half of the 1st Battalion being in the trenches under Colonel Norcott, the remainder, consisting of about 280 men under Lieutenant-Colonel Somerset, moved out of camp at eleven A.M. and took up a position in reserve on the Woronzow road.

The 2nd Battalion furnished a covering party for the assault of the Redan consisting of 100 men, under the command of Captain Fyers, who were to cover the advance of the ladder party, and to keep down the fire from the parapet; a party, also of 100 men, under Captain Balfour, occupied some broken ground and a Russian rifle-pit in front of and to the right of our most advanced works, who were also directed to keep down the fire from the parapet. With the same object two parties of 50 men each under Lieutenants Baillie and Playne, were stationed, one in the fifth parallel, and one in the Woronzow road. The remainder of the Battalion, about 230 men under the command of Lieutenant-Colonel Macdonell, took part in the general attack.

These men had to advance 150 yards, exposed to a most terrible fire in front and flank. This attack, most gallantly carried out, was not entirely successful; though, as is well known, the operations of this day led to the abandonment of the works by the Russians, and the fall of the place.

During the night following this attack Major Woodford (who had been slightly wounded) and Captain Balfour, with about 150 Riflemen, occupied the stone screen, the rifle pit, and the cave above mentioned. Major Woodford (it is said) had obtained a promise from Sir Colin Campbell that, if his Highlanders assaulted the Redan on the next morning, these men should again form a covering party. But the dawn of the 9th revealed the fact that the Russians were abandoning the flaming town; and the services of these Riflemen, utterly exhausted by the fighting and excitement of the assault, were not required.

The 2nd Battalion lost 2 officers, Captain Hammond and Lieutenant Ryder, 4 sergeants and 19 rank and file killed. And 8 officers, Major Woodford, Captain the Hon. B. R. Pellew, Lieutenants Eyre, Riley, Eccles, Moore, Borough and Playne, 8 sergeants, 1 bugler and 128 rank and file were wounded.[1]

The following interesting account of Captain Hammond and Lieutenant Ryder is extracted from a letter written by Staff Assistant-Surgeon Walter Clegg, dated September 9, 1855:

'With Captain Hammond's name you will be familiar, as I frequently mentioned to you the many acts of kindness I received from him when he commanded the Depôt at Fort Cumberland. A braver soldier never on that day mounted the Redan; a Christian of more unaffected piety never entered the presence of God.

'He had only been in the Crimea forty-eight hours when he was killed. When the Rifles were forming for the assault, a young subaltern, going into action for the first time, who had come out with Hammond, addressed him: "Captain Hammond, how fortunate we are! we are just in time for Sebastopol."

'Hammond's eye was gazing where the rays of the sun made a path of golden light over the sea, and his answer was short and remarkable, and accompanied by the quiet smile which those who knew him so well remember: "I am quite ready," said he.

'The next that was seen of Hammond was when his sword was flashing at one of the embrasures of the Redan. He was indeed at the head of his company, fighting to gain an entrance for them.

'A dozen bayonets were at his heart and once he was dragged in a prisoner. In a few minutes he was recognised again outside the embrasure, still hacking with his sword. The next morning at six o'clock Captain Balfour found him in the ditch beneath a dozen of the slain, with a bayonet wound through his heart.

'Hammond and Ryder were buried this afternoon in the burial-ground of the division, rendered sacred long ago by the

[1] Nineteen men of the 1st Battalion were wounded in action in September, of whom 2 died. One of these (William Hardinge) was so much injured about the head and face by the bursting of a shell (on September 5) that he died of lock-jaw on the 11th. And 25 men of the 2nd Battalion were killed, and 7 officers and 181 men were wounded in action, of whom 15 died of their wounds.

sepulture of brave men. Ryder was barely eighteen years old.

'Before the assault had lasted an hour he was shot in the throat and fell, and was carried to the rear and consigned to the surgeon. But as it happened the surgeon was engaged at the moment that Ryder was brought in, and the young Lieutenant tied his handkerchief round his throat, and was seen again on the ladder, and when he was found the next day in the ditch a bayonet thrust had transfixed his forehead.' [1]

The English troops now took possession of the Redan and the Karabelnaia district, and the Regiment took its share of the duty in Sebastopol during the destruction of the dock-yard and other works. Soon after the taking of the place a detachment of the 2nd Battalion, consisting of 8 officers, 12 sergeants and 200 men, under the command of Captain Fyers, proceeded to Head-quarters, where they acted as escort or body-guard to the Commander-in-Chief

On October 1 Colonel Norcott having proceeded to England, the command of the 1st Battalion devolved on Lieutenant-Colonel Somerset, who going to England on the 24th, Lord Alexander Russell took command. And on the 14th Colonel Hill having arrived from England, assumed command of the 2nd Battalion.

A great attack on the Inkerman side having been expected in consequence of telegraphic information from England, both Battalions were under arms at an early hour on the 16th and the following mornings for some time.

On the 26th Colour-Sergeant Noseley, who had been reported as killed at the battle of Inkerman, rejoined the 1st Battalion, he having been wounded and taken prisoner by the Russians He was the only man of the Battalion who was in the hands of the enemy during the campaign

The 1st Battalion continued to occupy the ground on which it was encamped. And early in November pannelled huts began to be erected

On November 15, about two o'clock in the afternoon, a tremendous explosion took place in the French siege train, situated at the head of a ravine which ran down towards

[1] 'Illustrated London News,' xxvii p. 394 A 'Memoir of Captain M. M. Hammond' was published in 1858.

Carecnage bay. Colour-Sergeant Pescott of the 1st Battalion, who had gone down in charge of a fatigue party, received injuries from a rocket, from the effects of which he died. And Lieutenant Eccles and several men of the 2nd Battalion were wounded, two of whom died from the injuries then inflicted.

On the 17th Lieutenant Borough, 2nd Battalion, died of fever.

On the 26th no one was reported sick in the 1st Battalion; this was the second time only that such an occurrence had taken place since its arrival in the East.

During the winter the Battalions were employed in road-making, in fetching up huts, in furnishing picquets, or guards in the town.

On February 24, 1856, the two Battalions (with the rest of the army) paraded on the Telegraph hill above Balaklava for the inspection of the Commander-in-Chief, General Codrington; Marshal Pelissier was also present.

Though the cold was very severe and much snow fell in the early part of this year, the Riflemen, having the protection of the huts and sufficient rations and fuel, were in far greater comfort than during the preceding winter. A theatre was erected with wood fetched from Sebastopol. Other amusements beguiled the time not required for duties, and in a foot race of the whole army on March 19, Lieutenant Palliser of the 1st Battalion won the officers' hurdle race, and Lieutenant Thomas, 2nd Battalion, came in second.

The whole English army paraded in the afternoon of April 17 for the inspection of the Russian General Luders. The Generals having gone down the line the troops marched past and returned to their camps.

On the 25th the 1st Battalion paraded for the inspection of General Vanlinsky, who had commanded the Russian troops on Mackenzie heights on September 25, 1854.

On May 9 a Rifleman (Private Connolly of the 1st Battalion) died from the effects of a wound received on April 26, by the explosion of a Russian shell, which was carelessly dropped by a soldier of another regiment, while they were gathering shells in Sebastopol

On the 24th the two Battalions were marched to Balaklava

plains to celebrate (with the rest of the troops) the Queen's birthday. On this occasion the medals granted by the Emperor of the French were distributed.

On June 4 the 1st Battalion marched to Balaklava at eight in the morning, and embarked immediately in H.M.S. 'Apollo,' and went out of harbour in tow of H.M.S. 'Medusa,' and after touching at Scutari, Malta, Algiers and Gibraltar, anchored off Corunna on the 27th. Here they were visited by Spanish Generals, soldiers, ladies (upward of fifty of whom came on board), and apparently everyone who could get a seat in a boat. A strange contrast to the scene forty-seven years before, when the Battalion embarked at Corunna!

Leaving Corunna on the 28th the Battalion landed at Portsmouth on July 7, and proceeding at once to Aldershot by rail, encamped there.

On June 8 the 2nd Battalion embarked at Balaklava on board the sailing transport 'King Philip,' and arrived at Portsmouth on July 11 and proceeded by rail to Aldershot.

On the 1st Battalion leaving the Crimea the following General Order was published by Major-General Garrett, K.H., commanding the 4th Division:

'Camp before Sebastopol, June 3, 1856. Division After-Order.

'Major-General Garrett regrets that the separation of the 1st Battalion Rifle Brigade from the 4th Division by their embarkation to-morrow for England, calls on him to take leave of them.

'The Major-General will look back with pride and pleasure to those eventful days when they were under his command, first as a Brigadier and afterwards commanding the Division, for upwards of a year and a half. During that period the willingness and smartness which the officers and the men invariably evinced, whether on duties in camp or in the trenches, clearly showed that that magnificent *esprit de corps* which descended from their predecessors, the old 95th, still animates the young soldiers, who were brought to supply the heavy casualties of the late campaign; which they quickly caught up from the fine old soldiers whose education had been formed in the rough and arduous enterprises of two Kaffir wars.

'That that noble *esprit de corps* may never fail them is the sincere wish of the Major-General, who hopes soon to see them exhibiting that spirit amongst their comrades in England.'

On July 8 the 1st Battalion was reviewed by the Queen, when the officers who disembarked with the Battalion, 8 sergeants, 7 buglers, 8 corporals and 9 privates, were selected to be addressed personally by Her Majesty. And being (with others) formed up round her carriage Her Majesty addressed them in the following words:

'Officers, Non-commissioned officers, and soldiers: I wish personally to convey to you, for the regiments assembled here this day, my hearty welcome on their return to England in health and full efficiency.

'Say to them, I have watched anxiously over their different trials and hardships which they have so nobly borne; that I mourn with deep sorrow for the brave men who have fallen for their country, and that I have felt proud of that valour, which with their gallant allies, they have displayed in the field. I thank God that your dangers are over whilst the glory of your deeds remains; but I know that should your services be again required, you will be animated by the same devotion which in the Crimea has rendered you invincible.'

And on the 16th the 2nd Battalion was reviewed by Her Majesty, when the 1st Battalion was also present. The appearance of the Riflemen, all of whom wore the Crimean Medal, with three or four clasps, many the Kaffir Medal, and some the Sardinian and other decorations, specially attracted attention.

The two Battalions were again reviewed by Her Majesty on July 30.

By letter from the War Office, dated August 11, the strength of the 1st Battalion was reduced from 109 sergeants, 41 buglers, and 2,000 rank and file, to 57 sergeants, 25 buglers, and 1,000 rank and file. A similar reduction took place in the 2nd Battalion.

On April 1, 1855, a 3rd Battalion was, a second time, added to the Regiment. They were formed at Haslar barracks, under Lieutenant-Colonel Bradford, by transfers from the Depôts of the 1st and 2nd Battalions; but as he very shortly afterwards exchanged with Colonel Hill,[1] to the Royal Canadian Rifle Regiment, Lieutenant-Colonel Horsford assumed the command and in fact made this new Battalion. They were inspected on June 25 by Major-General Breton, their strength then being 29 officers and 590 men.

On August 3 they moved by rail to Aldershot. And soon after 240 volunteers were received from the 1st Middlesex, 1st Surrey, and East Warwick, and on October 11, 180 volunteers from the Royal Elthorne, Militia regiments On the 22nd the Battalion was inspected by Major-General Knollys, when its strength had increased to 39 officers and 947 men. During the early part of 1856, volunteers continued to be received from several Militia regiments; and on June 9 the Battalion proceeded to Portsmouth, where, on their inspection by Major-General Breton, the strength of the Battalion had increased to 41 officers and 1,165 men.

On August 3 the Battalion was divided into Service and Depôt companies; the former returned to Aldershot, and the latter (two companies) proceeded to Winchester.

On September 30, in consequence of reductions, 170 men of the 1st and 2nd Battalions were transferred to the 3rd.

But on October 8 the establishment of the Battalion was reduced to 1,000 rank and file.

The 1st Battalion remained at Aldershot till July 27, 1857, when they proceeded by rail to Edinburgh, where they arrived on the 28th and occupied quarters in the Castle; one company (Brevet-Major Oxenden's) being detached to Greenlaw. This detachment was relieved monthly.

The following Brigade Order was issued by Major-General the Hon. A. A. Spencer on the Battalion leaving Aldershot:

'Major-General Spencer takes leave of Lieutenant-Colonel Somerset, the officers, non-commissioned officers and men of the 1st Battalion Rifle Brigade on their departure for Edinburgh, with much regret.

'It is now upwards of two years since he became acquainted and connected with the Battalion in the 4th Division before Sebastopol, during which time he has had opportunities of

[1] Major-General Percy Hill, C.B.

judging of their soldierlike qualities and habits of discipline.

'The greatest proofs of these are the success which always attended their separate important undertakings against the enemy, and also their speedy recovery from the effects of hardships they, as well as every other regiment in that army, experienced in the winters of 1854-5.

'The Major-General now bids them farewell, and trusts it may be his good fortune to meet them again in his military career.'

On August 5 a serious fire broke out in the old town of Edinburgh, which the Battalion succeeded with great exertions in extinguishing Their conduct on this occasion elicited the following letter to Lieutenant-Colonel Somerset from the Lord Provost:

'Edinburgh, August 11, 1857.

'Sir,—I have the honour to convey a resolution unanimously adopted by the magistrates and town council of this city at their meeting to-day, to express their warm and cordial thanks to the officers and men of your regiment for the valuable and effective aid rendered by you in extinguishing the late fire and preserving order.

'(Signed) JOHN MELVILL, Lord Provost.

'Lieutenant-Colonel Somerset, C B , Rifle Brigade'

During the time the Battalion was at Edinburgh the men received the short Enfield and resumed the armament of the sword bayonet, as of old.

Riots of the mill-hands being apprehended, three companies of the Battalion were hurriedly moved by rail to Glasgow on November 11 in aid of the Civil power; and these were reinforced by an additional company on December 1.

A few days afterwards the Head-quarters and remaining companies of the Battalion followed them to Glasgow, arriving there on the 10th and detaching two companies to Ayr.

The 2nd Battalion remained at Aldershot until June, on the 26th of which month they proceeded to London. And were present at the first distribution of the Victoria Cross by Her Majesty Queen Victoria. On which occasion the following officers and men of the Regiment received the cross from the hands of Her Majesty:

Brevet-Major the Hon. H. Clifford.
Brevet-Major C. T. Bourchier.
Captain William J. Cunninghame.
Lieutenant John Knox.
Private Francis Wheatley.
Private Joseph Bradshaw.
Private Roderic MacGregor.
Private John Humpston

After taking part in the review which followed this ceremony, the Battalion proceeded the same evening to Liverpool, where they embarked the following day for Dublin And on their arrival there Head-quarters and five companies occupied Beggar's-bush barracks, and the other three companies Linen-hall barracks.

A letter was issued from the War Office, dated September 22, 1857, by which a 4th Battalion was directed to be added to the Regiment. This Battalion was therefore immediately formed at Winchester under Lieutenant-Colonel Elrington, who was promoted from Senior Major on September 1.

Recruiting at once commenced, and transfers were received from the 1st and 2nd Battalions, and from some other regiments, so that by the end of the year the Battalion had attained a strength of 28 sergeants, 10 corporals, 15 buglers and 413 privates.

They proceeded by rail on December 15 from Winchester to Chichester.

Plate IV

RIFLE BRIGADE.
1856 TO 1860.

CHAPTER XI.

THE Sepoy Mutiny having broken out, and troops being despatched with all haste to quell it, the 2nd and 3rd Battalions received orders to embark immediately for India.

The 2nd Battalion embarked in three divisions:

The first under Brevet Lieutenant-Colonel Woodford, consisting of 3 captains, 5 subalterns, 21 sergeants, 7 buglers and 322 rank and file, proceeded by rail from Dublin to Cork on August 3, and embarked on board the 'Lady Jocelyn' screw steamer. The second under Brevet Lieutenant-Colonel Fyers, consisting of 2 captains, 2 subalterns, 9 sergeants, 3 buglers and 146 rank and file, proceeded by railway to Kingstown and embarked on board the 'United Kingdom' on August 4.

The Head-quarters with four companies under Lieutenant-Colonel Hill, consisting of 3 captains, 8 subalterns, 5 staff, 30 sergeants, 14 buglers and 292 rank and file, proceeded by railway to Kingstown on August 6, and embarking on board the 'Sussex,' hired transport, started for India on the next day.

The first of these detachments (Woodford's) arrived at Calcutta on November 3, and disembarked.

On the 7th they paraded at 3.30 to cross the Ganges, which they did in a steamer, and at 9.30 in the evening started by railroad for Raneegunge, where they arrived at 6.30 on the following morning.

From thence they proceeded on the 10th in carriages at three P.M. and arrived at Doomrhee at 7.30 on the next day; whence starting at 10.30 and passing through Brohal, the Dowah pass, and Bawa, reached Sherghotty at 8.45 A.M. on the morning of the 12th.

After a short halt there they started again at one P.M. for Barroon. Soon after which they crossed the river Sone, a most tedious process; the river here being about two miles broad and reached by a long plain of sand. The carriages had to be placed in boats; and having got over one bend of the river, another long sandy plain had to be traversed and then a still wider stream of water to be crossed. This occupied a very long time; from midnight to 5.30 in the morning; but having accomplished it they arrived at Sasseram at 8.45 A.M on the 13th. At five o'clock they started again, and travelling through the night, were about ten P.M. startled by an alarm that they were about to be attacked. The 'alarm' was sounded; rifles and revolvers were got into readiness, and some confusion occurred, but after a few minutes it was ascertained that the alarm, from wheresoever originating, was a false one. And on the 14th, about 10.20 in the morning, they reached Annabad, where they halted till five, when after passing Kurumnasa they reached the bank of the Ganges, and crossing it in boats arrived at the Mint at Benares about 4 45 on the morning of the 15th, where they halted till the 18th; this being the first occasion on which they had taken any of their things off since they left Raneegunge.

On the 18th they started again at 4 15 P.M. and reached Gopeegunge at 1 45 P.M. on the 19th, and after halting till 5.50 started again. Here Colonel Woodford was informed that a rebel force of 300 or 400 cavalry, 6,000 or 7,000 infantry and ten or twelve guns was encamped on his right, about twenty miles from Gopeegunge. The march, or rather the journey in bullock-carts, in the night was therefore made with great caution and with every preparation to resist an attack. But none was made, and on the 20th they reached the Ganges at Allahabad about twelve P.M, and after great difficulty in finding the camping-ground got into camp. On that night they again had a false alarm.

They halted at Allahabad till the 23rd, the intervening time being employed in getting clothing for the men.

Here the detachment under Lieutenant-Colonel Fyers, which had sailed in the 'United Kingdom,' joined them; and the whole started by rail at 8.30 on the 23rd and arrived at Lohunga at 12.30. Here they again divided; Colonel Woodford's detachment proceeding by bullock-carts and Colonel Fyers' by route march. Woodford's detachment started about five, and after delays by break-down of waggons and restive oxen, arrived at Futtehpore at 4.45 on the 24th. Starting again at eight they met a Sikh on the 25th bearing a message from General Windham urging them to push on, as they would be wanted. Making all speed therefore they reached Cawnpore at 6.45 P.M. and took up their quarters in the Theatre for the night, being warned to go to camp at four A.M. on the following morning.

On that morning (the 26th) they paraded at 2.30, and shortly afterwards marched to General Windham's camp, which was formed near the bridge, on the road from Cawnpore to Calpee, over the Ganges canal.

They reached it about seven; and no breakfast being provided, they received a dry biscuit and a ration of rum. Hence they moved out to attack the Gwalior contingent, which was posted in great force on the Pandoo Nuddee river. They advanced, the three companies[1] of Riflemen in front. On approaching the enemy's position the mutineers at once opened fire about 9.30. 'The battle on the part of the British began with the companies of the Rifle Brigade. These admirable troops at once advanced in skirmishing order on the right of the road. The country was a good deal encumbered with high standing corn, topes of trees, walls, &c.'[2] Some of the Riflemen got into ruined houses, and having got the range picked off the enemy's gunners. The Gwalior contingent however held their position—a strong one, on the right bank of the Pandoo Nuddee—for some time. But at last the men advanced with a rush, and crossing the almost dry bed of the river drove them back. The Riflemen pursued them for some miles. One man only (Wolfe) was killed in this day's fight: he was shot through the head. At a little before twelve the fight was over, and the Riflemen returned towards their camp. After they had retired some distance the mutineers pursued; and they were halted and deployed. During this halt a ration of rum was served out to the men. Resuming their march the Riflemen returned to Cawnpore, and pitched their camp near the city across the Calpee road and close to some brick-kilns. They arrived in this camp about four P.M.

[1] Forty men under Ensign Travers were left to guard the canal bridge.

[2] 'Defence of Cawnpore,' by Lieutenant-Colonel Adye, C.B., p. 19.

On the 27th there was a false alarm at six in the morning; but later it was found that the Gwalior contingent, with a strength of about 25,000 men and forty guns, had commenced a most determined attack on General Windham's position, both in front and on his right flank. The three companies of Riflemen, Nixon's, Dillon's and Earle's, were moved out about noon, and posted on the right of the road to Calpee at its junction with the Grand Trunk road to Delhi, and were immediately under fire. 'The heavy fighting in front, at the point of junction of the Calpee and Delhi roads, fell more especially upon the Rifle Brigade, ably commanded by Colonel Walpole.'[1]

However the enemy were too strong for them, and they were obliged to retire. Some officers and men occupied a small tope of trees, but they were soon out of ammunition, and Lieutenants George Curzon and Dugdale went back across the open, exposed to the fire of two guns which plied them with grape. However they succeeded in bringing up a camel with a supply. A second, third and fourth time Curzon passed the same ordeal in search of further ammunition or caps; and after some unsuccessful ventures obtained a supply from Captain Atherley of the 3rd Battalion, who with his company after a forced march from Futtehpore (to be presently more particularly mentioned) had arrived at Cawnpore.

This retreat was covered in a most masterly manner by the three companies under Woodford, who were extended in a line of skirmishers over a space of nearly a mile, and for a long time held back an enormous force of the enemy of all arms. And had it not been for the stand made by this detachment, it was generally supposed that the two guns of the Naval Brigade, which had been left unprotected, would have fallen into the enemy's hands.[2]

It was first observed by Corporal Suddlers of the 2nd Battalion that these guns were deserted, and they were with difficulty brought back by some Riflemen of Captain Nixon's company, under Lieutenant-Colonel Woodford, who took the slings off their rifles for that purpose.[3]

I have now to trace the march of Fyers' detachment of three

[1] General Windham's Despatch, November 30, 1857

[2] Letter from General Payn.

[3] Captain Curzon's notes.

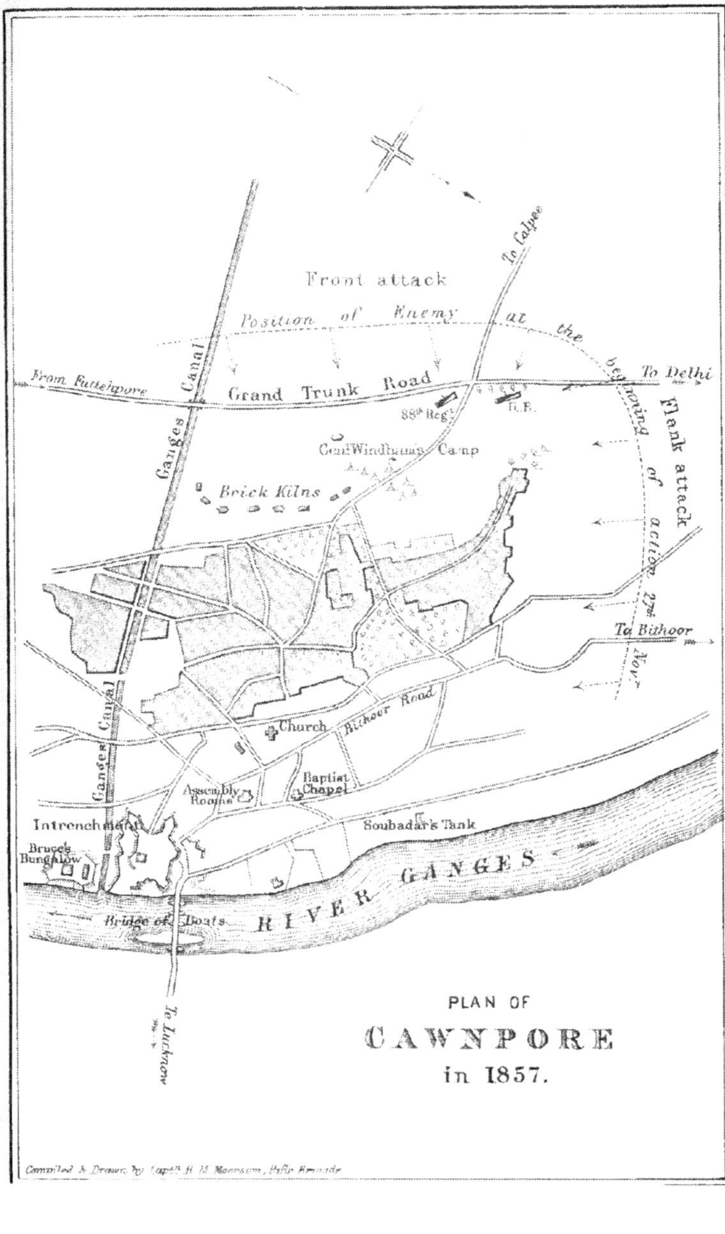

PLAN OF
CAWNPORE
in 1857.

companies, Captains the Hon. B. R. Pellew's (commanded by Lieutenant Grey[1]), Warren's, and the Hon. L. W. Milles',[2] whom we saw were together with Woodford's detachment at Allahabad. They marched from Lohunga at midnight on the 23rd–24th in charge of Commissariat stores; rum, rice, sugar and ammunition on donkeys. They marched about sixteen miles, and halted under a tope of trees till about two the next morning; when they proceeded to Futtehpore, about sixteen miles further, the stores in their charge being a great impediment to their progress. They left Futtehpore again on the 26th, and marched about seventeen miles. As the men were pitching their tents, a messenger on a camel (the same who had met Woodford) came in with a pencil note from General Windham, addressed to the officer commanding the detachment, urging him to make all speed, as troops were wanted. The few tents already pitched were immediately struck. Fyers placed the stores he was escorting in charge of the police, and directed the men to carry only what was absolutely necessary. After a halt of three hours in making these arrangements, he started again, placing the most footsore and the sick on elephants, and marched the men, weary as they already were, about nineteen miles further, allowing them short halts at intervals. Many of the men were so fatigued that when a 'halt' was sounded, they fell asleep almost as soon as they lay down on the ground. After a halt about midnight for one hour, during which a ration of rum was issued, falling in again, they marched forward till the morning, when Fyers gave them another halt of an hour to prepare some breakfast. Having had some tea and biscuit, they started again very weary and footsore; but now the sound of heavy guns and the rattle of musketry quickened the men. They pushed forward with increased vigour, and arrived at Cawnpore when the troops were retiring. They found the force engaged there in full retreat; a mixed multitude of soldiers and civilians, these last carrying property of various kinds, and endeavouring to make their way to the intrenchment.

The distance from Futtehpore to Cawnpore is forty-eight miles and three-quarters. It was marched in about twenty-

[1] Major Grey (retired), died December 11, 1874.
[2] The Hon. Major Milles, died June 7, 1871.

six hours, the first stage with all the impediment of the convoy of stores The men were wearing the European dress: cloth clothes and shakos The march of this detachment has never been exceeded in endurance and rapidity; and Dr. Reade, who accompanied it, states that 'all were well able for any service when the march was over.' It strikingly resembles in more points than one the march of the 1st Battalion (with the Light Division) from Calzada to Talavera in 1809. It differs from it in this, that Fyers' detachment came up in time to take part in the fight of which the sounds had quickened their advance.

For on reaching Cawnpore Windham met them, on his way from the front to the intrenchment, whither all were retreating; and putting himself at their head, he led them through the streets, ordering Fyers to fix swords, and prepare to defend the intrenchment. This they did well, gaining the high praise of General Windham, who then and long afterwards expressed in strong terms how important the arrival and the action of these companies had been to him. Footsore and weary as they were on their march, their fatigue was forgotten as soon as the sounds of fight told them that work was to be done; and they fought in Cawnpore and in defence of the intrenchment as if they were fresh from their camp. When they got to the intrenchment they were refreshed with an issue of grog, biscuits and tea, after which they were despatched on outpost duty: another parallel to the march to Talavera.

On this day Ensign Travers was wounded by a bullet in the shoulder, 2 sergeants and 4 men were also wounded.[1]

The companies took up their position for the night in a ruined house.

Captain Atherley's company of the 3rd Battalion also arrived at Cawnpore on the 27th. They had landed at Calcutta on the 8th, and on the next day started by rail for Raneegunge, and thence proceeded by bullock-cart up the country. On nearing Cawnpore a messenger met them with instructions that Atherley was not to advance, as the force at Cawnpore was in retreat, and he might be cut off. A second messenger informed him that he was to push on, as every

[1] Lieutenant Pemberton, of the 60th, temporarily attached to the Rifle companies, was also wounded.

man was wanted. A third soon followed with a repetition of the first message. All this time for many hours, and while marching many miles, the sound of heavy firing was heard. About six in the evening a youth (a cadet), mounted on a pony, met them, saying that the road was clear, and that they were to hasten on and reach the town if possible. He added that General Windham's force was getting the worst of it. Accordingly Atherley pushed on as fast as possible. The firing seemed to become heavier and more furious. As the company approached the bank of the canal, a mounted officer, extremely agitated, rode up and said, 'Leave all your carts, except the ammunition; fix your bayonets, and I will show you the way.' Atherley, with great *sang-froid*, said, 'We have not got any bayonets, we have swords.' 'Well,' said the other, 'fix what you have got.' Saying which he galloped off and they saw him no more. Neither as they advanced did they see any enemy, but they met some of the 2nd Battalion retiring in good order. Captain Atherley found General Windham in or near the intrenchment, and reported his arrival. Windham, expressing himself much pleased at being reinforced with a hundred 'fresh' Riflemen (they had just come off a fatiguing march), told him to patrol during the night, and guard the house in which he was living. He then asked if Atherley had had anything to eat; and being answered in the negative, he gave him a bone with some meat on it, which he and his two subalterns devoured in the verandah of Windham's quarters, cutting it off with their clasp knives.

They patrolled all night in front of the intrenchment, and guarded Major Bruce's house, which General Windham occupied. But the night passed without any attack from the Sepoys or any alarm.

On the 28th the Riflemen were ordered, about six in the morning, to come into an outwork of the intrenchment; where, having been supplied with some biscuit and tea, they were ordered out to resist the enemy, who were expected to make another attack. The Rifle companies, with part of the 82nd Regiment and Captain Greene's battery of Artillery, were posted on the left of the canal looking from the intrenchments. In moving to this position they were exposed to a heavy fire of musketry and grape. The action itself began about noon; and after hard fighting these troops repulsed the enemy. When they arrived at their position it was discovered that an ammunition waggon was missing, and Lieutenant Curzon had to go back (as on the previous day) a considerable distance in search of it, exposed to a heavy fire. It could not be found; but he succeeded in bringing up a camel loaded with ammunition. In the course of the fight, Colonel Woodford, Lieutenants Playne[1] and Nicholl, with three Riflemen, were in a dip in the ground, in front of the enemy's guns, and were making good practice in picking off the gunners; when Woodford, who was in the act of taking a shot with a rifle at a Sepoy, was shot through the head, and, uttering an exclamation, expired. A bugler, Bourne, carried him to a tope[2] of trees. Captain Dillon entered a house in which there were some Sepoys, and his revolver missing fire, he was bayonetted in the chest.

The Riflemen took two long eighteen-pounder guns, and the men having tackled to with ropes, drew them into the intrenchment, a distance of more than three miles. On their arrival they were greeted with a round of cheers for the guns, and another for the Rifles, and, amidst great excitement, civilians and soldiers pressed forward to offer congratulations and refreshment to the gallant captors.

Captain Atherley's company was ordered to patrol the native town and to clear it of any Sepoys who might be lurking there. About four o'clock Atherley, having heard of the death of Colonel Woodford, took his men to the front, leaving the native town in charge of the 82nd Regiment. General Windham ordered him to line the bank of the canal. Three guns were brought to bear on these Riflemen, and several round shot came amongst them, but without doing any hurt. Atherley made his men take shelter along the bank; and selecting two whom he knew to be excellent shots, he told them to pick off the gunners of these guns, which were annoying the troops from the bridges over the canal; and he desired some of their comrades to load for them, and to hand them up rifles as fast as they could. Thus aided, these Riflemen, creeping up near the bridges, picked off the gunners, and effectually silenced the guns.

[1] Captain F. C. Playne died at Hamilton, Canada West, December 18, 1863.
[2] *i.e.* a grove or clump.

As another instance of their excellence in shooting, I may add that Atherley, in the course of this day's fight, asked one of his men, named Robertson, how far he estimated the distance of the brick-kilns to be The Rifleman replied that he did not know; but calling Atherley's attention to a man standing on the top of the kiln, he put up his sight for 600 yards, fired, and the man fell. His body was examined the next day by Atherley, and the ball was found to have hit him in the stomach.

General Windham thus writes in his despatch of the conduct of the Riflemen:

'On the left advance Colonel Walpole,[1] with the Rifles, supported by Captain Greene's battery and part of the 82nd Regiment, achieved a complete victory, and captured two eighteen-pounder guns.

'The glory of this well-contested fight belongs entirely to the above-mentioned companies and artillery. It was owing to the gallantry of the men and officers, under the able leading of Colonel Walpole and of my lamented relative Lieutenant-Colonel Woodford, of the Rifle Brigade (who I deeply regret to say was killed), and of Lieutenant-Colonel Watson, 82nd, and of Captain Greene, R.A., that this hard-contested fight was won and brought to so profitable an end. I had nothing to do with it beyond sending them supports, and at the end of bringing some up myself.

'I repeat that the credit is entirely due to the above-mentioned officers and men'[2]

The loss of the Riflemen on this day was Lieutenant-Colonel Woodford and five men killed, and Captain Dillon (severely), Lieutenant Lawton, 1 bugler, and 18 men wounded, and 1 man missing

During the night of the 28th the enemy took entire possession of the town, and on the 29th began a heavy fire against the intrenchment, hitting the bridge of boats over the Ganges several times, damaging the Hospital and destroying stores. The Riflemen, who had during the night and morning occupied the principal outwork of the intrenchment, were ordered out by Sir Colin Campbell (who had arrived

[1] Lieutenant-General Sir Robert Walpole died July 12, 1876.

[2] General Windham's Despatch, November 30, 1857.

from Lucknow on the previous evening), to endeavour to take some guns which were doing much damage. Accordingly at three P.M. two companies of the 2nd Battalion and Atherley's company of the 3rd, under Lieutenant-Colonel Fyers, who had succeeded to the command on Woodford's death, made a sortie. Running out over some very uneven ground, they attacked some Sepoys who were in the Residency, and were for some time exposed to a very severe fire. However, after awhile they drove the enemy out of these buildings; and as these were escaping by the back of the compound, some Riflemen of Atherley's company crept round stealthily under the wall, and succeeded in catching the retreating rebels on their swords as they leapt over it. They thus slew a large number.

However, as they did not receive reinforcements, they were unable to take the guns, and returned to the intrenchment. On this occasion Captain the Hon. Lewis Milles was severely wounded, 1 man was killed, 1 sergeant and 6 privates were wounded, of whom 1 died on December 1, and 1 on December 7, and 1 was missing.[1]

The Riflemen, or some of them at least, had not had their clothes off since they left Allahabad; had been scantily fed, often being for twenty-four hours with only one meal, and sometimes that only of biscuit and tea or rum; exposed to heat by day and great cold by night, and suffering from sore feet. Yet they kept their spirits up, and did their work on these four hard-fought days in a manner to elicit General Windham's marked approval repeatedly expressed to them.

At this time the ladies and others rescued from Lucknow were crossing the bridge of boats, an operation which occupied about thirty hours, and Sir Colin with these and their escort encamped near the Old Dragoon lines.

From December 1 to 5 the Riflemen continued to occupy the outwork of the intrenchment; the enemy keeping up an occasional fire from guns planted about 450 yards from them.

On the evening of the 1st Captain Warren and Lieutenants Eccles and Grey went out with some men to recover

[1] Lieutenant Armstrong, who was attached to the Riflemen as interpreter, was also wounded in this sortie, being shot through both legs, one of which was amputated.

the body of Colonel Woodford, which they succeeded in doing, though fired at by the Sepoys; and he was buried on the morning of the 2nd in the intrenchment, where a tombstone was subsequently placed over his remains by his brother officers.

On the 5th the women and children having started, the Riflemen were ordered to move up to Sir Colin Campbell's camp. They started at four P.M., and did not reach their camping-ground till after dark. Having got their tents pitched they lay by their arms all night.

Before I describe the events of December 6, it is necessary that I should trace the movements of the 3rd Battalion which took part in them.

A detachment of that Battalion commanded by Lieutenant-Colonel Julius Glyn, consisting of Captain Alexander's[1] company and part of Captain Bourchier's company, proceeded from Aldershot and embarked on board the 'Barham' on July 1, and after experiencing very bad weather on September 30 when south of the Cape, and a hurricane from October 28 to 30 (during which seven of the crew were struck by lightning), arrived at Calcutta on November 8. They did not disembark till the 13th, and on the next day proceeded by railway to Raneegunge, where they arrived on the 15th at six A.M.

On the 16th they started at 3.30 A.M., part of the detachment being carried in bullock-carts, and part marching. They arrived at Gyra at nine in the morning of the 17th, after a march of thirty-eight miles. Leaving it again at three P.M. they made another march of thirty-eight miles, and reached Doomrhee at half-past ten in the morning of the 18th. Halting there till four P.M. they arrived at Burkutta at 6.30 the next morning, after a march of twenty-eight miles. Starting in the afternoon at 3.30 P.M. they reached Churparun at four in the morning of the 20th. At Churparun rifles were ordered to be loaded, and from thence they proceeded by daily marches through Sherghotty, Norunagabad, Sasseram, Annabad, Benares, Gopeegunge, to Allahabad, which they reached on the 27th. On the 30th, thence proceeding by rail, they encamped at Cheenee, the end of the railway then in course of

[1] Lieutenant-Colonel B. F. Alexander, retired.

construction. Proceeding thenceforward by route march, they left Cheenee on December 1, and encamped on the 2nd about six miles from Futtehpore. Starting from that in the evening they arrived on the evening of the 3rd at a bridge over the Pandoo Nuddee. Here they were to encamp; and the men were set to work to pitch their tents, which they were almost too tired to do, but which they had just accomplished, and turned in, when the bugle sounded for 'orders.' A message had been received from Sir Colin Campbell, directing the detachment to make all speed to the front, as he was about to engage the Gwalior contingent.

The word was given to strike tents and to 'fall in.' This the men did without a murmur, and resumed their march cheerfully, weary as they were, when they knew that active work was before them. Marching (of course with occasional halts) the remainder of that night and the whole of the day and night of the 4th, they arrived at Cawnpore at seven on the morning of the 5th.

This was a march of about seventy-five miles, accomplished in a very short time; and considering that this detachment consisted mostly of young soldiers, the Battalion having only been formed two years before; that these men had disembarked hardly three weeks, after being cooped up on board ship during a four months' voyage; that they had already made long and fatiguing marches up the country; this march, considering these circumstances of it, is perhaps hardly paralleled in military history.

The day of the 4th was very hot, and the men wore their cloth European clothing. They did not however carry their packs.

The Head-quarters of the 3rd Battalion, consisting of four companies, under Colonel Horsford, left Aldershot on July 22 by rail-road for Portsmouth, and embarking on board the 'Sutlej' sailing ship, sailed that afternoon and arrived at Calcutta on November 8. From thence they were forwarded to Raneegunge by rail-road, and thence proceeded in detachments, some by bullock-train, some by horse-dâk, and some by bearer-dâk, up the country by way of Benares and Allahabad. Thence, as we have seen, there was rail-road communication as far as Cheenee. I will trace from thence the progress of the Head-quarter division, consisting of 137 men with the Staff, under Major Ross, which left Allahabad on the 26th.

After leaving Cheenee by bullock-train, some delay took place on account of the badness of the road from this terminus of the railway to the Great Trunk road, but they reached Futtehpore at eight in the morning of the 27th. Major Ross had been directed by Brigadier Campbell before leaving Allahabad, in case the enemy were likely to interrupt him, not to proceed beyond Futtehpore, but, in this event, to fall back and reinforce a party of the 88th Regiment, which was escorting the guns of Major Smith's battery. These, however, he had passed in the night, and in reply to inquiries whether his escort was required, was informed by the Officer Commanding of Windham's engagement the day before, and assured that there was no reason why he should not move on.

Accordingly he proceeded at three in the afternoon, and they had advanced some twenty miles, when at about two in the morning a camel messenger met them, with orders that all troops moving up were to push on as fast as possible. This opened their eyes and quickened their pulse, for it meant that an enemy was in front. So Major Ross pushed on as fast as he could to the next bullock-changing station, got fresh bullocks, and gave his men some tea. Following the Brigadier's instructions, he awaited the artillery and 88th, which various native travellers assured him were only five or six miles behind him. Then he learned his first lesson of the falsehood of native reports. For he waited in some suspense, occupying a gravel pit, expecting every moment the appearance of the artillery; but he waited in vain, for they had never moved beyond Futtehpore. He had reduced at this place his *impedimenta* from thirty-four waggons to twenty-three by re-packing, but of these ten were filled with ammunition; rather an onerous charge had the enemy attacked, for of his small party about thirty were band and buglers without arms. While waiting here, and longing for the appearance of the guns, a messenger arrived about noon from the front, with peremptory orders from General Windham, superseding all others, to fall back on Futtehpore and to hold it to the last extremity before retiring further; and with intelligence that Windham was so hard pressed by the fire of the enemy's guns, that he could not meet them in the open till reinforced from Lucknow. Of course there was no alternative. Major Ross was obliged to march his detachment back the twenty-four miles they had come, to the no small disgust of the officers and men, who had been within hearing of the guns at Cawnpore (and in the night within sight of their flashes), and yet were not to take part in the fight. However, the soldier must obey, and they sorrowfully retraced their steps, keeping a sharp look-out, and reached Futtehpore at about two in the morning. They found that an attack was not unlooked for there; for Colonel Maxwell of the 88th ordered them to move their camp, which had been pitched about a mile and a half from the Great Trunk road, to a position in the open plain, where there had been a tank, now dry, the high banks of which formed an excellent intrenchment.

On December 1 came the joyful intelligence that they were to proceed at once to the front. Accordingly, at three in the morning of the 2nd they advanced (with the Head-quarters of the 88th and Smith's battery), and marching the greater part of that day and the whole of the night (except a two hours' halt) arrived in camp at Cawnpore at three o'clock next day; having done the distance in thirty-six hours. But during the last fifteen miles of the march the officers and men were very weary and footsore, and as they were overcome with drowsiness from fatigue and want of sleep, the scene was somewhat ludicrous; the men now and then lurching from side to side till brought up by their neighbour's shoulder, or missing that prop, occasionally falling forward in the road. The band, however, were wakeful enough to play for the last quarter of a mile, and the inspiriting strains of 'Ninety-five' carried them cheerfully into camp, which was pitched close to General Wheeler's intrenchment. Once in their tents the Riflemen were soon fast asleep. On the morning of the 5th Colonel Horsford came up with the remainder of the Battalion, 120 men. And that afternoon the 2nd Battalion moved from their intrenched camp and joined them.

On the 6th tents were struck at seven in the morning, and

the troops were formed in contiguous close columns, beyond the canal, near the Old Dragoon lines. Here they were halted till it was ascertained that Sir Colin Campbell was engaged with the enemy at the bridge on their left. Then about ten o'clock the two Battalions of Riflemen were ordered to cross the canal by a bridge near their position This they did at the double with a ringing cheer, Captain Nixon's company of the 2nd Battalion leading in gallant style, and forcing back the Sepoys. The 3rd Battalion were in quarter distance column; and the first round shot fired at them passed between the companies, doing no harm to them, but wounding some native camp followers who were on the reverse flank. However, the rebels had opened fire on them while halting in a walled enclosure near the bridge, and on their rushing out of the gate they were exposed to a sharp fire, which brought down only one man as they were crossing the bridge. Once over that the 3rd Battalion wheeled to the right, both Battalions deployed into line, and fixing swords advanced, and soon extended and cleared the woods and houses between the canal and the body of the town. As they advanced the enemy plied them with shot and shell, without however doing much mischief; but Colonel Horsford, who was leading his Battalion, was wounded by a fragment of a shell. He continued however to lead his Battalion. In about ten minutes the Riflemen had cleared the ground in their front, and not a rebel was to be seen there. They then moved towards their left to connect with the force which had crossed by the other bridge, and where the enemy had some guns and a body of infantry in open ground. As they approached the Riflemen saw the rebels flying towards their camp, pursued by Highlanders and other troops So continuing their advance in skirmishing order, the two Battalions swept the ground between the town and the Great Trunk road, passing the brick-field, and through suburbs and trees, till they came in view of the enemy's camp. They then closed to their left, in order to hold possession of the camp which the rebels had deserted, while other troops pushed on in pursuit.

However, later in the day, handing over the charge of the captured camp to some other troops, three companies of the

3rd Battalion and some of the 2nd Battalion started again, and bringing their left shoulders forward and extending, advanced to the Subahdar's tank, a position in rear of the enemy's left, and about a mile and a half in a direct line from the intrenchments through the old cantonments In front of the tank the enemy had some heavy guns; some distance on the right of the Riflemen was another gun, and two more a little to their left. These were well protected by earthworks or walls; a considerable body of rebels kept up a musketry fire from topes of trees and enclosures, and the Riflemen were exposed to showers of grape, canister and round shot. They advanced, extended, about 300 yards on each side of the road, slightly in advance of some heavy guns, while the 93rd were kept in reserve. The fire of these guns soon began to tell on the enemy. This, and the approach of the long line of extended Riflemen, soon disheartened the enemy, who began to give way immediately on the Riflemen passing through the enclosures to the right and broken ground to the left of the road. On reaching the entrance of the village, called the Soldiers' Burial Ground, the guns of Captain Middleton's battery were pushed through as rapidly as possible, the Riflemen running up to support them. They got very near the gun on their right and the two on their left, and were in hopes of capturing them; but they were so much delayed by having to climb over mud walls and pass through enclosures to get at them, that the rebels succeeded in removing them by the right and left, and took them among some houses which the Riflemen had orders not to pass.[1]

When it was getting late the Rifle Battalions, who were still in pursuit of the enemy, now completely routed, were ordered to halt, and got into some houses about five o'clock. The night was extremely cold, and the men had nothing but their usual clothing to cover them, not even their great-coats. The 3rd Battalion suffered from hunger too, as well as cold, being long without food. At last a lean cow was discovered, and immediately killed and cut up; and the men, roasting the tough morsels on the points of their swords, ate them half-raw. The 2nd Battalion were in this respect

[1] Colonel Ross' letters; and General Mansfield's Despatch, December 10, 1857. He specially mentions Brigadier Walpole, Lieutenant-Colonel Horsford, and Lieutenant-Colonel Fyers.

more fortunate. For they got hold of a good many sheep, and in fact regaled themselves so well on them, that they named the house where they passed the night Mutton Bungalow.

The casualties were: in the 2nd Battalion, 1 sergeant, 1 corporal and 6 Riflemen wounded, and 1 man was killed during the night in the town of Cawnpore, it was never known how; in the 3rd Battalion Colonel Horsford was slightly wounded, and 11 rank and file were wounded.

At night Captain Henry R. L. Newdigate's company, with Major Ross, was on picquet in a Bazaar on the Bithoor road, not far from the Subahdar's tank. They were suddenly startled by a noise in a large enclosure where some of the Riflemen were posted. It turned out that some of the rebels, mistaking their way, brought a string of camels laden with ammunition right up to the Riflemen. The sentry challenged rather too soon, and the mutineers fled and escaped; but they left their camels and 20,000 rounds of ammunition in the hands of the Riflemen. The next night the cartridges having been broken up on the ground, a grand illumination was produced by setting fire to the heap.

On the 7th the Riflemen continued in the houses they occupied: but some portion of the baggage of the 2nd Battalion companies having come up, they were rather more comfortable. The 3rd Battalion, however, were still without food, except what the men found in native houses, till towards evening when some rations were served out. The men were allowed to go out to *loot*; and found much, and took many arms and some prisoners. The night was again extremely cold; and men and officers, not on duty, slept under a heap of chopped straw in the hope of getting some warmth.

On the 8th the companies of the 2nd Battalion were ordered in the morning to come in and pitch camp, which they did about half a mile from the town. But they had hardly done so when they were ordered to move and to join Sir Colin Campbell's camp, some four miles in advance. They arrived there and pitched camp shortly before dark.

The 3rd Battalion also left the houses they had occupied since the action of the 6th, and joined Sir Colin Campbell's camp.

Before I describe the further operations of this force, I

must trace the movements of the Head-quarters of the 2nd Battalion. They had embarked at Kingstown on August 6 in the 'Sussex,' hired ship, consisting of 4 companies—17 officers and 336 of other ranks, under Colonel Percy Hill. Sailing the next day they arrived at Point de Galle, Ceylon, on October 29; and were transhipped to the 'Adventure' troop-ship, which started on November 1. The engines of this ship were in a very faulty condition. They were frequently stopped; and the services of a Rifleman named Adwick were constantly called into operation to repair them. This man had been bred an engine-maker or some such trade, and 'Pass the word for Adwick!' became a well-known signal that the engines were stopped and out of order.

In consequence of these defects of her engines, the 'Adventure' did not reach Calcutta till November 17. On disembarking the Riflemen went into quarters; and on the 20th they proceeded by railway to Raneegunge, where they encamped about a mile from the village and were detained for some days, and whence they moved up in detachments by bullock-carts to Benares. Here they were again detained. After which they moved on to Allahabad, whence there were some miles of railway towards Cawnpore, terminating at Cheenee.

The Head-quarters marched, as the other detachments had, from this point. Leaving Cheenee at two in the morning of the 11th December they arrived at Arrapore, a distance of fourteen miles. Leaving it next day at four in the morning, they reached Futtehpore at nine: from this they proceeded to Kutteanpore, where they arrived at nine in the morning of the 13th, after a march of seventeen miles and a half. On the next day they made another march of seventeen to Sirsour, and on the 15th arrived at Cawnpore, when they marched in and encamped about half-past nine in the morning. The whole of the Battalion were now reassembled; and great was the cheering with which the detached companies welcomed the new-comers; and with which these saluted their comrades, who had since their separation seen so much fighting.

On the 18th both Battalions, forming part of a force under Brigadier Walpole, marched from camp at Cawnpore and proceeded about twelve miles along the Calpee road to Churbiere, where they arrived at four in the afternoon, and halted in a capital camping-ground shaded by trees. Resuming the march next morning about half-past six, they had in the course of the day to cross the Pandoo Nuddee, the bridge over which was broken. The Engineers, with great want of forethought, had here placed two boats with one connecting plank, so that the men were obliged to cross in single file. There was ammunition in carts, and these, of course, had to be unloaded, and the ammunition carried over by the men, barrel by barrel. The consequence of this delay was that the baggage did not reach the camp till five in the evening. The march was about sixteen miles to Ukburpore, and the Riflemen encamped near a large tank and close to some trees Here they halted till the 23rd. But on the 25th the 3rd Battalion under Colonel Julius Glyn, with Captain Thynne's company of the 2nd Battalion, and some of the 9th Lancers, went out on an expedition against the rebels, and attacked two armed villages about eight miles distant At Putarah they were fired at, but captured five principal men. They started at four in the morning, and did not return till dark, having marched about eighteen miles, and taken eighteen prisoners; and on the 22nd Captain Wilmot's company, with some of the 9th Lancers, went out on a similar expedition, but returned to camp by ten o'clock. Among the prisoners made on the first of these occasions were a brigadier of the Gwalior contingent and his son, a man who had letters about him addressed to Nana Sahib, and the Nana's money-changer. The first of these was said to have taken an active part in the Cawnpore massacres. He was living in fancied security in this village some miles off the road from Cawnpore to Calpee, and must have been not a little disconcerted when he found his hiding-place surrounded by Lancers and Riflemen He and the other prisoners were executed by order of the Commissioner who accompanied the force.

On the 23rd, starting soon after six, the Riflemen marched eleven miles to Derapore, having in the way forded a branch of the river Jumna, and encamped near some jungle. The next day they made another march of about the same distance to Secundra, where they encamped on some excellent and well-wooded ground.

They halted on Christmas day, but Nixon's, Milles'

and Earle's companies went out at nine in the morning against the Rajah of Secundra, who was reported to be encamped near the Jumna with 2,000 men. The Riflemen started under the command of Colonel Fyers, but were joined about four miles on their road by Colonel Hill, who had gone out shooting, but who, on finding that an expedition was to be made, changed clothes with one of the subalterns, and assumed the command Some cavalry accompanied them, the whole being under Brigadier Walpole.

However, the enemy fled at their approach, the last boat-load crossing as the cavalry galloped up to the bank of the river; and the Riflemen returned to camp at five o'clock. A mess tent for their Christmas dinner was extemporised by joining two, and the men were regaled with an extra ration.

On the 26th, having struck tents at the usual hour, they marched eleven miles to Ooryah, which they reached at ten A.M. And on the next day made a march of fourteen miles to Serai Adjeet Mull, and encamped in a grain field.

On the 28th they made a further march of twelve miles to Buckbey Khanpore, where they encamped among some trees. On this march Lieutenant Buckley, with some men of the 3rd Battalion, found three armed rebels, who loaded to fire at them. They were taken and executed.

About midnight they received a sudden order to march immediately; and, falling in, started in a very cold morning for Etawah, where they arrived about half-past eight. It was expected that they would find a body of about 1,500 rebels with seventeen guns here; but they had heard of the approach of the force, and had disappeared, except a few who had shut themselves up in a fort. This was a quadrangular work, with a kind of tower-bastion at each corner, standing on a sand-hill on the bank of the Jumna Two companies of the 2nd Battalion, under the command of Colonel Hill, were ordered to take the fort. The gate was blown open by the blank fire of a gun which accompanied the force, and the Riflemen rushed in. It was then found that the rebels occupied one of the tower-bastions. Grey and Fryer with some men entered it. A long dark passage led to a small court in the centre of the bastion, which had dwellings round it As they threaded their way along this passage they received a fire of slugs, which whistled past, and they halted where a bend in the passage afforded some cover. Colour-Sergeant Andrews and some men climbed up on the flat roof of the dwelling; and as he was looking over into the court, he was severely wounded in the head, and also lost three fingers. Two other men were also severely wounded. Eventually the bastion was blown up, and its defenders made a rush out, but were all killed. It was then found that two or three of them were women.

The Riflemen halted at Etawah during the two following days in a very good camping-ground, the people of Etawah being friendly and well disposed. The force which had escaped, and the remnant of which had defended the fort, was part of the Nana's army, and had come into the district to levy tribute.

On January 1, 1858, the two Battalions marched from Etawah to Kurhul, a distance of eighteen miles, which they accomplished in little more than five hours, starting at five, and reaching their camping-ground soon after ten On the next day they made a march of the same distance in the same time to Mynpooree. And though they got in by half-past ten, the men were not encamped after their long march till one o'clock, the Quartermaster-General having at first selected wrong camping-ground, from which he moved them.

On the 3rd they started before six, and reached Bewur, a distance of fourteen miles, at ten, and passing through the town, encamped near a shady tope of trees.

On the 4th they started from Bewur soon after three in the morning, and, having crossed the Kallee Nuddee by a bridge of boats about two miles from their camp, halted for breakfast at the end of ten miles. After a halt of an hour and a half they resumed their march, and went on to Futteh-gurh, which they reached between four and five in the afternoon. The distance was twenty-six miles, and the day was extremely hot; yet very few men fell out. On their arrival here they joined the army under Sir Colin Campbell, and were pleasantly encamped in the pleasure-grounds and gardens of a Rajah's palace on the banks of the Ganges The Riflemen had marched seventy-six miles from Etawah to Futtehgurh in four days, or in about twenty-seven hours' marching

They halted here till the 13th; but during that time a detachment of the 3rd Battalion at Allahabad had been taken out (with some other troops) by Colonel Campbell of the Bays against some 300 Sepoys who were assembled in that neighbourhood, and whom they defeated, inflicting very heavy loss.

And on the 11th Captain Hill's company of the 3rd Battalion went out with some sappers on an expedition

On the 13th the two Battalions, forming part of a force under Brigadier Walpole, left Futtehgurh at nine in the morning, and crossed the Ganges by a bridge of boats, which the enemy had fortunately left uninjured. After a very fatiguing march of nine miles, part of it through the deep sand adjacent to the river, which in the rainy season it overflows, they reached Allygurh on the right bank of the Ramgunga at two in the afternoon, and found the enemy in force on the other side The march of the two companies on rear guard was most fatiguing. They could not start till an hour and a half after the Battalions had marched, as the elephants which were to carry the tents had not arrived. Then with very slow progress they arrived at the Ganges, which the native-carts took a long time to cross; and the elephants obstinately refused to enter the river, or to trust their ponderous weight to the planks connecting the boats of the bridge. The tents had therefore to be unloaded, and passed over in boats. However, the recreant elephants subsequently rejoined. The rear-guard had only made their way through the deep sand when night came upon them, and they halted at half-past six. Fortunately they found an old door near their halting-place, which furnished a camp-fire; for the night was exceedingly cold, and there was a high wind. Resuming their toilsome march at half-past six on the 14th, they reached the camp at Allygurh about noon, not having tasted food since early in the morning before.

At Allygurh the enemy had destroyed, a few days before the Rifle Battalions arrived there, the bridge of boats by which the road to Bareilly crossed the Ramgunga. Materials were therefore to be obtained in order to throw it across again. Accordingly on the 15th Colonel Hill was ordered to proceed down the river with a party of the 2nd Battalion, in order to collect flat-bottomed boats for this purpose. Captains Warren and Thynne, Lieutenant Grey, and others, proceeded on that duty. They collected a number of boats, and brought them up to within about two miles of Allygurh, when the enemy, who, as I have said, occupied the opposite bank, opened fire with such effect that a party under Grey, who were completely exposed to it, were obliged to retire from the bank until the enemy was driven back. This was no easy task, as the left bank which he held was high, and the right bank a level plain. Colonel Hill had received positive orders from the Brigadier not to cross the river, or the enemy might have been effectually repulsed; for the river was shallow, so much so, indeed, that the boats frequently ran aground.

Night coming on, the boats were secured, it not being possible to move them farther up in the dark, and the party bivouacked on the spot. At day-break the enemy brought up some guns, and opened fire upon them; and as the ground afforded no cover unless they had retired from the bank and left the boats, the Riflemen formed shelter-trenches in the sand. While making these they were exposed to fire, but none were hit. And as the enemy did not venture within range of their rifles, they were unable to return it. The fire was heard in camp, and a battery of Field Artillery was sent to the aid of the Riflemen. These guns soon silenced those of the rebels. Colonel Hill received orders not to attempt to take the boats farther up the river. And having passed a second night in bivouack, this party marched back to camp.

From this till the end of the month the two Rifle Battalions furnished picquets at the boats (occasionally relieved by the Line regiment which was in the brigade), some of the men occupying the rifle-pits or shelter-trenches, and exchanging shots with the Sepoys, who plied them with shot and shell as well as with musketry.

On February 1, Sir Colin Campbell having renounced his intention of crossing the Ramgunga into Rohilcund, the two Battalions returned to Futtehgurh, leaving Allygurh at 4.30, and arriving at their camping-ground at 7.30. Four companies of the 3rd Battalion, under Colonel Macdonell, were at this time detached to Oonao, on the road from Cawnpore to Lucknow, to keep open the communication. The 2nd Battalion and remaining companies of the 3rd halted at Futtehgurh till the 4th, on which day, marching at six, they reached Khodagunge, a distance of thirteen miles and a half, at ten. On the day following they reached Jellalabad, nine miles and a quarter, after crossing the Kallee Nuddee by the iron suspension bridge of Urhow. And on the 6th marched ten miles and a half to Meeranke Serai, a painful and tedious march; as the baggage which had started before the troops got mixed up with them on the road; and a halt of an hour and a half had to be made. When they proceeded, the dust was so thick that it was impossible to see many yards in front. So that, though they started at 4.30, they did not reach their camping-ground till nearly eleven.

On the 7th they started at six and marched nine miles and a half to Urroul, which they reached at nine. For the night had been extremely cold, and the morning was cool and fine, and the men got over the ground rapidly.

On the 8th they proceeded to Poorah, ten miles and a half; and on the day following to Chobeepore, thirteen miles and a half; and passing the town encamped about two miles beyond it. On the next day they marched to Kullianpore, nine miles. This was near Bithoor, the palace of the Nana; which however had been destroyed before the Riflemen visited it on this march.

On the 11th, starting at 5.45, they marched seven miles to Cawnpore, which they reached before nine; passing over the battle-fields of November 26, 27 and 28, and encamping on the ground where they had fought on the 27th. At this time the Oude force was formed, probably in number and efficiency the most formidable army that had ever assembled in British India. It consisted of one division (two brigades) of Cavalry, and of three divisions (six brigades) of Infantry, besides Artillery, etc.

It is sufficient for my purpose to record that the two Rifle Battalions (with a Punjaub native regiment) formed a brigade under Colonel Horsford in the division commanded by Brigadier Walpole, the Divisional General and the Brigadier being thus both Riflemen.

On February 13 the 2nd Battalion received a sudden order at six in the morning to march, with the object of intercepting or catching the Nana, who, it was supposed, was about to cross the Ganges. They started at 9.30, and retracing their steps made the march to Chobeepore, sixteen miles, in one day, arriving at 2.30. One man had a sunstroke on the road.

On the next day they marched at three in the morning, and arriving at Sheorajpore, halted for two hours before it was decided whether to continue the march or to remain there. Eventually, however, they encamped and halted there during the following day, it being reported that the Nana or his brother had crossed the river and got away.

On the 16th they resumed their march, and proceeding six miles encamped at Poorah on the ground they had occupied on the 8th.

On the day following they received a sudden order to march to Urroul. They started at 8.30, and passing by their old camping-ground they pitched tents about three miles beyond it, making the distance about thirteen miles. They arrived about two after a fatiguing march, the day being extremely hot.

They halted here till the 21st. On the 20th the women and children from Agra arrived, and passed through during the night; and on the next day the Battalion returned towards Cawnpore, halting that day at Poorah, on the next at Chobeepore; and reaching Cawnpore at nine o'clock on the morning of the 23rd, encamped on their former ground.

The 3rd Battalion during this expedition had remained at Cawnpore; but on the departure of the 2nd Battalion on the 13th, they had shifted their camp nearer to Head-quarters. They left Cawnpore on the 21st and marched to Oonao in Oude; and on the 22nd to Nawabgunge,[1] where they halted for some days.

Here they were reunited to their left wing, which they had not seen since before their embarkation in the July preceding. During their stay here numerous escorts were furnished by this Battalion, which was mainly employed in keeping open the road by which quantities of ammunition and stores were

[1] A different place from that of the same name, where the battle subsequently took place.

daily passing towards Lucknow. On the 28th, two companies of this Battalion, with some Horse Artillery, proceeded to a village about six miles distant, and brought in some of the principal men, the villagers having attacked and beaten the camel-drivers.

The 2nd Battalion remaining at Cawnpore, Captain Fremantle's company, made up to 100 men with Lieutenants Baillie[1] and Scriven, was sent as an escort with the ladies from Agra; and starting with them at four o'clock on the morning of the 25th, he marched to Maharajpore, ten miles, where he encamped that night; and on the next day made a further march of thirteen miles and a half, when he handed over his charge to an escort of the Madras Fusiliers, and encamped. On the next day he returned to Maharajpore, and on the 28th arrived at Cawnpore, which the Battalion had left; but Captains Thynne's and R. Glyn's[2] companies had remained there to await his arrival.

Sir Colin Campbell having decided to undertake the siege of Lucknow, the 2nd Battalion marched at five in the morning of February 27 to Oonao, a distance of thirteen miles, and on the following day to Nawabgunge, where they rejoined the 3rd Battalion.

The two Battalions marched on March 1 to Bunteerah, twelve miles, and encamped in a broad plain. About midday they were disturbed by an alarm that their enemy was close upon them; but it turned out to be a false alarm, no enemy appearing.

Here the three companies from Cawnpore came up with the Battalion. They had marched on the same day from Cawnpore at three in the morning to Nawabgunge, doing the twenty-three miles in one march, without the intermediate halt at Oonao. Rain had fallen in the night, and the morning was cool, and they reached Nawabgunge at 11.30. On March 2 they came on to Bunteerah, where, as I have said, they rejoined their Battalion.

On the 3rd the two Battalions received orders to march towards Lucknow. Four companies of the 3rd Battalion, under Major Bourchier, formed the advance, and starting at

[1] Lieutenant Henry D. Baillie, died November 1858, on passage home.

[2] Captain Riversdale R. Glyn, died at Aden, December 11, 1859.

six o'clock in the evening reached the Dilkoosha at two o'clock the next morning, a distance of twelve miles.

The Head-quarters of the two Battalions marched at 10 30 P.M, and reached their bivouack about three on the morning of the 4th. Four companies of the 2nd Battalion, Nixon's, Pellew's, Earle's, and Fremantle's, with two companies of the 3rd Battalion, formed the rear-guard: a most arduous duty. For the quantity of carts, laden with shot, shell, ammunition and provisions, was innumerable, and extended many miles. Though this rear-guard paraded with the Battalions it did not start until half-past three on the morning of the 4th, nor did they reach their destination till three o'clock on the following afternoon. This twelve miles' march was most harassing, and the dust was intolerable.

During this march, while the 2nd Battalion was halted in a tope, a curious circumstance took place. There were a number of skulls lying about, and bodies of rebels, killed, no doubt, in a former encounter; some were skeletons, some sun-dried and shrunk almost into mummies. A bugler gave one of them a kick, and hearing a rattle, stooped down and found in the body nine gold mohurs, wrapped in a rag. It was supposed that the man had carried them, as natives often do, in his cummerbund, and that this having perished, the coins and their envelope had fallen on or into the remains of the body. Sir Hope Grant, who mentions the circumstance,[1] supposes that the man had swallowed them in some panic or alarm, rag and all; which seems incredible.

The Battalions bivouacked near the Alumbagh from three till six A.M., when they were moved to near the Dilkoosha, where they encamped. But the ground was not good, and very dusty. They were exposed, too, to the enemy's fire from a battery about 700 yards off, near the Martinière.

On the 5th the Battalions furnished outlying picquets; and four companies of the 2nd Battalion marched back to Jellalabad (a small fort about three miles from the Dilkoosha), in order to look after some carts that had strayed away from the rear-guard the night before. They received there some of the horses, and returned to camp at three o'clock, where the 3rd Battalion had been under arms nearly all day.

[1] 'Sepoy War,' 245.

On the 6th the two Battalions struck tents at 1.30 in the morning, and marched an hour afterwards. They formed part of Sir James Outram's force, and crossed the Goomtee by a bridge of boats which Sir Colin Campbell had ordered to be thrown across, a little below the Dilkoosha By some error on the part of the Engineers, it was exposed to the fire of the guns in the Martinière, yet the enemy did not attempt to molest their passage. On reaching the left bank they moved along the river, which curves here, for some distance. Then four companies of the 2nd Battalion were sent to join the force under Brigadier Hope Grant. The two Rifle Battalions advanced extended in skirmishing order across a plain, the line regiments following in quarter-distance column. The appearance of this force was magnificent in the extreme. The men had their European clothing, and the helmets of the Bays shone, and the pennons of the 9th Lancers fluttered in the morning sun. They made a circuit of about five miles, keeping as near as possible to the river and the city. The Riflemen skirmished through some dâl[1] as high as their heads, but they saw no enemy. They then halted for breakfast and for the animals carrying ammunition to come up. They then advanced, circling more to the left, across a plain, till they came near the Fyzabad road.

Here they found the enemy in some number, who came out of the woods and villages on their left. The cavalry charged them, and in the pursuit Major Percy Smith of the Bays was killed. The Riflemen proceeding came upon some Sepoys, who fired at them with a gun, but without doing any mischief.

About half-past eleven they fell back and bivouacked in a tope, with a pond or tank in the middle of it, on the Fyzabad road, on the left bank of the Kookrail, a fordable tributary of the Goomtee, at Ishmaelgunge, about half a mile in advance of the village of Chinhut. But their baggage did not come up till long after dark. They formed outlying picquets and a guard or escort for the guns. On the left of their bivouack was a wood, and an occasional shot at the picquet sentries showed that it was occupied by the enemy.

Captains R. Glyn's and Dillon's companies of the 2nd Battalion and Captain Atherley's company of the 3rd Bat-

[1] A kind of pea, which grows very thick and tangled.

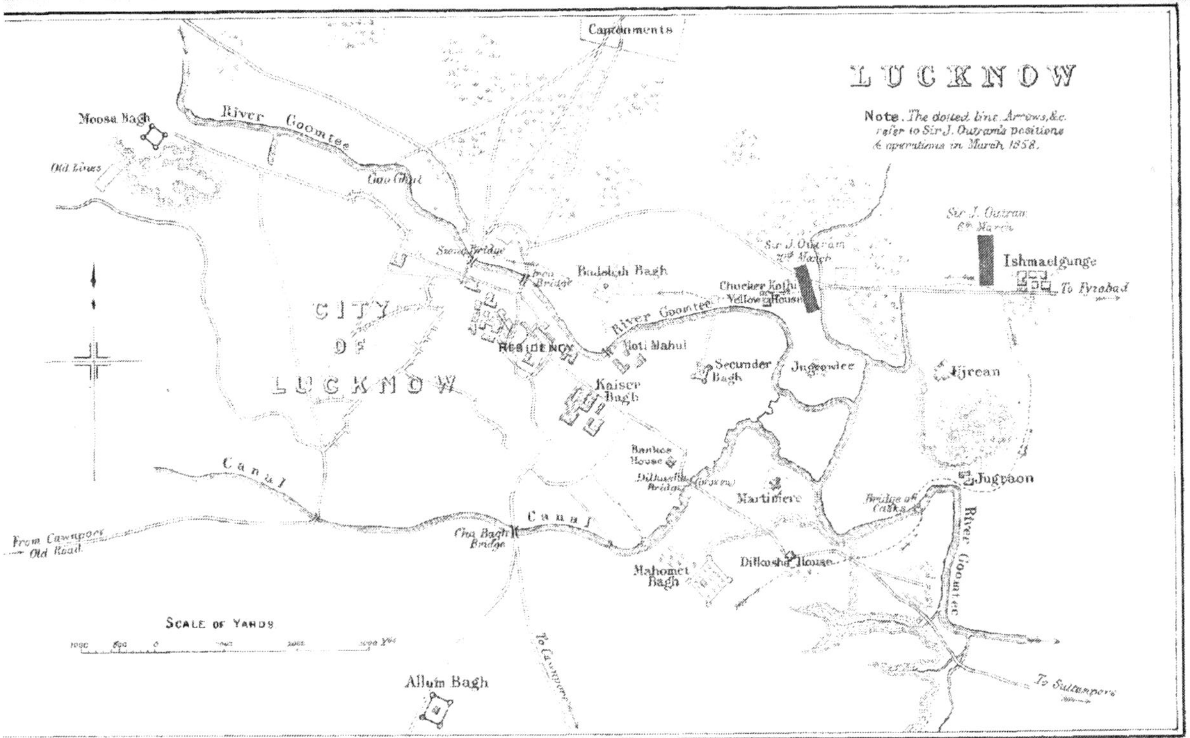

Drawn by Capt. H. M. Acherson, Rifle Brigade.

London, Chatto & Windus.

E. Weller, Lith.

talion were on picquet. In the course of the night Lieutenant Eyre, who was with this picquet, while out patrolling came upon the body of Major Smith, beheaded and mutilated. And in the morning of the 7th with a party of ten men, accompanied by Captain Dillon, he went out, found the body, and brought it in. They were fired at by the Sepoys, but did not suffer any damage. During the night there were several alarms, but without result; but about nine o'clock the enemy attacked this picquet in great force. They were said to be about 10,000 in number. They advanced, covered by the fire of three guns placed in a tope of trees. The picquet at once fell in, extended, and advanced, with two guns of the Royal Horse Artillery, and drove the enemy back into the town, capturing one ammunition waggon. The fire was very severe, but the casualties were only one man of the 3rd Battalion wounded. But there were some hair-breadth escapes. Lieutenant Baillie's sword was struck, and a Sergeant (Kemp) of the 2nd Battalion had his trousers torn, but without being wounded. The picquet continued to occupy the advanced position to which they had moved until the evening, when they were relieved about six o'clock.

The two Rifle Battalions had been moved up about 150 yards in front of their camp, into which the enemy pitched round shot; but they halted there in reserve, and were not actually engaged, the companies on picquet having repulsed the attack and disposed of their assailants On the morning of the 7th they pitched the tents which had come up the night before; and they continued in this camp during that day and the 8th.

On the morning of the 9th the two Battalions paraded at five at their alarm-posts. The object of the day's work was to drive the rebels out of the Yellow Bungalow, the key of their position, and from its neighbourhood. From the Kookrail to the Yellow Bungalow is a sandy plain, while the ground from the Bungalow to the Iron bridge is occupied by suburban villages and enclosed gardens. On the other side of the Fyzabad road the ground is wooded. The two Battalions advanced in skirmishing order, while other troops followed in contiguous columns, three companies of the 3rd Battalion under Colonel Macdonell, Lindsay's being extended, pivoting on their left, and an equal number of the 2nd Battalion prolonging the line. Moving forward, they forded the Kookrail river (about knee-deep), and soon after found the enemy. The Riflemen advanced to a small village in broken ground and well wooded, a very strong position if the enemy had availed himself of it, but the Sepoys retired without firing a shot. Colonel Fyers took his company to attack this village. The Riflemen then passed through this wooded ground at the double, and came out into the open. The skirmishers then brought their right shoulders forward, and advanced, the enemy retiring before them until the right of the line had moved up to the neighbourhood of the river. They then came to the Yellow Bungalow, and the Riflemen went at it with a rush. Lieutenant Cooper and Corporal Bradshaw, V.C., were the first over the wall of the compound surrounding it. There was a lane, with the Bungalow on one side, and some outhouses on the other. Some of the 2nd Battalion passed along the lane and came out in the open country beyond, wheie was a village on the right. Captain Nixon with part of his company passed through a lane which ran along the village, while the remainder, under G. Curzon, went forward. The Riflemen weie here exposed to a smart fire, but not of Artillery. There was a bungalow on the right, which a company of the 3rd Battalion under Captain Deedes occupied. Captain Fremantle, collecting as many men of his company as were near him, kept away to the right, clearing the houses in front of the guns, which were following him. This was disagreeable work, as it was impossible to tell how many of the Sepoys were in these houses; but the men backed him up, and the houses were cleared. The guns then opened at the gate of the Badshahbagh. Some additional guns moving to the right, Fremantle with his company covered their advance and lined a wall. They were here ordered to take a house in their front, which they did with a rush, and held it for an hour and a half, exposed to a heavy fire of musketry, till they were ordered by General Walpole to set fire to some villages, which they did under heavy fire, and then returned to and lined the former wall.

The enemy now gave way; and, though they showed some cavalry (Lancers with a green flag), on a battery being brought up and opening fire, they moved off in confusion along the bank of the river. Unfortunately, there was some space between the right of the line and the river, and some enclosures, and they got away. But they were pursued by some Horse Artillery; and Colonel Macdonell, carried away by the ardour of the moment, charged with them. Captain Nicholl killed one man with his revolver.

The Battalions halted from 8.30 till two in the afternoon, when they went under the shade of a tope; and they encamped for the night on the ground they had so gallantly won, in the open *à cheval* on the Fyzabad road, with their left 200 yards from the Goomtee.

The casualties of the 2nd Battalion were 5 men wounded.

On the 10th the Riflemen shifted their camp to near the Yellow Bungalow. A party under Lieutenants Grey and Dugdale, on escort to bring up the mortars, were engaged, when 1 sergeant (Richards) and 1 private were wounded. The two Battalions furnished outlying picquets, some of which were not relieved for forty-eight hours.

On the 11th the two Battalions paraded on the Fyzabad road a little before six, in order to make a reconnaissance in force to ascertain the possibility of crossing by a bridge to Lucknow. The Riflemen, leading in skirmishing order, were distributed among orchards, buildings of various kinds, and narrow streets. They skirmished through these as well as they could, each captain acting in a measure independently, and handling his company as he thought best. The streets were so intricate and the continuity of the Battalions so broken that no other system was possible. The Riflemen worked their way through these obstructions, and reached the mosque on the Old Cantonment road, which commands the approach to the Iron bridge. This bridge they were ordered not to cross. But, leaving the mosque in charge of other troops, they proceeded to fight their way to the Iron and Stone bridges. At one place the skirmishers came to a high wall, and dividing, passed some to the right and some to the left. And coming to the other side, they found themselves in a perfect labyrinth of streets, lanes and gardens. The enemy retreated before them, hiding among the buildings and enclosures, and were driven across the bridges. Major

Bourchier's company of the 3rd Battalion succeeded in getting a commanding position, and killed some fifty of the enemy. The camp of the rebel 15th Irregular Horse was surprised, and two guns and the standard of that regiment were captured by the Riflemen. As the 3rd Battalion were passing through the narrow street of a village which had been set on fire, they were blocked by one of the captured guns in their front sticking fast or being overturned, and had some difficulty in escaping the flames.

On approaching the Iron bridge Captain Wilmot, 2nd Battalion, found himself with only four men of his company at the end of a street opposed to a large force of the enemy. One of the men was shot through both legs, and was quite helpless. Corporal Nash and Private David Hawkes took him up and carried him to the rear; and though Hawkes was himself severely wounded, he continued to carry him under fire from the enemy, Captain Wilmot with his revolver keeping back the enemy and covering their retreat.[1] Eventually the Riflemen cleared the whole of the suburbs near the Old Cantonment road as far as the Iron bridge.

The casualties of the 2nd Battalion were considerable. Captain Thynne, while in a house drinking some water, was struck by a round shot, which shattered his arm and leg. The latter was at once amputated, but he died about two hours after. He was buried that evening in a tope of trees close to the camp of the Riflemen.

His loss was much regretted by his brother-officers, by whom he was much esteemed. 'No one in the whole regiment,' writes one of them, 'was more liked or could be more regretted. He was always a cheerful and agreeable companion, and a right good soldier besides.'

Lieutenant Cooper was also severely wounded in the neck; the ball passed out of his shoulder through the lung. He died on the 19th, and was buried at the Dilkoosha. Five privates were also wounded, of whom two died of their wounds

In his despatch Major-General Sir James Outram thus reports: 'The enemy held the ground in great strength in front

[1] Major Sir Henry Wilmot, Bart, received the Victoria Cross for his gallant conduct on this occasion. He has retired from the army. Nash and Hawkes also obtained the Cross.

of the Rifle skirmishers, commanded by Brevet-Major Warren, Captains Wilmot and Thynne, and Lieutenant Grey, who all behaved most gallantly. . . . The spirit and dash of the men during this critical operation was most remarkable, and merits my highest commendation.' He also mentions with especial commendation Brigadier-General Walpole, Brigadier Horsford, Lieutenant-Colonel Hill, commanding 2nd Battalion, and Lieutenant-Colonel Macdonell, commanding 3rd Battalion Rifle Brigade. Major Ross, Captain Nixon, and Lieutenant Eccles were also favourably mentioned in despatches.

On the 12th there was an attack, or a threatened attack, on the mortar batteries, and three companies of the 3rd Battalion were sent down to protect them. There was still, too, some fighting about the bridges. With this exception, the Rifle Battalions were not engaged on this or the following day; but furnished picquets and covering parties for guns.

The picquet duty at this time and till the end of the operations at Lucknow was very severe and harassing, the picquets being sometimes on for forty-eight hours; one, indeed, was not relieved for three days and nights. The weather too was very hot; and swarms of flies by day and of mosquitos by night made these duties anything but agreeable.

On the 14th (the day Sir Colin Campbell took the Imaumbarah and the Kaiserbagh), the two Battalions were suddenly turned out at three in the afternoon, and marched towards the Iron bridge, in order to prevent the Sepoys crossing it; but no enemy appearing, they returned to their camp at half-past five.

On the 16th some Sepoys who remained in the town attacked a picquet of the 3rd Battalion near the Iron bridge, but were driven back.

On the 18th the Riflemen moved their camp to near the Badshahbagh.

On the 19th the two Battalions were ordered, the 2nd to hold the Iron bridge, the 3rd the Stone bridge, while the force on the right bank cleared the town of Lucknow of the remaining rebels. They took up their position at 7.30 in the morning, and remained till 5.30 in the afternoon, when they returned to their camp, much exhausted by the great heat, but not having been actively engaged.

The casualties during the operations at Lucknow were: of the 2nd Battalion, Captain Thynne killed, and 13 men wounded; of the 3rd, 6 men wounded.[1]

On the 22nd the two Battalions were ordered to march on a secret expedition; and parading at half-past ten at night, moved to the Old Cantonment, about five miles from their camp, which was left standing. Here they joined the cavalry which was to act with them. Thence they proceeded in a very dark night for a considerable time, but were at last halted, and ordered to lie down in a dusty road ankle-deep in sand. The night was excessively cold. At five in the morning (March 23) the men having breakfasted, they marched on till eleven, when they were halted for three hours under the shade of a tope; and afterwards proceeded to the village of Koorsee, about sixteen miles from Lucknow, a strong position. But the enemy had for the most part evacuated it, and encamped about six miles farther on. However, the force had a brush, killed about 150 of the rebels, and took 15 guns, 70 camels, and 2 elephants, besides some carts loaded with ammunition, which was exploded during the night. The active part of this affair fell principally on the cavalry, but the Riflemen were drawn up in line, ready to support them if they had been wanted. In his despatch on this occasion Sir Hope Grant mentions Brigadier Horsford, commanding the infantry, Lieutenant-Colonel Hill, commanding the 2nd Battalion, and Lieutenant-Colonel Macdonell, commanding the 3rd Battalion. And on the 24th, the objects of the expedition having been accomplished, they started for their camp at seven, and halting as before during the hottest part of the day, returned to their camp at seven in the evening. Though the weather was very sultry, the men were not wearied; marching cheerfully and singing all the return march. This elicited the marked approval of General Grant, who was in command.

On the 30th the two Battalions moved camp to the Old Cantonment.

On April 5 the Camel Corps was formed by a draft of 4 officers and 100 men from each of the Battalions, and 200

[1] I cannot conclude the mention of Lucknow without noting that Havelock, whose name is indissolubly connected with it, was an old Rifleman. He entered the Army in the 1st Battalion July 20, 1815, and served in it till 1821.

Sikhs. The officers who were attached to it were Captain Nixon, Lieutenants Scriven, Eyre, and G. Curzon of the 2nd Battalion, and Major Ross, Captain H. Newdigate, Lieutenants Austin, Buckley, and Jeames of the 3rd Battalion.

On April 9 the 3rd Battalion moved camp to the Badshahbagh, and on the 15th, taking three days' provisions, six companies started on an expedition. They marched out beyond the Dilkoosha, and encamped. I cannot ascertain whether they engaged the enemy during the time they were in the field, but on the 24th these companies returned to the camp at the Badshahbagh. And the Battalion soon afterwards went into quarters at Lucknow.

During the fighting from Cawnpore to Lucknow this young Battalion had borne their part in action and in marching with great determination, valour and endurance. But now that excitement had passed away, and no amusement or interest took its place, sickness assailed these young soldiers Many, both men and officers, fell ill, and numbers of the men died. They were, therefore, left for some weeks in quarters at Lucknow, to recruit their health.

About this time the Riflemen gave up their European clothing, and received instead of it dust-coloured linen, with black facings.

On April 11 the 2nd Battalion (forming part of a field force under Sir Hope Grant) marched from Lucknow to Briesha Talow. They started at half-past four in the morning, and though the distance was but six miles, did not reach their camping-ground till eight, the road being bad, and the progress of the heavy guns consequently slow.

On the next day they continued their march to Utterah, thirteen miles, over a sandy track and through thick jungle, and did not encamp till noon. The day was exceedingly hot, with the thermometer at 110°.

On the 13th they started early, and as it was getting light, near Baree came on a force of the enemy with three guns, occupying a ridge at the end of a level plain. Three companies were immediately extended and advanced across it. The rebels opened fire of matchlocks at about 800 yards, and though it continued without intermission, no harm was done. Colonel Hill had intended to go in without returning this fire, but when the line of skirmishers was about 400 yards from the enemy, a hare started up, and one of the Riflemen, unable to resist his sporting propensities, fired at it. Nothing then remained but to go in with a rush, and the enemy at once broke and fled. The Riflemen pursued them till ten o'clock, when they encamped near the scene of the combat. There was a cavalry skirmish; but the ground was broken and unfavourable for them, and the rebels looted some of the baggage.

On the 14th they marched to Burassie, eight miles; on the 15th to Mamdabad, ten, on the 16th to Bilhir, also ten, where they halted one day; resuming their march on the 18th to Filwy, eight miles, they proceeded on the 19th to Ramnagurh, eight miles, where there was another halt of a day. On the 21st they moved to Massoulee, eight miles; and on the day following to Nawabgunge, six miles, where they halted. On the 23rd, 200 Riflemen, under the command of Colonel Fyers (with other troops) went with Brigadier Horsford to Jungerabad, about six miles from Nawabgunge, and took and destroyed the fort at that place.

Starting again on the 26th they marched thirteen miles to Chinhut, on the 27th to the Dilkoosha; and on the 28th to the Alumbagh; having in this expedition swept round that portion of Oude north of Lucknow.

But no rest was given the Battalion. On the day after they marched into Lucknow they marched out of it; now to the south, and halted at Bunnee bridge. On the next day they proceeded seven miles to Kantha; and after one day's halt there, on May 2 marched ten miles to Poorwah. Sir Hope Grant was anxious to come up with the force under the rebel general Beni Madhoo. So starting again on the 4th the Battalion marched seven miles to Moorawon. On the 5th they halted, but a reconnoitring party was sent out which took five hackeries laden with matchlocks and ammunition. On the 6th they marched seven miles to Dirgpalgunge, and on the 7th five miles to Parthan. Here they halted on the 8th. During this march the men had suffered much from the heat, many having died of sunstroke. The duties, picquets, &c., fell hard too on the officers; for three had been killed since their arrival in India, two had been sent home wounded, and one sick; two were on

General Walpole's Staff, two left sick at Lucknow, and one was sick in camp; so that there were only, besides the Lieutenant-Colonel, five captains and ten subalterns effective with the Battalion.

They marched on the 9th from Parthan to Nuggur, eight miles, and on the 10th to Doondia Khera, seven miles, where they encamped in a shady tope of mango trees.

From this place Sir Hope Grant thought that he could by a night march of some twenty miles, come upon the rebels under Beni Madhoo. Accordingly, at six in the evening the Battalion received orders to march at half-past eleven. But in the darkness of the night the various portions of the column missed each other, and not being able to make out the track, found themselves at daybreak near Nuggur, where they had encamped on the 9th. Here, accordingly, they halted and did not encamp till eight o'clock. They made a short halt there, striking tents at two, and parading in a grove of mango trees, marched at three in the afternoon. It was then fearfully hot, the thermometer marking 118° in the tent. The men were struck down by the sun every moment 'Shortly after we marched,' writes General Hill, 'the Surgeon, Fraser, rode up to me with the report, "There are fifteen men down; all the doolies[1] are full; what are we to do with the next?" It was a puzzling question, but I suggested elephants; and meanwhile sent to ask permission to make a sick depôt at the first convenient spot, and to leave one company to protect it. However, as the sun got lower the casualties were fewer, and we were enabled to keep on till the enemy were in sight and a halt was made.'

This was after a march of five miles. The Battalion advanced in skirmishing order; guns accompanying the skirmishers, galloping forward and firing two or three rounds until the Riflemen came up. Thus they went on to the bank of a large nullah, where they had orders to halt. Sir Hope Grant went off with the cavalry; and soon the sound of the enemy's baggage carts was so distinct that Colonel Hill asked permission to take on his Battalion to capture them. But it was too late, for the daylight only sufficed for a smart skirmish across the open. Meanwhile Colonel Fyers, with two com-

[1] Dooly, *i.e.* a litter.

panies, Earle's under Lieutenant Baillie, and R. Glyn's, had captured a gun. It was getting dark, the 'retire' had sounded, and all had joined the main body except these two companies. The gun was heavy, the ground bad; and the men worn out by heat and fatigue. They made little way with their gun, and it became quite dark. Then some horsemen appeared on the left. A question arose what they were. The general opinion was that they were Sikhs. At last they came near, and Colonel Fyers challenged; the reply was not satisfactory, and he fired his revolver. The Riflemen at once poured a volley into them at thirty yards which emptied half the saddles, and then fixed swords. But the horsemen fled, their leaders were seen through the darkness endeavouring to re-form them, but without success. The Riflemen, not without difficulty in the pitchy darkness, rejoined the Battalion.

In the course of this fight the enemy got in amongst our sick. A smart young Sergeant (Pitt) was being carried in a dooly insensible from sunstroke, when some of the enemy's troopers came upon it The bearers fled, and this poor fellow was beheaded; the rebels carrying off the head as a trophy. The mess baggage had also a narrow escape, the Sergeant in charge of it (Sergeant Cann) being obliged to run for his life.

I have said that the men were utterly exhausted by the heat, by their march, and by the fight. They bivouacked on the ground they occupied. But not to sleep the sleep of the weary; for in the night an extraordinary panic arose. Men cried out that the enemy were upon them. Some fired their rifles; some clubbed them and struck out at everyone near them. At last it wore itself out or was allayed; and except some broken heads no injuries were inflicted, at least in the Rifle Battalion. The origin of this panic remains a mystery; the most probable solution is that either some grass-cutters' ponies or some cavalry horses had got loose and knocked down the piled arms, and so caused an alarm The loss of the Battalion on this day was three men by sunstroke.

On the 13th they returned to their old camping-ground at Nuggur, where they halted two days Here Sir Hope Grant received intelligence of a large force of rebels being to the north of Lucknow; he therefore retraced his steps, and the Battalion marched on the 15th to Parthan and encamped under a tope of trees. They had not pitched their tents more than a couple of hours when they were ordered to turn out, the enemy having shown themselves and driven in the camels, which were out feeding. However, the rebels disappeared. On the next day the Battalion marched to Poorwah, seven miles; on the 17th they halted, but on a false alarm they were turned out under arms. On the 18th they moved to Mirree, seven miles; on the 19th to Bunnee, ten miles; thence on the 20th to the Alumbagh; and on the 21st to the Dilkoosha, where they pitched camp on the bank of the Goomtee. On their arrival at Lucknow they sent fifty-three men to hospital; among them the Sergeant-Major and the Quartermaster Sergeant.

They remained at Lucknow only three days, marching again on the 24th to Jellalabad, and on the 25th to Bunnee. In these marches, though the heat was very great, the Battalion did not lose a man, while the regiment with them (53rd) suffered much.

They halted for a week at Bunnee, a respite much needed after almost incessant marches for two months.

On May 11, an attack on Lucknow being apparently anticipated, a force took the field, in order to be ready to move on any point to repel it. Three companies of the 3rd Battalion, under Major Oxenden, therefore moved out of Lucknow and encamped on the Chinhut road. The heat was overpowering, and many men died every day during their stay here, which was but short. For on the 15th they broke up camp and returned to the Badshahbagh.

Early in June, in consequence of repeated alarms of attacks from the rebels, a camp was formed at Chinhut, about seven miles from Lucknow, and four companies of the 3rd Battalion were moved to this camp. On June 8, an attack being expected, they were under arms, but were not engaged, no enemy appearing.

The remainder of the Battalion, marching at about three on the morning of the 12th from Lucknow, were joined at Chinhut by these four companies, by the 2nd Battalion, and the other troops enumerated p. 386, and proceeding about two miles further on, encamped at Utterdowna. This march, for it was the hottest season of the year, was most fatiguing. Leaving the sick at Lucknow, this Battalion had started 702 strong And yet about 100 men out of that number were more or less disabled in this one march.

On June 1 the 2nd Battalion marched again at four in the morning to Meemteker, six miles, but on their arrival found that the enemy, whom it was expected to find there, had disappeared. They therefore halted in a tope. On the 2nd they proceeded five miles to Chumrowlee, a very hot and dusty march, and encamped in the open On the 3rd, starting at three, they made a march of eleven miles to Poorwah, where they halted for three days; on one of which they were paraded for the inspection of the Rajah of Kuppurthullah, who had arrived in camp with a force of his followers

Sir Hope Grant having received intelligence about this time that a large rebel force was assembling to the north of Lucknow, he resolved to leave the pursuit of Beni Madhoo, and the Riflemen began to retrace their steps towards Lucknow.

Starting again on the 7th early in the morning they marched to Mirzee, twelve miles, and on the 8th to Bunnee, five miles. These marches were by a different route from that by which they had marched through these places on former occasions On the 9th they marched to Bunteerah in a very hot wind; on the 10th to Jellalabad, and on the 11th to the Dilkoosha. On this occasion Brigadier Horsford had procured for the Battalion the permission to halt in Lucknow itself, and not merely to march through it as on some previous occasions; which gave them the opportunity of obtaining some much-needed supplies, which they had not had since landing in the country. But the time even for this was short; for on the afternoon of the 12th they marched at three o'clock to Utterdowna, about two miles beyond Chinhut. Here they were rejoined by the 3rd Battalion; and the force now consisted of these two Battalions, and a regiment of Punjaub rifles, part of the Bays, the 7th Hussars, and some Irregular (Hodson's) Horse.

They started again, after a very short halt of the 2nd Battalion, at about eleven at night. They took with them one day's rations, cooked, some rum, and all their ammunition. This march was one of the most fatiguing ever made. The men had been without rest the night before, and the heat of the tents by day was so intolerable that sleep was impossible. The road was bad, cut up, and damaged , there was no moon ; and the dust was suffocating. So weary were the men that whenever a halt occurred, by a block from a gun sticking fast or turning over, they sank down on the road, many inches deep with dust, and slept. Soon the water carried with the column was exhausted ; no wells were near or could be found ; and the cries of the men for water were pitiable in the extreme. Numbers of doolies accompanied the column (the 3rd Battalion had sixty); but these were soon filled, and the fainting soldiers were left on the road on the chance of being picked up by the Hospital staff of other regiments, or of rejoining when strength returned.

At last daylight appeared, and they found that by dint of marching all night they had arrived exactly where their chief, Sir Hope Grant, wished them to be, close to Nawabgunge.[1]

In this march and in the subsequent advance on the enemy's position, the 3rd Battalion led the column, not without some murmurs from their fellow-Riflemen of the 2nd, who held that as so much of the previous hard work had fallen to them, the post of honour ought to have been theirs. Nevertheless, honour and hard work were theirs before the day was over.

Having marched thus in darkness and suffering some nine miles, they turned off the road near Nawabgunge, for the enemy had seven guns in position, and halted.

They sat down, and water having been procured by some camels having come up, the men were given a dram of grog each.

Day having now fully broken, they fell in and advanced to a large square plain broken up with nullahs and uneven ground, and surrounded in the distance with topes of trees and villages. The cavalry and guns crossed a small river to the left, and were followed by the 3rd Battalion. This

[1] Called Nawabgunge-Burrabunkee to distinguish it from other places of the same name.

advanced guard was soon engaged, and forced the bridge. On crossing the river they came upon the enemy's position. They were formed in a kind of crescent, two regiments bearing green flags being drawn up in the centre. The Riflemen advanced in column, preceded by Major Bourchier's company extended in skirmishing order. As they approached the enemy Colonel Glyn, who was in command of the Battalion, directed the two rear companies to wheel to the right. These were Major Atherley's and one commanded by Lieutenant Cragg. As they got near the enemy, Atherley found himself facing one of the regiments with the green standard. He extended the companies, and after advancing some way ordered Cragg's company to lie down, sheltered by some rising ground, and directed Cragg if he saw him retiring, to pass through his files, and charge the enemy. Then forming up his own company in line, he fixed swords and charged the regiment in his front. These were drawn up in all the 'pomp and circumstance' of regular troops. They planted their green standard, shouted 'Deen, deen!' and stood their ground. The Riflemen engaged in a hand-to-hand conflict, killing many with their swords. It is said that 150 were thus disposed of One Rifleman having driven his sword fixed on his rifle through the shield of his opponent, was unable to draw it back, and the man making a cut at his hands, he was compelled to let it go, and it was never recovered. Some terrible drawing cuts were inflicted. One Rifleman's hand was cut off at a blow, the next cut severed the thumb and forefinger of the other hand, the third cut him across the stomach, and killed him. Meanwhile the enemy did not yield. Cragg's company had come up, and the Riflemen were nearly exhausted. Five of the enemy surrounded Atherley; four of them were shot by Percival with his revolver; the other was trampled on and disposed of by the pony on which Atherley was mounted, which was very vicious Percival having fired all six barrels of his revolver drew his sword, and resting it against his thigh, began to reload. At that instant, looking round, he saw a native aiming a lance at his side; he evaded it and the man was killed. This sort of thing could not last for ever. The Riflemen, whom the excitement of the fight had animated and borne up after their fatiguing night march, were becoming exhausted. Yet their courage and steadiness were not without their results, for their opponents began to break off and retire. Then Quartermaster Harvey,[1] who had accompanied these companies on his pony, galloped to some of Hodson's Horse who were near, and urged them to come and charge the regiment opposed to his comrades. He urged in vain. In vain did their officers give the word to advance. Not a man moved. It was well perhaps for him that they did not understand the epithets with which Harvey assailed them. But just then he saw some squadrons of the 7th Hussars approaching. He galloped to them, and told their commanding officer, Sir William Russell, who was leading, that the Riflemen could maintain the unequal fight no longer, and must be overpowered unless help was at hand. 'We'll soon clear them,' was the answer. And in an instant the Hussars were thundering along at the charge.[2] An instant more they were on the green-bannered regiment, cutting them up as they fled at their approach.

Meanwhile, in other parts of the field and against the other body with the green colours, the Riflemen of this Battalion waged an unequal conflict. For they were far outnumbered, and so weary from their night march and the fierce blaze of an Indian sun, that they were scarce able to load, and when loaded could fire only with a desultory aim. Many were struck down by the sun in the fight; and it was impossible to distinguish when a man fell, whether sunstroke or a wound brought him to the ground.

Sir Hope Grant, who commanded in this action, says: 'I have seen many battles in India, and many brave fellows fighting with a determination to conquer or die, but I never witnessed anything more magnificent than the conduct of these Zemindarees.'[3]

So far we have seen the part borne by the 3rd Battalion, which, as I have said, led the column. We must return to the opening of the battle, and to the 2nd Battalion. In front of it, as they drew near the field, were some large guns, and

[1] Major Harvey, Paymaster

[2] The officers of Hodson's Horse joined in this charge.

[3] 'Sepoy War,' 291.

the delay of getting them over the nullah allowed the other and leading Battalion to get a quarter or half a mile to the front. Before the 2nd Battalion had crossed, and while they were still expecting orders to advance, an alarm was given in the rear. A considerable force of the enemy had found their way to the rear round the right flank, and were cutting up the camp followers. The number of these was large, as the Bays had brought on their camp-equipage; and there was no rear-guard, so that the defence of all this baggage devolved on the 2nd Battalion. At this time, too, Lieutenant Ames, who was coming up with spare ammunition, was attacked. Colonel Hill immediately gave the word, 'Right-about turn,' and extended three companies in his now front, sending one under Lieutenant Baillie to protect his right flank, which was threatened. The camp followers were running in in a confused mass, to escape from their pursuers. As soon as these stragglers had passed the line of skirmishers and cleared the front, the skirmishers opened fire, and advancing to the nearest cover halted, awaiting the Artillery which Colonel Hill had sent to ask from the Brigadier. Meanwhile, the now left was enfiladed by two of the enemy's guns, and Captain Dillon was sent with two companies to take or to silence them.

The skirmishers were keeping up an incessant fire, which the enemy briskly returned, at a distance of about 400 yards, but as the Riflemen were well covered they did not much suffer. As no Artillery made its appearance, Colonel Hill ordered the men to make a rush on the enemy. They did so, and the rebels retired through a village; when the Riflemen were ordered to halt. Having waited there till the enemy had disappeared, the Battalion moved to a tope of mango trees not far from the river, and there awaited further orders.

Some time after, a large body of cavalry appeared in their rear (the proper rear of the column). These were at first taken for Hodson's Horse; but infantry soon appeared, and it was ascertained that they were enemies. Two companies of Riflemen moved down into a hollow which afforded good cover; and as the cavalry passed, gave them a volley at about 500 yards. This the infantry returned with a straggling fire and then turned and fled. The Battalion remained in the tope during the day and till about six in the evening, when they were ordered to join the rest of the column, then two or three miles in advance. They reached their camping-ground about seven, and pitched their tents.

I may here note some of the incidents of this fight. As some of the 3rd Battalion were advancing on the enemy, who were receiving them with a sharp fire, some hares were started between the opposing ranks. More than one Rifleman aimed and fired at the hares, not at the foe.[1]

One man, a Ghazee,[2] being cut off from his companions, seemed determined to make a desperate fight for it. Setting his back to a tree, he stood, sword in hand, glaring fiercely on his pursuers, for some officers and men had followed him into the tope. Some shots were taken at him, which he tried to avoid by dodging round the tree, but he was wounded and made more desperate. At last a Pioneer of the 3rd Battalion, Samuel Shaw, rushed at him and closed with him. The Ghazee wounded him on the head with his tulwar, but Shaw, drawing his Pioneer's sword, sawed at him with the serrated back and despatched him. Shaw rose from the ground covered with blood, but his opponent was slain. Many who witnessed it declared that this combat with a fanatic determined to sell his life to slay his foe, was the greatest instance of cool courage they ever saw. For this act Shaw received the Victoria Cross.

Quartermaster Harvey, on going into a tope of trees where the Battalion were about to encamp, came upon a man who seemed inclined to make off. On Harvey stopping him, he fell at his feet and offered, if his life were spared, to show him where a quantity of powder was concealed. Accordingly, Harvey and Percival followed him, and he brought them to a place where there was a bullock-cart laden with seven casks of powder. This was exploded and the bullocks taken possession of.

The casualties of the Regiment on this day were: of the 2nd Battalion, Lieutenant Lawton severely wounded, and 1

[1] An exact counterpart, or repetition rather, of what occurred at Sabugal. See p. 82.

[2] A champion who fights against infidels.

corporal and 2 privates wounded; in the 3rd Battalion, 1 corporal and 11 privates wounded, and 1 Rifleman missing.

But far worse than the injuries done by the enemy's fire, were the sufferings of the men from exposure to the sun. The 3rd Battalion lost 14 men from sunstroke: in the 2nd Battalion 1 man died of sunstroke, and many others suffered from it, of whom 2 died on the next day, and another on the 15th[1] Fortunately, the supply of water was plentiful, and the bheesties[2] assiduous in administering it. Some of the men were raving; some lying on their backs as if dead, while the bheesties sprinkled them with water So great was the exhaustion, that on Sir Hope Grant's giving an order that tents were to be pitched, Quartermaster Harvey went to Brigadier Horsford to say that in the 3rd Battalion the men were so utterly exhausted that they could not do it, and begged him to allow the men to lie down in the shade. The Brigadier replied that the General's order must be obeyed, but consented to take him to Sir Hope Grant, to make his report in person to him. Sir Hope insisted, and said 'the tents must and shall be pitched.' On Harvey's return to his Battalion the men turned to, and set about pitching the tents; but many fell down through sheer fatigue, and slept on the tents they were ordered to pitch. Yet they afterwards had reason to see the wisdom of General Grant's determination, for the shelter of the tents perhaps saved many lives; and as the enemy were still hovering about, and might again attack, it was essential that the regiments should be in some formation.

Thus at about six in the evening the two Battalions encamped on the field of Nawabgunge.

Sir Hope Grant, in his despatch dated June 17, 1858, speaks most favourably of the Rifle Battalions.

'Brigadier Horsford,' he writes, 'I am much indebted to for the very excellent way he led on the infantry, and for the support he gives me upon all occasions.'

He also mentions

'Lieutenant-Colonel Hill, who with his Battalion so gallantly and successfully protected our rear: a most important service.

[1] On the evening of the battle 24 men were buried in one grave.

[2] Water-carriers.

'Lieutenant-Colonel Glyn, a most excellent officer, and whose Battalion, the 3rd, behaved so well, being actively employed during the whole day.'

He also favourably notices '200 infantry under Major Oxenden,' and repeatedly mentions the 'two companies of the Rifles under Captain Atherley.'

Yet in his published work 'The Sepoy War,' Sir Hope Grant, or his editor, Captain Knollys, R.A., gives all the credit of these gallant deeds to the 60th, which was not near Nawabgunge at the time.

CHAPTER XII.

THE rains having come on, the 2nd Battalion was ordered to remain at Nawabgunge, and proceeded to build huts for shelter on raised platforms; but this was done but slowly, the supply of Coolies for the work being scanty, the Government having engaged them for other work, and before the huts were completed the Battalion was moved, as will be presently narrated.

The 3rd Battalion marched from Nawabgunge on the 21st at three in the morning, and proceeded to Chinhut, where they encamped. Here they had left their sick on the 12th, and it appeared that a fearful panic had occurred on the next day. For some irregular cavalry and camp followers had fled from the field while the battle was raging, and, passing through Chinhut to Lucknow, had spread a report that we had been cut up, and that the enemy were advancing. Some of the sick, terrified by this intelligence, left their beds or their doolies, and madly rushed about with scarce any clothing in the sun. This was attended in some cases with fatal results. However, these alarmists had better have faced the hostile fire on the field of Nawabgunge than the face of the General at Lucknow, who, knowing their reports to be false, ordered them to be soundly flogged.

On this march the Battalion brought with them five of the six guns taken at Nawabgunge; and as their carriages were old, and the road very bad, they much retarded their progress. However, they succeeded in pitching their tents before the sun was powerful.

On the 22nd they marched again at three A.M., and arrived at the Cantonments at Lucknow at nine, where they encamped. Soon after this the rains set in, with a violent thunderstorm which flooded the tents on July 8; and the men were employed to build huts, partly out of the remains of ruined bungalows which had been destroyed by the rebels, in order to shelter them during the rainy season. But no such provision was made for the officers, who continued in tents. Here the Battalion remained for more than three months, during which time the men suffered much from cholera and from their recent exposure to the weather.

On July 22 the 2nd Battalion left Nawabgunge for Fyzabad in order to assist Maun Singh, who was besieged by the rebels. They struck tents and marched eight miles to Dundirah, many men falling out from fatigue. On the next day they proceeded to Turkani, six miles, and on the 24th, intelligence having been received that Maun Singh could not hold out four days longer, they pushed forward to Derriabad, thirteen miles, instead of halting at the end of eight miles, as was intended. This was a most distressing march; the weather was very hot, the thermometer being at 105° in the tents; and numbers of men were taken ill on the way. They halted on the 25th, it having rained all night, but started again at four on the 26th, and encamped at Burehke Serai. On the next day they proceeded to Begumgunge, and on the 28th tents were struck at four in the morning; but in consequence of the heavy rain they did not start till half-past-six. They marched seven miles, and encamped at Samao, on the banks of the Gogra. On the 29th they reached Fyzabad after a march of thirteen miles, only to find that the rebels had left it that morning, and crossed the Gogra; however, the Horse Artillery got up to the bank in time to get a couple of shots at the last boat-loads. The Battalion halted at Fyzabad for a fortnight, during which time, on August 6, the camp was shifted to platforms on account of the rain; but while this was being done a violent storm came on, and the men were drenched before the tents could be pitched.

On the 9th Brigadier Horsford, with a portion of the 7th Hussars, the Madras Fusiliers, a troop of Horse Artillery, and some native troops, proceeded to Sultanpore; and the 2nd Battalion, being ordered to reinforce him, started soon after three on the morning of the 16th. It was a dreadful march. Soon after starting, they lost their way in the dark. The country being flooded from the rains, it was some time before they could find a track; and even on this the water was ankle-deep. Having marched about four miles, they halted for a rest. It came on to pour, and the rest of the way the men were up to their knees, sometimes to their middle, in water. The mud, too, on which they walked was slippery and fetid. Under these circumstances they did not reach their camping-ground at Butturpore, a distance of twelve miles, till one o'clock in the afternoon. Even then their sufferings were not at an end. The Commissariat carts were not up, and it was three o'clock before the drenched Riflemen got their tents pitched and broke their fast. On the 17th they marched to Perownee, nine miles, a repetition of the discomforts of the preceding day, save only that no rain fell. The men frequently fell into holes that had been made for planting trees; a source of merriment to his comrades, but of misery to the unfortunate diver himself. On arrival at Perownee there was considerable difficulty and delay in finding a spot dry enough to pitch a camp. At last some rocky eminences were fixed on, which cropped up above the plain and stood up above the flooded ground. Here the tents were pitched without order; for the men were obliged to place them wherever the scanty ground afforded room.

On the next day they marched to Burtenpore, six miles, with less discomfort, the day being fine and the road tolerably good. Here they halted on the 19th, to allow the Commissariat hackeries, which had fallen two marches behind, to come up. And on the 20th moved on to Sultanpore on the Goomtee, by a very good road. They found the enemy, with a force of about 10,000 men, occupying the opposite bank of the river, here not more than a hundred yards broad. They therefore halted, observing the enemy, and exchanging occasional shots with them, until General Grant came up on the 23rd with reinforcements. On the 25th the Madras Fusiliers began to cross the river without opposition This occupied some days. And on the 25th the 2nd Battalion was paraded at three o'clock to cross; but the Madras Fusiliers not having completed their passage, the Riflemen were ordered into bungalows for shelter. Later in the evening, however, Sir Hope Grant having received intelligence that the Madras Fusiliers were hard pressed, ordered the Battalion to cross immediately.

They were accordingly turned out at eight, and about two hours after began to cross the river, much swollen by the rains, on rafts. Of these there were only two, formed of old rum barrels, each calculated to convey twenty-four or thirty men. However, Colonel Hill got over as quickly as possible with two companies, who reached the opposite bank about midnight; and after a march of about two miles, reached the ridge occupied by the Madras Fusiliers. But it appeared to have been a false alarm, for there was no appearance of danger. The men, therefore, piled arms and bivouacked; and the night passed quietly, except that the rebels kept up a constant fire on the picquets. On the next morning a couple of tents were got over for the companies on the right bank, and the remainder of the Battalion crossed and encamped on the plain. On the 27th at sunset the enemy, who were about two miles or more distant, turned out as if for an attack; but they did not venture within 1,200 yards.

On the 28th the rebels, by giving a gun great elevation, and probably half burying it, contrived to throw a few shot into the Riflemen's camp; doing no damage to them, however, though they killed an old woman, and knocked over an elephant, by hitting him on the pad, but, except rolling him over, doing him no hurt.

On the 29th they paraded at two in the morning, and marched at three to the cantonments, making a circuit to get well round the enemy; but to their great disappointment the enemy had gone off during the night. The Riflemen waited under topes till the baggage came up, when they pitched their tents, heavy rain coming on just as they did so.

The Battalion halted at Sultanpore for some weeks with little change, such as, for instance, a company (under Lieutenant Sotheby) recrossing the Goomtee to protect the heavy guns.

On October 4 six companies of the 3rd Battalion, under Colonel Glyn, moved into Lucknow. And on the 5th Captain Alexander's company marched at nine in the evening to join an expedition to Sundeelah (about forty miles from Lucknow), commanded by Brigadier Barker.

This party, consisting of 100 men, was in charge of

Lieutenant Andrew Green,[1] and accompanied by Ensign Richards; for Captain Alexander had been ordered to take a detachment up the country.

On arrival at Sundeelah on the 7th, information was received that a large force of rebels were about four miles off at a place called Jamo.

At daybreak on the 8th, therefore, the column marched to Jamo. On approaching the enemy's position, which was a strong one, a village on high ground and surrounded with dense jungle, fire was opened on them from guns posted in the village and from matchlocks in the jungle. The Riflemen were extended in skirmishing order on the right, and entered the jungle Lieutenant Green had warned the men not to lose communication with their files; but in the thickness of the jungle three men got separated, and were surrounded and wounded by the enemy. Hearing firing, Lieutenant Green at once made for the place, and was immediately surrounded by six rebels He shot two with his revolver. As he was in the act of dismounting to attack the others, he was cut down and hacked at while on the ground. Springing to his feet, however, he managed to knock down two more of his assailants with the butt of his revolver, and drawing his sword, he kept the others at bay. While he was about to fall back in search of some of his men, he was attacked by three more of the enemy and a second time cut down. Again getting to his feet, he contrived with his wounded right hand to shoot another man, who was in the act of cutting at him with his tulwar, and whose blow, descending as he fell dead, inflicted a deep wound on Green's head. Colour-Sergeant Mansel,[2] meantime, had heard the firing, and was making his way to the part of the jungle the sounds seemed to proceed from, when he came on a Rifleman wounded and retiring, who informed him that Lieutenant Green had come to his assistance, and was then hard pressed by several Sepoys. Hurrying on in the direction the man had pointed out, the Sergeant soon was attacked by a rebel, whom he succeeded in shooting; but before he could reload his rifle he was set upon by another man, who cut at him with his tulwar.

[1] Lieutenant-Colonel Green, Captain of a company at Chelsea Hospital.

[2] Sergeant William Mansel was appointed Ensign in the 12th Foot, August 24, 1859.

After a severe struggle Sergeant Mansel knocked him over by a blow with the butt of his rifle, and soon after he came upon Green lying bathed in blood outside the jungle, and with the help of two Riflemen carried him fainting to the rear.

Green received fourteen sabre cuts and one gunshot wound. Four of these wounds were obliged to be sewn up on the ground, and as soon as he was brought back to camp his left arm was amputated below the elbow, and his right thumb was taken off. Faint from loss of blood and from excessive fatigue (for the Riflemen had been under arms from four in the morning till three in the afternoon), it was not thought that he could rally, and for some days his life was despaired of. He was, however, moved to Lucknow on the 21st.

Few men, probably, have ever survived so many and such severe wounds.

Besides Lieutenant Green, three Riflemen were (as I have said) wounded on this day.

It will be anticipated that Brigadier Barker speaks highly of this gallant deed in his despatch of October 9.

'The party of the Rifle Brigade, under Lieutenant Green,' he says, 'gallantly rushed up the high position in front of the village, and captured a six-pounder gun.' . . . 'Among the wounded (and I am sorry to say he is dangerously so) is Lieutenant Green, Rifle Brigade. . . . This officer had behaved so gallantly all through the day that I most deeply lament this misfortune.' Ensign Richards also was favourably mentioned in this despatch.

The Adjutant-General of the Army in India, also, in forwarding this despatch to the Secretary of the Government, by the direction of the Commander-in-Chief adds, 'I am also to request marked attention to the gallantry of Lieutenant Green of the Rifle Brigade, who has been dangerously wounded.' And the Governor-General in his General Order publishing these despatches, states his 'great satisfaction' at the conduct of Lieutenant Green.[1]

On the 12th Captain Alexander, who had returned to Lucknow on the previous day, proceeded to take command of his company, and arrived at Sundeelah on the 13th.

[1] 'London Gazette' and MS. Narratives of Colonel Green and Mr. Mansel.

On the 13th this company were engaged in a daur[1] to the fort of Mandaula, which was blown up, and three guns were taken. And on the 18th three more companies, Atherley's, Stephens', and H. Newdigate's, under command of Major Oxenden, marched from Lucknow and joined it at Sandeelah.

On the 21st the Brigade under Brigadier Barker proceeded to attack the fort of Birwah, which was held by Gholab Singh and about 700 rebels. The four companies of the 3rd Battalion, commanded by Captains Alexander and Stephens, and Lieutenants Percival and Cragg, and led by Major Oxenden, accompanied this force. They paraded at two A.M., and soon after marched in the direction of Birwah, and arrived before it about seven in the morning. Brigadier Barker had resolved to attack the west front. A few hundred yards from the fort was a village on a mound, which was intrenched and occupied by the enemy's picquets. It was surmised that, as in so many previous instances, the rebels would not have awaited the approach of the column. But the assailants were soon undeceived, for a puff of smoke issued from a large circular bamboo jungle on the right, and a round shot flew over the column. The Riflemen were then hurried to the front; and with some native police and an eighteen-pounder and mortars, gradually inclined to the right till they came to the village, from which they drove in the enemy's picquets, and it and the intrenchments were at once abandoned. They were then halted and ordered to lie down in a wood beyond the village. In front was an impenetrable bamboo jungle, out of which shots came now and then to show where the fort was, but so thick was the mass of bush and thorns that they could not see the walls; though from the reports of the guns they did not seem to be more than 100 yards off.

The mortars were placed in the village, and the gunners were directed to pitch their shells over the Riflemen, and to let them fall near a flag-staff which was supposed to mark the centre of the fort; but the enemy foreseeing this had moved the flag-staff to the further side, so that the shells went over the fort altogether. The fire of the mortars ap-

[1] *i.e.* An expedition, literally, a run.

pearing thus to produce no effect, the eighteen-pounder was brought to where the Riflemen were lying down among the trees, in order to endeavour to make a breach in the wall. Lieutenant Percival was sent with twenty men of the company in his charge into the jungle, with orders to move along the ditch, to mount the breastwork of the outer defences, and to clear it of the enemy. This was rapidly effected. They drove the enemy before them, who abandoned the outer works, leaving a gun in their hands, and escaping through the jungle, retired to the fort. In this service two Riflemen were killed.

At this time a shell fell near Major Oxenden, who was on horseback close behind the line of skirmishers, wounding his horse; wounding also Colour-Sergeant Mansel in two places, and knocking over one or two more Riflemen.

The eighteen-pounder continued to be fired point-blank through the jungle; and a lane was speedily cleared by its fire, and the wall of the fort was discovered about seventy yards distant.

As the fire of the mortars appeared to produce no effect, Brigadier Barker ordered the fort to be assaulted about half-past two in the afternoon. Captain Alexander's company, which had left camp fifty of all ranks, increased by a section of another company, was to act as the storming party; while 100 Riflemen were to keep down the fire from the place. At the same time another regiment (the 88th) was sent round to the opposite face of the fort, to force an entrance by blowing open the gate; while the native police were to occupy a gate on another side, by which it was anticipated the rebels might attempt to escape. Some of the native police who were left with the Riflemen were to carry the scaling ladders. Captain Goodenough, R.A. Brigade Major (who had joined the stormers as a volunteer), and Captain Alexander crept forward through the jungle, close up to the ditch, to reconnoitre it.

All being thus prepared, Alexander's company advanced through the jungle, the natives carrying the long bamboo ladders, till they came to a space clear of jungle, extending thirty or forty yards from the ditch. The enemy opened a heavy fire from the rampart, by which several Riflemen were shot down, Corporal Rudd being killed by a shot through the head. The native police dropped the ladders and disappeared, and the stormers had to carry them themselves. When they were placed in the ditch, which was here about twelve feet deep,[1] and the Riflemen began to descend them, the rungs gave way, and they had to let themselves down hand over hand The ladders were then tilted over to the other side to help the stormers to get up the breach, which was very imperfect and almost perpendicular. It seemed to them nearly forty feet to the top of the breach, and they were almost up to their waists in water in the ditch Richards was the first man at the top of the breach, and Sergeant Maloney closely followed him. Just before they got to the top of the breach a gun exploded over their heads, with which the enemy had no doubt intended to welcome them on arrival, but which was fired a few seconds too soon When the stormers reached the top of the wall the enemy ran away, and the Riflemen having waited a minute or two there to allow the remainder of the company to join them, moved forward, and found themselves in a kind of broad street with houses on the right-hand side, and the wall of the place on the left. At the further end, near the entrance to a courtyard, were four or five guns with some of the rebels near them. The Riflemen went at them as hard as they could, and took the guns before they could be discharged, and the enemy retreated into the courtyard, meaning probably to escape by the other gates. But at these the 88th and the native police met them and headed them back. Then it was that the hardest fighting took place. The rebels, being thus caught in a trap, fought bravely for a time. Many of the Riflemen were hit. Richards, while fighting hand to hand with a gigantic rebel, whom he succeeded in thrusting through the eye with his sword, was shot from a window, and received more than one wound. One ball traversed the thigh, and passed out at the back of the leg, just below the knee-joint. Sergeant Maloney picked him up and carried him away bathed in blood. This youth, barely eighteen years of age, had shown uncommon valour,

[1] It was found afterwards by measurement to be nearly forty feet wide, and thirty feet deep, with three or four feet of mud at the bottom.

both on this occasion and at Jamo a few days before. He died of these wounds at Lucknow on December 8 Captain Alexander was also slightly wounded at this time in the neck by a pistol bullet and in the left shoulder by an arrow.

The enemy broke up, however, and retreated into the different houses; and as these were loopholed and fortified, it was difficult to dislodge them. Some of the houses were broken open; and the Riflemen, taking advantage of whatever cover they could find, picked off the rebels whenever they showed themselves; which they did on the roofs of the houses, to hurl down stones or beams of wood on the assailants. A Rifleman had his sword, which was fixed on his rifle, bent nearly double by the blow of a great log of wood which fell on it. Thus the fighting went on till night. Gholab Singh, it was reported, and some of his followers had retreated to a house in the centre of the fort, from which a smart fire was kept up. This house was set on fire, and about ten o'clock the greater part of it was blown up by the Engineers. Yet Gholab Singh with twelve men escaped by making a rush, jumping from the wall, and getting into the jungle, though troops—not Riflemen—were left to prevent his escape. With this exception the defenders were all killed.

The casualties of the Riflemen were 2 officers (Alexander and Richards) wounded; 1 corporal killed, 2 others wounded, of whom 1 died; Colour-Sergeant Mansel dangerously wounded, arm amputated; 1 bugler severely wounded; 1 private killed, and 24 privates wounded: 3 dangerously and 12 severely. Captain Alexander and some of the men were wounded by barbed arrows. A long procession of doolies carrying these (and other) wounded soon after set out from Sundeelah to Lucknow.

Brigadier Barker, in his despatch dated October 24, 1858, thus speaks of the conduct of the Riflemen:

'Major Oxenden, commanding Rifle Brigade, deserves the greatest credit for the manner in which he handled his men, and disposed them for the assault of the breach. . . . Captain Alexander, Rifle Brigade, commanding the storming party, deserves the greatest credit; and Lieutenant Cragg and Ensign Richards, who accompanied him, displayed the greatest courage; the latter, as I have stated, was the first at the top of the breach, but I regret to say was shortly after dangerously wounded. . . . Assistant-Surgeon Storey, Rifle Brigade [and others], deserve the greatest praise for their attention to the wounded during the night. . . . The names of the men mentioned in the margin [1] have been brought to my notice by their commanding officers as having particularly distinguished themselves.'

I have now to resume the account of the movements of the 2nd Battalion after their halt of six weeks at Sultanpore. On the morning of October 11 this Battalion struck tents at four in the morning, and recrossing the Goomtee marched with a force under Sir Hope Grant to the north-east, in the direction of Tandah. They encamped that night at Itkowlie after a march of five miles; on the next day they proceeded to Rajahpore, nine miles; on the 13th, starting soon after three, they made a march of fifteen miles on a very hot day, and encamped at Dospore, where they halted till the 18th, when they moved to Akberpore, ten miles. After a halt of two days they resumed their march on the 21st; they encamped that night at Simree, nine miles; moved to Jasingpore, twelve miles, on the next day; and returned to Sultanpore, fourteen miles, on the 23rd.

They did not long remain here; for on the 26th they marched on an expedition towards the fort of Amethie. Starting at four in the morning, they encamped at Doadpore after an eleven miles' march. On the 27th they started at the same hour; four companies of the Battalion formed the advanced-guard; and as the rebels were expected to fight here, the Battalion formed up before entering the jungle. The enemy had erected two batteries on the road. There was a river running through, with a bridge which the batteries commanded. But before the troops came up, the enemy had deserted this position. The cavalry pursued them; but the country being full of jungle and intersected with ravines, could not come up with them. At the end of a twelve-mile march the Battalion encamped; but struck tents again at three in the afternoon, and marched five miles further to Jugdespore. They did not camp here till nine at night, when it was pitch

[1] '. . . . Rifle Brigade—Colour-Sergeant Maloney; Private Etteridge.'

dark; and the men were much wearied with their long and fatiguing march.

On the 28th, leaving their camp standing, they marched at four in the morning, about six miles into the jungle to a fort called Kataree. On arrival they found it deserted. The fort was blown up, and they took five guns, one brass and four iron The former had an inscription in Persian, stating that it had belonged to Rajah Buksh Ullah Khan Bahadoor. It had been employed in the Sikh campaign. The iron guns, being unserviceable, were destroyed.

It appeared from the traces on the ground that the rebels had occupied with considerable numbers the positions they had gone over in the late marches. Many of these were strong and commanding; and had the enemy dared to make a stand they might have harassed our people considerably; but their courage had failed them, and all were found unoccupied. The Battalion returned to their camp at Jugdespore about seven in the evening.

On the 29th they marched to Gooreabad, nine miles. A weary march, for the siege guns could not be got forward in consequence of the frequent occurrence of nullahs and aqueducts for irrigating the country. These were broken down by coolies; yet the progress was very slow, and they did not camp at Gooreabad, till after eleven.

On the 30th they started at four in the morning; and it was intended to make a march of seventeen miles. But from the same difficulties in moving the heavy guns as occurred the day before, the camp was pitched at Itterowah, after marching nine miles, which it took six hours to accomplish.

On the 31st the Battalion marched to Ettyah, eight miles, and halted there for some days.

On November 9 they marched at four o'clock in the morning. The country being cultivated there was great difficulty in getting the siege guns forward, and the treasure chest broke down. Thus hindered, it took the Battalion some thirteen hours to make a march of eighteen miles; and they did not encamp, about a mile and a half from the fort of Amethie, till five in the evening. Here they formed a junction with the Commander-in-Chief's army, which was encamped about five miles from them, on the north-east of the fort; while General Wetherall's force was on the south-west. The Riflemen expected to assault the fort on the morrow. But when that morrow came, Loll Madhoo, the Rajah of Amethie, came into camp and capitulated, declaring that he had no power over his people, and that he had been compelled, in order to save his own life, to fire on the English troops the day before.

But though the Rajah had himself surrendered, no doubt to secure his personal safety, the occupants of the fort evacuated it in the night, and disappeared through the jungle. Wherefore on the 11th the Battalion received an order to start in pursuit; and marched at three o'clock in the afternoon through very dusty roads nine miles to Gowriegunge, and did not reach their camping-ground till seven o'clock in the evening. On the 12th they proceeded to Ettyah, nine miles.

On the 13th, starting at six in the morning, they marched twelve miles to Pursaidepore, near Salone, where they arrived at twelve, having on the march crossed the river Sie. At eight o'clock at night they received a sudden order to move their camp further; and accordingly on the 14th, at five in the morning, marched four miles, and arriving at seven pitched their camp at Secrian, near the entrance of the jungle, and furnished strong outlying picquets.

On the next day, starting early in the morning, they marched fourteen miles by a very bad road and through clouds of dust to Shunkerpore. This was a stronghold of Beni Madhoo, and it was hoped that by concentrating the columns on it, he might be caught. But however there was a fresh disappointment. In the dark hours of the morning he managed to evade the picquets, and to escape with his followers, guns and baggage. As soon as his flight was discovered on the morning of the 16th, the Battalion received a sudden order to march in pursuit, and starting at seven o'clock proceeded to Roy Bareilly, where they pitched camp about two in the afternoon.

On the 17th they made a march of sixteen miles to Mohungunge, starting at six and not arriving till about two, several long halts having been made for guns to come up, the road leading through much thick jungle.

On the 18th they made a long and tedious march of fourteen miles to Jugdespore, where they halted for four days On the 20th they received an order to go on a reconnaissance, leaving their tents standing, and paraded for that purpose; but the order was countermanded.

On the 23rd they resumed their movements; and starting at six in the morning arrived at Inhona, after a short and easy march of seven miles, at a little after nine.

On the 24th the left wing of the Battalion, under Major Warren, received during the night orders to move (with part of the 7th Hussars and some guns) to the assistance of Colonel Galwey's column. That officer, it appeared, had come to some fort which had no guns; but on its occupants being called on to surrender they had refused, and had fired on and killed an Engineer officer and some men. The Riflemen marched at six in the morning to Koilee, twelve miles, but on arrival there found that the garrison of the fort had during the night crossed the Goomtee and disappeared. This wing, therefore, after a day's halt at Koilee, marched on the 26th to Bekta, seven miles; and on the 27th, after a short march of six miles, rejoined Head-quarters at Hydergurh.

These had in the meanwhile had an encounter with the enemy. For Brigadier Horsford had, before starting for Koilee, directed Colonel Hill to march towards Lucknow, taking with him the other wing of the Hussars and some Horse Artillery, and to attack a force of rebels supposed to be about two marches in that direction; and to protect the baggage of the entire column.

Colonel Hill came up with the rebels on the 26th near Hydergurh The Riflemen were first engaged, and as the enemy were making a running fight of it, the cavalry and Artillery galloped up through the skirmishers, and did considerable execution. The Riflemen took a gun; and the Hussars under Sir William Russell pursued the Sepoys and cut them up. The Riflemen then encamped at Hydergurh; and halted there till December 2, when they marched sixteen miles to Monshegunge, and encamped there for the night. And starting on the following morning at five o'clock, arrived at the Dilkoosha, Lucknow, after a fourteen-mile march, at half-past nine.

On December 5 the 2nd Battalion, forming part of a force under the command of Lord Clyde, started at six in the morning from Lucknow, and made a march of twenty miles, arriving at Newabgunge at about three or four in the afternoon, when the men got their breakfasts.

On the 6th they struck tents at five, and paraded at six, but did not get off till seven, when, making a very long march of twenty-two miles, they proceeded to Gunnespore, Byram Ghât, which they reached about three. The men were very tired and hungry, for they had had nothing to eat till about five, when they got their breakfast. On the way intelligence was received that the rebels were crossing the river. The cavalry and Horse Artillery pushed forward; and sixteen Riflemen and an officer (Lieutenant Sotheby[1]) were mounted on the limbers. They went as hard as they could go; but when they came to the Ghât they found the rebels had been too quick for them, and had crossed the river. However, the Riflemen got a few shots at them. The 7th Hussars after this chase were much astonished to hear the words, 'The Rifles to the front;' for they fancied the whole Battalion was coming up, and could not understand how they had kept up with such a pace as the Hussars and guns had been going. However, only Sotheby and his sixteen Riflemen then answered this call. For it had been a joke with these Hussars when they were an advanced guard with the Riflemen (and they had been on many): on the part of the troopers, 'that they could not get rid of these little fellows;' on the part of the Riflemen, that they 'marched the horsemen down,' and 'could not make them march fast enough.'

On the 7th some companies of the Battalion were suddenly paraded at half-past one, and with the 7th Hussars went five miles up the river in search of rebels; but returned unsuccessful at seven in the evening.

The great object was now to cross the Gogra; and as there was a difficulty in forming a boat-bridge at Byram Ghât, Lord Clyde determined to proceed to Fyzabad where a bridge already existed. Accordingly on the 8th the Battalion, starting at six in the morning, made a march of twenty miles to

[1] Brevet Lieutenant-Colonel Sotheby.

Derriabad, which they reached at three in the afternoon. On the next day they marched seventeen miles to Begumgunge, and on the 10th another long march of nineteen miles to Fyzabad. In these long marches few Riflemen, if any, fell out, though the marches lasted from six in the morning till two or three in the afternoon, the hottest hours of the day.

On the 11th the Battalion crossed the Gogra by a bridge of boats. The river is here about 600 yards broad, having a great expanse of sand on each side. The turn of the Battalion to cross came at four in the afternoon, and they afterwards marched about six miles on the other side to Newabgunge, where they encamped about six. On the 12th, starting at six in the morning, they arrived at Jamkapoorah at noon, and on the next day marched to Dheras, fifteen miles. On the 14th they proceeded to Secrora, another march of fifteen miles, and on the day following to Kurrunpore, eleven miles. Mr. Russell, the 'Times' correspondent, who was accompanying the Commander-in-Chief's column, thus writes of the Battalion under this date: 'The Rifle Brigade who are with us are as hard as nails; faces tanned brown, and muscles hardened into whipcord; and to see them step over the ground with their officers marching beside them is a very fine sight for those who have an eye for real first-rate soldiers. Lord Clyde is greatly pleased with the officers because they do not ride on ponies, as many officers of other regiments are accustomed to do.'[1]

On the 16th, though tents were struck at five in the morning, the Battalion did not march in consequence of rain till eleven, when they moved to Khariat, where, after a march of ten miles, they encamped at three.

On the next day they marched in heavy and constant rain to Baraitch, where camp was pitched in a very beautiful spot at eleven in the forenoon. Here they halted for five days: the first halt they had had since they left Lucknow, nearly a fortnight before; and very acceptable it was to the men, though not without its discomforts. For the night after their arrival was, as the day of their march had been, one of incessant rain. And tents and everything men and officers had on

[1] 'My Diary in India,' ii. 370.

or possessed were saturated with wet. The morning revealed a swamp, rather than a camp; many of the tents stood in pools of water in which the men waded ankle-deep. A dense fog, too, came down from the hills, and took away all hope of drying their clothes. Whether for this reason, or on account of the increasing cold which now began to be severely felt, the Riflemen resumed their cloth clothing on the next day. However, the remaining days of their halt at Baraitch were fine.

On the 23rd they again started at six in the morning; but soon after leaving Baraitch they were halted, and their route altered. They then made a march of fifteen miles, in the course of which they forded the river, and arrived at Jeta at two.

On the 24th the order was to march as usual in the morning; but as the men turned out rain came on, and the 'halt' was sounded, luckily before the tents were struck. Their halt here gave them an opportunity of making their arrangements for keeping Christmas on the morrow. But these were very near being useless; for Lord Clyde issued an order that the soldiers were to have their dinners at one, and march at two. Great was the consternation; and fears of all the good things they had provided being unconsumed or eaten half-raw pervaded everyone. However, before the dreaded hour, staff officers, who had been sent out to observe the roads, reported that they were in too bad a state from recent rains for the troops to move. The Commander-in-Chief, therefore, unwillingly postponed his intended march. Serenity was restored to hearts which knew no fear save that of losing the one good dinner long hoped for; and the day was spent happily, the more so as it was fine.

But after this recreation, hard work soon began again. The Battalion marched at six in the morning of the 26th. It was very foggy, but cleared up about eight. After marching some twelve miles, they were halted to allow them to eat their breakfast. Here they stayed about two hours, resuming their advance at half-past one. Two companies of the Battalion, under Captain Fremantle, with cavalry, formed the advanced guard.

On their arrival near a jungle Sir William Russell, who

commanded the advance, ordered these two companies to the front, and desired them to extend at the entrance of the jungle. They did so, and advanced, and about four in the afternoon found the enemy in a tope of trees, who opened upon them with two guns. The advanced companies then, with the cavalry, Horse Artillery, and five other companies of the Battalion, formed line and advanced. The cavalry and Horse Artillery soon distanced the Riflemen, and while the former attacked the flank of the enemy, the Riflemen brought their right shoulders forward, and went on at the double. They pursued the enemy, who did not make any stand, for five or six miles. The Battalion encamped at Churdah about eight o'clock, the men being very weary; for they had marched about twenty-one miles, and the latter part of it in pursuit of the rebels had been got over at a very quick pace. The Riflemen killed three Sepoys in this chase, and five guns were taken.

On the 27th it was understood that the Battalion was to halt; but at nine o'clock they received orders to march in an hour. They started, therefore, about ten, and after a march of about six miles, came to a thick jungle, and were ordered to assault the fort of Mejidia. The attack was confided to the Riflemen. Brigadier Horsford's orders to Colonel Hill were to advance to within 400 yards of the fort: then to open fire on the embrasures. Mortars and heavy guns were ordered to the front, and cavalry to the flanks. This took some time. Then the Battalion advanced to the front face; two companies skirmishing; two supporting them; two moved to the left; the remainder in support. A sharp fire was opened, and was returned for some time by a fire of grape from the fort. The Riflemen continued their fire for about two hours, picking off the gunners at the embrasures. After that time the fire from the place slackened; and Colonel Hill, having solicited and obtained permission to advance, the Battalion moved forward. A difficult thorny hedge interposed, which was soon cut down by the swords of the Riflemen, and entrance was effected into the fort, which was found to be evacuated. The Battalion took possession of the stores and muniments of war, powder, shot, etc., which were found there; and encamped in the evening after a very hard day's work. One sergeant and 6 rank and file were wounded, of whom one died on the next day.

On the 28th they were engaged in destroying the fort, and securing the stores of grain, etc., found in it. In the course of the day the Riflemen discovered two guns hidden in the jungle within the fort.

On the 29th the first orders were still to halt; but about eleven they received orders to march, and did so about noon, back to Nanparah, ten miles, but by a route different from that by which they had come on the 26th.

Here it was understood that they were to halt for three days. And accordingly on the 30th many officers of the Battalion went out shooting, the band played at five, and all things denoted a halt; when a sudden order was issued that the Battalion was to march at eight in the evening. They did so; half the men were carried on elephants, five on each, and half marched, turn about, ride and tie. The motion of the elephants was strange to the men; some were made sick by the motion, and some tumbled off; but gradually they settled down. The night was pitch dark, and those marching occasionally fell into holes and water-courses, undistinguishable in the darkness. So they moved on till four in the morning; when, it being ascertained that if they continued their march they would reach the enemy's position at Bankee (whither they were bound) before daylight, a halt was ordered. And they remained tormented by the cold and heavy dew; for no fires were allowed, for fear of alarming the enemy whom Lord Clyde hoped to surprise. This halt was probably continued too long. At any rate, a march of five miles remained to be got over; and the troops did not reach the enemy's position till eight. The cavalry (Carabiniers) were ordered to advance, and soon found themselves in front of a thick jungle occupied by the enemy's skirmishers and guns; to whose fire they offered an easy mark, without their being able to return it or to dislodge them They were therefore withdrawn; and the Riflemen were hurried to the front, and ordered to skirmish through the jungle. Three companies were extended under the command of Major Warren, Captain Singer and Lieutenant Lane,[1] accompanied and directed by Colonel Hill, who dis-

[1] Captain G. C. Lane, half-pay.

mounting accompanied the centre company, Lieutenant Lane's. On entering the wood they found a cart track, along which the enemy were endeavouring to withdraw a gun. The Riflemen pushed on at the double along this track, occasionally getting a glimpse of the gun in their front, while the enemy's skirmishers were retiring rapidly before them, and turning off into the jungle. Thus it happened that the advance of the Riflemen in the cart track was very rapid, while that of those in the jungle on each side of it was much slower, as they could not force their way through the tangled wood nearly so fast. The track was about a mile in length to the point where it reached the end of the jungle. By the time the Riflemen got there the gun had quite distanced them. On arriving at the end of this belt of jungle the whole of the enemy's force was seen on an undulating plain beyond, some few hundred paces distant.

The Riflemen, hurrying along the track in pursuit of the retreating gun, had arrived at the edge of the jungle completely out of breath; and Colonel Hill, on counting them, found himself accompanied by only twenty men, with Lieutenant Lane and a Colour-Sergeant (Piper).[1] As it was impossible to know where the remaining skirmishers and the supports were at the moment, it was necessary to act with caution; and the small party were ordered to remain hidden at the edge of the jungle, while the enemy's movements were observed. They seemed to be contemplating a retreat. At this time three officers rode up from the rear; and one of them, Sir Henry Norman, brought orders from Lord Clyde for the Riflemen to retire. Colonel Hill pointed out to him that the jungle was merely a belt; that if Lord Clyde was aware of this he would probably wish to push on; and that as the jungle was cleared, cavalry could now advance and act on the plain. The staff officers accordingly galloped off, and soon afterwards a squadron of the 7th Hussars came up. Meanwhile Major Warren's and Captain Singer's companies had made their way through the jungle, and joined their comrades at the edge of it. Sir William Mansfield soon came up, and by his permission Colonel Hill advanced with two companies, Warren's and Lane's, in skirmishing order. While the rest of

[1] Mr. Piper is now Paymaster of the 63rd Regiment.

the Battalion, which had passed through the jungle, were halted on the bank of a small but deep nullah, or river, which intersected the plain, successive squadrons of the 7th passed on their right flank; and though checked for a moment by the nullah, and exposed to the fire of a battery of six guns, which the enemy had placed on the opposite bank of the Raptee, charged the enemy's cavalry who were making for the ford of the Raptee, caught them on the bank, and engaged them in the river. The Riflemen, who were in an excellent position to observe this charge across the plain, saw with admiration this gallant feat of arms performed by their comrades of the 7th. Soon after this the Riflemen retired through the jungle, and pitched their camp about four o'clock two miles and a half from the scene of the action. But the men did not get settled till the evening, and it was eight o'clock before they got food. They had been under arms from eight o'clock the night before; had marched twenty-nine miles—most of it night marching—from Nanparah, and two and a half back to Bankee; and had been engaged from an early hour in the day.

In this affair the 2nd Battalion had one man wounded.

I have now to return to the 3rd Battalion, which we left at Lucknow, where they were stationed from the time of the battle of Nawabgunge The Head-quarters left Lucknow at four o'clock on the afternoon of November 22, four companies being still with Major Oxenden at Sundeelah. They marched to the Alumbagh, and halted there while the men had their tea and the officers their dinners. They started again about nine, and proceeded to Bunnee bridge, which they crossed, and then halted again from about 2.30 to 5.30 A.M. They then proceeded to Nawabgunge on the Cawnpore road, which they reached about nine and encamped. The object of this move was to intercept Beni Madhoo, who was said to be at the head of a very large force of rebels. Here they halted for a couple of days; and on the 26th they marched in light order and leaving their camp standing, to Busserutgunge. Soon after they had started, however, a note came in from Colonel Glyn, who was in charge of a party some twenty miles distant, conveying information of the supposed whereabouts of Beni Madhoo. This was opened by the Quartermaster, who was in charge of the camp, who despatched a messenger with it to Colonel Macdonell. The Battalion returned to Nawabgunge on the morning of the 27th, not having seen anything of Beni Madhoo or his army. On the 28th they marched to Bunteera, thirteen miles; and on the next day to the Alumbagh, where they encamped But in the afternoon they received orders to start again and march into the Cantonments at Lucknow, which they did not reach till eight o'clock at night, when they had to put up their tents in the dark. Their rest here was not long; for at four the next morning they received an order to march and join the Head-quarter division, a large force of the enemy being supposed to be near. They moved, therefore, to Buxee-ke-talou, and halted there on December 1 On that night, the detachment under Colonel Glyn, consisting of three companies, rejoined the Battalion, and the whole marched at daybreak the next morning for the fort of Oomria. They kept the road for some time, and then struck across country through thick jungle. On approaching the fort, which on account of the density of the wood surrounding it they could not see, they were attacked, but soon drove their assailants back. They then halted till the baggage came up. Later in the day, the 5th Fusiliers, supported by the Riflemen, approached the place, but were met by heavy fire from two of its faces, which caused some loss As the men had had a long march and it was late in the day, they were withdrawn; and arrangements were made to storm the fort on the next day. Camp was therefore pitched, but unfortunately within range of the guns of the fort. This made it uncomfortable, and some damage was done; but it was too late to move camp, and the men were tired. So they slept soundly, though an occasional shot fell among the tents. In the morning the usual discovery was made: the enemy had disappeared in the night, leaving behind him ammunition and most of his property. This fort had evidently been a residence of the Rajah; for many articles of women's furniture and belongings were found in some of the apartments: the property, no doubt, of some of his wives. It was as well that the Rajah and his troops had preferred discretion to valour;

for the works were very strong, one within the other, and with two deep ditches. The loss, therefore, must have been considerable if it had been defended with any tenacity.

The Riflemen halted on the 4th and 5th, and were engaged in demolishing the fort and blowing up the mud walls round some fortified villages near it. At one of these a gun was found concealed.

On the 6th they marched to Futtehpore, and just before their arrival there had a skirmish with some rebels, who appeared to be a rear-guard protecting a gun which had passed some time previously, and the tracks of which were plainly visible. It was an eighteen-mile march; and the skirmish at the end of it made the men weary enough. They did not reach their camping-ground, in a field of tall dâl, till after dark, and did not get their dinners till late at night. On the 7th they marched to Betwa, where was a strong fort which they found unoccupied, the enemy having evacuated it in the morning. Their fires were still burning when the Riflemen reached it in the afternoon. It was as usual surrounded by thick jungle. They halted on the 8th and 9th to demolish this fort.

On the 10th they marched sixteen miles to Nawabgunge on the Fyzabad road, the battle-field of June 13. In this march they passed several small forts and intrenchments, some of which had evidently been but recently evacuated; and some had been strengthened and repaired at the expense of much labour by those who had not the courage to defend them.

On the 11th they made a march of sixteen miles towards Derriabad, which they passed through on the following day, and after a dusty march of eighteen miles, halted for the night at Burehke Serai.

On the 13th they reached Mobaruckgunge on the Gogra at one in the afternoon, after a hot, dusty and fatiguing march of fifteen miles. For though the nights were cold, the mid-day sun was very hot.

On the 14th they marched to Fyzabad, and turning to the left before they entered that town, encamped on the bank of the river near a large mud fort.

On the next day they crossed the Gogra by the bridge of

boats, as their comrades of the 2nd Battalion had done four days before; both forming part of the army assembled under Lord Clyde, which was to drive the enemy into a corner, from which it was hoped if Jung Bahadoor, the Chief Minister of Nepaul, stood true to us, he could not escape, and so to terminate the war. After passing the river and marching three miles, they forded a river about three feet deep. This and its sandy banks much retarded the baggage, which also had been delayed by the obstinacy of the elephants, who would not venture on the bridge, and were made to swim the river under the lead or guidance of an old elephant. It was late, therefore, before their baggage came up and they encamped at Wuzeergunge.

On the 16th they made another long march to Gonda, where they encamped near some ruined bungalows, said to have been once occupied by the officers of a native regiment, who were murdered by their men.

Here they remained till after the close of the year without any incident of importance, save that two companies (Major Bourchier's and Captain Windham's) went out on a daur on the 21st and returned on the 23rd.

On January 3, 1859, the 2nd Battalion shifted camp to Purainee, about a mile from Bankee.

On the 6th they marched at seven in the morning to the bank of the Raptee, and encamped at Sudheeria Ghât[1] about ten.

On the 8th Lord Clyde and the greater part of the force quitted the frontier; leaving the 2nd Battalion, the 7th Hussars, and some native troops, under Brigadier Horsford, to watch the fords of the Raptee.

On the 12th the Battalion shifted camp to Ballapore, on the banks of a tributary of the Raptee; and at eleven at night three companies, Captains R. Glyn's, Blackett's and Dillon's, marched, under the command of Major Vaughan, of the 5th Punjaub Regiment, and crossing the Raptee, proceeded about sixteen miles, when they came on the rebels and killed twenty-five out of about thirty. They returned to camp on the 14th.

[1] This seems to have been called also Sidhonia Ghât.

On the 26th they again shifted camp close to the Raptee.

At last, on February 8, they received authority to cross the frontier into Nepaul, Jung Bahadoor having given consent to their entering that territory. On the 9th, therefore, they marched at five in the morning and crossed the Raptee. They then moved through about five miles of very dense jungle with very large trees, and passed a mark like a mile-stone, which denoted the boundary of Nepaul. They then went round the spur of the mountains, and debouched on a large plain. They went on some miles farther, when the Brigadier ordered Colonel Hill, with a wing of the Battalion and some native troops, to recross to the right bank of the Raptee, where, at a crossing called Sidka Ghât, the enemy were reported to be in force, with fifteen guns in position.

This force was told off: two companies to proceed along the river's bank; two under Major Warren to press through the jungle on the left, and to endeavour to intercept the enemy or to fall on their right flank; and the native troops under Major Vaughan to act in a similar manner, but on ground farther removed from the river.

The companies near the river extended in skirmishing order, the right file resting on the river's bank. After advancing some distance they found themselves in front of a hill, which they were obliged to file round along the water's edge. This was no easy work, for the ground was very difficult, and interspersed with rocks and great boulders. As they were thus proceeding, on reaching a bend of the river they found themselves in front of the guns of the enemy, who were in a strong position on some rising ground. These guns immediately opened on them with grape, but did little mischief, as the fire flew over their heads, wounding one man only. The Riflemen moved rapidly forward, and as soon as they were clear of the rocks formed and proceeded across the shingle, keeping up a smart fire which did much execution.

But the rebel gunners stood by their guns till the Riflemen were close upon them. Then they bolted and escaped into the jungle, giving the slip to Major Vaughan, whose force had been sent round to intercept them. They left fourteen guns and a mortar in the hands of Hill's force.

The other wing, with Brigadier Horsford, having given

the attacking party twenty minutes' start, moved on along the plain, keeping the Raptee on the left, till about three in the afternoon, when they entered a dense forest. The ground became hilly and the road bad. At half-past three they made another halt of twenty minutes, and were just falling in when they heard guns open in the front. They pushed forward, and soon came to a very steep hill, which they ran down, and found themselves on the bank of the river, and saw the skirmishers of the other wing entering the jungle on the opposite bank. They were ordered to halt; and after their fight the other wing recrossed the Raptee and joined them, and they then marched to camp, which they found pitched about four miles off, and which they did not reach till seven at night, after one of the hardest day's work they had ever had. For they had passed through dense and difficult jungle; had scrambled over rough rocks, and had moved over shingly and fatiguing ground; besides marching not less than twenty miles. A non-commissioned officer (Sergeant Braun) was very nearly drowned in crossing the Raptee. He fell twice, but one of the men on the right bank rescued him.

They remained in this camp till the 12th, when it was shifted to the tributary of the Raptee, near a jungle which seemed to be interminable. The rain was very heavy, and the camp-ground became a perfect swamp.

In his despatch reporting this action, Horsford favourably mentions Lieutenant-Colonel Hill, Major Dillon and Lieutenant Fryer.

On the 14th, very sudden orders were received at eleven P.M. for three companies, Captain Fremantle's, one under the command of Lieutenant Sotheby, and another, to start on an expedition under command of Major Ramsay of the Kumaon Battalion. These companies accordingly paraded at half-past three in the morning; but owing to a delay in the arrival of elephants did not move off till half-past four. They crossed the Raptee five times, and as it was deep and rapid, the men for the purpose of crossing were mounted on elephants. They then marched forward; and at about six arrived at the edge of the jungle and formed up They went on at a very brisk pace till half-past nine, when they halted for twenty minutes, sending on a spy to bring word if he could see anything of the enemy. Starting again, they marched through a gorge in the hill, and by the side and bed of a mountain stream, till half-past eleven ; when, it being suspected that they had missed their way, a Goorka was despatched, who soon returned with the intelligence that they were on a wrong track. They therefore retraced their steps, and soon meeting the spy, were disappointed at hearing from him that the enemy had departed. At one o'clock they came up to the ground they had occupied, and found the ashes of their fires still smouldering. Here the Riflemen bivouacked, no tents having been taken with this detachment ; but their rations did not come up till four o'clock. They had marched about sixteen miles over bad ground at a very rapid pace, and were much wearied.

On the 16th they returned to the camp of the Head-quarters, marching at half-past six, and arriving at one.

On the 17th the Battalion, starting at six in the morning, marched back to Sudheeria Ghât, where they camped about half-past eleven.

On the 21st the whole Battalion turned out early to take leave of their friends and comrades of the 7th Hussars, who had received the route for Umballa. They had been together for twelve months, and fought together in many brilliant affairs, and undergone together many weary days. Officers and men felt great regret at this parting ; for a feeling had grown up between them of such comradeship as is not usual between separate corps.

On the 26th the Battalion marched to a place about three miles on the other side of Bankee, and encamped there ; the whole march being about eight miles. On the next day, Brigadier Horsford, under whom they had so long served, started with his Staff for Gonda, to take command of the troops there, and the command of those on the Raptee devolved on Colonel Hill.

On the 28th the Battalion marched to Nanparah, fourteen miles, the country through which they passed being under water from daily rain. For the next few days this rain was so heavy, accompanied often by lightning and thunder, that though daily orders were given to march, they were as regularly countermanded. The camping-ground became first a swamp, then a perfect lake. At last, on March 6, they marched at ten in the forenoon, and arrived at their old camping-ground at Jeta at two in the afternoon. On the next day they proceeded to Baraitch, arriving there at half-past two in the afternoon. The rivers and nullahs, swollen by the rains, were up to a short man's hips.

They remained at Baraitch till the 28th, when they shifted camp; but the ground chosen being found to be infested with reptiles, they were moved back on the 30th to nearly their old ground.

On April 3 an order was received from Brigadier Horsford for two companies, with some native troops and guns, to proceed to Bankee to watch the ford there, and defend the line of the Raptee. Captain Singer and Lieutenant Nicholl went on this duty.

On the 4th two more companies were ordered to the Raptee; and at half-past four on the morning of the 5th Major Warren's and Captain R. Glyn's companies started, and after marching fourteen miles, halted to get something to eat. After which, marching about ten miles farther, they arrived at Bhinga Ghât on the Raptee, their destination. On the 6th they halted there, throwing out strong picquets. On the next day these companies moved back to a tope on the Baraitch road; and on the 8th they started on a reconnaissance at half-past eight, and marched about eight miles. No two villages which they passed through told the same tale. In one the inhabitants had seen the *budmashes* [1] in thousands; in the next they vowed that not one had been seen for six months. The companies got back to their camp at half-past three in the afternoon, having marched about sixteen miles in the heat of the day.

These companies halted during the 9th and 10th, and marched back to Baraitch and joined Head-quarters on the 11th.

In the meantime the remainder of the Battalion, with the exception of Captain Fremantle's company which was left at Baraitch, marched at five P.M. under Colonel Hill; and

[1] *i.e.* blackguards, scoundrels: a name applied by the soldiers and the loyal to the rebels.

after marching sixteen miles towards Rahdee, found that the enemy, whom they expected to find there, had fled. They therefore encamped about three A.M. And on the next day marched back at six in the evening to Baraitch, where they arrived the following morning at five. The men were very much fatigued, having had two nights' marching, and having been unable to sleep by day on account of the heat, the thermometer standing at 102°.

At midnight on the 8th–9th Captain Fremantle with his company, 2 Horse Artillery guns, 80 Punjaub rifles, and 150 native police, marched to join a force under Captain Cleveland, 98th Regiment, at Akouna. Halting every hour for ten minutes to rest the men, this force arrived at Akouna, and encamped in a tope at nine in the morning.

On the next day this detachment marched at half-past nine in the morning, some of the men being on gun-waggons and some on elephants, and arrived at Khagupore at half-past three. And on the following morning marched at six to Dahnapore, where they arrived at half-past eleven.

On the 12th they moved to Ramwapore, about five miles distant, and arrived there at eight in the morning.

In the afternoon reports came in that the rebels were encamped about three miles off, and would probably remain there during the night. Accordingly, Fremantle marched his detachment at three P.M., leaving his camp standing. After advancing for some time without seeing anything of rebels, they came on a picquet of Hodson's Horse, who were marching westward, and who reported that rebels were close at hand. It was then about six. They pushed on, and Captain Cleveland directed Fremantle to take his company, the guns, and some native horsemen round a jungle, and attack the rear of the enemy. After marching about a mile, they turned off the road into the jungle, and after about three quarters of a mile emerged into a kind of plain, though surrounded with jungle on all sides. Here the native guide said he could see a rebel vedette. Fremantle accordingly ordered the Punjaub men to form company and advance; and they had scarcely done so when a volley was poured into them at about forty yards. It was now half-past six, and nearly dark. The native police, who were leading, fled at the first fire, carrying away in their flight a section of the Punjaub men. The remainder of these sat down on the ground and fired at the enemy. Yet Fremantle could neither induce them to face the hill and attack the rebels, nor yet to clear off to the flank, and allow the guns and the Riflemen to act. At last he succeeded in getting them off to a flank; and then the guns opening with grape, and the Riflemen pouring in a steady fire, the flashes from the bushes and the hill in front soon ceased. Advancing up the hill, they found the camp of the rebels, their fires burning, and their bedding and grass for their horses unmoved; but not a man was there. This little affair lasted exactly half-an-hour. One Rifleman was severely wounded. Fremantle then went round the jungle; and, regaining the Fyzabad road, rejoined the main body under Captain Cleveland at nine. And the Riflemen reached their camp at half-past eleven, much fatigued by their marches and their fight.

On the 13th they halted, and on the next day marched back to Khagupore, and on the day following to Akouna, where they halted during the 16th. On the 17th this company marched to take up a position to cover the fords of the Raptee at Gunespore. Here they remained till the 22nd; when, being relieved by Sotheby's company, which had started from Baraitch the day before, they marched at 2.30 in the morning of the 23rd; and encamping during that day at a village, resumed their march at three o'clock the following morning, and rejoined the Battalion soon after seven on the 24th.

During this time, however, other expeditions had taken place. On the 9th one company, under Lieutenant Eccles, had marched about eighteen miles towards Nanparah, but returned on the 11th.

On the 20th Colonel Hill, having received Brigadier Horsford's orders to meet him at Nanparah, proceeded thither with three companies of the Battalion. The object was to clear the Jugdespore jungles of a number of rebels who had taken refuge there.

Accordingly, these three companies started from Baraitch in the afternoon of that day, and marched about seven miles. And on the 21st, marching early, they reached Nanparah, after a very long march, and found the Brigadier awaiting them.

On the next day they started soon after four, and marched sixteen miles; and on the 23rd made a further march of twelve miles to Hureeha, in the course of which they crossed the Surjoo river, and encamped on its banks.

On the 24th (Easter Sunday) they started soon after two in the morning, and made a march of eighteen miles, nearly half of it through thick jungle; and as the heat was now oppressive, the march was very wearisome. They had now got near the enemy, who was in a delta of the River Gogra. So that on the 25th they struck tents at two. Soon after starting they lost their way in the jungle, so that day broke before they were fairly started. Colonel Hill commanded the infantry of the force employed.

The Rifle companies marched on until they came to a ford of the Gogra. Here they were halted till the cavalry and guns, which had proceeded by another route, came up. On their arrival they crossed the river, which was at the ford waist-deep, holding their pouches up to their shoulders. They formed on the other side, and found the rebels in a large open space in front of a thick jungle. They were evidently surprised, and tried to make off. The Riflemen broke into extended order, and after a very smart skirmish, drove the enemy into a further jungle. Here Dr. Reade had a very narrow escape of his life, being attacked with great audacity by two of the enemy's Sowars immediately in rear of the supports. The rebels broke into three parties, and so gave the Riflemen some trouble, as they had to pursue them through jungle so thick that it seemed never to have been trodden by the foot of man. However, as the enemy had taken refuge in it, and it seemed impossible then to dislodge them, camp was pitched about eight o'clock, and the Riflemen rested for the night, weary and hungry; for they had received only half-a-pound of bread and a dram of rum till they reached their camp; and they had fought hard and marched far.

On the next day orders were given to clear the jungle. Accordingly Colonel Hill with his Riflemen scoured the whole of the delta, on which these jungles were situated, to the river's bank. But the rebels forded the river, and made good their escape. However, in the fight of the previous day a number (it is said 200) of them were killed, and some prisoners taken.

On the 27th, having effected the object of their expedition, they began their return, and marched eight miles. On the next day they marched the same distance to Hureeha, having recrossed the Gogra at a different point, where the water was deeper and the current very strong. Some men narrowly escaped drowning, and a bugler (Horton) saved the lives of three men. It was a difficult and dangerous ford, and a rifle and two swords were lost.

On the 29th they marched ten miles to Doobra; on the 30th fourteen miles, on May 1 twelve miles, and on the next day, after a march of sixteen miles, arrived at Nanparah.

Here they halted during the 3rd. And on the following day one company, accompanying the Brigadier and the cavalry, returned to Baraitch. The remaining two companies remained at Nanparah until June 6, when they started on their return to Baraitch.

I have now to return to the movements of Sotheby's company, which, as I have said, started from Baraitch on the 21st to relieve Captain Fremantle. On that day they marched twelve miles to Bamparah, and on the next seventeen miles to Gunespore. On the 28th they turned out at night, the picquets having been fired upon. From the 4th to the 10th May they patrolled about the neighbourhood. On the 4th they crossed the Raptee, and marched eight miles; on the 5th marched nine miles to Pepree Ghât; on the next day thirteen miles to Akouna, where they halted one day; and returned on the 8th to Pepree Ghât; and on the 10th marched back to their camp at Gunespore. On the 27th half the company proceeded to Bhinga, but finding no rebels there, returned to their camp the same evening. On June 2 the force under Captain Cleveland was broken up, and Sotheby, with the company under his command, marched for Baraitch, where they arrived on the 3rd, and joined Head-quarters of the Battalion.

The Mutiny was now virtually at an end. No enemy remained in the field, and only a few scattered fugitives skulked in the jungle, and these not in numbers sufficient to give uneasiness to our posts, or to necessitate keeping an army on the frontier or in the field. The 2nd Battalion, therefore, received on June 13 an order to march towards Lucknow, halting at Byram Ghât for Captain Singer's detachment of two companies, which was still watching the fords of the Raptee. On the 15th they left Baraitch at three in the morning, arriving at Puckerpore at half-past eight. The next day they were detained in the morning by heavy rains, but started at half-past four in the afternoon: the heat was intense, and it was like marching in a vapour bath, so that the men were much knocked up. The baggage, too, went astray, and on their arrival at their halting-place about nine at night, there were neither tents, rations, nor grog. The men lay down on the damp ground till two in the morning; and at three resumed their march without refreshment, and at daylight reached Hissampore; but no baggage appearing, they were obliged to set out in search of it, and at half-past eight arrived at a place where they halted, and sent for the baggage, having made a twenty-mile march. But no sooner was their camp pitched than a violent storm came on, blowing some of the tents clean away from the ropes, and leaving their inmates exposed to the full violence of the weather. On the 18th they started again at two in the morning, and arrived at Byram Ghât at seven. The river was much swollen, and there was no bridge. Two companies embarked at half-past seven, and attempted to cross; but the boats missed stays, and did not succeed in getting over. And as in consequence of the wind it was only practicable to cross in the morning or evening, they could not make a fresh attempt till six in the evening, when these two companies got across and landed at 6.20. The Regiment continued crossing on the 20th, and all got across on the 21st, Captain Singer's two companies from Bankee, which had arrived on the previous day, bringing up the rear. On the 22nd they marched at half-past four, and encamped beyond Ramnaghur, a march of six miles, soon after seven On the next day they proceeded seven miles On the 24th seven more, and encamped at Nawabgunge. On the 25th they were unable to continue their march on account of the violence of the rain; but on the next day they made a march of ten miles in the morning, and were ordered to march again at four in the afternoon; but rain poured down steadily, and continued all the evening. On the 27th they marched at half-past four in the morning, and arrived at the Yellow Bungalow at Lucknow at a quarter after eight. Here they encamped, but were ordered to parade again at four. It was so hot, however, that this was postponed till five, when they moved near the Dilkoosha. It had rained every day for some time, the country they had marched through was very wet, and the ground on which they now encamped was a perfect swamp.

Here they remained, furnishing a detachment of three companies to the Imaumbarah, till early in July, when the men were placed in barracks: a comfort few if any of them had enjoyed since they left Dublin two years before. The officers, however, continued in tents. The men now suffered much from their long exposure to the climate, and it is said that in August there were 200 men in hospital. But not till their work was over had they succumbed to fatigue, exposure, or climate For twenty months they had been in the field; often bivouacked in the open; never once in quarters. They had marched 1,745 miles in 161 marches (not including often shifting their camp to distances less than four miles), and every company-officer—save one who was lame—had accompanied his men on foot in these marches. They were, I believe, the only battalion which, from their landing in November 1857 to their cantonment at Lucknow in July 1859, had not at some time been in quarters; but had kept the field from the date of their arrival till the last day of the Mutiny.

Their casualties in that time may now be summed up.

Of officers, 2 had been killed in action; 4 had been severely wounded; 2 had died of their wounds; and 2 had died of disease. A total of 10 officers.

Of the Riflemen in the ranks there were

	Sergeants	Buglers	Privates	Total
Killed in action	...	...	10	10
Wounded severely	6	1	24	31
,, slightly	...	...	29	29
Died of wounds	...	...	7	7
,, disease	11	3	118	132
Invalided, and not included in the above	3	...	34	37
Grand total . . .	20	4	222	246

There had landed in India, either with the Battalion or

by drafts joining it, up to this period: 44 officers, 61 sergeants, 25 buglers, and 1,147 men. So that in this campaign nearly one-fourth of the officers, and a little more than one-fifth of other ranks, were killed, wounded, or invalided.

On October 22 Lord Canning, the Governor-General, made his entry into Lucknow; on which occasion the Battalion escorted him through the town, parading for that purpose at three A.M., and returning to their quarters at nine.

On the 29th they were inspected by the Commander-in-Chief, Lord Clyde, on which occasion there was a review and march-past. And on that evening the Governor-General, accompanied by their old Commander in the field, Sir Hope Grant, visited and went round their barracks.

We left the 3rd Battalion at Gonda in December 1858. On January 9, 1859, Head-quarters, with four companies, marched to Murajgunge, a distance of twenty-five miles; and on the 10th proceeded to the bank of the Raptee and encamped there. On the next day the Riflemen crossed the river on rafts, the baggage elephants and camels being made to wade across, and arrived at Tulsipore in the afternoon. The object of this march was to take over and escort the guns which had been taken at the Raptee and previously. Accordingly, on their arrival at Tulsipore they received from a company of Sikhs three guns and some treasure.

After a day's halt they started from Tulsipore on the 13th, and recrossing the Raptee arrived at Bulrampore after a fatiguing march of eighteen miles. On the 14th they proceeded to Cughai, seventeen miles; and on the next day rejoined the remainder of the Battalion at Gonda.

After one day's halt the Battalion started on the 17th for Agra, and passing through Secrora, recrossed the Gogra at Byram Ghât on the 20th. They proceeded to Nawabgunge on the 21st; and on the 23rd arrived at Lucknow. They marched from there on the 25th, and reached Bunteerah on the 27th, and Cawnpore on the 28th. Thence they proceeded by daily marches by Chobeepore, Poorah, Urroul, Mukrundnuggur, Chubramow, Bewar, Shekoabad, and Ferozabad to Agra, which they reached on February 12, and were there stationed.

CHAPTER XIII.

I HAVE now to give some account of the Camel Corps, which, as I have stated, was formed at Lucknow on April 5, 1858, by drafts of 100 men from the 2nd and 3rd Battalions, to which were eventually added 200 Sikhs. I have mentioned (p. 38) the names of the officers attached to this corps. The command of it was first proposed to Lieutenant-Colonel Julius Glyn of the 3rd Battalion; but on his declining it and preferring to serve with his Battalion, it was conferred on Major Ross[1] of that Battalion.

The men were to be mounted each on a camel, with a native driver to guide the animal. On April 7 they made their first attempt at camel-riding. The camel is, in fact, rather a difficult animal to sit, and the effects of this first lesson were rather ludicrous; the men clinging on in every possible position and appearing most uncomfortable. On the 8th they had two hours more of this drill, and the men began to sit much steadier; and this practice was repeated on the next day.

On the 10th the Camel Corps marched to the Dilkoosha at 5.30 in the morning, and encamped there for the completion of the formation of the Corps, and for camel-riding drill. But the ground on which they were encamped being found to be unhealthy—eight or ten men of the 3rd Battalion company having sickened—the camp was moved on the 12th at five in the afternoon to the front of and close to the Dilkoosha.

The men now made good progress in riding the camels; but with arms and accoutrements they found it harder to sit the camels, or to sling or dispose of their rifles. On the 16th Sir Colin Campbell inspected them, and seemed well pleased at their progress. The Camel Corps were all this time

[1] Now Brigadier-General John Ross, C B, commanding Brigade in Bengal, and lately commanding a Brigade in the Malay Peninsula.

without a surgeon; and as the men were sickening daily from the climate, without a regular hospital or medical officer, this was a serious evil.

On the 27th they left the Dilkoosha at five in the morning, and marched about five miles to Jellalabad, where they found mud huts and plenty of mango trees to shelter them from the sun.

While here, at about nine in the evening they experienced a dust storm, accompanied with vivid flashes of lightning. This was followed by a heavy fall of rain, which cleared and refreshed the atmosphere.

On the 28th the Corps marched at four in the morning eleven miles to Bunnee bridge. They halted on the 29th; and on the 30th struck tents at four in the morning, and marched seventeen miles to Bussarutgunge, and occupied some out-buildings of a mosque. On this march they loaded, as rebels were constantly crossing the road. It was found that the pace of the camels was a little over four miles an hour.[1]

On May 1 they marched to Cawnpore, fifteen miles, and occupied cantonments near Wheeler's intrenchment. They had marched from the Dilkoosha to Cawnpore with the 200 Riflemen only, and 250 camels. At the latter place they found 150 camels awaiting them, which made up the mount to 400; and steps were at once taken to raise the two companies of Sikhs, of 100 each, to complete the Corps to its full strength of 400 men.

While here Major Ross received a letter from Sir Colin Campbell, saying that the Camel Corps was a *Corps-d'élite*; and that the officers were to be very carefully picked, as there would be a great deal of independent command.

On the 4th they were ordered to march at midnight to Ukburpore, with stores for Sir Hugh Rose and mortars for the column commanded by Colonel Maxwell, 88th Regiment. The convoy did not arrive, however, till about two on the morning of the 5th, when they started and marched with a

[1] This walking pace was fast for the camel, whose walk does not generally exceed three English miles an hour. The Heirie (or swift camel) can travel, at a trot, eight or ten miles an hour, and maintain this speed for many hours; but that pace is very rough and fatiguing to the rider ('Illustrated Natural History,' by the Rev. J. G. Wood, i. 706). We shall see hereafter what long and what rapid marches were made by the Camel Corps.

long train of hackeries After proceeding fourteen miles they halted and pitched tents at eight in the morning. This day was most fearfully hot, the thermometer reaching 117°. At half-past eleven at night they struck tents, and marched at midnight. In about an hour they reached the Rind river and began crossing; but the convoy and train of hackeries was some two miles long, so that it was eight o'clock in the morning before all were got over. Then they continued their march to Ukburpore, about fourteen miles from their last halting-place, and reached it about 11.30. This day, like the last, was extremely hot; and as the men did not get in till near noon, and the rear-guard not till 1.30, they felt the heat extremely. They encamped on one side of the canal (then dry) in a white burning plain, without a tree on it, and only some small bushes.

On the 8th the Camel Corps was taken out at a trot, about two miles. The men were now beginning to get accustomed to the action of the strange beasts they bestrode, and they found sitting on them more easy.

Up to this time no General Order had been issued for the formation of the Camel Corps; one unpleasant consequence of which was that no pay, regimental or otherwise, was issued to the officers or to the men. They complained much, too, of their native camel-drivers; a most ruffianly and undisciplined set of men. As an instance of their ferocity, I may mention that on the 11th one of these men shot another with his carbine; and not content with thus wounding him, cut him over the back of the neck with his sword. The health, too, of the Rifle companies was unsatisfactory; sunstroke and apoplexy carried off several men; and their loss in the week ending May 12 was ten men.

On the 13th, striking tents at half-past three in the morning, they moved their camp about a mile and a half, in the hope of finding a more healthy situation for it.

On the 15th Colonel Maxwell, to whose column the Camel Corps was at that time attached, received a communication from Sir Hugh Rose, who was then advancing slowly towards Calpee, which was said to be occupied by 8,000 rebels with six guns In consequence of this the Camel Corps was ordered to march in the evening, but was afterwards countermanded. However, further messages having been received from Sir Hugh Rose, they were ordered off, and marched on the 16th about half-past two in the morning. They were to have marched about eight miles; but as the ammunition carts which the 88th Regiment had with them were not able to get across a river or nullah, the Camel Corps halted after a march of two miles and pitched tents. Captain Nixon's troop started again at half-past six in charge of the convoy; and having crossed the river, halted at about five miles and a half from the starting-place at half-past ten. Major Ross with the remainder of the Camel Corps came in about two. The whole halted till half-past four, when they trotted into their camping-ground, where they arrived by six o'clock. Lieutenant Eyre, who had charge of the convoy of ninety-five carts of ammunition, got them in with his escort about seven. The name of this halting-place was Bhogneepore. A good deal of firing had been heard in the direction of Calpee. They halted on the 17th, and on the next day the Riflemen of the Camel Corps were ordered to march at one the following morning, to take a fort about twelve miles off, in which it was reported that there were fifty or sixty fanatics; but the order was countermanded in the evening.

On the 19th a good deal of firing was heard. And the Camel Corps was ordered to cross the Jumna. They struck tents at half-past six, but as they were preparing to move off the order was countermanded; and they halted during the 20th. But Major Ross, with some of his officers, crossed the Jumna and visited Sir Hugh Rose's camp.

The Camel Corps moved at about one on the morning of the 21st, to join Sir Hugh Rose's force before Calpee. They crossed the Jumna at a ford so deep that it was up to the saddles of the camels. After crossing they joined the 2nd Brigade of the force under Sir Hugh Rose, and encamped about half-past seven.

The camp was very inconvenient, especially on account of the difficulty of getting water. For though they were not far from the river, yet the ravines which intersected the country and the steepness of the banks of the Jumna, made it impossible to obtain water without going two or three miles round. After the Riflemen had got over, 200 camels were sent back under Lieutenant Eyre, to bring over part of the 88th Regiment. Two Riflemen died of sunstroke on this march, for the heat was very great, the thermometer standing at 117° in the tents. The fort of Calpee, which stands on high ground, unapproachable from the river, and surrounded on all sides by ravines and a plain dotted only by a few topes of trees, gave them an occasional round-shot, just to let them realise that an enemy was close to them.

On the 22nd they had just sat down to breakfast, when an order came that they were to hold themselves in readiness to turn out at a moment's notice. That moment soon came; the 'assembly' sounded, and mounting their camels they formed up with the brigade to which they were attached. In front of them were thousands of rebels advancing. Soon an officer came up in great excitement, and ordered the two Rifle companies of the Camel Corps to advance to the right. On doing so they found the rebels driving before them the picquet, or rather they had already driven it in, and were almost on some heavy guns which were in position there. The rebels were steadily advancing and within a hundred yards. Then the Riflemen jumped off their camels, and doubling up to where the picquet was, extended as best they could, and with a ringing cheer went at the rebels. The fire of musketry was very heavy; and the rebels let the Riflemen get within eighty yards of them, but then they fled. In this way the Riflemen went on in pursuit, doubling through the ravines with which the country is much intersected, and availing themselves of such cover as there was; but there was very little. In this affair (called the battle of Goolowlee) the Rifle companies had but three men wounded, but twenty-five men were disabled by the sun, as was also one officer, Lieutenant Eyre. For the heat was fearful; and the pace the Riflemen went at up to the picquet, now charging, then pursuing the rebels, was very exhausting. Yet, weary as they were, the 2nd Battalion company of the Camel Corps had to remain on picquet.

The help of these Riflemen on this occasion was most opportune; for the enemy had crept up under cover of the ravines to the battery, which was placed 500 or 600 yards beyond the right of Sir Hugh Rose's position; the picquet posted there had given way; and the rebels would assuredly have had the guns, from which they were not more than fifty yards distant, and in good cover from a ravine.

On the 23rd, about two in the morning, 'rouse' sounded, and their camels came up; but they were without orders. After waiting about two hours a staff officer appeared, who informed them that they ought to have been with Sir Hugh Rose long before. They mounted their camels and the staff officer undertook to show them the way, but as he could not wait he left them to themselves. So proceeding in the dark as best they could, they happily fell in with Sir Hugh Rose about daybreak They made a long circuit to the left, and on arriving at a well which a cavalry picquet had just deserted, the rebels opened on them from two guns with a brisk fire of shot and shell; aiming well, but not hitting any of them. These guns were so well concealed in a ravine that our artillery could not touch them They then dismounted and covered the advance, Captain Nixon's company forming the reserve. They kept on advancing and returning the enemy's fire for some time. At length, when the rebels saw the skirmishers working round their right flank, they fled, and the Riflemen, on arriving at Calpee, about two miles distant, found that the Sepoys had disappeared and that the place was empty.

They reached Calpee about ten, and put up in a house till five in the afternoon, when they marched to their camping-ground, a dusty place, but with plenty of water. a luxury they had not had for some days. The force opposed to them was the Gwalior Contingent, the same the Riflemen had met at Cawnpore; and here, as there, they fought harder and stood longer than any other enemy they had encountered in India. They were commanded by Tantia Topee.

In this action the Riflemen had one sergeant and two privates wounded, one of them severely.

In his despatch reporting these engagements, dated, Gwalior, June 22, 1858, Sir Hugh Rose (Lord Strathnairn) writes thus:—

'The very important service rendered on this occasion by Major Ross, commanding Camel Corps, requires that I should make especial mention of the ability and resolute gallantry with which he led his brave Corps. . . . Lieutenant Buckley[1] of the same Corps attracted my attention by the spirit with which his party attacked and bayonetted rebels ; for which I beg to mention him specially.'

On the 24th, being the Queen's birthday, they paraded at sunrise, presented arms, and gave three cheers, while the English flag was hoisted on the fort of Calpee.

They halted during the next day ; and on the 26th they marched at two in the morning, and moving along through the ravines, reached the ford of the Jumna by which they had crossed on the 21st, but which was now (owing to rain on the preceding day) running with a strong current. Four natives were drowned in crossing. On reaching the other side they marched to Bhogneepore, which they reached about half-past eight, having made a march of about fifteen miles ; and they rejoined Maxwell's column.

On the 29th they marched to Ukburpore, about sixteen miles, and encamped in the same tope of trees they had occupied on their march from Cawnpore to Calpee.

On the 30th they marched to Suchendee, about fifteen miles, and arriving at about seven o'clock pitched their camp in a cool and pleasant place under some trees.

On the 31st they moved at the usual hour, and reached Cawnpore about half-past six. They occupied barracks near Wheeler's intrenchment.

They halted at Cawnpore for some weeks, during which time they received orders to equip for fresh service ; and Sikhs having now been enlisted, two companies of the 80th, which had been for a short time attached to the Camel Corps, now returned to their regiment. The camel-drivers were also drilled by non-commissioned officers sent from the Lahore regiments, and gradually became somewhat more like soldiers and obedient to discipline. The Riflemen were ordered to draw from Allahabad capes and yellow gaiters, which added somewhat to their appearance, and very much to their comfort.

On June 8 they were inspected by Sir Colin Campbell, who expressed himself well pleased with their appearance, and gave them final orders for their equipment and completion.

[1] Captain Buckley was killed by the accidental discharge of his gun, when out shooting November 1868.

He also complimented them on their conduct at Calpee. They had received up to this time 80 volunteers from Sikh regiments, and 50 Sikh recruits. And 180 Riflemen were effective.

It was intended that they should remain at Cawnpore during the rainy season; but the rains having been unusually late this year, they received a telegraphic message on July 20, directing them to be prepared to move at a moment's notice, as they were wanted for special service. And on the 22nd they marched at four in the morning, and encamped about thirteen miles on the road to Allahabad. On the next day (or rather in the night) they marched at midnight and made a march of about twenty miles. On the 24th they reached Futtehpore after a march of fifteen miles; and on the 25th proceeded to Khaga, about twenty miles. It had rained, and the roads were very slippery; one camel came down, and the long march had to be gone over carefully. On the 26th they made a march of sixteen miles. The rains had now set in, and their camp and their clothes were in a perpetual state of moisture. On the next day they marched seventeen miles; and on the 28th reached Allahabad after a march of twenty miles, and occupied barracks. On the 29th they were inspected by the Governor-General (Lord Canning) and Sir Colin Campbell, who expressed themselves well satisfied with their appearance and performances: a very satisfactory result of the pains they had taken with their drill and with their drivers while at Cawnpore.

On the 31st the Camel Corps began crossing the Ganges in boats, which, with the transfer of the baggage across the river, occupied the whole day and part of the next, for the Ganges is here about three miles broad. In this passage two or three camels were lost.

On August 2 they made a march of eighteen miles, which, being performed at a jog-trot, was soon got over; yet their tents were not pitched till eleven o'clock. On the 3rd they proceeded to Gopeegunge, about sixteen miles. On the next day they made a long march of twenty-four miles. And on the 5th reached Benares, after a march of fifteen miles, and encamped on the parade-ground in front of the cantonments.

They remained here during the 6th On the 7th the camels were got across the river, a slow and difficult operation, as the boats drifted some three miles down the stream from the strength of the current. And on the 9th they marched at five in the morning to the Raj Ghât, a distance of about four miles. On arrival there an order was received from Colonel Turner, commanding the force on the Great Trunk road, to send fifty men, with a proportionate number of officers, to Mohuneea, which was about thirty-seven miles distant, and to be there by twelve o'clock that night. Captain Newdigate, Lieutenants Austin and Eyre, were selected for this duty. They chose the best camels; and, having crossed the river, immediately started off. They halted for two hours at Noubutpore, twenty-seven miles south-east from Benares, having travelled at the rate of seven miles and a-half an hour: a great pace for even a swift camel to maintain. Remounting, they finished their march at Mohuneea, tired and wet through. They there found Colonel Turner, who had intended to start them off immediately for a place six miles farther, and across country. But a tremendous shower coming on about one o'clock in the morning (of the 9th), this intention was abandoned, or rather postponed. Besides, the camels were so tired that they could not have gone farther without rest. The officers and men, therefore, sought shelter and repose in carts, or wherever they could find it, till nine in the morning. They then started, having received some biscuit and tea; but they soon found the road impassable for the camels. In two miles they had six casualties, two camels having to be dug out of the mud. They therefore dismounted, and marched forward, up to their knees in mud and slush. After proceeding about two miles and a quarter farther they halted, having information that the enemy, who had intelligence of their approach, had disappeared Some cavalry were sent on to ascertain whether this report was correct, and on their return in about an hour with information that it was so, the camel detachment began to retrace their steps. And up to the middle in water, and with a burning sun beating on their heads, they marched back to Mohuneea. On their arrival there they had no change of clothes, so that they spent the rest of the day and night in great discomfort.

But at six in the morning of the 10th the remainder of the Camel Corps came up with their baggage. On the 11th they marched at half-past two in the morning, and proceeded fifteen miles and a half to Jehanabad, a large village, about fifteen miles from Sasseram. An order was received in the afternoon for two officers and fifty men to be left at this place, as the enemy was expected. Captain Nixon and Lieutenant Buckley remained with this party, which rejoined the Corps at the camp of Kurroundea on the 17th.

On the 12th the Camel Corps started at one in the morning, and marched twenty miles to Kurroundea, about four miles beyond Sasseram, where they formed a standing camp, and the Engineers built sheds for the men. The rebels were expected to cross the Great Trunk road, and to endeavour to escape into a range of hills about four miles from Sasseram. The camp stood close under a spur of these hills. A picquet, consisting of an officer and thirty men, was posted about a mile from the camp, to watch the road from the north. This picquet was relieved every third day. Altogether this standing camp of Kurroundea was a pleasant change for the officers and men; after their long moving about in the plains, the sight of hills was refreshing; and the grazing being excellent, the camels enjoyed the change as much as their riders.

On the 15th a detachment of the Camel Corps, consisting of twenty-five Riflemen and fifty Sikhs, under command of Lieutenant Eyre, marched from Kurroundea at six in the morning, *en route* for Shergotty. They proceeded on camels about six miles to Dearee, where they halted for breakfast. At three in the afternoon they crossed the river Sone in flat-bottomed boats It is here about three miles broad, and the crossing took about an hour and a half. On reaching the other side they found bullock-waggons awaiting them; into which the men being placed, four in each, with one walking beside every waggon as a guard, they proceeded through the night, and arrived at three in the morning of the 16th at Norungabad, about thirteen miles from the river.

They left it again at half-past three in the afternoon, and arrived at Shergotty about six in the morning of the 17th, where this detachment continued for some time

The Head-quarters of the Camel Corps continued at Kurroundea, and soon after, on the 20th, an order arrived at noon for every available man of the Camel Corps to accompany Colonel Turner. Accordingly eighty Riflemen and some Sikhs under Major Ross started from Kurroundea at half-past one in the afternoon, and marched about twenty miles to Nassreegunge on the Sone, where rebels were reported to have been sent by Oomar Singh to collect revenue. On arrival they found that 150 rebels had been at Nassreegunge in the morning, but had quitted it, leaving about twenty men behind in charge of the place. These were taken quite by surprise, and sixteen were killed; and two, who were slightly wounded, escaped. The Riflemen bivouacked near an old indigo plantation

In the night a detachment of the 37th Regiment arrived; and in the morning Colonel Turner started with twenty-five men of the Camel Corps on four elephants, under Lieutenant Austin, some Sikh Cavalry, and the party of the 37th But this party of the Camel Corps returned to Kurroundea on the 23rd, having only captured two or three prisoners. The other portion of the Camel Corps marched back from Nassreegunge to Kurroundea on the 21st.

On the 25th Lieutenant Jeames, with twenty-five men of the Camel Corps, marched on foot to Nassreegunge, as the rebels were expected to return and destroy it. This detachment returned to camp on the 30th

On September 3 Lieutenant Scriven was sent with thirty men to join Colonel Turner at Bikrumgunge, as the troops at that place had been attacked by the rebels, whom, however, they had driven off.

On September 5 Major Ross, with 50 of the Camel Corps, two guns, a few Sikh Cavalry, and 40 of the 37th Regiment, started from the camp to join Colonel Turner, who was twenty-six miles distant towards Jugdespore.[1] Their first day's march was about twenty miles to Sunjowlee Khas, and on the 6th they reached Bikrumgunge early in the morning, and effected their junction with Colonel Turner and the party under Scriven. After halting for breakfast, they paraded again at half-past ten, and leaving all their baggage under a guard, proceeded to a village, Surajpore, about five miles off. This was a large and strong place, and about 500 rebels occu-

[1] This (Jugdespore on the Sone) is a different place from Jugdespore in Oude, the scene of the operations of the 2nd Battalion in April, 1858.

pied it. But, notwithstanding the disparity of the attacking force, they abandoned it after firing a few shots at the advanced guard of cavalry. The Camel Corps pursued them as far as Kullanee, but could not come up with them. And the rebels having disappeared, they returned to Bikrum in the afternoon, where they halted during the next day. The Riflemen had a hard day's marching and skirmishing, sometimes up to their hips in water.

On the 8th, Colonel Turner having received intelligence that some rebels were likely to cross the main road about four miles farther towards Jugdespore, they started early to intercept them After about an hour and a half's march they came in sight of a large body of rebels posted in a village on the right. The Camel Corps, the cavalry, and the two guns started to attack them. But owing to the rains the roads were deep with mud; the rice fields on each side were under water, with a thick deposit of mud beneath it, and it was impossible for camels, or horses, or guns to move rapidly; so that the rebels escaped before these troops could reach them. Whilst they were engaged at this work, a party of the rebels made an attack on Bikrum, and came up within a few hundred yards of the trenches there thrown up for protection. However, several of them were killed or wounded, and amongst them the leader of the attack. On receiving intelligence of Bikrum being assailed, the force in the field fell back, and pitched their tents there just before dark; having been out from half-past three in the morning till six in the evening, during great part of which time the sun was extremely overpowering.

On the 9th they started about an hour before day on their return, and marched back ten miles to Nokah, and encamped; and on the 10th, after a march of sixteen miles, reached their camp at Kurroundea.

On the 12th Captain Nixon and Lieutenant Jeames, with 20 Riflemen and 30 Sikhs, were detached to Sunjowlee Khas, and did not rejoin Head-quarters at Kurroundea till October 26.

On the 23rd the Camel Corps (forming part of Colonel Turner's force) marched to Nassreegunge, where they halted on the 24th On the next day they moved to Behta, some miles farther up the Sone, and were occupied on that day and the 26th in destroying several boats which the rebels had concealed under boughs of trees and in the mud On the latter day Captain Newdigate, with thirty men of the Camel Corps, was sent to Sukreta, where a rebel Rissaldar, Unjoor Singh, was said to be. But he had left the evening before, and this detachment returned to Behta On the 27th, having intelligence that some rebels were not far off they marched some distance to Khurona, and a spy having come in while they were halting for breakfast, and having reported that the enemy were close at hand, they started in pursuit, the cavalry taking one direction and the Camel Corps another. The former, 120 Sikhs, under Mr Baker, found the rebels in a village, and by making a feint of retiring, drew them out into the open; when wheeling round, they attacked them, and succeeded in killing about 100, all mutinied Sepoys, with small loss to themselves. Their opponents numbered 700. The Camel Corps came up at the close of this engagement, but the rebels had then fled so far that it was useless to pursue them, and they encamped near Suhejne.

They halted on the 28th to allow supplies to come up from Bikrumgunge; and on the 29th marched to the westward and south of Jugdespore, in order to drive the rebels from the surrounding villages into that place; and in the afternoon came to Kooath, a village which had been occupied just before by some 300 of the enemy; but who, on hearing of their approach, had fled in such hot haste that it was impossible to overtake them. They encamped at Dawuth, where they halted on the 30th, and were occupied in collecting arms from the villages in the neighbourhood. During the last four days they had been exposed to heavy rains.

On October 1 they moved on to Roopsaugor, about thirty miles north of Sasseram, whence they moved towards Soombursa. But, as usual, the enemy fled at the first approach of the Camel Corps, and they returned to the camp at Roopsaugor.

And on the 3rd proceeded on their route to two large villages, Dinareh and Kochus, which were said to be occupied by rebels. They reached the former on the 4th, after a most fatiguing march, the country being under water and deep in mud, and on the 5th arrived at Kochus. Great difficulty was experienced in obtaining information. The populations of the villages, which in this part of the country are scattered about at distances of scarcely half a mile, were evidently friendly to the rebels; and all knowledge of their whereabouts or of having seen them was persistently denied. Yet it afterwards turned out that a body of rebels, under a chief they were in search of, were hiding in a village within a mile of their track. On arriving at Kochus it was ascertained that the darogah or headman of the village had been actively collecting supplies for Oomar Singh; and after pitching camp a visit was made to his house, which was full of grain. This having been given to the natives, his residence was burned. But they had no sooner marched from Kochus than Oomar Singh and his gang, who had been hiding in the high sugar-cane fields, entered it.

On the 7th the Camel Corps made a long march, and returned to their camp at Kurroundea. But their respite from work was not long; for on the 8th they were ordered to start again, and marched at four in the afternoon. And after halting at Nokah three or four hours during the night, reached Bikrumgunge at seven in the morning of the 9th. And on the next day moved towards Jugdespore; encamping that night at Deonar, and on the 11th at Sukreta. For the next fortnight the Camel Corps were on the move, often day and night, to harass the rebels in the Jugdespore jungles and the Kinsey hills, and to endeavour to prevent their escape from Jugdespore.

Thus on the 15th Newdigate started with 13 Riflemen and 13 Sikhs at a quarter to six for Nurainpore, about nine miles from Sukreta, with orders to bring in two rebel Zemindars; but he found that they had escaped. So after burning their houses, he returned to the camp at Sukreta.

On the 16th Brigadier Douglas entered Jugdespore, but the enemy eluded him and escaped. However, on the 18th they were driven out of the jungle. On the 20th Colonel Turner directed Colonel Ross to push on with part of the Camel Corps. Taking with him Major Newdigate and 2 other officers, and 55 Riflemen, he came on the enemy. As they approached them another body appeared on their right flank flying before some cavalry. The enemy were in force, upwards of 100 cavalry and 600 infantry. The Riflemen at once dismounted from their camels and skirmished up to the village of Sukreta, which the enemy occupied. Here they had a hard fight; for besides the superiority of the rebels in numbers, the village, being surrounded by bushes, formed a strong position; and the rebels, finding they could not get away, fought better than their usual wont.[1] This fight lasted for nearly an hour, when the rest of the Camel Corps and of Turner's column came up. Among these was Lieutenant Scriven of the 2nd Battalion, who, rushing up to the assistance of his comrades, was shot immediately. Besides his loss one Rifleman of the 2nd Battalion was killed and two were wounded severely, of whom one afterwards died; and of the 3rd Battalion two Riflemen were killed, and one sergeant and three privates wounded. The Adjutant of the Camel Corps (not a Rifleman) was also wounded. Of the enemy 70 dead, all rebel Sepoys, were counted in the village; and two or three times that number in the surrounding fields. The survivors fled towards the hills, and being pursued by some Horse under Major Havelock, were cut up and dispersed. On the next day the Camel Corps proceeded up the Sone and prevented the rebels crossing to the right bank of that river. They afterwards returned to their camp at Kurroundea.

Captain Newdigate, however, was detached with thirty-two Riflemen on camels, to join Major Havelock's force, which consisted of about 200 men of the Military Train, some Sikh Cavalry, and some of the 10th Foot mounted on ponies. The Riflemen had no baggage.

On the 21st they marched to Sydha, and after halting there two hours proceeded to Khooath Khas, where about four in the afternoon they came on the rebels, who fled at their approach; the Camel Corps pursued them till after dark, the cavalry cutting up a good many, and encamped at Sethan. At sunrise on the 22nd this detachment marched by Suhejne to Jendonee, whence, after a short halt, they proceeded to Dinareh. They there halted two hours, and on the 23rd reached Kochus, and thence proceeded to Kyree, where they halted for breakfast. But intelligence of rebels being in the vicinity being brought in they started without it. They found the rebels in about three miles, and on their flying lost trace of them for two or three hours, but again came upon them

[1] This affair is also said to have taken place at Nonadee ('London Gazette') or Hoadeh.

near Khurgurh. They pursued them till they fled across the Great Trunk road about nine miles to the north of Sasseram. This was the very place where they had been ordered to drive them across, and where they were to have been intercepted by the Native Cavalry; but unfortunately these had been deceived by false intelligence of the rebel movements, and were not in the right place. The Camel Corps detachment went on to Jehanabad, their camels being quite exhausted. Here Newdigate found Major Ross with 100 men of the Camel Corps; and leaving the greater part of his detachment there he proceeded to Kurroundea with the wearied camels and ten men.

The Camel Corps were soon again in pursuit of the rebels, who, after crossing the Great Trunk road, got into some hills above Sasseram On the 27th they marched, 120 Riflemen and 80 Sikhs, at half-past twelve to Akbarpore, near Rotas, where they arrived about ten at night. On the next day they marched to Khyrwa, where they breakfasted, and in the afternoon proceeded to Jeelokhur, and encamped; but Captain Nixon with about half the men went on to Nowadah. This detachment on the next day proceeded to Jadoonathpore, where they were followed on the 30th by the remainder of the Camel Corps. This place was about fifty miles from Sasseram, and on the Sone. Their position here was to guard one of the passes to the hills and to prevent the rebels coming down.

On November 3 and 4 the Camel Corps crossed the Sone, the bed of which is here some two miles broad and fringed with a range of high hills on each bank. On the 6th they marched to Purtee; on the 7th to Muktowar; on the 8th towards Kotah Ghât, when, finding rations running short, and no supplies likely to come up, they returned to some distance beyond their camping-ground of yesterday. On the 9th they marched to Pandoochoona; and on the following day recrossed the Sone to Jadoonathpore, and encamped, sending a detachment to Nowadah. On September 13 Newdigate was sent on a patrol to Jaca, about seven miles from the top of the pass through the hills. Incessantly moving in pursuit of the rebels, the Camel Corps again crossed the river on the 14th and 15th, marching on successive days to Pipra,

Gao Ghât, Hurdee, and Choopan. Leaving this on the 20th, they recrossed the river at daylight and marched to Robertgunge, where they arrived at half-past three in the afternoon, and leaving it again at ten at night, reached Pannoogunge at two in the morning of the 21st and encamped. Here patrols reported that the rebels had escaped into Oude; they therefore turned back to their camp at Kurroundea, where they arrived on the 30th. They were soon ordered to follow the rebels; and starting on December 3 in five days arrived at Benares, where they encamped and halted till the 10th.

They then marched with orders to join Sir Hope Grant's column at Fyzabad. They arrived at Jounpore on the 13th, and proceeded by Sultanpore to Fyzabad, which they reached on the 20th. Here a letter from the Chief of the Staff awaited Colonel Ross, directing him to join Brigadier Barker's column, about sixty miles north of Lucknow. They left Fyzabad, therefore, on the 21st, and marched into Lucknow on the 24th, where they halted for Christmas Day. They marched on the 26th, and encamped about eighteen miles north of Lucknow. The object of their movement was to watch the right bank of the Gogra, and while Lord Clyde and Sir Hope Grant were driving the rebels into a corner between Baraitch and the Nepaul frontier, to intercept any rebels who might attempt to cross the Gogra. However, on all this march the Corps was short of camels, many having died in the neighbourhood of Sasseram, where the climate is said to be very injurious to these animals. They were therefore ordered to Agra to procure remounts. They proceeded by Seetapore, Futtehgurh, and Mynpooree to Agra, where they arrived on January 23, 1859. Having obtained the camels they required to remount the Corps, they started again on the 26th, under Brigadier Showers, whose force consisted, besides the Camel Corps, of two squadrons of the Carabiniers and two squadrons of Irregular Cavalry. The object of this force was to capture Tantia Topee, who, with Ferozeshah and a force of some 3,000 or 4,000 horsemen, was giving trouble to the west and north-west of Agra. On the 27th the Camel Corps encamped at Bhurtpore. On February 4 they encamped at Loorkee in the Jeypore district. On the next day they marched at one in the morning, and reached their camping-ground at eleven. On the 6th they started again at midnight, and arrived at Futtehpore at half-past eleven, where they halted during the two following days. Tantia Topee now doubled behind them to the southward, passing by Nagpore, and with a portion of his followers gave his pursuers the slip, and it was for some time uncertain in what direction he had gone.

The Camel Corps, therefore, leaving Futtehpore on the 9th, moved southward, marching daily from twenty to thirty miles till the 15th, when they halted for that day at Burroo. Next day they made a march of twelve miles; and on the 17th, passing through the range of hills which runs from north-west to south-east through Rajpootana, arrived at Ajmeer. In all these marches they started about midnight, often marching till one or two o'clock the next day; and seldom halting for a day, and then only because the horses of the cavalry required rest. From Ajmeer the Camel Corps proceeded to Nusseerabad, where they halted for two days; and on the 21st marched still southward, and arrived at Boondee on the 26th.

Thence inclining to the south-east, they encamped at Barah in the Kotah district on March 2. They then moved towards Agra to receive some supplies forwarded from thence, and on the 13th were encamped at Madhoopoora in the Jeypore district. Thence retracing their steps and crossing the Chumbul river, they encamped on the 22nd at Etawah, and on the 29th at Bilowa in the Gwalior district This country was full of jungle, of which the rebels well knew how to take advantage; so that to trace them, or to dislodge them when tracked, was a most difficult operation. The Camel Corps marched into Goonah on April 7. On the 8th Tantia Topee was captured (by Colonel Meade's column) about ten miles from Goonah and four from the camp of the Camel Corps. Though he did not actually fall into their hands, there is no doubt that his inexorable pursuit by Brigadier Showers' force led to his capture, and so indeed he himself stated. For though reserved and uncommunicative to the officers, he spoke freely with the men, and said that had it not been for the incessant chase of Showers' force, which had run him to earth, he would have cared little for any other troops. He admitted that he had been so closely pressed by them that on one occasion he hid under a bridge they were actually passing over.

During their few days' halt at Goonah, Colonel Ross had the Riflemen's clothing, which was dilapidated and of many colours from patches, dyed.

The Camel Corps halted for a week at Goonah, and left it on the 14th at four o'clock in the afternoon to look for Ferozeshah, who with some force was about fifty miles to the south. They came upon him on the 16th near a village, and killed some of his followers; but the rebels scattered at once and with Ferozeshah escaped into the jungle. However, they took nine waggons laden with provisions and eleven prisoners, whom the Sikhs of the Camel Corps immediately shot. They then moved to Supree, where Tantia Topee had been hanged on the 15th. On their arrival there Brigadier Showers left them, and the cavalry which had hitherto formed part of the column also moved off, so that the Camel Corps, under Colonel Ross, alone began their march towards Agra They proceeded by Kallarus and Gwalior, where they arrived on the 30th, and reached Agra on May 5, where they went into quarters for about four months.

On September 15 they left Agra *en route* for Saugor, and passing through Muneeah and Dholpore encamped on the banks of the Chumbul on the morning of the 17th. Colonel Ross having endeavoured to find a ford with elephants, but without success, found it necessary to get his Corps across in boats; a difficult operation, as from the camels' dislike to water it is no easy matter to get them into boats. There were twenty-two boats, most of which held each three, and some few four camels. The stream was wide and rapid, and the ravines which border its banks (as they do many of the large rivers of India) had become water-courses; for much rain had recently fallen. On the morning of the 18th Colonel Ross took over a party with shovels and improved the landing-place, which was knee-deep with mud. He then passed over the two Sikh companies, to find fatigue parties and to establish a camp. This had to be pitched about two miles from the river's bank, as the ravines extend nearly that distance. Before dark he had succeeded in getting over the camels of three out of the four troops, besides many baggage-animals. Early on the 19th the two Rifle companies crossed; by four on that day the whole Corps, with its baggage, was in camp Thus, besides the men, 600 camels were got over in two days, and the baggage, which had to be unloaded on one bank and loaded on the other. And much time was lost by the rapidity of the current carrying the boats down-stream. On the 22nd they arrived at Gwalior, where they halted the next day. On the 26th they had some difficulty in crossing the Sinde river, for though the water was not deep the further bank was steep and slippery. On the 27th they encamped at Datia; and on the 28th arrived at Jhansi. On leaving it on the next day they had to cross the Betwa river, about six miles' distance, which, though less troublesome and tedious than the passage of the Chumbul, was not without its difficulties; and they encamped about four miles beyond it.

The Camel Corps arrived at Saugor on October 9.

The object of the operations now about to be commenced was to hunt all the jungles from the southward up towards the river Betwa, the line of which was to be closely watched. Ferozeshah was somewhere to the east of Saugor at the head of a body of rebels, or rather robbers and others of the evil classes, and was keeping the district in a state of unquiet.

With this view seven small columns were formed, and the command of one of them, consisting of his own Corps, an Irregular Cavalry Regiment, and a regiment of Punjaub Infantry, was conferred on Colonel Ross. Two companies of the Camel Corps, however, under Major Nixon, were attached to another column

Both portions of the Corps marched from Saugor on the 14th, and Colonel Ross moved to a position about fifty miles from it. The country through which he was to operate was covered with wild jungle, which clothed hills of moderate elevation, the valleys being watered by clear streams After pursuing the rebels in and through the jungle, where, from their invariably decamping as soon as the troops approached, and from their knowledge of the paths, it was impossible to catch or intercept them, Colonel Ross with his party reached Dergowah, about seventy miles to the north of Saugor, early in December. He proceeded to Heerapore on the 3rd, and halted till joined by Major Nixon with the other portion of the Camel Corps These had been attached to a column under Colonel Primrose of the 43rd Light Infantry, and on October 27 fifty men of the Camel Corps, twenty-five Riflemen and twenty-five Sikhs, under command of Lieutenant Ramsbottom, were engaged at the village of Mitharden, where some rebels were killed. The Riflemen on this occasion had not their camels, and fought dismounted.

The seven columns employed in scouring the jungle were broken up, and returned to their quarters; but the Camel Corps remained out still in pursuit of rebels.

Leaving a small detachment at Heerapore, the Camel Corps marched on December 11 to Shahgurh, nine miles, and leaving part of the Corps there, Colonel Ross with the remainder marched about sixteen miles further to the banks of the Dessaun river, where he encamped. Here he was joined by Captain Browne, the Assistant-Commissioner; and on the 12th, accompanied by him, marched at about seven in the morning They had advanced some way when a shot was heard in front, and near a village about a quarter of a mile distant. Word was also passed from the front that rebels were in the village Accordingly they pushed on with all speed, and soon spied a few mounted and some dismounted men in the jungle. After proceeding about a mile they came on a riding camel, belonging to the Assistant-Commissioner. Then the shot heard was explained: some rebels, headed by a noted miscreant, Dowlat Singh, had murdered the driver of the camel and the servant of the Commissioner riding behind him, whom he had sent forward with some despatches Colonel Ross requested the Assistant-Commissioner to send forward a few mounted police, to keep on the track of the rebels, and to hold them in check till the Camel Corps came up, as these police could ride faster than the pace of the camels But they soon returned, saying that the enemy were too many for them to approach them. If these men had done their duty the Camel Corps might have come up with them and caught many of the rebels As it was, they were delayed for some time in passing two ravines, the banks of which were thickly covered with jungle They followed them for a considerable distance, but could not come up with them The Camel Corps proceeded to Marowra, where they encamped.

They continued engaged in this jungle warfare, or rather harassing of the rebels, till April 1860, when, returning to Agra by the same route by which they had moved to Saugor, they arrived there on April 30

During the seven or eight months the Camel Corps were engaged in this service their duties were most harassing They marched at short notices in every direction, wherever and whenever they had intelligence of an enemy; and almost always without the satisfaction of finding or engaging one. Often detachments of forty or fifty men were ordered to mount at a moment's notice, and to ride thirty or forty miles as fast as they could, only to find that the enemy they expected to fight had fled before they approached his lair, or had scattered into jungle where it was hopeless to pursue.

Soon after their arrival at Agra they received information that the Camel Corps was to be broken up. They were disbanded on June 1 The company of the 3rd Battalion joined their Head-quarters at Agra, where the Battalion was quartered, the company of the 2nd Battalion proceeded by bullock-cart to Subathoo, where they joined Head-quarters of the Battalion on June 12 The men of the two Sikh companies were allowed to volunteer into any native corps they wished to join.

Colonel Ross, in alluding to his unsolicited and unexpected appointment to a Companionship of the Order of the Bath, assumes that it was meant as a recognition not only of his personal services, but of those of all who were in the Camel Corps; and adds this high testimony. 'And well do they deserve this recognition of their services. For we had lots of hard, tedious work, and never once all the time I was in command had I to speak a second time to either officers or men. Each seemed to take pleasure in doing what he had to do, and in assisting me in every way.' [1]

[1] Private letter, January 6, 1861 For this account of the actions and movements of the Camel Corps I am indebted to the journals of Captains George Curzon and Eyre; to information from Captain Austin, and Sergeants Carroll and Walsh; and especially to the letters of Colonel Ross.

CHAPTER XIV.

HAVING thus brought down the account of the services of the two Battalions in India, and of the companies of those Battalions which formed the Camel Corps, to the end of the Mutiny, I now resume the account of the movements of the other Battalions, which, in order not to interrupt the narrative of the operations in India, I had left aside.

The 1st Battalion moved from Glasgow to Newcastle-on-Tyne by rail on September 24, 1858, detaching four companies to Sunderland

On October 9 Lieutenant-General Sir Harry Smith, Colonel-Commandant of the Battalion, inspected it, and after the inspection and march past in the barrack-square, took them to the open ground near the barracks, where he put them through several rapid manœuvres. On their returning to the barracks, forming them in square, he addressed them as follows:

'Riflemen: I have had you out, and have given you some rough handling, but I find that I cannot take either Colonel Somerset or yourselves by surprise. I did this to see if the old stuff was still awake, for I saw that you could go steadily when you marched past in the square. This is the only Regiment or Battalion in which I took my place in the ranks. Your assistance at the Cape—in fact, in three quarters of the globe I have fought with you, and I always found you worthy of the green jacket. There is no one here who has soldiered so long as I have—fifty-three years Your hardships (which I heard of) in the Crimea, your comrades now in India, your doings in the Peninsula, when you still wore the green jacket; and, since that, in all quarters where fighting was to be done; your officers—your everything, in fact—will never be forgotten.' He then desired the men to let him get out of the square; observing that he well knew he never could get into it if they wished to prevent him.

The following letter was addressed to Sir Harry Smith by the Adjutant-General of the Forces:

'Horse Guards, November 2, 1858.

'Sir,—I have the honour to acknowledge the receipt of your highly favourable and creditable report for the second period of the current year upon the 1st Battalion Rifle Brigade.

'The General Commanding-in-Chief deems the absence of crime very remarkable; and desires me to express his satisfaction at your finding your old Corps so worthy of you; and further requests that you will assure Colonel Somerset and all the officers that they have merited His Royal Highness' warmest commendation.

'(Signed) W F. FOSTER, D.A.G

'Lieutenant-General Sir H Smith, Bart, G C B,
'Commanding Northern District'

Colonel Somerset having been appointed to the Staff, Lord Alexander Russell became Lieutenant-Colonel, and assumed command of the Battalion on December 17.

During the stay of the Battalion at Newcastle, the officers and men received the Turkish War Medal for service in the Crimea

The 4th Battalion at Chichester, having between January 1 and March 31 received 161 recruits, and 102 volunteers from the Militia, had attained a strength of 34 sergeants, 18 corporals, 15 buglers, and 649 privates On April 19 they proceeded from Chichester to Shorncliffe, and were quartered in that camp.

This Battalion was at first armed with the common or long Enfield rifle; but in June of this year received the short Enfield and sword

Having received a further increase of 86 recruits, and 24 volunteers from Militia regiments, they embarked in August for Malta, having then a strength of 756 non-commissioned officers and privates.

The Head-quarters, with eight companies, proceeded from Shorncliffe to Portsmouth by rail on August 11, and embarked on board the 'Urgent' troop-ship, and landed at Malta on the 22nd.

Two companies embarked at Portsmouth on board H.M.S. 'Perseverance' on the 13th, and reached Malta on August 25. The remaining two companies forming the Depôt proceeded to Winchester, and were attached to the Depôt Battalion there.

On May 6, 1859, the 1st Battalion was moved by rail from Newcastle and Sunderland to Portsmouth, where it arrived on the afternoon of the 7th, and occupied quarters: Anglesey barracks, two companies; Colewort barracks, two companies; Cambridge barracks, three companies, Clarence barracks, three companies

The 4th Battalion remained at Malta, moving its quarters in September from Lower St. Elmo barracks to Fort Ricasoli.

On March 27, 1860, the 1st Battalion removed by rail from Portsmouth to Aldershot, and occupied huts in the North Camp.

On which occasion the following order was issued by Major-General the Hon. Sir James Y. Scarlett, K.C.B.:

'Portsmouth, March 26, 1860.

'His Royal Highness the Commander-in-Chief, having ordered the 1st Battalion Rifle Brigade to be removed from this garrison and district to Aldershot, Major-General Sir James Scarlett cannot allow the Corps to quit his command without doing them that justice which is due to them, in expressing his great regret in parting with them, and offering his best thanks to Lieutenant-Colonel Lord Alexander Russell, and the officers and the men under his command, for the orderly and soldier-like conduct of the Battalion during the period they have served in this garrison (excelled by no Corps in smartness in the field and in quarters). The conduct of both officers and men has been such as to make their departure felt as a great loss, both in a military and a social point of view. They carry with them the best wishes of the Major-General wherever their duty may lead them; and he believes his feelings towards them are shared by both the civil and the military members of the garrison and the district

'By order.

'(Signed) J. C. THACKWELL, A.A.G.'

Their old companion-in-arms, Sir Harry Smith, having died in London on October 12, was succeeded as Colonel-Commandant of the Battalion by their former Lieutenant-Colonel, Major-General Sir George Buller, K.C.B.

The 2nd Battalion remained at Lucknow till January 3 in this year, when they marched *en route* for Delhi by the following route:

Jan.	3	to	Bunteerah	10 miles.
	4	„	Nawabgunge	12 „
	5	„	Oomao	13 „
	6	„	Cawnpore	12 „

Here they halted until the 19th, when, being relieved by the 52nd, they marched for Subathoo, to which station their destination was changed:

Jan	19	to	Kullianpore	8 miles
	20	„	Chobeepore	8 „
	21	„	Poorah	12 „
	22	„	Urrowl	13·3 „
	23	„	Meeran-ke-Serai	9·5 „
	24	„	Goorsuhagunge	13·3 „
	25	„	Chubramow	14·5 „
	27	„	Bewar	13·5 „
	28	„	Sultangunge	14·6 „
	29	„	Kurrowlee	8·3 „
	30	„	Mullown	12 „
	31	„	Eytah	11·1 „
Feb	2	„	Bhudwas	12·5 „
	3	„	Secundra Rao	9·2 „
	4	„	Akburabad	10·3 „
	6	„	Allygurh	13·6 „

Feb. 7	to	Somnagunge.	14·2 miles.
8	„	Khoorja	13·4 „
9	„	Chorla	8 „
10	„	Secundrabad	10 3 „
11	„	Dadree	10 1 „
12	„	Gazeeoodeenuggur	11·4 „
13	„	Delhi	12 4 „

They halted at Delhi till the 18th, when, resuming their march, they proceeded to Allypoor . . . 10 6 miles.

Feb. 19	to	Raie	10 „
20	„	Lursowlee	11·2 „
21	„	Sumalka	10·4 „
22	„	Paneeput	11 4 „
23	„	Gourrunda	9·6 „
24	„	Kurnal	11·1 „
26	„	Bootanah	10 6 „
27	„	Peeplie	8·7 „
28	„	Shahabad	13·3 „
29	„	Umballa	13 „

Leaving the left wing, 5 companies under Lieutenant-Colonel Fyers, at Umballa for target practice, the Head-quarters marched on March 2 for Subathoo, where they arrived on the 7th; and where the left wing joined them on the 30th The Battalion had thus made a march of more than 440 miles, from Lucknow to Subathoo

Here they remained until December, when, marching in three divisions on the 4th, 6th, and 12th, they arrived at Umballa on the 8th, 13th, and 16th respectively, and were there stationed for musketry instruction and target practice.

The 3rd Battalion remained at Agra during the whole of this year.

The 4th Battalion remained at Malta during this year.

In the latter part of this year the Regiment received a cloth shako of a new pattern, that known by the name of the 'Albert shako' being discontinued.

The 1st Battalion left Aldershot by rail on the afternoon of April 9, 1861, for Liverpool, where they embarked for Dublin, which they reached on the 10th, and landing on the 11th occupied Richmond barracks.

On the 29th they marched by route to Naas, and thence on the next day to the Curragh camp

During their stay at the Curragh they marched to Dunamase near Maryborough, where they encamped, using the '*tentes d'abri*' for the first time, and returned to the Curragh on the next day

On September 17 the Battalion left the Curragh, marching that day to Naas, and on the next to Dublin, where they re-occupied Richmond barracks.

During the time the Battalion was in the garrison of Dublin, a question arose as to the Castle guard, which is mounted at the residence of the Lord Lieutenant, when furnished by the Rifle Brigade carrying a colour. One of the colours of regiments of the line is 'trooped' and carried by this guard; but the Rifle Brigade having no colours, the attempt to make the subaltern for guard carry it was of course resisted Sir George Brown, who then commanded in Ireland, though he had served many years in the Regiment, wished to insist on the colour being carried. But the officer commanding the Battalion referred the matter to His Royal Highness the Colonel-in-Chief; and in consequence the following memorandum was issued from the Horse Guards June 10, 1861.—

'His Royal Highness the General Commanding-in-Chief has received the commands of the Queen to notify that Her Majesty is pleased to dispense with the use of colours when guards of honour or guards over the Royal person are furnished by Regiments which do not ordinarily carry colours.

'By command,

'(Signed) J. YORKE SCARLETT, A G.'

The American ship 'San Jacinto' having boarded the Royal Mail Packet 'Trent' and forcibly removed Messrs. Mason and Slidell, Commissioners from the Southern Confederate States proceeding to London and Paris, the Government, having resolved to demand reparation for this outrage on the British flag, ordered a force to proceed to Canada for the defence of that country in the event of a war. The Battalion was therefore ordered on December 4 to hold itself in readiness for active service, and having been inspected on the 7th by Major-General Ridley, embarked on the 11th at the North Wall, Dublin, in two divisions on board the 'Windsor' and 'Trafalgar,' under the command of Lord A. G Russell, for Liverpool. They arrived there on the following day and were immediately transferred to the hired steam-ship 'Australasian.' Their strength being

Field-officers	Captains	Subalterns	Staff	Staff-Sergeants	Sergeants	Buglers
3	10	21	6	5	38	16

Corporals	Privates	Total
37	738	874

At 7 P.M. on December 13 the 'Australasian' started, with orders to make the passage of the St. Lawrence, if possible; which was, however, doubtful in consequence of the ice in the depth of winter They had fair weather till the 23rd, when they sighted Cape Race. But at midnight it came on to blow a gale, with snow, or rather ice, falling so thick that it was impossible to see a foot before them. The 'Australasian' continued tacking all the 24th, and at midnight it was found she was off the southern coast of Anticosti. The captain now declaring that he was averse to trying to enter the St Lawrence in such weather, it was resolved (after consultation with the commanding officer and the officer of the Royal Navy on board) to make for Halifax, which, after a dangerous passage between Cape Ray and St. Paul's Island, they reached at midday on the 26th.

During the voyage each man was supplied with warm clothing.

On December 14 the lamented death of Field Marshal His Royal Highness the Prince Consort, Colonel-in-Chief, took place at Windsor Castle. He was succeeded by Field Marshal Lord Seaton; who, though not a Rifleman, had as colonel of their old comrades of the Light Division, the 52nd, and as commanding a brigade in the Peninsula and at Waterloo, fought beside the Riflemen in many actions.

The 2nd Battalion returned to Subathoo, marching from Umballa on March 11 and arriving at Subathoo on the 16th.

The 3rd Battalion marched from Agra on March 6 for Bareilly, where they arrived on the 21st and occupied quarters.

The 4th Battalion continued at Malta, changing their quarters from Fort Ricasoli to Fort Manoel, Valetta, on March 27.

By order dated Horse Guards, January 22, 1862, it was intimated that the Queen "desiring to perpetuate the remembrance of her beloved Husband's connection with the Rifle Brigade, and feeling sure that it will be gratifying to the Corps to have the name of one who, as its Colonel-in-Chief, took such deep and constant interest in its welfare, had been pleased to command that it should in future bear the designation of 'The Prince Consort's Own Rifle Brigade.'"

The 1st Battalion did not disembark at Halifax, and after remaining there a week in order to coal the ship, left it in the 'Australasian,' on January 1, 1862, and, after encountering another severe gale and snowstorm in the Bay of Fundy, reached St. John's, New Brunswick, on the 3rd at two P.M. and immediately landed, and occupied quarters in the permanent barracks. The heavy baggage was left in store at St John's; but the Battalion proceeded in detachments of five officers and about 100 men daily from the 6th to the 14th They were conveyed in sleighs: one for the officers, one for every eight men, and two for rations, ammunition and baggage The men received a field ration. Previous to starting they had breakfast and half their meat, at the midday halt a pint of tea and half the ration of grog; the remainder of their ration on their arrival at the halting place for the night. They were dressed in great-coats, fur caps and mocassins, with the accoutrements outside the coat the pouch being in front for the convenience of sitting in the sleighs; the cape of the great coat being turned up, and tied with a woollen comforter outside Over all a blanket with a hole cut for the head as a 'poncho'

The first day's journey was from St John's to Fredericton, 60 miles.

The second, Fredericton to Tilley's Hotel, Dumfries, 29 miles.

The third, Tilley's to Woodstock, 32 miles.

The fourth, Woodstock to Florenceville, 23 miles.

The fifth, Florenceville to Tobique, 23 miles.

The sixth, Tobique to Grand-Falls, 24 miles.

The seventh, Grand-Falls to Little-Falls, 36 miles.

The eighth, Little-Falls to Fort Ingall, 37 miles.

The ninth, Fort Ingall to Rivière-du-Loup, 42 miles

The men were placed at night in such rooms or shelter as the halting places afforded, lying down on pine branches Very great hospitality was manifested by the scattered inhabitants. Owing to the precautions taken no casualty occurred, save a few slight cases of frost-bite. One being that of Captain Playne, who, as well as two other officers who had recently joined from the Battalions in India, specially felt the extreme cold.

From Rivière-du-Loup, each detachment proceeded on the following morning by the Grand Trunk railway to Montreal, where the Battalion was assembled and occupied the College which had been given up by the Roman Catholic Bishop for the use of the troops.

The Head-quarters of the Battalion, consisting of 5 companies, left Montreal by special train at 8 45 A.M. on January 31, and arrived at Hamilton, Canada West, at 4 30 P.M. on the succeeding day, and were received with a perfect ovation by its inhabitants The left wing followed, leaving Montreal on February 10 and arriving at Hamilton on the next day.

As there were no barracks at Hamilton the Battalion was quartered in four different stores which had been hired for their occupation The overland journey from St John's to Hamilton was completed without the loss of a single man. This is most creditable to the Riflemen, as numerous agents of the United States offered them many temptations to desert.

The 2nd Battalion continued at Subathoo, sending detachments of two and three companies at a time to Umballa for musketry training during the months of December 1861, and January and February of this year. These having all returned the Battalion was again concentrated at Subathoo at the end of March, and continued there during the remainder of the year.

The 3rd Battalion continued at Bareilly, detaching one company to Loohoo Ghât on March 13

The 4th Battalion remained at Malta during the whole of this year

The Colonel-in-Chief, Field Marshal Lord Seaton, died on April 17, 1863, and was succeeded by General the Right Hon Sir George Brown, who had, as Lieutenant-Colonel, commanded the 2nd Battalion for seventeen years.

By a General Order, dated 'Horse Guards, September 3, 1863,' Her Majesty the Queen, in commemoration of the services of the Rifle Brigade in Her Majesty's Indian dominions, was graciously pleased to command that the word 'Lucknow' should be borne on the appointments of the Brigade.

The 1st Battalion remained at Hamilton during this year, its establishment being reduced on April 1 to—

Field Officers	Captains	Subalterns	Staff	Sergeants	Buglers	Corporals
3	12	24	5	58	25	50

Rank and File

750

On February 2 the 2nd Battalion marched from Subathoo, and arrived at Delhi on the 20th.

Three companies, under Captain F. Seymour, marched from Delhi to Meerut on November 22, and returned to Delhi on December 4

The 3rd Battalion marched from Bareilly on January 15 (the detachment from Loohoo Ghât having previously rejoined), and formed part of the Governor-General's escort at Agra on the 30th, and then marched to Umballa, where it was inspected by the Commander-in-Chief in India on March 30; after which it proceeded to Meon Meer, arriving there on April 16.

In the latter part of this year some of the tribes on the north-western frontier, between British India and Afghanistan, manifested a disposition to be troublesome; they made incursions into our territory, and pillaged some villages. A force under Sir Neville Chamberlain was therefore sent up to chastise them. Unfortunately, the difficult nature of the mountain passes, and the warlike nature of the tribes occupying these hills, proved insuperable obstacles to the troops originally sent forward. Reinforcements were required; and with this object the regiments at some of the adjacent stations were despatched to the frontier under Sir John Garvock. The 3rd Battalion was in consequence sent up to occupy the place of one of these regiments Accordingly they left Meon on November 25, and proceeded to Googerat, which they reached on December 1. On the 4th they arrived at Jhelum, on the 18th at Rawul Pindee, and on the 19th reached Hoti Murdan, a frontier fort situated beyond the Indus. About the middle of December Sir John Garvock, in two engagements, had completely defeated the offending tribes to the north, and had (as it was supposed) terminated this frontier war The Riflemen of the 3rd Battalion, therefore, not unnaturally concluded that their long and rapid march had been, so far as fighting went, to no purpose, and that they should return without having fired a shot. At any rate, they expected to eat their Christmas dinner at Hoti Murdan in peace. But on that very morning of the 25th, at three o'clock, they were startled by hearing the bugle sound for 'Orders.' They were to march at once for Shubkudder, another of the frontier forts, pushed up, indeed, to the very border of our north-eastern boundary The Mohmund tribe had shown signs of disquiet, and had not long before made an incursion to Shubkudder, and killed an officer of Irregular Cavalry, who attempted with a party to cut them off before they could return to their mountains. The Battalion started at once, and marched on Christmas Day eighteen miles to their camping-ground at Nowshera. On the 26th they made a double march of twenty-four miles to Peshawur, and on the 27th reached Shubkudder, after a march of twenty-one miles, where they encamped. The Fort of Shubkudder is situated at the foot of a spur of the Bajour mountains, in a fork formed by the junction of the Lundye river with the Cabool, and not very far to the north of the Khyber Pass.

On the 30th the Mohmund tribes were seen assembling on the low hills which bound the plain, and advancing in considerable numbers They did not, however, on that occasion come down from their mountain fastnesses; but the spies reported that an attack might be expected, as they had sworn to engage the force at Shubkudder.

Accordingly, on January 2, 1864, they were seen from the fort, early in the morning, descending the mountain paths, and collecting on a ridge about two miles off. Colonel Macdonell, who was in command of the force, sent Colonel Ross with a company of Riflemen and one of Ghoorkas, to occupy a village about 800 yards in front of the fort, to endeavour to entice them down. They accepted the invitation, and were soon seen creeping down from the hills in twos and threes; taking cover under every bank and inequality of the ground. They opened fire, which mostly whistled over the heads of the Riflemen, who returned it, probably with better effect. Meanwhile their main body came down towards our left, and planted their standards on a mound about 1,000 yards off Colonel Macdonell, seeing that they were not disposed to come on, sent a small body of cavalry[1] and some skirmishers to turn their right. Three guns were sent to the left of the village and opened on them. They could not stand their fire; the flags soon disappeared from the mound, and the Mohmunds retreated in a disordered crowd Then the remaining companies of the Battalion, with Ross's party and the Ghoorkas, formed a long line in extended order, and with the guns, advanced across the plain, and followed the retreating enemy over the ridge and to a valley beyond There the cavalry charged from the left right into them, and completed their defeat. The Riflemen gave them a hot fire as they ascended the passes into their hills Whilst the cavalry and guns withdrew, the Battalion retired in alternate lines of skirmishers; but the enemy were so disorganised and disheartened that they made no attempt to disturb their retreat On reaching the plain, the Riflemen closed; and they reached their camp at dusk The Mohmunds occupied an extent of some two miles from right to left, and are supposed to have numbered about 7,000[2]

[1] Colonel Macdonell had with him at Shubkudder three troops of the 7th Hussars and some Native Cavalry

[2] 'Colonel Ross' letters' While this sheet is passing through the press, a

The 4th Battalion left Malta on September 17, and landed at Gibraltar on the 21st, where they were inspected on December 18 by Major-General Sir Robert Walpole, K.C.B., who had so long served in the Regiment, and under whose command the Riflemen had often fought in India.

The 1st Battalion moved by rail on May 31, 1864, from Hamilton to Kingston, where they arrived on June 1 and were quartered, seven companies in Tête-de-Pont barracks, and three companies at Fort Henry.

During the stay of the Battalion at Kingston the men were allowed freely to boat on Lake Ontario, restrictions which had formerly been placed on the troops through fear of desertion being removed by the commanding officer, in perfect confidence in the loyalty of the Riflemen. Every company had a boat; and excursions on the lake and boat races were common among the men. Nor was this confidence misplaced, no desertions having, by this means, taken place.

Previous to leaving Hamilton the following Brigade-order was received:—

'Toronto, May 28, 1864.

'Major-General Napier cannot allow the 1st Battalion of the P. C. O. Rifle Brigade to leave his district without conveying to Colonel Lord Alexander Russell, the Officers, Non-commissioned Officers, and Privates, his unqualified approbation of the good conduct of the Regiment, during the time they have been serving under his command in Canada West. Major-General Napier has often served with the 1st Battalion, and in bidding them farewell for the present trusts that he may at some future period have the Regiment once more under his command.

'By order,

'(Signed) J. E. HALL.

'Major of Brigade.'

On September 8 and 9 the Battalion embarked at Kings-

letter has been received by the Officer Commanding the 3rd Battalion, informing him that a Medal will be granted for this action: a tardy recognition of the services of the Battalion, more than twelve years after the occurrence.

ton in two divisions on board the steam-boats 'Banshee' and 'Grecian,' and proceeded to Montreal, where they arrived on the 9th and 10th, and occupied quarters in the Victoria barracks. Where they were inspected on the 19th by Lieutenant-General Sir W F. Williams, Bart, K.C.B, Commanding British North America.

Colonel Julius Glyn, C.B, assumed command of the 2nd Battalion at Delhi on January 18, Colonel Hill having been appointed to the command of a brigade.

The Head-quarters marched from Delhi on March 26 to Meerut, where they arrived on the 29th. The left wing followed on April 1, and arrived at Meerut on the 4th.

We left the 3rd Battalion at the Camp of Shubkudder, after the fight of January 2 They remained there until the middle of February, when they moved to Rawul Pindee, where they arrived on the 15th. In about a month they left Rawul Pindee, and marching by Khairabad and Akorah, reached Peshawur on the 20th, and there occupied quarters.

On December 30 they moved to Nowshera, where they arrived on January 1, 1865.

The 4th Battalion remained at Gibraltar during the whole of the year.

In September Whitworth rifles were issued to the men of this Battalion, forty short Enfields being retained for the use of the sergeants.

The 1st Battalion continued in quarters at Montreal, where on March 9, 1865, a letter was received, of which the following is an extract:—

'Horse Guards, February 15, 1865

'The resistance of the men of the 1st Battalion Rifle Brigade to the great temptations held out to them to desert has elicited the expression of His Royal Highness's highest commendation.'[1]

[1] I may add the following extract from a letter to a former officer of the Regiment from an officer then serving in America. 'The only regiment which did not lose any men by desertion was the Rifles. Indeed, you have great reason of being proud of your Corps.'

On May 2 the Battalion embarked at Montreal in the steamboat 'Europa,' and proceeded to Quebec; and arriving there the following day, occupied the citadel

The Battalion having been inspected by Major-General the Hon. James Lindsay, a letter was received, which contained the following approval.—

'Horse Guards, August 11, 1865

'The Duke of Cambridge has received with much pleasure Major-General the Honourable James Lindsay's very favourable account of the 1st Battalion Rifle Brigade, which His Royal Highness desires may be highly commended, more particularly for the shooting.'

The 2nd Battalion remained at Meerut during the whole of the year.

On January 1 the 3rd Battalion arrived from Peshawur at Nowshera, and occupied quarters until December 13, when they left it for Rawul Pindee, where, arriving on the 19th, they occupied quarters.

The 4th Battalion embarked at Gibraltar on board the 'Himalaya' troop-ship on July 7 for Canada, and arrived at Point Levis on the 22nd, where they were encamped, and employed in erecting fortifications until October, on the 19th of which month they proceeded to Montreal, and occupied quarters in the Victoria barracks.

In this year the Regiment lost its Colonel-in-Chief, Sir George Brown, G.C.B., who died at Linkwood, Morayshire, on August 27 His remains were interred in the Cathedral burial-ground at Elgin on the 31st, being borne to the grave by five old Riflemen, who had served under him.

He was succeeded by Field-Marshal Sir Edward Blakeney, G.C.B., who had never served in, nor been connected with the Regiment.

The 1st Battalion remained in the citadel of Quebec during the whole of the year 1866.

On June 9 a railway-van, containing 2,000 pounds of ammunition, on its way from Quebec to Kingston, under charge of a sergeant and a guard of the Battalion, was discovered to be on fire on reaching Danville Station It had been ignited by a spark from the engine. The van was immediately shoved down the line away from the station, and the alarm given. The people living in the vicinity fled from their houses, in fear of the explosion. Private Timothy O'Hea of this guard ran down to the van, forced open the door, removed the covering from the ammunition, discovered the source of the fire, ran for water, and extinguished it. A braver or more daring act it is impossible to imagine. A subscription was immediately set on foot, and a purse handed to the brave Rifleman; and he subsequently received the Victoria Cross for this courageous act.

On October 14 occurred the great fire at Quebec; and the Riflemen took a very active part in endeavouring to suppress it, to save life, and to rescue property from the flames. One man of the Battalion, named William Berry, distinguished himself by rescuing a child from a house, which the engineers were about to blow up, to prevent the extension of the fire The train had been laid; and the fuse was already burning, when this brave man rushed in, and brought out the child in safety. For this gallant act Berry was recommended for the Victoria Cross, and though he did not obtain it, he was specially mentioned in General Orders issued at Montreal on May 7, 1867.

The 2nd Battalion continued at Meerut until November 2, when it moved *viâ* Ghazeeabad, to Agra, where it arrived on the 5th, and was encamped during the durbar held by the Governor-General, Sir John Lawrence; till December 1 to 5, when it proceeded in detachments, by rail, to Fort William, Calcutta

The 3rd Battalion continued at Rawul Pindee until the 1st, when they were employed in the construction of a road from Murree to Abbottabad. This work continued till November 5, and on the 10th they returned to Rawul Pindee.

The Battalion, having been ordered to be increased by 128 privates, received volunteers from the 34th, 51st, 97th and 98th Regiments

The 4th Battalion, continuing at Montreal, detached three

companies, with the band, to Ottawa on May 21, and they continued to be quartered there during the stay of His Excellency the Governor-General.

On the Fenians from the United States crossing the frontier into Canada, two companies proceeded from Montreal on June 2 to St. John's (Canada East), and were joined there by a company from Chambly, and were encamped at St John's till the 9th; when, being reinforced by the Head-quarters, consisting of four companies, under Major Nixon,[1] they proceeded by rail to St. Armand, and were about to encamp, when Lieutenant Acland,[2] who in the disguise of a *habitant* had gone amongst the Fenians, brought word that a considerable party of them had crossed the Canadian boundary. A small force, with two guns, to which Captains Norris'[3] and Moorsom's companies were attached, started to find them, but the Fenians seem to have had intelligence of their approach; for although the guns, escorted by a company of Riflemen, pushed on at a trot, they disappeared in the wood, or crossed the boundary. On Major Nixon, with the rest of the force, coming up, he led the skirmishers through some thick wood and cedar-swamp, and some shots were fired. A few Fenians, half-starved and partly armed, were taken prisoners. As it was then near evening, Colonel Elrington ordered the force back to St Armand; but Moorsom's company was sent to Freligsburgh, about 11 miles from St Armand. On arrival there, they found that the town had been sacked by the Fenians, and it was with some difficulty that the Riflemen obtained any provisions This company returned to St Armand on the 10th, but was again detached on the 15th to guard a block-house, in which the Fenian prisoners were confined, at Phillipsburgh, on Lake Champlain.

The whole of these companies, except one which proceeded to Chambly for musketry instruction, returned to Montreal on June 19.

On January 30, 1867, the 1st Battalion received the Snider breech-loading rifle.

[1] Colonel Elrington was in command of the whole force employed

[2] Lieutenant F G Dyke Acland, died Aug. 24, 1874

[3] Captain William Norris, died January 1874

The Battalion proceeded on June 10 across the St. Lawrence to Point Levis, leaving one company at Quebec. They encamped at Point Levis, and were employed during the summer in the construction of fortifications at that place.

On October 7 Head-quarters and two companies moved by rail to Ottawa, the remaining companies returning to Quebec. On November 20, however, two of these companies joined the Head-quarters at Ottawa.

The 2nd Battalion, having embarked at Calcutta on board H.M. Troop-ship 'Jumna,' proceeded to Suez. And re-embarking at Alexandria on board H.M Troop-ship 'Crocodile,' disembarked at Portsmouth on November 23, and proceeded at once by rail to Devonport, and occupied quarters.

The 3rd Battalion, being still at Rawul Pindee, on May 1 a working party of 238 privates, under a field officer, were employed, as in the preceding year, on the road from Murree to Abottabad, and rejoined Head-quarters at Rawul Pindee on November 3.

On January 4 the 4th Battalion at Montreal received the breech-loading short Snider, in place of the Whitworth rifle.

On September 5 the Battalion left Montreal, and on the next day embarked on board the Troop-ship 'Serapis,' and started for England. They arrived at Portsmouth on the 17th, and disembarked on the 18th, five companies with Head-quarters proceeding to Chichester, and three companies to Winchester, whence the Depôt companies joined Head-quarters. The Battalion made but a short stay in the south of England, for on December 23 the three companies at Winchester, with one from Chichester, moved to Weedon. And on the 26th the Head-quarters and remaining six companies followed, arriving at Weedon on the next day Three companies were detached to Leeds, and one to Northampton.

The Head-quarters of the 1st Battalion continued at Ottawa during the year 1868, where the companies remaining at Quebec joined on June 6.

In consequence of the proceedings of the Fenians in the United States, one company of the Battalion proceeded to

Coburg on October 1, and was followed by two other companies on the 5th.

The 2nd Battalion continued at Devonport during the whole year 1868.

On January 10 the 3rd Battalion left Rawul Pindee, and began its march to Moradabad and Seetapore. The left wing marched into quarters at Moradabad on March 14, and the right wing and Head-quarters at Seetapore on the 30th.

On November 30 the left wing, under Captain Moore, left Moradabad, and marched into quarters at Dinapore on December 14.

The 4th Battalion continued at Weedon, Leeds and Northampton, and furnished yet another detachment of one company to Warwick on January 14. The company at Northampton, however, joining Head-quarters at Weedon on February 7.

On May 21 the Head-quarters and five companies proceeded to Chester, and were quartered in the Castle; and the detachments from Leeds and Warwick joining the company left at Weedon formed the left wing, and were quartered there.

The Colonel-in-Chief, Sir Edward Blakeney, died on August 2, and the Regiment had the honour of receiving as his successor General His Royal Highness Albert Edward, Prince of Wales, who was appointed Colonel-in-Chief August 3.

The 1st Battalion, continuing at Ottawa, on March 1 and 15, 1869, furnished parties of 200 men each time to dig out the mail-trains imbedded in snow between Montreal and Ottawa, the *employés* of the railway being insufficient for that purpose The men carried their rations with them on these occasions.

On August 5 one company, and on the 17th a second company, proceeded by steamboat to Montreal on detachment. They were followed by the remainder of the Battalion in two divisions on September 9 and 10

On October 8 His Royal Highness Prince Arthur joined the Service companies at Montreal, having been appointed Lieutenant on August 3.

On the 24th five companies of the 2nd Battalion, under the command of Lieutenant-Colonel Walker, embarked at Plymouth on board H.M.S. 'Urgent' for Portsmouth, and on arrival there marched to Aldershot, *viâ* Bishop's Waltham and Alton.

And on the 14th the Head-quarters embarked on board H.M Troop-ship 'Simoom,' and arriving at Portsmouth, on the 16th, proceeded by rail to Farnborough; and marching to Cove Common, there encamped until the 23rd, when they occupied huts in the North Camp at Aldershot.

On July 14 the Battalion marched to Chobham, forming part of a flying column, under Major-General Sir Alfred Horsford. They encamped there that night, and on the next day marched to Bushy Park, and encamped Having taken part in a review at Wimbledon, they returned to Aldershot by the same route, and reached it on the 22nd, having taken part in a sham fight

On August 18 the Battalion, forming part of a flying column under Colonel Elrington of the 4th Battalion, marched to Bramshill Park, and encamped there, they remained there during the 19th, and on the 20th returned to Aldershot, having taken part in a sham fight on Hartfordbridge Flats on their way On October 1 the Glengarry cap was taken into wear, in place of the forage cap.

On January 7 the right wing and Head-quarters of the 3rd Battalion left Seetapore; and arriving at Dinapore on the 19th, marched into quarters on the 20th, and joined the left wing, which had arrived there from Moradabad in the previous month.

On May 17 two companies of the left wing of the 4th Battalion at Weedon left that station, proceeding by rail to Bicester, and thence marching by Oxford, Wallingford, and Reading to Aldershot, where they arrived on the 20th Two other companies followed on June 2, proceeding by the same route, and (with the fifth company, which proceeded by rail, and joined them at Reading) arrived at Aldershot on the 5th

The Head-quarters and right wing of this Battalion marched from Chester to Birkenhead on May 31; and embarked there on board the 'Urgent' Troop-ship for Portsmouth, where they landed on June 4, and proceeded to Farnborough. From whence they marched to Cove Common, where the Battalion encamped.

The Battalion was thus reunited for the first time since its arrival in England, its detachments having been widely separated; and for more than a year its two wings having been stationed 120 miles from each other.

This Battalion, as well as the 2nd, formed part of the flying column to Bramshill Park, mentioned above

On September 4 the Battalion removed from the camp at Cove Common, and occupied quarters in the Permanent barracks at Aldershot.

On April 1, 1870, the establishment of the 1st Battalion, then, at Montreal, was reduced to

Field Officers.	Captains.	Lieutenants [2]	Staff	Staff Sergeants	Sergeants
4 [1]	10	14	3	9	40

Buglers	Corporals	Privates.
21	40	460

On July 7 one company proceeded on detachment to Hochelaga.

On August 30 two companies proceeded, by the steamer 'Montreal,' to Quebec, and embarked on board H.M. Troopship 'Tamar' on the following morning. And on the 31st the Head-quarters and remaining companies, under the command of Lieutenant-Colonel Manningham Buller, embarked at Montreal on board the steamboat 'Quebec'; and arriving at Quebec, went on board the 'Tamar,' which started in the evening, and anchored a few miles down the river at nightfall On the following morning she proceeded on her course; but owing to heavy fogs and bad weather on September 3, did

[1] The Colonel-Commandant is included

[2] Four of the Lieutenants were on Ensign's pay.

not get clear of the Gulf of St Lawrence until the next day. After which the weather was favourable during the voyage, which ended on the 16th, when the 'Tamar' arrived at Portsmouth about ten A M Here orders were received to proceed to Gravesend, and at three P.M. she started, arriving there at midday on the 17th. But the Battalion did not disembark until the 19th (Monday), when they landed, partly in the ship's boats, and partly in a small steamer; and proceeded at once to Woolwich, where they occupied the Royal Marine barracks.

On August 24 the establishment of the Battalion was increased to 760 privates, other ranks remaining as before.

The 2nd Battalion remained in the North Camp, Aldershot; and on February 1 was equipped with the valise instead of the knapsack

On August 4 the Battalion marched (forming part of a flying column, under Major-General Dalrymple White) to Bramshill Park, where they encamped. And, as in the previous year, after remaining the next day, marched back to Aldershot on the 6th. On the intervening day the infantry of the column were put through a very pretty field-day by Colonel Elrington, of the 4th Battalion.

On August 24 the establishment of this Battalion was raised from 570 to 870 privates.

On the 30th the Battalion left Aldershot, and proceeded by rail to Dover, where they arrived the same afternoon, and were quartered, Head-quarters and five companies in the South-front barracks, and the remaining five companies (under Lieutenant-Colonel Walker) in the Castle Hill fort.

The following letter was communicated by Major-General Russell, Commanding at Dover, to Colonel Glyn:

'Horse Guards, August 31, 1870.

'Sir,—I am directed by the Field-Marshal Commanding-in-Chief to inform you that the Lieutenant-General Commanding at Aldershot has reported that the 2nd Battalion Rifle Brigade marched out with great regularity and sobriety, and maintained the high character of the Corps whilst in this command And I am to request that you will have the goodness to inform the officer commanding the Regiment of His Royal Highness' satisfaction at receiving so favourable a report.

'I have the honour, &c., &c.,

'(Signed) J. HOPE GRANT, Q.M.G.

'Major-General Russell, &c., &c.,
'Dover.'

On November 12 the left wing of the 3rd Battalion, under the command of Major Maclean, left Dinapore by rail for Allahabad, followed by the Head-quarters and right wing, under Colonel Ross, *en route* for Bombay, where they arrived on the 21st, and embarked on board H.M. Troop-ship 'Euphrates.' On the 30th they arrived at Aden, and two companies disembarked at Steamer-point. On December 1 the remainder of the Battalion disembarked; and they were stationed, two companies at Steamer-point, two at Isthmus position, and the remainder of the Battalion in cantonments.

The 4th Battalion continued to occupy quarters in the Permanent barracks, Aldershot.

On August 4 they formed part of the flying column, with the 2nd Battalion, which proceeded to Bramshill Park, and returned to Aldershot on the 6th.

They moved from Aldershot to Shorncliffe by rail on August 31.

In November this Battalion was again broken up, four companies proceeding to Chatham on the 11th, for duty in that garrison.

The 1st Battalion continued to occupy the Marine barracks at Woolwich; and on February 1, 1871, the number of privates was again altered, being reduced to 560.

On May 23 the Battalion was inspected by His Royal Highness the Duke of Cambridge.

On August 2 they proceeded by march-route to Wimbledon; on the next day to Hounslow, on the 4th to Chobham, and on the 5th to Aldershot, where they encamped on Cove Common. On each of these days they had encamped at their halting-places.

They remained here till September 12, when (taking part in the autumn manœuvres of that year) they marched to Chobham ridges; on the 13th to Chobham; and were employed in constructing field-works on the 14th. On the next day they marched to Pirbright; and after pitching camp proceeded to the Hog's-back and remained on outpost duty for the night. On the 16th they marched to Chobham ridges and remained there during the next day, Sunday, on the 18th they moved to Chobham and were encamped there till the 21st, when they returned to Cove Common and were encamped on their former ground.

During this time the Battalion daily took part in sham fights, and encamped at night, and in fact acted as in an actual campaign.

On September 27 the Battalion marched to Farnborough and proceeded by rail to Dover, and was quartered in the Shaft barracks.

The 2nd Battalion at Dover on February 1 had its establishment increased from 870 to 920 privates.

On September 26 the Head-quarters and three companies marched from Dover to Shorncliffe, and on the 29th three other companies followed, and the remaining four companies on October 2, and were there quartered.

The Service companies of the 3rd Battalion, under the command of Major Maclean, embarked at Aden on December 7, on board H.M. Troop-ship 'Serapis,' and arrived at Portsmouth on the 30th

The 4th Battalion continued at Shorncliffe, with four companies at Chatham; and on July 22 furnished another detachment of a company to Upnor Castle.

The Head-quarters and remaining five companies moved from Shorncliffe to Chatham on August 1; furnishing detachments to the Isle of Grain and to Gravesend.

At the commencement of the year, 1872, the head-dress of the Regiment was changed, the fur-busby with a bag being substituted for the shako.

RIFLE BRIGADE,
1871.

On the recovery of His Royal Highness the Colonel-in-Chief from his dangerous illness in the winter of 1871-2, Sir George Buller, Colonel-Commandant, addressed the following letter to the Comptroller of His Royal Highness's household:

'23 Bruton Street, Berkeley Square, March 5, 1872.

'Sir,—I have the honour by the desire of Lieutenant-Colonel Manningham-Buller, and the officers of the 1st Battalion Rifle Brigade, to request you will be pleased to lay before His Royal Highness the Prince of Wales, Colonel-in-Chief of the Rifle Brigade, their most respectful and sincere congratulations on the recovery of His Royal Highness from His late dangerous illness, and in which congratulations I beg to add that I most cordially concur.

'An unavoidable delay has occurred in the transmission of this address of the officers of the 1st Battalion Rifle Brigade in consequence of the letter on this subject having been sent to my house in London, and not forwarded to me by error.

'I have the honour to be,
&c. &c &c,

'(Signed) GEORGE BULLER

'General, Colonel-Commandant 1st Battalion
Rifle Brigade.

'General Sir William Knollys, K C.B
&c &c. &c'

To which the following gracious reply was received:

'Marlborough House, Pall Mall, March 9, 1872

'Sir,—I have the honour to inform you that in compliance with your request, I have laid before the Prince of Wales, Colonel-in-Chief of the Rifle Brigade, the congratulations which you have been good enough to forward of Colonel Manningham-Buller, and the officers of the 1st Battalion Rifle Brigade, on His Royal Highness's recovery from His late dangerous illness, with your own cordial concurrence in them.

'His Royal Highness requests you will accept for yourself and convey to Colonel Buller and the officers under his command His sincere thanks for their congratulations, and assures you how gratifying it is to His Royal Highness to receive them.

'I have the honour to be,
&c. &c. &c.

'(Signed) WILLIAM KNOLLYS,
'General

'General Sir George Buller, G C.B , Colonel-Commandant
1st Battalion Rifle Brigade'

On May 1 the establishment of the 1st Battalion was further reduced to 520 rank and file.

On May 25 the Battalion was inspected by Field-Marshal His Royal Highness the Duke of Cambridge.

The Battalion remained at the Shaft barracks, Dover, during the whole of this year.

The 2nd Battalion at Shorncliffe on May 1 received orders to reduce its establishment from 49 to 47 sergeants, 21 to 19 buglers; and from 850 rank and file to 820.

On August 16 Head-quarters and eight companies of the Battalion, under command of Major Stephens (Colonel Glyn having been selected to command a brigade) proceeded by rail to Aldershot, in order to take part in the autumn manœuvres On their arrival they encamped on Cove Common until the 26th, when they marched to Hazeley Heath and encamped. On the 27th they marched to Silchester, passing by Strathfieldsaye, where they marched past the monumental statue of their great Colonel-in-Chief, Arthur, Duke of Wellington. On the 28th they marched to Greenham Heath, where they halted next day, and on the 30th proceeded to camp near Wilton. On the following day they marched to camp at Rushall Park, where they remained till the commencement of the manœuvres on September 4

But on August 24 the two companies of the Battalion remaining at Shorncliffe, with the women, children and baggage, were conveyed by train from Shorncliffe to Dover and embarked on board H M. Troop-ship 'Tamar,' and arrived at Kingstown on the 29th, whence they proceeded on the same day by rail to Birr, there to await the arrival of the Battalion.

On September 4 the Head-quarters marched from Rushall Park to Stapleford, where they encamped until the 8th, during which time they were employed on outpost duties, and daily took part in sham-fights at Wishford, Steeple-Langford and Wiley. On the 9th they marched to Darrington-field On the 10th they took part in the defence of the river Avon, and on the 12th were in the march past, which concluded these autumn manœuvres.

During this time the Battalion was always encamped, as mentioned in the autumn manœuvres of the preceding year. They also furnished their regimental transport, having received waggons and field equipment at Woolwich, where a party of about 60 men with two officers had proceeded, after being instructed by the Land Transport Corps

On September 13 the Battalion marched from Darrington-field to Salisbury, and thence proceeded by train to Portsmouth, where they embarked in the evening, six companies on board H.M Troop-ship 'Orontes' and two on board H.M Troop-ship 'Jumna,' for conveyance to Ireland.

On the 16th they disembarked at Kingstown and proceeded by train to Birr, detaching a company and a half to Nenagh; a company to Roscrea; and half a company to Portumna

But the regimental transport marched from the camp at Darrington-field, by Andover, Basingstoke, Guildford, and Epsom to Woolwich, where they arrived and handed over equipment on the 25th. On the next day they marched with the horses to Aldershot, where they arrived on the 28th and remained till October 12, when they returned to Woolwich, arriving on the 16th; and after giving up the horses to the Control department were attached to the Army Service Corps at Woolwich till the 23rd They embarked on that day on board the 'Lady Eglinton,' and joined the Battalion on the 28th.

The 3rd Battalion, which had arrived from India on December 30, 1871, landed at Portsmouth on January 1, and occupied quarters in the Clarence barracks, and was joined by the Depôt companies from Chatham.

On February 27, 14 officers and 599 of other ranks of the 4th Battalion, under command of Colonel Elrington, proceeded from Chatham to London, to take part in the thanksgiving for the recovery of His Royal Highness, the Colonel-in-Chief

In June Colonel Elrington, who had formed the Battalion, and commanded it from its formation, retired on half-pay; and Colonel Ross, C.B, succeeded to the command.

The Head-quarters with eight companies removed from Chatham to Blandford by rail, and took part in the autumn manœuvres

The Battalion being destined for Ireland, the remaining two companies embarked at Sheerness on August 24, on board the 'Orontes' Troop-ship, and landed at Kingstown on the 28th, and proceeded to Richmond barracks.

At the conclusion of the autumn manœuvres the Head-quarters marched from camp near Amesbury to Salisbury on September 14, and thence proceeded by rail to Portsmouth and embarked on board the 'Jumna' Troop-ship They landed at Kingstown on the 16th and marched to Dublin, where for the remainder of the year they occupied Richmond, Ship-street, and Linen-hall barracks

The 1st Battalion proceeded by rail from Dover to Aldershot on June 5, 1873, and were encamped on Rushmoor bottom until July 28, when they occupied quarters in the Permanent barracks

On June 24 the Battalion proceeded by rail to Egham, and thence marched to Windsor Park and took part in a review before Her Majesty and the Shah of Persia. On this occasion His Royal Highness the Colonel-in-Chief marched past in the uniform of the Regiment, at the head of the Battalion. After the conclusion of the review they returned by the same route to their camp at Rushmoor which they reached about ten P.M.

The 2nd Battalion remained at Birr, occasionally relieving the detachments; and in June the establishment was reduced from 820 to 700 rank and file

On July 31 the Battalion and the detachments proceeded by rail to the Curragh for the autumn manœuvres, and encamped The Battalion returned to Birr on August 29, replacing the detachment at Portumna, the others being discontinued.

On September 3 the Battalion received orders to prepare for service on the Gold Coast of Africa, in the expedition against Ashantee under Sir Garnet Wolseley.

Colonel Glyn having been appointed Adjutant-General of Auxiliary Forces in Ireland, Lieutenant-Colonel Warren took command of the Battalion.

On November 13 they were inspected by Lieutenant-General Sir Thomas Steele, K.C.B., previous to embarkation; and on the next day they received definite orders to hold themselves in readiness to embark on any day after the 16th.

Accordingly, on the 21st, the Battalion proceeded by wings, by railway from Birr to Cork. The left wing, under the command of Major J Plumtre Glyn, started from Birr at three in the morning of that day; and the right wing, under Major Stephens, at half-past three for Cork, where they were to embark. Colonel Warren and the Staff of the Battalion accompanied the left wing.

The climate of the Coast of Africa necessitating the disuse of their European clothing, the men and officers were provided with two grey frocks, a pair of grey tweed trousers, a pair of duck trousers, two flannel shirts, two flannel belts, a pith helmet with *puggaree* attached, and a pair of canvas gaiters

On arrival at Cork they embarked on board the Troopship 'Himalaya,' and sailed at four in the afternoon. The officers who embarked were:—

Lieutenant-Colonel Warren; *Majors*, Stephens and Plumtre Glyn; *Brevet-Majors*, Nicholl and Sotheby; *Captains*, Slade, Dugdale, Somerset, Robinson, Cary and H. Lascelles; *Lieutenants*, the Honourable T. Scott, Stopford-Sackville,[1] Maberly,[2] Taylor, Hopwood, the Honourable A. Grosvenor, Thompson, (*Adjutant*), Harrington, Smyth,[1] the Honourable J. Constable-Maxwell,[1] Prideaux-Brune, Parke and Turnor, *Sub-Lieutenants*, the Honourable Otway Cuffe, Sherston, the Honourable E. Noel and the Honourable H O'C. Prittie.

Captain Harvey (*Paymaster*), Quarter-master Stanley, Surgeon-Major Wiles and Surgeon Macrobin.

[1] Volunteered from the 3rd Battalion, to complete the number of officer required.

[2] Volunteered from the 1st Battalion.

The 'Himalaya' arrived at Funchal, Madeira, on the 27th. Here they found in garrison at Funchal one of the regiments of Caçadores which had been brigaded with them sixty years before in the Peninsula. After coaling, the 'Himalaya' started on the evening of the same day, and reached St. Vincent on December 1, whence after coaling again, she started on the 2nd, and arrived at Cape Coast Castle on December 9. Here nothing was ready for their reception; and it was decided that the 'Himalaya' should put to sea again until the end of the month. Accordingly, on the 13th she started on a cruise. To be thus for three weeks longer cooped up on board ship under a tropical sun was a sore trial to the soldiers. However everything was done that could be done to amuse the men, and relieve the monotony of their enforced and unexpected cruise A newspaper was started, readings and theatricals were extemporised, and a *quasi* band which had been got up (the band of the Battalion having been left at the Depôt) played daily. At last on December 30, the 'Himalaya' arrived at Cape Coast Castle, and the Battalion was allowed to disembark

In the meanwhile Captain Robinson had been appointed Brigade-Major to Brigadier Sir Archibald Alison, commanding a brigade; and Captain Cope, who had been detailed for the Depôt, started on December 4 in the 'Sarmatian' (which took out the Brigadier and the 42nd Regiment), and having arrived at Cape Coast Castle on the 17th, awaited the arrival of the Battalion, and took over Captain Robinson's company on its landing.

On July 19 the 3rd Battalion left Portsmouth by rail-road for Exeter, and on arrival there encamped at Duck's Marsh, about two miles and a half from that station, until the 21st; on which day they proceeded by route march to Maiden Down; on the next to Merripit Hill, and on the 23rd to Yannaton Down, Dartmoor, encamping each day at their halting-places. They took part in the autumn manœuvres, being in the brigade commanded by Colonel Lord Alexander G Russell.

On the conclusion of the manœuvres, this Battalion was present at the review and march-past at Roborough Down on

August 22, before His Royal Highness, the Colonel-in-Chief. At its conclusion they marched seven miles to Plymouth, whence they proceeded at ten o'clock the same night, *viâ* Exeter, to Winchester, and arriving there on the morning of the 23rd, occupied barracks; detaching, on December 13, three companies to Portsmouth, who were quartered in the Clarence barracks.

The 4th Battalion continued in Dublin ; but were concentrated from the various quarters they occupied, in the Royal barracks in July.

Having received orders to embark for India, the Depôt and Service companies were formed, and transfers made and received to complete its establishment for foreign service (886 non-commissioned officers and privates). And on October 19 and 20 the Service companies proceeded by rail to Queenstown and embarked on the 21st in the 'Jumna.' They started on the 22nd and arrived at Bombay on November 23. They landed on the 24th and 25th, and proceeded by rail to Deolalee

From Deolalee they moved on November 28 and 30, and following day to Umballa, and on arrival occupied quarters there.

On March 12, 1874, the 1st Battalion proceeded by railroad from Aldershot to London, in order to be present at the entry of the Duke and Duchess of Edinburgh. They lined Regent Street during the progress of the Royal procession, and returned to their quarters at Aldershot in the evening.

On May 19 this Battalion was present at a review and march-past before the Emperor of Russia. The brigade to which they were attached was composed of three Battalions of the Regiment (the 1st, 2nd, and 3rd), and one of the 60th, and was commanded by Major-General Lord Alexander Russell, their former Lieutenant-Colonel

After taking part in the summer drills of this year, during the month of June, this Battalion proceeded to the forts on the Gosport side of Portsmouth harbour, which they occupied from July 3 and 4 until November 20, when they moved to Winchester, on the embarkation of the 2nd Battalion for Gibraltar, and were there quartered.

CHAPTER XV.

WE left the 2nd Battalion on board the 'Himalaya' at Cape Coast Castle. On January 1, 1874, 'rouse' sounded soon after midnight, and the parade was at 1.20 in the morning. The left wing, consisting of four companies (17 officers and 352 men), landed in surf boats, the first company reaching the shore at a quarter after three, the fourth company in about a quarter of an hour afterwards. The whole disembarkation occupied about forty minutes, and elicited the warm approval of the Brigadier, Sir Archibald Alison. The companies fell in immediately on landing, and at once marched for Inquabim, seven miles, which they reached about half-past six; the Battalion heading the advance up the country.

The right wing, consisting of the remaining four companies (16 officers and 300 men) disembarked at about the same hour on the morning of the 2nd, and started for Inquabim, which they reached about half-past five. On this march no men fell out. On their arrival they found an excellent encampment of bamboo huts, 65 men being in each hut.

The left wing had on this day preceded them to Accroful, another march of seven miles, to which the right wing proceeded on the 3rd, starting at half-past four, and arriving at half-past six, without a man falling out. On this day the left wing advanced to Yancoomassie-Fanti.

On the 4th the right wing, starting at the usual hour of half-past four, marched to Yancoomassie-Fanti, a distance of about ten miles and a quarter, where they arrived at eight o'clock. Not a man fell out; but the climate began already to tell on some of the officers, two of whom had to be carried during this day's march. The left wing had marched to Mansu, and it may suffice, once for all, to state that they preceded the march of the right wing by one day.

On the 5th the right wing started at a quarter to four, and after a fearfully hot march of eleven miles reached Mansu at eight The road was hilly, the weather extremely close, and four men fell out during the march.

It is well known that it is supposed that horses, mules and animals of carriage or draught will not live in the climate of this part of Africa. This idea is perhaps exaggerated. But its existence caused inconvenience to the mounted officers of the Regiment. Major Stephens, who was in command of the right wing, was obliged to content himself with a donkey, which had been brought up to Accroful by an officer of the Staff.

From Yancoomassie an officer with the Quarter-master-Sergeant started somewhat before the companies, to take over the camping ground. The sergeant started first, but soon returned with a tale that, in the darkness of the morning and of the woods, he had seen a monstrous beast which he took for a rhinoceros, that he had at first intended to shoot it, but had, on the whole, considering the size and probable fierceness of the animal, determined to retire However, re-inforced by the officer who was to accompany him, he started again. Both were determined, both held their revolvers ready to bring down the wild beast which barred the way. But when they came to the corner at which they were to find him, they stalked not a rhinoceros,—but the Major's charger.

On the 6th the right wing started at twenty minutes after three, and after a very cool and pleasant march of eleven miles, reached Sutah

On the 7th, having a long march before them, they started at half-past two in bright moonlight. The road was for the first four miles very bad, being across swamps, over which a path had been made of small trees laid down. The cooks had been sent on about six miles to Faisoowah to prepare breakfast, and the men were glad after this fatiguing march to find cocoa and biscuit ready for them. Resuming their march they found the remainder of the road good, the men marched well, and stepped out cheerfully; and they got into their camp at Yancoomassie-Assin at seven. The distance was about thirteen miles.

The right wing halted at this camp until the 19th. The

left wing also halted for some days at Barracoo, to which they had marched on the 7th During this time the Riflemen were engaged in clearing the bush and in other fatigue duties in the mornings and evenings. The desertion of the native carriers, the only means of transport, increased, and threatened serious evil ; and the Riflemen were ordered when on sentry over them to have their rifles loaded, and, if necessary, to shoot any carriers attempting to desert. Owing to this halt probably, and the want of interest and activity to the men, fever and dysentery, the scourges of the climate, began to make their appearance.

As it was found that the camp at Barracoo was from its situation particularly unhealthy, the left wing marched on the 17th to Prahsu, a distance of seven miles

But the right wing did not leave Yancoomassie-Assin till the 19th, when starting at five in the morning they reached their camp at Barracoo at half-past eight. They found it the worst camp they had hitherto occupied ; the huts very small, and the position, as has been above stated, very unhealthy. Seventeen men of these four companies were sent back, mostly ill with fever, and they found at Barracoo seven men of the other wing who had been left behind sick

On the 20th the right wing marched to Prahsu, and the whole Battalion was once more reunited On their march they heard in the front what they believed to be the report of three cannon, and much wondered why they should be fired. On arrival they found that these were the report of three volleys fired over the grave of Captain Huyshe of the 1st Battalion. He had died the day before of fever and dysentery. The left wing of the Battalion was at Prahsu, and paid the last sad honours to his remains

He was a man of great promise, and a most well-informed as well as talented officer The early part of his career had been in the 83rd Regiment, from which he exchanged into the Rifle Brigade He had accompanied Sir Garnet Wolseley in the expedition to the Red River in 1870, and had written an interesting account of it [1] He had entered the Staff College, and after a few months' study there, had, on the Ashantee Expedition being determined on, been offered the

[1] The 'Red River Expedition,' London, 1871.

post of Deputy-Assistant Quartermaster General of the force, which he most gladly accepted He had come to the Gold Coast with Sir Garnet Wolseley in September. He had started from Cape Coast with diarrhœa, had exposed himself a good deal to the weather in surveying and sketching country; and dysentery and fever supervened and carried him off. His talents, his fund of information, his sweetness of disposition, and his gentlemanly manners had endeared him to his brother officers, who have erected a handsome memorial to him in the Cathedral of Winchester; but to none more than to the writer of these lines.[1]

Hitherto the Battalion had found at their camping, or rather halting stations, huts built of bamboo, and thatched with plantain or palm leaves The men's huts contained about seventy men, those of the officers were, of course, smaller In all of them were bedsteads, constructed of bamboo, keeping the sleepers about two feet from the ground.

On the 21st the Battalion crossed a narrow bridge, which had been made across the Prah, here about eighty yards wide, and marched to Essiaman, about thirteen miles and a half. Cocoa had, however, been prepared for them at Attobiasse, about half-way. The morning was very dark when they started; but it was cooler, the bush much more open, and the road good On their arrival, they no longer found the huts which had been prepared for them on the other side of the Prah. At Essiaman the men were in long open sheds, covered with palm leaves, while the officers built themselves shelters of bushes and *tentes d'abri*, in which they could sling their field-hammocks.

On the 22nd, starting at half-past five, the Battalion marched to Accrofoomu, about fourteen miles, which they reached about a quarter to eleven. Some fourteen men fell out, mostly from fatigue, for the heat was excessive and the march long. The sheds here were insufficient to accommodate the Battalion; so that lean-tos had to be built and tents

[1] The funeral of Captain Huyshe is the subject of a water-colour picture by M Norie (from a drawing I believe by Colonel Colley) I am assured by those who were present that it is a faithful representation of the scene and of the surroundings.

pitched. As at Essiaman, the officers had to construct huts for themselves.

On the 23rd they started at a quarter to six, and marched to Moinsey, at the foot of the Adansi hills, a distance of about eight miles. It was a pleasant march, for the road was good, the bush much more open, and the air cooler. There were no huts nor sheds, and the men had to build them

The next day they started at the same hour, and ascended the Adansi range The ascent, which is steep, occupied about half an hour. They halted at the top, and saw the sun rise over the trees below, while the mists hanging between the hills had the appearance of lakes Resuming their march, they passed through Quisah, a large village about five miles on the way, deserted by the Ashantees. They arrived at Foomanah at about nine This was a considerable town, containing the house or palace of the King of Adansi The men and officers were quartered in the so-called houses, built of yellow baked clay, and rather resembling ovens with roofs over them In some of them were found dead bodies.

An envoy from the King of Ashantee had here met Sir Garnet Wolseley, and the Battalion, with the Naval Brigade, paraded at five in the afternoon, and lined the road north of the town, by which he was to return to Coomassie, the ranks facing inwards.

They halted at Foomanah till the 29th But on the 25th the Battalion was inspected by Sir Garnet Wolseley, and on the 26th Major Nicholl's company formed part of a reconnaissance in force to the village of Kiang Boassu, about four or five miles to the front, where Ashantee tom-toms had been heard the day before. The Riflemen on this reconnaissance were under the command of Major Stephens They started at a quarter to six, and returned soon after nine. The Ashantees fired on them ; they returned the compliment, killed two Ashantees, and made two prisoners, besides burning the village.

As usual during a halt, sickness again appeared. Captain Slade was sent down to the coast on the 28th, seriously ill from dysentery, and Lieutenant the Honourable Thomas Scott took command of his company.

On the 29th the Battalion paraded at half-past five, and

marched to Ahkankuassie, a distance of about ten miles. Here the men built huts for themselves ; while the officers, or some of them, found houses in the village. But these were filthy places, and overrun with lizards. The Battalion furnished an outlying picquet, Major Sotheby's company, at Adadwassie, about a mile and a half in advance of Ahkankuassie Rations were served out for the following day, which the men were to carry on the march.

On the 30th the Battalion moved forward to Insarfu, passing through Adadwassie, where the picquet joined them. The distance to Insarfu was only about four miles, and the Riflemen reached it about ten o'clock, having formed the rear-guard of the European brigade.

It being generally expected that the Ashantees would make a stand on the next day, and that there would be a fight, the Captains of the Battalion were assembled at the Commanding Officer's quarters, to receive instructions for the operations of the morrow. It was explained to them that they were to form the rear face of a hollow square, in which formation the Commanding General intended to advance Nor was this, they were informed, to be considered less the point of honour than the front, as the tactics of the Ashantees were to envelop the flanks and fall upon the rear. At evening parade these orders were explained by the Captains to the Riflemen, who listened with interest and eagerness to the information. Rations for the next day were issued. The men were camped under *tentes d'abri* in quarter-distance column in a plaintain ground ; the officers, some of them, built huts near their men ; some found shelter in the houses in the village, which, if less filthy than those at Ahkankuassie, were only a fraction of a degree nearer cleanliness.

On the 31st the Battalion paraded at twenty minutes after six, and about half-an-hour afterwards marched from Insarfu. The 42nd led, the Rifle Brigade forming the rear of the hollow square or order of battle, which was thus disposed :—

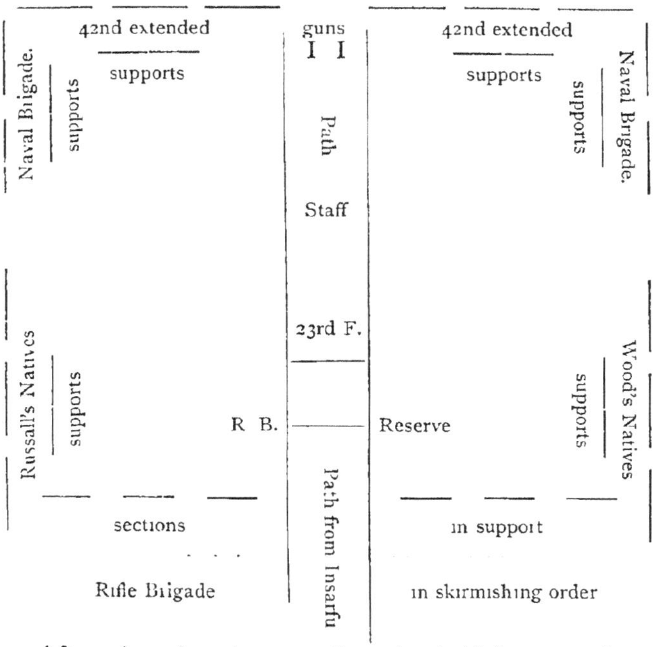

After advancing about a mile and a half, firing was heard in front, the 42nd having engaged the Ashantees, who were posted on ground rising from a muddy stream, which flowed through a swampy ravine. The action commenced about eight; but it was not till more than an hour and a half later that the Riflemen became engaged. Then Major Nicholl's company was sent to the right column, under Lieutenant-Colonel Wood, and Major Sotheby's and Captain Cope's companies were extended on the east and south-east of Egginassie, fire having been opened by the enemy from the bush in that direction. The bush was dense and thick; consisting of great cotton trees, with a high undergrowth, and interlaced everywhere with creepers, so that the men could not see more than fifteen or twenty yards before them, and had often to cut a way with their swords. Sotheby's left touched the Bonnymen of the right column, while the connection between his right and the road or path was kept up by Cope's com-

To face Plan of Battle

BATTLE OF AMOAFUL.

ABOUT 10 30 A M.

DETAILED DESCRIPTION.

CENTRE COLUMN.

The 42nd carrying the enemy's main position north of the swamp. Rait's artillery in action. 23rd in support.

Rifle Brigade.—No 1 company in action in the clearing to the east of the path (with the Right Column) No 3 company leaving Egginassie to support the 42nd. The remainder in action around Egginassie.

RIGHT COLUMN.

Naval Brigade engaged in the clearing east of the main path. (Lieut. Knox's rockets playing into a hollow to the north-east.)

Wood's Regiment in action round Egginassie.

LEFT COLUMN.

Russell's Regiment has taken the heights west of Egginassie.

Col M'Leod, with the Naval Brigade, is cutting his way to try and connect with the Centre Column.

RIFLE BRIGADE COMPANIES.

1. Nicholl, 2 Sotheby, 3. Somerset, 4 Dugdale, 5. Lascelles; 6 Cope; 7. Slade (Scott), 8. Cary.

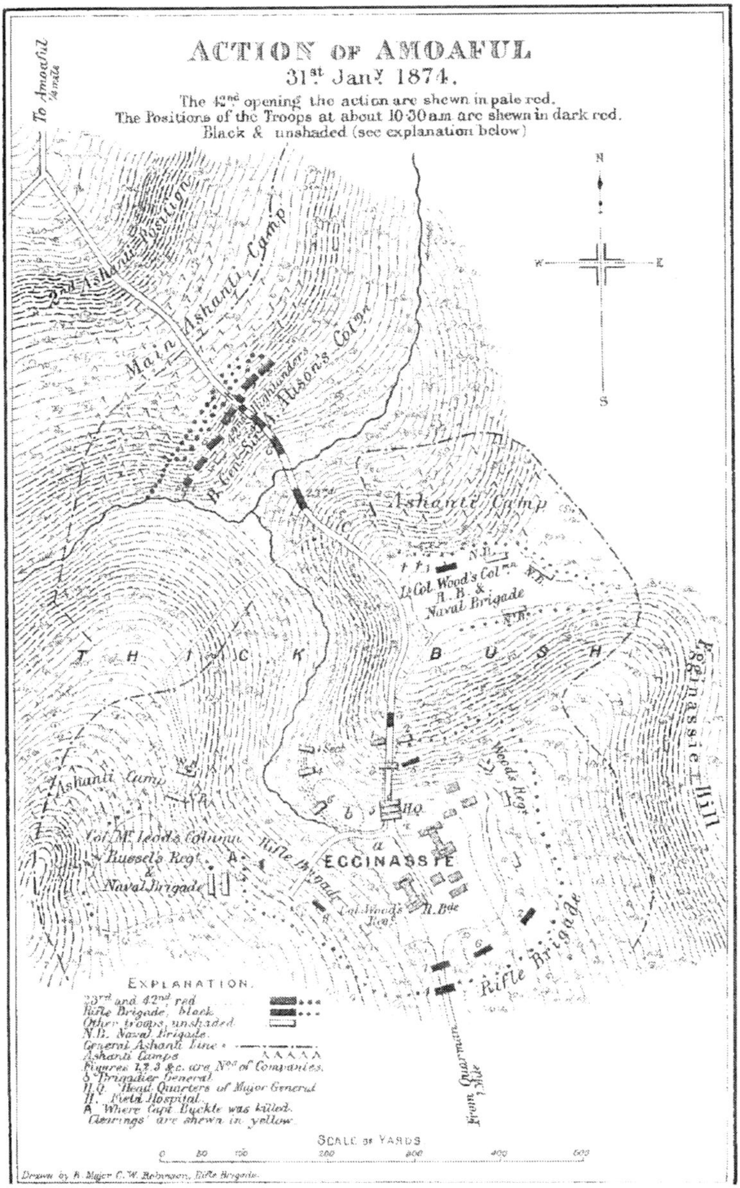
ACTION OF AMOAFUL
31st Jany 1874.
The 42nd opening the action are shewn in pale red.
The Positions of the Troops at about 10·30 a.m. are shewn in dark red.
Black & unshaded (see explanation below)
To Amoaful
N
S
W
E
2nd Ashanti Position
Main Ashanti Camp
Highlanders
Alison's Colm
Ashanti Camp
Lt Col. Wood's Colmn
R. B. &
Naval Brigade
N.B.
T H I C K B U S H
Egginassie Hill
Ashanti Camp
Col. Mc Leod's Column
Russel's Regt
&
Naval Brigade
Rifle Brigade
ECCINASSIE
H.Q.
Wood's Regt
Col. Wood's Regt
R. Bde
Rifle Brigade
From Quarman
EXPLANATION.
23rd and 42nd, red
Rifle Brigade, black
Other troops, unshaded
N.B. Naval Brigade.
General Ashanti Line
Ashanti Camps
Figures 1.2.3 &c. are Nos of Companies.
δ Brigadier General.
H.Q. Head Quarters of Major General
H. Field Hospital.
A Where Capt Buckle was killed.
Clearings are shewn in yellow
SCALE OF YARDS
0
50
100
200
300
400
500
Drawn by B. Major C. W. Robinson, Rifle Brigade.

pany, who entered the bush, and threw his right back to the road These companies were exposed to a heavy fire; and Lieutenant Sherston, one of Sotheby's subalterns, was very severely wounded through the right shoulder. Captain Cary was sent up to support a native company of the left wing on the left of Egginassie; but on Major Stephens reporting to Sir Garnet Wolseley that there was a gap between the left and centre columns, which ought to be filled, Lieutenant Taylor, with part of Cary's company, was sent to fill it up, while Captain Cary himself with the remainder moved towards the left flank, to support the native troops, which were hard pressed Captain Lascelles was directed by Sir Garnet Wolseley to take his company to occupy some heights to the north of Egginassie, and so to connect Wood's natives with the path. He passed through the bush, which had been partially cleared round the village by the Engineer labourers, and took up this position, extending three sections, and keeping the fourth in support under Lieutenant the Honourable E Noel[1]

Soon afterwards Sir Archibald Alison, who was in the front with the 42nd, asked for 'a support of half a Battalion of Rifles' The half-Battalion being, as we have seen, 'otherwise engaged,' Captain Somerset's company was sent forward by the road or path to him. Starting at the double, this company advanced to the swamp about half a mile in front, where Sir Archibald had fought his way with the 42nd. Here Somerset found Sir Archibald Alison, with the detachment of the 23rd Fusiliers, awaiting his arrival. The company was posted here to keep up communication with the rear, and to advance when required. Sir Archibald crossed the marsh with the Fusiliers, and advanced towards Amoaful. Somerset's company remained in this position till nearly the close of the day, keeping communication with the Fusiliers, who were some hundred yards to their north, and furnishing occasional escorts to staff officers passing along the path Somerset's men were exposed to the fire of Ashantees, who, creeping up to the edge of the bush, discharged their pieces at them. By

[1] This was in every case the position of all these companies of Riflemen acting more or less independently in this fight. a section at least being held in reserve while the greater part extended in skirmishing order

this fire Lieutenant Smyth was wounded in the thigh, and two other Riflemen were hit. But the Riflemen soon silenced this annoying fire; Sergeant Bills especially making good use of his rifle

But before Captain Somerset's company had moved up to the front, about twenty Riflemen had been detached from it, and attached to Major Nicholl's company, which, as we have seen, was on the right, supporting the Naval Brigade and the native levies under Colonel Wood. By noon the Ashantees had been driven from the ridge which they occupied beyond the stream, their camp had been taken, and the village of Amoaful carried by the 42nd Regiment. The direction of the combat was now changed; and, as far as the front and left faces of the square formation were concerned, it had terminated, and the fire, which had been kept up without cessation from eight in the morning, was now lulled. But about one it began again, and the brunt of the fight now fell on the Riflemen; for the Ashantees, pursuing their usual tactics, swept round and fell on the right flank and rear, attacking the village of Eggmassie on the north-east.

About one o'clock the fire was renewed Captain Cope's company was sent into the village, and lined one side; and Captain Cary, with a portion of his company, was sent through Eggmassie, and extended to the east of it. This attack of the Ashantees was most determined; they came up in numbers, and were shot down by the Riflemen. The din was tremendous Besides volleys and file-firing, and the heavy report of the Ashantee guns, tom-toms, horns, and the yells of the Ashantees and of the native troops, made the bush and all the surroundings hideous. In this fire a man of Cary's company was shot in the face by a slug fired by an Ashantee in a tree, but two of his comrades soon brought his assailant down, and killed him After about an hour of this work, during which the Ashantees kept up a fire as continuous and heavy as it had been during any part of the fight, their fire slackened. Then an advance was made by Major Sotheby's and Captain H Lascelles' companies, and part of Captain Cary's The line advanced towards the north-east up the valley; and pivoting on the left, bringing up the right, moved forward to the edge of a clearing, which had been made by the right column.

'This was admirably executed Skirmishing as quietly and steadily as if on parade, the men of the Rifle Brigade searched every bush with their bullets, and in five minutes from the commencement of the advance the Ashantees were in full and final retreat' [1]

The Ashantees having been thus driven from the high ground to the northward of Egginassie, Captains Lascelles' and Cary's companies were withdrawn, and passing by their left, regained the main path, and by it the village of Egginassie, which they at once began to entrench and fortify; the other portion of Cary's company, which had been detached under Lieutenant Taylor, being called in to assist in this work.

But the day was not over for the Riflemen Hardly had the firing lulled about Egginassie, when heavy firing was heard in the rear. A large force of Ashantees, sweeping round from the west, had attacked Quarman, about a mile to the south, on the line of communication, which was held by a detachment of the 2nd West India Regiment, and a few Europeans, under Captain Burnett, of the 15th Foot. Captain Dugdale's company, which formed the rear-guard of the Battalion, was at once ordered to Quarman, and on the way was somewhat exposed to the fire of the detachment there, who did not know of his approach to relieve them, and whose bullets whistled over the heads of the Riflemen as they passed through some low ground on the way. The bush had been cleared round Quarman, and Dugdale at once extended his company, and drove the Ashantees who were attacking it back into the bush with considerable loss He then entered the village, and being senior officer assumed the command. The position was very important, for it connected the front at Egginassie and Amoaful with Insarfu Soon after Dugdale had entered Quarman, Captain Slade's company, under Lieutenant the Honourable T. Scott,[2] joined him The attack was soon renewed; the Ashantees now not venturing into the clearing, but firing from the surrounding bush. This attack had just been repulsed, when Major Sotheby with his company reached Quarman. He had started from Egginassie, escorting a long

[1] Henty's 'March to Coomassie,' 384.

[2] Captain Slade had been sent back sick from Foomanah

train of hammocks containing wounded, and also some wounded men who were able to walk, and had passed through Quarman on his way to Insarfu, when he heard firing in his rear. Colonel Colley, who was passing through Quarman at this time, directed Captain Dugdale to take his company out; who, marching about half a mile towards Egginassie, and turning into the bush, outflanked the Ashantees, and fired several volleys which effectually drove them off. Major Sotheby, finding that Quarman was again attacked, turned back when near Insarfu His bearers flung down the wounded, and fled into the village Colonel Colley was also attacked as he was bringing up a convoy from Insarfu As soon as Dugdale knew of this attack, he detached Scott with his company to help him. The enemy occupied the side of the path and kept up a heavy fire, wounding two of Scott's men However, he kept up the fight till after six, when, as it was getting dark, Dugdale recalled him to Quarman, which these two companies occupied during the night. Thus Dugdale had saved and retained this important post, connecting the front with Insarfu, whence the supplies were to be drawn, and to which the wounded were to be escorted.[1]

Major Sotheby, finding that it was considered of importance that ammunition should be conveyed to the front from Insarfu, left that place about eight in the evening with his company, and having some carriers with him picked up some of the baggage abandoned by the cowardly bearers, and having parked it at Quarman, reached Egginassie at eleven at night. Here the Head-quarters and, on Sotheby's arrival, six companies of the Battalion were camped. For Somerset's company had been about six o'clock withdrawn from the marsh to higher ground in the rear, and had, with Nicholl's company, rejoined the Battalion about eight, while Cary's, Lascelles', and Cope's companies, after their fight, were employed in clearing the bush about Egginassie. This was very

[1] It is impossible to record this affair at Quarman without noticing that Captain Dugdale remains without any official recognition of his services on this occasion, while the officer whom he so materially assisted, or rather extricated from his dangerous position at Quarman, received the brevet of Major, Captain Dugdale obtained no promotion The former had then not thirteen years service; Dugdale had served nearly twenty years, and I have on more than one occasion noted in this record his services during the Indian mutiny. As promotion was

hard work. The men and officers had no food but the biscuit and sausage issued the day before, which they carried in their pockets But happily there was no hot sun, so that the Riflemen were able to clear a considerable space, and to throw up a breast-work Three officers, Major Stephens, Lieutenants Smyth and Sherston, and 6 Riflemen, were wounded on this day.

The main position of the Ashantees on this day was at the camp on the ridge north of the stream, which was carried by the 42nd ; and they had other advanced positions and smaller camps on the right and left of the path by which the troops advanced Their design seems to have been, while holding their main position, to turn the flanks and attack the rear. Directly the advance was made on the main position, the Ashantees attacked in strength against the left ; failing in this they fell on the right, and made a furious effort to get to Egginassie and so to establish themselves in rear Foiled at all these points, they attempted to capture Quarman, and cut the line of supplies. This attack was repelled by Captain Dugdale and his company

Though the central column forced the Ashantee camp and took the village of Amoaful, and so had the most conspicuous share in the events of the day, yet before the fight was over almost all the troops were engaged more or less , the Riflemen heavily and successfully before the close of it.

Six companies, as I have said, camped at Egginassie, Captain Lascelles' company being on outlying picquet ; and two occupied Quarman

During the night a panic took place among the native carriers, for a native sentry on outpost duty having fired his piece about four in the morning, the carriers were terrified. One officer was awakened by these cowards jumping over him ; another sleeping in a hammock was overset by them They knocked down the piled rifles, and were running in every direction in abject and contemptible terror. At last order was restored

dealt out with no unsparing hand for the Ashantee campaign, this neglect seems the more remarkable I may add that I make these remarks on the facts which I have recorded without any communication with Captain Dugdale, with whom, indeed, I am scarcely acquainted.

On February 1 the six companies of the Battalion at Egginassie were extended to line the road from that village to Insarfu (the 42nd continuing the line from Egginassie to Amoaful) in order to allow supplies to be brought up from Insarfu to the front On the same day the village of Becqua was destroyed by some of the other troops. In this affair the Battalion was to have been employed; but orders had been given to Colonel Warren as soon as he had assembled his six companies at Egginassie to ascertain if there was any force of Ashantees in the bush near the road between Quarman and Insarfu, and if they were found, to clear the bush with his Riflemen. No enemy were there; but in consequence of this delay, the Battalion did not reach Amoaful till after one o'clock, at which hour the expedition to Becqua had started. Part of the 42nd were therefore substituted for the Riflemen.

On their arrival at Amoaful they remained under arms in the broad street or central place until the destruction of Becqua was ascertained Then they were dismissed; and, after assisting in burying the dead Ashantees, encamped.

On the 2nd the Battalion advanced, Lord Gifford and his scouts preceding with some native troops, Captain Cary's company guarded Captain Rait's guns, and Captain Lascelles' company was in support. These formed the advanced guard under Colonel M'Leod The Battalion followed, Captain Somerset's company forming an escort to Sir Archibald Alison The other regiments brought up the rear. They moved off between six and seven o'clock, and soon came up with the rear of the Ashantees, on whom the native troops immediately opened fire, but with so little effect that Colonel M'Leod halted them and brought up Cary's company to the front But the enemy made no stand, merely firing wildly and then flying. The road was strewed with food, clothing, and weapons, evidencing the precipitate flight of the enemy. On the march, Cary's company still leading, the Riflemen passed through three villages and a camp all deserted by the Ashantees; though in some fires still burning and cooking materials at hand showed how short a time they had been abandoned As a flank attack was not unlikely, Somerset's company was extended and searched the forest paths on each side of the road. Sir Archibald Alison, as whose escort they had acted, signified through Captain Robinson, his Brigade-Major, his marked approval of the way in which they had skirmished, and of the individual intelligence of these Riflemen.

The Battalion reached Aggemamu, a distance of eight miles, about three in the afternoon, and halted there.

But Cary's and Lascelles' companies were pushed on about two miles and a half to the village of Adwabin, which they occupied.

Sir Garnet Wolseley having resolved to take on his forces to Coomassie as a flying column, determined to leave his baggage at Aggemamu, and to make that place a temporary base, through which his communications might be kept open with the rear The Battalion was therefore ordered to find a captain to take charge of this post, and the duty fell to Captain Cope. At Aggemamu the roads to Coomassie bifurcate; one leading to the right or east, and one the longer, but it was reported the best road, forking to the left. This Sir Garnet resolved to follow.

'The importance of Aggemamu could scarcely be over-estimated. From it two roads led to Coomassie, by the longer of which we were about to march, disregarding the shorter or easternmost of the two. It was of course of vital importance that the point at the junction of the roads should be securely held, as a base for our flying column, and as a point of support upon which, if necessary, to fall back'[1]

Lieutenants Bell and Hare, with native labourers, were engaged in the evening of this day, under the superintendence of Captain Home, in making a clearing round Aggemamu.

Sir Garnet Wolseley having thus determined to push on to Coomassie without *impedimenta*, enquired of the soldiers on this evening whether, as it might take six days to advance to Coomassie and to return to Aggemamu, and there were but four days' rations in hand, they were willing to do the six days' work on four days' rations The response was a unanimous assent. The General told them at the same time that they might probably get a fortnight sooner to the coast by this sacrifice than if they halted at Aggemamu for further supplies to come up. Eventually one day's additional ration of preserved meat, biscuit, and tea, came up.

[1] 'The Ashantee War,' by Captain Brackenbury, ii. 199.

On the 3rd the Battalion started at half-past five, Major Nicholl's company leading, and on reaching Adwabin, the advanced guard, with which were Cary's and Lascelles' companies which had passed the night there, were pushed forward They soon felt the enemy, with whom they became engaged about half-past eight. The first point at which he made a decided stand was in a hollow through which flowed a stream, a tributary of the Oidah The overloaded guns of the Ashantees carrying high, they chose positions, as in this case, below the attacking force. They were in cover behind a large fallen tree from which they kept up a heavy fire Nicholl's company was sent forward to reinforce the two companies already with the advance. On the road was a gun with an escort of part of Lascelles' company and some natives. On the left of the road was the remainder of Lascelles' company and Cary's ; further on the left was Nicholl's company, part advanced beyond the stream and part on its left bank. Lieutenant the Honourable T Scott's company was afterwards moved up in support, and these four companies were hotly engaged at this point, when about noon a flag of truce came in, and the firing ceased on our side, though the Ashantees continued their fire and actually wounded a native while the envoy was being passed to Head-quarters. However, his mission was fruitless, and he was very soon passed beyond the front. The fire was then renewed, and eventually slackened after lasting for about five hours. The advance then pushed on followed by the other troops ; but the progress was slow ; for the Ashantees, finding we could beat them fighting in the bush, now tried ambuscades, and a good many men were thus wounded. The other troops followed the advanced guard, which about three o'clock in the afternoon reached the bank of the river Oidah, here about three feet deep and forty yards wide Here they hutted themselves ; Captain Dugdale's company being on picquet.

In this affair eight Riflemen were wounded. The men carried their great-coats, which they found an incumbrance in skirmishing in the bush, and on the next day they were handed over to the carriers. Colonel M'Leod, who commanded the advance, praised the manner in which Cary's company had fought on this day.

Some captive Ashantees had stated that 10,000 of the enemy were around, and every precaution was taken to protect the camp from a sudden assault. A chain of sentries was posted at twenty yards apart at about 100 yards from the camp. A tremendous thunderstorm came on about six in the evening and lasted till two in the morning The Riflemen had indeed built huts, but as no banana, plantain, or palm leaves were at hand to thatch them, they afforded a very insufficient shelter against the storm However a cask of rum was brought in about three, and a ration of that spirit helped to revive the soldiers, while fires were lit to dry their clothes.

Meanwhile the Engineers and blue jackets had been busy in making a narrow bridge over the river, which was ready for their advance in the morning.

Accordingly, about seven in the morning of the 4th, the force crossed the bridge, the advance was led by some native troops; a gun with some rockets followed, with three companies of the Battalion, Captain Cope's commanded in his absence at Aggemamu by Lieutenant Stopford-Sackville, Captain Slade's under Lieutenant the Honourable T. Scott, and Major Sotheby's This advance was under the command of Colonel M'Leod. The rest of the troops followed, the remaining companies of the Battalion leading. Soon after passing the bridge the native troops became actively engaged. But as the native soldiers were firing wildly and ineffectively, Colonel M'Leod halted them, and passed Sackville's company through them to the front, and ordered him to extend to the right of the road The gun was also brought up with Scott's company in support on the road. As the first company was extending two or three men were wounded. One, Brown, was badly hit in the side, but refused for some time to go to the rear, and went on skirmishing. The road or path rose from the river, and after running for some distance along a ridge with ravines on each side, descended again, and finally rose to the village of Ordahsu. The gun having been brought up was fired up the road and into the bush on each side. It was advanced gradually by the native bearers as ground was gained, the Riflemen in support lying down on each side of it while it was in action, and then with it resuming the advance.

Colonel M'Leod had asked for and obtained a reinforcement of three companies of the Battalion, and Captain Cary's company was extended in the bush on the right of Sackville's. Sotheby's company was also sent by Colonel M'Leod into the bush on the left of the road.

Major Stephens with Scott's company pushed steadily on by the road, one section of this company supporting the gun. At last they reached the clearing which surrounded the village of Ordahsu. 'Then the Rifles gave a cheer, and with a sudden rush cleared the way to the open, and carried the village without a check.'[1] This was Scott's company, or part of it; and Lieutenant Harington, with the remainder, swept round the edge of the clearing, and having thus outflanked the Ashantees in the village, also rushed into it. The village was held by fifty or sixty of the enemy, who fought bravely, and were most of them killed. Major Stephens, with Scott and his portion of the company, passed through the village and to the edge of the clearing beyond it where the Riflemen lying down kept up a constant fire on the enemy. Sackville also brought up his company, one section being still with the gun, and as Scott's party had purposely left the road clear the gun made good practice to the front. It was afterwards taken forward beyond the village to where Major Stephens, with Scott and his party, were, and a heavy fire of shell and of rockets was kept up. The Ashantees here made a most determined resistance, coming up to the very edge of the clearing and discharging their pieces. Sackville shot one with one of the men's rifles. Meanwhile Major Sotheby was steadily advancing through the bush on the left of the road, and soon came up on the left of Scott's company. Here Private Taylor of Sotheby's company observed a chief and two other Ashantees in a tree about fifteen yards from him. He shot one man, and the other fled into the bush. The chief tried to hide himself in the leaves, and brought up his piece to his shoulder; but Taylor was too quick for him, and rushing up, ran him through with his sword before he could fire. For this act of valour Taylor received the medal for gallant conduct in the field.

Cary's company had at the same time been advancing on

[1] Henty's 'March to Coomassie,' 401

the extreme right, and was engaged in keeping back the Ashantees who were pressing on to the east of the village. This company was afterwards moved over to the left of the village, and the ground between it and Sotheby's on the extreme left was occupied by Captain Somerset's company; which, as well as Major Nicholl's, Captain Lascelles', and Captain Dugdale's, had been pushed on to Ordahsu.

It was now after eleven, and a halt was ordered, in order (it is said) that the baggage might be brought up to the village, and disposition made for its defence. But the enemy, who had been held or driven back until then, at once made a fresh and furious attack, rushing up as before to the very edge of the bush, shouting and yelling, and opening a very heavy fire. The Riflemen who were standing in the village or sheltering from the sun under the trees were at once extended, Dugdale's company on the right, and Nicholl's on the left of the village.

Sir Archibald Alison, considering that it would take too much time to withdraw the Riflemen from the bush round the village, and that as the enemy were making a vigorous attack it would be difficult to do so, brought up the 42nd to the front by the road the Riflemen had won, and were still guarding. The leading companies of the Riflemen, on seeing the 42nd advancing, sprang up, believing that a general advance was to be made, and were most anxious to push forward; but they were stopped by Colonel M'Leod, who advanced with his own regiment, the 42nd. But little more was done The Ashantees had had enough of it, and though the 42nd received some fire by which a few men were wounded, the enemy made no further stand in the front

Scott, with his company, followed the 42nd. And Lascelles and Sackville also advanced. And the firing about Ordahsu gradually ceased.

In these five hours' fighting the Battalion had 17 men wounded. Four officers were also hit: Major Sotheby in the face, Sackville in the leg, Scott on the right breast, and Surgeon Wiles. Sergeant-Major Stretch was also slightly wounded. But these officers, not wishing to add up a great list of casualties or to parade their wounds, were not reported as wounded, but went on with their work. One Sergeant

(Sumner) was missing. In the hard fighting between the river and Ordahsu he had sent two men to the rear with a wounded comrade; and probably in the gap thus formed in extended order the Ashantees had rushed in and killed him. He was never afterwards heard of.

Sir Archibald Alison, in a dispatch dated Ahkankuassie, February 9, 1874, thus speaks of the conduct of the Battalion at Ordahsu: 'This was the first day upon which (with the exception of one company) I had the pleasure of seeing the Rifle Brigade in action under my orders. It is needless for me to speak of the steadiness and high discipline of the Rifle Brigade; but I must express my satisfaction at the way in which they were handled by Lieutenant-Colonel Warren, and under him by Major Stephens and Major Glyn.

'On every occasion when I had an opportunity of seeing it, I had to remark on the excellent way in which the company officers commanded their companies.'

The Riflemen were much fatigued by their five or six hours' hard and incessant fighting under an African sun, and hungry too; for only a little biscuit had been served out, and few of them had had a meat ration the day before. But Coomassie was to be reached, and they pressed on from Ordahsu. Two rivers were forded in the way, and at the entrance of the town the road was through a marsh, and was covered with filthy water. At last Coomassie was entered about half-past five Many Ashantees were hanging about, watching the entrance of the English force, but they offered no resistance. Indeed, their courage did not then seem great. For the Battalion on marching in had formed quarter-distance column. When they were to wheel into line, of course they opened out to company-distance on the leading company. But this simple parade manœuvre struck terror into the surrounding Ashantees, who ran back as the rear companies retired.

When the line was formed, Sir Garnet Wolseley rode to the front, and three cheers were given for the Queen, which added wings to the flight of the gazing Ashantees. It was now nearly dark, and after the ceremony, the Riflemen were dismissed, and quarters told off to them, with orders not to leave their quarters, and to be ready to turn out at a moment's warning. A meat ration was served out, but many of the Riflemen were too tired to cook it. Captain Cary's company, made up to a hundred men by Riflemen of Captain Somerset's company, formed a guard over the King's palace. Captain Brackenbury was the staff officer appointed to accompany Captain Cary with orders for this guard. 'Some idea,' he says, 'of the size of the building, and of its irregularity, may be gained from the fact that we posted thirteen sentries in such positions that they were only just able to protect all the inlets to the building. After having apparently been all round the building once, we again marched round to see whether a sentry could not be economised; and though in one place we were enabled to remove one, we found that the whole of a long gallery, evidently the women's quarters, had been omitted, and we had to place another at the entrance of this. The guard of 100 men was placed in the great central court.'[1]

Captain Dugdale was the prize Commissioner on behalf of the European troops, and he and the other Commissioners worked all night in securing what articles of value they could find in the palace, or the carriers at their disposal enabled them to remove. Here were found, among other curious and costly articles, the gold masks, of which the 2nd Battalion subsequently purchased and possess one.

In the course of the night fires broke out in two or three places in Coomassie, which were kindled by the native followers, who were prowling about and plundering. Many of the Riflemen were turned out to assist in putting out these fires, and were engaged from two till four in the morning in assisting the Engineers to pull down houses and to extinguish the flames. This was hard work on the soldiers after their hard fight and march of the day before. One section of each company was ordered not to take their belts off, but to be ready to turn out instantly in case of an attack. In the course of the night the palace guard captured an Ashantee chief, who was endeavouring to escape with gold dust, nuggets, and jewels about him.

On the 5th the Battalion paraded at ten o'clock in the street of Coomassie. The wounded were sent down, escorted

[1] 'The Ashantee War,' ii. 236.

by Cope's company, under Lieutenant Sackville, and some native troops.

On the 6th the Battalion paraded at half-past six, and marched out of Coomassie about an hour afterwards. The palace was to be blown up, and the town burned. As soon as the Engineers reported that all was ready at the palace, the guard of the Rifle Brigade was marched off, with orders to rejoin its Battalion, and orders were given for the palace to be blown up.

Heavy rains had now set in. The marsh at the entrance of the town was knee deep, and the rivers, trifling streams on the march up, were now wide torrents, five feet deep in mid-channel The Engineers made a bridge with a felled tree, but the men had often to wade, almost waist deep. On arrival at Ordah about three in the afternoon, the bridge was found to be submerged some two or three feet deep, and the Riflemen had to wade across it. This was so slow a process that the rear companies did not get over till six. The Battalion then camped on the ground it had occupied on the 3rd.

They started at a quarter-past six on the morning of the 7th, and marched to Aggemamu. The stream before entering this village had been bridged over by Captain Cope, and steps had been cut by him in the steep path ascending from it.

We left him detailed to the charge of Aggemamu on the 2nd He had with him 17 sick or weakly Riflemen, and 15 sick men of the other regiments, 100 native troops, 50 or 60 labourers, under a sergeant of Engineers, a few native police, and 5 officers. But the men were so ill, that had he been attacked, he could barely have mustered 20 Europeans fit to fight. As soon as the force had marched, he set to work to make his post defensible. He pulled down the greater part of the village, keeping only a small square of houses, which he loop-holed; and built small redoubts and a kind of redan at the fork of the roads, in which he placed his native soldiers. He brought the baggage into his enclosure, and, indeed, used some of it in building his defences. In levelling the outside of the village, the native labourers most foolishly, and in direct violation of his orders, set fire to some houses. The fire came raging towards the intrenchment; but he happily succeeded in making a gap, and thus saving the stockade and the baggage from the flames Scouts informed him that the Ashantees were in force all round, and that he would most probably be attacked After the troops had left, he heard heavy firing in front, and his patrols brought in a prisoner, who stated that the king would fight at Kasie.

On the 4th he still continued his work of fortifying his post. No news came to him from the front, but heavy firing was heard to the north and north-west. Five prisoners were brought in. On the 5th he went on with his work, and sent some of his blacks out into the woods to gather plantains for food, thus utilising them as outposts; for on the approach of an enemy they would have fled back, and given the earliest intimation of danger. He was short of rations too, and was obliged to keep his men on half-rations He had another cause of anxiety, besides being without any intelligence from the front: that though the road was clear to the rear, no convoy of provisions came up; and he feared the troops on their return from Coomassie might find Aggemamu unprovisioned. He sent out a reconnaissance of 30 men, under Lieutenant de Hoghton, 10th Foot, who went three miles along the right-hand road, and brought in a good deal of corn. They burned a large village, but saw no Ashantees.

At last, in the middle of the night between the 5th and 6th, Colonel Colley came in from the front, 'in thunder, lightning, and in rain,' with intelligence of the proceedings of the last three days. This was the first communication Cope had received from the front since the troops left Aggemamu on the morning of the 3rd. It was a most anxious time; but his exertions were rewarded, for 'Sir Garnet on his return complimented Captain Cope much on the measures he had taken for defence; and added that they were so good that he could not have wished him better fortune than to have been attacked.'[1]

'We found,' says Colonel Brackenbury, 'that a perfect fortress had been constructed by Captain Cope, which would have defied the attacks of an army In the execution of his duty he had spared no person and no thing; and we shall not soon forget the despairing face of one non-combatant officer,

[1] 'Colburn's United Service Magazine,' September, 1874, p 74

who with tears in his eyes complained that his baggage had been built into the fortification, and that he was told he could not have it out.'[1]

In the same way Mr. Henty observes, 'I found [Aggemamu] changed beyond recognition; the whole place, in fact, having been levelled with the ground, except the principal group of houses, which had upon the way up been used as Head-quarters These had been loop-holed, and formed an interior citadel, which could have been defended by the garrison had the breast-work round the village been carried.'[2]

On Colonel Colley's information that the force was on its way back, Captain Cope set his people to build huts for the troops.

On the same day his company came in as escort to the wounded, and on the 7th proceeded to Biposu, and on the 8th to Ahkankuassie. On that day he started from Aggemamu with the Naval Brigade; and leaving them at Amoaful, pressed on and joined his company at Ahkankuassie. This was a march of about eighteen miles, a long one in that climate.

On the 11th he crossed the Prah. And on the 12th reached Barracoo with his convoy, who were thence to proceed by forced marches to Cape Coast, while he was ordered to take his company down by the regular marches by which they had come up to this point. Accordingly he reached Cape Coast at about half-past eight on the morning of the 19th, and at once embarked in surf-boats, and got on board the 'Himalaya' at half-past nine, where his company awaited the arrival of the Battalion.

They had moved from the camp at the Ordah as I have stated on the 7th, and marched to Aggemamu; whence, after a few hours' halt, Captain Somerset's company was sent forward as an escort of sick to Amoaful. But the convoy being large, and the progress slow, night fell while they were still some miles from Amoaful. And the road being bad, and the night very dark, great difficulty was experienced in getting through the forest.[3]

[1] 'The Ashantee War,' ii 246.
[2] 'March to Coomassie,' 417
[3] This difficulty is graphically described by Mr Henty, p 419

On the 8th the Battalion left Aggemamu, and proceeding by daily marches, with the same halting or camping-stages as on going up the country, reached Cape Coast Castle at six in the morning of the 22nd, where they embarked immediately on board the 'Himalaya.' The whole Battalion, with its baggage, was on board by half-past seven. The total strength of the Battalion on embarkation (including Captain Cope's company, which was already on board) was 22 officers, and 408 non-commissioned officers and private Riflemen, of whom only 16 officers and 277 of other ranks were reported as 'fit for duty.'[1]

The casualties of the campaign may be thus summarised:

	Officers	Non-commissioned officers and privates
Landed at Cape Coast Castle, fit for duty	33	652
Wounded	3	30
Died of wounds		2
Admitted in hospital while on the Coast	22	298
Invalided to England	3	47
Left sick on board the 'Victor Emmanuel'		42
Left sick at Gibraltar		48
Died on passage home		3
Landed in England	27	483[2]

Nor is this statement by any means a perfect record of what the Battalion suffered from this deadly climate. After their return to England, and even after their arrival at Gibraltar, many officers and men suffered from the effects of their African campaign, and some men died.

On the 23rd the 'Himalaya' sailed for England at six in the morning.

On March 4 she arrived at St. Vincent, where she remained till the 7th. On the 16th the green clothing was taken into wear again, and on the next day the 'Himalaya' arrived at Gibraltar. Here the Battalion was welcomed by Major-

[1] I derive the particulars of the Ashantee Expedition from the letters and journal of my son, Captain Cope; from three papers ('The Rifle Brigade in the Ashantee Expedition') in 'Colburn's United Service Journal,' July–September, 1874, and from a detailed MS Memoir on the Battle of Amoaful, kindly communicated to me by Major Robinson, Rifle Brigade, who has also favoured me with the plan.

[2] Of these ten men were at once sent to Netley Hospital.

General Somerset, an old Rifleman, who came off to see them, and during their stay showed them every attention. They left Gibraltar on the 20th. These stoppages had been made, and the rate of speed diminished purposely, in order not to bring the men from so hot a climate into the coldest portion of an English spring.

However, the 'Himalaya' reached Spithead about half-past two in the morning of the 26th. She came into harbour in the forenoon, the crews of the various ships manned the yards and cheered, their bands playing 'Ninety-five' The Battalion landed at the Dock-yard Wharf about half-past one, many officers of the 1st Battalion (then stationed in the Gosport Forts) and some old Riflemen being assembled to greet them. They marched thence through streets decorated with flags, and every disposable expression of welcome, to the 'Governor's Green,' where they were welcomed by Lieutenant-General Lord Templetown, Commanding at Portsmouth, the Mayor, and others Thence they marched to the station, where a repast had been provided for them. They left by special train for Winchester, where an ovation awaited them. A welcome from the Mayor and Corporation at the railway station; streets decorated with every flag, flower, and allusive ornament that could be put into requisition; and escorts of County Yeomanry and City Volunteers.

On the 28th the Battalion was inspected by His Royal Highness the Duke of Cambridge, who expressed himself much satisfied with the appearance of the Battalion. After they had marched past and formed square, His Royal Highness addressed some kind words to them; congratulating them on their conduct in the field and on their endurance on the march to and from Coomassie, adding that from what he then saw of their appearance, he considered that they were even now fit to go anywhere.

On the 30th the Battalion proceeded to Windsor, where the troops which had been employed in the Ashantee expedition were reviewed by Her Majesty the Queen The Prince of Wales (Colonel-in-Chief) and His Royal Highness Prince Arthur met the Battalion at the Windsor Station, and in a few kindly words the Colonel-in-Chief welcomed the Battalion home. His Royal Highness marched past at the head of the

Battalion. Sir Archibald Alison also addressed the Riflemen, and complimented them on the soldierlike qualities they had shown in the field while under his orders. The Battalion returned to Winchester that night at nine by rail.

Sir Archibald Alison issued the following order on resigning command of the Brigade After stating that he had amply complimented the 42nd Regiment in an order on board the 'Sarmatian' on his return voyage, he proceeds: 'Before now taking leave of the other regiments of the Brigade, he desires to express to Lieutenant-Colonel Mostyn, commanding 23rd Royal Welsh Fusiliers, and to Lieutenant-Colonel Warren, commanding 2nd Battalion Rifle Brigade, his appreciation of the gallantry displayed by their regiments in the field, and his perfect satisfaction with the excellent conduct which characterised them in camp and on the line of march. No words of his could convey more to these regiments than that, in his opinion, they fully sustained at Amoaful and Ordahsu, and throughout the campaign, the historical reputation with which they entered it In resigning his connection with the Brigade, the Brigadier-General desires to express his warm acknowledgment of the consistent support he has received from all ranks.'

An order was also received from His Royal Highness the Field-Marshal Commanding-in-Chief, conveying Her Majesty's approval of the conduct of her troops engaged on the Gold Coast.

On May 16 Sergeant Armstrong and Private Taylor received the Medal for distinguished conduct in the field from the hands of the Queen at Windsor; the former for having with some unarmed natives repelled an attack, and having himself killed two Ashantees on February 2, in the advance from Amoaful; and Taylor for his gallant conduct at Ordahsu, which I have already mentioned.

On May 19 the Battalion, consisting of 20 officers and 493 of other ranks, left Winchester at half-past five in the morning, by rail for Aldershot, and took part, with the 1st and 3rd Battalions, in a review before the Czar of Russia. They returned to Winchester the same evening, arriving at ten o'clock.

On October 24 the Battalion was armed with the Martini-Henry rifle.

They received orders to prepare for embarkation for Gibraltar, and two companies were selected to form the Depôt.

On November 7 Captain Dugdale's company embarked on board Her Majesty's Troop-ship 'Tamar' for Gibraltar. And on the 16th and 17th the remaining companies of the Battalion embarked at Portsmouth on board Her Majesty's Troop-ship 'Simoom,' and sailed for Gibraltar, where they arrived on the 24th, and on disembarkation were encamped at the North front until the 28th, when they moved to Buena Vista barracks, and were there quartered.

The total strength on disembarkation was 18 officers, 40 sergeants, 40 corporals, 17 buglers, and 585 private Riflemen.

The 3rd Battalion moved from Winchester and Portsmouth by rail-road on March 13, and occupied quarters in the Permanent barracks with the 1st Battalion. They took part in the summer drills held this year in June and July, and were encamped at Woolmer forest from the 20th to the 29th of the latter month. During the June drills the Battalion, with the 1st Battalion, one of the 60th, and a Militia battalion, formed a brigade commanded by Lord Alexander Russell.

The 4th Battalion remained at Umballa during this year, with the exception that, in consequence of an outbreak of fever at Umballa, they were moved out under canvas to camp at Jundlee, and afterwards nearer Umballa, from November 18 to December 12.

On February 24 and 25 they had been inspected by Major-General Percy Hill, and on August 8 by Lord Napier of Magdala, Commander-in-Chief in India.

The 1st Battalion continued at Winchester during the year 1875, moving to Aldershot for the summer manœuvres.

The 2nd Battalion remained at Gibraltar during the whole of the year.

Lieutenant-Colonel Nixon, commanding the 3rd Battalion, died near Aldershot on March 31, 1875. He had served in the Regiment twenty-eight years, and had accompanied the 2nd Battalion to the Crimea and India, and I have recorded his services and gallantry at Cawnpore and Lucknow, and with the Camel Corps, and the approval of those in command which they elicited. He was deservedly and universally esteemed by his brother officers, and his sudden premature death excited sincere regret. His funeral on April 5, at Hale Church, near Aldershot, was attended not only by the officers of the 1st Battalion, who also sent their band from Winchester, but by many old Riflemen. He was succeeded in the command of the Battalion by Lieutenant-Colonel Maclean, who was promoted from Senior Major.

This Battalion, after taking part in the summer drill and manœuvres near Aldershot in the months of June and July, including a review and march-past for the Sultan of Zanzibar before his Royal Highness the Prince of Wales, left Aldershot on July 27 for Chatham, where it occupied St. Mary's barracks, detaching (in November) one company to Upnor Castle.

The 4th Battalion left Umballa on March 3 for Delhi, where it arrived on the 13th, and formed part of the Governor-General, Lord Northbrook's, camp, during the durbar held there. It returned to Umballa on the 30th.

On the approach of the visit of the Prince of Wales to India, the 4th Battalion again marched from Umballa on November 26, and arrived at Delhi on December 8, in order to take part in the manœuvres to take place there during the Prince's stay. While His Royal Highness the Colonel-in-Chief was at Delhi, the Battalion furnished a personal guard of honour of 100 men, and on his visit to Agra a similar guard of honour accompanied him. After the review and march-past on January 12, 1876, the Prince gave a dinner to the men of both his regiments, the 10th Hussars and the 4th Battalion, on the 16th, and dined at the mess of the Battalion on the 13th.

The 1st Battalion left Winchester by rail-road on June 6, 1876, and embarking at Portsmouth on board the 'Simoom' Troop-ship, started on the same day for Dublin, where they arrived on the 9th, and occupy the Royal barracks, having a present strength of

Officers.	Sergeants.	Buglers.	Corporals	Privates.
33	46	18	40	758

The 2nd Battalion remain at Gibraltar, their strength being

Officers.	Sergeants.	Buglers.	Rank and File
33	39	17	624[1]

The 3rd Battalion left Chatham by rail-road on July 26, and proceeded to Shorncliffe camp, where they occupy quarters. Their strength on July 28, when inspected by Colonel the Hon. F. Thesiger, commanding that camp (who had served in the Regiment), being:—

Officers.	Sergeants	Buglers.	Rank and file.
30	45	19	528

On the conclusion of the manœuvres and the departure of the Prince of Wales from Delhi, the 4th Battalion returned on January 27 to Umballa, where they continue to be stationed; their strength being on the 1st October

Officers.	Sergeants	Buglers	Corporals.	Privates.
34	49	17	40	801 [1]

On October 7, 1876, His Royal Highness the Duke of Connaught, who had served upwards of four years in the 1st Battalion as Lieutenant and as Captain, and had left it in April 1874, took command of that Battalion at the Royal barracks, Dublin, as Lieutenant-Colonel.

On October 31 it was notified that Her Majesty had been graciously pleased to permit the word 'Ashantee' to be borne on the plates of the pouch-belts.

I have thus inadequately recorded the services of the Regiment, which as the Rifle Corps, as the 95th, and as the Rifle Brigade, has, in the seventy-five years of its existence, served in the field in Spain, Portugal, France, Belgium, Holland, Denmark, Germany, and Russia; in South and Western Africa, in North and South America; and in Asia. In these services it has been engaged in 22 General Actions, 30 Lesser Combats, 11 Sieges or Assaults of fortified places, and in skirmishes and affairs of posts too many to enumerate. In them it has won the commendation of all those commanders

[1] Exclusive of Depôt.

under whom it has served Nor have its discipline and conduct in quarters in more peaceful times less elicited the approbation of Generals who have commanded the stations it has occupied. And if I have not always recorded this, it is because I have been unwilling to load my pages with what no Rifleman can doubt, and what can scarcely interest any other reader.

Of the tone and *prestige* of its officers I need not speak. One honourable fact I must record: No officer of this Regiment has ever been brought to a Court-Martial.

Whatever future services it may be called to, whatever changes regiments or the army may undergo, I am confident that as long as the number 95 or the name Rifle Brigade exist in English Military History, the same love of the green jacket and the same *esprit-de-corps* which have animated its past, and animate its present, will still animate its future members—officers, non-commissioned officers, and private Riflemen.

APPENDIX I.

COLONELS-IN-CHIEF.

Colonel COOTE MANNINGHAM, August 25, 1800.

General SIR DAVID DUNDAS, August 31, 1809.

Field Marshal ARTHUR, DUKE OF WELLINGTON, K G., G.C.B., February 19, 1820.

Field Marshal H.R.H. ALBERT, PRINCE CONSORT, K.G., G C B , September 23, 1852.

Field Marshal JOHN, LORD SEATON, G.C.B., December 15, 1861.

General SIR GEORGE BROWN, G.C.B , April 18, 1863

Field Marshal SIR EDWARD BLAKENEY, G.C.B., August 28, 1865.

Field Marshal H.R.H. ALBERT EDWARD, PRINCE OF WALES, K G., G.C.B., August 3, 1868.

COLONELS COMMANDANT.

FORBES CHAMPAGNÉ, August 31, 1809. To 70th Foot, May 21, 1816

SIR BRENT SPENCER, G.C.B., August 31, 1809. To 40th Foot, July 2, 1818.

Hon. SIR WILLIAM STEWART, G.C.B., August 31, 1809. Died January 7, 1827.

SIR G. T. WALKER, G.C.B (*vice* CHAMPAGNÉ), May 21, 1816 To 34th Foot, May 13, 1820

SIR JOHN OSWALD, K.C.B. (*vice* SPENCER), July 2, 1818.

SIR EDWARD BARNES, K.C.B. (*vice* WALKER), May 13, 1820. To 78th Foot, August 25, 1822.

SIR ANDREW F. BARNARD, G.C.B. (*vice* BARNES), August 25, 1822 Died, January 17, 1855.

SIR T. S. BECKWITH, K.C.B. (*vice* STEWART), January 7, 1827. Died, January 19, 1831.

SIR GEORGE R. BINGHAM, K.C.B. (*vice* BECKWITH), June 18, 1831. Died, June 3, 1833.

SIR J. S. BARNES, K.C.B. (*vice* BINGHAM), January 7, 1833. To 20th Foot, April 25, 1842

SIR D. L. GILMOUR, K.C.B. (*vice* J. S. BARNES), April 25, 1842. Died, March 22, 1847.

SIR HARRY G W. SMITH, G.C.B. (*vice* GILMOUR), April 16, 1847. Died, October 12, 1860.

SIR GEORGE BROWN, G.C.B (*vice* BARNARD), January 18, 1855. To 32nd Foot, April 1, 1863.

SIR GEORGE BULLER, G.C.B. (*vice* SMITH), October 13, 1860

SIR CHARLES YORKE, G.C.B. (*vice* BROWN), April 1, 1863

*** The names in italics are those of officers who had not served in the Regiment

APPENDIX II.

ON THE ARMAMENT OF THE REGIMENT.

On the presentation of the report of Colonels Manningham and Stewart (see p. 1), a committee of field officers was directed to assemble at Woolwich on February 1, 1800, in order to select a rifle to be used by the Rifle Corps. The principal gun-makers in England were invited to attend; and rifles from America, France, Germany, Spain, and Holland were produced and tried. This committee reported in favour of a rifle submitted by Ezekiel Baker, a gun-maker in London, which was adopted for the Rifle Corps, and was known as the 'Baker rifle.' This arm was 2 feet 6 inches long in the barrel; seven-grooved, and rifled one quarter turn, the balls were 20 to the pound, and the weight of the arm was 9½ pounds. It had, of course, a flint lock. It was sighted to 100 yards, and by a folding sight to 200 yards. This rifle was loaded with some difficulty, and at first small wooden mallets were supplied to the Riflemen to assist in ramming down the ball. These were found inconvenient and an incumbrance to the soldier, and were soon discontinued. The Rifle Corps originally carried a horn for powder, as well as the pouch. The Baker rifle had a brass box in the stock to contain the greased rag in which the ball was wrapped.[1] A picker to clear the touch-hole and a brush were also carried by the Riflemen, suspended by brass chains to the waist-belt.

Ezekiel Baker, the inventor of this rifle, published in 1803 a book entitled 'Twenty-two Years' Practice with Rifle Guns,' a tenth edition of which, expanded from 8 pages of the original *brochure* to 238, appeared in 1829. His coloured prints of Riflemen aiming standing, kneeling, lying down on the face, and on the back, are curious, though the costume is rather fanciful. He gives diagrams showing that out of 34 shots at 100 yards with this rifle, 32 penetrated a human figure painted on a 6-ft. target; and of 24 shots at 200 yards, 22 penetrated

[1] The powder horn and the brass box in the stock are shown in Plate I. The Regulations for the exercise of Riflemen, issued in 1803, do not mention the mallet, which had probably been already discontinued; but they do mention 'the powder measure and the loose ball,' *i.e.* the using the powder-horn in loading.

a similar figure. Baker does not mention whether these were fired from the shoulder, or from a fixed rest.

To this rifle a triangular sword bayonet, 17 inches long in the blade, was affixed by a spring.

When the Rifle Corps was first formed, a few rifles were issued to it of the same bore as the musket then in use, viz. 14 balls to the pound; under the impression that there would be an advantage in the Riflemen being able to use the ammunition of soldiers of the line; but this arm was strongly objected to by Colonel Manningham and his officers, and was almost immediately done away with.

Some improvements were subsequently made in the Baker rifle; a chamber was introduced to hold the powder, and a flat-blade sword was substituted for that originally issued. With these and some other trifling changes, the Baker rifle continued till about the year 1837 or 1838 In the year 1836 a Board was assembled at Woolwich to report on various improved rifles. Of this Board Colonel Eeles, then commanding the 1st Battalion, was a member; and Captain Walpole, with a sergeant and twelve Riflemen of that Battalion, was sent to Woolwich to try the rifles submitted to the Board. These men fired daily for some weeks, and eventually the Brunswick rifle was fixed upon for the armament of the Rifle Brigade, and was issued to it (both Battalions being then at home) soon afterwards. This arm was 2 feet 6 inches long in the barrel, which was two-grooved, with complete turn in the length of the barrel, the ball was spherical and belted, and, to ensure the belt dropping into the grooves, two notches were cut at the muzzle. The ball weighed 557 grains, being about 12 to the pound. The rifle weighed nearly 2 pounds more than the Baker, its weight being 11 lbs. $5\frac{1}{2}$ oz. It had a detonating lock; a straight sword, 22 inches long, was affixed to it by a spring. The Brunswick rifle, like the Baker, had a brass box in the stock. It was sighted, by means of a folding sight, to 300 yards; and it was found, in the trials made at Woolwich, that it made as good practice at 300 yards as the Baker at 200.

This rifle continued in use for nearly twenty years; but it was found difficult to load, the belt of the ball being after much firing difficult to force down the grooves; and in action the necessity of fitting the belt to the grooves hindered rapidity of loading, notwithstanding the notches at the muzzle.

While the 1st Battalion were at the Cape, and at the conclusion of the war with the Kaffirs in 1846–7, Lancaster rifles were received at King William's-town for four or six men in each company. These were two-grooved, like the Brunswick, and of the same bore and length They had a patent breech; and were sighted to 900 yards. The ball was conical, with a flat base, and a rib on each side to fit the grooves. It was very heavy, and the flight was found to be uncertain. Nevertheless, these rifles were used with good effect against the Boers at Boem Plaatz, and against the Basutos at Berea. In the Kaffir War of 1851–2, the Riflemen armed with this Lancaster were occasionally formed into a party during night-marches, and on the attacks on the Waterkloof.

On the embarkation of the Regiment for the Crimea the Riflemen were armed with the Minié rifle, not differing from those carried by soldiers of line regiments. And while in the Crimea they received the long Enfield and bayonet, the same as those issued to troops of the line. These long weapons were also issued to the 3rd and 4th Battalions on their being raised. But subsequently, and before the embarkation of the 2nd and 3rd Battalions for India, the short Enfield and the sword was substituted. This was the three-grooved Enfield. But this being found an imperfect weapon, the five-grooved short Enfield, Naval pattern, a much superior arm, was issued to the various Battalions about the years 1861–2.

This continued in use till the issue of five-grooved short Enfields converted to breech-loaders on the Snider principle, which were afterwards replaced by the Snider proper, in 1867. The 4th Battalion, however, had received in 1864 Whitworth rifles in place of the short Enfield, and these were retained until the issue of breech-loaders in 1867.

The Snider was replaced by the Martini-Henry, which was issued to the several Battalions towards the close of the year 1874.

The various changes in the uniform of officers and men are sufficiently indicated by the plates in this volume, taken from the drawings deposited in the Adjutant-General's office, or from original drawings or portraits in my own possession.

The pouch-belt originally had only a whistle and chain affixed to a lion's head. I do not know when the Maltese cross was first adopted, probably when the names of victories were first granted to the Regiment. It was at first surmounted with a sitting figure of Fame; and it appears, from Sir W. Stewart's correspondence, that in 1821 it was in contemplation to replace this (which he calls an Angel) by 'an Eagle, or Britannia, or Minerva, or Amazon.'[1] An Eagle was, I believe, adopted for a time; but the Cross was soon after surmounted with a Royal Crown. When the present Imperial Crown was substituted I do not know. It has been in use, however, for forty years.

[1] Cumloden Papers, 131.

APPENDIX III.

ACTIONS AND CASUALTIES OF THE REGIMENT.

COLONEL LEACH, in concluding his 'Brief Sketch of the Field Services of the Rifle Brigade,' observes:—'I regret exceedingly that I am not in possession of returns of losses sustained by my old Corps in its numerous actions with the enemy, and by sickness. Such a document would have, perhaps, but few (if any) parallels in the Service; and it would be seen, moreover, that the Peninsular army had other formidable enemies to contend with besides the sword, in the form of pestilential fevers, ague, &c.'

No means, I believe, exist of giving any account of the losses of the Regiment by climate or disease; but I will endeavour to give an approximate return of the losses in the field, and at the same time I shall be able to enumerate the various actions in which the Regiment has been engaged.

Date	Action	Officers		Other ranks	
		Killed	Wounded	Killed	Wounded
August 25, 1800	Ferrol	...	1	...	...
August 26, 1800	Ferrol	...	3	...	8
April 2, 1801	Copenhagen	1	...	2	6
January 16, 1807	Maldonado	...	1	1	...
January 20, 1807	Suburbs of Monte Video	...	...	5	25
February 3, 1807	Monte Video	1	2	10	19
July 2, 1807	Passo Chico	...	1	3	22
June 7, 1807	San Pedro	...	2	...	27
July 4, 1807	Suburbs of Buenos Ayres	...	2	2	4
July 5, 1807	Buenos Ayres	1	9	90	129
August 17, 1807	Near Copenhagen	...	...	1	2
August 29, 1807	Kioge		A	few.	
August 15, 1808	Obidos	1	2	1	6
August 17, 1808	ROLEIA	...	3	17	30
August 21, 1808	VIMIERA	...	4	37	43
	Carried forward	4	30	169	321

Date	Action	Officers		Other ranks	
		Killed	Wounded	Killed	Wounded
Brought over		4	30	169	321
January 3, 1809	Cacabelos	1	1	19	...
January 4, 1809	Between Villa Franca		A	few.	
January 5, 1809	Constantino	...	...	1	...
January 10, 1809	Near Betanzos	...	...	1	...
January 12, 1809	El Burgo	...	...	...	...
January 16, 1809	Corunna	1	...	11	...
Returned to England		...	...	...	33
July 31, 1809	Near Flushing	...	1	...	10
August 9-15, 1809	Flushing	...	2	11	21
March 19, 1810	Barba del Puerco	1	...	3	10
July 4, 1810	Bridge of Marialva	...	...	...	...
July 24, 1810	The Coa	3	9	11	55
August 23-24, 1810	Celorico to Busaco	...	...	...	...
August 25, 1810	Mala Morta	...	...	...	...
August 26, 1810	Sula	...	...	...	...
August 27, 1810	BUSACO	...	...	...	...
September 10, 1810	Alemquer to Arruda	...	...	...	...
September 18, 1810	Alcalá de Gazules	...	...	...	...
October 14, 1810	Sobral	...	2	Seve	ral.
November 19, 1810	Valle		Slight	loss.	
December 20, 1810	Tarifa	...	...	2	16
December 31, 1810	Tarifa	...	...	1	1
March 5, 1811	BARROSA	1	5	19	76
March 8, 1811	Paialvo	...	...	...	...
March 9, 1811	. . . .	...	...	...	...
March 11, 1811	Pombal	...	1	...	...
March 12, 1811	Redinha	...	2	4	9*
March 14, 1811	Casal Nova	2	...	...	...*
March 15, 1811	Foz d'Aronce	...	2	..	...*
March 18, 1811	Ponte da Murcella	...	...	...	...
March 28, 1811	Freixadas	1	...	...	...*
April 3, 1811	Sabugal	1	2	2	14
April 12, 1811	San Pedro	...	...	1	...
April 23, 1811	Bridge of Marialva	...	...	...	...
May 2, 1811	Fuentes d'Onor	...	1	...	9
May 5, 1811	FUENTES D'ONOR	1	...	3	13
May 12, 1811	Near Espeja	...	...	...	...
September 27, 1811	Near Aldea de Ponte	...	...	...	...
January 8, 1812	San Francisco	1	...	1	7
January 19, 1812	CIUDAD RODRIGO	1	5	9	47
March 19, 1812	Before Badajos	...	1	...	...
March 26, 1812	La Picurina	...	...	...	...
April 6, 1812	BADAJOS	9	14	57	225
June 17, 1812	Rueda	...	...	...	...
July 17, 1812	Castrejon	...	...	...	...
July 19, 1812	On the march	...	...	1	...
July 22, 1812	SALAMANCA	...	...	3	24
Carried forward		27	78	329	891

* Return imperfect.

Date	Action	Officers		Other ranks	
		Killed	Wounded	Killed	Wounded
Brought over		27	78	329	891
July 23, 1812	Near the Tormes	...	...	...	...
August 24, 1812	San Lucar	...	...	...	...
August 26, 1812	Seville	...		...	...
October 29, 1812	Aranjuez	...	1	3	8
Nov. 15–19, 1812	Retreat to Portugal	...	...	3	11
June 12, 1813	Near the Hormuza	...	...	...	...
June 18, 1813	San Millan	...	1	4	13
June 21, 1813	VITTORIA	1	6	11	61
June 23, 1813	Echarri-Aranaz	...	...	...	...
June 24, 1813	On the Araquil	...	...	...	...
July 15, 1813	Sta. Barbara	...	...	...	...
August 1, 1813	Bridge of Yanci	...	1	A	few.
August 2, 1813	Echalar	...	...	...	...
August 31, 1813	ST. SEBASTIAN	...	2	8	16*
" "	Bridge of Vera	1	4	18	53
October 7, 1813	Pass of Vera	3	6	31	161
November 9, 1813	Nivelle	1	10	11	76
November 23, 1813	Arcangues	...	1	...	6
December 10, 1813	Nive	1	...	9	75
December 13, 1813	Bussassari	...	...	...	...
January 13, 1814	Before Antwerp	...	...	1	1
February 1, 1814	Donk	...	...	...	...
February 2, 1814	Merxem	...	4	3	6*
February 4, 1814	Sortie from Antwerp	...	...	...	...
February 24, 1814	Villeneuve	...	...	...	...
February 27, 1814	ORTHEZ	...	...	...	...
March 20, 1814	TARBES	1	11	6	75
March 27, 1814	Tournefeuille	...	...	A	few.
April 18, 1814	Toulouse	...	1	14	26*
December 22, 1814	Before New Orleans	...	3	23	59
December 28, 1814	Before New Orleans	...	...	1	4.
January 1, 1815	Before New Orleans	...	...	1	...
January 8, 1815	LINES OF NEW ORLEANS	1	6	11	94
June 16, 1815	QUATRE BRAS	2	3	8	51
June 18, 1815	WATERLOO	3	31	57	339
December 31, 1846	Near the Kei river	...	...	1	...
January 11, 1847	Near the Kei river	2	...	...	...
February, 1847	Patrol on the Fish river	...	...	...	...
August 29, 1847	Boem Plaatz	1	2	6	8
April 29, 1852	Mundell's Krantz	...	1	...	5
May 17, 1852	Mundell's Krantz	...	...	...	3
May 29, 1852	Ingilby's farm	...	...	...	4
July 8, 1852	Waterkloof	...	...	1	...
July 24, 1852	Waterkloof	...	...	...	2
September 14, 1852	Waterkloof	...	...	...	...
Carried forward		41	172	559	2048

* Return imperfect.

Date	Action	Officers		Other ranks	
		Killed	Wounded	Killed	Wounded
Brought over		44	172	559	2048
December 20, 1852	Berea	...	...	3	...
September 20, 1854	THE ALMA	...	1	11	38
October 14, 1854	Picquet	...	...	...	2
October 25, 1854	BALAKLAVA	...	...	...	1
October 26, 1854	Careenage ravine	...	...	...	5
October, 1854	In the trenches	..	1	11	27
November 5, 1854	INKERMAN	3	3	30	58
November 20, 1854	THE OVENS	1	...	9	17
April 9, 1855	Rifle pits	...	...	5	...
June 18, 1855	THE REDAN	2	3	33	89
July 3, 1855	In the trenches	...	...	8	5
September 1, 1855	In the trenches	1	...	1	15
September 8, 1855	SEBASTOPOL	2	8	23	137
November 15, 1855	Explosion	...	1	3	Several.
1854–5	In the trenches, or not otherwise accounted for	...	...	175	143*
November 26, 1857	Cawnpore	...	...	1	...
November 27, 1857	Cawnpore	...	1	...	6
November 28, 1857	Cawnpore	1	2	5	19
November 29, 1857	Cawnpore	...	1	3	5
December 1, 1857	Cawnpore	...	...	...	...
December 6, 1857	Cawnpore	...	1	1	19
December 25, 1857	Putarah	...	...	...	...
December 29, 1857	Etawah	...	...	...	3
January 1858	Near Allahabad	...	...	...	...
January 1858	On the Ramgunga	...	...	...	...
March 6–11, 1858	LUCKNOW	2	...	2	17
March 23, 1858	Koorsie	...	...	...	...
April 13, 1858	Baree	...	...	...	...
May 11, 1858	Nuggur	...	...	1	...
May 22, 1858	Goolowlie	...	...	3	...
May 23, 1858	Calpee	...	...	3	...
June 13, 1858	Nawabgunge	...	1	...	15
August 20, 1858	Nassreegunge	...	...	...	...
August 20–29, 1858	Sultanpore	...	...	...	...
September 6, 1858	Surajpore	...	...	...	...
September 8, 1858	Jamo	...	1	...	3
September 13, 1858	Mandaula	...	...	...	...
September 21, 1858	Fort of Birwah	1	1	3	27
October 20, 1858	Sukreta	1	...	4	5
October 21, 1858	Khooath Khas	...	...	...	...
October 23, 1858	Khurgurh	...	...	...	...
November 26, 1858	Hydergurh	...	...	...	...
December 3, 1858	Fort of Oomria	...	...	...	...
December 6, 1858	Futtehpore	...	...	...	...
Carried forward		58	197	897	2704

* Return of wounded imperfect. 648 Riflemen died of disease in the Crimea and in Turkey.—'Medical and Surgical History,' i. 449–57.

Date	Action	Officers		Other ranks	
		Killed	Wounded	Killed	Wounded
	Brought over	58	197	897	2704
December 6, 1858 .	Byram Ghât . . .	...	...	...	...
December 26, 1858	Near Churdah . .	...	...	...	...
December 27, 1858	Fort of Mejidia . .	...	...	1	6
December 31, 1858	Bankee	...	...	...	1
February 9, 1859 .	Sidka Ghât . . .	...	...	...	1
March 16, 1859 . .	Near Supree . . .	...	...	...	...
April 12, 1859 . .	Akouna	...	...	...	1
April 25-26, 1859 .	Jugdespore jungles.	...	...	...	...
	Not otherwise accounted for to this date*	...	...	2	2
October 27, 1859 .	Mitharden. . . .	...	...	...	...
December 11, 1859	Shahgurh	...	...	...	...
January 2, 1864 . .	Shubkudder . . .	...	...	...	...
January 31, 1874 .	Amoaful	...	3	...	6
February 2, 1874 .	Between Amoaful and Aggemamu .	...	...	...	...
February 3, 1874 .	Near the Ordah . .	...	...	...	8
February 4, 1874 .	Ordahsu	...	...	...	19
	Died of wounds	...	...	2	...
	Total	58	200	902	2748

* Two Officers and 132 Riflemen of other ranks of the 2nd Battalion died of disease during the Indian Mutiny Campaign.

NOTE.—In instances where no casualties are entered, it does not necessarily follow that there were no killed or wounded ; but that I have been unable to ascertain their number. In skirmishes (and occasionally in greater actions) aggregate returns have frequently been made, in which it was impossible to separate the losses of the Regiment. I have noted occasions only where the Riflemen have been engaged or under fire.

APPENDIX IV.

NAMES OF OFFICERS AND OTHER RIFLEMEN WHO HAVE OBTAINED SPECIAL MARKS OF DISTINCTION FOR SERVICES IN THE FIELD.

Name and Rank	Honour received	Action or Campaign for which granted
ANDREWS, Sergeant J.	Legion of Honour	Crimea
ANSON,* Lieut.-Col. Hon. A. H. A.	Medjidie	Crimea
ARMSTRONG, Sergeant	Medal for distinguished conduct in the Field	Ashantee
ARTHUR, NATHANIEL†	Distinguished conduct Medal	Crimea
BAILEY, H.	French military Medal	Crimea
BALVAIRD, Lieut.-Col. William	Gold Medal and Clasp, C.B.	Peninsula
BARNARD, Gen. Sir A. F.	Gold Medal ‡ and 4 Clasps, G.C.B., G.C.H., Maria Teresa (Austria), 4th class St. George (Russia)	Peninsula and Netherlands.
BECKWITH, Lieut.-Col. CHARLES	Gold Medal C.B.	Toulouse Waterloo
BECKWITH, Lieut.-Gen. Sir T. S.	Gold Medal and Clasp, K.C.B., Knight Commander of Tower and Sword (Portugal)	Peninsula
BEN, Corporal M.	French military Medal	Crimea
BLACKETT, Lieut.-Col. E. W.	Legion of Honour	Crimea

* Colonel Anson received the Victoria Cross for gallantry at Bolandshuhur, shortly after he had left the Rifle Brigade. I have noted only in this list the honours obtained by Riflemen while in the Regiment.

† Where no rank is indicated, the name is that of a Private Rifleman.

‡ These medals and crosses were granted to general and field officers (according to the recommendation of the Duke of Wellington), 'for important actions only, and to those engaged in them in a conspicuous manner,' Despatches, viii. 94. I have of course not recorded medals which were granted indiscriminately to all present in an action or campaign.

Name and Rank	Honour received	Action or Campaign for which granted
BOURCHIER, Col. C. T. .	Victoria Cross, Legion of Honour, Medjidie	The 'Ovens'
BRADSHAW, JOSEPH . .	Victoria Cross, French military Medal	Rifle-pit, Sebastopol
BRAMSTON, Capt. T. H.	Medjidie, Sardinian Medal	Crimea
BRETT, Lieut.-Col. J. .	Legion of Honour . . .	Crimea
BROWN, Gen. Sir GEORGE	G.C.B., Grand Cross of Legion of Honour, 1st class Medjidie, Sardinian Medal	Crimea
BROWN, J.	Distinguished conduct Medal	Crimea
BULLER, Gen. Sir GEO.	G.C.B., Commander of Legion of Honour, 2nd class Medjidie. .	Kaffraria and Crimea
BURGE, Sergeant T. . .	French military Medal .	Crimea
BURROWS, Sergeant J. .	Distinguished conduct Medal	Crimea
CAMERON, Major-Gen. Sir Alexander	Gold Medal and 2 Clasps, K.C.B., St. Anne 2nd class (Russia)	Peninsula and Netherlands
CHERRY, J.	Sardinian Medal . . .	Crimea
CLEMENTS, Corporal T. .	Distinguished conduct Medal	Crimea
CLIFFORD, Col. Hon. H. H.	Victoria Cross, C.B., Legion of Honour, Medjidie	Crimea
COLVILLE, Col. Hon. W. J.	Legion of Honour, Medjidie, Sardinian Medal	Crimea
COLLINS, TIMOTHY . .	Distinguished conduct Medal	Crimea
CORNELIUS, Sergt.-Major	French military Medal, Distinguished conduct Medal	Crimea
COX, Major-Gen. John .	K.H.	Peninsula and Netherlands
COX, Major-Gen. William	K.H.	Peninsula
CULLUM, Sergeant . .	Silver Medal for gallantry in the storming of	Monte Video
CUNINGHAME, Major Sir W. J. M., Bart.	Victoria Cross, Medjidie	The 'Ovens'
DAVIES, T.	French military Medal .	Crimea
DENSER, CHARLES . .	French military Medal .	Crimea
DILLON, Col. MARTIN .	C.B., C.S.I.	India, China, and Abyssinia
EAGLE, W.	French military Medal, Distinguished conduct Medal	Crimea

Name and Rank	Honour received	Action or Campaign for which granted
EELES, Lieut.-Col. W.	K.H.	Peninsula, Holland, and Waterloo
ELLIOT, Lieut.-Col. Hon. GILBERT	Medjidie, Sardinian Medal	Crimea
ELRINGTON, Major-General F. R.	C.B., Legion of Honour, Medjidie	Crimea
FAIR, Sergeant	Medal for gallantry	Monte Video
FISHER, Colour-Sergt. D.	French military Medal	Crimea
FITZMAURICE, Major-Gen. W.	K.H.	Peninsula and Netherlands
FITZROY, Capt. C. V.	Medjidie	Crimea
FRASER, Surg.-Gen. J.	Legion of Honour	Crimea
	C.B.	India
FREMANTLE, Lieut.-Col. FITZROY	Sardinian Medal	Crimea
FULLERTON, Col. J.	C.B., K.H.	Waterloo
FYERS, Col. W.	Legion of Honour, Medjidie	Crimea
	C.B.	India
GILMOUR, Major-Gen. Sir D. L.	Gold Cross, K.C.B.	Peninsula
GLYN, Major-Gen. J. R.	Legion of Honour, Medjidie	Crimea
	C.B.	India
HAINES, G.	Distinguished conduct Medal	Crimea
HANNAN, HUGH	Distinguished conduct Medal	Crimea
HARDINGE, Lieut.-Col. H.	Medjidie	Crimea
HARRINGTON, Quarter-Master Sergeant	Distinguished conduct Medal	Crimea
HARRYWOOD, Sergeant J.	French military Medal	Crimea
HARVEY,* Paymaster-Sergeant H.	Distinguished conduct Medal	Crimea
HAWKES, DAVID	Victoria Cross	Lucknow
HAWKESFORD, Sergt. T.	Distinguished conduct Medal	Crimea
HAWKINS, E.	French military Medal	Crimea
HICKS, Colour-Sergt. J.	French military Medal	The 'Ovens'
HILL, Major-Gen. PERCY	C.B.	India
HIMBURY, Sergt. JOHN	Silver Medal and Clasp for gallantry at	St. Sebastian
HOGGER, S.	Distinguished conduct Medal	Crimea
HOPE, Lieut.-Col. J. C.	K.H.	Peninsula and Netherlands
HORSFORD, Lieut.-Gen. Sir A. H.	G.C.B., Medjidie, Sardinian Medal	Crimea and India

* Captain Harvey, Paymaster.

Name and Rank	Honour received	Action or Campaign for which granted
HOUGH, CHARLES . .	French military Medal .	Crimea
HOULT, Sergeant . . .	Medal for gallantry . .	Monte Video
HUMPSTON, R.	Victoria Cross	Rifle-pit, Sebastopol
INGRAM, HENRY . . .	Distinguished conduct Medal	Crimea
KING, J.	French military Medal .	Crimea
KINGSCOTE, Capt. FITZ-H.	Medjidie	Crimea
KNOX, Capt. J. S. . . .	Victoria Cross, Legion of Honour	Crimea
LAWRENCE, Lieut.-Gen. Sir A. J.	K.C.B., Officer Legion of Honour, 3rd class Medjidie	Crimea
LEGGE, Hon. G. B. . .	Medjidie	Crimea
LEIGHFIELD, J. . . .	Distinguished conduct Medal	Crimea
LEWIS, P.	Distinguished conduct Medal	Crimea
MCCANN, P.	French military Medal .	Crimea
MCCORMICK, M. . . .	French military Medal .	Crimea
MCGIBBON, Sergeant .	Medal for gallantry . .	Monte Video
MCGREGOR, RODERICK	Victoria Cross	Rifle-pit, Sebastopol
MCKAY, Sergeant . . .	Medal for gallantry . .	Monte Video
MCKECHIE, Sergeant .	Medal for gallantry . .	Monte Video
MCLEOD, Major-Gen. NORMAN	C.B.	Corunna
MCMAHON, B.	French military Medal .	Crimea
MACDONELL, Major-Gen. A.	C.B., Legion of Honour, Medjidie, Sardinian Medal	Crimea
MANNERS, Lieut.-Col. H. H.	K.H.	Peninsula and Walcheren
MARRIOTT, E.	Distinguished conduct Medal	Crimea
MILLER, Col. GEORGE .	Gold Medal, C.B. . .	Peninsula and Netherlands
MITCHELL, Lieut.-Col. SAMUEL	Gold Medal and Clasp, C.B.	Peninsula and Netherlands
MOORE, Capt. J. C. . .	Sardinian Medal . . .	Crimea
MUNRO, Colour-Sergt. C. F.	French military Medal .	Crimea
MURPHY, Colour-Sergt. J.	Legion of Honour, Distinguished conduct Medal	Crimea
NASH, Corporal W. . .	Victoria Cross	Lucknow
NESBITT, Sergeant . .	Medal for gallantry . .	Monte Video
NEWDIGATE, Col. E. . .	Legion of Honour, Medjidie	Crimea
NIXON, Lieut.-Col. A. J.	Medjidie	Crimea

Name and Rank	Honour received	Action or Campaign for which granted
NORCOTT, Major-Gen. Sir AMOS G.	Medal and Clasp, C.B., K.C.H., St. Anne (Russia), Maximilian Joseph (Bavaria)	Peninsula and Netherlands
NORCOTT, Major-Gen. W. S. R.	C.B., Legion of Honour, Medjidie, Sardinian Medal	Crimea
NUTT, Sergeant JAMES .	Distinguished conduct Medal	Crimea
O'HARE, Major P. . .	Gold Medal	Peninsula
O'HEA, T.	Victoria Cross	Danville Station
PERCIVAL, Lieut.-Col. W.	Gold Medal and 2 Clasps, C.B.	Peninsula and Netherlands
PROMBY, Corporal H. .	Distinguished conduct Medal	Crimea
RAINES, CHARLES . .	Distinguished conduct Medal	Crimea
ROSS, Major-Gen. Sir JOHN	Cross, K.C.B., St. Wladimir 4th class (Russia), Wilhelm 4th class (Netherlands)	Peninsula and Netherlands
ROSS, Colonel JOHN . .	Medjidie	Crimea
	C.B.	India
ROSS, Sergeant. . . .	Medal for gallantry . .	Monte Video
RUSSELL, Major-General Lord A. G.	Medjidie, Sardinian Medal	Crimea
SAUNDERS, Capt. G. R.	Medjidie, Sardinian Medal	Crimea
SCOTT, Surgeon J. . .	Medjidie	Crimea
SHAW, Corporal SAML.	Distinguished conduct Medal	Crimea
	Victoria Cross	Nawabgunge
SMALL, Sergeant . . .	Medal for gallantry . .	Monte Video
SMITH, General Sir H. G. W.	G.C.B.	India and Kaffraria
SMYTH, Major-General Hon. L.	C.B., Legion of Honour, Medjidie, Sardinian Medal	Crimea
SOMERSET, Major-Gen. E. A.	C.B., Legion of Honour, Medjidie	Crimea
STAPLES, Sergeant . .	Medal for gallantry . .	Monte Video
STEWART, Major ARCHIBALD	K.H.	Peninsula and Netherlands
STEWART, Lieut.-Col. Hon. J. H. R.	Gold Medal and Clasp, C.B.	Peninsula
STEWART, Major John .	Gold Medal	Busaco
STEWART, Lieut.-Gen. Hon. Sir W.	Gold Medal and 2 Clasps, G.C.B. San Fernando (Spain), Tower and Sword (Portugal)	Peninsula
STRUCK, H..	Distinguished conduct Medal	Crimea

Name and Rank	Honour received	Action or Campaign for which granted
STUART, Lieut.-Colonel Hon. J.	Medjidie, Sardinian Medal	Crimea
TAINST, EDWARD . . .	Sardinian Medal . . .	Crimea
TAYLOR	Distinguished conduct Medal	Ashantee
THORPE, Sergeant . .	Medal for gallantry . .	Monte Video
TILBEY, T.	Distinguished conduct Medal	Crimea
TRAVERS, Major JAMES	K.H.	Peninsula and New Orleans
TRAVERS, Major-Gen. Sir R.	Gold Medal, C.B. . .	Peninsula
TURNER, Corporal W. .	Distinguished conduct Medal	Crimea
WADE, Colonel H. . .	Gold Medal, C.B. . .	Peninsula
WALKER-MYLN, Lieut.-Col. H.	Medjidie	Crimea
WALLER, Sergt.-Major .	French military Medal .	Crimea
WALPOLE, Lieut.-Gen. Sir R.	K.C.B.	India
WARREN, Lieut.-Col. A. F.	Medjidie	Crimea
	C.B.	Ashantee
WHEATLEY, FRANCIS .	**Victoria Cross**, Legion of Honour Distinguished conduct Medal	Trenches, Sebastopol
WILKINS, Lieut.-Col. G.	Gold Medal, C.B. . . .	Peninsula and Netherlands
WILMOT, Major Sir HENRY, Bart.	**Victoria Cross**	Lucknow
WISEMAN, Corporal R. .	Distinguished conduct Medal	Crimea
WOOD, JOSEPH . . .	Distinguished conduct Medal	Crimea
WOODFORD, Lieut.-Col. C. J.	Legion of Honour, Sardinian Medal	Crimea
YORKE, Gen. Sir CHAS.	G.C.B.	Peninsula and Waterloo

NOTE.—The non-commissioned officers and men of a detachment of the Rifle Corps engaged at Copenhagen in 1801 were presented with a Silver Medal specially given by Lord Nelson.

INDEX.

LONDON PRINTED BY
SPOTTISWOODE AND CO, NEW-STREET SQUARE
AND PARLIAMENT STREET

CPSIA information can be obtained
at www.ICGtesting.com
Printed in the USA
LVOW03*1505301015
460455LV00016B/188/P

9 781342 055521